THE MUSIC TRADE IN GEORGIAN ENGLAND

THE MUSIC TRADE IN GEORGIAN ENGLAND

Edited by
MICHAEL KASSLER

Routledge
Taylor & Francis Group
LONDON AND NEW YORK

First published 2011 by Ashgate Publishing

Published 2016 by Routledge
2 Park Square, Milton Park, Abingdon, Oxfordshire OX14 4RN
711 Third Avenue, New York, NY 10017, USA

First issued in paperback 2016

Routledge is an imprint of the Taylor & Francis Group, an informa business

British Library Cataloguing in Publication Data

The Music Trade in Georgian England.
1. Longman & Broderip – History. 2. Broderip & Wilkinson – History.
3. Clementi, Muzio, 1752–1832. 4. Music publishing – England – History –
18th century. 5. Music publishing – England – History – 19th century.
6. Musical instrument makers – England – History – 18th century. 7. Musical
instrument makers – England – History – 19th century. 8. Copyright –
Music – England – History – 18th century. 9. Copyright – Music – England –
History – 19th century. 10. Music printing – England – History.
I. Kassler, Michael, 1941–
381.4'5780942'09033-dc22

Library of Congress Cataloging-in-Publication Data

The Music Trade in Georgian England / [edited by] Michael Kassler.
p. cm.
Includes index.
1. Music trade – England – History – 18th century. 2. Music trade – England –
History – 19th century. I. Kassler, Michael, 1941–
ML3790.M755 2011
338.4'778094209033-dc22 2011008616

ISBN 13: 978-1-138-24903-5 (pbk)
ISBN 13: 978-0-7546-6065-1 (hbk)

CONTENTS

ILLUSTRATIONS AND MUSIC EXAMPLES

TABLES

PREFACE

The music trade in Georgian England was based upon shopkeepers called 'music sellers' who sold printed music and instruments on which it could be played. These persons—usually partnerships but sometimes sole traders—bought copyrights from composers, arranged for music to be engraved, printed and advertised, and organised the manufacture of musical instruments that they sold under their own names. They engaged external specialists to do the engraving, printing and much of the instrument making, although larger sellers acquired patent rights for instrument inventions and hired their own makers. Music sellers commonly carried out ancillary activities such as tuning and repairing instruments, importing music and retailing concert tickets and books about music. In his *A Complete Dictionary of Music*, published in 1801, Thomas Busby noted that 'the occupation of a music-seller ... has become an extensive, complex, and mysterious trade, and requires a capital, and a stock of information and experience, of which the music-sellers of the last age had no idea'. The trade was centred in London but distributed its goods and services widely.

As indicated by directories of instrument makers and music publishers, the trade employed thousands of people, and many more must have given music sellers custom. This book does not survey the entire trade but concentrates upon significant aspects of it.

The first part deals with Longman & Broderip, arguably the foremost English music seller in the late eighteenth century, and the firm's two successors—Broderip & Wilkinson and Muzio Clementi's variously styled partnerships—who carried on after Longman & Broderip's assets were divided in 1798. The next part shows how a rival music seller, John Bland, and his successors, used textual and thematic catalogues to advertise works that they published in periodically issued collections.

Like other shopkeepers, music sellers in the Georgian era were subject to various legal constraints, but the development of musical copyright, detailed in the third part, impinged upon them uniquely. The last part recounts Charles 3rd Earl Stanhope's efforts to change the ways in which music was printed and recorded, and describes Georg Jacob Vollweiler's endeavour to introduce the new technology of music lithography into England.

I am grateful to my colleagues who contributed to this book, to the librarians, archivists and scholars who answered our numerous queries, to Rachel Lynch (my editor at Ashgate for more than ten years), to her colleagues James McAllister and Kirsten Weissenberg who looked after the book's production, and to Felicity and Elizabeth Teague who copy-edited its text.

Michael Kassler
Northbridge, NSW, Australia
June 2011

ABBREVIATIONS AND CONVENTIONS

The following abbreviations are used in this book. Further abbreviations are defined at their first appearance in a chapter.

Baron	H. Baron collection of lithographed music, University of Reading Library
Beinecke	Beinecke Rare Book and Manuscript Library, Yale University, New Haven, Connecticut, USA
BL	British Library, London
BL Add. Ms	British Library Additional Manuscript
BM	British Museum, London
Bodleian	Bodleian Library, University of Oxford
CKS	Centre for Kentish Studies, Maidstone
CLRO	Corporation of London Records Office (records at Guildhall Library)
CMC	David Rowland (ed.), *The Correspondence of Muzio Clementi*, Bologna, 2010
col.	column number(s)
Coutts	Archivist's Department, Coutts & Co., London
CUL	Cambridge University Library
ER	*The English Reports* (Edinburgh, 178 volumes, 1900–1932)
ESH	Entered at Stationers' Hall (see below)
f	folio number(s)
fn	footnote
Guildhall	Guildhall Library, London
GUL	Glasgow University Library
IGI	FamilySearch.org (https://www.familysearch.org, including the International Genealogical Index of The Church of Jesus Christ of Latter-day Saints)
K	private collection of Jamie and Michael Kassler, Northbridge, NSW, Australia
Killerton	Killerton House, Broadclyst, Devon
LMA	London Metropolitan Archives

MESH	Michael Kassler, *Music Entries at Stationers' Hall, 1710–1818*, Aldershot, 2004
mf	microfiche or microfilm
ms	manuscript
NAL	National Art Library, Victoria and Albert Museum, London
n.s.	new series
NYPL	New York Public Library, New York, USA
OB	*The Proceedings of the Old Bailey, 1674–1913*: http://www.oldbaileyonline.org/ (see below)
p	page number(s)
pmk	postmark
RCM	Royal College of Music, London
RI	Royal Institution, London
RISM	*Répertoire International des Sources Musicales*: http://rism.ub.uni-frankfurt.de/
ser.	series
SRO	Somerset Record Office, Norton Fitzwarren, Somerset
TNA	The National Archives, Kew
UNE	University of New England Library, Armidale, NSW, Australia
v	volume number(s)
v	*versus* [in citations of legal cases]
wmk	watermark

Dates are presented in day/month/year format, i.e., the day precedes the month. The symbols '<' and '>' at the left of a date stand for 'before' and 'after', respectively. A letter is specified by using the format: Sender→Addressee, Date of the letter.

In transcriptions of texts the symbol '|' denotes a line break.

A work described by the acronym 'ESH' followed by a date was entered at Stationers' Hall on that day. If a work was published in London its day of entry there can be regarded as its publication date (see *MESH* p xxi). Symbols that follow the acronym 'OB' give the reference number on http://www.oldbaileyonline.org/ of the proceedings of a particular trial at London's central criminal court.

In this book a person born outside England generally is called by the name by which he or she was known in England.

~ I ~

LONGMAN, BRODERIP AND THEIR SUCCESSORS

CHRONOLOGY OF THE BUSINESS BEGUN BY JAMES LONGMAN

7/1768 James Longman commences business at 26 Cheapside as J. Longman & Co.

*c*1/8/1769 Charles Lukey joins James Longman as partner. Firm is restyled 'Longman, Lukey & Co.'

*c*12/1771–*c*3/1772 Firm relocates temporarily to 45 St Paul's Church Yard while 26 Cheapside is rebuilt

3–11/1773 Francis Fane Broderip joins the firm as a partner

*c*25/12/1774 Firm restyled 'Longman, Lukey & Broderip'

7/1776 Charles Lukey dies

<20/10/1776 Firm restyled 'Longman & Broderip'

<2/11/1782 Longman & Broderip acquire additional premises at 13 Haymarket

<16/4/1787 Longman & Broderip receive warrant from Prince of Wales

<29/9/1787 Longman & Broderip acquire additional premises in Tottenham Court Road for use as a musical instrument manufactory and timber yard

*c*1/1/1791 Longman & Broderip receive a further warrant from the royal family

23/5/1795 Commission of bankrupt awarded against James Longman and Francis Fane Broderip; the firm continues to trade under the control of the assignees

11/6/1795	Creditors of the firm asked to empower the assignees to carry on or to dispose of the business	
7/1795	Assignees decide to continue the business and hire James Longman to conduct its 26 Cheapside and Tottenham Court Road parts and Francis Fane Broderip to conduct its Haymarket part	
13/11/1795	James Longman and Francis Fane Broderip committed to the Fleet Prison because they are unable to repay debts to Culliford & Co. and others	
24/5/1796	Office of the Commissioners of Bankrupts grants certificates of conformity to James Longman and Francis Fane Broderip, permitting them to carry out new business activities without accounting for these to the firm's creditors	
2/11/1796	James Longman and Francis Fane Broderip released from the Fleet Prison and resume their work for the assignees	
6/4/1797	Creditors asked to empower the assignees to sell the Longman & Broderip business as a whole or in parts	
1/11/1798	Assignees sell Longman & Broderip's assets to the two partnerships named in the next row and the firm ceases to operate	
1/11/1798	Francis Fane Broderip and Charles Wilkinson Jr start Broderip & Wilkinson at 13 Haymarket	John Longman, Muzio Clementi, Josiah Banger, Frederick Augustus Hyde, Frederick William Collard and David Davis start Longman, Clementi & Co. at 26 Cheapside and Tottenham Court Road

6/3/1801		John Longman leaves partnership, which is restyled 'Clementi, Banger, Hyde, Collard & Davis' or (for short) 'Muzio Clementi & Co.' or 'Clementi & Co.'. John Longman's retirement from the partnership is backdated to 28/6/1800.
1/1/1805	George Wilkinson replaces Charles Wilkinson Jr as partner in Broderip & Wilkinson	
8/2/1807	Francis Fane Broderip dies. His share of the partnership purchased by George Wilkinson in instalments.	
20/3/1807		Tottenham Court Road premises damaged by fire but subsequently rebuilt
22/11/1807	George Wilkinson pays final instalment	
1/1/1808	Firm starts trading under the style 'Wilkinson & Co.'	
<28/7/1808	Firm acquires additional premises at 3 [Great] Windmill Street for use as a piano manufactory	

8/1809	Firm determines to exit by 12/1809 all business activities except piano making	
8–9/1810		William Frederick Collard becomes a partner before 18/8/1810. Frederick Augustus Hyde retires from the partnership on 31/8/1810. Firm restyled 'Clementi, Banger, Collard, Davis & Collard' before 18/8/1810.
1/1811	Wilkinson & Co. cease trading. George Wilkinson and Robert Wornum II form partnership styled 'Wilkinson & Wornum' at 315 Oxford Street to make pianos. Thomas Preston acquires Wilkinson & Co.'s music plates and copyrights.	
11/10/1812	Wilkinson & Wornum premises destroyed by fire	
*c*12/1812	George Wilkinson and Robert Wornum II start separate piano-making businesses	

24/6/1817	Josiah Banger retires from the partnership. Firm restyled 'Clementi, Collard, Davis & Collard'.
9/1/1822	David Davis dies. Firm restyled 'Clementi, Collard & Collard'.
24/6/1831	Muzio Clementi retires from the partnership. Firm restyled 'Collard & Collard'.

~ 1 ~

LONGMAN & BRODERIP

Jenny Nex

1.1 INTRODUCTION

As a centre of enlightened thought and the primary focus of commerce in Britain, London grew to become the largest city in Europe by the end of the eighteenth century. It was the hub of the British royal court, the legal system and the church, and a major port, and it attracted visitors and migrants from all over Britain, the European mainland and farther afield, its population rising from about 750,000 in 1700 to around 900,000 a century later. Furthermore, London was a major focus for intellectual and artistic pursuits, playing host both to the Royal Society—properly 'The Royal Society of London for the Promotion of Natural Knowledge', whose main concern was the furthering of 'scientific' activities—and to the Royal Academy of Arts, founded in 1768 to train artists and to guide wider artistic taste.[1] Inevitably, London became a centre of fashionable society, with royalty, nobility and gentry spending at least part of the year in the capital, attending the theatre, pleasure gardens and concerts. Music played a central role in both public and private entertainment, and the market for printed music and musical instruments grew as a consequence. This in turn led to an increase in the number of music sellers and other persons employed in the trade.

Newspapers at this time published notices that promoted individual firms and made the public aware of their importance. Although it generally is not known who placed such notices, in cases such as the following self-promotion seems the most likely motive:

---

[1] See Jeremy Black and Roy Porter (eds), *A Dictionary of Eighteenth-Century World History*, London, 1994, articles on 'London' (p 422), 'Royal Academy of Arts' (p 652) and 'Royal Society' (p 653).

> The proof of ENGLISH GENIUS is, in no instance evidenced more perceivably, than in the invention and improvement of MUSICAL INSTRUMENTS, which, within these few years, have become very considerable articles of export, whereas formerly, the *amateurs* imported from ITALY. But now LONDON has become as famous for every species of musical instruments, as CREMONA has been for exceeding in *violins*, and may boast of one manufactory which gives employment to several hundred workmen of different denominations. We allude to that of Mess. LONGMAN and BRODERIP.[2]

The activity of Longman and his partners that culminated in the firm of Longman & Broderip was central to musical life in London for thirty years from 1768, and their legacy can still be felt today. As their work encompassed many areas—instrument making and dealing, music publishing, selling concert tickets, entertaining visiting musicians and establishing property rights—they are often mentioned in books and articles about this period. However, due to the complexity of their situation and the lack of surviving company records, many misunderstandings and myths have become established by repetition. I hope that this chapter will lay to rest some of these inaccuracies.

The focus of this chapter is the instrument-making side of the firm, although it does not include an examination of the surviving instruments. That, together with detailed analysis of the firm's music publishing activities, lies outside the scope of this work.

Because of the scale of the firm's business, many individuals make an appearance in this chapter. However, the thread which runs through it all is in the shape of James Longman.

1.2 The Early Years

James Longman was born in Corton Denham in Somerset, the fourth and youngest son of Joseph and Susan(n)a(h). His baptism is recorded on 17 April 1745,[3] some ten years after that of his eldest brother Joseph Jr. Between the middle two brothers, George and John, a sister

---

[2] *The Times*, 31 January 1788, p 3.

[3] All dates have been converted to the Gregorian calendar, adopted in Britain in 1752. Before then, years began in March rather than January.

Ann was born, but she died at the age of three.[4] James lost both of his parents in his early years, his mother passing away only a year after his baptism and his father some four years later.[5] In his will, Joseph described himself as a linen weaver of Corton Denham. He bequeathed all his property to his four sons, the most to the eldest son Joseph Jr, who received land settled on his mother as well as the tools of his father's trade, including looms and engines and the use of the 'Brooken House and Water'. The younger three also received a share of Joseph's other 'lands and tenements' and were each to receive £490 when they reached the age of twenty-one years. Until then, the interest on these sums was to be paid for their maintenance and education.[6] Thus, a family of four boys aged fifteen, thirteen, eight and five were left without parental guidance but with the means to support themselves if they had the skill to do so. It is not known whether the boys' uncle William, executor of their father's will, stepped in to the breach, but the family seem to have been able to keep going without falling into poverty.

The next known appearance of James is in 1760, when he began his career in London. Why the profession of musical instrument maker was chosen by or for him is not clear, nor why he moved so far from his native land, but London certainly offered opportunities for him. Members of the wider Longman family were already established in the capital, so he could have been under the supervision of a kinsman.[7]

At a meeting of the Worshipful Company of Cooks on 7 June that year, James Longman, said to be 'aged 14', was bound

---

[4] Parish records for Corton Denham, SRO mf D\P\co.d.2/1/1 M4184/2, baptisms 1538–1760. Joseph was baptised on 2 March 1735, George on 18 October 1737, Ann on 6 February 1740 and John on 30 July 1742. All are recorded as children of Joseph and Susan(n)a(h). Ann was buried on 10 October 1743 (SRO mf D\P\co.d.2/1/1 M4184/4, burials 1560–1812).

[5] SRO mf D\P\co.d.2/1/1 M4184/4, burials 1560–1812. Susannah Longman was buried on 27 May 1746 and Joseph Longman on 29 November 1750.

[6] TNA PROB 11/786, court copy of will of Joseph Longman, written 31 July 1748, proved 13 February 1751. The executors named were Joseph's brother William and cousin Robert Longman.

[7] A detailed survey of the Longman family has been made by Dennis Longman. His unpublished notes are now housed at the Society of Genealogists in London.

apprentice to John Johnson, a 'citizen and cook', for seven years for the not inconsiderable sum of £105.[8] The records of the Cooks' Company confirm that this is indeed our James Longman as his father is described as 'Joseph Longman of Corton Denham in the County of Somerset, doulas maker', even though James's stated age differs by a year from his actual age as extrapolated from his christening date (not uncommon in archival sources of this period). Doulas is a cloth of coarse linen that was worn mainly by the lower classes, and fits with Joseph's occupation of linen-weaver as described in his will.[9] The description of John Johnson as a cook is also not problematic once it is realised that musical instrument makers did not have their own guild at this time, so it was necessary for one wishing to work within the City of London to belong to an established livery company. Musical instrument makers appear in a number of guilds, including the Cooks', Spectacle Makers', Turners', Glovers' and Haberdashers' Companies.[10] Johnson referred to himself as a musical instrument maker (his trade card is reproduced in *Figure 1.1*) and worked from a shop facing St Mary le Bow Church on Cheapside, at the sign of the Harp and Crown.[11]

What James learnt from his master is uncertain, but as Johnson made violins it is likely that James received some training as a luthier. Johnson's trade card states that he sold 'all sorts of musical instruments' as well as reeds, strings and harpsichord wire. In addition, he bought second-hand instruments and published music, so James would have seen how it was possible to combine different aspects of the music trade in order to make a living.

The composer Charles Dibdin records that his brother Thomas introduced him to Johnson's employ about 1756, 'by way of putting me in the road to church preferment'. As 'old Johnson ... kept a

---

[8] Worshipful Company of Cooks, Court Minutes, 1738–1784, Guildhall ms 3111/2 p 179.

[9] Ivor H. Evans (ed.), *Brewer's Dictionary of Phrase and Fable*, 14th ed., London, 1995, p 348.

[10] Cliff Webb, *London Livery Company Apprenticeship Registers*, 41 volumes, London, 1996–2007.

[11] John Milnes (ed.), *The British Violin*, Oxford, 2000, p 40.

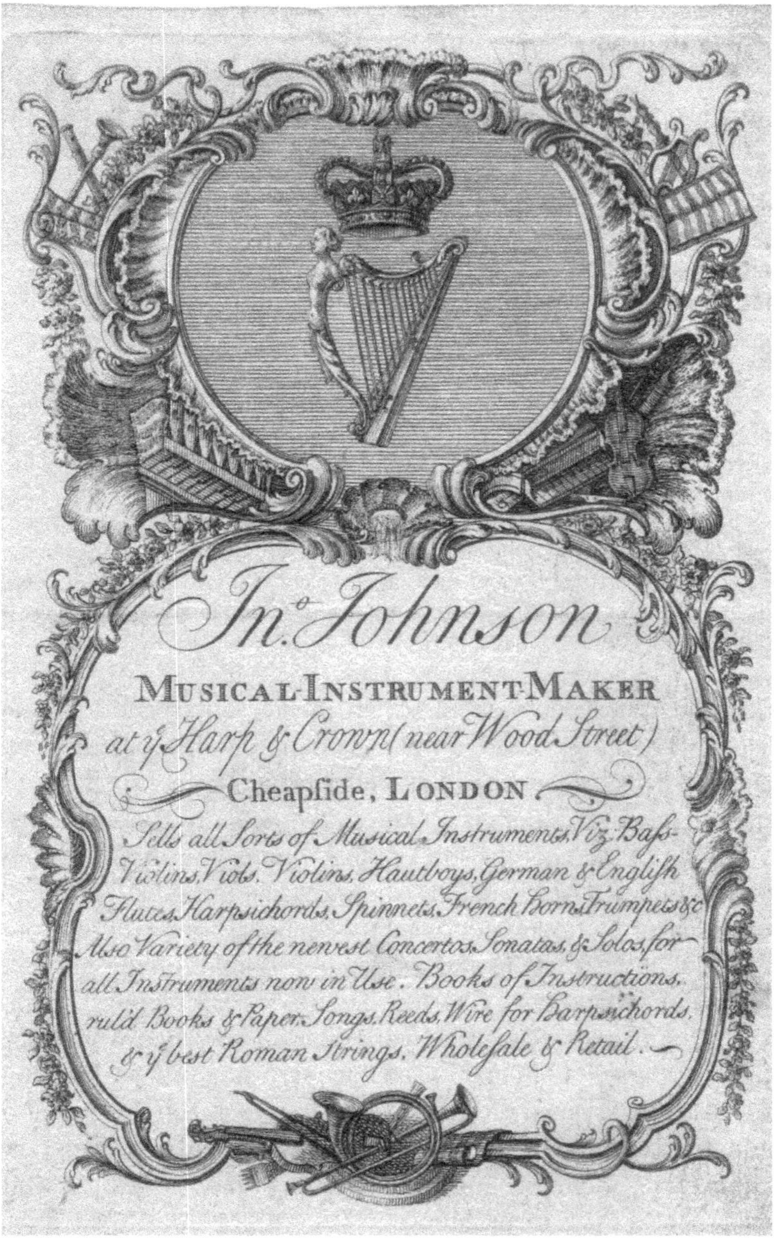

Figure 1.1 Trade card of John Johnson
(Tony Bingham Collection, London, by permission)

capital music-shop in Cheapside', Charles Dibdin started with a positive attitude, but soon

> grew tired of an attendance on him, for I saw no chance of advancement to the organ-loft; and he never failed, when I called, to set me down to tune harpsichords, a mere mechanical employment, not at all to my taste, which I buckled to with great reluctance, and considered as the height of indignity.[12]

He had more ambition than he saw could be fulfilled remaining where he was, so

> I began to look about me, and to consider how I might least infringe on my plan of independence. I saw plainly that I might have screwed up harpsichords in old Johnson's shop to all eternity without advancing my fortune; and, as to the songs and sonatas that I brought him for sale, they had not been performed at the theatres nor Vauxhall, nor any other place, nor introduced by music-masters at boarding-schools; besides, they came out under no patronage—and then, again, I am ready to allow they were puerile, imperfect and crude; but that, indeed, would have brought with it no objection, had they boasted the foregoing advantages.[13]

This demonstrates one way in which music sellers chose music to publish: if it was performed in the expanding public arena of theatres, pleasure gardens or concerts, they could promote it as such and hope to generate more sales than if it were sold purely on its own merits.

Dibdin also was frustrated that Johnson's friendship with Thomas Dibdin, a sea captain, was not more productive. He had helped Johnson by taking goods that were not selling well in London to the West Indies, where the market for London-made goods and music was expanding. Charles Dibdin's complaints, although interesting in themselves, are of particular significance when seen in the light of James Longman's later career. As well as learning to make instruments, he would have seen how a company operated both in the home market and in the increasing export market, supplying a range of goods including instruments and printed music as well as services such as instrument tuning.

---

[12] Charles Dibdin, *The Professional Life of Mr Dibdin, written by himself*, London, 1803, v 1 p 17.

[13] *ibid.*, v 1 p 18.

However, James did not serve his full term of seven years under Johnson. He died in 1761,[14] and his widow Ruth took over the firm, a common practice in eighteenth-century London. In 1767 there was a further hitch as James was 'discharged by judgement in the Outer Court'.[15] This meant that he was not able to gain his freedom of the City by servitude, as he was still three months short of completing his seven years' service. He appealed to a different livery company, the Spectacle Makers', to allow him to pay a fee and enter this company 'by redemption'. This he was permitted to do, and for the sum of £2/6/8 James was admitted into the Freedom of the City of London in the Company of Spectacle Makers on 5 March 1767.[16]

The year 1767 was significant also for James's inheritance. If we accept that a year was 'lost' before he began his apprenticeship, he would have been twenty-one around 17 April 1767, and whatever was left of the £490 and the share in the property bequeathed to him by his father would have come into his own control. Thus, within two months, he became able to work independently within the City of London and had some financial backing to help him to set up on his own. His first appearance in the Land Tax Assessment Books is in the Ward of Farringdon Within, St Matthew's precinct, where he is listed under Goldsmiths Row.[17] Although this street does not appear on contemporary maps such as Rocque's published in 1747 and Horwood's of 1799–1819,[18] Goldsmiths' Row was a group of houses

---

[14] TNA PROB 11/866, court copy of John Johnson's will, signed 19 January 1742, proved 8 June 1761. His sole legatee and executrix was his wife Ruth. No will in her name has been traced. The May 1762 date given for Johnson's death in the records of the Spectacle Makers' Company (CLRO CF1/943, ELJL/943/2) is incorrect.

[15] The reason for this judgement is not known as relevant records have not survived.

[16] Records of the Spectacle Makers' Company, *op. cit.* I am grateful to Nancy Mace for helping me to find this record.

[17] LMA, formerly Guildhall ms 11.316/205–89.

[18] John Rocque, *A Plan of the Cities of London and Westminster, and Borough of Southwark*, London, 1747, republished as *The A to Z of Georgian London*, Lympne Castle, Kent, 1981; and Richard Horwood, *Plan of the Cities of London and Westminster, with the Borough of Southwark...*, London, 1813, republished as *The A to Z of Regency London*, Lympne Castle, Kent, 1985.

on the south side of Cheapside near St Paul's Cathedral, on the other side of the road from Johnson's premises. It was so called because it was owned by the Worshipful Company of Goldsmiths, whose Hall is still located on Foster Lane, not far from the same end of Cheapside.[19] During this period of establishing himself, James Longman seems to have come to an arrangement with Ruth Johnson, for when she ceased to use the sign of the Harp and Crown inherited from her husband, it was taken over by him.[20]

The extent to which Longman used that sign is not clear from the historical record. Its appearances seem to have dwindled rapidly, and eventually another 'logo', of Apollo playing a lyre, was substituted (see *Figure 1.5* on page 60 below), although that too seems not to have been used for long.

The numbering of houses on Cheapside is confused. Although all other contemporary sources give Longman's address as 26 Cheapside, the Goldsmiths' rent books did not use that numbering until 1781: they record that Longman was responsible from 1769 for the rent of houses numbered 48 (or 49), 17 (called the Queen's Head) and part of 16.[21] His arrangement with the Goldsmiths' Company between 1767, when he began to pay Land Tax, and 28 August 1772, when his formal lease was signed, is not clear. The tenants previous to Longman were James Corneck at no. 17 and Edward Thorowgood at no. 48. Corneck, a hosier, apparently did not vacate his premises entirely when Longman took over, as he is recorded as still living

---

[19] Rent books of the Worshipful Company of Goldsmiths (in the Company's library) v 10, Lady Day 1763–1773. There are two series of rent books, for Lady Day (25 March) and Michaelmas Day (29 September), the rents being due every six months.

[20] *The Public Advertiser*, 4 May 1768, p 1, has the last located advertisement for 'Mrs Johnson, at the Harp and Crown, in Cheapside', while the first advertisement found with 'J. Longman and Co. at the Harp and Crown, No. 26, Cheapside' is in *The Public Advertiser*, 21 July 1768, p 3. Widow Johnson appears to have operated under the heading 'At the Old Music Shop, no. 110, in Cheapside', until her death in 1777. Her stock was advertised for sale at auction in July that year (*The Gazetteer and New Daily Advertiser*, 11 June 1777, p 3).

[21] 26 Cheapside was formed from what had been these three separate properties. Longman paid £7 'rent for the quarter to Lady Day 1769'.

there some years later.[22] This may have been a consequence of housing issues in London described by Adam Smith:

> The dearness of house-rent in London, arises, not only from those causes which render it dear in all great capitals, the dearness of labour, the dearness of all the materials of building, which must generally be bought from a great distance, and above all the dearness of ground-rent, every landlord acting the part of a monopolist, and frequently exacting a higher rent for a single acre of bad land in town, than can be had for a hundred of the best in the country; but it arises in part from the peculiar manners and customs of the people, which oblige every master of a family to hire a whole house from top to bottom.[23]

As a result

> A tradesman in London is obliged to hire a whole house in that part of the town where his customers live. His shop is upon the ground-floor, and he and his family sleep in the garret; and he endeavours to pay a part of his house-rent by letting the two middle stories to lodgers.[24]

1.3 Longman, Lukey & Co.

Between 20 July and 8 August 1769, James Longman took a business partner named Charles Lukey.[25] No information has come to light about the terms of their partnership or who had responsibility for particular activities. Like Longman, Lukey came up to London from the West Country. He was born in Falmouth in Cornwall where he was baptised on 5 November 1740, making him James's senior by five or six years.[26] Lukey was the third of at least six children and

---

[22] TNA PROB 10/2721, will of Charles Lukey, written February 1774 with a codicil dated 17 October 1775, proved 10 May 1777.

[23] Adam Smith, *An Inquiry into the Nature and Causes of the Wealth of Nations*, London, 1776, v 1 p 146.

[24] *ibid.*

[25] In *The Public Advertiser*, 20 July 1769, p 3, the firm is advertised as J. Longman and Co.; in *The Public Advertiser*, 8 August 1769, p 3, it is advertised as Longman, Lukey, and Co.

[26] IGI. His parents were named Charles and Grace.

probably the eldest son.[27] His father was a shopkeeper,[28] so would have had an idea of commercial practices. It is not known whether Lukey undertook a formal apprenticeship or when he removed to London, but he was admitted to the Worshipful Company of Musicians on 18 September 1772[29] and was made free of the City of London by redemption on 26 January 1773, paying, like Longman, £2/6/8 for this privilege.[30] It seems likely that Lukey was a subsidiary partner to Longman before then, as lack of the necessary freedom would have made it difficult for Lukey to be in charge of a business within the City of London.

In 1771 the partners decided that the premises at 26 Cheapside were not adequate for their purposes, so they removed temporarily to 45 St Paul's Church Yard, just up the road, while a building project was undertaken at no. 26.[31] This work did not go altogether to plan, as *The Public Advertiser* reported in August that 'yesterday morning a man fell from Longman and Co.'s house in Cheapside, which is repairing, and was taken up for dead'.[32] And in September:

> Yesterday morning, at the house Mr Longman is pulling down in Cheapside, there had like to have happened a second dreadful accident by the wall of the Nag's Head falling in; but owing to a cart not coming at the appointed time, eight men that were at work were saved by their going to breakfast half an hour before their time merely on that account.[33]

---

[27] The children of Charles Lukey Sr and Grace Lukey christened in Falmouth are listed in IGI as Prudence *bap*7/8/1736, Grace *bap*27/12/1738, Charles *bap*5/11/1740, Elizabeth *bap*24/10/1742, Mary *bap*1/3/1747 and Benjamin *bap*26/2/1749. Charles Lukey's (the son's) will (cited in note 22 above) also mentions a brother called Richard.

[28] CLRO, Worshipful Company of Musicians, Freedom Records, ELJL/1000/26.

[29] 'A List of the Court of Assistants of the Worshipful Company of Musicians', Guildhall ms 3098 p 62.

[30] Worshipful Company of Musicians, Freedom Records, *loc. cit.*

[31] *The Public Advertiser*, 9 December 1771, p 4.

[32] *The Public Advertiser*, 20 August 1771, p 2.

[33] *The Public Advertiser*, 27 September 1771, p 32.

It is somehow reassuring to note how little working habits have changed in two hundred years.

On their return to 26 Cheapside in 1772, Longman himself held the lease for the first time: it was for 60½ years from Lady Day 1772 to Michaelmas 1832 at the rate of £50/8/4 per year.[34] The lease makes clear what the building project involved, as it says that a rear section was added to the existing building at the cost of some £800, the two parts being numbered 17 and 48.[35] Having spent this large sum, it is understandable that James took out a policy with the Hand-in-Hand Fire Office on 29 April 1772 to insure the premises for £1,500.[36]

1.4 Longman, Lukey & Broderip

In 1773 a third partner joined the firm.[37] Francis Fane Broderip came from a family of musicians in Wells, Somerset. A son of John (the organist of Wells Cathedral) and Eleanor, he was received into the church on 1 November 1750 and was the youngest of three children recorded in the Cathedral registers from this union, Elizabeth being received in 1746 and William in 1748.[38] Like Lukey, Broderip was not free of the City when he joined the firm, but was admitted to the Freedom of the Worshipful Company of Spectacle Makers on 16 January 1777 by redemption.[39] Although Francis Broderip seems to

---

[34] Lady Day (the Feast of the Annunciation, 25 March), Midsummer's Day (21 June), Michaelmas (the Feast of St Michael, 29 September) and Christmas Day were the 'quarter days' which structured the business year.

[35] Lease between The Goldsmiths' Company and James Longman, 28 August 1772. The counterpart copy is in the Company's library at Goldsmiths' Hall.

[36] Policy no. 88125, LMA formerly Guildhall ms 8674/113 p 83.

[37] A document in the 1773 legal case *Bach v Longman* (TNA C12/71/22) indicates that Broderip joined the firm between March and November 1773.

[38] Transcripts of Wells Cathedral Registers of Baptisms, Marriages and Burials, 1660–1982 (SRO mf DD/WCL 69). Burials: 30/12/1770, John Broderip, organist of the Cathedral; 11/4/1785, Mrs Eleanor Broderip, widow of the late Mr John Broderip Organist of the Cathedral.

[39] I am grateful to Colin Eldridge, Honorary Archivist of the Spectacle Makers' Company, for advising that the Company's records corroborate Broderip's origins, as his father is described there as John Broderip of Wells, Somerset.

have lived at the Cheapside premises initially,[40] he later resided at Warwick Court with his family[41] and eventually became manager of the Haymarket branch that the firm established in 1782.[42]

All three partners married during the early years of the firm. Lukey was first, his wife Mary producing two children, Charles Jr on 19 September 1772 and Mary Jr on 6 September 1773,[43] both of whom feature in the firm's later history. The marriage was recorded in the Leominster parish register on 2 July 1771.[44] That these are indeed the correct people is evidenced by Charles's address in the 'Parish of Saint Michael le Querne, otherwise Foster Lane, London', in which 26 Cheapside is found.[45] While Charles was a bachelor, his wife Mary was widowed, her former husband Mr Broderip having died in the previous year. This was William Broderip, the Leominster organist, who appears to have been a relative, perhaps a cousin, of Francis. William had married Mary Woodhouse on 21 February 1770 in Leominster,[46] but details of her origins are not known.

Francis Broderip married Anne Longman on 12 January 1774 in West Drayton, Middlesex.[47] Again it is not possible to be certain of

[40] London Borough of Hillingdon, Parish of West Drayton, register of baptisms, marriages and burials, 1701–1813, LMA DRO1/A1/3, p 12. Broderip is recorded as being 'of the Parish of St Vedast Foster Lane', in which 26 Cheapside is situated.

[41] His four sons were baptised in the parish of St Andrew Holborn, from Warwick Court. LMA, formerly Guildhall ms 6667/12–13.

[42] In 1785 the 'gentleman composer' John Marsh wrote in his journal that after his quartet had been engraved and printed he 'desired some [copies] to be sent to Longman's in Cheapside for sale upon the usual terms, & as many to his partner Broderip in the Haymarket'. See Brian Robins (ed.), *The John Marsh Journals*, Stuyvesant, New York, 1998, p 348.

[43] Willoughby A. Littledale (ed.), *The Registers of St Vedast Forster Lane and St Michael le Querne*, Harleian Society registers no. 29, London, 1902, p 192 and p 282.

[44] In the Herefordshire Archive Service, Hereford.

[45] The parish of St Michael le Querne was united with the parish of Foster Lane after the Great Fire of 1666.

[46] IGI.

[47] *loc. cit.* in note 40 above.

Anne's familial connections with her husband's colleagues as none of their parents is named in the marriage record. The clergyman who married them was one J. Longman. The Rev. John Longman I came from North Cadbury in Somerset and was ordained by John Wynne, Bishop of Bath and Wells, on 23 September 1733.[48] North Cadbury is not far from Corton Denham, so it seems likely that James was related to the Rev. John Longman, who died at the Broderips' house in 1792.[49] To add to the confusion, Anne's brother was a second Rev. John Longman, who also died at the Broderips' house three years later.[50] Either the father or the son might have performed the marriage between Anne and Francis. It appears that Anne brought a legacy to the marriage since she had inherited £200 from an uncle in 1769. A second bequest brought her £400 in 1789,[51] a useful addition to the family finances since the Broderips' four sons, John, William, Charles and Francis, were born between 1775 and 1788.[52]

The last of the three men to take a wife, James Longman married Elizabeth Tomkyns, daughter of Packington and Elizabeth

[48] 'Clergy of the Church of England Database' (http://www.theclergydatabase.org.uk), record ID 46467.

[49] 'DIED. ... On Wednesday, at Mr Broderip's, in Bedford-row, the Rev. John Longman, father of Mrs Broderip, at the advanced age of eighty-four' (*The Morning Herald*, 9 June 1792, p 3).

[50] *The Star*, 2 March 1795, p 4. This death notice describes Rev. John Longman II as 'of Uxbridge, in the fifty-first year of his age'. Together with Francis Broderip, Mrs Broderip (presumably Anne), and their sons John and William (both then at Eton College), 'Rev. Mr Longman, Uxbridge' subscribed to Richard Eastcott, *Sketches of the Origin, Progress and Effects of Music*, Bath, 1793. Longman & Broderip also subscribed for six copies of this book, probably for sale to their customers.

[51] In the will of James Longman of Bristol, glassmaker, made 7/4/1768 and proved 16/3/1769, he left £200 each to Anne and her brother John. He also bequeathed £800 for the benefit of his sister Mary, which upon her death was to be divided equally between Anne and John. The will of Mary Longman of Bristol, spinster, was made 17/12/1788 and proved 14/2/1789. Information recorded from the *Transactions of the Bristol & Gloucestershire Archaeological Society* by Dennis Longman in his Longman family study (see note 7 above).

[52] IGI. They were all christened at Saint Andrew Holborn: John *bap*12/1/1775, William *bap*26/3/1778, Charles *bap*1/3/1781 and Francis *bap*27/3/1788. Their careers are briefly described in the next chapter.

Tomkyns at St Anne's, Soho, on 7 April 1775.[53] The Tomkyns family were wine merchants of Oxford Street and were of sufficient wealth that, on the death of her father, Elizabeth had her own income from his estate.[54] This included a sum in the three per cent consolidated annuities which brought her a total of £144/14/15 between 17 July 1779 and 25 January 1785.[55] That this income did not automatically pass to her husband, as would have been the general case, is due to the clause in her father's will that bequeathed the funds to his

> daughter Elizabeth Longman and her assigns for and during the term of her natural life for her own sole and separate use and benefit and not to be subject or liable to the debts engagements or controul of her present husband and so that he may not have any thing to do or intermeddle therewith.[56]

While this strong language might appear at first to show a dislike or distrust of Longman by his father-in-law, it was the usual wording in documents where a father wished to secure the financial future of his daughter. Otherwise, the law was such that any property received by a wife belonged to her husband.[57]

The triumvirate of Longman, Lukey & Broderip, cemented not only through business but also through familial ties, existed for less than three years, as Lukey died in his home town of Falmouth in July 1776. In his will, written in 1774, he bequeathed £10 each plus some personal effects to his mother Grace and his four siblings Richard, Elizabeth (Betsey), Grace and Prudence. However, a codicil of October 1775 stated that Richard and Betsey 'shall not receive more than one shilling from my property', that which was previously

[53] IGI.

[54] TNA E/112/1787/6238, *Longman v Assignees*, 1802.

[55] TNA C12/1703/6, *Longman v Tomkyns*, 1785.

[56] TNA PROB 11/1041, court copy of the will of Packington Tomkyns, made 3 August 1775, proved 7 April 1778. See also TNA PROB 11/1274, court copy of the will of Elizabeth Tomkyns, made 12 January 1789, proved 9 April 1796.

[57] It was not until the Married Women's Property Act in 1857 and subsequent legislation that married British women were able to own property independently of their husbands. See John Belchem and Richard Price (eds), *The Penguin Dictionary of Nineteenth-Century History*, London, 1996, p 365–367.

designed for them going instead to Charles Jr. The cause of this change of heart is not recorded. As well as the three central legatees—his wife Mary and their two children—Lukey bequeathed mourning rings, each of the value of one guinea, to James Longman, Francis Broderip, George Eltoft (their clerk),[58] James Corneck and Ely Dyson, all of Cheapside and probably all residing at number 26. The latter two men, both hosiers, also acted as the executors and trustees of the will. Lukey's wife Mary was nominated as guardian of the children and also received his 'two reels or machines for silvering strings and also my household goods plate china and linnen of every kind to be possessed and enjoyed by her for her own use'.[59]

The mention of machines for silvering strings is significant as it indicates one of the operations which the firm undertook itself rather than by hiring outsiders. As women at this time often were left widowed with children to care for, it was important that they could support themselves if the need arose, and this bequest enabled Lukey's wife to earn a living after he died.

1.5 Longman and Broderip as Partners

Lukey's death left the firm with two partners, James Longman and Francis Fane Broderip, the way it remained, at least in appearance, until 1798, when its assets were divided and sold to Broderip & Wilkinson and Longman, Clementi & Co. The partnership was not an equal one as Longman owned a three-quarter share and Broderip the remainder.[60] They allowed themselves £10/10/– to be drawn from their business each week, giving Longman a weekly wage of £7/17/6 and Broderip £2/12/6.[61] This equalled an annual salary of £136/10/– for Broderip and £409/10/– for Longman, and compares favourably

[58] Office of the Commission of Bankrupts and Successors: Order books relating to petitions against declarations of bankruptcy, TNA B1/93, 1795–1796, p 68–73, 28 July 1796.

[59] TNA PROB 10/2721, court copy of will of Charles Lukey, written February 1774, proved 10 May 1777, codicil dated 17 October 1775.

[60] TNA C12/178/48, *Smith v Longman*, 1791.

[61] *ibid.*

with tradesmen, who earned about £40, army officers, who were paid up to about £100, and lawyers, who earned about £200 per year. Successful manufacturers and tradesmen in London earned between £200 and £600 per year.[62] These numbers also show that, together with the £50/8/4 paid to the Goldsmiths' Company for the premises at 26 Cheapside,[63] the firm spent some £600 per annum on rent and the salaries of the two partners alone.

One of the few references to the characters of the partners is found in the Rev. William Peters's description of members of the Prince of Wales's Lodge of Freemasons in 1788, where Broderip, then aged 37, is described as 'a good, jolly fellow'.[64] He was initiated into this Lodge on 16 April 1787 and seems to have been an energetic member, acting as secretary in March 1788 and providing the lodge with 'an elegant and useful desk, and a chest for the use of the secretary of this lodge', for which he was given the 'thanks of this lodge ... for his generous donation'. He became a deputy warden in 1790, proposed members and seconded the appointment of others.[65]

Longman and Broderip supported the Whig party, as in the Westminster polls of 1784, 1788 and 1790 they both voted for Samuel Lord Hood and Charles James Fox.[66] Both partners also signed in 1792 the declaration:

> of our determined Resolution to support, by every Means in our Power, the ancient and most excellent Constitution of Great Britain, and a

---

[62] Liza Picard, *Dr Johnson's London*, London, 2000, p 55. These amounts are based upon statistics of average family incomes compiled by the economist Joseph Massie in 1759.

[63] James Longman's 28 August 1772 lease (see note 35 above).

[64] See Henry Sadler, *Thomas Dunkerley, his Life, Labours, and Letters*, London, 1891, p 131–132. Peters was secretary of the lodge. I am grateful for Michael Kassler for this reference.

[65] I thank Diane Clements, director, The Library and Museum of Freemasonry, London, for searching the Lodge's archive, and Michael Kassler for forwarding the results of the search to me. Thanks also to the Prince of Wales's Lodge, no. 259, for permitting these references to be cited.

[66] LMA, Westminster Poll Books, WR/PP1784/22 & 24 (1784); WR/PP1788/15 & 16 (1788); WR/PP1790/10 & 11 (1790). My thanks to Lance Whitehead for this information.

> Government by King, Lords, and Commons; and to exert our best Endeavours to impress on the Minds of those connected with us, a Reverence for, and a due Submission to the Laws of their Country, which have hitherto preserved the Liberty, protected the Property, and increased the Enjoyments of a free and prosperous People.[67]

Longman and Broderip may have felt obliged to sign this declaration because they had held an appointment to the Prince of Wales for a number of years. Newspaper advertisements claiming this warrant have not been found before December 1787,[68] but for Broderip to join the Prince of Wales's Lodge he would have needed such an appointment, so it must have preceded 16 April 1787.[69] The firm must later have received additional royal appointments, as from January 1791 they advertised that they were 'Manufacturers of Musical Instruments, and Music Sellers to their Majesties, His Royal Highness the Prince of Wales and all the Royal Family'.[70]

1.6 Music Publishing and Legal Issues

As mentioned, music publishing was a core activity of James Longman and his partners from the outset. Nearly 700 Longman & Broderip publications were entered at Stationers' Hall.[71] Because musical instruments were bought only occasionally it was good for music sellers to have another string to their bow. An ongoing service

---

[67] *Declaration of the Merchants, Bankers, Traders, and other Inhabitants of London, made at Merchant Taylors' Hall, December 5th, 1792...*, London, 1793, p 4 (copy at BL 1141.d.6(5)): 'Frans. Broderip' (p 12), 'James Longman' (p 43).

[68] In *The Daily Universal Register*, 7 December 1787, p 1, they advertised that they were 'music-sellers, and musical instrument-makers, to His Royal Highness the Prince of Wales'.

[69] I thank Diane Clements for this information.

[70] *The World*, 24 January 1791, p 1. Only their appointment to the Prince of Wales was noted in their advertisement in *The World*, 31 December 1790, p 1.

[71] See *MESH* and Nancy A. Mace, 'The market for music in the late eighteenth century and the entry books of the Stationers' Company', *The Library* v 10 no. 2 (June 2009) p 157–187 at p 162–163.

of providing music to instrument owners could generate further sales over a long term.

Works published and sold by Longman & Broderip included solo and chamber music, songs with easy accompaniments for the amateur, and favourite pieces arranged from the popular operas of the day. They also sold tutors that taught people to play instruments that they had purchased. Between 1770 and 1790, the firm issued instruction books for the harpsichord, piano, flute, oboe, bassoon, clarinet, bagpipe, violin, guitar, mandoline, harp, cistre (cittern) and tenor (viola).[72] Their July 1789 eight-page catalogue listed about 500 works for sale, including their own publications and editions imported 'from different parts of Europe'.[73]

It seems likely that the firm used external engravers and printers to produce their publications, but few such tradesmen can be definitely linked with them. In 1791 John Williams said that he had known Longman and Broderip for some twenty years and had printed music for them.[74] His proximity to their Cheapside shop in 1780 is recorded in the policy that insured his dwelling house, utensils, stock and other goods at 7 Fountain Court for £300.[75] Williams is not mentioned in standard reference books, but Humphries and Smith include Lucy Williams of Fountain Court, a music and copperplate printer who started printing in 1808 and printed some music for Clementi & Co., which succeeded Longman, Clementi & Co.[76]

---

[72] See Adrienne Simpson, 'A short-title list of printed English instrumental tutors up to 1800, held in British libraries', *RMA Research Chronicle* no. 6 (1966) p 24–50.

[73] Imagery of the copy of this catalogue at BL RB.23.b.2153 is in the database *Eighteenth Century Collections Online.*

[74] TNA E133/54/55, *Forster v Longman*, 1791.

[75] LMA, formerly Guildhall ms 11936/287 p 18, Sun Fire Office policy no. 432842, 12 September 1780.

[76] Charles Humphries and William C. Smith, *Music Publishing in the British Isles*, 2nd ed., Oxford, 1970, p 335. Her will shows that her business had multiple locations in 1843: 123 Cheapside, 17 St Martins le Grand, and no. 72 and no. 21 of the Pantheon on Oxford Street (TNA PROB 11/1994, p 97–98, court copy of the will of Lucy Williams, made 1 September 1843, proved 2 February 1844).

Robert Williamson, a music printer,[77] and James Freeman, a music engraver, gave evidence in court saying that they knew Longman and Broderip, but neither testified that he had worked for them.[78]

In the 1780s the King's Theatre in the Haymarket appears to have granted the benefit of publishing music performed there to its copyist Leopoldo di Micheli, who in turn sold this right to Longman & Broderip for about £40 per season.[79] This enabled the firm to publish music which would be bought by the theatre-going public who wished to keep up with the latest fashions. However, this was not as simple an arrangement as it might seem. The law of musical copyright was not well established at this time, and it was unclear whether copyright in a composition was owned by the composer, the performer or the copyist.[80] This led to trouble, as all three parties could sell rights in a composition to different persons, bringing composers and rival publishers into conflict with one another. For example, a case concerning ownership of copyright was brought by the composer Stephen Storace after Longman & Broderip published a song from his opera *Il Re Teodoro*. Here, the question of ownership was between Storace, his sister Nancy who sang the aria, and di Micheli, who sold it to Longman & Broderip. Stephen Storace won the case in July 1789 and was awarded an injunction against Longman & Broderip publishing the aria in question, a token 1/– compensation and legal costs.[81]

Perhaps the most significant occurrences during the Longman, Lukey & Co. years from the point of view of their long-term and wide-ranging impact are the court cases discussed in Chapter 6 that were brought against the firm by the composers John Christian Bach and Charles Frederick Abel in 1773. Joseph Haydn, through the

---

[77] TNA E113/82/27, *Longman v Blundell*, 1781.

[78] TNA E113/54/55, *Forster v Longman*, 1791.

[79] See Curtis Price, Judith Milhous and Robert D Hume, *Italian Opera in Late Eighteenth-Century London: Volume I: The King's Theatre, Haymarket*, Oxford, 1995, p 38, quoting 21 July 1789 testimony of Sir John Andrew Gallini, a trustee of the opera company, in TNA C107/201.

[80] A detailed survey of this subject is given in Chapter 6 below.

[81] Jane Girdham, *English Opera in Late Eighteenth-Century London: Stephen Storace at Drury Lane*, Oxford, 1997, p 89.

London music sellers William Forster & Son, also was involved in legal wrangling with Longman & Broderip. This case rested on the identification of the composer of two trios that Haydn had sent to William Forster I in 1784, which Longman & Broderip had separately acquired as compositions by Ignace Pleyel. Each publisher sued the other and it became vital to establish who the composer was.[82] A full discussion of this dispute has been published, and it appears that the parties eventually settled out of court.[83]

After buying the stock and music plates of the music seller Mary Hughes *otherwise* Welcker at auction after her death in 1778,[84] James Longman sued her executors, James Blundell, John Henry Moze and William Sherlock. Although Longman had been assured that all remaining copies in her stock of music were included in the sale, James Blundell had kept back over £500 worth of music which legally belonged to Longman.[85] Another court case was brought by Longman & Broderip against the music seller Samuel Babb in 1784.[86] The issue here was whether parts of a published work could be extracted and used in a lesson book or teaching aid without infringing the copyright of the original composer and publisher.[87]

Some injured parties decided to publicise a perceived infringement of copyright by advertising the matter in newspapers. An example inserted by Joseph Tacet reads as follows:

---

[82] Documentation of the *Forster v Longman* cases is found in TNA E133/54/54–55, E133/54/55, E127/49, E112/1746/4924 and E112/1724/4329.

[83] Nancy A. Mace, 'Haydn and the London music sellers: Forster v. Longman & Broderip', *Music and Letters* v 77 no. 4 (November 1996) p 527–541. For Longman & Broderip's dealings with other London publishers see Ian Woodfield, 'John Bland: London retailer of the music of Haydn and Mozart', *Music and Letters* v 81 no. 2 (2000) p 210–244.

[84] Mary Hughes cohabited with the music seller Peter Welcker, whom she succeeded after his death in 1775. She was known as 'Mrs Welcker', but they never married.

[85] TNA E113/82/27, *Longman v Blundell*, 1781.

[86] TNA E133/82/26, *Longman v Babb*, 1784.

[87] One witness, the musical instrument maker Peter Thompson II, a partner of the music sellers Samuel, Ann & Peter Thompson, testified that it was common and agreed practice that, after a work had been published over a year, extracts from it could be used as examples in such books. See page 374 below.

MUSIC

Mr Tacet begs leave to inform all lovers of honesty as well as music, that Mess. Longman and Lukey, music printers, in Cheapside, people entirely unknown to him, have taken the honest means of printing a book, as they are pleased to intitle, Thirty-six Preludes in different Keys, with Minuets, and Variations, &c. by Mr Tacet: Mr Tacet thinks it his duty to inform the public, that those worthy gentlemen Longman and Lukey never had his permission to pirate his works, which they have done in respect of the minuets and variations; and as to the Preludes, Mr Tacet declares he never saw them till after published, and thinks those miserable productions a disgrace to the Name of any Musician.

J. TACET.[88]

Longman, Lukey & Co. replied to this charge in an advertisement a few days later, denying that Tacet was the composer.[89]

Longman & Broderip also crossed swords with contemporaries regarding rights to innovations in musical instruments. This is exemplified in the case of Christian Clauss, a maker of English guittars,[90] who patented the addition of a small keyboard to that instruments in 1783, and termed the result a 'piano forte guittar'. In April 1784 he advertised that:[91]

so particularly excellent are the improvements, and so distinguished the honor and reward the Patentee has received that it is not wonderful to find the trade attempting to impose an imitation of the Patent Instrument upon the public, and even attempting, by public advertisement, to call in question the solemn decision of the High Court of Chancery, made upon an inspection and comparison of the genuine and spurious instruments, their separate properties, and an investigation of the facts adduced in

---

[88] *The Public Advertiser*, 31 January 1771, p 1.

[89] *The Public Advertiser*, 6 February 1771, p 1.

[90] The English guittar is a type of cittern, a wire-strung instrument usually plucked with the fingers, which was popular in England during the second half of the eighteenth century. See Robert Spencer and Ian Harwood, 'English guitar', in Stanley Sadie (ed.), *The New Grove Dictionary of Musical Instruments*, London, 1984, v 1 p 706–707. The spelling 'guittar' is adopted here as it was widely used at the time and distinguishes this instrument from the Spanish guitar.

[91] This patent subsequently was numbered 1394. See B[ennet] Woodcroft (ed.), *Patents for Inventions: Abridgments of specifications relating to music and musical instruments, 1694–1866*, 2nd ed., London, 1871, p 14.

> support of them. To prevent however any further controversy, and to place the question beyond all possibility of doubt, Mr Clauss takes the liberty to subjoin an extract from the order made by the Court on this occasion. It is as follows, viz. 'That the caveat asked by Charles Pinto and James Longman be withdrawn, and that the Patent of the said Christian Clauss do pass the Great Seal of Great Britain.'—After this the Patentee flatters himself the candour of a generous public will readily determine whose instrument most deserves their attention.[92]

It seems that Clauss's problems were not resolved by that advertisement. A year later he brought a legal challenge against Longman & Broderip for infringing his 1783 patent rights.[93] Unfortunately, the outcome of this case is not known. Clauss clearly was keen to establish his rights and seems to have tried other means to do so: in July 1786, he was bound over, together with Mr Brawns, a tailor, and Henry Walther, a bookbinder,[94] to keep the peace towards his partner or former partner Joseph Levy, a jeweller and goldsmith.[95] Clauss and Levy also argued (more properly) in the courts about their partnership and its termination.[96] However, Clauss may have been clutching at financial straws, as he was declared bankrupt in 1787.[97]

Charles Pinto, mentioned in the advertisement just quoted, is not recorded in modern literature about the music trade. He left no will and, as his heirs were (like himself) illegitimate, a probate inventory was made of his property in 1792, which provides a fascinating insight into the living conditions of someone who appears

---

[92] *The Morning Herald and Daily Advertiser*, 17 April 1784, p 3. This advertisement was repeated multiple times.

[93] TNA C217/134, *Clauss v Longman*, 1785.

[94] Walther, who succeeded his better-known relative John Ernst Baumgarten in 1782, also supplied 'a powder to kill and destroy the book-worm' (advertisement, *The Morning Post, and Daily Advertiser*, 3 August 1782, p 1).

[95] LMA Middlesex Sessions of the Peace, MJ/SP/1786/07/032. Clauss and Levy are described as 'patent musical instrument makers' in *Bailey's British Directory; or, Merchant's & Trader's Useful Companion*, London, 2nd ed., 1785, v 1 p 64 (copy at Guildhall).

[96] TNA C12/154/35, *Clauss v Levy*, 1786.

[97] *The London Gazette*, 31 July 1787, p 367.

to have been involved in dealing, making or repairing instruments.[98] Besides twenty harpsichords, four pianos, three harps, five organs, some sixty guitars, ninety bowed stringed instruments, seventy bows and 'a bell instrument', Pinto possessed a work bench, eleven stoves and many pieces of wood and metal (presumably for making or repairing instruments). One guitar listed is described as 'a patent guitar by Longman & Co.', suggesting that he might have worked for them. No connection is known between him and the musicians Thomas and George Frederick Pinto.[99]

In 1796 Longman & Broderip warned the public of infringements to their rights to use William Southwell's 1794 piano patent (subsequently numbered 2017):

> The Musical Dilettanti are particularly requested by LONGMAN and BRODERIP, to be cautious in respect to places where they may apply for the purchase of Mr SOUTHWELL's new invented Patent Piano Forte, with additional Keys, as those manufactured and sold by them at their respective houses, No. 26, Cheapside, No. 13, Haymarket, and No. 141, Tottenham Court Road, are universally allowed to be infinitely superior in point of tone, touch, and quality, to those which are attempted to be offered to the Public, under the idea of the same invention and improvements, yet differing widely in their actuating principles.[100]

In a busy marketplace, makers and dealers tried to gain advantage over their competitors by fair means or foul, with each party setting his own standard of ethical behaviour. Some chose to commence legal proceedings when they felt others had gone too far. However, as Southwell found, the law at this time did not have much strength to resolve what now are regarded as intellectual property disputes. Although Longman & Broderip were involved in numerous legal actions, their activities appear to have been within the bounds of commercial practice of the time.

---

[98] TNA PROB 31/821/151.

[99] I am grateful to Nicholas Temperley for help with this matter.

[100] *The True Briton*, 8 January 1796, p 4. Details of Southwell's difficulties in benefiting from this patent are given in George S. Bozarth and Margaret Debenham, 'Piano wars: the legal machinations of London pianoforte makers 1795–1806', *Royal Musical Association Research Chronicle* v 42 (2009) p 45–108.

1.7 Workers and Working Practices

Because Longman & Broderip's business records have not survived it is difficult to find information about their employees.[101] However, other documents reveal some names of people who supplied instruments to the firm or who contributed to its daily running in one way or another. The 1788 newspaper notice quoted on page 10 above said that Longman & Broderip gave 'employment to several hundred workmen of different denominations'. Although this phrase is imprecise it gives an order of magnitude of the size of the workforce.

To obtain musical instruments for their customers Longman & Broderip appear to have had four types of business relationship with workers. Some people were directly employed by the firm and worked in their premises. A number of external contractors made instruments exclusively for the firm which bore the firm's label. Other instruments were bought in and resold under the original makers' names. A 'putting-out' system also was used, in which all the necessary materials were given to external makers who constructed instruments in their own premises for an agreed fee. Such diversity of approach was common during the latter years of the eighteenth century. This was a time of both continuity and change in industrial production, and it is not surprising that some traditional methods were in use while more modern procedures were being adopted.

In conformity with the sales practices of merchants of their time, Longman & Broderip used a credit system in which proprietors of other music shops could pay at a later date,[102] and dealers in

---

[101] Some of these records may have been destroyed in one or another fire that affected the firm's successors. An 1807 fire at one of the premises of Clementi & Co., described in Chapter 3, burnt some of their property. The brothers Frederick William Collard and William Frederick Collard, who took over after Clementi retired, suffered a major fire in 1851 when their newly completed factory burnt to the ground. They were able to rebuild and were bought out by Chappell's in 1929. They were lessees of Queen's Hall when it was destroyed by enemy action in 1941, and a fire in 1964 ruined their premises in New Bond Street. (See the obituary of Louis Dreyfus, head of Chappell & Co., in *The Times*, 5 May 1967, p 12.) As noted in Chapter 2, the premises of Wilkinson & Wornum, a successor of Broderip & Wilkinson, were destroyed by fire in 1812.

[102] As evidenced in the 1783 legal case *Wynne v Longman* (Parliamentary Archives, Main Papers, HL/PO/JO/10/2/58).

musical instruments were allowed to take instruments on a 'sale or return' basis.[103] Cash was accepted, which in the Haymarket branch that the firm opened in 1782 was kept in a money drawer and a till which contained a bowl for coins. The till was kept locked and only Broderip, Joseph Serle (a young shopman) and one other person had keys.[104]

The Spectacle Makers' Company records show that James Longman took on twelve apprentices between 1770 and 1789, namely:

- John Crowther (son of Ralph, St James Westminster, Middlesex) 9/7/1770
- John Barrow (son of John, St James Clerkenwell, Middlesex, waiter) 29/10/1771
- Joseph Longman (son of George, Milborne Port, Somerset, farmer) 10/9/1785
- George Read (son of John of Putney, Surrey, gardener) 3/4/1786
- George Smith (son of George, St Swithin, London, hairdresser) 15/8/1786
- Charles Lukey (son of Charles, Cheapside, London, musician) 3/10/1786
- William Naughan (son of Philip, St Luke, Middlesex, soap-maker) 9/5/1787
- George Garrett (son of Robert, Panton Street, Haymarket, stationer) 23/10/1787
- George Gough (son of George) 28/6/1788
- John Allan (son of John, Castle Street, Oxford Market, Middlesex, musical instrument maker) 31/7/1789
- Elizabeth Gough (d[aughter of] …, Little Red Lion Court, Charterhouse Lane) 5/8/1789
- James Edwards (son of Lloyd Pittell, Abergavenny, Monmouthsire, bookbinder) 16/9/1789[105]

It is interesting that the first two apprentices were bound early in the firm's existence while the others were taken on between 1785 and 1789, the last three at monthly intervals in 1789. The reasons for this temporal distribution are not known. It is conceivable that the firm

---

[103] Trial of John Bates, 6 April 1796, OB t17960406-85. David Davis, superintendent of Longman & Broderip, and Thomas Young, a former employee, testified in this trial that the firm had operated on a 'sale or return' basis, but not since bankruptcy proceedings began in 1795.

[104] Trial of James Jones *otherwise* Sandy, 27 February 1788, OB t17880227-1, testimony of Broderip and Serle.

[105] These records are transcribed in Cliff Webb, *London Livery Company Apprenticeship Registers* v 14: *Spectaclemakers' Company 1666–1800…*, London, 1998.

had grown so large by the mid-1780s that many basic chores needed to be done. The idea that Longman needed the fees that apprentices often brought as lump sums from their parents or guardians is contradicted by the circumstance that none of his apprentices came with a 'consideration'. By training apprentices he enabled members of the next generation to climb onto the first rung of the music trade in the expanding London market.

Charles Lukey Jr was the son of Longman's former partner, whose premature death had left his wife and children vulnerable. Joseph Longman of Milborne Port (close to Corton Denham) probably was a son of James's brother George. He is recorded as having two sons called Joseph, the first passing away at the age of four. The second Joseph was born in 1768, so would have been in 1785 a relatively old apprentice at seventeen years.[106]

The inclusion of a female apprentice, Elizabeth Gough, is unusual but not unheard of. Women did undertake formal apprenticeships but these were usually in the 'female trades' such as millinery and dressmaking. Elizabeth is not listed as being made free of the Spectacle Makers' Company, so it is not known what her work was within the firm, although it could have included minding the shop, keeping accounts, or lighter aspects of instrument making such as string making or the silking of pianos. Only two of the apprentices' fathers were recorded as having music-related occupations,[107] showing that Longman was of high enough standing for people not otherwise involved in instrument making to want to send their children to him to learn a trade.

The records of the Spectacle Makers' Company also show that Broderip took on two apprentices: William Moore, son of Stephen Moore, tailor of Panton Street, on 12 March 1787, and George Wilkinson, son of Charles Wilkinson Sr of Islington, on 4 November 1797.[108] The latter relationship, discussed in the next chapter, grew in

---

[106] Dennis Longman notes (described in note 7 above).

[107] Although Lloyd Pittell Edwards was listed as a bookbinder he was also a schoolmaster and an organist. See the article by Raymond B. Davies on Edwards' son, the artist Sydenham Teast Edwards, in the *Oxford Dictionary of National Biography*.

[108] Cliff Webb, *op. cit.*

significance. The former entry may have been incorrectly recorded, because a pamphlet published in Aberdeen in 1800 establishes that Broderip had an apprentice named Stephen Moore.[109]

Despite claims he apparently made that his apprenticeship lasted for a full term, Stephen Moore served Broderip for only three years and 'was not employed during that time in the manufactory of musical instruments, or organ work'.[110] Moore later made at least one piano in London, as a square piano with a nameboard inscribed 'Stephen Moore and Co., Panton Square, Haymarket, Patent, London 1796' was sold in 1982,[111] but he had to leave London by 1798. In a letter written *c*1799, the Longman & Broderip employee Frederick Augustus Hyde recalled that:

> Mr Moore lived at the Hay Market with Messrs Longman and Broderip, but never to my recollection received any lessons from Mr Clementi, who is now by my side, and does not even remember him by name. Mr Moore's unfortunate situation in life obliged him, I believe, to leave this country, since which he has been in Edinburgh; and Mr Watlen can inform you of every particular respecting him.[112]

Moore and the music seller John Watlen had become partners so that Moore could make pianos in Edinburgh, 'but none he ever made was good, of course he broke deep in debt, which he will never be able to pay'.[113] Their partnership lasted only for six months and led to litigation between them.[114] Moore then tuned and repaired pianos and

---

[109] [Alexander Anderson], *A Detail of the Facts, respecting the late attempt, made by Mr Stephen Moore, to tune and repair the organ of St Paul's Chapel, Aberdeen*, Aberdeen, [1800].

[110] Francis Fane Broderip→unnamed recipient in Dundee, 28 July 1799, quoted in *ibid.*, p 7.

[111] *Important Musical Instruments*, Sotheby's, London, 7 April 1982, lot 88, p 26–27.

[112] Frederick Augustus Hyde→unnamed recipient, *c*1799, quoted in [Anderson], *A Detail of the Facts…*, *op. cit.*, p 7. Hyde's career is described below and in Chapter 3.

[113] John Hamilton [music seller in Edinburgh]→unnamed recipient, 4 September 1799, quoted in *ibid.*, p 8.

[114] *ibid.*, p 9–10; *Moore v Watlen*, 1799.

organs in Scotland, to general dissatisfaction.[115] He returned to London, spent time in the Fleet Prison for debt,[116] and died in 1803.[117]

One of the best known suppliers of harpsichords and pianos to Longman & Broderip was Thomas Culliford.[118] Another west-country man, he was born in Penzance, Cornwall in 1747. The earliest surviving Longman & Broderip instrument which bears his name is dated 1779.[119] In July 1789 John Marsh referred to him as 'foreman to Longman & Broderip'.[120] Culliford used a range of premises, including the workshops in Fountain Court behind 26 Cheapside, for which he paid an annual rent of some £70.[121] On 29 September 1784 he entered into a fourteen-year partnership with William Rolfe, John Goldsworth and Thomas Bradford, and on 2 January 1786 they signed a contract with Longman & Broderip, agreeing not to sell instruments to other customers nor to tune instruments unless under Longman & Broderip's name, and to supply Longman & Broderip with £5,000 worth of instruments per year.[122] By 1789, the partners had changed—the firm was now run by Thomas Culliford, William Rolfe and Charles Barrow—but the contract remained in force.[123] In order for these partners to supply what was probably hundreds of

---

[115] As detailed in [Anderson], *op. cit.*

[116] *The London Gazette*, 4 July 1801, p 765; 7 July 1801, p 795; 14 July 1801, p 867.

[117] Court copy of will of Stephen Moore, 'piano maker in Upper James Street, Golden Square', made 20 December 1802, proved 27 October 1803, TNA PROB 11/1400. I am grateful to Michael Kassler for information about Moore.

[118] For a detailed analysis of his life and work see Jenny Nex, 'Culliford and Company: keyboard instrument makers in Georgian London', *Early Keyboard Journal* v 22 (2004) p 7–48.

[119] Donald H. Boalch, *Makers of the Harpsichord and Clavichord 1440–1840*, 3rd ed. by Charles Mould, Oxford, 1995, p 483–490.

[120] Brian Robins (ed.), *The John Marsh Journals*, *op. cit.*, p 457.

[121] TNA E112/1771/5631, *Longman v Culliford*, 1795. I am very grateful to Margaret Debenham for her assistance in untangling the complexities of this legal case.

[122] *ibid.*

[123] *ibid.*

instruments every year, Culliford & Co. would have needed a considerable workforce who though employed by that company worked indirectly for Longman & Broderip. Although we do not have a list of all of Culliford & Co.'s employees, the internal parts of some of their instruments bear the names of workmen who presumably were responsible for a whole instrument or made the part on which their name rests.

J. Hanson's signature appears in the keywell of a harpsichord dated 1783.[124] The names 'Cairns' and 'Glen' are on the keyboard of a harpsichord sold as lot 14 by Christie's on 13 November 2002. Cairns's signature is found on the keyboards of instruments by both Broadwood and Houston, suggesting that Cairns specialised in making keyboards and either moved from one firm to another or sold his keyboards to multiple customers.[125] The names 'Mcfarlane' and 'Kaisor' are on the back of one nameboard,[126] while 'Glen', 'Grey' and 'J Spiessegger Jr' (apparently a mistake for 'J. Speissegger Jr') are on keys of a harpsichord dated 1787 now at the Horniman Museum in London.[127] Within three years Speissegger Jr had gone home to Charleston, South Carolina, where he set up on his own.[128] In a 1790 advertisement 'John Speisseger, jun.' said that he was 'late from Messrs Longman & Broderip's, London' and that, as well as having for sale a 'variety of instruments and every other article in the musical line', he had 'an excellent harpsichord, with a celestiniel stop, made by Longman and Broderip' and 'a neat assortment of hosiery, haberdashery, and various other articles' available for sale.[129]

---

[124] Boalch, *op. cit.*, p 485. This instrument is now in private ownership in Maidenhead, Berkshire.

[125] My thanks to John Watson of Colonial Williamsburg for this information.

[126] Boalch, *op. cit.*, p 489. It is now in private ownership in the United States.

[127] I thank Mimi Waitzman for providing imagery of Speissegger's signature.

[128] His father John Speissegger Sr, who died in 1793, was an organ builder in Charleston from the 1760s to the 1780s and belonged to a family of organ builders. John Snetzler, well known for the organs he built in England, was a cousin of another member of this family, Johann Conrad Speissegger, and served his apprenticeship with him in Schaffhausen, Switzerland.

[129] *The City Gazette and Daily Advertiser*, Charleston, 1 March 1790, p 2. I am grateful to Michael Kassler for bringing this advertisement to my attention.

Thomas Pringle's name appears on the action of a Longman & Broderip square piano made about 1785.[130] Thomas Young, who described himself as a 'harpsichord and piano-forte maker', testified in 1796 that he 'was formerly in the employ of Messrs Longman and Broderip'.[131]

In addition to these workers, whose status with Culliford & Co. is not clear, that partnership employed a foreman named James Stevenson (who was a carpenter) and a porter named John Griffiths.[132] They also took on apprentices. Culliford was master to Charles May from 1779,[133] Samuel Davies from 1784 and Samuel's brother Joseph from 1788.[134] William Rolfe took on John Hunter in 1787[135] as well as his own four sons Robert, Nicholas, Thomas Hall, and James Longman Rolfe over subsequent years.[136] Besides these individuals who probably were directly involved in manufacturing, Culliford had a 'servant' named Samuel Allen who had come over from America,[137] and may have been the Samuel Allen who later testified that he had worked for 'Ellison and Oakley' in Fountain Court in 1796 who 'make instruments for Longman & Broderip'.[138] His reference presumably was to Thomas Allison and John Oakey, named in a 1795 legal case as 'two of the principal finishers and workmen' employed by Culliford & Co.[139] Even from this small

---

[130] *ibid.*, p 222.

[131] Trial of John Bates, 6 April 1796, OB t17960406-85.

[132] Trial of John Griffiths, 14 January 1789, OB t17890114-7. I thank Lance Whitehead for bringing this source to my attention.

[133] TNA IR 1/30 (Board of Stamps, Apprenticeship Books 9/1778–1/1781).

[134] Glovers' Company records, Guildhall ms 4591/3–4. For further details of the Davies brothers see Jenny Nex, 'Culliford and Company…', *op. cit.*, p 21.

[135] TNA IR 1/33 (Board of Stamps, Apprenticeship Books 2/1786–8/1788).

[136] TNA PROB 10/5138 (will of William Rolfe, proved 22 January 1830, names his sons) and Cliff Webb, *London Livery Company Apprenticeship Registers* v 4: *The Glovers' Company 1675–1804*, London, 1996, p 17.

[137] Trial of William Martin and Benjamin Williams, 12 December 1787, OB t17871212-21.

[138] Trial of Richard Geast, 6 April 1796, OB t17960406-83.

[139] TNA E112/1771/5631, *Longman v Culliford*, 1795.

sample it appears that an entire structure of workers carried out the daily business of that company. During the time of their exclusive contract with Longman & Broderip these workers could be regarded as part of the latter's empire.

Further information about people directly employed by Longman & Broderip can be gleaned from various historical documents. A number of persons, when setting up on their own or promoting their services, stated that they had previously worked for the firm. Their advertisements show that this connection was positive and indicate the firm's status. Examples include George Grant Mann, a harpsichord and violin teacher who opened a shop in Loll Bazaar, Calcutta in 1786, and advertised that he had 'just arrived from Messrs Longman and Broderip's at their music warehouses No. 26 Cheapside, and No. 13 Haymarket London', where he had 'presided over' the 'repair and hire of all kinds of musical instruments'.[140] With his partner Mr Russell, Mann offered a music-selling and tuning service, a combination he would have been familiar with from his previous employers. William Phillips advertised in 1793 that he was 'from Longman & Broderip' but was now based at 3 Manor Row, Little Tower Hill, where he worked as a music seller and offered a tuning and repair service.[141] Humphries and Smith report that P[eter] Evans, a music seller at 102 High Holborn in the 1770s and 80s, had previously worked for Longman, Lukey and Co., but give no reference to support this claim.[142]

Some singers augmented the income they earned as performers by working for Longman & Broderip during the day. They include James Cooke, a 'new singer at Drury Lane' in 1791, who soon after his début there was described as 'an articled clerk to Messrs Longman

---

[140] *The Calcutta Gazette; or, Oriental Advertiser*, 27 July 1786, p 3. He arrived at Calcutta in 1785 (*The East India Kalendar; or, Asiatic Register ... for the year 1791*, London, 1791, p 73) and was listed as a musician in Cawnpore (now Kanpur, Uttar Pradesh) in John Mathison and Alexander Way Mason (eds), *An East-India Register and Directory for 1803*, London, [1802], p 122. His 'only relative' advertised in *The Morning Post*, London, 4 January 1804, p 1, for information about him.

[141] *The Times*, 28 December 1793, p 1.

[142] Humphries and Smith, *Music Publishing in the British Isles*, *op. cit.*, p 142.

and Broderip'.[143] A 1796 publication contains the interesting assertion that Cooke had 'procured an engagement at Drury-lane, as chorus singer, by the interest of Messrs Longman and Broderip, musical instrument makers, by whom he was employed, to introduce their songs [i.e., songs that they published] into choral societies'.[144] Joseph Ward, a tenor whose address given in a 1794 directory was Longman & Broderip's Tottenham Court Road premises, may have had similar duties.[145]

Two men are known to have worked for the firm as tuners: Richard Geast[146] and Henry Banks, the latter a son of the Salisbury-based violin maker Benjamin Banks who provided the firm with instruments.[147] Other employees known to have had specific jobs include Thomas Baskerville, a porter and packer,[148] and David Davis,[149] who testified in 1796 that he was superintendent of the firm's works and had lived there 'near ten years'.[150] Whether his role was solely managerial or included organ-making is not clear. Some individuals had less formal relationships with the firm. John Bates, identified in a trial as a musician, appears to have dealt in instruments from Longman & Broderip on a 'sale or return' basis until the relationship went sour in the late 1790s.[151] The music seller George

---

143 *The Times*, 6 January 1791, p 2.

144 J[ohn] Roach, *Roach's Authentic Memoirs of the Green Room...*, London, 1796, p 18.

145 J[oseph] Doane, *A Musical Directory for the Year 1794*, London, *c*1794 (reprinted London, 1993), p 67.

146 Trial of Richard Geast, 6 April 1796, OB t17960406-83, testimony of the music seller William Phillips.

147 See John Milnes, *The British Violin*, Oxford, 2000, p 49.

148 Trial of John Bates, 6 April 1796, OB t17960406-85.

149 Two pairs of brothers with similar surnames—James and David Davis, and Samuel and Joseph Davies—made keyboard instruments at this time. Although their surnames have been spelt inconsistently with and without an 'e', to avoid confusion each name is spelt here as in the last sentence, the most common spellings. No link between the two pairs has been established.

150 Trial of Richard Geast, *op. cit.*

151 Trial of John Bates, *op. cit.*, evidence of David Davis.

Wynne, who seems to have worked in Cambridge in the 1780s,[152] had goods from the firm on credit and was sued for unpaid debts of £170.[153]

Several others who made musical instruments for the firm are known but many more remain unknown. In some cases the position of a person identified as a musical instrument maker, such as William Wallis, is unclear: he is known only from a 1791 Sun Fire Office policy in which he insured his utensils in Longman's Fountain Court workshop for £10.[154]

Allison and Oakey have been mentioned as 'principal finishers' for Culliford & Co. Thomas Allison was a musical instrument maker based in Haberdashers Walk, Shoreditch. His will, proved in 1813,[155] mentions no family beyond his wife Ann, but a younger Thomas Allison of the piano makers Allison & Allison in Soho perhaps was a relative. 'Oakey' was the name of another piano-making family active in London at this time. Although John, the first known member, called himself a 'gentleman' in his own will,[156] that of his widow Elizabeth describes him as a musical instrument maker 'late of Cheapside London and Pentonville, Middlesex',[157] which ties him nicely to the Longman firm and the legal case mentioned above. In addition, when John Oakey sold off his furniture, stock in trade and lease of his premises in London, he stated that he was 'from Clementi's', so his association with one of the firm's successors continued beyond the turn of the century.[158]

---

[152] See advertisements in the *Whitehall Evening Post*, 30 May 1782, p 1, and *The World*, 14 January 1788, p 1.

[153] As recorded in Wynne's appeal *Wynne v Longman*, cited in note 102 above.

[154] LMA, formerly Guildhall ms 11936/376 p 67, policy number 581644, total value £300. See Lance Whitehead and Jenny Nex, 'Keyboard instrument building in London and the Sun Insurance records, 1775–87', *Early Music* v 30 no. 1 (2002) p 4–25 at p 13.

[155] Court copy at TNA PROB 11/1546. The will was signed on 24/10/1812 and proved on 9/7/1813.

[156] Court copy at TNA PROB 11/1791A, made 4/7/1829, proved 12/10/1831.

[157] Court copy at TNA PROB 11/2059, signed 18/8/1841, proved 5/7/1847.

[158] *The Times*, 30 June 1829, p 4.

Longman & Broderip had links with some of the period's foremost piano designers and makers and appear to have sold more pianos than any other instrument. John Geib came to London from near Saarbrücken, where his family were organ builders. He received two English patents in 1786 and 1792 and left London in 1797 to settle in New York.[159] Evidence that Geib worked for Longman & Broderip in 1785 is found in the records of a trial concerning the theft of green silk. He testified that 'I use green silk in my business, in the inside of my instruments, for my piano fortes'. When asked 'Do you keep an open shop?', he replied 'No, I work for Mr Longman & Co., Cheapside'. Furthermore, he acknowledged that Longman & Broderip supplied him with the silk in question, as they 'furnish[ed him] with materials for making instruments' and that he was 'paid only for the workmanship'—an example of the 'putting out' way of working mentioned on page 32 above.[160] Although this practice can be efficient it caused problems when workers used their masters' assets unscrupulously, and for this reason tended to be used less as the eighteenth century drew to a close.[161]

Geib's 1786 patent probably was granted when he was working for Longman & Broderip. It concerns 'improvements' to pianos and harpsichords 'by which the same can be more easily tuned and played upon'.[162] He subsequently advertised that he was 'the inventor of the first patent piano fortes in England, for which a patent was obtained by him though the instruments were sold in the name of Longman and Broderip'.[163]

---

[159] For his biography see Margaret Cranmer, Barbara Owen, W. Thomas Marrocco and Mark Jacobs, 'Geib, John', in Stanley Sadie (ed.), *The New Grove Dictionary of Musical Instruments*, London, 1984, v 2, p 31–32.

[160] Trial of Edward Johnson, 11 May 1785, OB t17850511-14.

[161] J[ames] A[nthony] Sharpe, *Early Modern England: A social history 1550–1760*, London, 1987, p 144. Further information about Geib's London years is given in Thomas Strange and Jenny Nex, 'John Geib: beyond the footnote', *Eighteenth-Century Music* v 7 no. 1 (2010) p 81–103.

[162] See B[ennet] Woodcroft, *op. cit.* in note 91 above, p 18–19. Geib's patent subsequently was numbered 1571.

[163] *The Evening Post*, New York, 7 June 1805, p 2. I am grateful to Michael Kassler for this reference.

Longman & Broderip signed an agreement with William Southwell on 29 October 1794 to use his recent English patent in their pianos, for which they agreed to pay an initial sum of £100 plus 10/6 for every instrument in which these inventions were incorporated.[164] Southwell's inventions claimed to improve piano mechanisms so that the tones 'are rendered more distinct and perfect, and the players playing on such instruments have a power to produce the gradation of tones from piano to forte with greater effect than they were able'. His inventions also provided 'an additional number' of treble keys and 'a new mode of using the dampers'.[165] *Figure 1.2* on page 44 reproduces Longman & Broderip's *c*1795 print promoting this 'new invented patent piano-forte'. As shown in *Figure 1.3* on page 45, Broderip & Wilkinson later reissued this print (after altering its engraving) when they sold pianos incorporating Southwell's 1794 patent.[166]

Unlike Southwell, the piano maker Christopher Ganer worked directly for Longman & Broderip. Between 1778 and 1783 regular payments from 'Longman & Co.' totalling £1,680/3/– were credited to Ganer's account with the bankers Drummond & Co.[167] As he had his own warehouse and workshop adjacent to his dwelling at 47 Broad Street,[168] he may have made pianos that were sold on to

---

[164] TNA C13/29/34, *Longman v Clementi*, 1803. The patent was granted on 18 October 1794.

[165] B[ennet] Woodcroft, *op. cit.*, p 28–29.

[166] The upper portion of the drawing in *Figure 1.2* was copied from the figure enrolled with Southwell's patent specification. As will be seen, Broderip & Wilkinson reused the same engraved plate after altering it to substitute their name and address for that of Longman & Broderip; they also filled in the leftmost F♯ black key in the drawing that was left unfilled both in Southwell's specification and in the Longman & Broderip drawing. The illustration in *Figure 1.2* lacks the text line at the bottom of *Figure 1.3* and seems likely to have been trimmed.

[167] Archives of the Royal Bank of Scotland plc, Drummonds Bank customer account ledgers. In 1778 Ganer received £290, in 1779 £410, in 1780 £369, in 1781 £211/3, in 1782 £200 and in 1783 £200 from Longman & Broderip.

[168] According to Sun Fire Office insurance policies issued between October 1780 and 1783 (in LMA, formerly Guildhall ms 11936; an endorsement is in LMA, formerly Guildhall ms 12160).

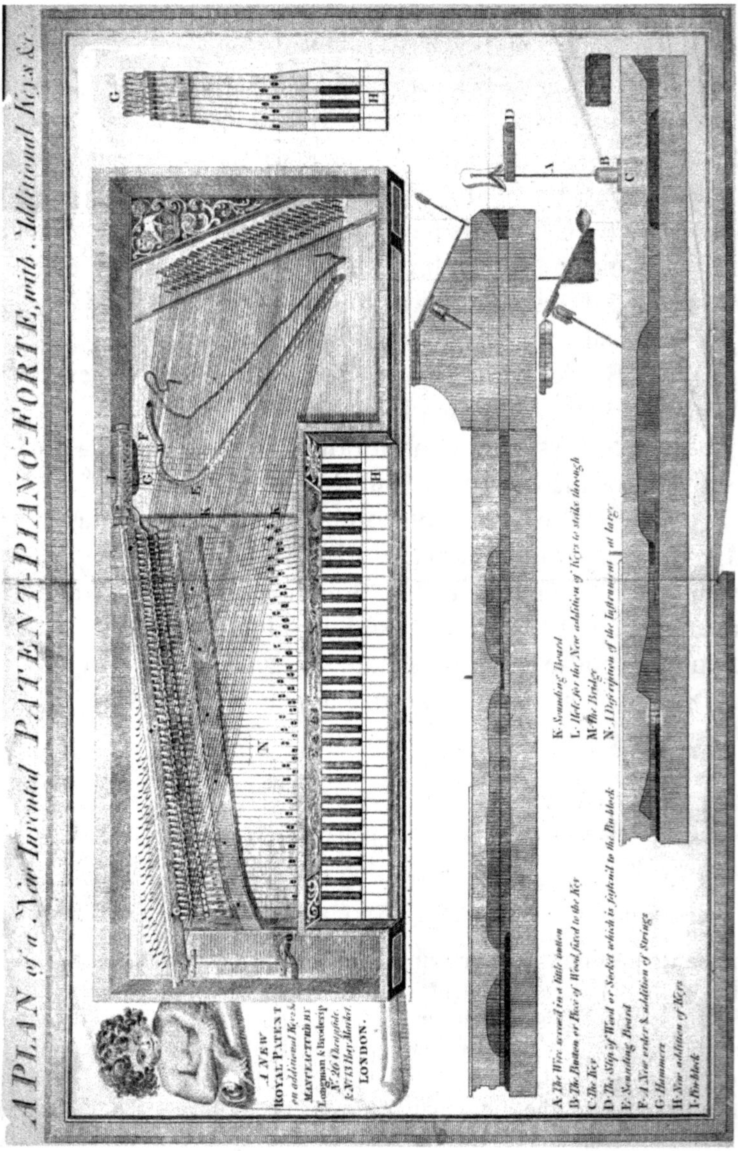

Figure 1.2 Plan of a Longman & Broderip piano forte incorporating inventions patented by William Southwell (by permission of the Bodleian Library, University of Oxford, John Johnson Collection, in Musical Instruments 1)

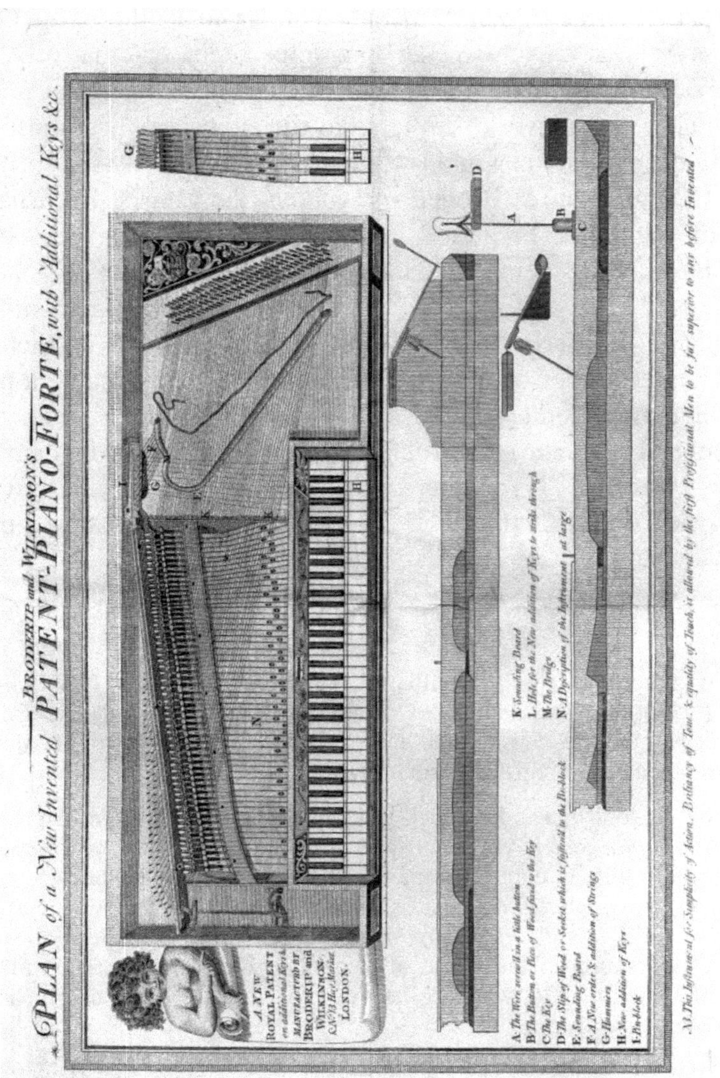

Figure 1.3 Plan of a Broderip & Wilkinson piano forte incorporating the same Southwell inventions (British Museum Department of Prints and Drawings D,2.2617, Trade cards Banks 88.8, © Trustees of the British Museum)

Longman & Broderip in a manner similar to Culliford & Co., or perhaps he was an out-worker like John Geib. Alternatively, since Ganer described himself in one of his insurance policies as a 'piano forte maker and inlayer', he might have been a specialist whose focus was the decorative inlay on instruments.[169]

Of Longman & Broderip's workers the longest-lived name is that of Collard. Frederick William Collard was baptised in Wiveliscombe, Somerset on 21 June 1772,[170] and came to London in November 1791, where he 'entered into an engagement' with Longman & Broderip 'as an assistant' and 'remained with them until that firm became insolvent' in 1795.[171] In 1798 he became a partner in Longman, Clementi & Co., investing £2,000,[172] and on 30 November 1799 he married Mary Lukey, daughter of Longman's first partner Charles.[173] Together with his younger brother William Frederick Collard (baptised 25 August 1776), who became a partner

---

[169] Sun Fire Office policy 463403 dated 8 August 1782, LMA, formerly Guildhall ms 11936/303 p 561–562.

[170] He was the ninth child of William Collard and Thamosin (Thomasine) née Tutley (or Lutley). Data about the Collard family have been collected from IGI, SRO, census returns (TNA) and David Cheek's transcript of St Andrew's, Wiveliscombe parish registers (http://www.pbenyon1.plus.com).

[171] According to 'The late Frederick William Collard', letter from 'Alpha' to the editor of *The Musical World*, published in v 38 no. 17 of that periodical on 28 April 1860, p 265. G[eorge] C[lement] Boase's article on Collard in the 1887 *Dictionary of National Biography*, substantially reprinted in the recent *Oxford Dictionary of National Biography*, states that Collard 'at the age of fourteen, obtained a situation in the house of Longman, Lukey, and Broderip', but as Lukey had died in 1776, when Collard was four, Boase's account is inaccurate in at least this one detail.

[172] See the 24 January 1811 balance sheet of Clementi & Co. partnership accounts transcribed in *CMC* p 423–425 at p 424.

[173] Willoughby A. Littledale (ed.), *The Registers of St Vedast Foster Lane and of St Michael le Quern*, Harleian Society registers no. 30, London, 1903, p 94. Ely Dyson, a witness to the marriage, was one of the executors of Charles Lukey's will. Clementi seems to have appreciated Mary's virtues, since he wrote to Frederick William Collard on 4 August 1804, 'Now I must beg a favour of you, my dear Collard, to choose for me—not a wife, no, that I'd rather do myself, though your good luck in your own case would make any man's mouth water'. (Clementi→Frederick William Collard, 4 August 1804, transcribed in *CMC* p 120–122 at p 122).

of Clementi & Co. in 1810, Frederick William played a major role in developing that company. After Clementi's retirement in 1831 the company was restyled 'Collard & Collard'.[174]

Longman & Broderip also built and sold organs. A typical advertisement offered 'portable finger and barrel organs, harpsichords, ditto organised, upright harpsichords with a curious new invented swell, and warranted to stand in tune; piano fortes, ditto organised'.[175] A finger organ, in contrast to a barrel organ, was actuated by a player's fingers; an 'organised' harpsichord or piano combined a harpsichord or piano with an organ. Although few of the latter survive, they were not uncommon.[176] Extant barrel organs include examples by both Longman, Lukey & Co.[177] and Longman & Broderip.[178] In addition to organs for domestic or concert use, Longman & Broderip made church organs. 'A fine new organ, erected by Messrs Longman and Broderip, was opened by Doctor [Benjamin] Cooke' at St George's Church, Old Fish-street on New Year's Day 1786,[179] and an advertisement in the following year said that 'at their manufactory in Tottenham Court-road, they have ready

---

174 From 1834 Collard & Collard concentrated upon making pianos and other musical instruments. The business subsequently was carried on by two sons, Charles Lukey Collard and William Frederick Collard Jr, of Frederick William's sister Phoebe and her husband, a tailor also named William Collard who probably was Frederick William Collard's cousin. The story of the Collard family's involvement in piano making is fascinating but outside the scope of this book.

175 *The Daily Universal Register*, 4 May 1786, p 1.

176 A square Longman & Broderip organised piano is preserved in the Nydahl Collection, Stockholm, instrument no. IKL012. A similar 'claviorganum' made by Joseph Merlin is in the Colt Clavier Collection, Bethersden, Kent and is described in Frances Palmer, 'Merlin and music', in the exhibition catalogue *John Joseph Merlin, The Ingenious Mechanick*, London, 1985, p 85–110 at p 105–106.

177 RCM Museum of Instruments, Freddy Hill collection, no. RCM 808. Three barrels for this organ survive.

178 Victoria and Albert Museum, London, no. 2155 and A-1899. See Raymond Russell, *Catalogue of Musical Instruments [in the] Victoria and Albert Museum*, London, 1968, v 1 p 70.

179 *The Daily Universal Register*, 3 January 1786, p 2.

for inspection, a capital large finger organ, built by them for the new church at Barbadoes'.[180]

A number of organ builders had ties with the firm. Henry Holland, 'nephew and successor to Mr [George] Pyke, organ builder to His Majesty',[181] had his own business as a musical instrument maker from at least 1779 until his bankruptcy in 1793.[182] He resumed working after then, as he testified in 1796 that 'I am an organ-builder; in the month of February last, I was employed in the organ line for the assignees of Longman and Broderip'.[183] For this work he used one of the warehouses behind their Cheapside premises, no. 8 in Fountain Court.[184] Christopher Hayman, an organ builder based at 8 Eagle Court off the Strand, worked for the firm and insured his utensils and other goods in the Fountain Court premises for £200 in 1782.[185] Another organ builder, William Gater, had been with the firm for sixteen years when he was indicted in 1796 for theft of a piano forte.[186]

A small organ by John Kelly dated 1790, preserved at the Bowes Museum, Barnard Castle, Co. Durham, bears the Longman & Broderip name. Kelly is better known as a partner of Benjamin Flight, and the terms of the relationship between Kelly and Longman & Broderip are unclear. The brothers David and James Davis, originally

---

[180] *The Daily Universal Register*, 3 November 1787, p 1. See also Gerald Hudson, 'Longman & Broderip: a Barbados organ', letter to the editor, *The Musical Times* v 77 no. 1124 (October 1936) p 928.

[181] Advertisement, *The Daily Universal Register*, 26 November 1785, p 1. See also Donovan Dawe, 'The mysterious Pyke, organ builder', *The Musical Times* v 115 no. 1571 (January 1974) p 68–70.

[182] Sun Fire Office policy 418688, LMA, formerly Guildhall ms 11936/277 p 531, dated 25 September 1779; *The London Gazette*, 29 October 1793, p 969.

[183] Trial of William Gater, 6 April 1796, OB t17960406-84.

[184] See Joan Jeffery, 'Organ-builder history from fire insurance policies', *BIOS Journal* v 26 (2002) p 76–135 at p 126. Holland's troubles were ongoing and he was admitted in 1800 to the Fleet Prison where he remained for five months, being released on 15 July, a pauper (TNA PRIS 1/18, 10/92 and 3/7).

[185] Sun Fire Office policy 458600, LMA, formerly Guildhall ms 11936/301 p 377, dated 27 April 1782.

[186] Trial of William Gater, *op. cit.*, testimony of David Davis.

from Lancashire, worked as organ builders for Longman & Broderip, and in 1798 David Davis became a partner of Longman, Clementi & Co.[187] He reputedly bequeathed £12,000 to his brother James, who then retired.[188] James Davis is best known for his organ erected in Wymondham Abbey, Norfolk in 1793. His letter concerning this instrument to John Clarke Stoughton, churchwarden of the Abbey, is reproduced in *Figure 1.4* on page 50.[189] The Abbey accounts record that James was paid 'for his masters Longman & Broderip', affirming that he was their employee then and not an independent organ builder.[190]

Several makers of violins, violas or cellos had connections with Longman & Broderip. They include John Carter, whose work was sold through 'Duke, Merlin, Betts and Longman & Broderip',[191] and David Furber, whose instruments rarely display his name, although an example with both his label inside and the brand of Longman & Co. survives.[192] All these makers seem to have built instruments at their own premises for subsequent sale by the firm. In most cases the firm's stamp appears on the instrument, occasionally accompanied by the stamp or label of the original maker.

---

[187] Reports in some secondary sources that David Davis was a partner of Longman & Broderip have not been substantiated.

[188] See Michael I. Wilson, *The Chamber Organ in Britain, 1600–1830*, Aldershot, 2001, p 183; David C. Wickens, 'Renn re-visited: an appreciation of "Samuel Renn—English organ builder", with reference to some recent findings', *BIOS Journal* v 32 (2008) p 163–178; and Michael Sayer, 'James Davis and the Lancashire organ builders', *The Musical Times* v 111 no. 1528 (June 1970) p 645–649. Renn was James Davis's foreman and nephew.

[189] Stoughton recorded in his memorandum book that the organ 'came down' on 24 July 1793. See Paul Cattermole (ed.), *Wymondham Abbey: A history of the monastery and parish church*, Wymondham, 2007, p 244. I am grateful to Paula Lucas, Honorary Archivist of Wymondham Abbey, for this reference.

[190] Paul Tindall, 'Research notes', *BIOS Reporter* v 26 no. 1 (January 2002) p 33–34, referring to Maxwell Betts, *A Jewel or Ornament*, 2nd ed., East Harling, Norfolk, 1997, p 10.

[191] John Milnes (ed.), *The British Violin*, Oxford, 2000, p 44.

[192] *ibid.*, p 53.

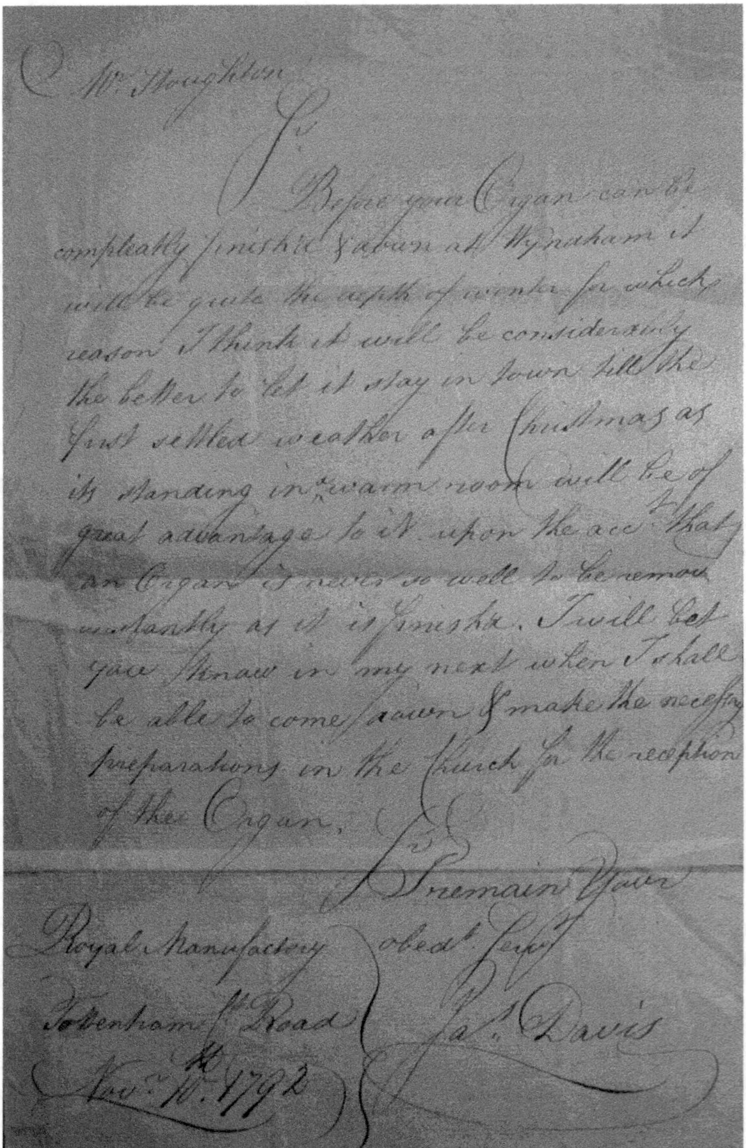

Mr Stoughton

Sir

Before your Organ can be compleatly finish'd & [illegible] at Wymondham it will be quite the depth of winter for which reason I think it will be considerably the better to let it stay in town till the first settled weather after Christmas as its standing in a warm room will be of great advantage to it upon the acct that an Organ is never so well to be remov'd instantly as it is finish'd. I will let you know in my next when I shall be able to come down & make the necessary preparations in the Church for the reception of the Organ,

Sir I remain Your obedt Servt

Jas Davis

Royal Manufactory
Tottenham Ct Road
Novr 10th 1792

Figure 1.4 10 November 1792 letter from James Davis to John Clarke Stoughton regarding the Longman & Broderip organ for Wymondham Abbey (Royal College of Music, Museum of Instruments RCM 800, by permission)

At least one of Richard Duke's instruments and a cello made by Joseph Hill I (the first of a famous and long lasting family of violin makers) passed through Longman, Lukey & Co.'s shop.[193] Of course they might have been bought in by the firm rather than commissioned. A similar situation can be seen in relation to a cello branded 'Longman & Broderip London' below its button and labelled 'Made and sold by Chas and Saml Thompson St Paul's church yard London 1784'.[194] It seems likely that this instrument passed through Longman & Broderip's shop as new or second-hand and was given their label even though it originated in another workshop. Henry Jay also reportedly made instruments for Longman & Broderip.[195]

Lockey Hill, a son of Joseph Hill I, also is said to have provided Longman & Broderip with instruments.[196] In 1795 he was tried at the Old Bailey for stealing a horse.[197] He hoped to call James Longman as a character witness, but James was unable to be there on the right day because he was occupied by business. Hill was found guilty and sentenced to death. He was held at Newgate Prison until February 1796, and was executed by hanging on the 24th of that month.[198]

---

[193] The Duke instrument was auctioned by Sotheby's in London on 30 March 1988, lot 258. It is branded 'Longman & Lukey, Cheapside, London' and labelled 'Richard Duke, Maker, Holborn, London, Anno 1769'. The Hill cello was sold by Sotheby's on 9 March 2010, lot 97. It is labelled 'Joseph Hill and Sons, Makers at the Harp and Flute, in the Hay Market, 1771' and branded 'Longman, Lukey & Co., No. 26 Cheapside, London' by the button. I am grateful to Duncan Lockie for his assistance in searching Sotheby's catalogues.

[194] Sotheby's auction, London, 28 February 2006, lot 118.

[195] Willibald Leo von Lütgendorff, *Die Geigen- und Lautenmacher vom Mittelalter bis zur Gegenwart*, Nendeln, Liechtenstein, 1968, v 2 p 241: 'Er arbeitete gut nach italienischen Meistern, oft für die Firma Longman & Broderip'.

[196] John Milnes (ed.), *The British Violin, op. cit.*, p 85.

[197] Trial of Lockey Hill, 2 December 1795, OB t17951202-53. See Jenny Nex, 'Luthier and thief', *The Strad* v 121 no. 1444 (August 2010) p 48–52, and Jenny Nex and Lance Whitehead, 'Musical instrument making in Georgian London, 1753–1809: Evidence from the Proceedings of the Old Bailey and the Middlesex Sessions of the Peace', *Eighteenth Century Music* v 2 no. 2 (2005) p 251–272 at p 255.

[198] Newgate Prison Calendar, TNA HO 77/3. This corrects prior assertions that Hill died in 1810. Before his execution he 'addressed the populace who attended

The Salisbury violin maker Benjamin Banks seems to have had a reciprocal arrangement with Longman & Broderip. As he ran his own shop in a provincial city it made sense for him to supply the London firm with stringed instruments while they sent him other types of instrument, probably including keyboard instruments, for sale in Salisbury.[199]

As well as bowed stringed instruments, Longman & Broderip sold plucked instruments such as the harp and the English guittar. John Goldsworth, a partner of Culliford & Co. mentioned above, made English guittars and may have done this under the Longman & Broderip label while he was employed by Culliford. His 1785 patent (granted while Culliford were contracted to sell instruments to Longman & Broderip) added a small keyboard and hammer action to the guittar (a different improvement from that patented by Clauss a year earlier).[200] Goldsworth left Culliford & Co. to form a partnership with John Geib, which lasted until the end of March 1793.[201] Unfortunately, on the day their business arrangement was terminated, bankruptcy proceedings were commenced against Goldsworth.[202]

The music seller John Preston made English guittars. One example has 'PRESTON' on the front face of what remains of its tuning head and bears a stamp on its button which reads 'LONGMAN LUKEY & Co | N° 26 CHEAPSIDE | LONDON'.[203] It is not known how this instrument gained these labels. Charles Pinto had many

---

on this melancholy occasion in a very impressive manner; and though declaring his innocence for the crime for which he suffered, he exhorted them to beware of evil company, which, if followed, would in the end bring them to the same untimely fate' (*The Whitehall Evening Post*, 25 February 1796, p 2).

199 Milnes, *op. cit.*, p 47.

200 B[ennet] Woodcroft, *op. cit.* in note 91 above, p 15–16. Goldsworth's patent subsequently was numbered 1491. An example of such an instrument, attributed to him, survives in Venice. See Franco Rossi, 'Gli strumenti musicali dei Musei Civici Veneziani', *Bollettino dei Musei Civici Veneziani* ser. 3 no. 1 (2006) [http://www.museiciviciveneziani.it/images/Int89990.pdf] p 11–69 at p 55–56.

201 *The London Gazette*, 2 April 1793, p 273.

202 *The London Gazette*, 30 March 1793, p 266.

203 RCM Museum of Instruments, RCM 315, dated *c*1770. See Elizabeth Wells and Christopher Nobbs, *Royal College of Music Museum of Instruments Catalogue Part III: European stringed instruments*, London, 2007, p 96.

guittars in his possession when he died and, as noted on page 30 above, he and James Longman jointly issued a caveat against Christian Clauss's guittar patent.[204] A hint that Clauss supplied guittars to Longman & Broderip perhaps may be gathered from a 1786 statement by his former partner Joseph Levy that he had advised Longman, Broderip and Culliford to have no dealings with Clauss.[205]

Longman & Broderip bought harps in from other makers. When trade laws permitted, they imported them from Europe, as stated in their 1789 announcement:

> HARPS
> Just imported from France,
> By LONGMAN and BRODERIP,
> No. 26, Cheapside, and No. 13, Hay-market, London.
> THESE HARPS are from the Manufactories of Naderman, Cousineau and Son, and other Eminent Makers, upon the newest and most approved principles, particularly the last invention, with a Swell which gives an uncommon brilliancy and effect to the performance.[206]

In 1797 the firm advertised that they had 'engaged workmen regularly brought up in the manufactories in France, and men of the most experienced abilities, who have now brought these instruments [pedal harps] to the greatest perfection'.[207] Because of the Revolutionary wars trade with France was restricted at this time. Although it is dangerous to speculate about the identity of these men with such little evidence, it is worth noting that Sébastien Erard came to London in the early 1790s. It is conceivable that he supplied harps to Longman & Broderip,[208] although the extant harp sales ledgers of the Erard manufactory in London do not begin until 1798.[209]

---

[204] Pinto's 1792 probate inventory is at TNA PROB 31/821/151.

[205] TNA C12/154/35, *Clauss v Levy*, 1786.

[206] *The Times*, 17 November 1789, p 1.

[207] *The Star*, 8 March 1797, p 1.

[208] See Ann Griffiths, 'Erard', in Stanley Sadie (ed.), *The New Grove Dictionary of Musical Instruments*, London, 1984, v 1, p 715.

[209] Sales ledgers of the London Erard harp manufactory, RCM Museum of Instruments, RCM 497. Broderip & Wilkinson's purchase of a harp from them in 1800 is noted in the next chapter.

Longman & Broderip also sold a wide range of wind and brass instruments. Their four-page *c*1780 catalogue[210] mentioned:

French Horns
Ear Horns
Glove Horns
Hunting Horns
Trumpets
Kettle Drums
Bassoons
Tenoroons, or Vauxhumanes
Bagpipes, Scotch or Irish
German Flutes, Ivory, Ebony, Cocoa and Box, tipp'd or plain
Hautboys tipp'd or plain
Clarinets ditto
English Flutes ditto, all sizes
Bird Flutes ditto
Flagelets ditto
Fifes of all sorts ditto
Pipes and Tabors
Sticcado Pastorales or Metallic Armonicas
Pitch Pipes, all sizes

Although a clarinet stamped 'Longman & Broderip' appears to resemble the work of George Miller, it has not been possible to identify the makers of these instruments with any certainty.[211] Surviving instruments with the stamp of Longman & Broderip do not display the name of their manufacturer.

According to a letter written in 1798 concerning the Frampton Volunteers of Gloucestershire, clarinets made by John Cramer were sold by both Longman & Broderip and Preston & Son.[212] James Longman appears to have had some connection with the trumpet maker William Shaw who brought a bill of complaint against James's

---

[210] The copy of this catalogue at BL 7896.h.40.(7) is reproduced in the database *Eighteenth Century Collections Online.*

[211] This clarinet was sold at Sotheby's auction, London, 30 April 1987, lot 201. Its keys are thought to be by John Hale.

[212] J[ohn] Pearce→Nathaniel Winchcombe *later* Clifford, *c*August 1798, Gloucestershire Archives D149/X21/15, quoted in David Lasocki, 'New light on eighteenth-century English woodwind makers from newspaper advertisements', *The Galpin Society Journal* v 63 (2010) p 73–142 at p 125–126.

assignees concerning patent rights that James allegedly had signed over to him.[213] This might suggest that James owed Shaw money, perhaps for instruments, and had transferred these patent rights to try to placate Shaw.

Information about Longman & Broderip was given as evidence in legal cases. Frederick Augustus Hyde, who features later in this story, was hired by the firm in 1786 at the age of eighteen and progressed to be a shopman by 1791.[214] He is likely to have been a family friend of Longman's from Somerset as he was baptised in Milborne Port on 28 May 1767.[215] Charles Mitchell [Michcell] was a shopman from 1786 when he was twenty-three years old, and William Jones was an employee from 1787 when he was twenty-seven. John Barrow, mentioned above as one of Longman's apprentices, lived in Longman & Broderip's premises from the age of twelve in 1771, was made free of the Spectacle Makers' Company on 10 May 1785 and advanced to shopman ten years later. He was still in that position in 1790 and in 1792 described himself as a shopman and music seller, aged thirty-two.

Joseph Serle *or* Searle served customers at the Haymarket shop.[216] Henry Thorowgood was a shopman for about five years from 1783, when he was forty-three years old.[217] Interestingly, while working for Longman & Broderip in 1786, he took on an apprentice,

---

[213] TNA C/13/70/42, *Shaw v Longman*, 1806. Although this document does not say that the complainant William Shaw made brass instruments, his Red Lion Street address matches that known for the trumpet maker. See William Waterhouse, *The New Langwill Index*, London, 1993, p 372 and p 393.

[214] TNA E133/54/55, *Forster v Longman*, 1791.

[215] IGI.

[216] Trial of James Jones *otherwise* Sandy, 27 February 1788, OB t17880227-1.

[217] From 1762 to about 1780 he was (initially in partnership with Robert Horne and then as sole proprietor) a music seller and musical instrument maker, particularly of Aeolian harps. See Jamie Croy Kassler, *The Science of Music in Britain, 1714–1830, A catalogue of writings, lectures and inventions*, New York, 1979, v 2 p 1016–1017. Conceivably he was a relation of Edward Thorowgood, who had rented one of the three houses amalgamated into 26 Cheapside (see page 16 above). Curiously, a musical instrument maker named Edward Thorowgood died in Cheapside in November 1768 (*The St James's Chronicle; or, The British Evening-Post*, 17–19 November 1768, p 3).

George Taylor, and was described in that context as a musical instrument maker.[218]

When testifying in the firm's 1784 suit against Samuel Babb, one of Longman & Broderip's clerks, Richard Bride, said that he was aged fifty-one and had been with the firm for nine years, working as a music copyist alongside 'divers persons at divers times'.[219] In another case in the following year, Bride was described as a 'shopman'.[220] Documents of that case name Joseph Searle as a servant aged twenty-two (presumably the man just mentioned who served customers at the Haymarket shop) and refer to John Jeanes of Corton Denham (Longman's home town), whose role is not given but who had left the firm in 1784. Another clerk, Ambrose Moore, is mentioned in the case between Longman & Broderip and Culliford, Rolfe & Barrow, during which process he was asked to examine accounts.[221]

To obtain materials for making instruments Longman & Broderip required regular suppliers. Two of these have come to light. Charles Drake supplied the green silk that John Geib used in his pianos.[222] Thomas Culliford got ivory for his keyboards from Thomas Fauntleroy, a dealer in Tooley Street, Potter's Fields.[223] Since Culliford & Co. had a smith's shop at their premises in Pelican Court,

---

[218] Cliff Webb, *London Livery Company Apprenticeship Registers* v 28: *The Farriers' Company, 1619–1800*, London, 1999, p 28. Thorowgood's other apprentices included his son Henry Jr in 1775, William Wallis in 1774 (mentioned above for insuring his utensils at Longman's in 1791) and Richard Yours in 1791 (*ibid.*, p 62, p 65 and p 71).

[219] TNA E133/82/26, *Longman v Babb*, 1784. See also p 373–374 below.

[220] TNA E133/104/67, *Rennett v Longman*, 1785. A detailed discussion of this case is in Nancy A. Mace, 'Charles Rennett and the London music-sellers in the 1780s: testing the ownership of reversionary copyrights', *Journal of the Royal Musical Association* v 129 no. 1 (spring 2004) p 1–23. A summary of Rennett's activities is given in Chapter 6 on p 371–374 below.

[221] TNA E112/1771/5631, *Longman v Culliford*, 1795.

[222] Trial of Edward Johnson, 11 May 1785, OB t17850511-14.

[223] Trial of John Griffiths, 14 January 1789, OB t17890114-7. Thomas Fauntleroy appears in various directories (e.g., in *A Supplement to the British Directory of Trade, Commerce, and Manufacture, 1792*, London, [1798], reprinted in v 5 of *The Universal British Directory 1793–1798*, King's Lynn, Norfolk, 1993).

Little Britain,[224] they could have supplied Longman & Broderip with hinges, pins and other metalware, but evidence of this is lacking. No further names of the firm's suppliers are known.

1.8 Services and Premises

As well as new musical instruments Longman & Broderip sold second-hand ones. Highlights of the latter included 'two fine toned Cremona violins, in excellent preservation'[225] and

> a large assortment of harpsichords, grand piano fortes, portable grand and small piano fortes, spinnets, organs; ditto in tables and bookcases; organized piano fortes, &c. &c. Among which are two very fine, by Kirckman, Shudi, Baker, Harris, &c.
>
> N.B. The above instruments will be sold on very low terms (for ready money only), having been taken in exchange for their new improved patent grand and small piano fortes; specimens of which may be seen at the manufactory ... [in Tottenham Court Road], and at their shops, no. 26, Cheapside, and no. 13, Hay-market.[226]

In 1773 or 1774 Longman, Lukey & Broderip purchased 'the prime instruments of the late ingenious Mahoon'—i.e., Joseph Mahoon, harpsichord maker to King George III—and offered them to the public at 'fifty per cent under [Mahoon's] usual prices'.[227] They

---

[224] LMA, formerly Guildhall ms 11936/331 p 87, Sun Fire Office insurance policy 507215, transcribed in Jenny Nex, 'Culliford and Company…', *op. cit.* in note 118 above, p 38.

[225] Advertised in *The Daily Universal Register*, 7 December 1787, p 1.

[226] *The Times*, 25 December 1793, p 1. The phrase 'two very fine, by Kirckman, Shudi, Baker, Harris, &c.' is confusing. Longman & Broderip may have meant to say that they had two very fine instruments for sale without naming their makers, and that instruments available for purchase had been made by Kirkman, Shudi and others. The comma in this advertisement between 'Baker' and 'Harris' is erroneous, as Baker Harris was one person.

[227] Longman, Lukey & Broderip advertisement included in their reissue of Richard Langdon (ed.), *Divine Harmony; Being a collection in score of psalms and anthems…*, London, Longman & Lukey, 1774, copy at RCM D760/1. The advertisement is reproduced in Boalch, *op. cit.* in note 119 above, p 119.

also bought 'the most valuable part of the old stock of Mr [James] Lewer, the successor of the late Mr [John] Tyther, in Moorfields, (the oldest shop in London)'.[228] The firm accepted old instruments as part payment of new ones, as shown in the 1794 accounts of the Earl of Verulam who, when Lord Dunboyne, gave the firm a harpsichord valued at £10/10 towards the £27/6 purchase price of a piano forte.[229]

In addition to instruments and printed music, the firm offered for sale 'every other article in the musical way, wholesale, retail, and for exportation', including:

Steel Forks for tuning Harpsicords, Spinnets, Violins, Guitars, &c.
Harpsicord and Spinnet Hammers
Crow and Raven Quills
Desks for Harpsicords
New invented portable Music Desks
Rosin Boxes, Wood or Ivory
Mutes, Brass, Box or Ivory
Mouth-Pieces for French Horns or Trumpets, Brass or Ivory
Mouth-Pieces for German Flutes
Pens to rule Music Paper
Ruled Books of all sizes
Ruled Paper of all sorts
Bows for Violins, Kits,[230] Tenors, Violoncellos, and Viol de Gambos
Bridges for Violins, Kits, Tenors, Violoncellos, Viol de Gambos, Guitars, &c.
Pegs, or Pins and Tail Pieces for ditto
Hinges and Locks for Harpsichords and Spinnets
Reeds for Bassoons, Hautboys, Clarinets, Vaux-humanes and Bagpipes
Cases for Reeds, all sorts
Cases for Flutes and Hautboys
Cases for Violins, Violoncellos and Guitars[231]

Mahoon died on 17 November 1773 (*The Gentleman's Magazine* v 43 (November 1773) p 582).

[228] Longman, Lukey & Broderip advertisement, *op. cit.* Lewer's stock in trade was sold at auction on 13 May 1774 (*The Gazetteer and New Daily Advertiser*, 13 May 1774, p 3); he died fifteen days later (*The Middlesex Journal, and Evening Advertiser*, 31 May–2 June 1774, p 3).

[229] Historical Manuscripts Commission, *Report on the Manuscripts of the Earl of Verulam, preserved at Gorhambury*, London, 1906, p.209.

[230] A kit was a small fiddle.

[231] Longman & Broderip *c*1780 catalogue, see note 210 above.

Longman & Broderip also imported 'monthly':

> The best Italian Strings for Violins, Tenors, Violoncellos, Double Basses, Welch Harps, &c.
> Genuine German Wire for Harpsicords, Spinnets, Piano Fortes, Guitars, Irish Harps, Dulcimers, &c.
> Italian Catgut and Wire strings silver'd in the completest Manner, and well proportioned for Violins, Basses, Guitars, and Piano Fortes, &c.[232]

The firm's capability of supplying everything that a musician might need is indicated in their trade card reproduced in *Figure 1.5* on page 60, which was issued some time after their Haymarket branch opened in 1782. In addition to the items mentioned on that card, their timber yard also supplied wood for makers of musical instruments:

> Mahagony, Beech, Deals. Clap-boards,[233] mahogany panel boards, black and white holly, black ebony, King's and tulip wood, and all sorts of veneers; American pine deals 30 inches wide, and 20 feet long, without a knot, with every other article in the timber way, on the lowest terms by LONGMAN and BRODERIP, at their timber yard, Tottenham Court Road.[234]

Although this advertisement does not say that Longman & Broderip sold timber exclusively to musical instrument makers, the types of wood mentioned in the advertisement could help to determine whether part of a surviving instrument is original and where its material came from.

The firm also invented and sold musical items that might appeal to persons who were not serious musicians. A 1770 advertisement included a set of country-dances and cotillions (French social dances) printed on playing cards:

---

[232] *ibid.*

[233] Deals were boards sawn from logs; 'clapboards' refers to a small size of split oak, imported from America or Germany.

[234] *The Times*, 15 January 1788, p 1.

Figure 1.5 Trade card of Longman & Broderip (Tony Bingham Collection, London, by permission)

NEW MUSIC.
This Day was published,
LONGMAN and LUKEY's complete pack of favourite Country-Dances and Cotillions, with proper directions to each tune, curiously engraved, and printed on cards for the pocket, not larger than a common pack. Price 2s. 6d.

The invention of these cards is quite new, and exceeding useful, being contrived in so small a compass, that the whole pack will lay in a common card-case, and far preferable to any books, being no trouble in turning over, are handy to shuffle or cut for a dance, also to see the figure at a view without the least incumbrance; and of great service for learners, as they may keep the card, with the dance and figure in their hands, without the least inconveniency.

Invented and sold at their Music-shop, No. 26, Cheapside. Where may be had Cases for the above, likewise their new-invented Pocket-cases for German flutes (of all sizes) which preserve them in excessive hot or immoderate damp climates, keep them free from dust, and from all danger of breaking.[235]

Another product not directed to professional musicians was advertised in 1788:

THE REAL *OPERA FAN*
The sole invention of Signor Carinvalle, to be had of Messrs. LONGMAN and BRODERIP, No. 26, Cheapside, and No. 13, Haymarket. This elegant *trifle* presents at one view the *interior elevation* of the Opera House, as it now stands with the additional Boxes and other improvements. One side gives a full and satisfactory account of the Boxes, as held by the *original proprietors*—The other, of the different *Subscribers* to each Box, for the years 1787 and 1788. Consequently any person unacquainted with the Opera may, by the assistance of this Fan, be perfect master of all the situations of the *present occupants*, in a few minutes.

N.B. It is sold by Messrs. Longman and Broderip ONLY.[236]

This advertisement attests to the practice of attending the theatre as much to be seen as to see the performance. Knowing who was present was of great importance to those who cared about being in the right places with the right people. If the inventor of the fan was in fact

---

[235] *The General Evening Post (London)*, 20–23 January 1770, p 1. A *c*1775 set of *Longman and Lukey's complete Pack of new Cotillons* [sic] ..., wanting the ace of spades, is at BL K.1.c.26.

[236] *The Times*, 9 January 1788, p 1.

Pietro Carnevale, deputy manager of the Opera at the King's Theatre, he would have been ideally placed to compile the information on it.[237]

Besides selling objects, Longman & Broderip sold services. Harpsichords, spinets and pianos could be rented by the month, quarter or year, and the firm offered to tune instruments per time or on a quarterly or yearly basis.[238] Workers journeyed beyond London to provide these services. Thomas Culliford, for instance, travelled to large towns in the south of England such as Chichester, where he tuned and mended the harpsichord used in the concerts there. John Marsh wrote that in July 1789:

> The Concert harpsichord being got into a very bad condition, for want of having a proper place to stand when not used at the Concert; I on the 23d. employed Mr Culliford, foreman to Longman & Broderip (who was on his way from Portsmouth to Brighton) to repair it & put it into good condition which he did, & afterw'ds tuned most of the piano fortes etc. in Chichester where there was then no tuner other than Walond who was by no means a good one & was rather indifferent about it.[239]

This instrument seems to have been rather vulnerable to abuse because of its position in a public space, and Marsh took responsibility to have it repaired on more than one occasion:

> As I had forseen the crowd wo'd be very great at these balls, I had desired Triggs the porter of the Concert ether to remove the Concert harpsichord quite, or else to set it on it's back upon the floor in a corner against the wall with it's sloping edge upwards; but he undertaking that it sho'd not be hurt, left it in the lobby where some men for want of other seats, sitting upon it, the lid was crack'd quite thro' in 2 or 3 places, thro' which some negus[240] spilt thereon got into the harpsichord upon the soundboard, which it stain'd very much & upon w'ch it lay to dry itself without being wiped afterwards, in consequence of which, before the next winter we were oblig'd to have Culliford down to repair & put it to rights again.[241]

---

[237] I thank Michael Kassler for this suggestion.

[238] Longman & Broderip *c*1780 catalogue, see note 210 above.

[239] Brian Robins (ed.), *The John Marsh Journals*, *op. cit.*, p 457.

[240] A drink made of wine and hot water with sugar and lemon.

[241] *The John Marsh Journals*, p 612, referring to May 1796. The harpsichord had also been dropped two years previously, when 'half the strings broke at

This service of the firm clearly was important to provincial musicians, particularly when no local resident had sufficient skill to maintain their instruments. Longman & Broderip also addressed one challenge faced by those without easy access to specialist help by selling 'patent tuning machines, so peculiarly constructed, that ladies and gentlemen may tune their own instruments with the greatest ease.'[242] Of course, expert help still would have been required to carry out repairs such as the ones described by Marsh.

A further service offered was a musical circulating library. This opened at the firm's Cheapside shop in 1782 and offered subscribers 'every publication, ancient and modern, that England, France, Holland, and Germany have produced, or may in future'.[243] The same service became available through the Haymarket shop soon afterwards.[244] The firm also offered to recommend 'judicious masters' to 'teach all instruments',[245] so it benefited musicians to be on friendly terms with them. In addition, they held free public demonstrations of new instruments at their Tottenham Court Road manufactory, notably in June 1790 when Abbé Georg Joseph Vogler, who was then visiting London, gave several performances exemplifying the stops of a large organ that the firm's 'principal builder' John Geib had just completed for St Mary, Stafford.[246]

---

once & the movements became too much strain'd that it cost us a guinea & a half to get it repair'd again' (*ibid.*).

[242] *The Daily Universal Register*, 2 March 1787, p 1. Alexander Mackenzie of Ord and Kenneth Mobbs, 'The musical enigma of Longman and Broderip's monochord *c*1790', *The Galpin Society Journal* v 57 (2004) p 46–52 and p 206, describes such a machine now in the Horniman Museum, London.

[243] *The London Courant, Morning Gazette, and Daily Advertiser*, 21 March 1782, p 1.

[244] *Parker's General Advertiser, and Morning Intelligencer*, 27 January 1783, p 1.

[245] *The World*, 8 December 1790, p 2.

[246] See advertisements in *The Public Advertiser*, 3 June 1790, p 1, and *The Gazetteer and New Daily Advertiser*, 12 June 1790, p 1; also, a letter to Henry Sampson Woodfall, editor of *The Public Advertiser*, signed 'Friends to Merit', published in that newspaper on 30 June 1790, p 1–2. The organ cost £820 (National Pipe Organ Register survey N04932 at www.npor.org.uk). John Marsh and his wife Elizabeth heard Vogler play this organ at the Longman &

The firm also appraised the value of music collections. This is evidenced by the 'Calculation of the Value of the Collection of Manuscript & Printed Musick Books belonging to William, James, & Granville Sharp, according to the prices set opposite to each Article by Messrs Longman and Broderip, Musick Sellers in Cheapside'.[247]

Beyond their direct impact on musical life in late eighteenth-century London, Longman & Broderip had sufficient status to achieve wider social significance. An anonymous commentator wrote of the shopfront of their recently opened manufactory that

> Among the many ornamental fronts in the different parts of London, we know of nothing so elegant, and withal so professionally *appropriate*, as that which appears to the manufactory of Messrs. *Longman* and *Broderip*, in Tottenham-Court Road.—We think its taste and contrivance of that merit, as to wish it were a decoration to one of the principal streets of the metropolis.[248]

Of course this might have been self-promotion.

In 1789, the firm joined other merchants by illuminating their shopfronts to mark the restoration of the King's health. *The Times* said of the firm's Haymarket shop that 'Longman and Broderip were also, as usual, distinguishable for an elegant and various display of beautiful lamps, with the addition of a most brilliant transparency', and the illuminations in front of their Cheapside shop were also noticed in that story.[249] In June that year the firm's illuminations 'added much to the celebration' of the King's birthday.[250]

Politically important visitors to London were taken to Longman & Broderip's premises about this time. In November 1787, Charles

---

Broderip manufactory on 5 June 1790 (Brian Robins (ed.), *The John Marsh Journals*, *op. cit.*, p 474).

[247] NYPL Drexel 1022, unpaginated. The text quoted appears on a page marked 'G'. Although the title-page of this manuscript is dated 1759, presumably the year when this collection started to be listed, its contents include works published in the early 1780s. The collection probably was valued by Longman & Broderip about that time. I thank Michael Kassler for this information.

[248] *The Daily Universal Register*, 24 October 1787, p 3.

[249] *The Times*, 12 March 1789, p 3.

[250] According to *The Morning Star*, 5 June 1789, p 3.

Alexandre de Calonne, who had served as French controller-general of finances from 1783 until April 1787,[251] visited the firm's Cheapside shop and, accompanied by 'a French lady of quality', was shown the 'magazine of musical instruments'. Both reportedly were 'highly pleased not only with the great variety in the firm's warehouses but also with the attention shown to them.'[252] In 1790 six Cherokee chiefs were taken to that shop. The Cherokee nation had sided with the British during fighting with Spain and France over territories in North America, and fought alongside British forces in the American War of Independence.[253] Therefore, it was perhaps of international significance that the pleasure these chiefs 'expressed on hearing' the firm's 'Grand Piano Fortes, was only equalled by their admiration of the mechanism, which they very minutely examined, and, which appeared to give them great satisfaction'.[254]

As well as such high-status activities the firm contributed to the welfare of contemporaries. For instance, they allowed 26 Cheapside to be used as a contact address. Respondents to advertisements in 1787 for a 'servant who is not above his business' and for 'a snug cabbin or neat house, furnished' were directed there.[255] In 1772 Longman, Lukey & Co. were in a long list of retailers from whom William Bailey's drops to cure scurvy could be bought.[256] In 1788 Longman & Broderip collected funds for William Donn, a doulas and tick maker from West Chinnock, Somersetshire who, because of a fire, lost uninsured property valued at more than £1,000.[257] West Chinnock is about ten miles from James Longman's home village and as his father and Donn had the same occupation it seems likely that

---

[251] See Jeremy Black and Roy Porter (eds), *A Dictionary of Eighteenth-Century World History, op. cit.* in note 1 above, p 111. A few months later, following the failure of his plans for economic reform in France, Viscount de Calonne made a prolonged visit to England.

[252] *The Daily Universal Register*, 12 November 1787, p 2.

[253] Theda Perdue, *The Cherokee*, New York, 1989, p 32–35.

[254] *The Times*, 12 November 1790, p 2.

[255] *The World, Fashionable Advertiser*, 20 June 1787, p 4.

[256] *The Morning Chronicle, and London Advertiser*, 19 June 1772, p 1.

[257] Tick is a stout cloth that was used for covering bedding.

James knew him.[258] These actions outside the firm's core activities gave them publicity and may have attracted customers.

Musicians visiting London also gained from the firm's goodwill. Ignace Pleyel stayed at their Haymarket premises during his visit to London in 1791–1792.[259] John Marsh relied on the firm's hospitality on several occasions. On the morning of 26 May 1784 he tried to find somewhere to eat before the first Commemoration of Handel performance at Westminster Abbey but could not locate a coffee house that served before nine o'clock. However,

> it occurring to me that I might get a slice of bread & butter & a little milk & water at Longman & Broderips in the Haymarket, I stept there & mentioning to a young man in the shop how I was circumstanc'd he order'd the maid to get what I wanted; but my difficulties however were not to end here as on bringing the bread & butter she brought word that the milk was not then brought & that there was not a drop in the house, I therefore hastily swallowed 2 or 3 slices of the bread & butter & washing down with a glass of *cold* water pursued my walk to the Abbey doors...[260]

Marsh also attended more formal mealtime gatherings in the firm's premises, such as on 25 June 1791 when he was invited to dinner at Cheapside. The other diners were

> Mr Snow (formerly a celebrated harpsichord player), Blewit, a blind organist, Greatorex (father of the celebrated organ player) etc. whose very free & licentious conversation I was very glad after dinner to find interrupted by a piece called for on the piano forte by Snow (whose fingers however were now so distorted by the gout that he gave but a poor specimen of his former abilities) & one on the organ (of w'ch Longman had one in a recess behind the sideboard) by Blewit, after which I took my leave...[261]

This entertainment did not put Marsh off from further visits, and on 9 November 1797 he hoped to view the Lord Mayor's Show from the

---

[258] *The World*, 26 March 1788, p 2.

[259] TNA E133/54/54, *Forster v Longman*, 1791; Nancy A. Mace, 'Haydn and the London music sellers', *op. cit.* in note 83 above, p 539.

[260] Brian Robins (ed.), *The John Marsh Journals*, *op. cit.*, p 316–317.

[261] *ibid.*, p 487. Robins identifies the other guests as Jonathon Snow, Jonas Blewitt and Anthony Greatorex, father of Thomas Greatorex.

front windows of the firm's Cheapside shop. However, fate was again not his friend: 'finding the fore rooms there full of company, I went over to Culliford Rolfe & Barrows opposite Bow Church where I had a window to myself in their dining room'.[262] As noted in the next chapter, Haydn met Charles Burney at the firm's Haymarket shop.[263]

Longman & Broderip advertised in September 1789 that they had 'opened a shop at Margate and Brighthelmstone [now Brighton] for the sale or hire of musical instruments' during 'the watering season'.[264] They also had business associates in the provinces and Europe. As mentioned, Benjamin Banks sold the firm's instruments in Salisbury. A nameboard in the National Museum of Ireland, which probably came from a square piano, records that this instrument was made for the firm and sold by E. Lee of Dublin.[265] The firm served as London agent of the Viennese music publishers Artaria & Co. and imported or republished their editions of music by Haydn, Mozart, Rosetti, Vanhal and Boccherini.[266] Artaria, in return, sold Longman & Broderip instruments: a harpsichord and piano from their workshop are mentioned in an Artaria advertisement of November 1784.[267] The firm's instruments also were exported to France: a 1793 inventory of

---

[262] *ibid.*, p 657.

[263] See pages 109–110 below.

[264] *The Oracle, Bell's New World*, 11 September 1789, p 1.

[265] The nameboard (uncatalogued) reads: 'BY ROYAL PATENT | LONGMAN & BRODERIP | MUSICAL INSTRUMENT MAKERS | N° 26 CHEAPSIDE & N° 13 HAYMARKET | LONDON | SOLD BY E. LEE N° 2 DAME STREET | DUBLIN'. Edmund Lee, son of the violinist, music publisher and instrument maker Samuel Lee (*d*1776), took over his parents' business following the withdrawal of his mother Anne in 1788 (see Brian Boydell, *A Dublin Musical Calendar, 1700–1760*, Dublin, 1988, Appendix 1, p 259 and p 283).

[266] David Wyn Jones, 'From Artaria to Longman & Broderip: Mozart's music on sale in London', in Otto Biba and David Wyn Jones (eds), *Studies in Music History Presented to H. C. Robbins Landon on his Seventieth Birthday*, London, 1996, p 105–114. Longman & Broderip affixed their label to the front page of copies of imported editions. For an example of this see pages 101–102 below.

[267] Richard Maunder, *Keyboard Instruments in Eighteenth-Century Vienna*, Oxford 1999, p 155.

Pascal Taskin's workshop included a 'forte piano' by 'Longuemann'.[268]

Some individuals travelling overseas bought instruments from Longman & Broderip to take with them. For instance, in 1798 Edward Clive (son of the famous 'Clive of India') bought a piano forte together with packing cases for this and other instruments.[269] The firm offered a 'large allowance to merchants, captains of ships, & others who take for sale',[270] and their instruments are known to have travelled to Jamaica, some probably though Culliford & Co., as one of that company's partners, Thomas Bradford, resided in Kingston.[271]

None of Longman & Broderip's three London establishments has survived, but archival records provide data about their design and construction. James Longman's lease of 26 Cheapside, dated 28 August 1772, includes a plan of the premises reproduced in *Figure 1.6*.[272] The site measurements are given as 20 ft 2 in. (20 ft 3 in. on the south side) × 60 ft, and the plan shows two sets of stairs, presumably one for each of two previously separate buildings. The names of Longman's neighbours are amplified in *The London Directory for the Year 1772*, which lists John Hooker, linen draper, 18 Cheapside; Thomas Symonds, goldsmith, 27 Cheapside; and Hodgson & Donaldson, chinamen, 28 Cheapside.[273]

Longman's 29 April 1772 £1,500 insurance policy with the Hand-in-Hand Fire Office shows that no. 26 was the tenth house westwards from Friday Street, measured 18 × 58 ft and consisted of

---

[268] Frank Hubbard, *Three Centuries of Harpsichord Making*, Cambridge, Mass., 1965, p 298.

[269] He paid nearly £40 for all this (BL mss Eur IOR Neg 4383, transcribed in Ian Woodfield, *Music of the Raj: A social and economic history of music in late eighteenth-century Anglo-Indian Society*, *op. cit.*, p 17).

[270] Longman & Broderip trade card reproduced in *Figure 1.5* on page 60 above. Captains and other ship officers sometimes bought items in London as an investment that they auctioned when they arrived at a distant port.

[271] TNA E112/1771/5631, *Longman v Culliford*, 1795.

[272] See note 35 above.

[273] London, *c*1772 (reproduced in the database *Eighteenth Century Collections Online*).

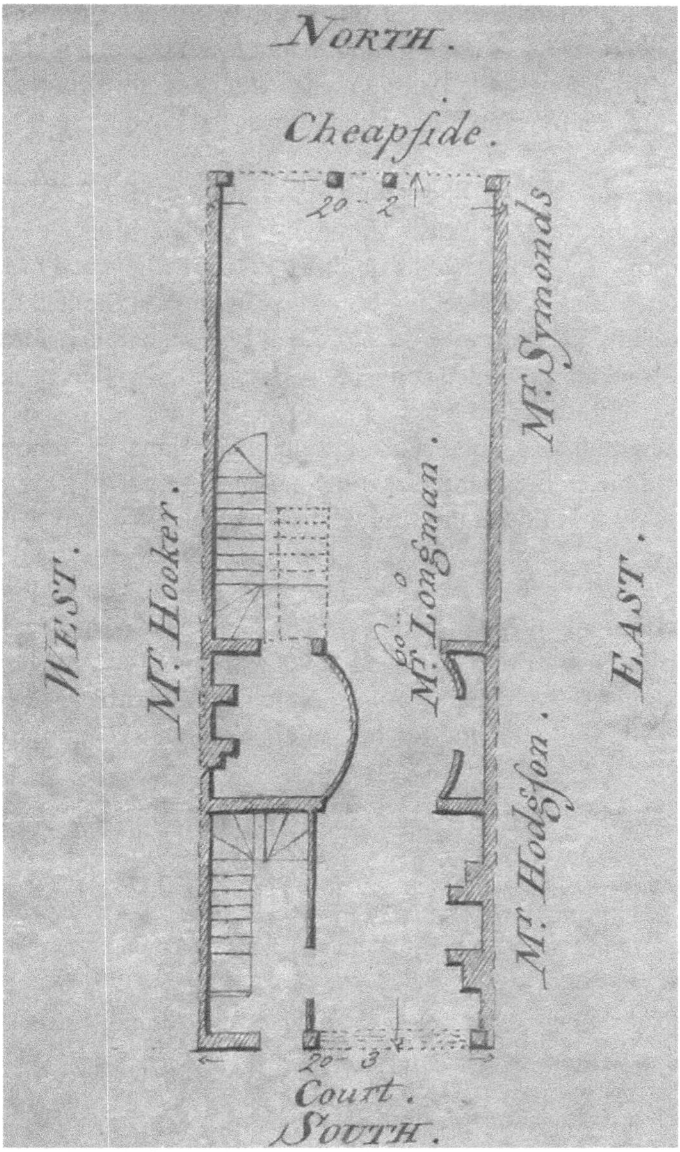

Figure 1.6 Drawing of Longman, Lukey & Co. premises at 26 Cheapside in lease dated 28 August 1772 between The Worshipful Company of Goldsmiths and James Longman (© The Worshipful Company of Goldsmiths)

five stories built of brick. The discrepancy in measurements might have come from one source giving external dimensions and the other internal. No. 26 is called Longman's 'intended dwelling house' in that policy, confirming that when it was taken out he was living elsewhere.[274]

The renovation cost Longman about £800, and for this investment the Goldsmiths' Company allowed him eleven days' discount on his rent.[275] When he renewed the policy in 1773, no. 26 was described as 'his dwelling house', showing that he had moved in by then.[276] In 1774, further development was undertaken for the sum of £800, which included opening up a door at the back of 26 Cheapside into the court behind.

Longman took out a second policy with Hand-in-Hand in 1777, covering four-storey warehouses behind 26 Cheapside. This property was 38 × 29 ft with a cellar projecting a further 8 feet (area 38 × 8 ft) and was valued at £1,000.[277] The records of the Goldsmiths' Company show that he invested a further £2,000 during the construction of these premises. The address was recorded as 'Goldsmiths' Court' but became known as Fountain Court because of the fountain at its centre. A house, which seems to have been added about 1780, was attached to the warehouses and Longman himself

---

[274] In the trial of John Norton, 12 January 1774, OB t17740112-54, Longman testified that 'in the year 1772 I lived in St Paul's Church Yard, while my present house in Cheapside was rebuilding'. For this temporary move see page 18 above.

[275] Goldsmiths' Company records in their library at Goldsmith's Hall, London.

[276] Policy no. 88125 dated 29/4/1772 (LMA, formerly Guildhall ms 8674/113 p 83), renewed 2/6/1773 (LMA, formerly Guildhall ms 8674/144 p 274). This policy was again renewed on 19/8/1800 by John Longman, Muzio Clementi and Josiah Banger, three partners of Longman, Clementi & Co., by which time further alterations and additions to the premises had been made.

[277] Hand-in-Hand Fire Office policy no. 90109, April 1777 (LMA, formerly Guildhall ms 8674/119 p 220), renewed 22/12/1778 (ms 8674/121 p 250), 7/6/1780 (ms 8674/123 p 133), 2/7/1787 (ms 8674/130 p 37), 28/7/1790 (ms 8674/132 p 186) and 25/4/1792 (ms 8674/133 p 292). This policy subsequently was renewed by John Longman and Muzio Clementi on 25/4/1799 (ms 8674/138 p 118).

used two warehouses.[278] The gradual expansion of the buildings at the Cheapside site is reflected in land tax records.[279]

There is frustratingly little evidence about the use of these spaces. We know that Culliford used one of the upper floors for 'finishing' instruments, which would probably include the relatively clean operations of polishing and tuning. There was also a 'fiddle room', presumably where violins and other bowed stringed instruments were available for customers to try.[280] No picture of the Cheapside buildings during the time of Longman's occupancy is known to have survived. A plan of the area is found in Richard Horwood's map of London and Westminster published in 1813.[281]

Little information is available about Longman & Broderip's second outlet at 13 Haymarket. It appears to have been primarily a shop with living accommodation on the upper floors, and to have had no warehouse or workshop. Longman & Co. are named in the paving rates for these premises from Michaelmas 1782 until 1802, when Broderip & Wilkinson are named instead.[282] The Tottenham Court

---

[278] This four-storey brick house 'on south side of Fountain Court, the last house eastwards' was insured on 7/3/1780 for £1,000. Hand-in-Hand policy no. 91129 (LMA, formerly Guildhall ms 8674/123 p 45), renewed 15/11/1787 (ms 8674/130 p 148).

[279] In 1767, Longman made a single payment of £13/4; in 1778-1779, there are two entries for which he was responsible; and in 1781 a third entry, also for £13/4, was added. (Land tax assessment books in the ward of Farringdon Within, St Matthews precinct, 1767–1768 (LMA, formerly Guildhall, ms 11316/205); 1778–1779 (ms 11316/239); 1779–1780 (ms 11316/242); 1781–1782 (ms 11316/247); 1798–1799 (ms 11316/298); 1791–1792 (ms 11316/277).)

[280] Trial of Richard Geast, 6 April 1796, OB t17960406-83.

[281] Reproduced in *The A to Z of Regency London*, Lympne Castle, Kent, 1985, map 15, p 30–31.

[282] Westminster City Archives, paving rates for the parish of St Martin in the Fields, Haymarket east side, Suffolk Street ward, mf1791 F2941 (1782), F2948 (30/7/1783) and F2957 (14/9/1785); mf1799 F3038 (8/4/1802) and F3065 (14/4/1803); mf1800 F3073 (10/4/1806), F3078 (14/4/1807 and 14/4/1809) and F3086 (12/4/1810). Presumably the writer of the post-1798 entries was late in noting the change of the occupants' name.

Road premises included a timber yard which in 1788 probably was guarded by dogs.[283]

In 1796 David Davis testified that the firm had 'a warehouse in Fountain-court, and another in Trinity-lane', and land tax records confirm that James Longman was responsible for premises in Great Trinity Lane from 1794–1795 to 1802–1803.[284] Items were transferred between the firm's locations in two ways. Smaller goods were carried by porters employed by the firm or by 'ticket-porters' hired by the job. Larger items or large quantities of items were carried in 'vans'[285] or in a 'machine', a horse-drawn covered wagon with the name of the firm painted on its sides—apparently an invention of the firm.[286]

1.9 Financial Problems and Bankruptcy

Notwithstanding the success of their business for nearly three decades, Longman & Broderip succumbed to bankruptcy in 1795, brought on by the widespread depression of the 1790s that resulted from Britain's war liabilities. The firm appears to have contravened Benjamin Franklin's ethic that, if one is reliable in paying one's debts

---

283 *The Morning Herald*, 15 August 1788, p 4, advertised the sale of 'a well-bred grey mare' and 'two very fine large yard dogs'. All could be seen at the firm's Tottenham Court Road manufactory.

284 Trial of Richard Geast, 6 April 1796, OB t17960406-83; land tax assessment books for the ward of Bread Street, St Mildred Lower Precinct, Great Trinity Lane, 1794–1795 (LMA, formerly Guildhall ms 11316/285) until 1802–1803 (ms 11316/309).

285 Trial of John Bates, 6 April 1796, OB t17960406-85.

286 Thomas Busby asserted (in *Concert Room and Orchestra Anecdotes of Music and Musicians Ancient and Modern*, London, 1825, v 1 p 82–83) that James Longman was the first 'to build a close caravan, … to paint his name, business, and address, in large letters, on each side of the machine, and to have it driven empty from morning till night through the town, in order to persuade the public that he was driving what is called a *roaring* trade'. The firm advertised in *The St James's Chronicle; or, British Evening-Post*, 8 December 1781, p 2, that their keyboard instruments were 'conveyed in a machine built on a peculiar construction, to prevent their being put out of order by carriage'.

on time, further loans will be easily obtained.[287] Longman seems to have borrowed large sums of money[288] and, while his capitalist spirit helped to create a huge business empire whose influence stretched to Europe, India, the United States and the West Indies, he could not pay his debts when the cash crisis of the 1790s hit London businesses.

Some problems faced by Longman & Broderip are revealed in their advertisements and in documentation of various court cases in which they were involved. Commercial activities at this time relied on an extensive credit system, and while this could work to the trade's advantage, once there was any degree of uncertainty, things could go wrong fairly rapidly. It could take over a year for customers to settle their accounts with tradesmen.[289] It was therefore advantageous for an instrument maker to maintain contact with their customers by providing services such as tuning.

Longman & Broderip tried to avoid some outstanding debts, as shown in their 1792 advertisement:

> To prevent the trouble and difficulty attending the collecting of cash due for tuning, and the frequent disputes respecting the same, it is humbly presumed that Ladies and Gentlemen cannot be offended if payment is required at the time, by the Tuner, except of those who agree by the year.[290]

However, some customers defaulted. In the 1780s Longman & Broderip sued George Wynne, a music seller who had been based in London but apparently moved to Cambridge, for nonpayment of £164/16/2, the residue of transactions relating to 'divers goods wares

[287] See Max Weber, *The Protestant Ethic and the Spirit of Capitalism*, London, 2002, p 14–15.

[288] TNA B1/93, Office of the Commission of Bankrupts and Successors: Order books relating to petitions against declarations of bankruptcy, 1795–1796, p 68–73.

[289] For instance, the layout of the copy of the account book of the Dublin harpsichord and organ builder Ferdinand Weber indicates that some customers only settled up after four or five years. See Jenny Nex and Lance Whitehead, 'A copy of Ferdinand Weber's account book', *Royal Musical Association Research Chronicle* no. 33 (2000) p 89–150.

[290] *The Star*, 25 January 1792, p 1.

and merchandizes', 'divers materials and things necessary' as well as 'work and labour'.[291] Longman & Broderip won the case as well as their expenses, although Wynne appealed, and not all records of the proceedings survive.

As well as problems of cash flow, the firm's finances were impacted by robbery. Instruments worth a total of between £300 and £400 were stolen from Longman, Lukey & Co. in 1772. Two years later John Norton was found guilty for stealing seven wooden flutes from a lot which Longman had spotted in James Wheeler's flute shop on High Holborn. Longman identified these flutes by matching them with spare joints (*corps de rechange*) that had not been stolen.[292] The theft of a cello was reported in 1786:

> Yesterday Thomas Franklin was fully committed to Newgate by the Lord Mayor [Thomas Wright] on the oath of Mr James Longman, for feloniously stealing one violincello, the property of the said James Longman and Francis Broderip, musical instrument-makers, in Cheapside.[293]

In 1793 Benjamin Hart was accused of receiving a stolen harp belonging to Longman & Broderip, although he was acquitted.[294] Materials also were taken such as the 59½ yards of green silk, valued at £2/10/–, which the firm had given to John Geib for use in his pianos.[295]

James Jones *otherwise* Sandy was sentenced in 1788 to transportation for seven years for stealing cash from the Haymarket shop.[296] John Griffiths was found guilty in 1789 of stealing ivory weighing 66 lb and valued at £8/5/– while it was being carried from Culliford & Co.'s Pelican Court workshop to their Fountain Court

[291] As evidenced in *Wynne v Longman*, see note 102 above.

[292] Trial of John Norton, 12 January 1774, OB t17740112-54.

[293] *The Universal Daily Register*, 27 October 1786, p 3.

[294] LMA MJ/SP/1793/09/047.

[295] Trial of Edward Johnson, 11 May 1785, OB t17850511-14. He was found guilty and sentenced to transportation for seven years.

[296] Trial of James Jones *otherwise* Sandy, 27 February 1788, OB t17880227-1.

shop.[297] This could have impacted Longman & Broderip, as Culliford & Co. were providing them with instruments then.

During the bankruptcy proceedings the number of thefts from Longman & Broderip apparently grew, perhaps because thieves thought there would be easy pickings. Three such cases, supported by Longman, Broderip and the firm's assignees, were brought before the Old Bailey on 6 April 1796. Richard Geast was indicted for stealing a piano worth £10, another piano worth £8, a spinet valued at £3, a violin of 16/– and five bows worth 18/–. William Gater was charged with the theft of a piano valued at £12, and John Bates with stealing a piano worth £10.[298]

Archival sources indicate that the firm had financial difficulties from the mid-1780s because of insufficient ready cash to pay off debts. When James Longman removed to 26 Cheapside, he became friendly with his neighbour, the china seller Thomas Hodgson, and from about 1774 regularly borrowed money from him.[299] James used this money to invest £2,500 in a mortgage, £1,000 in 5% stock, some £2,721 in 4% stock and £3,000 in 3% stock, making a total of £7,271/2/4, of which he endeavoured to repay about £1,000 per annum, including interest. By September 1785, the amount of money he owed was so great that he offered Hodgson a share in Longman & Broderip, essentially as a 'sleeping partner'. Longman had a three-quarter share in the firm and offered Hodgson one-third of that, a quarter of the whole business.

Naturally Hodgson and his advisers needed to assess whether this offer was fair, so the business was valued as at 1 August 1783 and its value on that day was deemed to be £29,377/11/11. This was a substantial amount and demonstrates the extent of the business that Longman and his partners had built up.

Before the situation was resolved, Hodgson died, having appointed as his executors James Longman, Payler Donaldson (Hodgson's partner in the china business) and the Rev. Richard

---

[297] Trial of John Griffiths, 14 January 1789, OB t17890114-7.

[298] OB t17960406-83, t17960406-84 and t17960406-85.

[299] TNA B1/94, 1797–1798, p 111–114.

Burleigh (Hodgson's nephew).[300] In December 1769 Sarah Smith, a young lady of some fortune, had given Hodgson £3,200 to invest on her behalf, and she sent his executors an account of the money she claimed he owed her. In the litigation that followed Longman deposed that he was unable to determine how much money Longman & Broderip owed to Hodgson for his share in the firm.[301]

James clearly was worried about having to pay off a large debt in a single payment. He argued that

> although the said business is very lucrative and profitable yet from the very great extent thereof and of the capital required therein it hath not been and would not be practicable with any degree of convenience or advisable to draw out thereupon so much as would be necessary to pay at once the amount of the said one fourth part of the said trade and stock so assigned to the said testator...

He added that it

> is impracticable if not impossible for him to pay the same in any other manner than as directed and allowed to this defendant by the said testator's said will without greatly distressing if not materially injuring the said trade.[302]

Further evidence of Longman's financial activities is found in records of the Bedford Estate.[303] In February 1788 Longman bought several properties from Payler Donaldson.[304] Later that year Longman

---

[300] Burleigh was based in Chilton Candover, Hampshire, when he signed his own will on 12 January 1798 (court copy at TNA PROB 11/304, proved 21 April 1798).

[301] TNA C12/178/48, *Smith v Longman*, 1791; C12/185/38, *Smith v Longman*, 1792. Donaldson replied that he had paid off some of this debt and that Smith was receiving £200 per annum from property belonging to the Hodgson estate. James also believed that Smith's claim was for more than was actually due her. He also said that he had made many payments as Hodgson's executor and had paid out more on behalf of the estate than he had received.

[302] TNA C12/185/38, *Smith v Longman*, 1792.

[303] LMA E/BER/CG/T/III/007/8–30 (summarised in 30). I am grateful to Lance Whitehead for bringing these records to my attention.

[304] TNA C12/178/48, *Smith v Longman*, 1791. These properties, which Donaldson had inherited from his father Colin, included a house at the corner of

together with Broderip 'having occasion for money' borrowed £500 from the attorney William Herne, using these properties as security. Herne apparently required repayment in September, so Longman was obliged to look elsewhere for money. Together with his wife Elizabeth and Broderip, he then entered into a contract with James Vashon, a naval captain in command of the ship *Europa*.

Vashon was not paid back until 1791, when Longman applied to Sir James Sanderson, Robert Harrison, John Brenchley, Matthew Bloxam and Robert Parker to act as the firm's bankers, 'the better enabling [Longman] together with Francis Fane Broderip his partner to carry on their business with credit and advantage'.[305] The bankers, based in Southwark, agreed and granted a mortgage at a rate of 5%, on condition that Longman insured the Middlesex premises against fire. He took out such a policy with Hand-in-Hand on 11 October 1790.[306] By November 1791, he had repaid the mortgage loan and interest, and in August 1792 he finally sold all the properties he had bought from Donaldson to Francis, Duke of Bedford, for £1,100.

While Longman's financial dealings enabled him to enlarge his business when all was going well, they brought court cases on his shoulders and caused problems that led ultimately to his firm's bankruptcy. To be declared bankrupt, three conditions had to be met: the debtor had to be a trader, the trader had to commit an 'act of bankruptcy' such as delaying his creditors, and the creditors had to prove that a total of £100 was owed to one creditor, £150 to two creditors or £200 to three or more creditors.[307] Although it was not always in the creditors' interest to press a debtor into bankruptcy, as they risked losing all chance of repayment,[308] Longman and Broderip

Russell Street and Drury Lane, a second property in Russell Street, a cottage in Bishell, Pontefract, premises in Allhallowgate, Ripon, and numerous meadows and fields on the edge of Ripon. Payler Donaldson was experiencing financial problems that ultimately led to his bankruptcy in February 1789.

[305] *ibid.* For this banking company, which originated about 1785, see F. G. Hilton Price, *A Handbook of London Bankers*, London, 1876, p 114–115, entry for Sir C[harles] Price & Co.

[306] LMA, formerly Guildhall ms 8674/132 p 246, policy no. 79260.

[307] See Sheila Marriner, 'English bankruptcy records and statistics before 1850', *Economic History Review* v 33 no. 3 (August 1980) p 351–366 at p 357.

[308] Roy Porter, *English Society in the Eighteenth Century*, London, 1990, p 139.

met all three conditions (otherwise they would have been declared insolvent debtors, a less desirable state to be in over the longer term).

The two partners first appeared in a bankruptcy docket on 23 May 1795, with separate suits brought against them by James Pearce (an attorney then in partnership with William Herne) and by the administrator of Joseph Spooner, deceased.[309] Two further suits followed, both brought by Culliford, Rolfe and Barrow: in November 1795 for £1,000, and in Easter term 1796 for a further £627.[310]

The London Gazette, where it was obligatory to announce bankruptcies and the meetings of bankruptcy commissioners, reported on 23 May 1795 that Longman and Broderip were required to

> surrender themselves to the Commissioners in the said Commission [of Bankrupt] ... on the 30th day of May instant, on the 6th day of June next, and on the 7th day of July following, at one in the afternoon on each of the said days, at Guildhall, London, and make a full discovery and disclosure of their estate and effects; when and where the creditors are to come prepared to prove their debts, and at the second sitting to chuse assignees, and at the last sitting the said bankrupts are required to finish their examination, and the creditors are to assent to or dissent from the allowance of their Certificate [of conformity with the statutory requirements of bankruptcy, after which they could undertake business activities without accounting to the assignees or the commissioners]. All persons indebted to the said bankrupts, or that have any of their effects, are not to pay or deliver the same but to whom the Commissioners shall appoint, but give notice to Mess. Herne and Pearce, Paternoster-Row, London.[311]

The assignees chosen were:

- William Bloxam of Lombard Street, merchant
- William Blake of Aldersgate Street, banker
- Josiah Banger of Hackney, gentleman
- Muzio Clementi of Upper Mary Bone Street, gentleman

---

[309] TNA B4/24, p 84. Spooner's connection with Longman & Broderip has not been determined.

[310] Fleet Prison commitment books (admissions registers detailing the commitment of debtors to prison), TNA PRIS 1/16, 9/2/1795–16/11/1796 p 134; Fleet Prison commitment files, TNA PRIS 2/73, 5/1795–12/11/1795.

[311] *The London Gazette*, 23 May 1795, p 522–523.

- John Wood of Foster Lane, Cheapside, jeweller[312]

William Bloxam was a brother of the firm's banker Matthew Bloxam (who served as MP for Maidstone from 1788 to 1806). At different times both brothers were in partnership with various members of the Fourdrinier family in what was described *c*1801 as 'the leading firm of London wholesale stationers'.[313] More information about the five assignees is given in the following two chapters.

The assignees decided that the business would continue to trade,[314] and appointed David Davis, who had worked for the firm for around ten years, to manage it on their behalf.[315] They also decided that it would benefit the creditors to engage Longman and Broderip to help run the business under the assignees' direction.[316] Each of Longman and Broderip was to be paid £300 per year or one sixteenth of the annual profits, whichever was greater, and each was given particular responsibilities: from July 1795 Broderip worked only at

---

[312] As listed in TNA C13/33/13, *Wood v Norman*, 1803. This legal case related to ownership of various lands in which James Longman was involved. The assignees are named in TNA B1/93 p 68–73, 28 July 1796.

[313] D[onald] C[uthbert] Coleman, *The British Paper Industry: A study in industrial growth*, Oxford, 1958, p 181. It is not known whether Longman & Broderip bought paper from this Lombard Street firm, which in the 1790s was styled 'Fourdrinier, Bloxam and Fourdriniers'. In 1792 Henry Fourdrinier, William Bloxam, Henry Fourdriner Jr and Charles Fourdrinier insured their partnership's stock and goods in London for £42,000 (Alfred H[enry] Shorter, *Paper Making in the British Isles: An historical and geographical study*, New York, 1972, p 85). The well-known Fourdrinier paper-making machine was financed later by three of Henry Fourdrinier's sons. William Bloxam was a wealthy man. According to evidence by his son Charles John Bloxam given to the House of Commons on 9 May 1837, the firm's profit for the year ended 30 June 1801 was in excess of £14,215, and when William Bloxam retired from the partnership in 1803 (because he objected to so much of the firm's capital being spent to develop the paper-making machine) he left a capital investment of £16,000 with the firm (*Report from the Select Committee on Fourdrinier's Patent…*, House of Commons Parliamentary Paper no. 351, London, 1 June 1837, p 2).

[314] *The London Gazette*, 23 May 1795, p 518.

[315] Testimony of David Davis in the trials of Richard Geast and William Gater, 6 April 1796, OB t17960406-83 and t17960406-84.

[316] TNA E112/1771/5631, *Longman v Culliford*, 1795.

the Haymarket shop and Longman only at the Cheapside and Tottenham Court Road premises.[317]

In April 1796 the bankruptcy commissioners announced that Longman's and Broderip's certificates of conformity 'will be allowed and confirmed ... unless cause be shewn to the contrary on or before the 14th day of May next.'[318] Apparently no contrary cause was established, as both Longman and Broderip received their certificates on 24 May 1796.[319] On that day, however, both of them were residing in the Fleet Prison, having been committed there on 13 November 1795 because they had not paid debts owed to Culliford, Rolfe and Barrow. After Longman and Broderip received their certificates of conformity they applied to the Court of Common Pleas to be discharged from their debt of £627 to Culliford and his partners,[320] but their application was refused and they remained in prison for nearly a year, being released on 2 November 1796[321] after the assignees had lent each of them £300 so that this debt could be paid.[322]

Prisoners were not put in the Fleet as punishment for a crime but were held in confinement, obliged to remain within a certain area or allowed out on day release, until they had paid off their debts or settled with their creditors. Residing in prison in the eighteenth century was not cheap. There were many fees to be paid, including a commitment fee and a discharge fee. On entering, you first sat for

---

[317] TNA E112/1787/6238, *Longman v Assignees*, 1802. One of the assignees, John Wood, had died in 1800.

[318] *The London Gazette*, 23 April 1796, p 384.

[319] TNA B6/9 (Certificates of Conformity, 1/7/1795–30/10/1798), p 55.

[320] TNA E112/1787/6238, *Longman v Assignees*, 1802. The Court of Common Pleas had assessed this amount of damages on 8 February 1796 (TNA CP41/163, *Culliford v Longman*, 1796, transcribed in Jenny Nex, 'Culliford and Company...', *op. cit.* in note 118 above, p 41–44).

[321] Entry books for discharges, TNA PRIS 10/52; Discharges, TNA PRIS 3/5. Several associates of Longman & Broderip also spent time in the Fleet Prison. Culliford and Barrow were committed there on 13 November 1798 but released four days later. The organ builder Henry Holland was committed on 11 February 1800 and released on 5 July in the same year.

[322] TNA E112/1787/6238, *Longman v Assignees*, 1802.

half an hour before the prison wardens so that they would recognise you if you tried to slip out with prison visitors. Then, you were obliged to chose either the master's side, for which in the 1790s you paid either 8/4 for an unfurnished or £1/1 for a furnished room, or the common side, which was for poor prisoners. Rooms were shared. Prisoners were obliged to support themselves, and most relied on friends or family to provide them with food and money. Visitors were freely admitted, and it was possible for families to move in with a prisoner or for wives (legal or otherwise) to stay overnight.[323]

On 28 July 1796 Richard Burleigh (Hodgson's executor and legatee) together with Payler Donaldson's assignees (appointed after his own bankruptcy) pressed Longman for the debts owed to Hodgson. Surviving documents reveal further details of their dealings. It had taken George Eltoft (Longman & Broderip's clerk) and Donaldson nearly three years to examine the many transactions between Longman and Hodgson before concluding in September 1794 that Longman owed Hodgson £3,879/7/11, the residue of borrowings and notes totalling 'near a million of money'.[324] Longman apparently had paid off small amounts of this debt before 1795, and it had been assumed that the full repayment would gradually follow, but the situation changed when he and Broderip became bankrupt. Burleigh and Richard Somersall (one of Payler Donaldson's assignees) were obliged to present evidence of their debt to the bankruptcy commissioners in order to receive a dividend along with the other creditors.[325] This matter was still not resolved in August 1798, when they appealed again to be allowed to prove debts owing both to Hodgson's private estate and to the Hodgson & Donaldson partnership. It was ordered that Burleigh and Somersall should be admitted as creditors and should receive a dividend in proportion to that received by other Longman & Broderip creditors.[326]

---

[323] See Roger Lee Brown, *A History of the Fleet Prison, London: The anatomy of the Fleet*, Lewiston, New York, 1996, p 181–296.

[324] TNA B1/93.

[325] TNA B1/93, B1/94, B1/96 and B1/97.

[326] TNA B1/97.

1.10 James Longman's Final Years

Following their release from prison in 1796, Longman and Broderip returned to work on behalf of the assignees. They continued to do so (Longman at Cheapside and Tottenham Court Road, Broderip at Haymarket) until 1 November 1798 when—as detailed in the next two chapters of this book—the assignees divided the business and sold it in two separate parts. Earlier that year, the stock of second-hand instruments in all three premises was offered to the public 'at very reduced prices' for 'ready money only', presumably to free up finances and space before the division and sale of the firm.[327]

After the sale, Broderip carried on at the Haymarket shop with a new partner, Charles Wilkinson Jr, who was a brother of Broderip's apprentice George Wilkinson. Longman's part of the business was bought by John Longman, Muzio Clementi (musician), Frederick Augustus Hyde (a former employee of Longman & Broderip), Frederick William Collard (piano maker), Josiah Banger (one of the assignees) and David Davis (organ builder and former employee of Longman & Broderip, who had managed the firm for the assignees). This John Longman was James's brother[328] who lived in Somerset in 1803[329] and may have continued living there until his death in 1819.[330] According to documents provided in an 1803 legal case, John did not settle in London in 1798 but remained in Milborne Port, where he had his own business; instead, he had his brother James act for him in London.[331]

It appears therefore that John became a partner of Longman, Clementi & Co. to help his brother but did not take an active part in the company's daily affairs. Presumably John could pay the capital

---

327 *The Star*, 23 April 1798, p 1.

328 TNA C/13/70/42, *Shaw v Longman*, 1806.

329 TNA C13/29/34, *Longman v Clementi*, 1803.

330 The age (77) of a John Longman buried on 12 June 1819 at St John the Evangelist, Milborne Port, coincides with that of James Longman's brother John, who was baptised on 30 July 1742 (National Burial Index—see http://www.ancestor-search.info/SRC-NationalBurial.htm; parish records for Corton Denham, SRO mf D\P\co.d.2/1/1 M4184/2, baptisms 1538–1760).

331 TNA C13/29/34, *Longman v Clementi*, 1803.

required of partners but James could not, and John preferred to invest directly in the partnership than to lend money to his brother so that James could provide the required capital. James was to receive £200 per year for his work for the company and was to inherit John's share of the business should he die first. In addition, James was to receive £1/1/– for every piano sold by the company that made use of William Southwell's patent, or £315 per annum, whichever was greater. Furthermore, once John had been reimbursed for his initial investment, James was to take over his share in the business.[332]

From the estimates given in Chapter 3 of the partners' investments in Longman, Clementi & Co. it appears that they paid £12,000 for the Cheapside and Tottenham Court Road part of the Longman & Broderip business.[333] As the entire firm, including its Haymarket branch, had been valued at £29,377/11/11 in 1783,[334] Longman, Clementi & Co. seem to have got a good deal from the assignees.

Unfortunately, James Longman's financial problems were not solved by the 1798 sale and the agreement he made with Longman, Clementi & Co. Frederick Hyde reportedly added a clause to the draft of that agreement stating that if James were imprisoned he would not receive the £200 annuity, as he would be unable to work for the company.[335] James was supposed to work solely for that company but was accused of 'undertaking business for his own benefit', trying to 'seduce' manufacturers and workmen away from the company, and going into a business with a Doctor Barton.[336] These accusations are considered in the next section.

Since James had apparently ceased to co-operate with Longman, Clementi & Co. its partners decided to bypass his interest in the Southwell patent, which they regarded as important for their business, and to go instead to Broderip, who had a similar right. They

---

332 *ibid.*

333 See page 133 below.

334 TNA B1/94, 1797–1798, p 111–114.

335 TNA C13/2333/6, *Longman v Banger*, 1803. This case refers to the same issues as TNA C13/29/34, *Longman v Clementi*.

336 TNA C13/29/34, *Longman v Clementi*.

paid Broderip £157/10/– for a licence to continue making pianos based upon that patent, thereby stopping James's threat to withdraw their ability to make such instruments by depriving them of the use of his licence from Southwell.[337] As James still was in debt, he assigned in January 1802 his rights relating to the Southwell patent to William Styan, Richard Hovil and Joseph James.[338] They became discontented when the money amounted to little because of widespread adoption of Southwell's ideas without payment to him or his assignees.[339]

In the event, Hyde's clause proved significant. James could not pay his debts and was readmitted into the Fleet Prison on 26 January 1803 for want of bail in four cases, totalling about £460.[340] This time, however, he did not leave alive. According to the prison inquest he was taken ill on 8 November 1803 with 'a pleurisy in his side attended with fever and a cold'. He was attended by Mr Box, a surgeon, and was prescribed 'medicine and other necessary things'.[341] Sadly, however, he died shortly before midnight on 11 November 1803, aged sixty-three.[342] Thirteen men from the parish of St Bride's Fleet Street, along with the coroner, Thomas Shelton, attended his body and witnessed that he had died a natural death. His remains were interred in the lower ground of St Bride's church, Fleet Street, on 15 November.[343]

His death was noticed in *The Times*[344] and in *The Gentleman's Magazine*,[345] which published a longer obituary of him in the following month:

---

337 TNA C13/2333/6, *Longman v Banger*, 1803.

338 In TNA C13/29/34, *Longman v Clementi*, 1803, Hovil is called Henry, but in TNA C13/2333/6, *Longman v Banger*, 1803, he is referred to as Richard Hovil 'in the said bill called Henry Hovill'.

339 Bozarth and Debenham, 'Piano wars', *op. cit.* in note 100 above.

340 TNA PRIS 1/26, p 49; PRIS 2/88.

341 Probably William Hutchinson Box, surgeon of Newgate Prison and other city institutions. At this time the Fleet Prison had no resident medical staff.

342 Corporation of London Record Office, Prison Inquests, 12 November 1803.

343 St Bride's Fleet Street burials, LMA, formerly Guildhall ms 6543/1.

344 *The Times*, 16 November 1803, p 3.

345 *The Gentleman's Magazine* v 123 (November 1803) p 1098.

> Mr Longman served his time at Johnstone's [sic] musick-warehouse, opposite Bow church, Cheapside. Without the advantage of education, by superior sagacity and strength of intellect, he established a musical connexion superior to any other in Europe; and likewise introduced into celebrity a number of capital performers, &c. His finances, however, were affected by the common misfortunes of the Continent. Mr Longman, who, according to his own account, had 70,000*l*. owing to his establishment in Cheapside, Tottenham Court road, &c. was compelled to have recourse to a statute of bankruptcy; a remaining contingent of which immured him in the Fleet prison, where, borne down by the severe pressure of 'a wounded spirit', he was suddenly seized with a pleuritic complaint, which terminated in his dissolution.[346]

This offers a further explanation for James Longman's financial problems. The French wars had led to widespread economic difficulties and a sharp decline in foreign trade in the 1790s, resulting in a British recession in 1797.[347] The figure of £70,000 appears on first perusal to be very high, but it is not out of proportion to Longman's dealings with Hodgson, or the valuation of the firm made twenty years earlier.

Another obituary notice ended thus:

> borne down by the mortification of an afflicted mind, he was seized with a pleuritic complaint, which hastened his dissolution; a striking instance of the capriciousness of fortune, and furnishing another proof that however, the enlarged spirit of commercial adventure may tend to the promulgation of the liberal sciences: It too often fails of procuring for its possessor that pecuniary state of comfort so much more attained by the plain ungifted tradesman![348]

1.11 LEGACY

The activities of Longman & Broderip's two successors, Broderip & Wilkinson and Longman, Clementi & Co., are described in the next

---

[346] *The Gentleman's Magazine* v 123 (December 1803) p 1183–1184.

[347] George Rudé, *Hanoverian London 1714–1808*, London, 1971, p 228.

[348] *Hampshire Telegraph, and Sussex Chronicle; Or, Portsmouth and Chichester Advertiser*, 21 November 1803, p 4.

two chapters. For a full picture of Longman & Broderip's legacy some smaller offshoots of the firm need to be mentioned.

The third most significant music-selling business involving the Longman family was that of John Longman at 131 Cheapside. It must be stressed that he was not James Longman's brother who was a partner of Longman, Clementi & Co.,[349] nor was he James Longman's son. In an 1806 legal case this John testified that he was 'of Cheapside in the City of London organ builder',[350] and noted that he had obtained a patent relating to barrel organs on 27 January 1801.[351] He stated that he knew the brothers James and John well, was a relation of theirs and had worked for a time as an instrument maker for Longman, Clementi & Co.[352] It may be more than a coincidence that when the elder John resigned from the Longman, Clementi & Co. partnership in March 1801 the younger John set up on his own, but evidence has not been found that these events were directly connected.[353]

---

[349] Contrary to Humphries and Smith, *Music Publishing in the British Isles*, *op. cit.*, p 217–218.

[350] TNA C/13/70/42, *Shaw v Longman*, 1806.

[351] Subsequently numbered 2468. See B[ennet] Woodcroft, *op. cit.* in note 91 above, p 38. One of John Longman's barrel organs, now in the Scott Polar Research Institute, University of Cambridge, was taken by Rear-Admiral Sir William Edward Parry on his Arctic expeditions in the early nineteenth century and has been restored and recorded. See Clive Holland and F. F. Hill, 'Sir William Edward Parry's barrel organ', *Polar Record* v 16 no. 102 (September 1972) p 413–414, and Clive Holland and F. F. Hill, *Parry's Barrel Organ: John Longman's new invented patent barrel organ with bells, drums and triangle*, booklet accompanying Saydisc Records Stereo CD-SDL 234, 1972.

[352] This connection is confirmed by an advertisement in *The Morning Post and Gazetteer*, 9 December 1801, p 2, by 'Longman and Co. No. 131, Cheapside (from 26)'.

[353] Advertisements indicate that in September 1801 only one music seller, Longman, Clementi & Co., was trading under the Longman name. *The Times*, 10 September 1801, p 1, advertised 'tickets ... from Messrs Longman, Clementi, & Co. Cheapside'. By the end of October the Longman name was used by a different music seller. *The Times*, 27 October 1801, p 1, advertised tickets from 'Clementi, & Co. Cheapside' and 'Longman, No. 131, Cheapside'. After the elder John Longman withdrew from the Longman, Clementi & Co. partnership that company was restyled 'Clementi & Co.', enabling the younger John

It appears that James had encouraged the younger John Longman and had offered to support him once the entanglement with Longman, Clementi & Co. was resolved. The accusation mentioned in the last section that James was seducing manufacturers and workmen away from that company and for his own benefit seems consistent with efforts he may have made to help the new Longman & Co. at 131 Cheapside. The Dr Barton with whom James is said to have had business ties at this time seems likely to have been Joseph Barton of 7 Berners Street,[354] who in 1800 and 1801 marketed a product he had developed called 'vital wine'.[355] However, the younger John Longman remained disappointed because of James's ongoing financial difficulties and death.

The younger John appears to have got financial support for his business from another source. A partnership 'lately subsisting between John Longman, Richard Hovil and Joseph Seel[e]y, of Cheapside, London, musical instrument makers and carried out under the Firm of Longman and Co.' was dissolved on 26 May 1804.[356] As Richard Hovil and Joseph Seeley are recorded elsewhere as coopers of Great Hermitage Street, Wapping,[357] it seems unlikely that they were actively involved in musical instrument making, so their principal roles in the business may have been as investors. The younger John Longman subsequently formed a partnership with Thomas Thompson that was dissolved on 5 April 1805.[358] They

---

Longman to trade under the Longman name without confusion with other music sellers.

[354] No other Dr Barton is listed in the editions of *Boyle's Fashionable Court and Country Guide* published in London in 1800 and 1801.

[355] Barton sold this product through Messrs Ching & Butler, apothecaries, who had premises at 2 Cheapside (advertisement, *The Morning Chronicle*, 19 July 1800, p 1). Although that address suggests how James Longman and Barton might have made contact, no details of their relationship are known.

[356] *The London Gazette*, 2 June 1804, p 692.

[357] *The London Gazette*, 28 June 1803, p 777; 5 January 1808, p 44; and 14 June 1808, p 841. These notices show that two Richard Hovils were involved, senior and junior. Whether they were related to, or one was the same person as, the Richard Hovil to whom James Longman sold his rights to Southwell's patent is not clear.

[358] *The London Gazette*, 2 April 1805, p 441.

appear to have been related by marriage, as a John Longman married Sarai [sic] Thompson at St Matthew, Friday Street (near Cheapside) in 1803, and one of the witnesses was Thomas Thompson Jr.[359]

The scope of the younger John Longman's publishing activities is indicated by his three-page *A Catalogue of Songs printed by John Longman & Co.* issued about 1810, which also included some instrumental music.[360] A viola labelled 'John Longman ... 131 Cheapside' was auctioned in London in 2008.[361]

Three further Longmans appear in subsequent years as musical instrument makers, but their relationships are hazy. About 1816 the younger John Longman was succeeded at 131 Cheapside by Giles Longman,[362] who worked as a music seller with James Herron until their partnership was dissolved on 24 June 1822.[363] In the following year Giles and Theodore Charles Bates became partners, the announcement of which suggests that Giles and John were brothers:

> G. Longman, late of 131, Cheapside, begs to return his sincere thanks to his friends and the public for the many favours conferred on himself and his late brother, and at the same time to inform them he has commenced partnership with Mr Bates, at 19 and 20, St. John's-square, near Smithfield, where they continue to manufacture church, chamber, and barrel organs, cabinet, square, and self-acting pianofortes, of the most superior description. As G. Longman superintends the manufacturing and finishing of every instrument himself, his friends and the public may with the most implicit confidence rely upon every instrument purchased at their manufactory, being, in point of elegance of make, freedom of touch, and brilliancy of tone, equal to any, and superior to most, that can be obtained at any house in London.[364]

---

359 A[lice] M[ay] Bruce Bannerman (ed.), *The Register of St Matthew, Friday Street, London ... marriages, 1754–1812*, Harleian Society registers no. 63, London, 1933, p 107.

360 Copy at BL 7896.h.40(10).

361 Bonhams sale of *Fine Musical Instruments*, 24 June 2008, lot 124.

362 The succession certainly occurred before the 1818 legal case *Birchall v Longman* (TNA C13/729/6), in which the music seller Robert Birchall sought to enjoin Longman & Herron from selling their publication of a Beethoven sonata because Birchall had bought its English copyright and had published the music.

363 *The London Gazette*, 25 June 1822, p 1061.

364 *The Times*, 16 August 1823, p 1.

Although this advertisement gives Giles's first initial only, the notice of the dissolution of Longman & Bates on 1 August 1829 included the full names of both partners.[365] Soon after then they were joined by the music seller Samuel Chappell and traded as Chappell, Longman & Bates.[366]

During the time of these two partnerships 131 Cheapside was occupied by the music seller Robert William Keith, first as sole trader and then as the partnership Keith, Prowse & Co.[367] However, in the 1830s another George Longman, a son of the younger John and Sarai, returned to 131 Cheapside and made musical instruments there.[368]

A Richard Longman (whose relationship to the other Longmans is not known) worked as a musical instrument maker in Tottenham Court Road by 1802. He, like James, suffered bankruptcy in 1803 and was committed to the Fleet Prison on 27 April 1803.[369] He subsequently spent time in Newgate Prison.[370] Almost certainly he was not the son of John and Sarai mentioned in her will, as his dates do not correlate with theirs.

James Longman's marriage to Elizabeth *née* Tomkyns produced no children,[371] and it seems that they separated, at least informally, as James's will left everything to his executrix Frances

---

[365] *The London Gazette*, 25 August 1829, p 1592.

[366] Humphries and Smith, *op. cit.*, p 215–216.

[367] *ibid.*, p 198. Keith's partner was the music seller William Prowse.

[368] Sarai Longman's will, made 16 January 1840, proved 15 December 1853 (court copy at TNA PROB 11/2182), said that she was a widow of High Street Kensington, Middlesex. She left everything to her three sons: John Thomas Longman, Richard Longman and George Longman.

[369] According to debtors schedules in LMA CLA/047/LJ/17/084 concerning Richard Longman 'formerly of Tottenham Court Road and late of Tottenham Court New Road in the County of Middlesex musical instrument maker'.

[370] *The London Gazette*, 13 July 1811, p 1315–1316, where the prisoner is described as 'Richard Longman, formerly of Tottenham-Court, New-Road, and late of No. 23, Grafton-Street, Fitzroy-Square, … carpenter'.

[371] Evidenced in the 1818 legal case *Doe dem. Tomkyns v Willan*, reported in Richard Vaughan Barnewall and Edward Hall Alderson, *Reports of Cases argued and determined in the Court of King's Bench* v 2, London, 1819, p 84–93 at p 86.

Loftis *otherwise* St John, spinster 'with whom I have cohabited several years and by whom I have living two children'.[372] Although he did not name these children in his will, information about them appears in Frances's 1806 appeal on behalf of herself and her children to the parish of St Clement Danes for poor relief.[373] James John St John Smith Clementi Longman was born on 26 July 1796 at 11 Royal Row, Lambeth;[374] his younger brother John Sykes Longman was born on 1 August 1803 in Thorney Street, Bloomsbury. As the poor were the responsibility of the parish in which they were born, it was ordered that James should be removed to Lambeth while the three-year old John was sent to Bloomsbury. What their mother decided to do is not recorded, but she was living with her mother then so one can hope that she had some familial support at a difficult time.

Frances was said to have been about thirty years old then, which makes her James's junior by about thirty-five years. When their first child was born she was aged about twenty. Assuming that both pregnancies were full term, each child was conceived within weeks before their father was admitted to the Fleet Prison. John would barely have known his father as he died in the Fleet when John was only three months old. It is not known what the young Longmans did with their lives, or how long they lived, but young James married one Mary Dimes in 1838.[375]

No clear link has been established between the Longmans involved in the music trade and the better-known side of the family who worked in the book trade, although Anne Broderip *née* Longman appears to provide a connection. Her branch of the Longman family

---

[372] James Longman's will, made 11 November 1803, proved 20 February 1804 (TNA PROB 11/1405 p 26–27). Elizabeth Longman's will, made 10 April 1816, proved 13 February 1817 (TNA PROB 11/1589 p 214–215) named Frederick William Collard Jr as one of her executors, and included both her friend William Frederick Collard and Mary, the wife of Frederick William Collard, as beneficiaries of her estate.

[373] City of Westminster Archives Centre STC/B/1/3/1194, St Clement Danes poor relief examination books 1/1/1805–17/10/1806, p 146.

[374] But baptised almost five years later on 29 June 1801 at St Anne Soho (IGI, which records 'Smythe' instead of 'Smith').

[375] Marriages at St James, Clerkenwell (information from www.ancestry.com). The banns were read on 11, 18 and 25 February 1838.

moved to Bristol from Somerset to make soap.[376] Thomas Longman I, who moved to London in 1716 where he later started the Longman & Co. bookselling and publishing business, belonged to that branch.[377]

James Longman's importance is not widely recognised today, in part because of the prejudice with which his bankruptcy has been interpreted. His achievements, however, were admired by nineteenth-century commentators. In 1825 Thomas Busby wrote that:

> It was the ambition of the late James Longman, not only to render himself, if possible, the greatest music-seller existing, but to raise the credit and importance of the trade he exercised. One of the methods he employed for effecting this purpose was, to buy up the plates of all the songs then in circulation, and to persuade the different publishers to burn all their three-halfpenny and three-penny ballads and cantatas, and, in future, not to sell even the shortest melody under sixpence.[378]

Furthermore,

> The musical genius of this country was much promoted by the liberal spirit of the house of Longman and Broderip, which flourished between the years 1780 and 1800, and still continues under the firm of Clementi, Collard, and Co. Those tradesmen, by bringing a respectable capital and extensive credit to bear on the interests of music, not only improved every kind of musical instrument, and created a commerce in them with every part of the world, but gave prices for copy-rights, far surpassing any thing that had been anticipated by the previous generation. ... Nor was the benefit to the musical profession, derived from these gentlemen, confined merely to the purse; but they conferred a nearly equal service by keeping an open table at which professors and amateurs, from every part of the world, had the opportunity of meeting,

---

[376] According to Dennis Longman's notes (see note 7 above).

[377] For the Longman bookselling family see Philip Wallis, *At the Sign of the Ship, Notes on the House of Longman 1724–1974*, Burnt Mill, Harlow, Essex, 1974. The relationship of Thomas Longman I to Anne Broderip is not clarified in Dennis Longman's notes.

[378] Busby, *Concert Room and Orchestra Anecdotes…*, *op. cit.* in note 286 above, v 1 p 82–83. As this book was co-published by Clementi & Co. it is plausible that some of its anecdotes were confirmed by partners of that company who had been involved in Longman & Broderip's activities.

and of eliciting from each other information of mutual and considerable advantage.[379]

1.12 Conclusions

Longman & Broderip appear to have been the foremost and largest of the music sellers who sprang up in London during the latter part of the eighteenth century. James Longman developed the import and export of musical instruments in the colonies and Europe and coupled this with the publication and sale of music and other paraphernalia for use with those instruments. An active social network of men and women was based in and around the Cheapside, Haymarket and Tottenham Court Road premises of the firm. Their litigation made an important contribution towards establishing the law of copyright in relation to music.

The financial problems of the firm and hence their sometimes shady reputation in modern times seem to have been a result of James's somewhat loose financial dealings. This can be interpreted as deliberate misconduct or simply as an individual out of his depth in a business which grew too large for him to manage. Perhaps in the light of recent financial crises, his activities may be viewed more kindly than has sometimes been the case.

As well as selling musical instruments, Longman and Broderip may personally have contributed to their making, but due to the loss of the firm's records we may never know what each of them did. Their situation is little different from the 'great' contemporary piano makers such as Kirkman and Broadwood who are unlikely to have been able to oversee the making of every instrument that bore their names.

James Longman and his partners had a major impact on the musical world of Britain and its colonies at a time when social, industrial and economic uncertainties affected many kinds of business in unprecedented ways. Industrialisation changed some industries beyond recognition, while the developing global market created opportunities for those willing to take risks. Longman seems to have been a risk-taker and although his entrepreneurial spirit sometimes

[379] *ibid.*, v 1 p 126–127.

paid off it nevertheless caused trouble for some of those around him. Ultimately, though, he suffered most himself, dying within the Fleet Prison. It is for their entrepreneurship, the size and extent of the business empire they built up and the networks they helped to establish in the musical community that the eighteenth-century firm of Longman & Broderip should be remembered.

~ 2 ~

BRODERIP & WILKINSON

Michael Kassler

On 1 November 1798 the following advertisement appeared on the front page of *The Times*:

> FRANCIS BRODERIP respectfully informs the Nobility, Gentry, and the Public in general, that the Musical Business lately carried on under the Firm of LONGMAN and BRODERIP is now separated; and that he has no connection whatever with Mr Longman, or with the Houses in Cheapside and Tottenham Court Road, but will in future carry on the Business in the Haymarket only, in conjunction with Mr C. Wilkinson. He gratefully acknowledges the favours which have already been conferred on the House, and assures the Public that all Orders in the Musical Line, directed to BRODERIP and WILKINSON, No. 13, HAYMARKET, will be executed with the utmost punctuality and attention.
>
> The separation of the Concern having been long in contemplation, F. B. has some time since established a separate Manufactory, and has engaged Workmen, who have been under his direction for many years, and whose superior abilities in the excellent workmanship and fine tone of their Instruments, particularly of the new invented Patent Piano Fortes with additional Keys, have been long known and acknowledged.[1]

The successors to James Longman's side of the former partnership, led by his brother John Longman and Muzio Clementi, replied in an advertisement two days later:

> LONGMAN, CLEMENTI, and Company, as Successors to LONGMAN and BRODERIP, No. 26, Cheapside, and in Tottenham-Court-Road, beg leave to announce to the Nobility and Public in general, that they have established an extensive and liberal Plan for carrying on the Trade of Musical Instrument Makers, also for printing, publishing, and vending all Musical Productions worthy of notice. ...

---

[1] *The Times*, 1 November 1798. This advertisement was repeated several times and also was placed in other newspapers that month.

> LONGMAN, CLEMENTI, and Company, request all Orders intended for them may be addressed to No. 26, Cheapside, as they have no connexion whatever with Mr Broderip, in the Haymarket.[2]

As noted in the last chapter, the assignees of Longman & Broderip, appointed after the 1795 bankruptcy of James Longman and Francis Fane Broderip, allowed the business to continue to trade.[3] On 6 April 1797 the firm's creditors were asked to empower these assignees

> to sell and dispose of the Stock and good Will of the Houses and Manufactories at Cheapside, the Haymarket and Tottenham-Court Road, either together or separate, by private Contract, to any Person or Persons who may come forward to purchase the same.[4]

The creditors must have agreed to this, as the assignees 'disposed of the stock and trade, in Cheapside, to Messrs John Longman, Clementi, and Co. and the stock and trade, in the Haymarket, to Messrs Broderip and Wilkinson' on 1 November 1798.[5]

The capital that enabled the Haymarket stock and trade to be bought was provided by Charles Wilkinson Sr, a wealthy man who worked at the Custom House and lived at 17 Highbury Place, Islington.[6] As one of the assignees—the stationer William Bloxam—resided a block away at Highbury Grove, Islington,[7] it seems

---

[2] Advertisement, *The Times*, 3 November 1798, p 1, repeated several times and also published in other newspapers. The full advertisement is quoted on page 128–129 below.

[3] See page 79 above.

[4] *The London Gazette*, 28 March 1797, p 303.

[5] *The London Gazette*, 2 April 1799, p 319.

[6] His wealth is indicated by his subscription of £2,000 towards the Bank of England loan for 1797. See [Bank of England], *A List of the Names and Residencies of the Subscribers to the Loan of £18,000,000 for the Service of the Year 1797*, London, 1797, p 25.

[7] Wilkinson lived at 17 Highbury Place from at least 1795: see Ann Wilkinson (his daughter)→[Sylvanus] Urban (pseudonym of the editor of *The Gentleman's Magazine*), 22 January 1853, printed in *The Gentleman's Magazine* n.s. v 39 (February 1853) p 114. The Highbury addresses of both Bloxam and Wilkinson are listed in *Boyle's City Companion to the Court Guide for the Year 1799*,

plausible that he informed Wilkinson of the assignees' desire to sell the Longman & Broderip assets, and that Wilkinson then pursued this opportunity. He must have made contact with Broderip before November 1797, as on the fourth of that month Wilkinson's youngest son George was bound apprentice to Broderip for seven years.[8]

A condition of Wilkinson's investment was that his eldest son Charles Wilkinson Jr be made an equal partner to Broderip in the enterprise styled 'Broderip & Wilkinson' that began trading on 1 November 1798.[9] Charles Jr's musical interests and the role that he played in the firm are not known.[10] His brother George, however, showed much greater affinity to the business and on 1 January 1805, soon after completing his apprenticeship and reaching the age of twenty-one, he replaced Charles Jr as Broderip's partner,[11] and Charles Jr went on to do other things.[12]

London, [1799], part 2 p 45–46. The preface of this book is dated 20 January 1799, suggesting that Bloxam lived in Highbury Grove in the latter part of 1798 although not establishing that he was there in 1797.

[8] See Henry Broadhurst Wilkinson, *Souvenir of the Broadhurst Wilkinsons: Descendants of Joseph Edmondson, Esq., F.S.A. Mowbray Herald Extraordinary, 1764*, Manchester, privately printed, 1902, p 22 (online at http://contentdm.lib.byu.edu/cdm4/document.php?CISOROOT=/FH1&CISOPTR=9805&REC=14). See also Michael Kassler, 'Broderip, Wilkinson and the first English edition of the "48"', *The Musical Times* v 147 no. 1895 (summer 2006) p 67–76 at p 71.

[9] Henry Broadhurst Wilkinson wrote (*loc. cit.*) that his grandfather Charles Wilkinson Sr 'bought for his eldest son, Charles, a half share in Mr Broderip's business'.

[10] The only manuscript document relating to Broderip & Wilkinson known to have survived from the time when Charles Jr was a partner is a bond dated 30 January 1800 guaranteeing the satisfactory service of Richard Taylor as collecting clerk to Francis Fane Broderip and Charles Wilkinson (i.e., Charles Jr) 'in their trade as musicsellers'. I am grateful to David Bramwell for sending me a photocopy of this bond and also to Neil Robertson for putting me in contact with him.

[11] Henry Broadhurst Wilkinson, *loc. cit.* The change of partnership is recorded in *The London Gazette*, 12 January 1805, p 71.

[12] In 1806 he operated a warehouse in Basing Lane with a partner, William Stephenson, but left when their partnership was dissolved on 31 December 1807 (*The London Gazette*, 31 May 1808, p 778, and 28 June 1808, p 918). Charles

As none of the three Wilkinsons had prior experience in the music trade, Broderip & Wilkinson must have relied initially upon Francis Broderip's knowledge to carry on and develop the new enterprise. The range of their activities—which is similar to that previously undertaken by Longman & Broderip—is detailed in two notices that were printed for Broderip & Wilkinson shortly after the partnership began trading.

The title-page of their edition of Ignace Pleyel's 'Six duetts for two violins', op. 18, announced that it was

> *Printed by* BRODERIP *&* WILKINSON *No. 13 Hay-market. | Music Sellers & Musical Instrument Makers to their Majesties :& His Royal Highness | The Prince of Wales. —— Where Musical Instruments in General | are Manufactured & Sold Wholesale & for Exportation, on very Advantageous | Terms —— Likewise Engrave, Print, Import & Sell every Musical Publica- | tion of this Country & every other Part of Europe —— NB Organs, Piano Fortes, | Harpsichords &c. Lent out, Convey'd. & Tuned in Town & Country on the | shortest notice &c&c&c.*[13]

The second notice was placed inside a barrel organ made for the firm:

> BY [Royal crest] ROYAL [Prince of Wales crest] PATENT. | MUSICAL INSTRUMENTS AND MUSICAL ARTICLES | MANUFACTURED & SOLD | WHOLESALE, RETAIL, AND FOR EXPORTATION, | BY | BRODERIP AND WILKINSON, | No. 13, Hay - Market, London; | MUSICAL INSTRUMENT MAKERS, AND MUSIC-SELLERS | TO | THEIR MAJESTIES, | HIS ROYAL HIGHNESS THE PRINCE OF WALES, | AND | ALL THE ROYAL FAMILY, | WHERE ARE MANUFACTURED AND SOLD, | Their Patent Grand, & Square Piano Fortes, with & without additional Keys, | And THEIR NEW IMPROVED PEDAL HARPS, | Also, imported best Italian and Roman Strings, for Violins, Tenors, Mandolines, Violincellos, Double Basses, | Welsh Harps &c. German Wire for Harpsichords, Spinnets, Piano Fortes, Guitars &c. Italian Catgut and | Wire Strings,

---

Wilkinson Jr's address is given as Basing Lane in the 14 June 1806 legal document cited in note 37 below.

[13] The copy of this edition in the University of Iowa music library, catalogue no. rare book FOLIO M287.P44 B.519–524 1798, is printed on paper watermarked '1798' (Rita Benton, *Ignace Pleyel: A thematic catalogue of his compositions*, New York, 1977, p 247). On the title-pages of each violin part the opus number is given by an engraved roman numeral 'X' followed by an arabic numeral '8' written in ink.

silvered in the completest Manner, and well proportioned for Violins, Basses, Guitars, and | Piano Fortes. | Regiments supplied with complete Sets of the best Military Instruments, warranted. | ALSO | Chamber Organs. | Barrel Organs, with Drums and | Harp Stops, and Triangle | Guitars | Piano Forte Guitars. | Eolian Harps. | Violincellos. | Tenors. | Violins of all Sorts. | Kits | Bows of every Description | German Flutes, from one key to | six, tipt or plain, with silver | or Brass Keys. | English Flutes of all sorts | Flageolets. | Bird Pipes. | Pipes and Tabors. | Bassoons. | Clarinets, tipt. and plain. | Hautboys, tipt and plain. | Fifes of all Kinds. | Concert Horns. | E. Flat ditto. | Concert Trumpets | E. Flat ditto. | Tambourins for Ladies. | Kettle Drums. | Bass Drums. | Military Tambourins. | Common ditto. | Cymbals. | Triangles. | Bugle Horns, large & small. | Hunting Horns. | Tuning Hammers and Forks. | Brass Mutes. | Ivory and Wood ditto. | Violin, Tenor, and Violincello | Pegs. | Cases for Violins, Guitars, | Flutes | &c. &c. | Violin, Tenor, and Violincello | Tail-Pieces. | Violin, Tenor, and Violincello | Bridges. | Rosin Boxes. | Rosin Rolls. | French Horn Mouth-Pieces. | Trumpet ditto. | German Flute ditto. | Hautboy Reeds. | Clarinet ditto. | Bassoon ditto. | Reed Cases of all Sorts. | Harpsichord and Piano Forte Wire. | Covered Strings for Guitars, &c. | &c. | Best Roman Strings. | A great variety of Eolian Harps constantly on Sale. | Instruments lent on Hire, and repaired or tuned, in Town and Country, at the shortest Notice, and | in the best Manner. | Merchants, and Captains of Ships supplied on the most advantageous Terms. | N.B. MUSIC NEATLY ENGRAVED AND PRINTED. | Where may be had, also, every New Musical Publication, as soon as printed. | Second Hand Musical Instruments, of every Description, by the most eminent Makers.[14]

Although neither of these notices is dated, their claims that the partnership held a warrant to supply the royal family indicate that they were printed before March 1799. Such claims can be traced to Francis Broderip's initiation on 16 April 1787 as a foundation member of the Prince of Wales's Masonic lodge, which consisted then 'wholly of those who were honoured with appointments under His Royal Highness or men firmly attached to His Royal Highness's

[14] This barrel organ, now RCM Museum of Instruments no. RCM 103, is described and illustrated in Elizabeth Wells (ed.), *The Royal College of Music Museum of Instruments Catalogue: Part II. Keyboard Instruments*, London, 2000, p 137. Lydnesay G. Langwill and Noel Boston, *Church and Chamber Barrel-Organs*, Edinburgh, 2nd ed., 1970, p 46, list ten other barrel organs of differing specifications that were made for Broderip & Wilkinson; one of these is pictured in *The Music Box* no. 4 (Christmas, 1963) p 17.

person and interests'.[15] This initiation clearly was related to Longman & Broderip's appointment as 'music-sellers to his Royal Highness the Prince of Wales', which they began to advertise about January 1788.[16] The lodge's minute-book does not record Broderip's membership after Longman & Broderip's bankruptcy,[17] but he must have believed that his old firm's royal warrants were transferable to his new firm, as they advertised soon after starting business that they were 'music-sellers to their Majesties and his Royal Highness the Prince of Wales'.[18] However, their assertion that the prince permitted Broderip & Wilkinson to use his name seems to have been incorrect, as they apparently stopped advertising any royal ties after February 1799.[19]

---

[15] Thomas Fenn *et al.* (compilers), *Prince of Wales's Lodge, No. 259. List of Members...*, London, 1910, p 11–15. The Prince of Wales was initiated on the same day. In 1788–1789 Broderip actively supported the lodge's efforts to establish the Royal Cumberland Free Mason School for 'female children of indigent free masons' (advertisements, *The Times*, 26 September 1788, p 1; and 24 March 1789, p 1; and *St James's Chronicle*, 16 May 1789, p 1). In 1799 both 'Mrs Broderip' and 'Mrs Longman' were governesses of the school, and the annual subscribers included 'F. Broderip' and 'Longman' (advertisement, *Morning Star*, 4 May 1789, p 1).

[16] For instance, in *The World*, 5 January 1788, p 2, and in their July 1788 and July 1789 'complete registers' of published and imported music (copies at BL 1609/5257 and BL 1601/587). James Longman was not a member of this lodge. As shown in the letter reproduced in *Figure 1.4* on page 50 above, a Longman & Broderip employee referred to their Tottenham Court Road manufactory in 1792 as a 'royal manufactory'.

[17] I am very grateful to Diane Clements of The Library and Museum of Freemasonry, London for transcribing entries of the lodge's minute book relating to Broderip, and to lodge no. 259 for allowing a transcript to be made.

[18] See, for instance, their advertisement in *E. Johnson's British Gazette and Sunday Monitor*, 2 December 1788, p 1.

[19] The Prince of Wales is mentioned in their advertisement in *The Star*, 9 February 1799, p 2, but all later Broderip & Wilkinson advertisements seen do not refer to the prince or to other members of the royal family. Although Wells, *loc. cit.*, dates the RCM 103 barrel organ *c*1805, the reference to a patent from the Prince of Wales in the notice inside the organ suggests that 1798–1799 is a more likely date. It may be relevant that on 19 March 1800 Monzani & Cimador advertised (*The Star*, p 1) that they were 'music-sellers to his Royal Highness the Prince of Wales', and they continued to use this style for several years.

In addition to the activities mentioned in the two quoted notices, Broderip & Wilkinson retailed accessories such as pens which (they said) were particularly suited to composers and copyists of music,[20] collected subscriptions and sold tickets for concerts,[21] received subscriptions for publications of music[22] and books about music,[23] and supported authors who retained the copyright of their works by subscribing for six copies in advance of publication.[24]

The international aspect of their business is documented on their printed label

> Imported & Sold | by | Broderip & Wilkinson | Musical Instrument Makers & Music Sellers | At their Warehouse. 13 Hay market | London | Who have a regular Correspondence with all the Most Eminent Professors & publishers of Music in every part of Europe

affixed to a copy of Josef Gelinek's 'Variazioni del Duetto La ci darem la mano Nell'Opera Il D. Giovanni' that was published by Artaria & Co. in Vienna about 1791.[25] As this Broderip & Wilkinson label is pasted over a similarly worded Longman & Broderip label placed over Artaria's name on the title-page, it appears that Longman & Broderip imported this copy into England but had not sold it when

---

[20] Advertisement, *The Morning Chronicle*, 17 July 1801, p 1.

[21] See, for instance, the New Musical Fund's advertisement in *The Morning Post and Gazetteer*, 4 February 1799, p 1.

[22] See, for instance, the advertisement in *The True Briton*, 30 May 1800, p 2, seeking London subscribers to the publication of William Crotch's 'Ode to Fancy', his exercise for the degree of Doctor of Music at Oxford.

[23] Such as Matthew Peter King's *A General Treatise on Music*; see the advertisement in *The Times*, 9 November 1799, p 2.

[24] This is shown, for example, in the printed lists of subscribers to Augustus F. C. Kollmann, *An Essay on Practical Musical Composition*, London, 1799, p v, and to John Sale, *A Collection of New Glees*, London, *c*1800.

[25] Beinecke M27 G317 L1+ OVERSIZE. I thank Eva Wrightson for information about this copy, which bears Artaria's plate number 339. (Dates of Artaria plate numbers are given in Otto Erich Deutsch, *Musikverlags Nummern*, 2nd ed., Berlin, 1961, p 7–8.) I am grateful to Dale Gilligan for the information that a copy of Ignace Pleyel's 'Sinfonie périodique' in the Henry Watson Music Library, Manchester Central Library, shelfmark BR580 PR328, bears the same Broderip & Wilkinson label.

the assignees took control, and that it belonged to the part of their stock that the assignees sold to Broderip & Wilkinson.[26]

One of Francis Broderip's first tasks for his new firm was to secure rights for them to publish music that they could sell profitably. Although his manuscript correspondence unfortunately has not survived, he is known to have approached one composer with whom he had been in contact when working for Longman & Broderip. Leopold Koželuch, then living in Vienna, received a letter from Broderip on 14 November 1798, who

> tells him that the Partnership is desolved [sic] & that he is at Nr. 13 Haymarket & wishes to have his [Koželuch's] Composition [sic] to Publish alone for England. Promissing to be very punctual in paym[en]t[27]

Broderip's wish was not granted. John Bland, who also had published Koželuch's music in England and whose advice he valued, apparently directed him to another music seller, Robert Birchall.[28] However, Broderip did secure for his new partnership compositions by the Bristol organist Robert Broderip, who seems to have been Francis's brother and whose works Longman & Broderip had published from at least 1785.[29]

---

[26] Such a Longman & Broderip label is reproduced in David Wyn Jones, 'From Artaria to Longman & Broderip: Mozart's music on sale in London', in Otto Biba and David Wyn Jones (eds), *Studies in Music History Presented to H. C. Robbins Landon on his Seventieth Birthday*, London, 1996, p 105–114 at p 109, *Figure 1.*

[27] Broderip's letter is summarised in F. Oliver→John Bland, 14 November 1798, Österreichische Nationalbibliothek ms 355/60–2, transcribed in Christa Flamm, 'Ein Verlegerbriefwechsel zur Beethovenzeit', *Beethoven-Studien* v 11 (1970), p 57–110 at p 71–72, from which this quotation is taken. Oliver, who lived in Vienna at that time, served as an intermediary in Koželuch's dealings with English music publishers including Longman & Broderip and John Bland.

[28] See Flamm, *op. cit.*, p 76–107. In 1797 (as noted on page 206 below) Birchall had acquired some engraved music plates that formerly belonged to Bland. On 1 December 1818 Christopher Lonsdale, who was then employed by Birchall, described Bland as 'a great friend' of both Birchall and Koželuch (Flamm, p 99).

[29] In the will (court copy at TNA PROB 11/1058) of Robert's uncle Edmund Broderip, who died in 1779, Robert (who succeeded Edmund as organist of the Mayor's Chapel, Bristol, in 1780) is called a 'son of my late brother John

Francis Broderip also arranged for musical instruments to be made for sale that bore the partnership's name. As implied by the advertisements quoted at the start of this chapter, the Tottenham Court Road premises that Longman & Broderip had used to build pianos were sold by the assignees to Longman, Clementi & Co. and were unavailable to Broderip & Wilkinson. To secure piano fortes for his new partnership, Broderip therefore 'established a separate manufactory'.[30] This establishment, at 27 Tottenham Street, which began to operate about the same time as Broderip & Wilkinson, seems to have been set up by the music seller George Astor to make pianos both for his own firm and for Broderip & Wilkinson, who apparently agreed to buy sufficiently many pianos to justify Astor's investment. Up to 21 October 1798 Astor had advertised that his 'grand piano fortes, with additional keys' could be bought at his warehouse at 79 Cornhill,[31] but from 15 November 1798 he advertised that they could be bought at his two warehouses, 79 Cornhill and 27 Tottenham Street.[32]

According to George Wilkinson's son Henry Broadhurst Wilkinson, who saw documents no longer extant, 'in 1798' Broderip 'entered into an arrangement with Astor and Leukenfeld to make pianos for him, on the Irish patent belonging to Mr Southwell, to whom he paid a royalty'.[33] 'Leukenfeld' is a mistranscription of the

---

Broderip'. However, unlike Francis and his two older siblings Elizabeth and William, Robert's baptism was not recorded in the Wells Cathedral register (I am grateful to Anne Crawford for this information). Some Broderip family relationships are given in Graham Hooper, 'The Broderips', letter to the editor, *The Musical Times* v 111 no. 1534 (December 1970) p 1220. Longman & Broderip entered Robert Broderip's ballad 'The sailor's return' at Stationers' Hall on 22 July 1785 (*MESH* p 54).

[30] Broderip & Wilkinson advertisement, *The Times*, 1 November 1798, p 1, quoted on page 95 above.

[31] *The Observer*, 21 October 1798, p 1. These pianos could be had there for 55 guineas and were available from 'other houses' for 70 guineas. Grand piano fortes without the additional keys could be purchased for £5 less.

[32] *The Morning Herald*, 15 November 1798, p 1; *The Star*, 15 November 1798, p 1. See also Astor's 1799 catalogue of musical instruments and music (at BL 1609/4276, reproduced in the database *Eighteenth Century Collections Online*).

[33] Henry Broadhurst Wilkinson, *op. cit.*, p 23. The phrase 'Irish patent' is a misnomer—see note 40 below.

variously spelt name of the piano forte maker Ludewig Augustus Leukfeld. About 1801 he became sole proprietor of the 27 Tottenham Street manufactory, presumably because Astor had decided to concentrate his attention on other parts of his business. This had included a separate venture with Broderip & Wilkinson in 1799, when the two firms published, together with William Hodsoll, Beethoven's 'A favourite canzonetta for the piano forte' composed to English words by William Wennington.[34]

Broderip and Leukfeld presumably met before 1798, as Leukfeld was in partnership up to 18 February 1796 with the piano maker John Geib, who made many pianos for Longman & Broderip.[35] Moreover, Broderip and Leukfeld had a mutual friend: the wine merchant and amateur musician Charles Bertram.[36]

Henry Broadhurst Wilkinson's intimation that Astor and Leukfeld worked together in 1798 is plausible. On 27 January 1801 Broderip and Charles Wilkinson Jr signed an agreement with Leukfeld that superseded their earlier contract with Astor and mentioned 'a former agreement made between' Leukfeld and Broderip & Wilkinson.[37] Astor's connection with Leukfeld also is

---

[34] Wennington entered this edition at Stationers' Hall on 12 December 1799. Although Beethoven's authorship of this canzonetta was questioned by Alan Tyson in his *The Authentic English Editions of Beethoven*, London, 1963, p 41, he subsequently confirmed that Beethoven did compose it. See Alan Tyson, 'Beethoven's English canzonetta', *The Musical Times* v 112 no. 1536 (February 1971) p 122–123.

[35] The end of their partnership is noticed in *The London Gazette*, 20 February 1796, p 188, where Leukfeld's surname is misspelled 'Lenkfeld'. As Geib was in partnership with another piano maker, John Goldsworth, until 30 March 1793 (*The London Gazette*, 2 April 1793, p 273), Geib's partnership with Leukfeld presumably began after then. For Geib's career see Thomas Strange and Jenny Nex, 'John Geib: beyond the footnote', *Eighteenth-Century Music* v 7 no. 1 (2010) p 81–103, and page 42 above.

[36] Bertram introduced the musician Charles Frederick Horn to Broderip in 1782 (see Michael Kassler, *Charles Edward Horn's Memoirs of his Father and Himself*, Aldershot and London, 2003, p 2–4) and was a trustee and executor of Leukfeld's will proved on 1 December 1810 (court copy at TNA PROB 11/1517). Astor, Bertram, Geib, Horn and Leukfeld all were German-born.

[37] The 1798 and 1801 agreements are not extant, so it is not clear whether Leukfeld was a signatory to Broderip & Wilkinson's 1798 agreement with Astor

evidenced by the circumstance that Astor advertised 27 Tottenham Street under his own name in 1798 and reoccupied these premises after Leukfeld's 1810 death.[38] Leukfeld expanded the manufactory which, from the picture reproduced in *Figure 2.1* on page 107, appears to have been quite substantial.

The 1801 agreement provided that Leukfeld would make pianos exclusively for Astor and Broderip & Wilkinson, and that Broderip & Wilkinson would purchase at least three pianos a week from Leukfeld for the next seven years. This contract was breached because Broderip & Wilkinson failed to buy the number of pianos they had promised, and Leukfeld subsequently sold some of his pianos under his own name to other persons.[39]

The Dublin piano maker William Southwell received an English patent on 18 October 1794 for 'improvements in the construction' of pianos, including a novel placement of additional treble keys.[40] He granted rights to manufacture these pianos to

---

or whether Leukfeld signed a separate agreement with Broderip & Wilkinson before 1801. Information about the 1801 agreement is found in a bill of complaint that Broderip and Charles Wilkinson Jr filed against Leukfeld in the Court of Chancery on 14 June 1806, and in Leukfeld's answer (which refers to a 'former agreement' with him) that was filed on 20 October 1806. The 1806 complaint and answer are both in TNA C13/2415/7.

[38] Astor insured 27 Tottenham Street in Sun Fire Office insurance policy dated 10 December 1812 (LMA, formerly Guildhall ms 11936/455/877308). In 1820, after Astor's death, 27 Tottenham Street was one of three addresses from which Astor & Co. operated (advertisement, *The Times*, 14 July 1820, p 4).

[39] According to the 1806 complaint and answer cited in note 37. A piano with the nameplate '*Leukfeld* | MANUFACTURER | TOTTENHAM STREET | *London*' is now in Ireland in the private collection of Nigel Barnes, to whom I am grateful for information about it. Another piano with the nameplate '*Leukfeld* | PIANO FORTE MAKER, | 27 | *Tottenham Street* | *FITZROY SQUARE* | *London*' is in the Beurmann collection in the Museum für Kunst und Gewerbe, Hamburg (see Andreas E[rich] Beurmann, *Klingende Kostbarkeiten, Tasteninstrumente der Sammlung Beurmann*, Lübeck, 2000, p 81–82).

[40] This patent, subsequently numbered 2017, commonly was referred to as the 'Irish patent' (e.g., in the documents cited in note 37 above and in Henry Broadhurst Wilkinson, *op. cit.*, p 23). Although records relating to Irish patents of this time were destroyed by fire in 1922 (see Stephen van Dulken, *British Patents of Invention, 1617–1977*, London, 1999, p 15), Southwell's name is not in the manuscript index (in the BL Business & IP Centre) to Irish patent specifications from 1789 to 1853 (I thank Sonya Pinnock for this information).

Longman & Broderip,[41] who advertised in 1795 the sale of 'Southwell's new invented Patent Piano Fortes, with additional Keys'[42] and warned the public away from others who used the 'idea' of his patent but made instruments with different 'actuating principles'.[43] Further evidence of Southwell's connection with Longman & Broderip is found in the latter's *c*1795 advertisement of 'A Plan for a New Invented Patent Piano-Forte with Additional Keys &c.', reproduced in *Figure 1.2* on page 44 above, in which the engraved picture illustrating the keyboard and strings of this piano was copied from the drawing that Southwell submitted in support of his piano patent, except that the nameboard above the strings was changed from 'Southwell | Dublin' to 'Longman | Broderip'.[44]

On 16 July 1796, following Longman & Broderip's bankruptcy, Southwell granted rights to use his 1794 patent to each of the two former partners,[45] and Broderip brought his rights to his new firm. As shown in *Figure 1.3* on page 45, Broderip & Wilkinson retained the engraved plate from which the Longman & Broderip advertisement for the new piano had been printed, and had this plate altered—removing 'Longman' from the nameboard and substituting 'Broderip & Wilkinson' for 'Longman & Broderip' in the text—to create their own advertisement of this piano.

Broderip later passed his long-term connection with Southwell on to George Wilkinson, and in 1808 Wilkinson & Co., which

---

An Irish patent at this time would have had no validity in England. The misnomer presumably arose from the circumstance that Southwell had made pianos in Dublin before his English patent was granted (see Terry de Valera, 'Two eighteenth-century musical instrument makers', *Dublin Historical Record* v 36 no. 4 (1983) p 122–131 at p 127).

[41] See page 43 above.

[42] *The Morning Post*, 15 October 1795, p 1.

[43] *The True Briton*, 18 January 1796, p 4, quoted on page 31 above.

[44] The drawing enrolled with Southwell's patent was first published as part of the specification of this patent that was printed by Eyre & Spottiswoode in London in 1856.

[45] See George S. Bozarth and Margaret Debenham, 'Piano wars: the legal machinations of London pianoforte makers, 1795–1806', *Royal Musical Association Research Chronicle* v 42 (2009) p 45–108 at p 83.

Figure 2.1 Ludewig Augustus Leukfeld's piano forte manufactory at 27 Tottenham Street (British Museum Department of Prints and Drawings, Trade cards Heal 88.54, by permission)

succeeded Broderip & Wilkinson after Broderip's death in 1807, became proprietors of a new 'cabinet piano forte' that Southwell patented that year.[46] Probably because the agreement with Leukfeld to

[46] Southwell received this English patent, subsequently numbered 3029, on 8 April 1807. According to *Some Notes made by J[ames] S[hudi] Broadwood,*

manufacture Broderip & Wilkinson's pianos had ended in dispute, Wilkinson & Co. established their own manufactory in 1808 at 3 [Great] Windmill Street, where their cabinet pianos were finished under Southwell's 'immediate inspection'.[47] This part of the company's business proved so successful that Wilkinson & Co. relinquished selling and publishing music in 1809 to concentrate exclusively upon piano-making.[48]

About 1800 Broderip & Wilkinson bought a harp from the Erard firm, presumably for resale.[49] They dealt with various other makers to obtain their stock of musical instruments—for instance, a violin stamped 'Broderip & Wilkinson' auctioned by Sotheby's in London in 1982[50]—but records of these dealings have not been found.

In addition to copies of printed music, Longman & Broderip's assets when the firm ceased trading included some of the engraved plates that had been used to print their publications. The assignees sold part of these assets to Broderip & Wilkinson and the remainder to Longman, Clementi & Co.,[51] although it is not known why particular stock passed to one or the other successor.[52] After the successor's name and address were substituted for that of Longman &

1838, with Observations & Elucidations by H[enry] F[owler] Broadwood, 1862, London, 1862 (photocopy at BL LD.31 b.657), p 9, Southwell produced the cabinet piano 'from a sketch given him by James Broadwood about 1804', but 'so little was it then appreciated, that the first manufactory in the line [presumably the Broadwood firm] refused to purchase the patent he took out'.

[47] Advertisement, *The Morning Chronicle*, 28 July 1808, p 1.

[48] See Michael Kassler, 'Broderip, Wilkinson and the first English edition of the "48"', *op. cit.* in note 8 above, p 75.

[49] Erard harp no. 331 (Erard ledger, RCM Museum of Musical Instruments ms 497, v 1 p 83). I am grateful to Jenny Nex for this information.

[50] *Important Musical Instruments*, 7 April 1982, in lot 140, p 42.

[51] The sale of copies is indicated by labels pasted over Longman & Broderip's name, as noted on page 101 above. The sale of plates is demonstrated by a comparison of *Figures 1.2* and *1.3* on pages 44–45 above.

[52] Curiously, many Longman & Broderip plates of Muzio Clementi's compositions were acquired by Broderip & Wilkinson rather than by Longman, Clementi & Co., of which he was a partner. See pages 159–162 below.

Broderip, works were reprinted from some of these plates.[53] Broderip & Wilkinson also had new plates engraved to print music that Longman & Broderip had issued, presumably because the original plates were unavailable or had deteriorated.[54]

Almost immediately after their establishment Broderip & Wilkinson began publishing works by Mozart,[55] and in February 1800 they announced that they would 'speedily' produce a 'complete collection of his works for the piano forte'.[56] This collection, which ultimately comprised twenty books, included works both for piano solo and for piano accompanied by other instruments.[57]

The firm's interest in Mozart's music seems to have been animated by a conversation—recorded by two witnesses—that Broderip had with Haydn after Mozart's death in December 1791. Charles Burney wrote:

> After his [Mozart's] decease, when Haydn was asked in our hearing by Broderip, in his [Longman & Broderip] music-shop, whether Mozart had left any MS. compositions behind him that were worth purchasing, as his widow had offered his unedited papers at a high price to the principal publishers of music throughout Europe; Haydn eagerly said; 'purchase them by all means. He was truly a great musician. I have been

[53] For instance, the plates from which Longman & Broderip printed Griffith Jones's translation of Book IV of Jean-Philippe Rameau's *A Treatise on Harmony* (which they entered at Stationers' Hall on 24 April 1792) were reused about 1804 by Clementi, Banger, Hyde, Collard & Davis (successor to Longman, Clementi & Co.) with just such a change in the title-page plate. Copies of both editions are in K.

[54] For example, new title-page and music plates were engraved for the Broderip & Wilkinson four-hand piano arrangement of Johann Paul Aegidius Martini's 'Overture to Henry the Fourth' (copy in K). The engraver's source appears, from the music layout, to have been the Longman & Broderip edition of this arrangement (copy in University of New South Wales library, catalogue no. VQ 780/MAR/N-1).

[55] In November 1798, their first month of operation, Broderip & Wilkinson entered eight compositions at Stationers' Hall, of which three were by Mozart (*MESH* p 380–383).

[56] Advertisement, *The Star*, 14 February 1800, p 1.

[57] When reissued by Thomas Preston in 1811 or 1812, the twenty books could be had individually or bound in five volumes (advertisement, *The Times*, 20 August 1812, p 2).

> often flattered by my friends with having some genius; but he was much my superior.'[58]

And Richard John Samuel Stevens corroborated that Haydn had

> called on Broderip in the Haymarket, and 'urged him to purchase *all Mozart's compositions*. Such a genius he never knew'. I [Stevens] *saw Haydn* leave Broderip's shop, after he had made this declaration. Mr Broderip mentioned Haydn's words to me.[59]

It seems likely that Broderip & Wilkinson's considerable effort to promote Mozart's music was influenced by their loss of access to new works by Haydn. The Viennese firm Artaria & Co.—a principal publisher of music by Haydn and Mozart—had enjoyed a long-standing connection with Longman & Broderip.[60] However, after that firm's bankruptcy, Frederick Augustus Hyde, who had worked for them as a shopman,[61] signed a contract with Haydn in 1796, in which he agreed to sell numerous itemised works that he proposed to

---

[58] [Charles Burney], 'Mozart', in Abraham Rees *et al.*, *The Cyclopædia; or, Universal Dictionary…*, v 24 (London, 1819), unpaginated. The section of *The Cyclopædia* that included this article was first issued in 1813.

[59] According to J[ohn] B[rande] Trend, 'R. J. S. Stevens (1757–1837) and his contemporaries', *Music and Letters* v 13 no. 2 (April 1933) p 128–137 at p 130. Haydn's discussions with Broderip must have taken place before 15 August 1795, when Haydn left England for the last time (H[oward] C[handler] Robbins Landon, *Haydn in England 1791–1795*, London, 1976, p 319).

[60] See David Wyn Jones, 'From Artaria to Longman & Broderip: Mozart's music on sale in London', *op. cit.* in note 26 above.

[61] In a 24 June 1791 deposition (TNA E133/54/55) in the case of *Forster v Longman*, Hyde testified that he was twenty-three years old and 'now lives as shopman to the def[endan]ts & has lived with them in that & other capacities for 5 years says he has been during that time & now is accustomed to serve sell & deliver out their publications as music printers & music sellers'. I am grateful to Jenny Nex for this transcript. This legal case is described in Nancy A. Mace, 'Haydn and the London music sellers: Forster v. Longman & Broderip', *Music and Letters* v 77 no. 4 (November 1996) p 527–541. Hyde left Longman & Broderip before their bankruptcy. Between 1793 and 1795 he was in partnership with John Lewis Vautier Sollicoffre and James Henry Houston, trading under the name Lewis, Houston & Hyde; this partnership acquired the business of John Bland.

compose during the next five years exclusively to him.[62] This contract presumably was a major reason why Hyde was invited to join Longman, Clementi & Co. as a partner.

Broderip & Wilkinson's decision to publish a 'complete edition' of Mozart's piano music imitated the attempt by the Leipzig music publishers Breitkopf & Härtel to produce a 'complete and elegant edition' of Mozart's works—news of which was reported in London in January 1799.[63] Indeed, as *Figures 2.2* and *2.3* on pages 112–113 show, Broderip & Wilkinson had their engraver etch into the series title-page plate of their edition an illustration that copied the picture (of a woman mourning at a portrait of Mozart) that Breitkopf & Härtel had put on a series title-page of their edition, although the London copy suppressed the names of the artist and engraver of the Leipzig illustration. However, the order in which the London edition appeared differed from that of the Leipzig edition, and further research is required to determine the sources that Broderip & Wilkinson used to compile their edition.[64]

Broderip & Wilkinson issued seven printed catalogues of their music publications. Each of these catalogues was engraved on a single plate that was printed in some of their published music and perhaps also on single sheets that could be shown or given to potential purchasers. Several catalogues were updated by engraving the titles and prices of recent publications into the catalogue's existing plate and thus were printed in more than one state.[65]

---

[62] This document is reproduced, transcribed and discussed in Albi Rosenthal, 'The contract between Joseph Haydn and Frederick Augustus Hyde (1796)', in Otto Biba and David Wyn Jones (eds), *Studies in Music History…*, *op. cit.* in note 26 above, p 72–81.

[63] *The Monthly Magazine* v 7 no. 41 (January 1799) p 56.

[64] This edition appears to have been ignored by Mozart scholars. It is not mentioned either in Ludwig von Köchel *et al*, *Chronologisch-thematisches Verzeichnis sämtlicher Tonwerke Wolfgang Amadé Mozarts*, 7th ed., Wiesbaden, 1965, 'Anhang D: Gesamtausgaben', p 915–925, nor in Wolfgang Rehm (translated by Faye Ferguson), 'Collected editions', in H[oward] C[handler] Robbins Landon (ed.), *The Mozart Compendium*, London, 1990, p 422–428.

[65] I am grateful to Yu Lee An and Peter Ward Jones for information about Broderip & Wilkinson's catalogues.

Figure 2.2 A series title-page of Breitkopf & Härtel's Complete Edition of Mozart's Music (by permission of the Royal College of Music)

The firm's first catalogue, reproduced in *Figure 2.4* on page 114, was devoted to music by Mozart. It listed the first seventeen of the books in their projected 'complete collection' of his piano music, together with other works by Mozart that they published. As this catalogue was printed in Book 2 of *A Collection of Original Songs with an Accompaniment for the Piano Forte or Harp* by Mozart, which Broderip & Wilkinson entered at Stationers' Hall on 24 January 1801,[66] it must have been engraved before then, but after their 29 July 1800 newspaper advertisement which announced that

[66] *MESH* p 446. A copy of Book 2 that Broderip & Wilkinson deposited at Stationers' Hall is at Bodleian Mus. Voc. I, 41 (81).

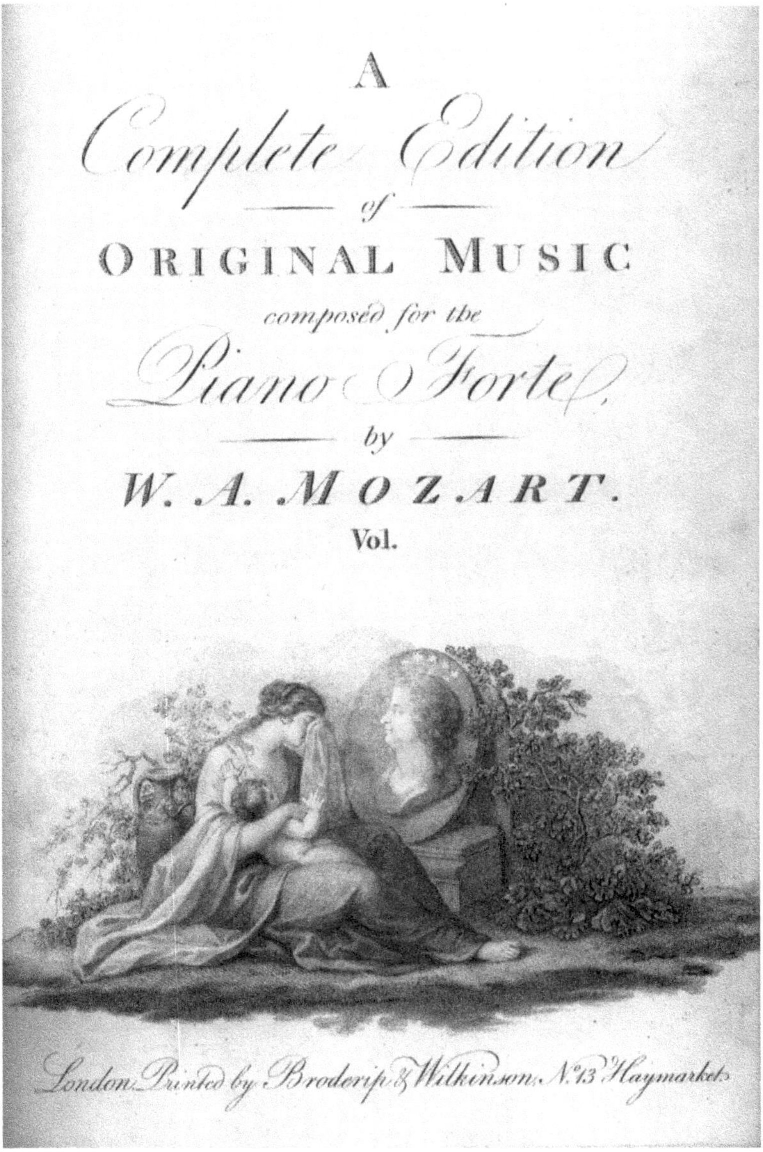

Figure 2.3 Series title-page of Broderip & Wilkinson's Complete Edition of Mozart's Piano Music (by permission of the Archives and Rare Book Library, University of Cincinnati, USA)

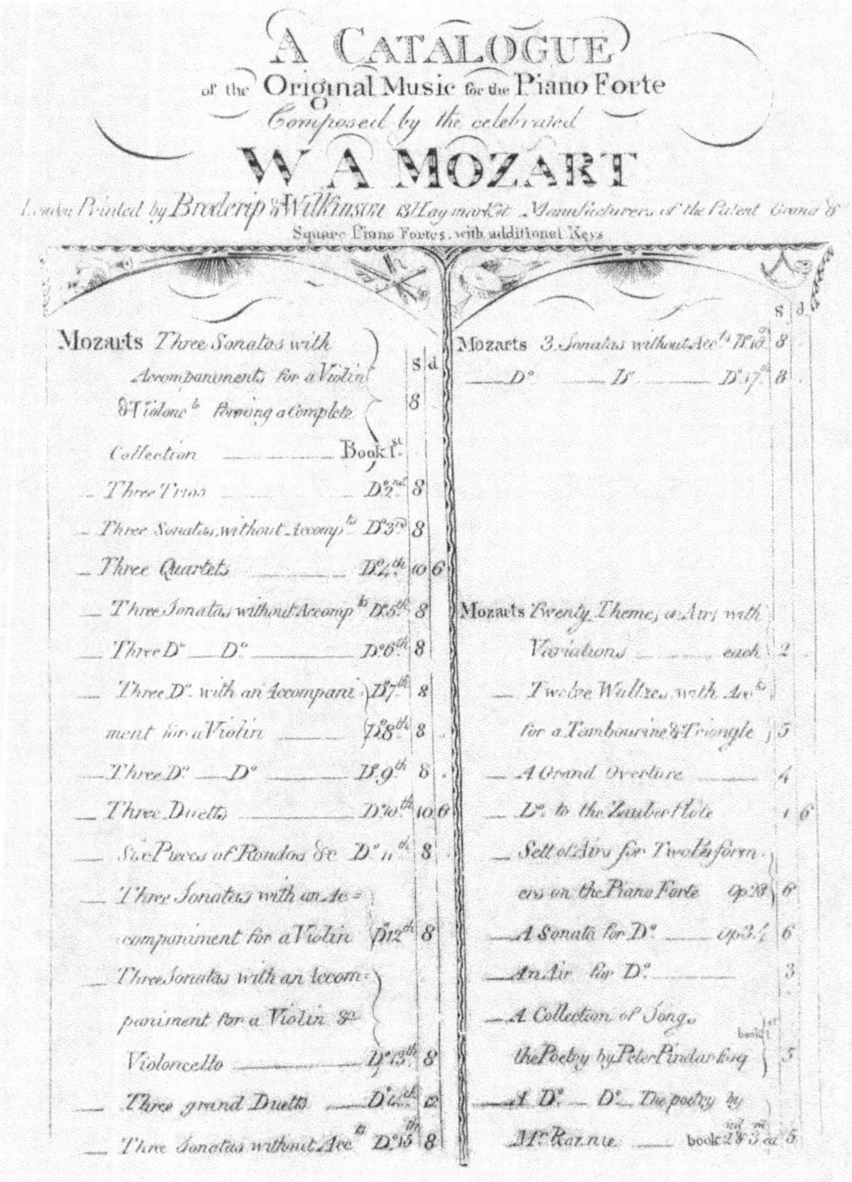

A CATALOGUE
of the Original Music for the Piano Forte
Composed by the celebrated
W A MOZART
London Printed by Broderip & Wilkinson 13 Haymarket Manufacturers of the Patent Grand & Square Piano Fortes, with additional Keys

	s	d
Mozarts Three Sonatas with Accompaniments for a Violin & Violonc[lo] Forming a Complete Collection — Book 1st	8	
— Three Trios — Do 2nd	8	
— Three Sonatas without Accomp[ts] Do 3rd	8	
— Three Quartets — Do 4th	10	6
— Three Sonatas without Accomp[ts] Do 5th	8	
— Three Do — Do — Do 6th	8	
— Three Do with an Accompaniment for a Violin Do 7th	8	
Do 8th	8	
— Three Do — Do — Do 9th	8	
— Three Duetts — Do 10th	10	6
— Six Pieces of Rondos &c Do 11th	8	
— Three Sonatas with an Accompaniment for a Violin Do 12th	8	
— Three Sonatas with an Accompaniment for a Violin & Violoncello — Do 13th	8	
— Three grand Duetts — Do 14th	12	
— Three Sonatas without Acc[ts] Do 15th	8	

	s	d
Mozarts 3 Sonatas without Acc[ts] No 16	8	
— Do — Do — Do 17th	8	
Mozarts Twenty Themes or Airs with Variations — each	2	
— Twelve Waltzes with Acc[ts] for a Tambourine & Triangle	5	
— A Grand Overture	4	
— Do to the Zauber Flote	1	6
— Sett of Airs for Two Performers on the Piano Forte Op 28		6
— A Sonata for Do — Op 34		6
— An Air for Do		3
— A Collection of Songs the Poetry by Peter Pindar Esq book 1st	5	
— A Do — Do — The poetry by Mr Rannie — book 2nd & 3rd at	5	

Figure 2.4 Broderip & Wilkinson's first catalogue c1800 (by permission of the Department of Special Collections, Glasgow University Library)

Books 1–14 of their 'complete collection' of Mozart's piano music were available for sale but did not mention higher-numbered books.[67]

The catalogues subsequently issued by Broderip & Wilkinson listed music by a variety of composers that was printed in England or imported from Europe. Their second catalogue, of piano forte compositions for one or two performers, reproduced in *Figure 2.5* on page 116, was headed 'N°. 1. | A Catalogue of Music | of the most esteemed Authors, Published by Broderip & Wilkinson'. Like their previous catalogue, it emphasised that the firm were 'Manufacturers of the Patent Grand & Square Piano Forte with additional Keys &c.', thus informing readers that they could buy at 13 Haymarket not only piano music but also an instrument on which it could be played.

Works in this catalogue that were entered at Stationers' Hall were registered there between 13 November 1798 (Mozart's 'Air') and 29 October 1801 (Jan Ladislav Dussek's 'Two sonatas for the piano forte'). The catalogue probably was printed about September 1801 when Dussek's 'Two sonatas' was still in production, as the firm's agent in Exeter, the bookseller Philip Hedgeland, advertised on 17 September 1801 that 'a general catalogue of Broderip and Wilkinson's publications' could be seen at his shop.[68] The catalogue included music that Longman & Broderip had entered at Stationers' Hall before Broderip & Wilkinson began trading, e.g., Adalbert Gyrowetz's 'Notturno', Op. 21 (ESH 8/9/1797) and Girolamo Masi's 'Waltzes' (ESH 18/3/1799), as well as much music that was never entered at Stationers' Hall.

The firm did not produce a catalogue numbered 2, but issued three catalogues of vocal music as well as an 'Additional Catalogue of New Music' for each of the years 1806 and 1807. Although the 1806 catalogue included older compositions,[69] most of its music that was entered at Stationers' Hall was first published between 1804 and

[67] *The Morning Herald*, 29 July 1800, p 1.

[68] *Trewman's Exeter Flying Post*, 17 September 1801, p 3. Besides copies of many Broderip & Wilkinson publications Hedgeland also had for sale 'one of their last [i.e., latest] Patent Piano Fortes, with the additional Keys'.

[69] Louis von Esch's sonata 'Le Retour de Wandsworth' (ESH 15/6/1801) appears both in it and in catalogue 'N°. 1'.

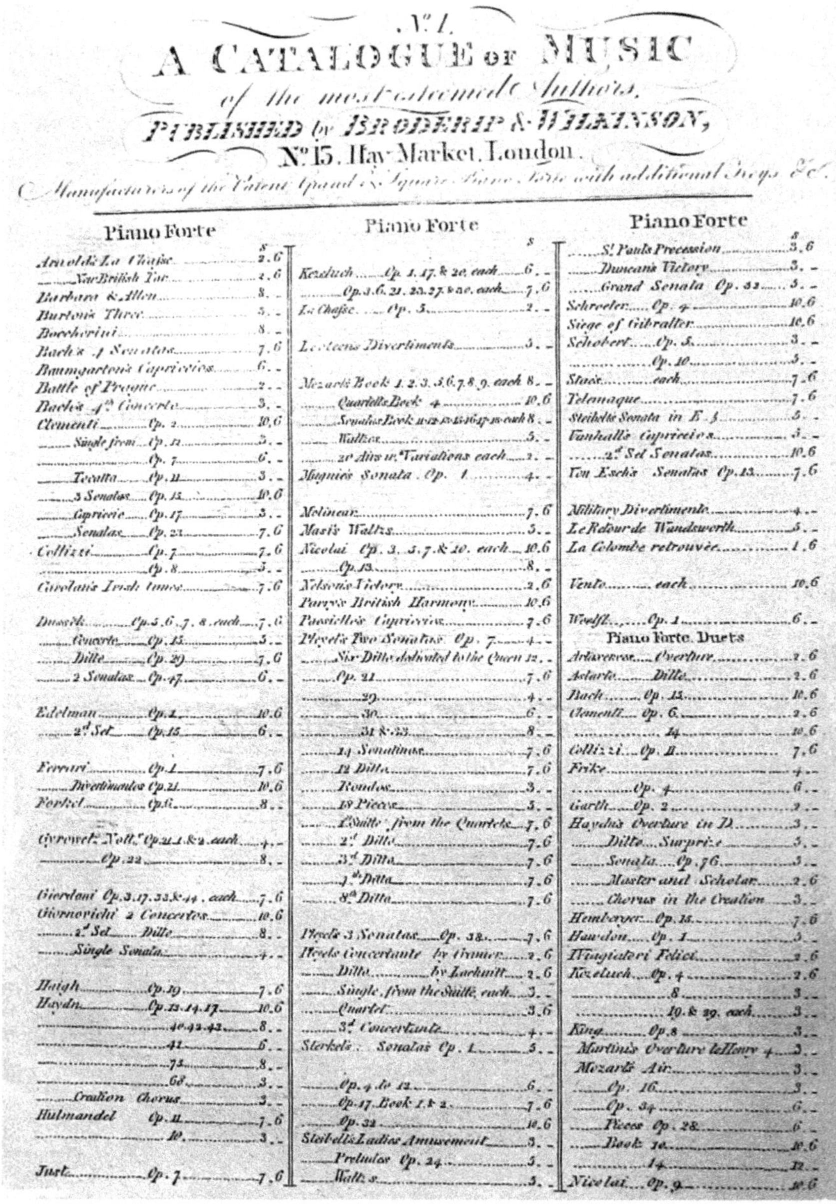

N.º 1.
A CATALOGUE OF MUSIC
of the most esteemed Authors,
PUBLISHED by BRODERIP & WILKINSON,
N.º 13, Hay Market, London.
Manufacturers of the Patent Grand & Square Piano Forte with additional Keys &c.

Piano Forte	s	Piano Forte	s	Piano Forte	s
Arnold's La Chaise	2.6	Kozeluch ... Op. 1. 17. & 20. each	6.-	St. Pauls Procession	3.6
... New British Tar	2.6	... Op. 3. 6. 21. 23. 27. & 30. each	7.6	... Duncans Victory	3.-
Barbara & Allen	8.-	La Chasse ... Op. 5	2.-	... Grand Sonata Op. 32	5.-
Burton's Three	5.-			Schroeter ... Op. 4	10.6
Boccherini	8.-			Siege of Gibralter	10.6
Bach's 4 Sonatas	7.6	Lesteens Divertiments	5.-	Schobert ... Op. 5	3.-
Baumgarten's Capriccios	6.-			... Op. 10	5.-
Battle of Prague	2.-	Mozart's Book 1. 2. 3. 5. 6. 7. 8. 9. each	8.-	Stacks ... each	7.6
Bach's 4th Concerto	3.-	... Quartetts Book 4	10.6	Telemaque	7.6
Clementi ... Op. 2	10.6	... Sonatas Book [illegible] each	8.-	Steibelts Sonata in E ♭	5.-
... Single from ... Op. 11	3.-	... Waltzes	5.-	Vanhalls Capriccios	5.-
... Op. 7	6.-	... 20 Airs w. Variations each	2.-	... 2d Set Sonatas	10.6
... Toccata ... Op. 11	3.-	Mugnie's Sonata Op. 1	4.-	Von Esch's Sonatas Op. 13	7.6
... 3 Sonatas ... Op. 15	10.6				
... Capriccio ... Op. 17	5.-	Molineux	7.6	Military Divertimento	4.-
... Sonatas ... Op. 23	7.6	Mast's Waltzs	5.-	Le Retour de Wandsworth	5.-
Collizzi ... Op. 7	7.6	Nicolai Op. 3. 5. 7. & 10. each	10.6	La Colombe retrouvée	1.6
... Op. 8	5.-	... Op. 13	8.-		
Carolan's Irish tunes	7.6	Nelson's Victory	2.6	Vento ... each	10.6
		Parry's British Harmony	10.6		
Dussek ... Op. 5. 6. 7. 8. each	7.6	Paesiello's Capriccios	7.6	Woelfl ... Op. 1	6.-
... Concerto ... Op. 15	5.-	Pleyel's Two Sonatas Op. 7	4.-	Piano Forte. Duets	
... Ditto ... Op. 29	7.6	... Six Ditto dedicated to the Queen 12	2.-	Artaxerxes ... Overture	2.6
... 2 Sonatas ... Op. 47	6.-	... Op. 21	7.6	Astarte ... Ditto	2.6
		... 29	4.-	Bach ... Op. 15	10.6
Edelman ... Op. 1	10.6	... 30	6.-	Clementi ... Op. 6	2.6
... 2d Set ... Op. 15	6.-	... 31 & 33	8.-	... 14	10.6
		... 14 Sonatinas	7.6	Collizzi ... Op. 11	7.6
Ferrari ... Op. 1	7.6	... 12 Ditto	7.6	Frike	4.-
... Divertimentos Op. 21	10.6	... Rondos	3.-	... Op. 4	6.-
Forkel ... Op. 6	8.-	... 18 Pieces	5.-	Garth ... Op. 2	7.-
		... 1st Suitte from the Quartetts	7.6	Haydn's Overture in D	3.-
Gyrowetz Nott.° Op. 21. 1. & 2. each	4.-	... 2d Ditto	7.6	... Ditto ... Surprise	3.-
... Op. 22	8.-	... 3d Ditto	7.6	... Sonata ... Op. 76	3.-
		... 4th Ditto	7.6	... Master and Scholar	2.6
Giordani Op. 3. 17. 33. & 44. each	7.6	... 8th Ditto	7.6	... Chorus in the Creation	3.-
Giornovichi 2 Concertos	10.6			Hemberger ... Op. 15	7.6
... 2d Set ... Ditto	8.-	Pleyel's 3 Sonatas ... Op. 38	7.6	Hawdon ... Op. 1	5.-
... Single Sonata	4.-	Pleyels Concertante by Graiser	2.6	Winglateri Felici	2.6
		... Ditto ... by Lachnitt	2.6	Kozeluch ... Op. 4	2.6
Haigh ... Op. 19	7.6	... Single from the Suitte each	3.-	... 8	3.-
Haydn ... Op. 13. 14. 17	10.6	... Quartet	3.6	... 19. & 29. each	3.-
... 40. 42. 43	8.-	... 3d Concertante	4.-	King ... Op. 8	3.-
... 41	6.-	Sterkels Sonatas Op. 1	5.-	Martini's Overture le Henry 4	3.-
... 75	8.-			Mozart's Air	3.-
... 68	3.-	... Op. 4 to 12	6.-	... Op. 16	3.-
... Creation Chorus	3.-	... Op. 17 Book 1. & 2	7.6	... Op. 34	6.-
Hulmandel Op. 11	7.6	... Op. 32	10.6	... Pieces Op. 28	6.-
... 10	3.-	Steibelts Ladies Amusement	3.-	... Book 10	10.6
		... Preludes Op. 24	5.-	... 14	12.-
Just ... Op. 7	7.6	... Waltzs	5.-	Nicolai ... Op. 9	10.6

Figure 2.5 Broderip & Wilkinson's second catalogue c1801 (by permission of Jamie and Michael Kassler, Northbridge, NSW, Australia)

6 May 1806,[70] suggesting that this catalogue was issued in May or June 1806. Besides piano music it promoted 'new songs', 'military music', 'cathedral music' and two items of 'imported music': Luigi Boccherini's 'quintetts for piano forte' and a piano-forte arrangement of Mozart's *Don Giovanni*.

The 1807 catalogue gave the titles of twenty-four compositions (including piano and vocal music), of which the ten that were entered at Stationers' Hall were registered there between 5 January and 12 January 1807. The body of this catalogue was formatted in three columns, of which the last is empty. The firm obviously planned to update it later that year, but after Broderip's death on 8 February 1807 did not do so.

To reach customers outside London, Broderip & Wilkinson co-operated with music shops in the provinces. An 1806 advertisement named thirteen provincial shops from which their 'new piano forte music' and other new publications could be had, and noted that 'all other music shops in England, Scotland and Ireland' could obtain them.[71]

Broderip & Wilkinson published numerous compositions by Louis von Esch. Of German descent, he was educated in France by the Duke and Duchess de Choiseul and came to England at the time of the French revolution. The firm's interest in publishing his music conceivably was related to Broderip's earlier connection with the Prince of Wales, as von Esch was appointed by him in 1801 'for the musical education' of his daughter, Princess Charlotte.[72]

In 1802 Broderip & Wilkinson published works by J. S. Bach and Haydn. Both of these editions had Paris connections. On 14 June the firm advertised that Book I of part 2 of Bach's '48' was 'just

---

[70] Masi's divertimento 'L'Automne' was entered on that day.

[71] *The Morning Chronicle*, 26 July 1806, p 1.

[72] *The Times*, 15 August 1801, p 5; and 15 March 1829, p 5 (von Esch's death notice). He appears to have taught Princess Charlotte until 1806, when he was replaced by Jane Mary Miles *née* Guest. His teaching appears to have succeeded: on 30 May 1816 Princess Charlotte 'delighted her guests' at a dinner party 'by the performance of some beautiful sonatas on the piano-forte, composed by … Mr von Esch' (Robert Huish, *Memoirs of Her Late Royal Highness Charlotte Augusta, Princess of Wales…*, London, 1818, p 320).

printed'.[73] Its musical and title-page text (the latter in the French language, with a dedication to the Conservatoire de Musique in Paris) were copied from an edition that Nicolaus Simrock had published in Paris and Bonn in 1801, but its plates were re-engraved, presumably in London.[74] The 1802 Broderip & Wilkinson edition was the first English printing of multiple preludes and fugues from the '48'.[75]

A few weeks later the firm advertised as 'ready for delivery' the first six symphonies of 'A new and complete edition of the symphonies of Doctor Haydn, in score, elegantly and correctly engraved, under the direction of Mr Cherubini'.[76] Luigi Cherubini had been appointed an inspector of education in the Paris Conservatoire when it was founded in 1795,[77] and the Conservatoire's music shop ('magasin de musique') published some of his music.[78]

---

[73] *The Times*, 14 June 1802, p 1. Only one copy of the 1802 issue—at the Riemenschneider Memorial Bach Library, Baldwin-Wallace College, Berea, Ohio—is known to have survived; as mentioned below, it was reprinted in 1808 from the same plates by the firm's successor, Wilkinson & Co. See Yo Tomita, 'The dawn of the English Bach Awakening manifested in sources of the "48"', in Michael Kassler (ed.), *The English Bach Awakening, Knowledge of J. S. Bach and his Music in England, 1750–1830*, Aldershot, 2004, p 35–167 at p 143–144.

[74] See Michael Kassler, 'Broderip, Wilkinson and the first English edition of the "48"', *op. cit.* in note 8 above. I am grateful to Yo Tomita for confirming the relationship of these two editions. Their dedication to the Paris Conservatoire may reflect the circumstance that Simrock's brother Henri was a teacher there.

[75] Two preludes and one fugue from the '48' had been published earlier in England: Augustus F. C. Kollmann included a prelude and fugue in his *An Essay on Practical Musical Composition* (London, 1799), and William Shield presented another prelude in his *An Introduction to Harmony* (London, 1800). See Michael Kassler (ed.), *The English Bach Awakening, op. cit.*, p 12. As Kollmann (*op. cit.*, p 97–98) had announced his intention to publish an 'analysed' edition of the '48', and as Broderip & Wilkinson had subscribed to Kollmann's *Essay*, it is plausible that, when they received a copy of the Simrock edition of part 2 of the '48', perhaps in May or June 1801, they decided to engrave and print the first twelve preludes and fugues in part 2 before Kollmann could produce the edition he had announced.

[76] *The Morning Chronicle*, 3 July 1802, p 1.

[77] Constant Pierre, *B. Sarrette et les origines du Conservatoire national de musique et de déclamation*, Paris, 1895, p 129.

[78] These compositions are listed in Constant Pierre, *Le Magasin de musique à l'usage des fêtes nationales et du Conservatoire*, Paris, 1895, p 117–164 *passim*.

No copies of the Haydn edition advertised by Broderip & Wilkinson are known to be extant, although it seems likely (from the reference to Cherubini) to have been imported or re-engraved from a Paris edition,[79] perhaps that of Pierre Leduc which started in 1801.[80] Cherubini's interests in the music trade led him to form a company with Étienne-Nicolas Méhul and other Conservatoire associates in August 1802 that published music and operated a music shop in Paris separate from the Conservatoire's.[81]

Although most Broderip & Wilkinson title-pages consisted solely of lettering, and many of their editions of short musical compositions had no separate title-page, for a few special publications they commissioned title-page illustrations that presumably were etched into comparatively expensive copper plates. *Figure 2.6* on page 120 reproduces one such title-page whose artwork was engraved by T. King.[82]

---

[79] This hypothesis appears to be supported by the circumstance that 'proposals for a complete edition of the symphonies of Dr Haydn, in score to be published in numbers' were issued about the same time by Laurent Louis Deconchy, a French bookseller resident in London (see *The Monthly Epitome* v 1 (July 1802) p 448). Broderip & Wilkinson sold their numbers at 6/– 'on common paper' and 7/6 'on wove vellum' (advertisement, *The Morning Chronicle*, 3 July 1802, p 1), whereas Deconchy proposed to sell numbers of Haydn symphonies for 5/– and 6/– each.

[80] I thank Dr Armin Raab of the Haydn-Institut, Vienna, for this suggestion. The Leduc edition is described in Anthony van Hoboken, *Joseph Haydn Thematisch-bibliographisches Werkverzeichnis* v 3, Mainz, 1978, p 19–21, catalogue no. Coll.Sy.8a. I am grateful to Kathy Adamson and Richard Andrewes for advising that neither of the two copies (at the Royal Academy of Music and Cambridge University Library) of the 1801 Leduc edition listed in the COPAC on-line catalogue of British and Irish academic and research libraries shows evidence of having been sold by Broderip & Wilkinson. The several Leducs in the Parisian music trade are discussed in Anik Devriès, 'Deux dynasties d'éditeurs et de musiciens: les Leduc', *Revue belge de musicologie* v 28–30 (1974–1976) p 195–213.

[81] For the music sellers Cherubini, Méhul et Cie see Constant Pierre, *Le magasin de musique…*, *op. cit.*, p 105–115, and Anik Devriès and François Lesure, *Dictionnaire des éditeurs de musique français*, Geneva, v 1, 1979, p 116–117.

[82] This work was advertised as 'just published' in *The Morning Chronicle*, 14 June 1802, p 2.

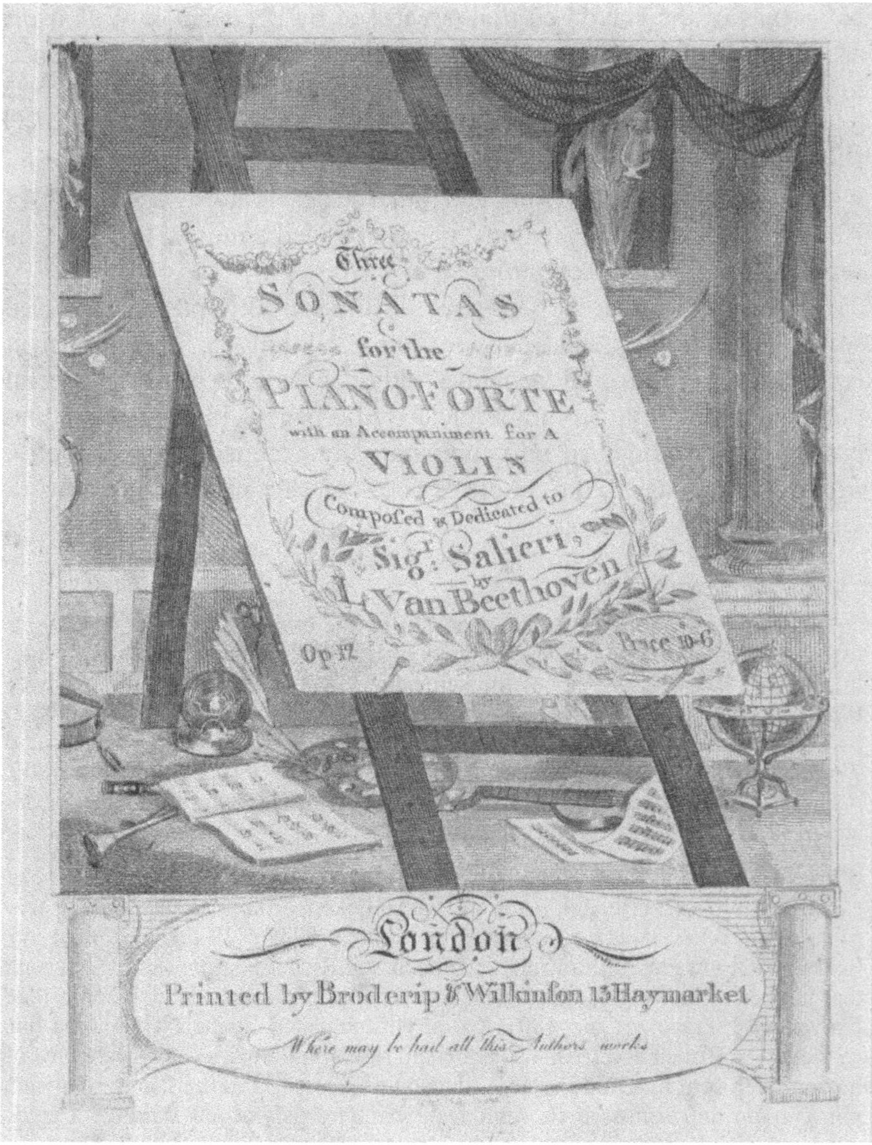

Figure 2.6 Elaborate Broderip & Wilkinson title-page c1802 (National Library of Australia catalogue no. MUS mb 785.28192 B415, by permission)

In his will, dated 27 February 1805, Francis Fane Broderip bequeathed his house and possessions in Upper Fitzroy Street to his wife Anne and the remainder of his estate to her and their four sons. After he died, his share of the Broderip & Wilkinson partnership was bought by George Wilkinson in instalments that he paid initially to Anne Broderip and—after her 9 June 1807 death—to her eldest son John, who received the final payment on 22 November 1807.[83] The firm's name then was changed to Wilkinson & Co., under which it began trading in January 1808.[84] The business records of Broderip & Wilkinson presumably stayed with George Wilkinson rather than with Broderip's children (none of whom married),[85] and—as these records have not survived[86]—conceivably were consumed in the 'dreadful fire' of 11 October 1812 that destroyed the premises of Wilkinson & Wornum, the successor of Wilkinson & Co.[87]

---

[83] Henry Broadhurst Wilkinson, *op. cit.* in note 8 above, p 22.

[84] The last entries at Stationers' Hall of music published by Broderip & Wilkinson were made on 1 January 1808. The first Wilkinson & Co. entries were made on 1 February 1808. See *MESH* p xx.

[85] John Broderip, a tutor at King's College, Cambridge, where he graduated M.A. in 1801, left his property to his brothers. Charles Broderip received four English patents relating to steam engines and was elected Fellow of the Royal Society in 1816. His work is described in *Brief Statement of Facts, connected with the scientific Pursuits of the late Charles Broderip...,* London, 1829. He left his property to his executor, Lt-Col. Joseph d'Arcy. William Broderip, a solicitor, bequeathed his property to his last surviving brother, Francis Broderip, a solicitor and collector and a benefactor of Middlesex Hospital, which subsequently merged with University College London Hospital, which today has no documents relating to the Broderip family. Neither William John Broderip, F.R.S., barrister, court reporter, police magistrate and renowned geologist, nor the author Frances Freeling Broderip were immediate relations of Francis Fane Broderip.

[86] A few records of payments to Broderip & Wilkinson are preserved in accounts of their customers. For instance, Dorothea Banks (wife of Sir Joseph Banks) paid 'Mr Broderip & Wilkinson's Bill' of £2/14/– on 17 January 1803 and their bill of 18/– on 9 January 1804 (account book of Lady Banks, CKS U951/A75). She appears to have paid her creditors annually (including her music teacher Dr Charles Burney, with whom she had about sixty lessons a year at a cost of 10/6 per lesson).

[87] *The Times*, 13 October 1812, p 2; *The Morning Chronicle*, 13 October 1812, p 3.

In addition to publishing new music under their own name, Wilkinson & Co. reprinted music from plates that had been engraved and printed for Broderip & Wilkinson, generally without incurring the cost of altering the title-page plate to show that the name of the firm had changed. For example, when issuing Book I of part 2 of Bach's '48' in 1808, Wilkinson & Co. reprinted without change the title-page plate and music plates originally engraved for Broderip & Wilkinson, and they used the same title-page plate again for their edition of Book II of part 2 of the '48', which Broderip & Wilkinson had not published.[88]

Wilkinson & Co. were so successful in selling cabinet piano fortes made upon William Southwell's 1807 patent that they 'determined to relinquish all ... branches of the music line' other than the manufacture of piano fortes by 30 November 1809, and offered for sale 'the whole of their very large and valuable stock of foreign and English music, at half the original price'.[89] At the end of 1810, Charles Wilkinson Sr supplied a further £12,000 to enable George to establish an expanded piano-making firm in partnership with his foreman Robert Wornum II,[90] and Wilkinson & Co. then ceased trading. When the underinsured Wilkinson & Wornum business was burnt down it owed £16,640 to Charles Wilkinson Sr, which he agreed not to claim.[91] The partnership of Wilkinson and Wornum was dissolved on 3 March 1813,[92] and the two partners subsequently sold pianos separately.

On 11 January 1811 the music seller Thomas Preston advertised that he had

---

[88] Michael Kassler, 'Broderip, Wilkinson and the first English edition of the "48"', *op. cit.*, p 72.

[89] Advertisement, *The Morning Chronicle*, 3 August 1809, p 2. This advertisement was repeated several times.

[90] Henry Broadhurst Wilkinson, *op. cit.*, p 25. See also Michael Kassler, 'Broderip, Wilkinson and the first English edition of the "48"', *op. cit.*, p 75. Robert Wornum II was the son of the music seller Robert Wornum.

[91] Henry Broadhurst Wilkinson, p 25–26. Because of this generosity it seems likely that Charles Wilkinson Sr also helped George to buy the half share of the Broderip & Wilkinson partnership that Francis Broderip had owned.

[92] *The London Gazette*, 6 March 1813, p 489.

> just purchased the entire and extensive stock of music plates, and copy-right, the property of Wilkinson and Co. (late Broderip and Wilkinson) of the Haymarket; consisting of the finest works of Mozart, Beethoven, Haydn, Pleyel, Von Esch, Handel, Corelli, and others of the esteemed Classic Authors: new editions of which are now prepared....[93]

About this time he issued a four-page printed list of *Musical Publications selected from the Catalogue published by Broderip and Wilkinson, lately purchased, and now printed and sold by Preston.*[94] It comprised about 750 titles and indicates the extent of Broderip & Wilkinson's publishing progamme.

Preston continued to reprint music from Broderip & Wilkinson's plates when copies were still in demand but their stock was low or exhausted.[95] For some reprints, such as part 2 of the '48', the title-page plate was altered to substitute Preston's name and address for that of Broderip & Wilkinson but their music plates were reused without change.[96] Preston died on 1 July 1834 and was succeeded by the partnership of Charles Coventry and John Hollier, who again reprinted Broderip & Wilkinson's and Wilkinson & Co.'s music plates of part 2 of the '48' but updated the imprint on the title-page plate to 'Coventry & Hollier'.[97]

---

[93] *The Morning Chronicle*, 11 January 1811, p 1.

[94] A copy of this list is in BL Hirsch iv.1113.(10.). It includes works first published by Wilkinson & Co. as well as a much larger number of works that Wilkinson & Co. acquired from Broderip & Wilkinson. Preston mentioned the availability of this list in his 11 January 1811 advertisement, which was repeated several times.

[95] For an example of this see Patricia Stroh, 'Evolution of an edition: the case of Beethoven's opus 2', part 2, *Notes* v 60 no. 1 (September 2003) p 46–129 at p 61, p 88 and p 107.

[96] Michael Kassler, 'Broderip, Wilkinson and the first English edition of the "48"', *op. cit.*, p 76.

[97] See Yo Tomita, 'The dawn of the English Bach Awakening...', *op. cit.* in note 73 above, p 142.

~ 3 ~

CLEMENTI'S MUSIC BUSINESS

David Rowland

On 1 November 1798 the Cheapside and Tottenham Court Road assets of Longman & Broderip were acquired by Longman, Clementi & Co. With the exception of John Longman, each of the six partners of the new company—the others were Muzio Clementi, Josiah Banger, Frederick William Collard, David Davis and Frederick Augustus Hyde—knew Longman & Broderip's business well. Collard, Davis and Hyde had worked for the firm, and when its partners became bankrupt in May 1795 Banger and Clementi were appointed two of its assignees. Davis was particularly knowledgeable of the firm as he managed it while it was under the assignees' control.

As noted in Chapter 1, John Longman seems to have become a partner of Longman, Clementi & Co. as a favour to his brother James, who had been the senior partner of Longman & Broderip but presumably was unable to raise the capital required of partners in the new company. During the less than two years of John's partnership he resided in Milborne Port, Somerset, where he ran his own business unrelated to the music trade and had James act for him in London.[1]

Muzio Clementi was the new company's best-known partner. From the mid-1770s, when he first came to London, he developed rapidly into one of its most prominent keyboard players, conductors, composers and teachers.[2] He had early experience of the music business, sometimes publishing his works 'for the author' at his own address and sometimes relinquishing their copyrights to music sellers for a fee. This experience taught him some difficult truths about the trade, as he complained in a 1784 letter to his father:

---

[1] See pages 82–83 above.

[2] I give a biographical sketch of Clementi in *CMC* p liii–lxxvii.

Figure 3.1 Portrait of Muzio Clementi published by William Richardson on 1 January 1803 (Beinecke Rare Book and Manuscript Library, Yale University, Osborn collection, in folder 3328, by permission)

> a certain Welcker who was very well-known throughout Europe and who used to have a music shop in London, went bankrupt three or four years ago, and he had over 300 guineas of mine.... Blundel was a music merchant from the Hay Market who went bankrupt about a year ago, and he owed me about 40 guineas.[3]

About the same time Clementi also suffered from seeing his work printed in a rogue edition in Paris:

> On his return to England [from the continent in the early 1780s] he deemed it necessary to publish his celebrated Toccata, with a Sonata, Op. 11, a surreptitious copy, full of errors, having been printed without his knowledge in France.[4]

He quickly overcame these setbacks and became known throughout Europe as a performer and composer. During the 1780s and 1790s his music was published frequently in Paris and Vienna,[5] and he was approached by music sellers elsewhere in Europe who wanted to sell some of his compositions that he had published in London. Around the time of his appointment as a Longman & Broderip assignee he withdrew from playing the piano in public, but continued to conduct, to compose and to teach.

Clementi's association with Longman & Broderip dates from at least 1786, when they published his *La Chasse*, Op. 16.[6] From then until the firm's bankruptcy he continued to publish with them,

---

[3] Muzio Clementi→Nicola Clementi, 1 August 1784, transcribed and translated in *CMC* p 13–16. John Welcker, who was declared bankrupt in 1780 (*The London Gazette*, 25–28 March 1780, p 4), had published Clementi's Op. 2–3 in 1779 and on Clementi's behalf had arranged for the printing and selling of his Op. 4 in 1780 (see Alan Tyson, *Thematic Catalogue of the Works of Muzio Clementi*, Tutzing, 1967, p 36–39). James Blundell, Welcker's brother-in-law, was declared bankrupt in 1782 (*The London Gazette*, 28 September–1 October 1782, p 4). He reprinted Clementi's Op. 4 *c*1781 (Tyson, *op. cit.*, p 39).

[4] 'Mr Clementi', *Quarterly Musical Magazine and Review* v 2 no. 7 (1820) p 308–316 at p 311. Clementi's son Charles confirmed (in Charles Clementi→ John Davis Sainsbury, 20 January 1824, *CMC* p 309–312) that his father agreed with this anonymous memoir 'in the principal parts'.

[5] Tyson, *op. cit.*, gives details of publications of Clementi's music on the continent.

[6] It was entered at Stationers' Hall on 10 July 1786 (*MESH* p 66).

although not exclusively. He also was commissioned by the firm to make arrangements of other composers' works, including two Haydn symphonies and some quartets by Pleyel.[7]

Clementi thus brought to Longman, Clementi & Co. a wealth of publishing experience and impressive musical contacts with individuals and music sellers throughout Europe. In addition, he brought expertise in the making and retailing of keyboard instruments. He was a friend of John Broadwood, who had entrusted his eldest son James Shudi Broadwood to Clementi's care in Paris,[8] where Clementi appears to have acted as the elder Broadwood's agent, selling a harpsichord and square piano of his there in 1781.[9] In 1791 an edition that Clementi made and published of Domenico 'Scarlatti's Chefs-d'Oeuvre, for the harpsichord or piano-forte' was 'to be had at Mr Broadwood's harpsichord maker'.[10]

Two days after it began trading, the new company's first advertisement appeared in *The Times*:

> LONGMAN, CLEMENTI, and Company, as Successors to LONGMAN and BRODERIP, No. 26, Cheapside, and in Tottenham-Court-Road, beg leave to announce to the Nobility and Public in general, that they have established an extensive and liberal Plan for carrying on the Trade of Musical Instrument Makers, also printing, publishing, and vending all Musical Productions worthy of notice, and have settled a Correspondence for importing all Foreign Compositions that possess a sufficiency of merit to deserve recommendation. From the regular system they have adopted for the managing and conducting every branch of their trade, all orders committed to their care will be executed with the greatest punctuality, and every possible attention used for giving complete satisfaction to every person who may indulge them with their favors. LONGMAN, CLEMENTI, and Company, beg leave to declare, that they are now employing, in the manufacture of Piano Fortes and other Musical

---

[7] Tyson, *op. cit.*, p 129–130.

[8] David Wainwright, *Broadwood, by Appointment: A history*, London, 1982, p 65.

[9] William Dale, *Tschudi the Harpsichord Maker*, London, 1913, p 8. Because these instruments arrived after Clementi had been in Paris for several months and shortly before he left, it is likely that he was selling them to others and taking a cut for himself, a common way at this time for keyboard players to fund their activities.

[10] Tyson, p 130–131.

> Instruments, workmen they have selected of the first rate genius and abilities, and are resolved to give generous encouragement to every new Invention that can be produced for improving Musical Instruments, and for gratifying the lovers of harmony. And they conceive it would be a want of duty to themselves, if they neglected to observe, that as Mr Clementi intends to devote a considerable portion of his time for superintending and directing the finishing of grand and small Piano Fortes, with additional keys, &c. they may, without hazard to their reputation, be reasonably allowed to assert, that from his known skill, experience, and judgment, their Instruments for richness, evenness and brilliancy of tone, and pleasantness of touch, will be equal, if not superior to any before offered to the Public.
>
> LONGMAN, CLEMENTI, and Company, request all Orders intended for them may be addressed to No. 26, Cheapside, as they have no connexion whatever with Mr Broderip, in the Haymarket.[11]

As is evident from Clementi's correspondence while he toured Europe in the early years of the nineteenth century, the announcement that 'Mr Clementi intends to devote a considerable portion of his time for superintending and directing the finishing of grand and small piano fortes' was a genuine statement of intent rather than mere sales talk. He frequently referred to details of piano making and claimed in 1806 to have invented a new mechanism to produce 'a grand effect'.[12]

Josiah Banger of Hackney, the other Longman & Broderip assignee who became a partner of Longman, Clementi & Co., is said to have had financial expertise.[13] In 1803 and again in 1805 the creditors of Longman & Broderip were asked by the assignees to

[11] *The Times*, 3 November 1798, p 1.

[12] Clementi→Frederick William Collard, 9/21 June 1806, *CMC* p 164–165. On 8 March 1821 Collard received an English patent (subsequently numbered 4542) for applying to piano soundboards a novel 'bridge of reverberation', which may have been influenced by Clementi's idea.

[13] According to testimony given in the 1802 legal case *Longman v Assignees* (TNA E112/1787/6238, answer of the assignees) he was 'particularly acquainted with the accounts' of Longman & Broderip. In 1789 he had been appointed treasurer of a society to support Sunday schools in Hackney (see V. W., 'Account of the Sunday and daily schools in connexion with St Thomas's Square Chapel, Hackney, Middlesex', *The Sunday School Teachers' Magazine, and Journal of Education* 4th ser. v 2 (1851) p 641–646 at p 642).

consider what, if any, allowance he should be paid for his services and expenses while the bankrupts' business was carried on.[14]

As mentioned, and as summarised in Chapter 1, each of Frederick William Collard, David Davis and Frederick Augustus Hyde had worked for Longman & Broderip.[15] Hyde appears to have left their employment by December 1793 and formed an association with the music seller Joseph Buchinger *or* Buckinger, for songs that Buchinger published were entered at Stationers' Hall by Hyde on 14 December 1793 and again on 21 March 1794.[16] Not long after that, he formed a partnership with John Lewis Vautier Sollicoffre and James Henry Houston, known as Lewis, Houston & Hyde, which bought the business of the music seller John Bland. This short-lived partnership entered music at Stationers' Hall between 18 March 1795 and 10 October 1795 but was dissolved on 1 December 1795 and its business was continued by Francis Linley.[17]

Hyde subsequently engaged Longman & Broderip (then under the control of the assignees) to arrange the printing and selling of three works in which he had a financial interest. William Shield's *A Collection of Canzonetts and an Elegy*, 'printed for the author' by Longman & Broderip, was entered at Stationers' Hall on 9 May 1796 by both Shield and Hyde, suggesting that Hyde had bought half its copyright from Shield. Another publication, which was 'compiled by' Hyde, entitled *A Miscellaneous Collection of Songs, Ballads, Canzonets, Duets, Trios, Glees, & Elegies ... The glees harmonized ... by Mr* [Samuel] *Webbe* [Sr], *and the Italian airs adapted by Mr Shield* was 'printed for' its proprietors—Hyde, Frederick William Collard and David Davis—by Longman & Broderip. And Hyde entered a song, 'Sylvia again is true and kind', written and composed by Richard Suett and 'printed by' Longman & Broderip, at

---

[14] *The London Gazette*, 18 June 1803, p 731, and 6 April 1805, p 472.

[15] For Collard see pages 46–47 above, for Davis pages 48–49 and 79, and for Hyde page 55.

[16] The songs were 'The tint on the cheek of my love' composed by Charles Thomas Carter (copy at BL G.364.(15) and 'The gentle shepherdess' composed by Thomas Welsh (copy at BL G.365.(43)).

[17] *The London Gazette*, 3 December 1795, p 1350, transcribed on pages 204–205 below.

Stationers' Hall on 2 August 1798. Hyde thus had contact with the firm on several occasions between 1796 and 1798, certainly with Collard and Davis and conceivably with Clementi. Their ability to work together would have been important when the partnership of Longman, Clementi & Co. was determined. Another factor must have strengthened Hyde's position: on 30 July 1796 he had signed a contract with Haydn (discussed in the next chapter) to publish the composer's music in England.

With the exception of John Longman all the partners of Longman, Clementi & Co. had significant expertise in music publishing and musical instrument making, and Longman's lack of experience was compensated by his brother James acting for him. Acquisition of Longman & Broderip's Tottenham Court Road manufactory meant that Longman, Clementi & Co. were well equipped to run a musical instrument business. Longman & Broderip's stock of engraved plates was divided between the two successor firms, even to the extent that the plates of a number of Clementi's works went to Broderip & Wilkinson.[18]

The advertisement quoted above gives a strong indication that the scope of Longman, Clementi & Co.'s activities was to be at least as extensive as Longman & Broderip's. Subsequent newspaper notices show that the company regularly sold London concert tickets, as had its predecessor. The advertisement also shows that although John Longman and Muzio Clementi had equal status in the name of the new company, Clementi was the public face of the business.

Although Longman's name was dropped in 1801 following his withdrawal and the partnership underwent several subsequent changes, Clementi continued as a partner until 24 June 1831, less than a year before his death.[19] *The London Gazette* announced John Longman's departure in May 1801:

> Notice is hereby given, that the Partnership between John Longman, Muzio Clementi, Frederick Augustus Hyde, Frederick William Collard, Josiah Banger, and David Davis, of Cheapside, London, Manufacturers of Musical Instruments and Music-Sellers, is and stands dissolved from the 28th June last, 1800. All Bills, Notes, or other Demands on the same

[18] See pages 159–162 below.

[19] *The London Gazette*, 8 July 1831, p 1369.

> Partnership will be paid by Messrs Clementi, Hyde, Collard, Banger, and Davis, who continue to carry on Business on their own Account; and all Debts due to the said Partnership are to be paid to them, who are fully authorised to receive the same, and by whom all Accounts concerning the same Partnership are to be adjusted and settled. Witness our Hands this 24th of April 1801.
>
> N.B. Clementi, Banger, Hyde, Collard, and Davis, beg Leave to acquaint their Friends and the Public, that their Trade as Manufacturers of Musical Instruments and Music-Sellers, is now carried on under the firm of Muzio Clementi and Co.[20]

The next partnership change occurred in 1810, when William Frederick Collard (a younger brother of Frederick William) entered and Hyde departed. The former event occurred before 18 August 1810, as on that date Beethoven's 'Thema, with variations for the piano forte' was entered at Stationers' Hall by Clementi, Banger, Collard, Davis & Collard.[21] Hyde's retirement from the partnership 'by mutual consent' took effect on 21 September 1810.[22]

William Frederick Collard was baptised in Wiveliscombe, Somerset on 25 August 1776. He followed his brother to London where he married Sarah Dean at the Old Church, St Pancras, on 26 December 1810.[23] He appears to have been an engaging individual with wider interests than his brother. Charlotte Moscheles relates that her husband Ignaz described William Frederick as 'one of the most intelligent men he ever came across',[24] and Clementi referred in 1829 to William Frederick's 'enlivening society'.[25] He wrote the texts of several songs that were published by the company.

Other partnership changes resulted from the retirement of Josiah Banger in 1817 and the death of David Davis in 1822. As

---

[20] *The London Gazette*, 12 May 1801, p 542. However, numerous publications of the firm listed the surnames of all its partners.

[21] *MESH* p 657.

[22] *The London Gazette*, 22 September 1810, p 1501.

[23] IGI.

[24] [Charlotte Moscheles], *Life of Moscheles, with selections from his diaries and correspondence by his wife, adapted from the original German by A[rthur] D[uke] Coleridge*, London, 1873, p 109.

[25] Clementi→Frederick William Collard, 2 February 1829, *CMC* p 352.

William Frederick Collard was the only new partner taken on in the three decades following the formation of Longman, Clementi & Co. in 1798, he and his brother Frederick William were the only remaining partners when Clementi stepped down in 1831 and the company was restyled 'Collard & Collard'.

A balance sheet dated 24 June 1811 of Clementi & Co.—the only such document to have survived—shows that the partners then held the following capital in the firm:[26]

Muzio Clementi	£ 3,000
Josiah Banger	£ 2,000
Frederick William Collard	£ 2,000
David Davis	£ 2,000
William Frederick Collard	£ 1,000

In addition to their capital investment the first four of these partners had advanced various amounts to the firm, and its value then was said to be £111,922/0/8.

It seems plausible that each of the six partners of Longman, Clementi & Co. had invested £2,000 in 1798, making the firm's initial capitalisation £12,000. When John Longman left in 1801 he was to receive £2,830/12/–, which could have come from his suggested initial investment plus a share in the profits made while he was a partner.[27] This would allow for Clementi and William Frederick Collard buying out John Longman's share at £1,000 each, but unfortunately we do not know what the actual arrangement was.

This balance sheet also shows that, for the approximately ten months from 1 September 1810 to 24 June 1811, Clementi & Co.'s profits (excluding bad or doubtful debts) totalled £5,631/1/4, of which £1,689/6/5 accrued to Clementi, £1,126/4/3 to each of Banger, Frederick William Collard and Davis, and £563/2/2 to William

[26] This document, now in the possession of John Collard, is transcribed in *CMC* p 423–425.

[27] TNA C13/29/34, *Longman v Clementi*, 1803. The 24 June 1811 balance sheet gives £3,000 as the 'amount paid Fr. A. Hyde for retiring and to be liquidated by instalments yearly' and shows an additional £9,187/10/– that he had lent to the partnership which presumably was due to be paid back to him with interest at some future time.

Frederick Collard. If this level of profitability continued or increased, it helps to explain how David Davis could have bequeathed £12,000 to his brother James in 1822, who then retired from building organs.[28]

The partners of Longman, Clementi & Co. took several initiatives at the start to give momentum to the company's activities. Many new editions of music by a range of composers were produced, including some extremely saleable works and collections by Clementi himself, notably his *Introduction to the Art of Playing on the Piano Forte* of 1801 and his *Practical Harmony*, the first of whose four parts was published in the same year. The introduction of new works and the rationalisation of stock acquired from Longman & Broderip necessitated the production of a catalogue. This was achieved within a few months—by June 1799—and evidently was needed for the new company to establish the exchange of business with British and foreign music sellers that had been a feature of Longman & Broderip's operations.

Clementi's correspondence with the Viennese music publisher Artaria & Co. shows one of the uses to which the new catalogue was put.[29] He wrote to them on 21 December 1798:

> Being an associate of Longman, Hyde, and others, it would give me great pleasure to enter into correspondence with you, to the mutual advantage of both parties. But first of all, might we ask you to send us your catalogue, and we will send you ours as soon as it is ready. We have a range of excellent new works, and I hope that if we do enter into trading business with each other, both of us will find it mutually beneficial.[30]

---

[28] See page 49 above.

[29] Clementi was used to dealing with foreign publishers. His own music had been published by Artaria and Torricella in Vienna, Bailleux in Paris and Castaud in Lyons, and he had corresponded on this subject with Hans Georg Nägeli in Zurich. See Nägeli→Clementi, 18 January 1794 and 19 November 1794 (*CMC* p 19–23).

[30] *CMC* p 31–32. Artaria & Co. had had a long-standing relationship with Longman & Broderip. See David Wyn Jones, 'From Artaria to Longman & Broderip: Mozart's music on sale in London', in Otto Biba and David Wyn Jones (eds), *Studies in Music History Presented to H. C. Robbins Landon on his Seventieth Birthday*, London, 1996, p 105–114.

On 24 June 1799 Clementi wrote that his 'illustrious pupil' John Baptist Cramer was about to set off for Europe with a catalogue, which he subsequently delivered to Artaria.[31]

On 21 December 1798 Clementi also wrote to his brother Gaetano in Rome. Unsurprisingly, the letter refers to family matters, but it deals as well with purchasing violin, violoncello and harp strings for the new company:

> We are very much in need at the moment of gut strings called strings for violin, bass and harp, and we have written to Messrs Pica, Toffani and company requesting a large quantity, and seeing as these strings are to become my property on behalf of the Company, I beg you to use your eloquence with the aforementioned Messrs Pica & Co. so that they might send our strings as soon as possible; and I ask you at the same time to check that they are *good merchandise*, seeing as they are, as you would say, for your blood brother. And seeing as we will pay in cash, my associates hope that the aforementioned merchants will be so good as to give us a discount in proportion with the order, which is considerable. We have not received any reply from them since after the beginning of the year 1797.[32]

This request eventually bore fruit, because the company advertised on 18 April 1800 that

> John Longman, Clementi, & Co. beg leave to acquaint the musical profession, and the public in general, that they have just imported a quantity of excellent ROMAN STRINGS, which are now ready for sale at their music warehouse, No. 26, Cheapside....[33]

Clementi had almost certainly known Ignace Pleyel in London in the early 1790s before Pleyel moved to Paris, where he established a music-selling business in 1795 named 'Maison Pleyel'. On 2 August 1799 Longman, Clementi & Co. signed a contract with them

---

[31] Clementi→Artaria & Co., 24 June 1799 and 29 November 1799 (*CMC* p 34–38). This catalogue does not appear to be extant. For extant Longman, Clementi & Co. catalogues see page 164 below.

[32] *CMC* p 27–30. Pica, Toffani & Co. were string makers in Rome: see Remo Giazotto, *Muzio Clementi Epistolario 1781–1831*, Milan, 2002, p 35–39. Their name is transcribed incorrectly in *CMC*.

[33] *The Oracle, and the Daily Advertiser*, 18 April 1800, p 1.

concerning the publication of Haydn's quartets op. 76.[34] Correspondence between the firms followed, but ceased after 1802 because of trading difficulties between England and France at that time.[35] In the meantime Longman, Clementi & Co. seem to have sold instruments through Pleyel's firm. In the summer of 1800, during a period of quiet in the fractious relationship between England and France, Clementi's friend Rev. John Cleaver Banks visited Paris and reported in an account of his visit that the Parisians

> are very far advanced [in instrumental music], if I may except the piano-forte, which is an instrument very imperfectly understood at Paris. The manufacture of that instrument is much in arrear. Mr Pleyel told me that he could easily sell a good instrument of Clementi's or Broadwood's manufacture for more than 100 Louis.[36]

Pleyel might have heard of Clementi's problems with buying strings from Italy, as he wrote to him in September 1801 that 'I have received for 20,000 livres the best quality strings from Naples, if you need any I could let you have some'.[37]

So fruitful was their relationship that Clementi contemplated opening a piano factory in France with Pleyel's help. On 20 October 1801, within a few days of the preliminary agreement which led to the Peace of Amiens and a brief period of better relations between England and France, Clementi wrote to Pleyel to explore the possibility of a factory, or at least to secure an agency for Clementi & Co.'s pianos in the country.[38] But the venture came to nothing, no doubt in part because of France's protectionist attitude to industry.

---

[34] Max Unger, *Muzio Clementis Leben*, Langensalza, 1914, p 102.

[35] See *CMC*. For further details of the relationship between the French and English piano industries see David Rowland, 'Piano businesses in England and France', in Christophe Coin, Éric de Visscher and Florence Gétreau (eds), *Le pianoforte en France 1780–1820*, Paris, 2009, p 127–135.

[36] J[ohn] C[leaver] B[anks]→Editor, *Monthly Magazine and British Register*, 9/2/1801, printed as part 3 of 'An accurate account of the present state of the French Republic', *Monthly Magazine and British Register* v 11 no. 2 = no. 70 (1 March 1801) p 105–106 at p 105.

[37] Pleyel→Clementi, 25 September 1801, *CMC* p 75–76.

[38] See *CMC* p 77.

Evidence of how difficult it was to export British goods to France is found in various sources. For example, the pianist Friedrich Himmel, who was acting as an agent for Clementi & Co. on the continent, wrote from Paris on 18 May 1802:

> I am writing to you concerning an upright fortepiano for Mr de Grisenoy, Director of the famous Concert de Cléry here. While Mr de Grisenoy has wanted to have one of these magnificent instruments, he will have to be patient, because the French government, in order to protect French factories, has given the order that no English instrument is to enter France, and Mr de Grisenoy sees no other way than to have it sent from London to Hamburg, and in Hamburg to aim to get hold of a document which authenticates that this instrument belongs to a person who wishes to reside and remain in France. This is the great difficulty for your instruments in France. Mr de Grisenoy will correspond with you on this subject, but the difficulty seems to me insuperable.[39]

Later in the same year, on 26 October, the French piano makers Jean-Baptiste Erard and Sébastien Erard wrote to the French Ministry of the Interior, concerned that there might be some relaxation of the government's protectionist stance on imports, but they need not have worried: the Ministry replied giving an assurance that English pianos would be kept out of France.[40]

Another important relationship began in the late 1790s between Longman, Clementi & Co. and Breitkopf & Härtel in Leipzig. The two firms apparently exchanged letters in 1799–1800,[41] but their relationship does not seem to have developed substantially until Clementi met Gottfried Härtel or another representative of Breitkopf & Härtel in Dresden early in 1804.[42] On 11 September 1804 Clementi felt free to write to Härtel asking for accommodation in Leipzig for a

---

[39] *CMC* p 85–87. Clementi & Co. made both upright grand and upright square pianos at this time.

[40] Archives Nationales, Paris, F 12-1966 G. See Malou Haine, *Les facteurs d'instruments de musique à Paris au XIXe siècle*, Brussels, 1985, p 61–62.

[41] Max Unger, *Muzio Clementis Leben, op. cit.*, p 99.

[42] See Breitkopf & Härtel→Clementi & Co., 13 February 1804, *CMC* p 113–114.

day or two.[43] In 1802 Pleyel offered Clementi accommodation during a planned visit to Paris and Clementi's company returned the favour by inviting Pleyel to stay at their premises in London.[44] Clementi and Domenico Artaria also became friends, presumably during the time that Clementi spent in Vienna during the first decade of the century. He wrote to Artaria on 6 August 1827 to secure rooms in Vienna for himself, his wife Emma and their daughter Cecilia Susanna.[45]

The personal relationships that Clementi established with Artaria, Härtel and Pleyel seem to have been the most significant and closest during the early days of Clementi's company, but contacts with other continental music sellers followed. Clementi had dealings with the Erard family,[46] although how close the two firms became is not known. He probably met Giovanni Ricordi on his European travels in the first decade of the century and by the time Clementi was in his seventies the two men were good friends, Clementi asking Ricordi to take care of some personal business in Italy on his behalf.[47] Through Artaria, Clementi also knew the Viennese piano maker Johann Andreas Streicher, who supplied Clementi & Co. with leather for hammer coverings in the 1820s.[48]

Clementi & Co. also traded outside Europe. According to an 1809 letter from Daniel Stewart in New York to James Shudi Broadwood, 'Clementi & Co have sold a good many instruments to people in this country'.[49] Perhaps these sales had something to do

---

[43] *CMC* p 125–126. Härtel offered hospitality to Clementi again in 1822 (see *CMC* p 291).

[44] Pleyel→Clementi, 3 June 1802, *CMC* p 89; Clementi & Co.→Pleyel, 30 September 1802, extract quoted in *CMC* p 98.

[45] *CMC* p 345–346. Artaria also made practical arrangements for the Clementi family's return trip (see Clementi→Domenico Artaria, 17 September 1827, *CMC* p 347–348).

[46] See Clementi→Gottfried Härtel, 12 April 1818, *CMC* p 254–256 at p 255.

[47] See Clementi→Ricordi, 27 June 1830, *CMC* p 363–364.

[48] See Clementi & Co.→Streicher, 21 May 1831, *CMC* p 367–368. This letter was signed by Frederick William Collard.

[49] Daniel Stewart→James Shudi Broadwood, 4 September 1809, Broadwood archive, Surrey History Centre, quoted in David Wainwright, *Broadwood by Appointment*, London, 1982, p 108.

with Adam Stewart, an employee of Clementi & Co. who emigrated to Baltimore, Maryland and set up in business as a piano maker in 1810.[50] Clementi & Co. later described themselves as musical instrument makers and music sellers 'to His Majesty, all the Royal Family and to the Honble East India Company'.[51] The last relationship may have been aided by Josiah Banger, who was a long-time stockholder of that company.[52]

Clementi's efforts to establish the company in international markets went hand-in-hand with activities designed to secure the firm's position as one of the largest British music traders. The company's relationship with provincial agents is shown in an August 1800 Longman, Clementi & Co. advertisement that:

> The above works may be had at all the music-sellers in England, Scotland, and Ireland; but particularly of Messrs Linterns, Bath [i.e., James and Walter Lintern]; Howell, Bristol; Hodges, Bristol; Hime, Liverpool; Knapton, York; Porter, Leeds; Holden, Wakefield; Woodward, Birmingham; [Henry and James] Banks, Salisbury; Wellman and Hammond, Southampton; Christiana, Southampton; Taylor, Chester; Stewart and Co.[,] Edinburgh; Muir, Wood, and Co.[,] Edinburgh; White [i.e., Whyte], Edinburgh; Urbane [i.e., Urbani] and Liston, Edinburgh; McGown [i.e., McGoun], Glasgow; McFadyn [i.e., McFadyen],

---

[50] In 1812 Adam Stewart was joined in business in Baltimore by his brother James, who later worked with Jonas Chickering and then returned to London in 1826 to work as a foreman for Clementi, Collard & Collard. See Cynthia Adams Hoover, 'Stewart, James', in *Oxford Music Online*.

[51] This wording appears on an invoice dated 31 December 1823 attached to Thomas Lindsay→John Gough, 5 January 1824, *CMC* p 307. Lindsay was then employed by Clementi & Co. and responsible for some of their correspondence.

[52] Banger's name appears in the company's printed lists of members at least between 1789 and 1816. Between 1811 and 1815 his address was given as 26 Cheapside (Clementi & Co.'s address) as well as Hackney. In the 1815 membership list Michael Banger, presumably Josiah's son of that name, is entered at the address 'Cheapside' without a house number, but it is not known whether he worked for Clementi & Co. Muzio Clementi is listed as a shareholder of the East India Company in 1813 (*A List of the Names of the Members of the United Company of Merchants of England, trading to the East-Indies, who stood qualified as voters on the company's books, 13th April 1813*, [London], 1813, p 17) and subsequently, and held stock in the company when he wrote his will on 2 January 1832 (TNA PROB 10/5307, transcribed in *CMC* p 430–434).

> Glasgow; Anderson, Perth; Hime, Dublin; Lee, Dublin; Rhames, Dublin; Corbett, Cork; Corbett, Limerick; and Brown, Dungannon [Ireland].—Longman, Clementi, and Co.'s new patent piano fortes, with or without additional keys, may be seen at any of the above warehouses.[53]

The firm's goods were transported around the British Isles by road, canal, river and sea. During the eighteenth century there had been significant improvements in the nation's roads as the result of the establishment of hundreds of turnpike trusts which maintained major routes in exchange for tolls. By the end of the century a comprehensive road network existed and commercial haulage firms regularly ran wagons between all major centres. By 1798 many canals had been built but a fully coherent system of waterways was yet to be established. The Grand Junction Canal, for example, which later formed part of the Grand Union Canal, and which significantly cut the cost of north-south traffic by establishing a direct route between Birmingham and London, was completed in 1805. The canals and river systems joined with established sea routes followed by boats that regularly left the Thames wharfs.[54]

A number of factors influenced what means of transport was chosen. A sea voyage to Bristol, for example, was substantially longer than either of the other two modes of transport and during French Revolutionary and Napoleonic times was potentially at risk from foreign warships. Road transport, on the other hand, was quicker and more secure but comparatively expensive if the goods carried were heavy.

The company's correspondence shows how various forms of transport were used. On 29 March 1798 Clementi wrote to Harriet Frances Alpe:

> There seems to be a great scarcity of good musical works of late, so that I am reduced to the poverty of a single concerto by Cramer and my

[53] *The Times*, 1 August 1800, p 2. Lee of Dublin could refer to Edmund Lee (who was an agent of Longman & Broderip, see page 67 above) or to his brother John, who had an independent business.

[54] General information on transport in this period is found in Derek H. Aldcroft and Michael J. Freeman (eds.), *Transport in the Industrial Revolution*, Manchester, 1983.

> op. 37th[55] which I sent this evening by the Expedition coach from the Bell and Crown, directed as you desired.[56]

These were not heavy goods, so the use of a regular road service is easily understandable. Three years later, on 1 December 1801, a piano was sent by road to a Miss Penny in Weymouth: 'at last the instrument is chosen, packt up, and it set off last night by Russell's wagon, from the Bell Inn, Friday Street'.[57] In this letter Clementi comments that 'a pedal to raise the dampers I took care should be fixed to it', suggesting that the piano was a square rather than a grand, since grands routinely had pedals whereas squares at that time did not. If it were a square this could explain why it was sent by road rather than by water. Alternatively, perhaps it was sent by road because it needed to be sent quickly; the letter suggests that the recipient had already waited some time for its delivery.

Other instruments went by boat. On 18 February 1805 John Erskine, who ran a music shop in York, wrote to Clementi & Co.:

> I have had very good luck with the two last piano Fortes & if you will always send good ones I don't fear having the same in general, I have to request the favour of Mr Davies [i.e., Clementi's partner David Davis] choosing me a *Couple*—provided they are approved of when they

---

[55] Probably the edition for 'piano forte only' of John Baptist Cramer's 'Second Grand Concerto' in D minor, advertised as just published by Robert Birchall in *The Times*, 4 July 1797, p 2. See Thomas B. Milligan, *Johann Baptist Cramer (1771–1858): A thematic catalogue of his works*, Stuyvesant, New York, 1994, p 2. Clementi's piano sonatas op. 37 were entered at Stationers' Hall by Longman & Broderip on 8 February 1798.

[56] *CMC* p 24–25. Although the recipient's name does not appear in this letter its previous owner, Arthur F. Hill, identified her as Mrs Alpe when he lent it to the Musicians' Company for their 1904 exhibition (see Worshipful Company of Musicians, *Catalogue of the Loan Exhibition held in Fishmongers' Hall*, London, 1904, p 43, exhibit no. 486). The letter was sold in lot 277 of the posthumous sale of Hill's collection by Sotheby's (London, 16–17 June 1947), whose auction catalogue prints (p 37) the following note that Hill put in the album of other Clementi manuscripts that then contained this letter: 'I obtained this ms and letters from Mrs Sconce of … Kensington. They were given by Clementi to a Mrs Alpe of Hardingham Hall, near Attleborough, Norfolk, of whom Mrs Sconce is a grand-daughter'. The Expedition coach travelled between London and Norwich.

[57] Partly transcribed in *CMC* p 78.

> arrive, I shall sell one directly—send them to Gun & Shot Wharf [on the south bank of the Thames in Southwark], to come by one of the York Traders.[58]

Goods regularly were sent to and from York via the North Sea, and Erskine's piano presumably travelled up the Humber estuary and on through the river network to York. Thomas Lindsay, who worked for Clementi & Co. in 1823 and 1824, mentioned an 1824 shipment of a grand piano: 'The case is sent by Crowley's Boat to Wolverhampton',[59] indicating that it travelled there via the canal network.

Trade with Ireland was important throughout the early nineteenth century. In January 1800 Philip Cogan wrote to Clementi requesting a piano for a customer in Dublin, adding that

> I shou'd be enabled to sell more Instroments [sic] but for the delay, if you think Commissions from Dublin worth your attention, I now Inform you, that some of the first proffesors [sic] have promis'd me to get their Instruments from you.[60]

In 1813 John Bernard Logier wrote from Dublin to John Green, then an employee of Clementi & Co.:

> I hope you have received the 6 Kent bugles & trumpets, the boat containing 24 more has arrived at Liverpool....
>
> Send me the [word(s) unclear]—directed to the care of Mr Owens—HolyHead on a small boat.[61]

Instruments and other goods were transported between Dublin and London via sea to Holyhead and then to Liverpool, and from there to London, probably via the canal network or by road.

The good reputation of Clementi & Co.'s pianos in Dublin is shown by a newspaper advertisement of an 1814 legal case:

---

[58] *CMC* p 137.

[59] Thomas Lindsay→John Gough, 5 January 1824, *CMC* p 307.

[60] Cogan→Clementi, 20 January 1800, *CMC* p 50.

[61] Logier→John Green, 10 December 1813, *CMC* p 214–215. A Kent bugle was a novel keyed bugle.

> WHEREAS, it has been discovered that some obscure Persons in Dublin, have lately made piano fortes, and put upon them the names of respectable Houses in London, as if manufactured by them.
>
> And, whereas several auctioneers and others have been in the habit of selling these spurious instruments, thereby grossly deceiving the public, to the material injury of the said Houses.
>
> Notice is hereby given, that actions at law are commenced on the part of Messrs Clementi and Company, Cheapside, London, against M. Larkin, Grafton-street, Thomas Kelly, Clarendon-street, John Byrne, Ship-street, and others; and that any person, hereafter detected, making use of the name of Clementi and Company upon any instruments not manufactured by them, will, in like manner, be immediately proceeded against....
>
> Dublin, July 8, 1814.[62]

Clementi & Co. seem still to have been trading in Ireland a decade later.[63]

Few names of workers in Clementi's music business are known, but one anecdote about a Longman, Clementi & Co. employee is worth repeating. An 1823 dictionary of slang compiled by John Badcock, who used the pseudonym 'Jon Bee', has the following entry for the expression 'Hookey Walker':

> *Hookey*, *Hookey Walker*—and '*with a hook*', usually accompanied by a significant upliftment of the hand and crooking of the fore-finger, implying that what is said is a lie, or is to be taken contrary-wise. One tells a long-yarn-story that asks for the disbelief of his auditory; whereupon another cries out 'Hookey Walker!' having previously shewn *the sign* above described, or another more elaborate still, which may be looked upon as a counter-sign, viz. spread the fingers of both hands wide open, apply one thumb to the tip of the nose, and the other to the point of the little finger of the first hand—this signifies *a clincher*. *History*: John Walker was an out-door clerk at Longman, Clementi, & Co.'s in Cheapside, where a great number of persons were employed, and 'old Jack', who had a crooked or *hook nose*, occupied also the post of spy upon their aberrations (which were manifold). Of course, it was for the interests of the surveillants, to throw discredit upon all Jack's reports to the nobs of the firm, and numbers could attest that those reports were fabrications, however true; Jack was constantly out-voted, his evidence

---

[62] *The Freeman's Journal, and Daily Commercial Advertiser*, Dublin, 13 July 1814, p 1.

[63] William Horsley→Clementi, 20 August 1824, *CMC* p 317–322, states that William [Frederick] Collard had recently 'set off for Ireland'.

> overlaid, and of course disbelieved, when his occupation ceased, but not so the fame of 'Hookey Walker'.[64]

Although this identification of the origin of the expression has been considered 'unlikely to be more than a folk etymology',[65] the inclusion of a specific firm's name, and that denoting an instrument maker, gives it the ring of truth, since a musical instrument-making firm would not be the obvious choice if one were fabricating a story. Interestingly, near the end of Charles Dickens's *A Christmas Carol* (1843), when Scrooge tells the small boy to go and buy the big turkey, he replies 'Walk-ER!'[66] Since Dickens was the great-grandson of Thomas Culliford and grandson of his son-in-law and partner Charles Barrow, who worked for Longman & Broderip,[67] it is conceivable that he had heard of Walker's activities at Longman, Clementi & Co., adding credibility to Badcock's explanation.

By the middle of 1802 Clementi must have been confident that his company's activities were on a secure footing, because he left London on an extended business trip to Europe to collect new music, to establish relationships with other music publishers and to sell the company's instruments on the continent. He must have trusted his partners' abilities, because even the major fire that consumed many of the buildings and much of the stock in Tottenham Court Road in 1807 was insufficient to bring him back to London until 1810.

---

[64] 'Jon Bee', *Slang. A Dictionary of the Turf, the Ring, the Chase, the Pit, of Bon-ton, and the Varieties of Life*, London, 1823, p 99.

[65] See the entry for 'Walker, *int.* (and *n.*^{2})' in the *Oxford English Dictionary Online*. The earliest occurrence recorded there—'*Hookee Walker*, an expression signifying that the story is not true'—dates from 1811 ([Francis] Grose *et al*, *Lexicon Balatronicum. A Dictionary of Buckish Slang, University Wit, and Pickpocket Eloquence*, London, 1811, unpaginated).

[66] Charles Dickens, *A Christmas Carol. In prose. Being a ghost story of Christmas*, London, 1843, p 156. Dickens had used the expression 'Walker!' five years earlier (*Oxford English Dictionary Online*, *loc. cit.*).

[67] See pages 35–36 above and Jenny Nex, 'Culliford and Company: keyboard instrument makers in Georgian London', *Early Keyboard Journal* v 22 (2004) p 7–48 at p 35–36. Dickens's eldest son was christened Charles Culliford Boz Dickens in 1837.

The fire took place on 20 March 1807 and *The Star* printed the following account of it on the same day:

> FIRE.—About five o'clock this morning, a fire was discovered on the premises of Messrs. Clementi & Co, musical instrument makers, Tottenham Court Road. In the course of an hour, the conflagration became awfully grand, and threatened the destruction of the whole of the adjoining neighbourhood. — Happily the prompt arrival of the engines, and the timely exertions of the firemen prevented the spreading calamity; but exclusive of the front of the building, scarcely a vestige remains standing of this once extensive manufactory. We understand a similar accident took place on these premises about ten years ago.[68]

A report published the next day describes some materials used in the firm's instrument making:

> Mr Whitfield's [sic] Tabernacle, and the burial-ground belonging to it, being directly opposite, several valuable pieces of mahogany, Turkish box, limewood, &c. were carried out of the fire, it might almost be said, and deposited in the church-yard, where a party of volunteers did constant duty all day.[69] ... The workshops, ware-rooms, with a great number of instruments nearly finished, and the yard full of timber, were all consumed. ... It is said that almost every working man in the factory lost from 30 to 40*l*. worth of tools. The loss of Mr Clementi and his partners must be immense, his premises were so extensive and so well filled, and it is said that his insurance was but to a comparatively small amount. ... The fire was, on opening the gates, seen to proceed from the part of the premises where the block-room (a sawing place) was across the yard, to a sort of gallery that was piled up with a vast number of most valuable planks of mahogany.[70]

Further newspaper announcements said that 'the tools of every workman in that immense concern were destroyed, by which means a great number of families must be left destitute', and advised that donations to help these families would 'be received by Messrs Sansom, Blake and Postle[th]waite, 65, Lombard-street, and at

---

[68] The texts of several contemporary reports of this fire are reproduced in *CMC* p 417–419.

[69] The reference is to the chapel in Tottenham Court Road built in 1756 for Rev. George Whitefield.

[70] *The Morning Chronicle*, 21 March 1807, p 3.

Mr Kimber's, 194 Tottenham-court Road, next door to the manufactory'.[71] William Blake, the assignee of Longman & Broderip, was a partner of this bank, which appears to have had a continuing relationship with Clementi & Co.[72]

The fire, though serious, did not stop the company trading. Advertisements assuring the firm's continuing activities were printed in newspapers in the week beginning 24 March, presenting the following information:

> FIRE. Clementi and Co. having unfortunately had their premises, in Tottenham-court-road, destroyed by fire, beg to inform the public, that through the generous exertions of their neighbours and friends, they have saved their grand and square piano-forte cases, and also a principal part of their dry manufactured and unmanufactured stock. It also affords them great consolation, under the pressure of their severe loss, to be enabled to state, that the finishing part of their manufacture has always been conducted at their extensive premises, no. 26, Cheapside, where their stock of grand and small piano-fortes, organs, &c. in an advanced state, will enable them to serve the public with every article of their trade in that perfection which has hitherto secured them general approbation....
>
> 26, Cheapside. March 23, 1807.[73]

Although the company continued trading, concerns about the levels of their insurances had been raised as early as *The Morning Chronicle*'s account of 21 March quoted above. *The Gentleman's Magazine* reported that 'the damage is estimated at 40,000*l.*; 15,000*l.* of which is insured'.[74] It has been impossible to verify these figures, but surviving evidence shows that the risk on Clementi & Co.'s Tottenham Court Road premises was shared between at least two and

[71] *The Morning Post*, 28 March 1807, p 1. This advertisement noted 'the great liberality of their employers, Clementi and Co. in support of this subscription'. A total of £633/12/2 was subscribed, enabling each workman to receive 18/11 in the pound for his loss (*The Morning Post*, 4 June 1807, p 1). Thomas Kimber was a coffin maker and undertaker.

[72] In 1816, after Blake's death, Sansom & Co. (i.e., Sansom, Postlethwaite & Sansom) received a £21 subscription from Clementi, Banger & Co. towards alleviating extreme distress in Spitalfields (*The Morning Chronicle*, 5 December 1816, p 2).

[73] *The Times*, 24 March 1807, p 1.

[74] *The Gentleman's Magazine*, March 1807, p 271.

probably more companies. A cash book of the London Assurance Corporation records: 'May 7th Paid Muzio Clementi & Co. £7000 for Loss & Damage by fire'.[75] In one of the general ledgers of the Phoenix Insurance Company is a similar note under 'losses': '1807... April 23 Cash M. Clementi & Co. £2,000'.[76] These sums enabled the firm to rebuild, and on 1 December 1807 Clementi & Co. took out new insurance with the Hand-in-Hand Fire Office on a house and several other buildings in Tottenham-Court Road.[77]

It was obviously essential for the buildings to be replaced but new materials and tools were also needed. It has been suggested that the rival John Broadwood & Son firm helped Clementi & Co., but the nature of any such help is not known.[78] It may have been at this time that the company went in search of wood around the country. In the early years of the century they reportedly bought an avenue of lime trees at Kentwell Hall (Long Melford, Suffolk):

> The avenue of lime trees, ¾ of a mile long, was sold by Mr [Richard] Moore to Clementi the musical instrument maker for £500, & he took down 5 trees: Mr Moore's mother [Mary] redeemed the rest by the sacrifice of a farm which belonged to her, & which she gave to her son, but which Mr Moore immediately sold.[79]

By the end of 1807 Clementi & Co. had buildings in which to pursue their manufacturing and had also re-stocked, at least to some extent, for insurance of £1000 for 'stock & utensils' at the premises in Tottenham Court Road was added on 22 December to the Hand-in-Hand policy. A note was made on this document that insurance on the buildings and contents was shared with three other insurance

---

[75] LMA formerly Guildhall, London Assurance Corporation archives, Fire Charter Cash Books, v 3, shelfmark 8745, May 1807. The policy itself no longer survives.

[76] CUL, Phoenix Insurance Company archives, General Ledger C, shelfmark PX12 p 254. The policy itself no longer survives.

[77] LMA formerly Guildhall, Hand-in-Hand Fire Office records, policy registers, supplemental sequnce, v 1 shelfmark 8675, p 117.

[78] According to David Wainwright, *Broadwood by Appointment*, London, 1982,, p 173.

[79] BL Add. Ms 19078 f 37^{v}, notes made by David Elisha Davy.

companies (£3000 with the Hope, £5000 with the Albion and £5000 with the Eagle).[80]

The accounts of the fire reveal not only the devastation that was caused and the company's speedy return to normal business but also several details of the firm's manufacturing processes. *The Morning Chronicle* account of 21 March, quoted above, reveals that the company had stored large stocks of wood in the yard (mahogany, Turkish box and lime were specifically mentioned) and that some wood was seasoned in a gallery. Some sawing evidently took place on the premises, as did instrument making, which was undertaken by workmen using their own tools. The wood stored was not exclusively for keyboard instrument manufacture, since boxwood was not a major component of keyboard instruments. Rather, it was a very common material for woodwind instruments, the implication being that the firm's woodwind instruments were made on site, or the wood stored on site and then handed out to the firm's subcontractors to make wind instruments on their own premises. The references to 'nearly finished' instruments and 'square pianoforte cases' in the newspaper reports suggest that all of the piano manufacturing process took place at Tottenham Court Road with the exception of the 'finishing', which was done at Cheapside, where all kinds of finished and almost-finished instruments were housed.

As mentioned, Clementi was in continental Europe at the time of the fire and heard nothing of it until many weeks later. It was only on 19 May 1807 that his partners wrote to him about it,[81] and, given the speed with which mail travelled at the time, it is unlikely that he would have heard anything about the fire before June. In the meantime he was as busy as ever, securing a valuable contract with Beethoven (described in the next chapter) and continuing the firm's work around the continent. He became increasingly frustrated, however, at difficulties caused by war. Following a brief period of peace in the early years of the decade, France had been at war with

---

[80] LMA formerly Guildhall, Hand-in-Hand Fire Office records, fire insurance policy registers for goods and stock in trade, v 1 shelfmark 8676, p 26.

[81] This letter does not survive, but information about it is found in Clementi→ Frederick William Collard and co-partners (Banger, Hyde and David Davis), 28 December 1808, *CMC* p 187–188.

England since 1803. A subsequent naval blockade was designed to keep English goods out of Europe and a system of trading inaugurated by Napoléon—the so-called 'continental system'—encouraged French trade with continental Europe. The effect of this activity was to weaken economies throughout Europe and to frustrate the activities of English exporters. By 1810 Clementi had had enough of the miserable conditions that affected not only trade but also travel, and returned to London.

Evidence that trade with Europe diminished significantly at this time is found in the company's correspondence. It proved impossible to maintain the close links that had been forged with his European partners at the end of the eighteenth century, and once peace was restored in 1815 those relationships needed to be re-established. Clementi turned again to letter-writing and within a short while renewed contact with many old friends on the continent, including Artaria and Härtel. Earlier patterns of exchanging publications were used once again, as noted in the next chapter, and the company endeavoured to sell its instruments abroad.

Instrument sales were difficult, however. One reason was the success of foreign piano makers. Whereas in the late eighteenth century English piano makers had led the way in many aspects of instrument design, the situation changed rapidly towards the 1820s. On 20 October 1801 Clementi & Co. had canvassed the possibility of opening a piano factory in France or at least an agency for the company there, and had hoped that Maison Pleyel would take up such an offer.[82] This followed the spectacular success of English pianos in France in the late eighteenth century, when makers such as Johannes Zumpe had a large proportion of the French market. However, when Camille Pleyel, Ignace's son, visited London in 1815, instead of buying pianos he bought mahogany wood and samples of ivory keys for their piano manufactory, Pleyel et Cie, in Paris.[83] Another obstacle

---

[82] According to Max Unger, *Muzio Clementis Leben*, *op. cit.* in note 34 above, p 102–103; see *CMC* p 77.

[83] See Rita Benton, 'London music in 1815, as seen by Camille Pleyel', *Music & Letters* v 47 no. 1 (January 1966) p 34–47. In 1815 Ignace and Camille Pleyel were partners in Pleyel et Cie. For the relationship between English and French piano makers at this time see David Rowland, 'Piano businesses in England and

was economic. From 1817 onwards Clementi & Co. had a protracted correspondence with Breitkopf & Härtel about the sale of pianos, but had little or no success because of exchange rates. English pianos were simply too expensive for German customers.

Like Longman & Broderip, Clementi & Co. sold many kinds of musical instruments and accessories. Their 1823 catalogue listed twenty-three types of piano, seventeen types of barrel organ and barrel harp, three types of pedal harp, ninety-two types of flute and piccolo, twenty-three types of fife, twelve types of clarinet, twenty-seven types of flageolet, nine types of oboe, six types of French horn, eighteen types of bugle, a range of bassoons, vox humanes, serpents, pandean pipes, castinets, triangles, cymbals, tambourines, drums, eolian [sic] harps, guitars, lyres, lutes, violins, violas, cellos, bass horns, trumpets, trombones and various parts for all these instruments such as strings and mouth pieces.[84]

Pianos formed the most important part of the company's instrument trade. Many survive and Clementi's correspondence shows that the sale and quality control of pianos were among his major preoccupations. During his European travels of 1802–1810 his correspondence with Frederick William Collard is full of detail of piano sales in Germany, Russia and elsewhere. For much of this time Clementi was assisted by pupils who acted as demonstrators and salesmen, on commission.

John Field, who was apprenticed to Clementi in 1793 at the age of eleven for seven years, demonstrated Longman & Broderip instruments almost from the start of his apprenticeship,[85] and after that firm's demise he performed a similar role for Longman, Clementi & Co., who published his op. 1 sonatas, dedicated to Clementi, in 1801. Field accompanied Clementi to Russia in 1802 and played the company's pianos there at the private concerts and assemblies of the

---

France', in Christoph Coin, Éric de Visscher and Florence Gétreau (eds), *Le pianoforte en France 1780–1820*, Paris, 2009, p 127–135.

[84] *A Catalogue of Instrumental and Vocal Music, printed by Clementi, Collard & Collard*, London, 1823 (copy in Library of Congress, Washington, catalogue no. ML145.C5).

[85] See Patrick Piggott, *The Life and Music of John Field*, Berkeley, 1973, p 11. On 21 May 1793 he performed in public on a Longman & Broderip 'grand piano forte harpsichord' (*The World*, 15 May 1793, p 1).

nobility. Louis Spohr recorded one such event in St Petersburg in December 1802:

> *Clementi* ... liked much to converse with me.... In the evening, I sometimes accompanied him to his large pianoforte warehouse, where *Field* was often obliged to play for hours, to display the instruments to the best advantage to the purchasers.[86]

In the middle of 1803 Clementi left for Germany, leaving Field in Russia, and although there is no definitive evidence it seems likely that he continued to act as an agent for Clementi & Co.'s pianos there. It was certainly the company's practice to encourage Clementi's pupils and acquaintances to buy pianos at discounted rates in order to encourage sales. Evidence survives showing that the company had this sort of relationship with Ludwig Berger, Dussek, Himmel, August Alexander Klengel and Karl Traugott Zeuner. Dussek advised Longman, Clementi & Co. on 16 May 1800 that he had recently received a piano from them.[87] He proceeded to perform on the instrument to a number of people in Hamburg and was confident of selling two grand pianos there. His confidence was well-placed, because one month later he mentioned two 'gentlemen' who wanted to buy the instruments.[88] On 9/21 June 1806 Clementi wrote to Frederick William Collard from St Petersburg that Berger and Klengel had secured a number of pupils and would therefore need to purchase pianos from the firm from time to time at the usual discounted rate.[89] In 1807 Clementi stated that another pupil, Zeuner, was returning to Russia and 'perhaps will send for instruments' to sell locally.[90] Himmel's parallel activities in Paris have been noted on page 137 above. One way or another, Clementi took the opportunities that came his way to promote and to sell the firm's pianos in Europe.

---

[86] *Louis Spohr's Autobiography translated from the German*, London, 1865, p 39.

[87] Dussek→Longman, Clementi & Co., 16 May 1800, *CMC* p 53–54.

[88] Dussek→Longman, Clementi & Co., 12 June 1800, *CMC* p 60–61.

[89] *CMC* p 164–165. 9 June, the 'old style' date then used in St Petersburg, was 21 June in London.

[90] Clementi→Frederick William Collard, 22 April 1807, *CMC* p 182–185.

During Clementi's travels he became very well acquainted with European piano manufacture. His correspondence mentions specific features such as the lighter action preferred by many continental pianists, and his awareness of differences between English and continental pianos must have influenced his company's piano designs.

There were difficulties for the company because English and continental keyboard compasses were not always the same.[91] This was no problem when pianists and composers used just five-and-a-half octaves: English and continental makers installed exactly the same keys, from FF to c^4. However, English and continental six-octave compasses did not match. When Broadwood started making six-octave pianos in the 1790s he chose a compass based on C, but in continental Europe the six-octave compass was based on F. Strangely, the anomalous situation of two parallel six-octave compasses persisted for many years so that, for example, the six-octave piano that Beethoven received from John Broadwood & Sons in 1818 was out of step with the six-octave instruments made by local makers. Although some English makers persisted with their own six-octave compass, after Clementi arrived back in London in the summer of 1810 his company began to produce continental-style six-octave instruments. A number of works that the company published at this time commented on the title-page that the work was written for the piano 'with additional keys up to F, & also arranged for the piano forte up to C', including the first edition of Beethoven's fifth piano concerto, op. 73, which was published in London in November 1810, several months before it appeared on the continent.[92]

Components for the company's pianos came from various sources. In 1804 Clementi referred to '500lb of steel and brass wire' that he had bought from Johann Dietz, a wire drawer in Berlin.[93] The

---

[91] For a more detailed account of the development of the piano's compass at the end of the eighteenth and beginning of the nineteenth centuries see David Rowland (ed.), *The Cambridge Companion to the Piano*, Cambridge, 1998, chapters 1 and 2.

[92] See Alan Tyson, *The Authentic English Editions of Beethoven*, London, 1963, p 79.

[93] Clementi→Frederick William Collard, 11 September 1804, *CMC* p 127–129. The transaction is further discussed in Clementi→Frederick William Collard, 16 July 1805, *CMC* p 145–149.

firm's purchase of leather for hammer-covering from Streicher in Vienna has been mentioned on page 138 above. The different kinds of wood noted in newspaper reports of the 1807 fire could have been sourced from some of the numerous cargo ships that sailed up the Thames. Clementi also helped out other makers. In his letter of 16 July 1805 he asked Frederick William Collard to send two elephant tusks to the Berlin keyboard instrument maker Carl Ludwig Steibelt, presumably to be used as ivory in his keyboards.[94]

Like Longman & Broderip, Clementi & Co. dealt in various types of organ, including barrel organs, chamber organs and church organs.[95] The organ builder James Davis, brother of David, made organs for the firm, as he had for Longman & Broderip.[96] In 1803 Clementi met the German organ builder Johann Gabrahn in St Petersburg and invited him to work for the company in London, but Gabrahn offered the excuse of being too old.[97] James Chapman Bishop supplied a number of organs to the company around 1820 and when James Davis retired in 1822 took over his business.[98] A December 1823 letter gives details of an organ for clients on whose behalf Clementi & Co. evidently were negotiating.[99]

The company sold many different types of woodwind instrument, but there can be no doubt that they sold more flutes than any other such instrument. In 1823 a reviewer of flute compositions commented:

---

[94] Clementi→Frederick William Collard, 11 September 1804, *CMC* p 127–129.

[95] Organs bearing the company's name are listed in Michael Wilson, *The English Chamber Organ*, Oxford, 1968; Lyndesay G[raham] Langwill and Noel Boston, *Church and Chamber Barrel-Organs*, Edinburgh, 2nd ed., 1970; Michael Sayer, *Samuel Renn, English organ builder*, London, 1974; and Arthur W[olfgang] J[ulius] G[erald] Ord-Hume, *Barrel Organ*, London, 1978.

[96] See pages 49–50 above.

[97] Clementi→Frederick William Collard, 17 August 1803, *CMC* p 104–110 at p 108.

[98] See Laurence Elvin, *Bishop and Son, Organ Builders*, Lincoln, 1984, and Nicholas Thistlethwaite, 'The early career of J. C. Bishop, organ-builder, 1807–29', *BIOS Journal* v 25 (2001) p 6–29 at p 10.

[99] Thomas Lindsay→James Chapman Bishop, 22 December 1823, *CMC* p 305–306.

> In what estimation the flute was held should however most appear from the fact, that Ismenias, a musician of Thebes, gave three talents, or something more than 580*l.* for an instrument. Messrs Clementi and Co. would be most happy, we suspect, to furnish a ship-load at a fiftieth part of the price, and yet we question whether Ismenias's purchase had half the excellences of those made by these worthy manufacturers, after the model of Mr Nicholson's celebrated instrument.[100]

Many flutes sold by Clementi & Co. were of Charles Nicholson's design, who commented in his flute tutor that 'Clementi & Co. were the first who undertook to manufacture flutes under my superintendence, and I had great difficulty in overcoming the prejudices of their workmen'.[101] The quantity of flutes made to his design that the company sold indicates that they were produced by several makers, of whom George Miller,[102] Thomas Prowse Sr and Samuel Potter are known.[103] Some flutes may have been made by Clementi & Co.'s employee Thomas Lindsay, who opened his own music shop in 1825 and published his *The Elements of Flute-Playing*, in which he describes himself as a flute maker.

Clarinets were manufactured for the company according to William Gutteridge's 1824 patent,[104] and bugles according to the system of Thomas Harper Sr.[105] Presumably many of the wind

---

[100] *Quarterly Musical Magazine and Review* v 5 no. 17 (1823) p 83.

[101] Charles Nicholson, *A School for the Flute*, New York, [1836], p 6.

[102] William Waterhouse, *The New Langwill Index: A dictionary of musical wind-instrument makers and inventors*, London, 1993, p 240, mentions a flute that Miller made for Longman, Clementi & Co.

[103] See Jeremy Montagu, 'Instruments', *Early Music* v 25 no. 3 (August 1997) p 533–537 at p 536, and 'As like as two peas', *FoMRHIQ* [*Fellowship of Makers and Researchers of Historical Musical Instruments Quarterly*] no. 92 (July 1998), comm[unication] 1588, online at http://jeremymontagu.co.uk/twopeas.pdf.

[104] On 19 January 1824 Gutteridge was granted the English patent subsequently numbered 4890 for 'improvements on the clarionet'. Clementi & Co.'s manufacture of this instrument was advertised in 1825 (e.g., *The Morning Chronicle*, 18 July 1825, p 1). The company also published about this time *Introduction to the Art of Playing on Gutteridge's new patent Clarinet*.

[105] Waterhouse, *The New Langwill Index*, p 161.

instruments were made from wood held at the company's Tottenham Court Road premises.

As mentioned, Clementi & Co. traded in brass instruments made in Ireland,[106] but extant documentation of these arrangements does not show how important or extensive this arm of the firm's operations was. Evidence of that can be gleaned from the company's 1823 catalogue, which advertised four different types of Kent bugle (with six, seven, eight or nine keys) and many other brass instruments. These instruments must have been used by military and other bands and the company expected that they would sometimes be purchased in sets, as the following statement shows:

> Bands furnished with complete sets to any extent, on the shortest notice.—The appointment of Clementi and Co. to supply the Honourable East India Company with these instruments is a sufficient warranty of their excellence.[107]

The company's harps came from various sources. In an 1803 letter Clementi describes a request from Petr L'vovich Davydov for a harp, saying, 'I told him he may rely on me; that is, if ours without the least partiality be not as good *now* as Erard's, we shall send him one of his'.[108] Problems with the quality of Clementi & Co.'s harps *c*1805 were indicated by the actress and singer Dora Jordan, who described her instrument as 'so very bad'.[109] The musical instrument maker Henry Faveryear, who was in St Petersburg in 1803 but planning to return to London,[110] seems to have acted as an agent for Clementi,[111] and appears in Erard's ledger for having purchased a

---

[106] See page 142 above.

[107] *A Catalogue of Instrumental and Vocal Music, printed by Clementi, Collard & Collard*, London, 1823, p xiv.

[108] Clementi→Frederick William Collard, 17 August 1803, *CMC* p 104–110 at p 107–108.

[109] Dora Jordan→Frederick Augustus Hyde, wmk 1805, *CMC* p 378.

[110] Clementi→Frederick William Collard, 17 August 1803, *CMC* p 104–110 at p 105.

[111] Clementi & Co.'s 24 June 1811 balance sheet (see page 133 above) records £400 as the 'amount of Faveryear's interest' (*CMC* p 424).

number of harps shortly afterwards.[112] Clementi & Co. bought harps directly from Erard in London in 1815 and 1824.[113]

Longman, Clementi & Co. and Clementi & Co. were worthy successors to Longman & Broderip. In range of activity and international reach it is hard to imagine that there were any more significant music sellers in London at the time, and their domestic and overseas connections made their musical instruments known to some of the most important musicians of the era. Their premises in Cheapside continued to be a centre to which musicians were drawn,[114] and private performances of piano music sometimes took place in their Tottenham Court Road manufactory.[115] Much of their success resulted from the activities of their senior partner, Muzio Clementi, who all but retired from performing on the piano in order to develop the company. He became influential in London's musical institutions and was a founding member of the Philharmonic Society in 1813.

His role in the company's affairs is underscored by its contraction of activities after he stepped down from the partnership in his late seventies, less than a year before his death, leaving the company in the hands of the Collard brothers, who decided three years later to exit the side of their business that published and sold printed music. On 1 July 1834 they advertised:

> IMPORTANT to the MUSIC TRADE.—To be SOLD, the extensive and important COPYRIGHT, and new COPYRIGHT MUSIC and PLATES of the works contained in the Catalogue of the late firm of Muzio Clementi and Co., consisting of instrumental and vocal compositions of the most eminent and popular authors. Printed catalogues are preparing, and the days of sale will be shortly announced; in the mean time proposals will be received for purchases by private contract of the above, as well as of a variety of violins, violoncellos, guitars, bugle horns, &c. &c. &c. ... N.B. The retail printed music business, carried on for the late firm of Clementi and Co., will be closed at the time of sale, and the

---

112 Erard ledger, RCM Museum of Musical Instruments.

113 *ibid.*

114 See the quotations from Thomas Busby's 1825 book on pages 91–92 above.

115 For a description of one such event see Samuel Wesley→Robert Glenn, 22 July 1814, transcribed in Philip Olleson (ed.), *The Letters of Samuel Wesley, Professional and Social Correspondence, 1797–1837*, Oxford, 2001, p 233.

warehouses at 26, Cheapside, solely occupied by Messrs Collard and Collard as manufacturers of pianofortes.[116]

On 13–16 January 1835 'the very valuable stock in trade of the late firm of Muzio Clementi & Co. comprising upwards of 40,000 engraved music plates, a great proportion of which are copyright' was auctioned by Mr [T. H.] Watson in London.[117] About this time the 'retail printed music' side of the business was taken over by Thomas Edward Purday, who had previously worked for Collard & Collard.[118]

The Collard & Collard piano-making partnership, which other members of the Collard family subsequently joined, continued until 1929, when it was taken over by the Chappell Piano Company. Production of pianos bearing the Collard & Collard name ceased in 1971, and the company's records were destroyed in a fire in 1964.[119]

---

116 *The Morning Chronicle*, 1 July 1834, p 1.

117 A copy of the sale catalogue is in the library of the State University of New York at Buffalo, catalogue no. ML152.W287 C2864. It includes some plates that must have been inherited from Longman & Broderip. The same auctioneer had sold 'a select portion of the library of the late celebrated Muzio Clementi' in London on 19–21 December 1832. I thank Michael Kassler for the information that a copy of this catalogue is in NYPL Performing Arts collection Drexel 830.

118 On a 1 August 1834 lease (counterpart in Lincolnshire Archives 2 PG 1/5/3) Purday is described as 'late of 26 Cheapside but now of 50 St Paul's Churchyard, music seller'. Purday advertised (on an unpaginated advertising sheet distributed with the *The Musical World* v 1 no. 3 (1 April 1836)) that he was 'successor (in this branch of the business)'—i.e., publishing and selling printed music—'to Collard & Collard, late Clementi & Co.'.

119 See note 101 on page 32 above.

CLEMENTI AS PUBLISHER

David Rowland

In January 1824 Charles Clementi answered a request from Sainsbury & Co. for biographical information about his father Muzio, for inclusion in their forthcoming *Dictionary of Musicians*.[1] Charles enclosed with his reply the list of his father's works reproduced in *Figure 4.1*. Its latter three columns give the opus numbers, titles and dedicatees of these works, but the first column is the most intriguing: next to fourteen works—Clementi's Op. 2, 7, 11, 12, 16, 17, 19, 21, 22, 23, 24, 26, 28 and 35—the name 'Preston' appears, crossed out in all but one instance. These entries indicated works by Clementi that were published not by his company but by Thomas Preston, a rival music seller. Presumably the *Dictionary*'s compilers struck through the word 'Preston' repeatedly, as the list of Clementi's works printed in the *Dictionary* omitted their publishers' names.

Preston acquired the copyrights and engraved plates for these works in two ways. His father John Preston had published the first edition of Op. 12, and their subsequent partnership Preston & Son issued editions of Op. 24, 26, 28 and 35.[2] The firm presumably retained the engraved plates of all of these publications. Thomas Preston bought the plates of Op. 2, 7, 11, 16, 17, 19, 21, 22 and 23 in January 1811 when he 'purchased the entire and extensive stock of music plates, and copy-right, the property of Wilkinson and Co. (late

---

[1] Charles Clementi→John Davis Sainsbury, 20 January 1824 (GUL ms Euing R.d.85/43, transcribed in *CMC* p 309). *A Dictionary of Musicians, from the Earliest Ages to the Present Time* was published in London later that year.

[2] See Alan Tyson, *Thematic Catalogue of the Works of Muzio Clementi*, Tutzing, 1967, p 49, p 63, p 65, p 67 and p 75.

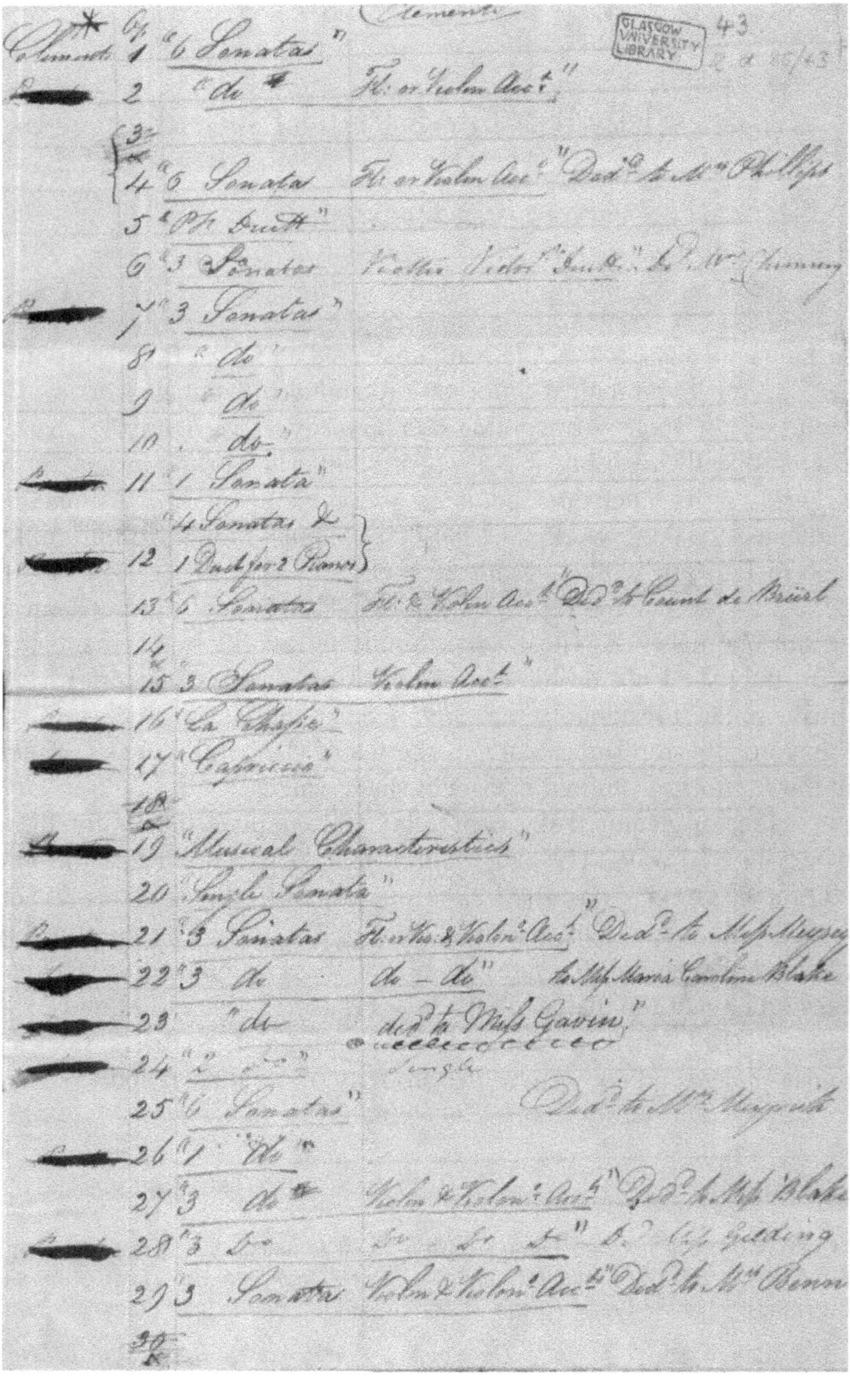
Clementi
GLASGOW UNIVERSITY LIBRARY
43
Op. 1 "6 Sonatas"
2 "do Fl. or Violin Acct."
3
4 "6 Sonatas Fl. or Violin Acct." Ded. to Mr Phillips
5 "P.F. Duett"
6 "3 Sonatas Violin Violoncello "Duets" Ded. to Mr Chinnery
7 "3 Sonatas"
8 "do"
9 "do"
10 "do"
11 "1 Sonata"
12 "4 Sonatas & 1 Duet for 2 Pianos"
13 "6 Sonatas Fl. & Violin Acct. Ded. to Count de Brühl
14
15 "3 Sonatas Violin Acct."
16 "La Chasse"
17 "Capriccio"
18
19 "Musical Characteristics"
20 "Single Sonata"
21 "3 Sonatas Fl. or Ho. & Violon. Acct." Ded. to Miss Meyer
22 "3 do do – do" to Miss Maria Caroline Blake
23 "do ded. to Miss Gavin"
24 "2 do" single
25 "6 Sonatas" Ded. to Mrs Meyrick
26 "1 do"
27 "3 do Violin & Violon. Acct." Ded. to Miss Blake
28 "3 do do do do" Ded. Miss Gilding
29 "3 Sonatas Violin & Violon. Acct." Ded. to Mrs Bonn
30

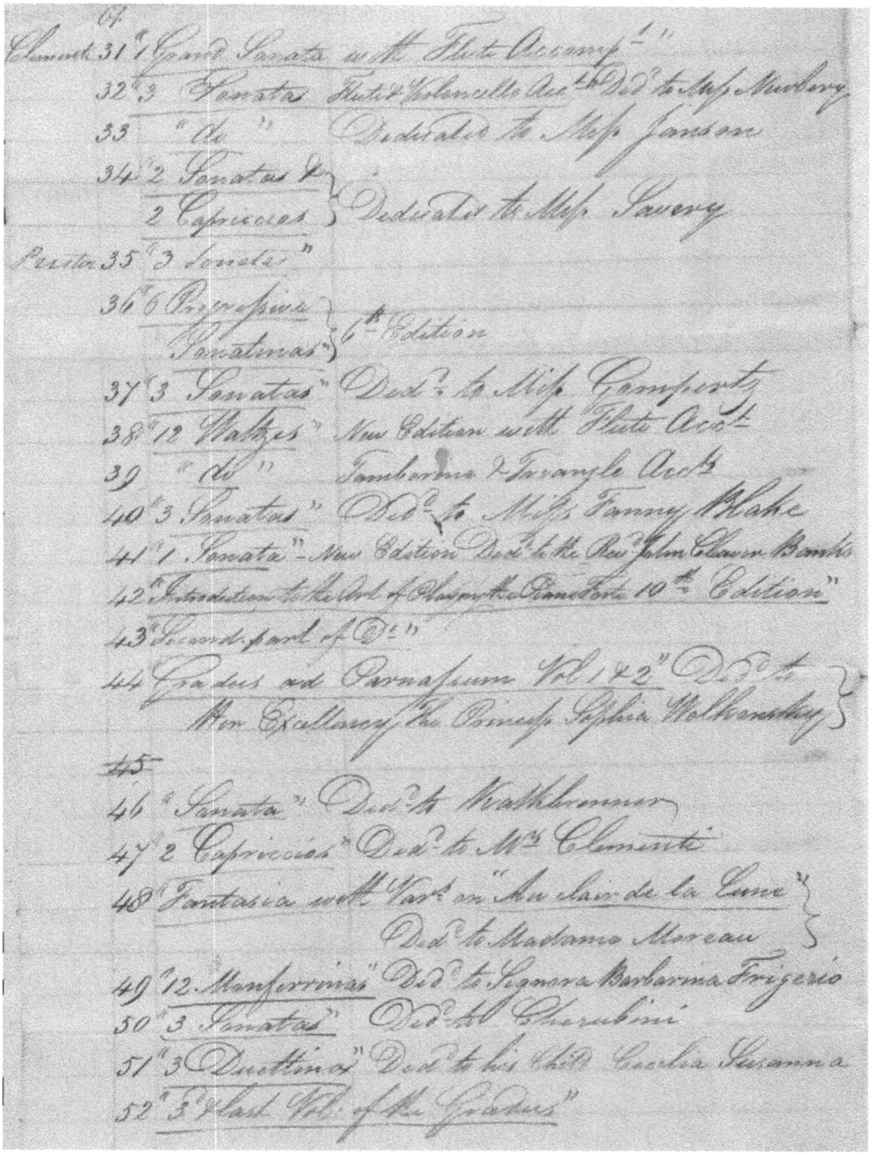
Op.
Clementi 31 "1 Grand Sonata with the Flute Accomp^t"
32 "3 Sonatas Flute & Violoncello Acc^t Ded^d to Miss Mudbury
33 "do" Dedicated to Miss Janson
34 "2 Sonatas & 2 Capriccios" Dedicated to Miss Savery
Pirater 35 "3 Sonate"
36 "6 Progressive Sonatinas" 6th Edition
37 "3 Sonatas" Ded^d to Miss Gamperty
38 "12 Waltzes" New Edition with Flute Acc^t
39 "do" Tambarine & Triangle Acc^ts
40 "3 Sonatas" Ded^d to Miss Fanny Blake
41 "1 Sonata" New Edition Ded^d to the Revd John Clowes Banks
42 "Introduction to the Art of Playing the Piano Forte 10th Edition"
43 "Second part of D^o"
44 Gradus ad Parnassum Vol 1 & 2" Ded^d to Her Excellency the Princess Sophia Wolkonsky
45
46 "Sonata" Ded^d to Kalkbrenner
47 "2 Capriccios" Ded^d to Mrs Clementi
48 "Fantasia with Var^s on "Au clair de la Lune" Ded^d to Madame Moreau
49 "12 Monferrinas" Ded^d to Signora Barbarina Frigerio
50 "3 Sonatas" Ded^d to Cherubini
51 "3 Duettinos" Ded^d to his Child Caecilia Susanna
52 "3^d & last Vol. of the Gradus"

Figure 4.1 List of Muzio Clementi's Works sent in 1824 by Charles Clementi to the compilers of the Sainsbury & Co. Dictionary of Musicians *(by permission of the Department of Special Collections, Glasgow University Library)*

Broderip and Wilkinson)'.[3] Each of the latter editions is mentioned in *Musical Publications selected from the Catalogue published by Broderip and Wilkinson, lately purchased, and now printed and sold by Preston.*[4]

Broderip & Wilkinson almost certainly acquired the plates of some of these works on 1 November 1798, when Longman & Broderip's assets were divided between Broderip & Wilkinson and Longman, Clementi & Co. Clementi's Op. 23 sonatas, which were first published by Longman & Broderip in 1790, were later reprinted from the same plates by Broderip & Wilkinson, who had the title-page plate altered to substitute their name and address.[5] Their catalogue no. 1, issued about September 1801 and reproduced in *Figure 2.5* on page 116 above, advertised their editions of Clementi's Op. 2, 7, 12 (one sonata only), 15, 17 and 23.

As Clementi was a partner of Longman, Clementi & Co. it is curious that his company did not acquire all of Longman & Broderip's editions of his music. Conceivably he was prepared to part with some editions because he had already revised them, or was in the process of doing so, and therefore had no need of the old versions. Joseph Dale had published a revised version 'corrected and fingered by the author, 1792' of the sonata and toccata of Op. 11 (later reissued by Clementi & Co.) and the third trio of Op. 22.[6] Clementi & Co. published a revised version of Op. 17, probably in 1801 or 1802.[7] Op. 21, changed minimally to take advantage of the extended compass of five-and-a-half octave pianos, was published by them in the first decade of the new century.[8] Part of Op. 23 was revised in Clementi's *Introduction to the Art of Playing on the Piano Forte*,

---

[3] Thomas Preston advertisement, *The Morning Chronicle*, 11 January 1811, p 1.

[4] This catalogue (a copy is in BL Hirsch iv.1113.(10.)) lists only the first sonata in Clementi's Op. 12. However, John Preston entered the complete Op. 12 at Stationers' Hall on 10 May 1784 (*MESH* p 43).

[5] Copies of the two editions are in CUL Mus. 3.54(1) and CUL MR340.a.75.55(5) respectively.

[6] Tyson, *op. cit.*, p 47–48 and p 60.

[7] *ibid.*, p 55.

[8] *ibid.*, p 59.

which they published in 1801. Broderip & Wilkinson presumably held the plates of the unrevised versions of all these compositions, as well as Clementi's Op. 2 sonatas, which were later revised on a number of occasions.

The situation was different with Op. 16 and Op. 19, which Clementi did not revise. Their plates were initially retained by Longman, Clementi & Co.—copies exist with their imprint[9]—but passed on to Broderip & Wilkinson at an unknown later date. The plates of Op. 19 remained with Clementi & Co. after John Longman left the partnership, as an edition was issued with their imprint (rather than that of Longman, Clementi & Co.).[10] No further details are known about the only other work transferred to Broderip & Wilkinson, the Op. 7 sonatas.

Whatever the circumstances of the transfer of these plates and copyrights, it is clear that Clementi did not part with any of his more recent works, which were more up-to-date in style and therefore more likely to sell than his earlier works. In particular, the three Clementi compositions that Longman & Broderip published while he was an assignee of that firm—Op. 36–38, entered at Stationers' Hall in 1797 and 1798—passed to Longman, Clementi & Co., who reprinted the latter two from the original plates.[11]

The plates of Haydn's music that Longman & Broderip had used were divided between both of its successors, as can be deduced from the numerous reprints that each of them made.[12] The stock of other composers' music and plates presumably were also distributed, although whether the split was equal, or favoured one company over the other, has not been ascertained.

The first catalogues of the two new companies arose from the division of Longman & Broderip's stock and probably lacked coherence. It must therefore have been important for Longman, Clementi & Co to publish freshly commissioned works as soon as

---

[9] *ibid.*, p 54 and p 57.

[10] *ibid.*, p 57.

[11] *ibid.*, p 76–78. Op. 36 was reprinted by Clementi & Co. from the original plates.

[12] See David Rowland, 'Haydn's music and Clementi's publishing circle', forthcoming.

possible, yet it was more than two months before they issued anything new. They advertised no new works and entered nothing at Stationers' Hall in November and December 1798: their only press announcements during these months concerned their changed ownership. By contrast, Broderip & Wilkinson registered music at Stationers' Hall as early as 13 November 1798.

The following year was full of activity for Longman, Clementi & Co. Their first Stationers' Hall entry was made on 4 January 1799 and press advertisements of new publications followed later in the month. Well over forty new works had been advertised by the time John Baptist Cramer set off with a catalogue to the continent at the end of June,[13] and a similar rate of production continued during the rest of the year, so that 1799 saw a total of around 100 new publications in all. The content of that catalogue is unknown. Only three Longman, Clementi & Co. catalogues survive and none of them listed any new publications. Each of these three had originally been issued by Longman & Broderip, and the only change Longman, Clementi & Co. made was to substitute their name and address for the name and address of their predecessor.[14]

The new company worked hard to ensure that their publications came to the public's attention. Although only twenty of their 1799 publications were entered at Stationers' Hall virtually all of them were advertised in the press. At first, works were advertised around the same time in three, four, or even five newspapers—typically *The Morning Chronicle*, *The Morning Herald*, *The Morning Post*, *The Oracle* and *The Times*. Towards the end of that year, advertisements were usually confined to two or three newspapers.

The new works published during the company's first year were extremely varied in genre and in the status of their composers. In this respect, Longman, Clementi & Co. differed little from Longman & Broderip. Several new sonatas appeared—some for harp, some for piano solo, and some with accompaniment of violin or violin and cello—as well as other instrumental works with piano. The first set of Haydn's Op. 76 quartets was published in April and there were

[13] According to Clementi→Artaria & Co., 24 June 1799, *CMC* p 34–35.

[14] I thank Yu Lee An for this information. After John Longman's departure Clementi & Co. produced new catalogues of their recent publications.

further chamber works for a variety of combinations that did not include the piano. A steady stream of songs with piano accompaniment was published as well as glees and arrangements of a few larger-scale vocal works such as Daniel Steibelt's and Thomas Attwood's pasticcio *Albert and Adelaide* and Thomas John Dibdin's comedy *Five Thousand a Year*. Some military music was advertised along with various piano arrangements of orchestral overtures, dances and other works. There was also Clementi's arrangement of twelve trios by Corelli, the first of several editions of music by earlier composers published by the new company.

The piano and chamber music was composed mainly by Clementi's friends, including substantial works by Cramer, Dussek, Haydn, Steibelt and Viotti. Other publications mostly were by less well-known composers. Musicians such as Charles Dignum, James Sanderson and Reginald Spofforth, who wrote mostly songs and glees, feature frequently alongside several other composers of similar repertoire. Notably absent, however, are sonatas and quartets by lesser-known composers. Clementi was in a position to be able to turn down works of this nature, as his correspondence with Adalbert Gyrowetz and Gabriel Nezot shows,[15] relying instead on more famous figures who were personally known to him. Also notable by their absence during the first year were orchestral parts for symphonies.

Clementi himself contributed works to his firm's developing catalogue, including a modest amount of piano music. His second set of waltzes, Op. 39, was advertised in *The Morning Post* on 8 April 1800; his sonatas Op. 40 were entered at Stationers' Hall on 11 September 1802; and *The Morning Post* of 9 April 1804 advertised that his sonata Op. 41 would shortly be published. No other similar compositions by Clementi were published until the 1820s. Instead, he began to produce didactic works with popular appeal, starting with his *Introduction to the Art of Playing on the Piano Forte*, entered at Stationers' Hall on 26 October 1801. It comprised instructional text

---

[15] In Gyrowetz→Clementi, 26 December 1799 (*CMC* p 40–42) Gyrowetz offered his 'new quartets' to Clementi, an offer that Longman, Clementi & Co. apparently did not accept. In Clementi→Nezot, 27 October 1800 (*CMC* p 67), Clementi wrote that after consultation with his partners the firm had to refuse Nezot's 'beautiful sonatinas' because they had more manuscripts 'than we are able to bring forward for these 2 years'.

and fifty simple pieces for beginners and clearly was designed to have wide appeal, given Clementi's reputation as a teacher and the growing number of piano pupils in the country. Its success is shown by the fact that it was published in numerous editions in England as well as in French, German and Spanish in the early 1800s.[16]

Clementi reordered and revised some material for an Appendix to the *Introduction* in 1811, and the Appendix itself was subsequently further revised, appearing around 1821 as the *Second Part of Clementi's Introduction....* The whole enterprise must have been one of his company's most profitable. He subsequently added to his company's didactic literature by producing the more advanced *Gradus ad Parnassum* in three volumes from 1817 to 1826.

In addition to these instructional works Clementi edited anthologies of music by other composers, notably his four-volume *Selection of Practical Harmony* published from 1801 to *c*1815 and his *Selection from the Melodies of different Nations*, published in 1814. Not only were these publications likely to capture a large market, but they also played an important role in keeping music of earlier generations in the repertoire of contemporary keyboard players.

Clementi's interest in earlier music ensured that his firm was a leader in its publication. The first of his editions of eighteenth-century music had been 'printed for the editor, Muzio Clementi' in 1791 under the title 'Scarlatti's Chefs-d'Oeuvre': it contained ten sonatas by Domenico Scarlatti, one by Antonio Soler and an unidentified composition. The title-page noted that these works had been 'selected from an elegant collection of manuscripts, in the possession of Muzio Clementi'. This was followed by his piano arrangement of some Corelli trio sonatas in 1799.

Thirty of the fifty lessons in *Introduction to the Art of Playing on the Piano Forte* are by Baroque composers. Such a high proportion of early works was unusual for a didactic volume at this time. The only other keyboard tutor published around this time with a significant number of early works was Louis Adam's *Méthode de*

---

[16] Details of all editions of this work and its Appendix are given in the 'new introduction' by Sandra P. Rosenblum to a facsimile reprint (New York, 1974, p v–xxxix) of one of the work's early editions.

piano du Conservatoire (Paris, 1804), six of whose fifty *leçons* were by J. S. Bach, Handel and Scarlatti. Clementi's *Introduction* contained two movements from Bach's E-major 'French' suite, one of which was its first publication anywhere, eleven arrangements of Corelli movements, ten arrangements of Handel instrumental and vocal movements and four sonatas by Scarlatti. Most unusually, the *Introduction* included three works by Couperin and one by Rameau. The former were the only editions of Couperin's music issued between his death in 1733 and the 1830s, excepting *Le Réveil-matin* (*Ordre* 4), which Marpurg had published in 1762.[17] Clementi's *Practical Harmony*, which appeared within a month or so of his *Introduction*, was intended primarily for organists and comprises works by a wide range of early eighteenth-century composers.

Clementi's editorial policy with regard to earlier music was relatively restrained. The most heavily edited were the Scarlatti sonatas published in 1791, which contain some expression marks, directions for *piano* and *forte*, some *crescendos* and *diminuendos*, the occasional *sforzando* and a few articulation markings. In contrast, the works published a decade later appear in 'cleaner' editions, with only an occasional articulation marking or extended slur. This approach was distinctly different from the way in which he updated some of his own compositions in line with contemporary performing trends,[18] an approach also seen in the music of some other composers published by the firm in revised editions, such as those by Dussek and Cramer discussed below.

Besides new editions, Longman, Clementi & Co. reissued works from plates acquired from Longman & Broderip. That firm had published about 100 works by Haydn, and each of the two companies that succeeded them received some of the plates from which those works had been printed. More than half of these editions were reissued by the two successors, Clementi's company publishing rather

---

[17] English publications of J. S. Bach's music in the Georgian era are listed in Michael Kassler (ed.), *The English Bach Awakening: Knowledge of J. S. Bach and his music in England, 1750–1830*, Aldershot, 2004. Further details of the publication of Couperin's and Rameau's works are given in David Rowland, 'Nineteenth-century pianists and Baroque music', forthcoming.

[18] David Rowland, 'From harpsichordist to "Father of the Pianoforte"; changes in the performance styles in the lifetime of Muzio Clementi', forthcoming.

more than Broderip & Wilkinson. Most of the Haydn works reissued by Longman, Clementi & Co. or Clementi & Co. had been published by Longman & Broderip in the late 1780s or 1790s. By far the most popular genres were string quartets and piano trios; seventeen string quartets were reprinted along with twelve piano trios, reflecting the popularity of domestic music in England around the year 1800. Whereas the company reprinted twelve of Haydn's earlier quartets in addition to publishing nine new works in the period 1798 to 1806, quartets by other composers barely feature in the company's catalogue, indicating that the publisher or the musical public had a special affection for quartets by Haydn.

Clementi & Co. also acquired engraved plates from Corri, Dussek & Co. For instance, Dussek's *Grand Military Concerto*, Op. 40, performed on 23 February 1798,[19] was published by Corri, Dussek & Co. in the winter or spring of 1798/1799,[20] and Clementi & Co. reprinted the piano and orchestral parts from Corri & Dussek's plates, except for the title-page, which was re-engraved.[21] Similarly, J. B. Cramer's three sonatas Op. 12, first published by Corri, Dussek & Co. and entered at Stationers' Hall on 21 October 1796, were later issued by Clementi & Co. from the same music plates; again, the title-page plate was re-engraved.[22] Clementi & Co. updated the music plates to add many more slurs, dynamic markings, octave transpositions (to take advantage of the piano's newly extended keyboard) and pedalling indications. Presumably these changes were sanctioned by the composer, although there is no acknowledgement of this in the edition.

In common with other music sellers of the period, Clementi & Co. sometimes re-engraved music that other firms had published. For

---

[19] Advertisement, *The Times*, 16 February 1798, p 1. See also Howard Allen Craw, *A Biography and Thematic Catalog of the Works of J. L. Dussek (1760–1812)*, Ph.D. dissertation, University of Southern California, 1964.

[20] It was customary at this time to publish concertos in the season following their first performance.

[21] A copy of the Corri, Dussek & Co. edition is at BL g.452.p.(2); a copy of the Clementi & Co. edition is at BL g.452.a.(12).

[22] A copy of the Corri, Dussek & Co. edition is at CUL Mus.3.95(2); a copy of the Clementi & Co. edition is at CUL MRS.1.404(6).

example, Dussek's three sonatas, Op. 31, were initially issued by Corri, Dussek & Co. *c*1795. Their edition included versions for five- and five-and-a-half octave piano fortes in which the 'additional notes' for pianos of the latter range were printed above the staff, as was usual at the time. When Clementi & Co. had the work re-engraved they presented only the five-and-a-half octave version and omitted the chord-spreading indications given in the first edition.[23]

Clementi & Co.'s output predominantly comprised domestic music but included a comparatively small amount of music for larger numbers of performers. The company's 180-page 1823 catalogue shows that the balance of their publishing output did not change essentially over the years, although a great many works were added.[24] The 1823 catalogue listed around 6000 items in fifty-nine categories:

> [It] begins with music for the piano, the first nine sections, from p 1 to p 47; there are over 500 sonatas and over 600 'rondos and Airs with variations', works that catered mainly for the huge amateur market of the time; the number of duets, 165, is striking too. ... On p 74–79, to complement the emphasis on piano music, Clementi advertises treatises on keyboard playing.... As well as several by Clementi himself, including the first two volumes of *Gradus ad Parnassum*, older treatises by Pasquali (*Thorough-bass made Easy*) and Rameau (*Treatise on Harmony*) are advertised.
>
> Even more aimed at the English drawing room than the piano music is the vast quantity of vocal music in the catalogue, from arrangements of British folksongs, through adaptations of opera arias (in Italian and French, as well as English) to original songs, a total of over 3500 items. The vocal items advertised from p 92 through to p 104, catches, glees and canons, are part of a British tradition that can be traced back to the seventeenth century. Indicative of changing attitudes, especially the

[23] Dussek's Op. 31 sonatas must have been particularly popular, since the third prelude and the sonata in C were both published later in a re-engraved issue by Lewis Lavenu.

[24] *A Catalogue of Instrumental and Vocal Music, printed by Clementi, Collard & Collard*, London, 1823 (copy in Library of Congress, Washington, catalogue no. ML145.C5). The catalogue is discussed in David Wyn Jones, 'Some aspects of Clementi's career as a publisher', in Bianca Maria Antolini and Costantino Mastroprimiano (eds), *Muzio Clementi compositore, (forte)pianista, editore*, Lucca, 2006, p 3–19, and in Rudolf Rasch, 'Muzio Clementi: the last composer–publisher', in Roberto Illiano, Luca Sala and Massimiliano Sala (eds), *Muzio Clementi Studies and Prospects*, Bologna, 2002, p 355–366. Rasch also lists and discusses other, smaller, catalogues of the company.

> increasing piety of nineteenth-century English society, are the two sections headed 'Sacred Music', p 108–116. The first section (beginning on p 108) contains music designed for the Anglican church service, anthems, hymns, chants and psalm tunes; the following section (beginning on p 113) details the contents of two volumes of arias, duets and trios with piano accompaniment arranged from Handel oratorios.[25]

Several pages in this catalogue are devoted to chamber music without piano, but there is nothing like the same amount of orchestral music: no symphonies by Mozart or Beethoven and only a few by Haydn. The entries for orchestral music are outnumbered by the entries for military band music and 'Highland and Irish' music, which occupy one or two pages each. The conclusion must be that Clementi & Co.'s success as music publishers lay chiefly in producing domestic and church music as well as didactic works, with smaller markets in other areas such as military band repertoire.

Clementi was scrupulous in his attempts to stay within the law, no doubt aware that others before him—not least Longman & Broderip—had spent a considerable amount of time in the courts. On 10 June 1804, during an eight-year tour of Europe from 1802 to 1810 when he was drumming up business on the firm's behalf, he wrote to his partner Frederick William Collard: 'I wish to know when [Joseph] Dale *1st* published my Op. 2nd with the *new* Adagio or Larghetto in the Sonata in C. I think ye 14 years must be over'.[26] Clementi probably was contemplating the publication of yet another revision of his popular sonata Op. 2 no. 2. As Dale had entered the revised edition of that sonata 'with new accompaniments, an additional movement and alterations' at Stationers' Hall on 10 July 1794, its copyright would have lasted until 1808. A further revision of the work exists in a manuscript in the Library of Congress, containing a few bars of the first movement and a complete rewriting of the slow movement, which Alan Tyson tentatively dated 1807,[27] suggesting that Clementi may have been preparing a new version of the work for publication when Dale's copyright ran out.

---

[25] David Wyn Jones, *op. cit.*, p 7–8.

[26] *CMC* p 117–119 at p 118.

[27] Alan Tyson, *Thematic Catalogue*, *op. cit.* in note 2 above, p 69 and p 115.

Whereas Longman & Broderip were involved in numerous legal disputes, Clementi & Co. were party to just a few. Two of these cases demonstrate difficulties with copyright law in the period. *Clementi v Goulding* (1809) concerned the publication of a single-sheet song, 'Heigh-ho!' from the opera *Two Faces under a Hood* by William Shield. This song had been so popular that Goulding, Phipps, d'Almaine & Co. had extracted it from the opera and published it as a single sheet, of which they had printed 1000 copies and had sold 500 by the time the case went to court. Appealing to the wording of the Copyright Act of 1710 which protected 'books and other writings', the defendants contended that single-sheet music compositions were not covered by the Act because they could not be regarded as books. After much time and discussion the court found in favour of Clementi & Co., but not unanimously.[28]

Another case, *Clementi v Walker* (1824), was brought by Clementi & Co. against the music seller George Walker Sr. In June 1814 Maison Pleyel in Paris had published Frederick William Kalkbrenner's 'Introduction and variations on *Vive Henri Quatre*' in France and deposited five copies with the French copyright authorities. Kalkbrenner then travelled to England where on 12 July 1814 he verbally agreed to sell British rights to this composition to Clementi & Co., which they published. In 1818, Walker's son (presumably George Walker Jr) bought a copy of the Pleyel edition in Paris and took it back to England, from which Walker Sr had the music re-engraved and printed 2000 copies that he published in December of that year. On 24 January 1822 Kalkbrenner, back in London again, signed a retrospective agreement with Clementi & Co. for publication of this work. The court determined that because there had been no written assignment of copyright from Kalkbrenner to Clementi & Co. when they published the work in 1814, and as French copyright had no jurisdiction in Britain, the work had no copyright protection there. Accordingly, the court found in favour of Walker Sr.

Although Clementi & Co.'s entry of Kalkbrenner's work at Stationers' Hall on 20 July 1815 did not stop Walker Sr from publishing it, the decision in this case highlighted the need for music sellers to keep records in good order. At the time of the 1824 case the

---

[28] This case is further discussed on pages 380–381 below.

company was careful to register works at Stationers' Hall, but it had not always been so. While Clementi was absent on the continent from 1802 to the summer of 1810 there was a decline in registration. In 1802 the firm entered six works; in 1803 and 1804 that number rose slightly to eight; and nine works were entered in 1805. However, there were no entries in 1806 or 1807 and only one in 1808, but when Clementi returned there was an immediate increase in the number of entries: fifteen from 31 August 1810 to the end of the year. Twelve of these were for works by Beethoven and one was for a Haydn work, so it may have been the particular importance of that repertory, or its foreign origin, that convinced him to take legal care of the works. A similar pattern occurred in 1811, when six of the eleven registered works were by Beethoven. Thereafter the company returned to its more relaxed ways, registering nothing in 1812 and one work in each of 1813 and 1814. Numbers of registrations were higher during the next seven years, but did not reflect anything like the firm's output of works, and it was only in 1822 that the number of registrations approached representative levels with forty-five entries.

Only two contracts relating to Clementi's publishing business—those with Haydn and Beethoven—are known to survive, although extant correspondence shows that there were more. The contract between Haydn and Frederick Augustus Hyde was signed on 10 August 1796, after Hyde had left Longman & Broderip and was in business on his own.[29] Its existence probably assured Hyde's place as a partner in Longman, Clementi & Co., as the whole firm stood to be beneficiaries of it. The contract was for five years, and under its terms Haydn agreed to write and deliver to Hyde 'new and original' music on an annual basis. Hyde would become outright owner of this music and Haydn agreed not to provide copies of this music to anyone else. Hyde of course could not appeal to British courts if Haydn arranged for works to be published on the continent, but could withhold payment to him in such circumstances. Hyde guaranteed to purchase

[29] This contract (now BL ms Mus. 1713) is reproduced in facsimile, transcribed and discussed in Albi Rosenthal, 'The contract between Joseph Haydn and Frederick Augustus Hyde (1796)', in Otto Biba and David Wyn Jones (eds), *Studies in Music History Presented to H. C. Robins Landon on his Seventieth Birthday*, London, 1996, p 72–81. It is also transcribed in *CMC* p 405–407. For Hyde see pages 130–131 above.

and publish music annually up to the value of £150 according to prices set out in the contract and had the option to buy more, should he wish. Haydn had the right if he came to London 'to produce' any symphonies and quartets that he composed under this agreement. Hyde could terminate the contract at the end of three years if he gave three months' notice of so doing and paid £300. The contract ends with a price list of works ranging from keyboard sonatas and violin solos to quartets, symphonies, concertos, trios, quintets and sextets, as well as several different categories of vocal works.

The purpose of the agreement is clear enough: by owning rights to Haydn's creative output, so long as it fell within the categories listed at the end of the contract, Hyde attempted to create a monopoly. The list should be regarded not as a set of works that Haydn promised to complete in the five-year period, but as a kind of menu from which the works that he was to compose would be drawn.

In the event, very little of Haydn's music was published in London during the contract's five-year term. His piano trio sonatas dedicated to Theresa Bartolozzi *née* Jansen were entered at Stationers' Hall by Longman & Broderip on 27 April 1797, as Op. 75. Longman, Clementi & Co. subsequently published Haydn's Op. 76 quartets. The first set of three, which appeared in London in the spring of 1799, was made from an authentic manuscript of the work that differed from the one used for the Artaria & Co. edition in Vienna. The second set of three was published in the middle of the following year, apparently from the same copy that was used for the Vienna edition.[30] Meanwhile, Haydn had sent another work to London for publication; on 29 October 1799, Longman, Clementi & Co. announced in the press the forthcoming publication of their authentic edition of the piano sonata in E♭, no. 52, also dedicated to Theresa Bartolozzi. Haydn's *Battle of the Nile* was published, probably in 1801; it therefore may or may not have been published within the five-year period of the Hyde/Haydn contract, and the Op. 77 quartets may also have been published by Clementi within that time frame.

---

[30] Details of the manuscripts and early editions of these quartets are given in Joseph Haydn (ed. by Horst Walter), *Streichquartette 'Opus 76', 'Opus 77' und 'Opus 103'*, Munich, 2003, p 182.

At best, therefore, only a little over £300 worth of music can have been published within the period of the contract, perhaps less, and certainly nothing like the £750-plus that the contract was set up to achieve. Why was so little published? The reason is revealed in a letter that Georg August Griesinger wrote to Gottfried Christoph Härtel on 12 June 1799. It refers to someone called 'Mr Bay', but from the context Griesinger clearly is referring to Hyde:

> His [Haydn's] publisher in England is a Mr Bay, a rather unimportant man as Haydn said, but associated with Clementi and Broderip. His agreement is for five years, of which three are now finished, and Bay has agreed to take everything he composes, and the price for every psalm, sonata, etc. has been established beforehand. But because of the great amount of work on his [Haydn's] shoulders, he has only delivered some quartets in these three years, and these were sent to England quite recently. Bay is pushing him especially hard for piano sonatas, but up to now he hasn't been able to fulfil his wish.[31]

This letter makes no mention of the piano trio sonatas published by Longman & Broderip in 1797, but does refer to the string quartets and piano sonatas. It shows that the reason why Haydn sent so few new compositions to London was simply one of workload. He was busy at this time composing *The Creation*, *The Seasons* and the late masses.

Haydn's concerns about producing sufficient music for Hyde were compounded by worries over the terms of the contract and the remuneration it provided. According to the contract no other music seller should have been able to publish the Op. 76 quartets without dealing with Hyde. Whether Artaria & Co. had made any such deal or was considered to be exempt from these terms is unknown, but on 15 August 1799 Haydn wrote to them concerning Op. 76:

> I sent the first 3 quartets as early as 27th March and the last 3 on 15th June. If the publication in Vienna should be earlier than that in London (which I hope will not be the case), and if the gentlemen were to discover that you at once received the same 3 quartets from me, I should lose £75 Sterling, which would be a serious matter. You must therefore

[31] Edward Olleson, 'Georg August Griesinger's correspondence with Breitkopf & Härtel', *The Haydn Yearbook* v 3 (1965) p 5–53 at p 10–11, translated in H[oward] C[handler] Robbins Landon, *Haydn:Tthe years of 'The Creation' 1796–1800*, London, 1977, p 469–470.

> take immediate action, *sub rosa*, to ascertain positively whether the first 3 are out, and likewise approximately when the last 3 will appear, so that I won't have a double fine imposed on me.[32]

Whatever arrangement may or may not have been made with Artaria, Haydn evidently thought that the quartets needed to be published first in London in order to fulfil his contractual obligations, and since the price for a group of any three such works was £75 he was worried that he would receive no fee if Artaria published them first.

According to the terms of the Haydn/Hyde contract Longman, Clementi & Co. paid a high premium for Haydn's music. When Gyrowetz offered three quartets to Clementi in December 1799 their price was much lower:

> Those who were present at the rehearsal of my quartets say that among my works these quartets are my best, and they call them the *King* of my quartets. As I hope that this might be an opportunity to extend my reputation I ask you no other price than 20 guineas together with the Nocturne[33] which Mrs Mathew will give you, after you have paid her the 20 guineas. I hope, however, that another time I will be able to count more on the generosity of your gentlemen partners. In truth, you should pay me at least 25 guineas for the quartets alone, or rather the usual price which is 30 guineas, but in order not to waste time and to make known to you the esteem and friendship I have for you and for your great talent, without regard for my own interests, I ask such a small, truly pitiful price. However, if perhaps it is within your power, I hope that you would pay me more.[34]

Longman, Clementi & Co. never published Gyrowetz's quartets, but went on to publish Haydn's Op. 77 and Op. 103.

---

[32] Haydn→Artaria & Co., 15 August 1799, transcribed in H[oward] C[handler] Robbins Landon and Dénes Bartha (eds), *Joseph Haydn Gesammelte Briefe und Aufzeichnungen*, Kassel, 1965, p 332–333; English translation in Landon, *The Collected Correspondence and London Notebooks of Joseph Haydn*, London, 1959, p 162–163.

[33] Probably Gyrowetz's Notturno for piano, violin or flute, and cello, Op. 26, which is listed in Clementi & Co. catalogues.

[34] Gyrowetz→Clementi, 26 December 1799, *CMC* p 40–42. Mrs Mathew has not been identified. Gyrowetz dedicated his 'Eight Italian Ariettes' to 'Miss Mathew', presumably her daughter (*MESH* p 277 and p 282).

Since Longman, Clementi & Co. paid a high price for Haydn's works it is not surprising that they set out to capitalise on their investment. The contract with Hyde effectively allowed him to choose who published the works it covered and enabled Longman, Clementi & Co. to sign a contract with Maison Pleyel on 2 August 1799 for the publication of Haydn's Op. 76 quartets in France.[35] It seems that Maison Pleyel also had an agreement for Haydn's Op. 77 quartets, which they published in Paris in 1803 or 1804.[36]

Longman, Clementi & Co. tried to make similar deals with other prominent composers. They signed a contract with Jan Ladislav Dussek on 3 or 4 November 1799. From 1794 he had been a partner of the rival music seller Corri, Dussek & Co., but that company failed and he fled overseas in late 1799 or early 1800, shortly before his partner and father-in-law Domenico Corri was declared bankrupt. Although the contract is not extant, Clementi told Artaria & Co. on 29 November 1799 that 'we have entered into a contract with Dussek for everything he will compose in the future',[37] and Dussek informed the music seller Robert Birchall in October 1806 that 'my contract with Clementi & Co. finishes the 4th November this year'.[38] This proved to be a quite profitable agreement, leading to the publication by Clementi & Co. of some of Dussek's finest and most prestigious later works, including the sonatas Op. 43–45, the duos Op. 48 and 50, the concerto Op. 49, the quartet Op. 56, the Fantasia and Fugue dedicated to Cramer, six canzonets and a small number of minor works. Like the Hyde/Haydn contract, the agreement with Dussek must have given Clementi & Co. the right to sell his music to other publishers as Clementi wrote to Pleyel in these terms. A 6 March 1801 letter concerned rights to Dussek's Op. 46; a 9 December 1801 letter offered another work.[39] Consequently, many Dussek works that

---

[35] See Max Unger, *Muzio Clementis Leben*, Langensalza, 1914, p 102. The details of this contract are not known, as it is in private hands and not available for public consultation.

[36] See Clementi & Co.→Pleyel, 26 October 1802, *CMC* p 99.

[37] Clementi→Artaria & Co., 29 November 1799, *CMC* p 37–38.

[38] Dussek→Birchall, 8 October 1806, BL Add. Ms 33965 f 200.

[39] See Clementi & Co.→[Maison] Pleyel, 9 December 1801, *CMC* p 79–80.

Clementi & Co. published while he was contracted to them also were published by Maison Pleyel.

Whether the contract with Dussek turned out to be as exclusive as Clementi & Co. intended is open to question. Some of his works dating from the period of the contract were published by other London music sellers, such as two sonatas Op. 47 published by Broderip & Wilkinson, and the *New Year's Gift* comprising six waltzes for the piano, accompanied by flute or violin, published by Montague P. Corri & Co. Conceivably these works were sold by Dussek before he signed the contract with Longman, Clementi & Co., or perhaps they declined to publish these pieces, or maybe Dussek breached the terms of his contract, a plausible scenario since Clementi referred to him in somewhat derogatory terms in an 1804 letter, a paragraph of which begins: 'Now return to *honest* Dussek'.[40] A cooling of relations with Clementi may explain why Dussek was investigating a change of London publishers after his contract with Clementi expired in 1806.

Clementi wrote to Pleyel in June 1802, hoping to become his English publisher:

> My intention in coming to Paris was to negotiate for manuscripts of *your* composition, but as I cannot (at present) make this journey, I beg you to write to me as soon as possible with your terms, so that I can make the necessary arrangements. I should like to have a book of 3 sonatas for the piano; and if you wish to compose 6 sonatas for the piano with some Scottish airs for Adagios Andantes or Rondos you would do me the greatest pleasure, if I might also ask you to let me know the price, whether in money or in instruments. Finally, I hope that you will grant me preference for London, for everything you will compose.[41]

Clementi & Co. also were eager to secure Viotti's works. Although he seems never to have been under contract to them, their 9 December 1801 letter to Pleyel noted that they had 'Viotti's positive assurance that no other publisher shall possess his works'.[42]

---

[40] Clementi→Frederick William Collard, 10 June 1804, *CMC* p 117–119 at p 119.

[41] Clementi→Pleyel, 29 June 1802, *CMC* p 90–91.

[42] *CMC* p 79–80 at p 80.

He seems to have been as good as his word, as virtually all of his subsequent works issued in London were published by the company.

The company's initial contractual model bought exclusive rights to a composer's works for a set time and then capitalised on this purchase by selling rights to publish these works in other countries. But when Clementi began to negotiate for Beethoven's music in 1804, a different arrangement was proposed. The intention to secure rights to all of Beethoven's music for a period of time remained, but rather than setting up an exclusive contract with him Clementi & Co. collaborated with Breitkopf & Härtel, who were to be the lead partner.

Clementi visited Gottfried Christoph Härtel (the owner of Breitkopf & Härtel) in Leipzig in 1804 and on 10 June wrote from there to Frederick William Collard in London:

> With regard to Beethoven I have laid a still better plan than before to possess all his MSS. for as he is *well* (by miracle, for he quarrels w[ith] almost every living creature) I say as he is *well* w[ith] Härtel, I have engaged with this last that he shall contract for all the former's compositions in MS. for the future; & whatever (*reasonable*) price he shall pay him, I'll go halves w[ith] him for the copy-right in y[e] *British Dominions*. And by contracting for all Härtel is sure we shall possess his works at a *tolerably easy* rate; for he is otherwise very exorbitant.[43]

On 4 August 1804, Clementi wrote again to Collard:

> He [Härtel] has promised me to engage Beethoven to send him *all* his new MSS, & we shall have them for the *British Dominions* for *half the price he gives him*. He is to have all that Haydn means to publish, & has likewise promised to send you whatever he gets *from* his pen.... Writing to *him* or *Beethoven* is now become superfluous to say no more, since my conference w[ith] Härtel, for now with *less* trouble & *much less* expense we shall get all we want.[44]

Beethoven and Haydn were not the only composers with whom Clementi wanted to work in co-operation with an overseas music seller. On 11 September 1804 he wrote to Collard about publishing a cello tutor by Jean-Louis Duport: 'Duport expects 200 Louis

---

[43] *CMC* p 117–119 at p 118.

[44] *CMC* p 120–122 at p 120–121.

(Prussian money) for his school for the violoncello. I shall talk to Härtel about it, and if he will go halves for Germany & France I think we should accept.'[45] However, Clementi & Co. never published Duport's *Essai sur le doigté du violoncelle et sur le conduite de l'archet*, which instead appeared in Paris in 1806.

Meanwhile, negotiations with Beethoven were progressing. On 4 September 1804 Breitkopf & Härtel reported to Clementi & Co.:

> Beethoven offers to us the following 4 new Works:
> 1. An Oratorio on religious subject with german words.
> 2. 1 Symphony for full Orchester.
> 3. Concertante for Violin, Violoncello and Pianoforte with full Orchester.
> 4. 3 Sonatas for Pianoforte.
>
> He asks for this 4 works 2000 florins, which amounts to 157 £ St[e]rl[ing]. As the Oratorio will be of no utility to us both, we propose to offer to him the amount of 80 £ Strl. for the 3 works sub N. 2. 3. 4. if you consent to contribute for the propriety of them 40 £ St[erling]. for your part.[46]

By this time the basis of the agreement had shifted. Beethoven cannot have been comfortable with being tied to two music sellers and instead began to negotiate the publication of individual works. Such deals were not unusual. Viotti, who had resisted Clementi's attempt to tie him to the firm, had the sort of contract with two music sellers that Beethoven proposed to Clementi.[47] Perhaps this was more usual; the rarity of extant composer contracts from this time makes it impossible to say.

Within a few years Clementi's and Härtel's plans had to be modified further and it eventually became impossible for their companies to continue to work together on a contract with Beethoven. On 20 January 1807 Härtel informed Clementi that Beethoven's proposals were unacceptable 'because of the war',[48] and as a result

---

[45] *CMC* p 127–129 at p 128.

[46] *CMC* p 124.

[47] François Lesure, 'Deux contrats d'édition de Viotti (1796–1802)', in Rudolf Elvers (ed.), *Festschrift Albi Rosenthal*, Tutzing, 1984, p 221–226.

[48] This passage is quoted in Clementi→Härtel, 22 April 1807, transcribed in *CMC* p 179–181.

Clementi moved swiftly to make his own arrangements with Beethoven, signing on 20 April 1807 a contract with him in Vienna.[49] Although Härtel was not a party to this contract Clementi ensured that he knew of its progress, writing to him on 22 April 1807:

> We have reached an agreement whereby he grants me the rights in the British Dominions[50] for 3 quartets, a symphony, an overture, a violin concerto and a pianoforte concerto. I made this agreement with him following on from your letter dated 20 January, in which you told me you were *unable to accept* his proposals because of the war. I asked him to deal with you regarding Germany, etc., etc.[51]

On the same day, Clementi wrote to Frederick William Collard outlining the events in Vienna that led to the signing of the contract. The detail is sufficiently colourful to warrant extensive quotation:

> By a little management, and without committing myself, I have at last made a compleat conquest of that *haughty beauty*, Beethoven; who first began at public places to grin and coquet with me, which of course I took care not to discourage; then slid into familiar chat, till meeting him by chance one day in the street, — where do you lodge? says he; I have not seen you this *long* while! — Upon which I gave him my address. Two days after I find on my table his card, brought by himself, from the maid's description of his lovely form. This will do, thought I. Three days after that, he calls again and finds me at home. Conceive then the mutual extasy of such a meeting! I took pretty good care to improve it to *our house's* advantage, therefore as soon as decency would allow, after praising very handsomely some of his compositions, — Are you engaged with any publisher in London? — No, says he. — Suppose then, you prefer *me* — With all my heart — Done —. What have you ready? — I'll bring you a list. — In short, I agreed with him to take in M.S. *three Quartetts*, A *Symphony*, an *overture*, a *concerto for the violin* which is beautiful, and which, at my request, he will adapt for the pianoforte with and without additional keys; and a *concerto for the Pianoforte*: for *all* which we are to pay him two hundred pounds sterling. The property however is only for the British Dominions. Today sets off a Courier for London thro[ugh] Russia, and he will bring over to you 2 or 3 of the

---

[49] The contract, in the French language (now Staatsbibliothek zu Berlin, Mus. ms autogr. Beethoven 35,8), is transcribed and translated in *CMC* p 408–410.

[50] The contract refers to 'les royaumes unis britaniques', i.e., the United Kingdom.

[51] Clementi→Härtel, 22 April 1807, transcribed in *CMC* p 179–181.

> mentioned articles. Remember that the Violin concerto he will adapt himself and send it as soon as he can. The Quartetts &c: you may get Cramer or some other very clever fellow to adapt for the P[iano]-Forte. The Symphony and the Overture are wonderfully fine, so that I think I have made a very good bargain. What do you think? — I have likewise engaged him to compose 2 sonatas and a Fantasia for the P[iano]Forte, which he is to deliver to our house for sixty pounds sterling (mind I have treated for Pounds not Guineas). In short he has promised to treat with no one but me for the British Dominions. In proportion as you receive his compositions, you are to remit him the money; that is, he considers the whole as consisting of six articles, viz: 3 *quart[ets]: Symph[ony]: Overt[ure]: Pianoforte-concerto, violin-concerto*, and the *adaptation* of the said conc[erto]: for which he is to receive £200. — For three articles you'll remit £100, and so on, in proportion. The agreement says also that as soon as you receive the compositions you are to pay into the hands of Messrs R. W. & E. Lee the stated sum, who are to authorise Messrs J. G. Schuller & comp[any]. in Vienna to pay to Mr Van Beethoven the value of the said sum, according to the course of exchange, and the said Messrs. Schuller & co: are to reimburse themselves on Messrs R. W. & E. Lee.
>
> On account of the impediments by war &c. I begged Beethoven to allow us 4 months (after the setting off of his MS.S.) to publish in. He said he would write to your house in French *stating the time*, for of course he sends them likewise to Paris &c: &c: and they must appear on the same day. — You are also by agreement to send Beethoven, by a *convenient* opportunity, *two* sets of each of the new compositions you print of his.[52]

Clementi's letter summarises most of the contract. The only substantive detail missing is that Beethoven explicitly reserved the right to publish the works in question outside the United Kingdom and agreed that publication in London would not take place before September 1807.

Barry Cooper's examination of correspondence relating to the contract and to the publication of the works mentioned therein concludes that three works were sent from Vienna in April 1807—the fourth piano concerto, Op. 58; the fourth symphony, Op. 60; and the Coriolan Overture, Op. 62—but were lost *en route*, which would account for Clementi & Co. never issuing them.[53] He suggests that

---

[52] *CMC* p 182–185.

[53] Barry Cooper, 'The Clementi–Beethoven contract of 1807: a reinvestigation', in Roberto Illiano, Luca Sala and Massimiliano Sala (eds), *Muzio Clementi Studies and Prospects*, *op. cit.* in note 24 above, p 337–353.

manuscripts of the quartets Op. 59 and the parts for the violin concerto Op. 61 along with its piano arrangement were sent in September 1807 or a little later but may not have arrived in London for over a year. This would explain why Clementi & Co. did not publish these works until much later than originally intended.

None of these editions was entered at Stationers' Hall and their publication dates are uncertain. The imprint of Op. 59 lists Hyde among the company's partners, so predates 31 August 1810, when he retired, and almost certainly predates 18 August 1810, as an edition of Beethoven's Op. 76 'Thema, with Variations' was entered that day by 'Clementi, Banger, Collard, Davis & Collard', the style used after Hyde's departure. The latter style also appears on the title-page of the piano arrangement of the violin concerto. The title-page of Op. 61 has the generic imprint 'Clementi & Co.', so a precise publishing date cannot be assigned. Clementi was back in London about this time and almost certainly brought with him several more works by Beethoven. Those that were entered at Stationers' Hall in the last few months of 1810 were Op. 73–80, as well as a few other minor works. In the early weeks of 1811 Op. 81 and Op. 81a were registered there. Clementi's efforts thus resulted in a good number of authentic English editions of Beethoven's music.[54]

Shortly before returning to London Clementi concluded an agreement with Härtel for the publication of Clementi's own Op. 50 sonatas. The composer proposed that Breitkopf & Härtel buy the rights for all of Europe except the British Isles, which Clementi would retain.[55] It is not known whether the deal lasted through the tortuous final stages of preparation for the works' publication. The sonatas were not published until 1821, when they appeared simultaneously in Leipzig, London, Paris and Vienna.

Clementi's just-quoted letter to Frederick William Collard said that British and European editions of a Beethoven composition 'must appear on the same day'. As we have seen, imported foreign publications could affect sales of London editions without infringing British copyright law. For this reason Clementi arranged for

---

[54] See Alan Tyson, *The Authentic English Editions of Beethoven*, London, 1963.

[55] Clementi→Härtel, 20 December 1809 and 23 May 1810, *CMC* p 196–198 and p 200–201.

Beethoven to send three works to London in April 1807 to be published a few months later, while begging him to ensure that they were not published in continental Europe for at least four months after dispatch. These timings would have ensured that sales in England were not adversely affected by legitimate foreign imports, a circumstance with which Clementi was familiar.

As far back as 1784 a work by Clementi had been published on the continent before he could arrange for it to be printed in London. His toccata Op. 11 was published by Antoine Bailleux (who had also published Clementi's Op. 1, Op. 5 and Op. 6) and advertised in the *Journal de Paris* on 24 April 1784. Under English law Clementi could not stop the sale of Bailleux's edition in London so he prepared a new edition of his toccata 'corrected by the author', a familiar formula designed to persuade buyers that they were purchasing the authentic version. The London edition, advertised on 8 May 1784, was published by John Kerpen together with a Clementi sonata.[56]

Clementi's later works all appeared first in London, sometimes simultaneously with continental editions, with the exception of sonata Op. 41, which had an unusual publication history. His sonatas Op. 40 provide a typical example of Clementi's later practice. The London edition was entered at Stationers' Hall on 11 September 1802, Maison Pleyel's Paris edition was registered on 23 October 1802, and T. Mollo & Co.'s Vienna edition was announced in the *Wiener Zeitung* on 17 November 1802.[57] Many other works in the closing decades of the eighteenth century and beginning of the nineteenth were published according to a similar pattern, including works by Cramer, Dussek and Haydn, to name three composers with whom Clementi was well acquainted. Publication of a composition in England, France and Germany within two or three months was usual.

Production according to this timescale could easily be achieved using the postal system. For example, Haydn sent the first three of his Op. 76 quartets to London on 27 March 1799.[58] They must have reached Hyde within a few weeks, because Longman, Clementi & Co.'s edition of them was entered at Stationers' Hall on 11 June, less

---

[56] *The Morning Herald, and Daily Advertiser*, 8 May 1784, p 2.

[57] Alan Tyson, *Thematic Catalogue*, *op. cit.* in note 2 above, p 80–81.

[58] Haydn→Artaria & Co., 15 August 1799, *op. cit.* in note 32 above.

than three months later. We can therefore understand the timings that Clementi negotiated with Beethoven in 1807: the four-month interval stipulated between the dispatch of his compositions to England and the appearance of parallel editions in other countries was a slightly stretched version of the usual schedule, because the war could cause delays.[59]

Clementi had experienced such delays well before 1807. Haydn sent his second set of three quartets from Op. 76 from Vienna on 15 June 1799, but they were not advertised in London newspapers until 1 August 1800. Haydn was surprised and concerned by this delay, suggesting to Artaria & Co. on 15 August 1799 that his normal expectations about timing were not met:

> I should have delivered the third quartet [i.e., op. 76 no. 6 = Artaria's op. 76 no. 3] to you, but certain doubts hold me back from doing so: I have not yet received an answer as to the last three quartets which I sent to London, and I fear that if the gentlemen issue all 6 quartets together and not divided—i.e., if they have not yet announced them—your edition and announcement could appear earlier than that in London; though that is difficult to believe, for I sent the first 3 quartets as early as 27th March and the last 3 on 15th June.[60]

Frustration also surrounded delays in distributing subscribers' copies of the edition of the full score of Haydn's *The Creation* which the publisher, Artaria & Co., sent to Longman, Clementi & Co. in 1800. This prompted a strained correspondence with Charles Burney, who was co-ordinating the distribution of copies to English subscribers.[61] Similar problems were experienced over the publication of Vincenzo Righini's Op. 10 *Twelve Exercises for the Voice.* He wrote indignantly to Clementi & Co. on 9 November 1804, protesting that he had fulfilled his side of their agreement:

---

[59] See Clementi→Frederick William Collard, 22 April 1807, quoted on pages 180–181 above.

[60] Haydn→Artaria & Co., 15 August 1799, *op. cit.* in note 32 above.

[61] See Burney→Longman, Clementi & Co., 11 January 1800; Burney→ Clementi, 26 May 1800; and Burney→Longman, Clementi & Co., 25 July 1800; transcribed in *CMC* p 46–48, p 55–56 and p 63–64.

> Regarding the complaints you make of having heard that the same composition has been advertised in Germany, I had informed you in my letter that I would be selling it to a music dealer, according to the agreement which I had made with Mr Clementi, with the condition of being able to sell it, not only in Germany but also in France and Italy, and you will find that this music only appeared at the Easter Fair in Leipzig, much later than I had written in my letter to you; and it is not my fault if you did not have it engraved sooner.[62]

These examples show that parallel publication of music across Europe became more hazardous from around 1800 onwards. While Haydn and Clementi may have expected that a two- or three-month time scale, or a slightly stretched version of it, could be maintained during the Napoleonic wars, the evidence increasingly suggested otherwise. As mentioned, on 20 January 1807 Härtel told Clementi that Beethoven's proposals were unacceptable 'because of the war'. Significant delays in publishing Beethoven's music in London and the complete loss of some of his compositions en route to London probably explain why Clementi broke off his correspondence with Artaria & Co., Breitkopf & Härtel and Maison Pleyel in the course of the first decade of the new century, to initiate it once more (as noted in the previous chapter) only after peace was restored in 1815.

Clementi seems at this time to have become more insistent that the time difference between publication in various European countries should be minimal, and that works preferably should be published on the same day. This had been Beethoven's aspiration in 1807, but was then an impossible goal. However, starting with *Gradus ad Parnassum*, whose first volume appeared in 1817, Clementi took great pains to ensure that his works were published either on the same day in different countries, or at least within a few days of each other. This was a remarkable achievement, not least because many later composers who routinely published internationally never achieved Clementi's degree of simultaneity in European publishing.[63]

---

[62] *CMC* p 131–132. Righini's Op. 10 was published in Leipzig by the Bureau de Musique chez Hoffmeister & Kühnel and by Nicolaus Simrock and Henri Simrock in Bonn and Paris respectively.

[63] See Jeffrey Kallberg, 'Chopin in the marketplace: aspects of the international music publishing industry in the first half of the nineteenth century. Part I:

As early as 19 December 1815 Clementi was planning to publish the first volume of *Gradus ad Parnassum*,[64] and by 29 December 1816 he had fixed 1 March 1817 as its publication date in London, Paris and Leipzig.[65] His 19 March 1819 letter to Härtel said that the publication date for volume 2 would be 15 April 1819;[66] it was registered that day in France and on the following day at Stationers' Hall. Volume 3 was registered on 31 October 1826 in London and Paris, but only after Clementi had moved the publication date forward by a day to accommodate a public holiday in France.[67] He exercised similarly tight control over the publication of his other late works. He may have been obsessive about simultaneous publication of his works around Europe (it is not clear whether his company achieved similar results with other composers' music), but he demonstrated that it could be done and that it was the best possible guard against foreign copies of a work competing against English publication of the same work.

While Clementi was refining the process of simultaneous publication in Europe he engaged in collaborative publishing activities at home. From 1817 until 1830, when his involvement in the company was all but finished, Clementi & Co. published several works together with another London music seller, both publishers' names appearing on the title-pages. These collaborators included Birchall, Cramer (like his teacher Clementi, a music seller as well as a pianist and composer), Goulding & d'Almaine and Goulding & Co., but Clementi appears to have collaborated most with Chappell.[68] Occasionally, the list of publishers printed on a Clementi & Co. title-page included foreign ones. For instance, the imprint on the title-page of Ferdinand Ries's 'The thirty second sonata', Op. 47, entered at

France and England', *Notes* 2nd ser. v 39 no. 3 (March 1983) p 535–569 at p 536–539.

[64] See *CMC* p 227.

[65] See *CMC* p 243. The first volume was registered on that day in London and Paris. Records of its German registration no longer survive.

[66] See *CMC* p 261.

[67] *CMC* p 331.

[68] Several examples are given in Cecil Hill, *Ferdinand Ries: A thematic catalogue*, Armidale NSW, Australia, 1977.

Stationers' Hall on 19 April 1817, states: 'Printed by Clementi & Co. 26, Cheapside, Chappell & Co. No. 124, New Bond Street, & C. F. Peters, Leipsic'.[69]

What was the purpose of these dual publishing arrangements? There was no change in the law that prompted them, so the reason must have been purely commercial. It was not unprecedented, as isolated works had been published by more than one music seller in London prior to 1817. The benefits from the composer's point of view must have been better dissemination and from the publisher's point of view cost: only one firm had to bear the expenses of production, but all co-publishers shared ownership of the work. In a letter of 26 August 1819, Breitkopf & Härtel offered Clementi & Co. the option of a dual publication arrangement as an alternative to a straightforward copyright deal:

> At present we can offer you *Gabrielsky*'s Opus 39, 3. Duos for 2 fl[ute]s. of which we have bought the manuscript. We offer you the option either for us to send you the original manuscript to engrave it for which you would pay us £5 Sterl[ing]: or for you to take 200 copies of this work (which will have about 54 pages and the marked price of which will be 2 Saxon Reichsthaler) at 60% discount or for 2/5 of the marked price. In this case the frontispiece would bear the name of your firm.[70]

In this instance Clementi chose to acquire the copyright and to have the works printed in London. Copies of Gabrielsky's Op. 39 have only Clementi & Co.'s name on the title-page.

Clementi & Co.'s business involved different sorts of transactions. The simplest were cash payments, used at the company's Cheapside shop where music and instruments were sold. Other arrangements often were employed where transactions took place elsewhere.

Companies who did business internationally at this time relied upon a network of money transferers. As we have seen, when setting up arrangements to pay Beethoven after he sent works to London, Clementi instructed Frederick William Collard to pay money to the merchants Messrs R. W. & E. Lee, who would then transfer the

---

[69] *ibid.*, p 41.

[70] *CMC* p 262–263.

amount to the Vienna wholesaler J. G. Schuller & Co., who would pay Beethoven the equivalent in local currency.[71]

Composers sometimes agreed to non-cash transactions. When Dussek sent some of his music from Hamburg to London in May 1800 he expressed a preference to be paid in pianos rather than cash:

> A Friend of mine, a Man of respectability is going over to London in a few Days, he will bring, and deliver to You Three Sonatas, with wich I hope You will be pleased. I have also mostly finished the Three Concertionos, wich You shall receive in the Course of a Forthnight, — I have at Last received the Forte Piano in a pretty good state, and having played upon it to several Amateurs, some of them are very anxious of possessing a Like instrument, therefore I hope it will be no objection with You to pay me the Two above mentioned works with Instruments (at Professors' rate) as the exchange from England is very disadvantageous, by this I will not only save the Discount wich [sic] is considerable, but gain at the same time the Allowance.[72]

In 1802 Clementi offered to pay Pleyel 'in money or in instruments':

> I should like to have a book of 3 sonatas for the piano; and if you wish to compose 6 sonatas for the piano with some Scottish airs for Adagios Andantes or Rondos you would do me the greatest pleasure, if I might also ask you to let me know the price, whether in money or in instruments.[73]

An exchange of instruments for new music seems to be contemplated in an 1803 letter from Friedrich Heinrich Himmel.[74] In 1816 August Alexander Klengel wanted two Clementi & Co. pianos and offered to pay for them half in 'ready money' and half in compositions.[75] Publication rights also were transferred. On 6 March 1801 Clementi wrote to Maison Pleyel about exchanging the rights to Haydn's Op. 77 Quartets and a work identified as Dussek's Op. 46

---

[71] Clementi→Frederick William Collard, 22 April 1807, quoted on page 181 above.

[72] Dussek→Longman, Clementi & Co., 16 May 1800, *CMC* p 53–54.

[73] Clementi→Pleyel, 29 June 1802, *CMC* p 90–91.

[74] Himmel→Clementi & Co., 9 July 1803, *CMC* p 101–102.

[75] Klengel→Clementi & Co., 20 November 1816, *CMC* p 238–240.

for some quartets by Pleyel.[76] On 10 June 1804 Clementi wrote to Frederick William Collard:

> I think you may venture to send immediately by the post his [Dussek's] three sonatas, if they be in the *grand* style, to Nägeli, at Zurich, as I mentioned in my last, for which he is to send you Beethoven's grand sonata in E flat and a sonata by Woelfl in C minor.[77]

Other forms of transaction were used for quantities of print music. Clementi wrote to Artaria & Co. on 21 December 1798 proposing that their companies enter into a mutually beneficial arrangement based on exchanges from their catalogues.[78] His 29 November 1799 letter reveals a little more of what he had in mind:

> whatever you take from our catalogue we ask you to send us the equivalent from your catalogue. You could send us two copies of every popular publication that you have printed in the past twelve months, and especially vocal music, military music, sonatas for pianoforte and Haydn's new symphonies for full orchestra.[79]

On 7 May 1817 Clementi & Co. asked Artaria & Co. to renew the agreement they had prior to the Napoleonic wars, whereby they exchanged music on a page-for-page basis.[80]

Clementi & Co.'s correspondence with Breitkopf & Härtel is extensive and provides many examples of how the two firms did business together. For instance, Breitkopf & Härtel wrote on 13 February 1804:

> We can offer you works from our collection, for which we enclose a catalogue, at a 50% reduction on the advertised prices and with a six month payment term, or, if the number of transactions is more considerable, we can offer a twelve month payment term.... And because in our music shop we also stock all the other publishers from Germany,

---

[76] See Max Unger, *Muzio Clementis Leben*, *op. cit.* in note 35 above, p 102.

[77] *CMC* p 117–119 at p 119.

[78] *CMC* p 31–32.

[79] *CMC* p 37–38.

[80] *CMC* p 246. This letter appears to be in the handwriting of Frederick William Collard.

> Switzerland etc., and the major publishers from Paris, we can also offer you these at a 20% reduction on the advertised prices.[81]

An 1819 letter indicates the extent of their business:

> The items you request were dispatched on 18 August in a crate … to M^essrs Beyer and Ferber in Hamburg, whom we have asked to have it reach you by the swiftest route. The value of the dispatch for insurance purposes was given to them as 500 Marks-Banco of Hamburg. You will want to add to your account the net total of 234.– Saxon Reichsthaler as per the enclosed account.[82]

An important aspect of Clementi & Co.'s activities which has received little attention is their publication of specially produced arrangements. Numerous musicians arranged music for the company, including John Field, Frederick Kalkbrenner, Ferdinand Ries and Samuel Webbe Jr.[83] Clementi himself was not above taking on the task when the work in question was of high profile or when he knew the composer personally, and he provided arrangements for the company throughout his partnership (as he had done previously for Longman & Broderip). The most significant of his arrangements were vocal scores of Haydn's *The Creation* (published in 1800) and *The Seasons* (in 1813), but he also arranged a number of Haydn's and Mozart's symphonies for piano, flute, violin and cello.[84]

---

[81] *CMC* p 113–114.

[82] Breitkopf & Härtel→Clementi & Co., 26 August 1819, *CMC* p 262–264.

[83] Others whose arrangements were published by the company included Thomas Attwood, Jonathan Blewitt, John Freckleton Burrowes, Thomas Simpson Cooke, John Thomas Craven, Christopher Frederick Eley, S. Goadby, Thomas Haigh, George Frederick Harris, Matthias von Holst and his son Gustavus Valentin von Holst, Benjamin Jacob, Thomas Killick Sr, Christian Kramer, William Thomas Ling, Augustus Meves Sr, Charles Nicholson, Joseph de Pinnaina, Johann Peter Pixis, Thomas Augustus Rawlings, Charles Michel Alexis Solá, William Turle, Thomas Valentine, William Watts, John Michael Weippert and John Wilkins. Many of these people arranged only one or two works that the company issued, but some seem to have had fairly regular employment as arrangers.

[84] A fuller list of Clementi's arrangements is given in Alan Tyson, *Thematic Catalogue, op. cit.* in note 2 above, p 129–131. Clementi was not unique in making arrangements: Cramer did the same for his own firm. See Thomas B.

Like Longman & Broderip, Longman, Clementi & Co. and Clementi & Co. appear to have relied upon external engravers and printers to produce their publications. Little has been documented about these persons, but both Richard Skarratt and his son Richard Thomas Skarratt are known to have engraved many works for Clementi's company.[85]

A successful music publisher at the beginning of the nineteenth century required a number of skills and a good deal of experience. Knowledge of the international musical environment was essential and it helped to have personal contacts that would bring new commissions and favourable deals with other publishers. Because Clementi had an international network of relationships with composers and music sellers when he began his partnership he was in a strong position to build his new company, but legal and financial expertise also was needed. Clementi must have developed some of this but doubtless relied heavily on the help of his fellow partners. Nevertheless, the impression gained from source documents is that the success of his company depended particularly upon his drive and ability. Once he had retired, Collard & Collard never achieved the commercial and musical influence that the company exercised under Clementi's leadership.

Milligan, *Johann Baptist Cramer (1771–1858): A thematic catalogue of his works*, Stuyvesant, New York, 1994, Appendix A.

[85] See Michael Kassler, 'The Horn/Wesley edition of Bach's "trio" sonatas', in Michael Kassler (ed.), *The English Bach Awakening: Knowledge of J. S. Bach and his music in England 1750–1830*, Aldershot, 2004, p 417–429 at p 426–429, which points out that a characteristic of the Skarratts' engraving style from about 1801 was the use of right-opening bass clefs. About 1820 Clementi & Co. published a 'Divertimento, for two performers on the piano forte' by T. Skarratt, presumably Richard Thomas Skarratt (it is known only from its review in *The Quarterly Musical Magazine and Review* v 3 no. 9 (January 1821) p 112).

~ II ~

MUSIC SELLERS' CATALOGUES: A CASE STUDY

~ 5 ~

THE PERIODICAL MUSIC COLLECTIONS OF JOHN BLAND AND HIS SUCCESSORS

Yu Lee An

5.1 INTRODUCTION

Music sellers in Georgian England produced catalogues to advertise music available for purchase. They were the most practical and efficient means of promoting simultaneously a large number of new or old publications and were more cost-effective than other existing channels of advertising.

This indispensable tool of the Georgian music trade now provides us with evidence of the activities of major and minor music sellers. Some enterprises flourished for several decades. But many were short-lived small operations, and for the majority of these, business records have vanished along with the publishers. Even for large and longer-surviving firms, little of their correspondence, contracts, stock-books, ledgers, bills and receipts is extant.[1] Yet, thanks to the persistent custom of printing catalogues on inner pages of music publications that otherwise would have been blank,[2] a

[1] Georgian music sellers with some surviving business records include the firms of Preston and Birchall. Receipts issued for one-off payments by John and Thomas Preston and their successors Coventry & Hollier for music copyrights and other items are collected in an album now at BL Add. Ms 63814. They are the subject of Katharine Hogg, *Music Publishing in London, 1773–1834: The Preston firm*, MA thesis, University of Sheffield, 1988. A scrapbook of original receipts issued by the publisher Robert Birchall and his successor Christopher Lonsdale to composers from 1781 to 1864 is in the Newberry Library, Chicago, Case ms fV 209.52. The binder's title on this scrapbook reads *Musical and Dramatic Curiosities exhibited by C. Lonsdale*.

[2] Catalogues included in music publications usually were printed on the verso of the title-page or on the verso of the last leaf. They can also be found on the recto

wealth of catalogues is available from this period.[3] They often present the comprehensive output of individual publishers and provide a detailed account of their activities that is unparalleled by any other primary source of information.

Catalogues do more than reveal the extent of a music publisher's business and the types of music in which the publisher specialised.[4] They may show distribution networks (agencies in provincial towns and abroad), musical instruments manufactured or sold (if the publisher did this), and other subsidiary services offered, such as engraving, printing, and retailing music on behalf of self-publishing composers. Comparing the contents of catalogues issued by related firms illuminates the nature of their relationships.

Catalogues also help to establish when works were issued. Much music printed during the eighteenth and early nineteenth centuries does not bear a printed date, and the almost universal use of engraved plates which allowed publishers to reprint music on demand in small print runs has compounded the situation.[5] However, a majority of catalogues were regularly updated to include items newly published or 'in the press'. Examining a large number of catalogues in conjunction with Stationers' Hall copyright entries, contemporary

---

of the second leaf, with its verso containing the first page of music. Music was rarely printed on the verso of the title-page.

[3] From the collections of the British Library, the Bodleian Library and the Cambridge University Library I have unearthed nearly 600 catalogues issued in more than 1100 states by over 100 London music publishers from 1780 to 1837. See Yu Lee An, *Music Publishing in London from 1780 to 1837 as reflected in Music Publishers' Catalogues of Music for Sale: A bibliography and commentary*, Ph.D. dissertation, University of Canterbury [New Zealand], 2008, online at http://ir.canterbury.ac.nz/handle/10092/4197.

[4] Large stand-alone accumulative catalogues issued by the Goulding and Clementi firms are particularly useful as they present the publications of each firm over a considerable period of time. Clementi's 1823 catalogue comprises 189 pages (BL Mic.A.2054, microfilm of a copy in the Library of Congress); Goulding & Co.'s catalogues issued in 1800 (BL 1570/3597), 1808 (Bodleian Johnson d. 1704 (13)) and 1820 (BL Hirsch IV. 1116) consist of 40, 80 and 50 pages respectively.

[5] A rather loose dating of reprinted music can be obtained from changes of publisher's imprint. As many Georgian music publishers also were music retailers, having their current address on title-pages was essential for communicating where their music could be inspected and purchased.

press advertisements, watermark dates and rather haphazardly employed plate numbers shows that most publishers revised their catalogues promptly, in some instances within a couple of months. Such reissues can pinpoint publication dates quite accurately.

Although music sellers employed catalogues as a commercial device to cultivate and exploit public taste, they tailored their catalogues' content and appearance to accommodate perceived changes in the preferences of their intended customers. Catalogues therefore help us to reconstruct not only the histories of Georgian music publishers but also the role they played in accommodating, influencing, expanding and educating contemporary musical taste.

5.2 John Bland's Periodical Collections of Music

As a case study to illustrate these points, this chapter discusses catalogues of the following six so-called periodical collections[6] that were begun by the music seller John Bland and continued by later purchasers of these collections:[7]

A. *Bland's Collection of Periodical Duetts for two performers on one harpsichord or piano forte* (hereafter *Periodical Duetts*) (began *c*1782)
B. *Bland's Le tout Ensemble pour le Forte-Piano ou Clavecin, avec Accompagnemens* (hereafter *Le tout Ensemble*) (began January 1789)
C. *Bland's Collection of Sonatas, Lessons, Overtures, Capriccios, Divertimentos, &c. &c. for the harpsichord or piano forte, without accompaniments* (hereafter *Harpsichord Collection*) (began January 1790)
D. *Bland's Periodical Italian Song* (began *c*1782)

---

[6] The term 'periodical' was used to describe collections that appeared from time to time, usually at irregular intervals.

[7] Bland also issued 'Periodical Overtures'. They have been excluded from this study as they were not continued by any later publisher.

E. *Bland's Collection of Ladies' Glees, Catches, and Canons* (hereafter *Ladies' Glees*) (began *c*1780)
F. *Bland's Collection of Divine Music* (began *c*1793)

Our primary focus is upon the catalogues that were devoted to these collections, although more general, broad-ranging catalogues by Bland and his successors that list these collections are considered. The involvement of five publishers—Bland, Robert Birchall, George Goulding, Francis Linley and the firm Lewis, Houston & Hyde—offers an opportunity to study how music sellers bought and sold copyrights and music plates and how purchased collections were treated by those who acquired them.

These six periodical collections represent Bland at the height of his career, rising to become a formidable rival to Longman & Broderip in what was becoming an increasingly competitive and lucrative music market. They exemplify the most fashionable instrumental music (A, B and C) and vocal music (D, E and F) of late eighteenth- and early nineteenth-century England, and were products of an innovative and experimental method of publishing music in periodically appearing series.

Bland did not invent this concept: Robert Bremner's *Periodical Overture*, issued in eight instrumental parts, appeared in June 1763 in response to the public's interest in concerted music.[8] But it was Bland who introduced periodical collections of diverse instrumental and vocal repertoires into England, which he aimed at the largest market for Georgian music publishers: domestic, amateur performers. For each of the six collections he issued one or more catalogues that were dedicated to it, and he also promoted his periodical collections in his general catalogues. This two-pronged approach to the market is significant because most of his contemporaries produced only general catalogues that listed a large number of compositions scored for a variety of voices or instruments.

Bland issued nine catalogues that were devoted to his periodical collections. All but one of these were reprinted more than once with updated information. Five of the nine were thematic

---

[8] See David Wyn Jones, 'Robert Bremner and *The Periodical Overture*', *Soundings* [Cardiff, Wales] no. 7 (1978) p 63–84 at p 64–65.

catalogues; four were 'title catalogues' that gave only the title, composer and price of each work.

With the exception of the *Ladies' Glees* collection, which Bland promoted only by a title catalogue, each collection was advertised both in a thematic catalogue and in a title catalogue. Thematic catalogues were relatively new to England.[9] John Corri, a son of Domenico Corri working in Edinburgh, issued one, *A Select Collection of the most admired Songs, Duets, etc. from operas of the highest esteem, etc.*, as early as 1779, and William Forster I devoted a thematic catalogue to the works of Joseph Haydn in late 1787.[10] But these were isolated examples. Bland was the only English music publisher to make extensive and consistent use of thematic catalogues in the eighteenth century. It is highly likely that, for many of his customers, this type of catalogue was a novelty.

John Bland issued many catalogues during his business career. Those dedicated to one or more of his periodical collections are described in *Table 5.1* on pages 200–201. The numeral or numerals following the abbreviation 'BlJ' (for 'John Bland') show the chronological order of the first state of each catalogue; the letter after a numeral specifies the the chronological 'state' of the catalogue's printing. Printed catalogues have different states if they differ textually; for instance, if a new entry has been added. Catalogue BlJ 3a therefore preceded catalogues BlJ 3b and BlJ 5a but, as shown in the table, catalogue BlJ 3f (the sixth state of catalogue BlJ 3) appeared after BlJ 5a.

Unless marked by the symbol ♪ to indicate a thematic catalogue, each of the following catalogues listed the titles of compositions only. Excepting catalogue BlJ 3d, which was typeset, all catalogues listed in *Table 5.1* were printed from engraved plates. The dating of catalogues is approximate and has been derived chiefly from newspaper advertisements of works mentioned therein. A library location is given for each catalogue.

---

[9] Yu Lee An, 'Thematic catalogues in London music publishing 1780–1837', *Brio* v 44 no. 2 (autumn/winter 2007) p 19–36.

[10] See Barry S. Brook, 'A tale of thematic catalogues', *Notes* v 29 no. 3 (March 1973) p 407–415 at p 412, and Barry S. Brook, *Thematic Catalogues in Music: An annotated bibliography*, Hillsdale, New York, 1972, p 57.

BlJ 3a	*A Catalogue of Catches, Glees, Canzonetts, Canons, &c.* (lists *Ladies Glees* 2–5) [BL G.424.g.(2)]	late 1784
BlJ 3b	*Catalogue of Glees, Catches, Canons, Canzonetts, &c. &c.* (lists *Ladies Glees* 2–8) [BL E.207.d.(2)]	early 1785
BlJ 3c	*A Catalogue of Catches, Glees, Canons, Canzonetts, &c. &c.* (lists *Ladies Glees* 1–12) [BL RM 13.d.(30)]	1787
BlJ 3d	*Catalogue of Glees, Canons, Canzonets, &c.* (lists *Ladies Glees* 1–17) [RCM D.77, p 7–8]	early 1789
BlJ 3e	*Index to Blands 2 Vols. of Catches, Glees, Canons, Canzonets, Madrigals, &c. &c.* (lists *Ladies Glees* 1–24) [Bodleian Mus. 2 c.63]	mid 1789
BlJ 3f	*Index to 3d & 4th Vol. of Catches Glees Canons Canzonets Madrigals &c.* (lists *Ladies Glees* 25–36) [Bodleian Harding Mus. E 649]	mid 1791
BlJ 5a	*Periodical Duetts* (lists 1–10) [BL h.3691, no. 2]	late 1788 or early 1789
BlJ 5b	*Periodical Duetts* (lists 1–18) [BL h.3691, no. 3]	mid 1790
BlJ 5c	*Periodical Duetts* (lists 1–22) [BL h.3961, no. 1]	1793
BlJ 6a	*Le tout Ensemble* (lists 1–4) [BL h.1497, no. 3]	early 1789
BlJ 6b	*Le tout Ensemble* (lists 1–12) [Bodleian Mus. Instr. I,110]	mid 1790
BlJ 6c	*Le tout Ensemble* (lists 1–13) [Bodleian Mus. 61 c.159 (1)]	mid 1790
BlJ 6d	*Le tout Ensemble* (lists 1–22) [BL RM 17.d.1, no. 28]	early 1792
BlJ 6e	*Le tout Ensemble* (lists 1–29) [BL RM 17.d.1, no. 12]	mid 1792
BlJ 6f	*Le tout Ensemble* (lists 1–36) [BL RM 17.d.1, no. 3]	late 1794 or early 1795
BlJ 12a	*Periodical Italian Song* (lists 1–40 and eleven other compositions) [Bodleian Johnson Mus. c.21]	mid 1789
BlJ 12b	*Periodical Italian Song* (lists 1–49 and fifteen other compositions) [BL G.206.n.(15)]	early 1791
BlJ 12c	*Periodical Italian Song* (lists 1–53 and fifteen other compositions) [Bodleian Harding Mus. H 8 (14)]	1793
BlJ 12d	*Periodical Italian Song* (lists 1–60 and seventeen other compositions) [BL G.811.n.(10)]	late 1794 or early 1795

BlJ 13a ♪	*Catalogue of Subjects or Beginnings of Italian Songs* (lists 1–49 and sixteen other compositions) [BL E.601.k.(11)]	mid 1791
BlJ 13b ♪	*Catalogue of Subjects or Beginnings of Italian Songs* (lists 1–49 and eighteen other compositions) [Bodleian Mus. 301 c.94(7)]	mid 1791
BlJ 13c ♪	*Catalogue of Subjects or Beginnings of Italian Songs* (lists 1–53 and eighteen other compositions) [BL G.811.n.(10)]	1794
BlJ 15a ♪	*Catalogue of Subjects or Beginnings of 2 Periodical Works* (lists 1–22 of *Le tout Ensemble* and 1–28 of the *Harpsichord Collection*) [BL g.445.i.(2), *Le tout Ensemble* no. 12]	early 1792
BlJ 15b ♪	*Catalogue of Subjects or Beginnings of 2 Periodical Works* (lists 1–26 of *Le tout Ensemble* and 1–30 of the *Harpsichord Collection*) [BL RM 17.d.1, *Le tout Ensemble* no. 28]	mid 1792
BlJ 15c ♪	*Index to 48 Nos. of Bland's Harpsichord Collection* (lists 1–37) [BL g.12, *Harpsichord Coll.* no. 17]	early 1793
BlJ 15d ♪	*Index to 48 Nos. of Bland's Harpsichord Collection* (lists 1–48) [BL g.12, *Harpsichord Coll.* no. 4]	>11/1793
BlJ 17a ♪	*Index to Le tout Ensemble* and *Index to Duetts* (lists 1–30 of *Le tout Ensemble* and 1–22 of *Periodical Duetts*) [BL RM 17.d.1, *Le tout Ensemble* no. 27]	mid 1793
BlJ 17b ♪	*Index to Le tout Ensemble* and *Index to Duetts* (lists 1–33 of *Le tout Ensemble* and 1–25 of *Periodical Duetts*) [BL RM 17.d.1, *Le tout Ensemble* no. 19]	mid 1794
BlJ 17c ♪	*Index to Le tout Ensemble* and *Index to Duetts* (lists 1–37 of *Le tout Ensemble* and 1–25 of *Periodical Duetts*) [BL RM 17.d.1, *Le tout Ensemble* no. 3]	early 1795
BlJ 18a ♪	*Catalogue of Subjects or Beginnings of Blands Collection of Divine Music* (lists 1–12) [BL H.817]	early 1795

Table 5.1 John Bland's Title and Thematic Catalogues relating to his Periodical Collections

The six periodical collections form a coherent study because they were designed, promoted and marketed in a similar manner not only by Bland but also by the music sellers who continued these collections after he sold his business in 1795. From the outset, he planned each collection to be consistent and homogeneous in style, length and price. The *Ladies' Glees*, the *Harpsichord Collection* and *Bland's Collection of Divine Music* were to be published in numbers 'containing 10 pages at 1s.6d. each'.[11] While such rigidity may seem extreme, it assured his customers of value for money, with ten pages of music guaranteed to be included in each new issue. His catalogues for *Le tout Ensemble*, the *Periodical Italian Song* and the *Periodical Duetts* were incorporated into their respective series' title-pages, giving these collections visual unity.

The six collections also share other characteristics that distinguish them as 'series': continuous pagination is used throughout each collection, and successive issues within each collection are numbered serially. More importantly, these collections were intended from their inception to be ongoing and to appear more or less regularly.[12]

For example, the thematic catalogue devoted to the *Harpsichord Collection* said that each new number will be 'Publish'd the 1st day of every Month'.[13] '6 Numbers of Glees will come out Annually at 1s.6d. each' was printed at the foot of the mid-1789 catalogue of the *Ladies' Glees*.[14] When this collection reached its seventeenth number Bland changed to quarterly issues,[15] but he resumed bimonthly publication about the middle of 1791.[16]

---

[11] The quotation is from the title of Bland's catalogue BlJ 3f.

[12] Although individual volumes of a collection were 'completed' after six or twelve numbers were issued it was planned that each volume would be followed by another volume in the same collection.

[13] This appears just below the title of catalogue BlJ 15.

[14] 'Index to Bland's 2 Vols of [Ladies] Catches, Glees, Canons, Canzonets, Madrigals, &c.' (catalogue BlJ 3e).

[15] His general catalogue issued in January 1789 (copy at RCM D.77) said: 'N.B. 1 number of the above is published every 3 Months'.

[16] Bland announced in the catalogue devoted to the third and fourth volumes (BlJ 3f) that '6 Nos. will be Published Yearly at 1s.6d. each'.

'Periodical' was applied more loosely to *Le tout Ensemble* and the *Periodical Duetts*, whose numbers appeared irregularly.[17] Initially, *Le tout Ensemble* was intended as a monthly periodical,[18] but it seems that Bland could not achieve that schedule and was forced into a looser frequency of issue. His *Collection of Divine Music* also was originally planned as a monthly publication[19] but never came out on a regular basis.

Whether they appeared regularly or not, periodical collections were conceived as publications with no predetermined end. They were designed to entice customers to purchase successive numbers, and their existence relied on the continued consumption of the music-buying public. To take an example from Bland's most regular issue, the *Harpsichord Collection*, Franziska Le Brun's first two sonatas from her op. 1 set constituted no. 44 of the collection; the third and fourth sonatas no. 45; and the fifth and sixth sonatas no. 46. Instead of issuing a set of six sonatas in one publication like most publishers of the period, Bland had his customers wait a month after the initial issue to purchase two further sonatas, and yet another month to complete the set. This delayed release may have improved sales, as those reluctant to spend 4/6 for a set of six new sonatas may have succumbed to buying three instalments at 1/6 per month.

Bland devised four of the six collections as sets and offered bound volumes when a set was complete. Twelve numbers made up a set of the *Ladies' Glees*, the *Harpsichord Collection* and the *Collection of Divine Music*; six numbers completed a set of the *Periodical Duetts*.

The six collections and their associated catalogues form a microcosm that epitomises various idiosyncratic characteristics of the Georgian music trade. They also illustrate Bland's attempts to exploit the market for the most fashionable music through the new means of

---

[17] Bland's *Theme Catalogue of French Songs*, issued *c*1793 (copy at BL H.1601.c.(11)), included the notice: 'Bland's Harps^{d}. Duetts Pub^{d} Occasion^{y}. each 1^{s}/_' and 'Le tout Ensemble Harp^{d}. with Acc^{ts}. Occasion^{y}. ea. 2^{s}/6^{d}'.

[18] In his January 1789 general catalogue Bland noted immediately after entries of its first six numbers: 'N.B. This will be continued monthly.'

[19] This appears in Bland's *c*1794 catalogue of vocal music (copy in v 2 of BL H.817).

single-medium catalogues.[20] Details are given below for each of the six collections.

Succeeding issuers of Bland's collections continued to promote them as 'Bland's collection', often adding a phrase such as 'continued by F. Linley' or 'Birchall's continuation of'. The circumstance that Birchall and Goulding carried on Bland's collections into the early nineteenth century shows their extended popularity and underscores his astute judgement of the English music market.

5.3 John Bland and his Successors

Before turning to the individual collections, a brief discussion of John Bland and his successors, and the disposition of his stock-in-trade, is essential.

John Bland established a music-selling business in London 'by 1776' and was succeeded in March 1795 by the newly formed partnership of Lewis, Houston & Hyde,[21] who made their first entries of music at Stationers' Hall on 18 March 1795.[22] This partnership was short-lived and was succeeded by Francis Linley on 1 December 1795, as noticed in *The London Gazette*:[23]

> The partnership lately subsisting between John Lewis Vautier Sollicoffre, James Henry Houston, and Frederick Hyde, of No. 45, Holborn, in the County of Middlesex, in the business of music-sellers, under the firm of Lewis, Houston and Hyde, was this day dissolved by mutual consent: all debts due from and to the said partnership will be

---

[20] Although catalogues limited to a single medium (e.g., keyboard music) first appeared in 1790 they were not commonly issued before the nineteenth century.

[21] Frank Kidson, William C[harles] Smith and Peter Ward Jones, 'Bland, John', *Oxford Music Online* database.

[22] *MESH* p 254. The imprint on a Stationers' Hall deposit copy of one of these ([Charles] Thomas Carter's 'The loyal Tar', copy at Bodleian Mus. Voc. I, 12 (44)) reads 'Lewis, Houston and Hyde (Successors to Mr. Bland) No. 45 Holborn', indicating that acquisition of Bland's business was a purpose of the new partnership from its outset. The first advertisement located that mentions this partnership appeared in *The Morning Chronicle*, 26 March 1795, p 1.

[23] *The London Gazette*, 3 December 1795, p 1350. Statements in reference sources that this succession took place in 1797 are incorrect.

paid and received by their successor Mr Francis Linley, who will in future conduct the business on his own account: witness our hands this 1st day of December, 1795.

John Lewis Vautier Sollicoffre.
James Henry Houston.
Fred. Hyde.
Fra. Linley.

On 30 December 1795 Linley entered four compositions at Stationers' Hall. Copies of three of them bear Linley's imprint as 'Successor to Mr Bland, No. 45 Holborn',[24] and it is noteworthy that Linley identified himself as 'late Bland' rather than as 'successor to Lewis, Houston & Hyde'.[25] By January 1797 Linley was bankrupt,[26] and to repay his creditors his stock was auctioned on 21–22 September, as announced in the following advertisement:

CAPITAL MUSIC STOCK.
To MUSIC-SELLERS, PUBLISHERS, and the PUBLIC.
By Mr GRAHAM,

On the Premises. No. 45, High Holborn, on Thursday the 21st instant, and following day, at eleven o'clock,

ALL the extensive STOCK, consisting of near twelve thousand engraved Music Plates, with the remaining Copies attached to each work, and the valuable Copyrights of Printing and Publishing some of the most popular productions, by Composers of the greatest celebrity, originally purchased at an immense expense, to command a regular and extensive sale; the whole late the property of Mr F. LINLEY, a Bankrupt.

Catalogues may be now had, on the Premises, and of Mr Graham, No. 17, Holborn.

And on the 23d will be sold, a large collection of the most esteemed Music imported and printed by other Houses, in Lots, suitable for the Trade, or private use, together with a variety of grand and square Piano Fortes, capital Finger and Barrel Organs, the curious Aiuton, or ever-

[24] *MESH* p 282–283. The fourth item—Four sonatinas for the pedal harp, by Giacomo Gotifredo Ferrari, Op. 2, copy at BL g.192.a.(10.)—bears Lewis, Houston & Hyde's imprint, so may have been printed just prior to the sale of the business.

[25] For instance, an advertisement in *The Morning Chronicle*, 20 January 1796, p 1, said that concert tickets could be bought at 'Linley's (late Bland) 45, Holborn'.

[26] *The London Gazette*, 31 January 1797, p 114.

> tuned Organ, exhibited by Mr Claggett, a great number of Violins, Violoncellos and other Articles in the Musical line.
>
> Catalogues will be ready for delivery on the 16th instant.
>
> N. B. Approved Bills at three and seven months, will be taken, or a liberal discount allowed on prompt payment.
>
> *** The Premises may now be had upon very low and desirable terms, for the above or any other Business, but in the musical line, the advantages are peculiarly striking, it having been for many years one of the first houses, and the taker may enter at once upon an extensive trade, both at home and abroad.[27]

Unlike the two earlier transitions, this auction dispersed Bland's stock-in-trade to more than one buyer. No copy of the sale catalogue has been found, but from later advertisements, catalogues and printed music it seems that major London music sellers participated, including Robert Birchall, George Goulding and William Hodsoll. Bland himself, who—as noted on page 102 above—appears to have worked closely with Birchall about this time, also seems likely to have attended the auction.

Birchall was the principal purchaser of the Bland/Linley stock of periodical collections and continued four of them: *Bland's Collection of Divine Music*, the *Harpsichord Collection*, the *Ladies' Glees* and the *Periodical Duetts*. Goulding—who became Goulding, Phipps & d'Almaine in 1798—acquired *Le tout Ensemble* and the *Periodical Italian Song*.

William Hodsoll played no part in continuing Bland's collections but took over his premises at 45 Holborn no later than February 1798,[28] presumably acquiring them at the 'very low and desirable terms' mentioned in the auction advertisement. Although Hodsoll has been described as Linley's successor,[29] this refers principally to his doing business at the same address and not to his carrying on Bland's or Linley's publishing programmes.

On 15 July 1806 Bland sold the music plates and copyrights of a Haydn cantata and three works by Samuel Webbe Sr to Birchall for

---

27 *The Morning Chronicle*, 13 September 1797, p 4.

28 Hodsoll appears at that address in an advertisement in *The Morning Chronicle*, 7 February 1798, p 1.

29 For instance, by Charles Humphries and William C[harles] Smith, *Music Publishing in the British Isles*, 2nd ed., Oxford, 1970, p 182 and p 213.

£30.[30] It is not known whether Bland had withheld these items from the sale of his stock to Lewis, Houston & Hyde or had repurchased them at the Linley auction.

5.4 The Influence of Engraving Practice on the Georgian Music Trade

A comparison of Bland's periodical collections and catalogues he devoted to them with those published by the purchasers of these collections shows that, in most cases, the latter collections and catalogues were reprinted from Bland's plates, with only the imprint and sometimes part of the content altered. A large majority of the 'near twelve thousand engraved music plates' offered for sale in Linley's auction probably originated with Bland.

Although some of Bland's catalogues were typeset, those of the six collections considered here predominantly were engraved. Because these collections were intended to grow, their catalogues were designed with expansion in mind, a point well illustrated by his title catalogues for the *Periodical Duetts* and *Le tout Ensemble*. In both cases the numerals 1 to 48 were incised into the plate at the outset, and in earlier printed states the titles are only partly filled in. Non-final states of his thematic catalogues show staves engraved without notes, in anticipation that themes would be added later to these staves.

For such 'expanding' catalogues, engraving was a better option than typesetting because the process permitted easy updating. Updating a letterpress catalogue would have required storing the type that had been set to print it or, if the type had been distributed, resetting the catalogue from scratch.[31]

As is evident from the many catalogues of music sellers that were printed in multiple states from the same plate, engraved plates

---

[30] Bland's receipt for this transaction is in the Newberry Library, Chicago, Case ms fV 209.52. The cantata presumably was Haydn's *Ariana a Naxos*, which was issued by both Bland and Birchall.

[31] Accordingly, catalogues printed from type normally do not contain blank spaces for later addition of items.

could be impressed repeatedly until worn out or damaged. Besides allowing new entries to be added into an existing plate, the engraving process enabled minor changes, such as altering a publisher's imprint, to be made easily and quickly.[32] The heavy reuse of engraved plates by Bland and his successors, exemplified below, shows the qualities of permanency and flexibility that endeared the engraving process to Georgian music publishers.

The portability of plates and the lack of additional materials such as sets of type made them a very saleable commodity. Publishers could store plates without taking up much room and, aside from cleaning their surface after printing, their maintenance was minimal.

5.5 General Remarks on the six Periodical Collections

Bland's instrumental collections contained music for the harpsichord or piano forte, the primary instruments for domestic music-making at the time. The wording 'harpsichord or piano forte' in each of their titles shows that the two instruments were interchangeable then: the piano did not replace the harpsichord until the first decade of the nineteenth century. Bland's tripartite division of keyboard music—collection A has four-hand music, B has keyboard music with required accompaniments,[33] and C has keyboard music without accompaniments—is typical of publishing practice of late eighteenth-century England. The titles of these three collections make clear the centrality of keyboard over other instruments: all three consisted fundamentally of keyboard repertory.

The genres selected for both *Le tout Ensemble* and the *Harpsichord Collection* are worth noting. 'Sonatas' (also called 'lessons') were the most favoured type of keyboard music at the time. This may have led Bland to describe items from his *Periodical Duetts*

---

[32] The reverse face of a plate was flattened at the appropriate place with a hammer. After polishing, the printing surface was ready for re-engraving.

[33] Half of the first forty-eight numbers in *Le tout Ensemble* are keyboard trio sonatas with violin and cello accompaniments; eleven have violin or flute accompaniments; seven have violin accompaniments; and three have accompaniments for flute and cello.

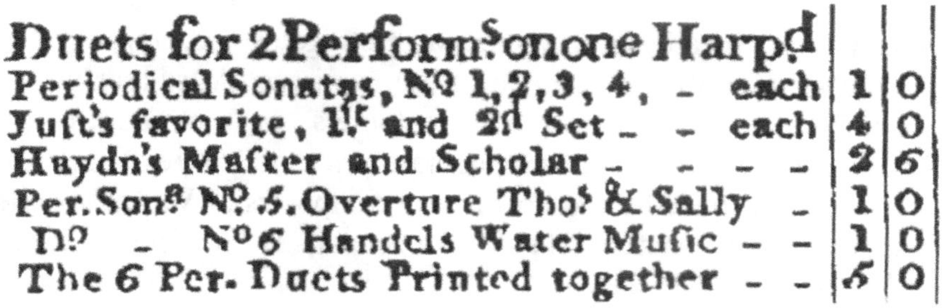

Duets for 2 Perform^s^ on one Harp^d^		
Periodical Sonatas, N° 1, 2, 3, 4, - each	1	0
Just's favorite, 1st and 2^d^ Set - - each	4	0
Haydn's Master and Scholar - - - -	2	6
Per. Son^a^ N° 5. Overture Thos & Sally -	1	0
D^o^ - N° 6 Handels Water Music - -	1	0
The 6 Per. Duets Printed together - -	5	0

Figure 5.1 Extract from John Bland's c1783 *general catalogue (BL h.70.b.(9), by permission of the British Library)*

as 'periodical sonatas' in his various general catalogues (see *Figure 5.1*).[34] That he applied this term, rather incongruously, to four-hand arrangements of Arne's operatic overture *Thomas and Sally* and Handel's *Water Music*, underscores the status of the sonata genre in the late eighteenth century.

Between the *Periodical Duetts* begun *c*1782 and *Le tout Ensemble*, which started in 1789, Bland issued *Bland's Collection of Lessons, Divertimentos, Sonatas, Overtures, Concertos, Duets, &c. with and without Accompaniments, selected from the Works of the first Composers* 'containing at least 50 pages of music per issue at 5s.0d', which was to be continued monthly. The first six numbers were advertised in November 1787.[35] Only six numbers from this collection were listed in his general catalogues, suggesting that he discontinued the collection after issuing the first volume and offering the first six numbers, bound, at £1/11/6. Perhaps he found the challenge of producing a monthly publication of fifty pages too formidable. But its early demise may have come from the lack of public interest in so diverse a collection, or from its rather high price.

---

[34] In his catalogues devoted to this collection, most individual numbers simply appear as 'No. [1] easy'. Arrangements are given the title of the original works, e.g., 'No. 5, Overture to Thomas and Sally', 'No. 6, Handel's Water Music'.

[35] *The Daily Universal Register*, 28 November 1787, p 1, where the work is described as 'Bland's Harpsichord Collection, No. 1 to 6, each 5s'.

On his next attempt—*Le tout Ensemble*—Bland launched a collection specifically for keyboard with obligatory accompaniments at a much more affordable price of 2/6 per issue. After receiving a favourable response from his customers he introduced the *Harpsichord Collection* at the moderate price of 1/6 per issue. For these two collections he chose works by composers of Viennese-style chamber music, namely Haydn, Koželuch, Hoffmeister, Pleyel, Sterkel, Vanhal and Lentz.

The three vocal music collections are more diverse in nature. Italian vocal music was almost ubiquitous in Georgian music publishers' catalogues. The strong preference—principally by the cultured upper class—for Italian vocal music and acceptance of Italian texts in this period is demonstrated by the early appearance of catalogues solely devoted to this. Glees and catches were genres indigenous to England and, unsurprisingly, the *Ladies' Glees* collection is dominated by English composers. The music in *Bland's Collection of Divine Music*—anthems and hymns for liturgical use—also was mostly written by English composers.

5.6 THE *PERIODICAL DUETTS*

A1 (Bland) ⇨(LHH) ⇨A2 (Linley) ⇨A3 (Birchall)

Collection A—the *Periodical Duetts*—was the property of four successive music sellers. As no music or catalogue of this collection has been found with a Lewis, Houston & Hyde (LHH) imprint (although they presumably sold copies of the duets from stock they had acquired from Bland), the ownership of this collection can be documented in three stages:

Stage A1. Bland began to list the *Periodical Duetts* in the third state of his first general catalogue printed *c*1782, in which the first six numbers were entered.[36] *Figure 5.1* on page 209 reproduces an extract from the ninth state of that catalogue *c*1783, which shows that these duets could be bought both singly and together. Bland's first title catalogue of this collection (BlJ 5a in *Table 5.1* above) was the

[36] A copy of this catalogue is in BL g.443.(1).

first issued for any of his periodical collections and also his first catalogue devoted to a single medium (keyboard duets). Its appearance indicates the demand for such music in the late eighteenth century, notably from genteel young ladies who were rapidly taking up the favoured domestic instrument.

About 1793, Bland issued a thematic catalogue (BlJ 17a) of both this collection and *Le tout Ensemble*. This coincided with the introduction by major English manufacturers—notably Broadwood and Longman & Broderip—of pianos with 'additional keys', which encouraged composers to exploit the new five-and-a-half octave compass of this instrument.[37] Even though thematic catalogues cost more to produce and required more space than text-only title catalogues, Bland clearly was willing to invest the extra amount to obtain the advantage of this attention-grabbing format. It may be significant that he stopped updating his title catalogue at the twenty-second number of this collection and listed the next three numbers in a thematic catalogue only. When he updated the thematic catalogue of *Le tout Ensemble* about the middle of 1794 (BlJ 17b), he added incipits for these three numbers of the *Periodical Duetts.*

Stage A2. Francis Linley resurrected the series, reissuing Bland's title catalogue (BlJ 5c) without troubling to enter the last three numbers of the series (23 to 25) that Bland had added to his thematic catalogue. Linley's handling of this collection and its title catalogue was inconsequential: he merely altered its title and replaced Bland's imprint.[38] The 'Continued' in Linley's amended title never went beyond reprinting the music plates he had inherited from Bland, presumably via Lewis, Houston & Hyde. Linley kept Bland's pricing; offering the collection in sets of six numbers at 5/– and each single number at 1/–.

Stage A3. Robert Birchall reprinted Bland's title catalogue *c*1798, using the plate acquired from Linley, and expanded the collection immediately to twenty-seven numbers and more slowly to

[37] See David Rowland, 'Piano music and keyboard compass in the 1790s', *Early Music* v 27 no. 2 (May 1999) p 283–293.

[38] It is conceivable that Linley did not acquire the plate of the thematic catalogue of this collection (BlJ 17). As only no. 6 and no. 8 of this collection have been located with Linley's imprint, it seems unlikely that he had the time or the need to reprint the whole collection.

thirty-one. The engraver who replaced Linley's imprint with Birchall's left the three-line advertisement following the imprint unchanged. The reference to *Le tout Ensemble*—which had been bought by Goulding—therefore remained; the convenient reuse of the catalogue plate producing a small bibliographical mishap. However, 'Price One Shilling' was removed from the first line of the plate because Birchall raised the price of a number of items by six pence,[39] and no longer offered the collection in sets at a reduced price.[40] Both Bland and Linley had sold the first set of six numbers at 5/–; Birchall's price was 6/– and the second set was raised to 7/6, a 50% increase in the price. It is curious that the prices of only some items were adjusted, as their choice appears to be random. If Birchall had to re-engrave these items because of plate wear, he might have raised their prices to recover those costs. Alternatively, the increases might indicate such continued popularity of the *Periodical Duetts* that reprints of 'old' music published in the 1780s could be marketed at higher prices.

Birchall had published keyboard duets before issuing the *Periodical Duetts*, but not as a collection. While continually reusing Bland's title catalogue, he also included the *Periodical Duetts* in other catalogues. In 1806 he published the first edition of John Wall Callcott's *A Musical Grammar*, and second and third editions of this commercially successful typeset instruction book followed in 1809 and 1817.[41] Each of these editions was printed by Buchanan Macmillan and contained a catalogue of Birchall's publications. The catalogues in the second and third editions listed, in the category of piano forte duets, 'Bland's Periodical Collection, No. 1 to 31, each 1/0',[42] although curiously this is absent from the catalogue in the first edition. Birchall's promotion of the *Periodical Duetts* as late as 1817

---

[39] For numbers 1, 9, 10, 11, 18 and 25. Birchall also increased the price of each number in the *Harpsichord Collection* from 1/6 to 2/–.

[40] Indicated by removal of the phrase that had stood at the foot of the catalogue: 'NB. The Above may be had in Setts of Six, at five Shillg^{s} each'.

[41] According to Callcott's agreement with Birchall (in Newberry Library, Chicago, Case ms fV 209.52), the first edition had a press run of 1500 copies.

[42] Apparently forgetting to note that the price of some duets had been raised to 1/6.

confirms the sustained popularity of the collection, even though he stopped expanding it after no. 31 in 1801.

About 1807 Birchall issued a three-column catalogue of four-hand duets.[43] The *Periodical Duetts*, including his own six additions to the collection, are listed in the right column, but the left and central columns record other duets he had published.

5.7 *Le tout Ensemble*

B1 (Bland) ⇨(LHH) ⇨B2 (Linley) ⇨B3 (Goulding)

As with the *Periodical Duetts*, no Lewis, Houston & Hyde imprints or stickers have been found on music or catalogues of this collection.

Stage B1. Bland listed the first six numbers of *Le tout Ensemble* in his title catalogue dated January 1789 which he issued after returning from four months on the continent. The main purpose of his tour was to establish personal connections with publishers and composers in order to acquire music previously unavailable in England and to outdo his rival, Longman & Broderip, in supplying the English market with fashionable Viennese chamber music by esteemed composers of the time.44 After establishing a business connection with the Viennese music publisher Franz Anton Hoffmeister, Bland launched a periodical collection of Viennese chamber music that was modelled in some respects upon Hoffmeister's 'Praenumeration' series.

As indicated by that word, Hoffmeister published his series by subscription, a widespread practice that reduced the risk of publishing by ensuring that income pledged by subscribers would cover engraving, printing and other costs. Persons were encouraged to subscribe by the offer of a discount upon publication, and the number of copies subscribed (if sufficient for publication to proceed) was a major determinant of the print run. Bland was well aware of this

---

[43] Copy in BL h.275.(15).

[44] See Ian Woodfield, 'John Bland: London retailer of the music of Haydn and Mozart', *Music and Letters* v 81 no. 2 (May 200) p 210–244 at p 212.

system, having received subscriptions at his shop for works that their composers planned to publish.[45]

However, he did not adopt this method for *Le tout Ensemble*. Knowing that chamber music by Haydn, Koželuch, Pleyel, Sterkel and other 'Viennese' composers was in vogue in England, and having Hoffmeister as his supplier and direct access to the London music buying public, Bland was confident that his new collection would be commercially successful and chose to market it as a non-subscription series.

He devoted one title catalogue to the collection (BlJ 6), which was engraved as part of the series title-page included with each number;[46] and he published two thematic catalogues that advertised *Le tout Ensemble* next to another periodical collection. In BlJ 15 it was paired with the *Harpsichord Collection*; in BlJ 17, with the *Periodical Duetts*. In the first two states of BlJ 15, *Le tout Ensemble* was allocated only one of the four columns. In the newly engraved penultimate state of BlJ 15 it was sacrificed entirely for additional numbers of the *Harpsichord Collection*. In all three states of BlJ 17, forty single-staff incipits very closely printed were packed into the two columns allocated to *Le tout Ensemble*. Both thematic catalogues were printed in various issues of his three keyboard periodical collections and also in some of his non-periodical publications. That *Le tout Ensemble* was promoted so variously shows his vigour in marketing the collection.

Thirty-eight numbers of the collection were published with Bland's imprint over six years. For the last two numbers, presumably issued shortly before he sold his business, Bland reused the series title-page BlJ 6f (whose catalogue stops at no. 36) without endeavouring to update it.

Stages B2 and B3. Linley and Goulding both reprinted Bland's title catalogue BlJ 6f with additional entries. About 1798 Goulding had a new thematic catalogue engraved, *Index to Le tout Ensemble*,

---

[45] See the advertisements to receive subscriptions for Samuel Webbe Sr's 'Eighth book of glees' (in *The World, Fashionable Advertiser*, 21 November 1787, p 4) and John Danby's 'Second book of catches, canons and glees' (in *Stuart's Star and Evening Advertiser*, 28 February 1789, p 1).

[46] This title-page has the printed text 'N^{o}:' after which the composition's number in the series was written in ink.

which comfortably accommodated the eight titles added after the last state of BlJ 17. More importantly, the *Harpsichord Collection* and *Periodical Duetts*—with which *Le tout Ensemble* had always appeared in Bland's catalogues—now were Birchall's property.[47] Bland's catalogue plates that mentioned the *Periodical Duetts* were of no use to Goulding.

The first state of Goulding's new thematic catalogue contained incipits of forty-five works followed by fifteen empty staves. The titles and the prices of the first thirty-seven numbers are the same as in BlJ 17c, and the pagination of these numbers, given at the right of each staff, matches Bland's. However, the new plate is readily distinguished by its engraving style, misspellings of the names of Haydn and Pleyel,[48] and a difference in the theme of no. 3 (a quartet by Pleyel). Bland's catalogue mistakenly presented the theme as:

Goulding's catalogue corrected this incipit to:

It is clear that Goulding's engraver worked from a print of BlJ 17, as he copied the advertisement at the bottom of that catalogue and its position on the plate, revising only the music seller's name. However, this advertisement then was about four years out of date and three of its titles—the *Harpsichord Collection*, the *Divine Music*, and the *Ladies' Glees*—were not Goulding's property. As this is the only mention of those three collections in his catalogues it is remarkable that the mistake went undetected when the plate was

[47] Goulding's purchase of *Le tout Ensemble* probably did not include the plates of catalogues BlJ 15 and BlJ 17. Birchall never reissued BlJ 17c, as Goulding now owned *Le tout Ensemble.*

[48] Both catalogues misspell Hoffmeister's name as 'Hoffmiester'.

updated some time before 1800. The second state of Goulding's thematic catalogue, in which three themes were added, is reproduced in *Figure 5.2*.

Goulding seems not to have extended Bland's *Le tout Ensemble* beyond no. 51. Both the 1800 and 1808 cumulative catalogues of Goulding, Phipps & d'Almaine[49] list fifty-one numbers. They subsequently abandoned *Le tout Ensemble* to concentrate on lightweight genres such as airs with variations, rondos on popular tunes, and potpourris, all appealing to the mass market of amateur domestic performers.

However, about a decade later, they resumed the collection as *Le tout Ensemble (New Series)*. The first two numbers of this are listed in Goulding, d'Almaine, Potter & Co.'s cumulative catalogue issued *c*1822.[50] Extant copies suggest that this partnership brought out at least twelve numbers, but the series was never graced with its own catalogue. The collection was 'new' in the sense that the considerable time lapse disconnected it from its predecessor. But most significantly it was 'new' in the nature of its contents, which included works of the rising generation of composers such as Ferdinand Ries, Ignaz Moscheles and Victor Dourlen. Their compositions were no longer 'accompanied' but for piano forte alone. Perhaps in an act of homage, the publishers kept the French title *Le tout Ensemble* but married it with 'for the piano forte, consisting of favorite selections from the works of various composers'.

5.8 THE *HARPSICHORD COLLECTION*

C1 (Bland) ⇨C2 (LHH) ⇨C3 (Linley) ⇨C4 (Birchall)

Stage C1. The 'advertisement' that Bland placed on his series title-pages of the *Harpsichord Collection* offers insight into his approach to the market:

---

[49] Copies in BL 1570/3579 and Bodleian Johnson d.1704(13) respectively.

[50] Copy at BL Hirsch IV.1106. 'Goulding' then was George Goulding's widow and successor Sarah Dennis Goulding.

Figure 5.2 George Goulding's thematic catalogue of Le tout Ensemble *(Bodleian Tyson Mus. 750, by permission of the Bodleian Library)*

> Advertisement. The very flattering success of my Periodical Works with Accompani^{nts}, "Le tout Ensemble" par les plus Grand Maitres & the Duetts for two Performers on One Harpsichord, has induced me to undertake this, which shall consist of 10 Pages of the most Esteemed Compositions selected from works already Published in Books of a High Price or from M.S. by Haydn, Kozeluch, Hoffmeister, Mozart, Vanhall, &c. &c. having personally settled a Connection with those Composers; the whole to be well & correctly Engrav'd & Printed on the best Paper.[51]

When saying that the contents were 'already published in books of a high price', Bland probably was referring to Hoffmeister's 'Praenumeration' series, and perhaps also to music that Bland had published earlier, but this was never clarified. He shrewdly noted that 'the publisher will be at all times thankful of information of any new or good work which may have escaped his notice', effectively professing that he would comply with and publish to customer demand.

The title of the *Harpsichord Collection* said that its music was 'for keyboard without accompaniments'. However, Bland stated in his thematic catalogue BlJ 15 that these works 'have accompaniments ad libitum and may be had as above.'[52] Although this seems to cater for both possibilities and to broaden the market as much as possible, the collection may reflect Bland's desire to appeal to keyboard performers who occasionally played together with other musicians. BlJ 15c—the third state, issued in early 1793, of catalogue BlJ 15—is reproduced in *Figure 5.3*.

Stage C2. Direct evidence of Lewis, Houston & Hyde's involvement is found in a copy of one number of this collection which bears their imprint.[53]

---

[51] Copies at Bodleian Tyson Mus. 551, and BL Hirsch M. 1408. Unlike collections A. and B., the catalogue for collection C. was not used as a series title-page.

[52] For instance, Nicolai's sonatas from op. 3 which appear in Nos. 5, 8, 13, 34, 35, 36 (1st, 5th, 2nd, 4th, 3rd and 6th Sonatas) in Bland's Harpsichord Collection, also listed as 'with Violin Accompaniment' in Bland's general catalogues under the category 'Sonatas with Accompaniments'.

[53] CUL MRA.340.75.78 is a reprint of Bland's no. 48 from this collection in which the imprint has been changed to Lewis, Houston & Hyde.

Figure 5.3 John Bland's catalogue of the Harpsichord Collection *(BL g.12, by permission of the British Library)*

Stage C3. Linley reprinted the last state of Bland's catalogue of this collection (BlJ 15d) from the same plate, changing only the imprint and the title (from 'INDEX to 48 N^os^. of BLAND's Harpsichord Collection' to 'INDEX to *Bland's (continued by F. Linley)* Harpsichord Collection').

Stage C4. Birchall again reprinted the same catalogue. Beyond modifying the imprint and the title to 'INDEX to *Bland's (continued by Rt. Birchall)* Harpsichord Collection', he made several minor changes, increasing the price of each number from '1s.6d.' to '2s.0d.' and bound volumes from '18s.' to '£1.4s (24s)'. He removed the frequency-of-issue detail but provided no substitute and curiously left unaltered at the bottom of the catalogue Bland's three-line, outdated notice advertising only twenty-four numbers of *Periodical Duetts*, and forty-eight numbers of *Ladies' Glees*. Although Birchall had augmented the collection before reprinting this catalogue, he reused a plate that listed the first forty-eight numbers and had no room for additions.

After the collection reached sixty numbers, offered in five volumes, Birchall included it in his fifth general title catalogue that was issued in twelve states between *c*1798 and *c*1803.[54] His promotion of the *Harpsichord Collection* was less vigorous than Bland's, who, from the outset, promoted the collection in thematic catalogues. Even in title catalogues that mentioned the collection, Bland always detailed individual items, usually two to four from each number. Such details were absent from Birchall's catalogues, the collection merely appearing as 'Bland 1st. vol. [or 2d, 3d, 4th and 5th] bound containing 120 pages published from MSS or Selected from the most Favorite Authors 24s.0d.'

Birchall's reuse of Bland's series title-page for the collection may have deluded unwary buyers. Although Birchall inserted '(continued by Rt. Birchall)' in the space between the second (*Bland's Collection*) and the third lines (*SONATAS, LESSONS, OVERTURES*) of the title, he left Bland's advertisement quoted above 'The very flattering success of my Periodical Works…' intact, thereby directing, intentionally or otherwise, the 'my' to himself. Moreover, the list of publications at the foot of Bland's title-page, although partially

---

54 A copy of the first state of this catalogue is in BL h.3200.(8).

modified to accommodate Birchall's new publications and his prices for Bland's collections, still contained *Le tout Ensemble* and the *Periodical Italian Songs*, of which Goulding was the proprietor.

5.9 THE *PERIODICAL ITALIAN SONGS*

D1 (Bland) ⇨D2 (LHH) ⇨(Linley) ⇨D3 (Goulding)

Bland's *Periodical Italian Song* collection, begun about 1781, did not corner the field. His rival, Longman & Broderip, started their own collection of *Periodical Italian Songs, Duets, &c. c*1786 and issued a title catalogue of it in 1794.[55] In the meantime, Bland's collection was reprinted and continued by Lewis, Houston & Hyde and Goulding. The latter's effort competed directly with Theobald Monzani's *c*1799–1802 *A Collection of Periodical Italian Songs, Duets, Trios, &c.* and with Lewis Lavenu's *A Collection of Periodical Italian Songs, Duetts, &c.* published *c*1800. No prints or catalogues of this collection have been found with Linley's imprint.

Stage D1. As usual, Bland's title catalogue for this collection was presented in an engraved title-page for the series. Its earliest known state (BlJ 12a, issued mid-1789) lists forty numbers. Before then he advertised the progress of this collection in his general title catalogues. BlJ 12a was updated three times, its last state (BlJ 12d, shown in *Figure 5.4* on page 222) listing all sixty numbers. As can be seen, Bland included in this catalogue a small but slowly expanding number of songs not part of the collection, labelling them 'Miscellaneous'. In mid-1791 he issued a thematic catalogue of this collection (BlJ 13). This apparently was the first thematic catalogue he produced, and reinforces the immense popularity of Italian vocal music at this time.

Stages D2 and D3. Lewis, Houston & Hyde reprinted Bland's title catalogue BlJ 12d and his thematic catalogue BlJ 13c, adding to

---

[55] *A Collection of Periodical Italian Songs, Duets, &c.* A copy of this catalogue is at BL G.811.(2.) in no. 79 of that collection: '*Moriamo mia Vita*, a favorite song, sung by Madame [Brigitta] Banti in the opera of *Zenobia in Palmira*, composed by [Pasquale] Anfossi'.

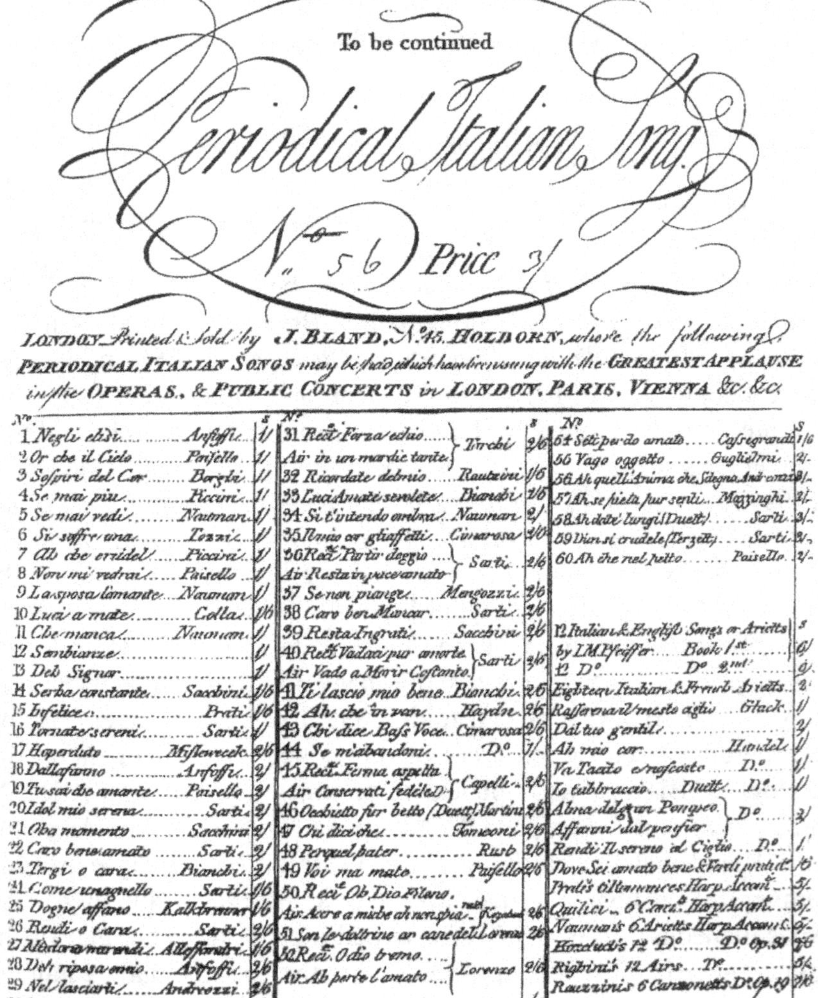

To be continued

Periodical Italian Songs

No. 56 Price 3/

LONDON Printed & Sold by J. BLAND, No. 45, HOLBORN, where the following PERIODICAL ITALIAN SONGS may be had which have been sung with the GREATEST APPLAUSE in the OPERAS, & PUBLIC CONCERTS in LONDON, PARIS, VIENNA &c. &c.

No.			s
1	Negli elisi	Anfossi	1/
2	Or che il Cielo	Paisello	1/
3	Sospiri del Cor	Borghi	1/
4	Se mai piu	Piccini	1/
5	Se mai vedi	Nauman	1/
6	Si soffre una	Tozzi	1/
7	Ah che crudel	Piccini	1/
8	Non mi vedrai	Paisello	1/
9	La sposa l'amante	Nauman	1/
10	Luci amate	Colla	1/6
11	Che manca	Nauman	1/
12	Sembianze		1/
13	Deh Signor		1/
14	Serba costante	Sacchini	1/6
15	Infelice	Prati	1/6
16	Tornate sereni	Sarti	1/
17	Ho perduto	Misliwecek	2/6
18	Dalla sfiorno	Anfossi	2/
19	Tu sai che amante	Paisello	2/
20	Idol mio serena	Sarti	2/
21	Oh a momento	Sacchini	2/
22	Caro bene amato	Sarti	2/
23	Tergi o cara	Bianchi	2/
24	Come un agnello	Sarti	1/6
25	D'ogni affano	Kalkbrenner	1/6
26	Rendi o Cara	Sarti	2/6
27	Alessandro ma rendi	Allessandri	1/6
28	Deh riposa o mio	Anfossi	2/6
29	Nel lasciarti	Andreozzi	2/6
30	Partiro dal caro	Cimarosa	2/6

No.			s
31	Recit. Forza e duo / Air in un mar che tante	Tirchi	2/6
32	Ricordate del mio	Rauzzini	1/6
33	Luci Amate se volete	Bianchi	1/6
34	Si t'intendo ombra	Nauman	2/
35	Il mio cor gli affetti	Cimarosa	2/0
36	Recit. Partir deggio / Air Resta in pace amato	Sarti	2/6
37	Se non piange	Mengozzi	2/6
38	Caro ben Morcar	Sarti	2/6
39	Resta Ingrato	Sacchini	2/6
40	Recit. Vado pur a morte / Air Vado a Morir Costante	Sarti	3/6
41	Ti lascio mio bene	Bianchi	2/6
42	Ah che in van	Haydn	2/6
43	Chi dice Bass Voce	Cimarosa	2/6
44	Se m'abandoni	Do.	1/
45	Recit. Ferma aspetta / Air Conservati fedele Do.	Capelli	2/6
46	Occhietto fur bello (Duett)	Martini	2/6
47	Chi dice che	Tomeoni	2/6
48	Perque l pater	Rush	2/6
49	Voi ma mato	Paisello	2/6
50	Recit. Oh Dio Filano / Air Accre a mirbe ah non spia	Kegnoton	2/6
51	Son le dottrine ar care del Lamma		2/6
52	Recit. O dio tremo / Air Ah parte l'amato	Lorenzo	2/6
53	Deh lascia mi in pace	Vito	1/6

No.			s
54	Seti perdo amato	Cassegrandi	1/6
56	Vago oggetto	Guglielmi	2/-
56	Ah quell'Anima che Sdegna	Andreozzi	3/-
57	Ah se pieta pur senti	Mazzinghi	2/-
58	Ah dite lungi (Duett)	Sarti	3/-
59	Dio si crudele (Terzett)	Sarti	2/-
60	Ah che nel petto	Paisello	2/-
	12 Italian & English Songs or Arietts by I. M. Pfeiffer Book 1st		6/
	12 Do. Do. 2nd		6/
	Eighteen Italian & French Arietts		2/
	Rasserena il mesto ciglio	Gluck	1/
	Dal tuo gentil		2/
	Ah mio cor	Handel	1/
	Va Tacito e nascosto	Do.	1/
	Io t'abbraccio Duett	Do.	1/
	Alma del gran Pompeo / Affanni del pensier	Do.	3/
	Rendi il sereno al Ciglio	Do.	1/
	Dove Sei amato bene & Verdi prati &c.		1/6
	Prati's 6 Romances Harp Accomt.		5/
	Quilici 6 Canzs. Harp Accomt.		5/
	Nauman's 6 Arietts Harp Accomt. &c.		6/
	Hoeducci's 12 Do. Do. Op. 31		7/6
	Righini's 12 Airs Do.		5/
	Rauzzini's 6 Canzonetts Do. Op. 19		7/6

Figure 5.4 John Bland's catalogue issued in late 1794 or early 1795 of Periodical Italian Songs *(BL G.811.n.(10), by permission of the British Library)*

the latter the themes of no. 54 to no. 60. These songs were not additions to the collection, as they had appeared in Bland's title catalogue BlJ 12d. Lewis, Houston & Hyde's engraver showed ingenuity in accommodating new information within the title catalogue's limited space, curtailing 'Printed & Sold' to 'Printed by' so that 'J. Bland' could be replaced by the new firm's longer name. Similar manoeuvrings were made on the plate of the thematic catalogue. Goulding similarly reprinted Bland's title catalogue *c*1798, using the same plate. When the collection grew beyond eighty-two numbers, which filled that plate, a second plate was engraved to accommodate the additions.

In the general catalogues issued in 1800 and subsequently Goulding, Phipps & d'Almaine adopted a more user-friendly layout, ordering this collection alphabetically by title. Thus 'Negli elisi' by Anfossi—the first entry in the earlier title catalogues (BlJ 12 and its reprints by Lewis, Houston & Hyde and Goulding)—became no. 44 of the 102 items of this collection listed in the 1800 catalogue. When the collection expanded to 153 numbers in Goulding, Phipps, d'Almaine & Co.'s catalogue of 1808, this song became no. 75.

5.10 THE *LADIES' GLEES*

E1 (Bland) ⇨E2 (LHH) ⇨E3 (Linley) ⇨E4 (Birchall)

Stage E1. Although the *Ladies' Glees* collection constitutes a large portion of Bland's title catalogue BlJ 3, its first four states included gentlemen's glees as well as collections of glees by Samuel Webbe Sr and John Danby. From BlJ 3e, issued mid-1789 and shown in *Figure 5.5*, this catalogue promoted only the *Ladies' Glees*, although neither BlJ 3e nor BlJ 3f makes this apparent. This move may show the commercial acumen of a publisher alert to the changing social context of glees around the turn of the nineteenth century, when they began to move out of their original settings in gentlemen's clubs or 'societies' (which met regularly in taverns, where catches and glees were typically sung by an all-male company) and to infiltrate domestic music-making in which women participated.

INDEX to BLAND'S 2 Vol.s of CATCHES, GLEES, CANONS, CANZONETS, MADRIGALS &c.
and which are also Printed & Sold in No.s at 1/6 each, by him at his Music Warehouse No. 45. Holborn London
N.B. Gl means Glee. Ch Catches. M Madrigals. Cn Canons. Ct Canzonett. D Duetts. R Rounds. E Elegy. V.1 or 2. Vol.s 1st or 2d

		No.	Page
A			
All in the Downs V.1.	Gl	5	48
A generous friendſhip	Gl	6	53
All into ſervice	Ch	6	55
Amen amen	Cn	7	68
+Adieu to the Village	Gl	8	72
A blooming Youth	Ch	10	92
Adieu ye verdant	D	10	99
Adieu my Love	D	11	111
+As I ſaw fair Clora	D	12	120
+Amo amas V.2.	Gl	16	152
+Awake Æolian Lyre	Gl	18	172
Awake my fair	Gl	18	174
Antient Phillis	Ch	18	176
+And muſt we part	D	22	220
B			
Bow down thine ear	Cn	1	6
Buz quoth the blue fly	Ch	4	33
+Bevi amo tutti tre	Gl	5	42
+By Greenwood Tree	Gl	11	104
By Pipe and Pot	Ch	11	110
Briſk Wine & lovely V.2.	D	21	205
+Britons ſtrike home	D	21	209
C			
+Care thou canker V.1.	Ch	1	5
Come my Heroes	Gl	1	9
Come hither Boy	Ch	3	22
Comincio Solo	Ch	3	28
Che mai diminique	Ch	3	28
Colla bottiglia	G	3	28
Come come pull away	Ch	4	36
+Come come all noble	Gl	4	38
Come honeſt friends	Ch	4	39
Come hither Tom	Ch	4	39
Curſt be the Wretch	Ch	5	45
Come lets all a maying	Ch	7	66
+Come Shepherds well	Gl	9	82
Chairs to mend	Ch	9	84
Compana che ſuona	Gl	10	96
+Come live with me	Gl	11	102
+Canſt thou love V.2.	Ct	14	136
+Cupid no more	Gl	18	180
Cuckoo good neighbours	Ch	18	181
+Che dolce Liquore	Gl	20	200
+Cupid my pleaſure	Gl	21	201
+Come fill the board	Gl	22	212
+Come ye party	Gl	23	222
D			
+Down in a Valley V.1.	M	1	2
Do re mi fa	Ch	4	33
Divine Cecelia	Ch	9	85
Doubtleſs the pleaſure	Ch	10	98
+Drink to me only	Ch	12	119
+Damon and Clora	D	12	121
Did Celia's perſon V.2.	Ch	18	176
Diſſi al'amatamia	Ct	22	216
Dove ſon dove vado	M	23	228
F			
Fill fill a briming V.1.	Ch	2	23
Faireſt Iſle	Gl	3	24
Fye nay prithee John	Ch	5	46
+From the fair Lavinian	Gl	7	65
+Fear no danger	Gl	7	69
Flora wilt thou tormen	Ct	8	77
From tyrant Laws	D	9	86
Faireſt flower	Gl	11	106
+Fair Flora decks V.2.	Gl	14	139
Fourteen Cows	Ch	18	177
+Fill all the Glaſſes	Gl	18	177

		No.	Page
Follow follow me	Ch	19	183
Fill me a bowl	D	24	235
G			
Go gentle Breezes V.1.	Ch	2	18
+Gently touch the warbling	G	2	19
Go ye my Canzonetts	C	5	51
Go Damon go Amarillis	Ch	7	68
Gather your Roſe buds	Gl	7	70
Gently hear me	Gl	10	97
+Go Damon go Amarillis	Gl	12	113
Gently hear me V.2.	Gl	16	154
+Great God of Sleep	Gl	24	239
H			
Help us O God V.1.	Cn	1	6
How happy are we now	Ch	1	8
Haſte ye ſoft gales	Ch	1	9
+How merrily we live	Gl	1	10
+How great is the pleaſure	Ch	2	18
+Huſh to peace	Gl	2	20
Have you any work	Ch	3	22
Hark the bonny	Ch	3	23
How ſoft the delights	Ch	5	50
Here lieth Sr John Guiſe	E	6	55
Here lies old Bridges	E	6	55
+Hail ſocial pleaſure	Gl	7	62
Hail flow'ry Meads	Ch	7	68
Hark hark how the woods	Ch	7	70
Hail ever pleaſing	Gl	8	80
Hated by fools	Ch	9	84
Hail green fields	Ch	10	92
Here Innocence & Beauty	E	10	93
Happy the Youth	Ch	11	110
+Here in cooll grot	Gl	11	104
+Hark the hollow woods V.2.	Gl	13	124
How imperfect	D	17	170
How ſleep the brave	E	19	182
Here's a Bowl will drown	Ch	19	183
Help me each harmonis	Gl	19	191
How ſhall we ſpeak	R	23	227
I & J			
I like a Bee V.1.	Ch	3	25
Joan ſaid to John	Ch	4	36
If you truſt before you	R	6	54
I ſaw fair Cloris	Gl	7	67
I charge you O ye	R	7	70
Jack and Gill	Ch	8	77
In drinking full Bumpers	Ch	9	84
Inſpire us genius of the	Gl	9	90
If my miſtreſs fix her	Gl	10	93
If neither braſs nor marble	Ch	11	108
+In thee each joy V.2.	D	14	134
+If love and all the World	Gl	16	156
+I my dear was born	Ct	16	159
+If 'tis joy to wound	Gl	17	168
I know that my Redeemer	Cn	19	190
+If muſic can charm	Gl	20	197
+I ſwore I lov'd	Gl	20	198
L			
Let us be merry V.1.	Ch	3	23
Life's a jeſt	Ch	4	33
Let's live good honeſt	Ch	5	50
Let's drink & be	Ch	6	54
Let Ceſar & Urania	D	6	56
Lightly tread	Gl	7	66
Leave now mine eyes	Ct	8	76
Let's drink & let's ſing	Cn	9	86
Let Ambition fire	Gl	9	89
Love's a gentle gen'rous	D	9	90
Long live King George	Ch	10	92

		No.	Page
L'avare eſt toujours	Ch	11	109
Look Neighbours look	Ch	12	119
+Let the ſage Hermit V.2.	Gl	24	[illegible]
M			
+Melting Airs V.1.	Gl	2	17
Mercy and truth	Ch	5	48
Mr. Speaker	Ch	6	54
Make haſte O God	Cn	6	55
Mortals learn your	Ch	11	108
My Dame has in her hut	Ch	11	109
May the God of Wit		12	112
N			
Now God be with old	Ch	1	7
Now kiſs the Cup	Ch	2	18
+Non nobis Domine	Cn	4	32
Now we are met	Ch	4	34
+Now is the Month of	Gl	4	40
Ne'er trouble thyſelf	Gl	5	43
Now we are met lets	Gl	5	46
No more ye warbling	D	8	73
Now that the Spring	Ch	10	95
Nayons dans ce bon	Ch	11	108
No longer Orpheus	Ch	11	110
Now we are met V.2.	Gl	17	167
O			
+O beauteous eyes V.1.	Ch	2	19
O my Clariſſa	Gl	3	26
O Abſalom my Son	R	4	38
On thy ſweet lips	Ch	6	52
+Oh. how fleeting	D	7	71
O Nymph divine	Gl	9	85
On the poor confin'd	Ch	10	98
Our God is great	Cn	12	119
+O thou wert born V.2.	D	14	132
+Oh come o bella	Gl	15	142
Of all the brave Birds	Gl	17	166
O be joyful	Cn	19	190
P			
Poor Johnny's dead V.1.	Ch	1	5
Pour prix du ſang	Ch	1	7
Perche vezzoſi rai	Ch	2	18
Phillis my faireſt	Ch	3	31
Plenty Mirth	D	5	49
Prepare your hearts	Ch	7	67
Pale faces ſtand by	Ch	9	84
Peace thou white rob'd	Gl	9	86
Prithee fooliſh Boy	Ch	11	109
Praiſe the Lord	Cn	12	119
Poco ne ſan V.2.	Ch	20	199
R			
+Return my lovely V.2.	Gl	15	149
Remember in your ways	Ch	20	192
S			
Su cantiamo V.1.	Ch	1	6
+Soft Cupid	Gl	2	14
Senza dite	Ch	3	27
Sweet Enſlaver	Ch	3	27
Still ſtill in our ears	Ch	4	32
Sweet Nymph	Ct	4	33
+Sweet are the banks	Gl	4	35
Sweet Tyranneſs	Gl	5	47
So che vanti	Ch	6	55
+Says Pontius in rage	Ct	8	74
So peaceful reſts	Ch	10	98
Sum up all the delights	Ch	11	108
Stay Daphne ſtay V.2.	Ch	15	143
Sir youre a comical	Ch	16	153

		No.	Page
Since firſt I ſaw your	Gl	17	[illegible]
+Sigh no more Ladies	Gl	19	[illegible]
T			
'Tis Amarillis walking	Ch	1	7
The Silver Swan	Ch	1	8
+The Nightingale	Gl	2	12
+Turn Amarillis to thy	Gl	3	30
This Tomb be thine	R	4	34
To heal the wound	Gl	4	37
'Tis thus & thus farewell		5	46
The Silver Swan	Gl	4	4
Turn Amarillis	Ch	7	63
Tu ſei pazzo	Ch	8	75
The Morning is charmg	Gl	9	87
Thou'rt gone away	Gl	10	94
The very Bees	Ch	10	95
+Turn Amarillis 4 Voc	Gl	10	100
To our Muſical Club	Ch	10	97
+The glories of our	Gl	12	116
+Turn fair Clora	D	12	121
+To Love & Wine V.2.	Gl	13	126
+The Dying Chriſtian	Gl	13	129
+The Curfew tolls	E		130
+Tell me thou dear	Gl	15	140
+The mighty Conqueror	Gl	17	169
Te Deum Laudamus	Ch	18	176
Thus to the Muſes	Ct	19	187
+To Arms	D	21	206
+To Bacchus	Gl	21	[illegible]
+Take Oh take thoſe Lips	R	22	[illegible]
U & V			
Uxor mea V.1.	Ch	4	34
Up and down	Ch	4	34
+Viva tutti le vezzoſe	Gl	8	75
W			
When here Lucinda V.2.	Gl	1	5
Where the Bee ſucks	Gl	1	8
When Chloe's kind	Ch	1	9
+Winde gentle evergreen	Ch	2	18
We be Soldiers three	Gl	4	38
+Which is the propereſt	Gl	5	44
Wilt thou lend me	Ch	5	48
Would you ſing	Ch	6	52
White Sand grey Sand	Ch	6	55
+Welcome ſweet pleaſure	M	6	58
+We be 3 poor Mariners	Gl	6	59
+When all alone	M	6	60
Will you hear how	Gl	7	64
Will Cloris caſt her	Gl	7	67
When Troy Town	Ch	7	69
What ſhall he have	Ch	7	70
Where weeping Ews	E	8	79
Where is pity's melting	D	11	107
When for the Worlds	Gl	10	93
Would you know	Ch	11	109
+When Sappho tun'd V.2.	Gl	13	122
+What is this abſorbs	Gl	13	129
+Who was it that ſat	Ch	15	144
+When Phoebus the tops	D	17	171
+When gay Bacchus	Gl	19	184
When with good Wine	D	22	218
+When gen'rous Wine	Gl	24	236
Y			
You beat your Pate V.1.	Ch	1	7
Ye Heav'ns if Innocence	Ch	2	17
Ye chearful Virgins	Gl	10	98
Ye woods & ye mountains V.2.	E	14	140
+You aſk me dear Jack	Gl	23	[illegible]

N.B. 6 Numbers of Glees will come out Annually at 1s. 6d. each in which ſhall be the moſt favorite Pieces both antient and modern.

+ The Works marked (+) may be had ſeparately.

Figure 5.5 John Bland's catalogue issued mid-1789 of the Ladies' Glees *(BL G.325, by permission of the British Library)*

The *Ladies' Glees* is the only one of Bland's six collections not promoted in a thematic catalogue, an understandable decision because each number contained up to eighteen songs. Printing the collection's incipits would have required a single folio sheet for every four or five numbers. Bland opted for the practical solution.

However, he made a major change to present the collection to the best advantage. In states BlJ 3a–3d individual items are listed under their respective numbers. The last two states (BLJ 3e–3f) present the items alphabetically, befitting the concept of the catalogue as an 'index' to volumes. Additionally, items are denoted by genre (Gl. for glees, Ch. for catches, M. for madrigals, Cn. for canons, Ct. for canzonets, D. for duets, and R. for rounds, and E. for elegys [sic]); the individual number in which each item is to be found is given, as is the relevant volume and the page number. This arrangement would have been useful to owners of bound volumes of the *Ladies' Glees*, as it facilitated locating particular songs. Despite the availability of bound volumes, numbers in the collection as well as selected songs within individual numbers could still be purchased individually—a more practical option for performance.

Stages E2 and E3. Both Lewis, Houston & Hyde and Linley reprinted Bland's catalogue BlJ 3e. Quite unusually, Linley followed that reprint with a three-page letterpress catalogue, his most ambitious cataloguing effort. Its title begins boldly 'FRANCIS LINLEY, Successor to Mr Bland' yet the imprint remains 'Printed and Sold by J. Bland'. It is perhaps Linley's honest admission that he was selling Bland's stock; more likely, the collection had gained its reputation under Bland and was still generally known as 'Bland's Collection'.

The first two pages of Linley's catalogue contain the first forty-eight numbers of the *Ladies' Glees* which Bland had published; its third page lists the first two numbers of Bland's *Gentlemens' Collections* and miscellaneous collections by Samuel Webbe Sr, John Danby, Richard Langdon and Dr (*later* Sir) John Stevenson, all previously published by Bland. Bland is known to have issued no. 49 of the *Ladies' Glees* and Linley may have issued no. 50, but he seems not to have added further numbers.

Stage E4. Birchall completed the fifth volume and added a sixth volume to the *Ladies' Glees*. His volumes bear his imprint on the collection's title-page but occasionally contain odd items with Bland's or Linley's imprint, indicating that Birchall did not always update the music plates he had purchased from Linley.[56] *Figure 5.6*, for example, is reproduced from a volume that has Birchall's name on the title-page and Bland's and Linley's names (but not Birchall's) on this music page. As no variation of paper has been noticed within these volumes, it seems unlikely that leftover printed stock from either Bland or Linley was sewn together with Birchall's reprints.

As with the *Periodical Duetts* and the *Harpsichord Collection*, Birchall raised the price of each number from Bland's 1/6 to 2/–, not only for his own publications in the fifth and sixth volumes but also for the single numbers in earlier volumes.

5.11 *The Collection of Divine Music*

F1 (Bland) ⇨(LHH) ⇨F2 (Linley) ⇨F3 (Birchall)

Stage F1. This is the last and probably the least popular of the six periodical collections examined in this chapter. As far as is known, Bland published only fourteen numbers of this collection and issued only one catalogue of it (BlJ18a, in early 1795), a thematic catalogue of the first twelve numbers shown in *Figure 5.7* on page 228. Nevertheless, with seventy-two incipits, the catalogue is quite substantial. No imprints showing Lewis, Houston & Hyde's involvement with this collection have been found.

Stage F2. Linley issued a similarly titled catalogue that was printed from a newly engraved plate containing the same seventy-two incipits. In both Bland's and Linley's catalogues the incipits are identical in engraving style and the shape of the music punches, suggesting that the two plates were prepared from the same set of punches. As each incipit terminates at the same place in both catalogues and the page numbers are unchanged, the question arises why Linley bothered to have the catalogue re-engraved.

---

[56] These odd items also were sold singly.

Figure 5.6 First page of a Ladies' Glee *composed by John Moulds and published consecutively by John Bland, Francis Linley and Robert Birchall (BL G.352.a* v 5 p 484, *by permission of the British Library)*

Figure 5.7 John Bland's catalogue issued early in 1795 of Divine Music *(BL H.817, by permission of the British Library)*

Linley is not known to have issued a catalogue of numbers of the collection after no. 12, although extant music with his imprint extends to no. 20.[57] Although he changed the collection's title to *Linley's Continuation of Bland's Collection of Divine Music*,[58] his name is absent from his newly engraved catalogue that was included in no. 20 of the collection. Its imprint simply reads 'Printed at No. 45 Holborn'.

Stage F3. Birchall retained Bland's *Divine Music* in his catalogues until at least 1817, but did not add to the collection after issuing no. 24 in 1797. His neglect of the collection may reflect a lack of a sizeable market and perhaps may be a commentary on the merit and standard of performance of church music at this time. In cathedrals—the most likely purchasers of liturgical settings and anthems—music was at its nadir.[59] Neither composers nor publishers would have been stimulated to produce new repertoire for this audience.

---

[57] Perhaps he was waiting until the collection reached no. 24 to do this.

[58] This title or a variant appears both on the title-pages and at the bottom of every music page.

[59] See Peter le Huray and John Harper, 'Anthem: England. 5. History *c*1770–*c*1890', and Nicolas Temperley, 'Anglican and Episcopalian church music. 5. English Cathedral Music, 1660–1830', both in *Oxford Music Online*.

~ III~

THE LEGAL CONTEXT

~ 6 ~

THE DEVELOPMENT OF MUSICAL COPYRIGHT

John Small

in memory of Rachel

Musical copyright is a product of the Georgian period. During the eighteenth and early nineteenth centuries British composers and music sellers began to seek copyright protection for music, a firm legal basis was established for copyright in music and various questions in copyright law with particular relevance to music were first addressed. These events were part of a much larger process of legal development that began well before the accession of George I.[1]

Under the Licensing Act of 1662 the London-based booksellers' organisation, the Worshipful Company of Stationers, controlled the English book trade on behalf of the government (section 6.1). While this Act was in force the law courts (section 6.2) made the first reported legal decisions to do with the book trade. At this time two kinds of copyright protection were in official use: royal printing grants, and registration with the Stationers' Company in accordance with the Licensing Act. The Company also acted as if copyright existed at common law (section 6.3). Law reports and other sources give some indication of how contemporary lawyers saw privileges and might have seen common-law copyright (section 6.4). For various reasons, the idea of copyright in music had not yet developed (section 6.5).

---

[1] For their interest, comments, criticism, advice (not always followed), encouragement and help, I am grateful to many people and especially to Jean Callaghan, Graeme Haigh, Jamie Kassler, Michael Kassler, Genevieve Lloyd, Nancy Mace, Prue Neidorf and Graham Pont.

The Copyright Act of 1710, which filled the legislative vacuum left when the Licensing Act lapsed, was concerned with the book trade and did not mention music (section 6.6). Composers and music sellers ignored the Act's registration provisions almost completely, but a series of musicians and a few publishers and editors obtained privileges giving them exclusive publication rights to their music (section 6.7). Two attempts in the 1730s to replace the Copyright Act and to extend statutory copyright protection to music were failures, but some legal decisions about books made from the 1740s onwards were relevant to practices in the music trade (section 6.8).

From the 1740s onwards a major legal dispute developed between English booksellers, who claimed that the common law protected their publications after statutory protection came to an end, and Scottish booksellers, who denied the existence of common-law copyright. In 1769 the King's Bench endorsed the English booksellers' view, but not unanimously (section 6.9).

Early lawsuits over the right to publish musical works ended inconclusively (section 6.10). After two more music lawsuits were launched in the early 1770s (sections 6.11–6.12), the House of Lords in effect reversed the 1769 King's Bench decision and further unsuccessful attempts were made to replace the Copyright Act and to have statutory copyright extended to music (section 6.13). The first of the two music lawsuits was promptly settled. Then, in a non-musical case, a decision was made which meant that privileges had no legal basis (section 6.14). The second music lawsuit went ahead and led to a decision in 1777 that music was within the scope of the 1710 Copyright Act (section 6.15). Later cases dealt with some legal questions which had particular relevance to the music trade, but the 1777 decision remained the basis of copyright in music until a new Copyright Act became law in 1842 (section 6.16).

6.1 THE LICENSING ACT; THE STATIONERS' REGISTER

During the sixteenth and seventeenth centuries English governments exercised strict control over printing and publishing in order to prevent the dissemination of blasphemous, seditious or otherwise unacceptable printed material. The trade was controlled by Star

Chamber decree until the prerogative courts were abolished in 1641, and then by Parliamentary act or ordinance until the government of the newly restored monarchy imposed controls on printing and publishing by Act of Parliament in 1662. Based largely on the Star Chamber decree of 1637, the statute 13&14 Charles II c.33 is known as the Licensing Act because it provided that new books had to be licensed by appropriate public officials or their delegates—books on English law by the Lord Chancellor or a senior judge, history books by a Secretary of State, and so on—and that each book's licence had to be printed at the front of the book.

Under the Licensing Act, as under earlier measures, day-to-day supervision of the book trade was the responsibility of the Stationers' Company, which, in return for administering government policy, was allowed to run the trade in the interests of its members. The Act permitted only Stationers, their sons or their former apprentices to trade in books without first getting permission from the local bishop. New books had to be entered in a register maintained by the Company; and as the Company was not obliged to register books submitted to it for registration, this provision gave the Company control over what books were published and by whom. (Stationers were not always punctilious about registration, but the law did not need to be observed to the letter to achieve its aims.) The Act prohibited the importation of books in English; it forbade importation of books into ports other than London, or by non-Stationers, without permission from the church authorities; and it provided that imported books were to be inspected by church and Company representatives. The Act contained detailed provisions limiting the numbers of printers and printing presses, and provided that presses were not to be set up, or printing equipment produced or imported, without notice to the Company. The Act empowered the Company as well as the civil authorities to search for and impound illegally produced material. And it required the Company to obtain three copies of each new book and to distribute them to the royal library and the university libraries of Cambridge and Oxford. The only printing and publishing not supervised by the Company took place in the universities, which had long had their own printing presses, and at York, where printing had been permitted since 1649. The universities and the Archbishop of York were also given limited licensing powers.

The Stationers' register, as well as having an official function, was the Company's internal record of which Stationer or Stationers had the right to publish a particular book. Thus the role given to the register by the Licensing Act enabled the Company to enforce its practice of treating the right to print a particular book—the 'copy' or, as it was coming to be called, the 'copyright'—as exclusive.[2] Being exclusive, printing rights could be treated as a form of property; late-seventeenth-century entries in the register take this for granted, usually beginning with some such phrase as 'Entred [sic] then for his booke or coppy' or 'Entred for his copie'.[3] There was no time limit on the rights recorded in the register, and Stationers' copyright was bought and sold, bequeathed and inherited, in whole or in part, like any other kind of lasting property.

The role of the Stationers' Company under the Licensing Act was anachronistic. The old civic trade organisations had long been in decline—a process accelerated by the hostility of Parliament and the law courts to trade monopolies—and the Company had retained its power only because it had a unique national role which governments

---

[2] The term 'copyright' (or 'copy right' or 'copy-right') was used in 1678 by the Stationers' Company in its orders, rules and ordinances (see John Feather, *Publishing, Piracy and Politics: An historical study of copyright in Britain*, London, 1994, p 46, and H. Tomás Gómez-Arostegui, 'What history teaches us about copyright injunctions and the inadequate-remedy-at-law requirement', *Southern California Law Review* v 81 (2008) p 1197–1280 at p 1258). It was used again in the Stationers' register on 31 May 1701 and 6 August 1703 (Mark Rose, *Authors and Owners: the invention of copyright*, Cambridge, Mass., 1993, p 58). The term appeared in print in Daniel Defoe's periodical *A Review of the State of the British Nation* v 8 no. 2 (29 March 1711) p 7, and in the report of the 1683 legal case *Company of Stationers v Lee* in Bartholomew Shower, *The Second Part of the Reports of Cases and Special Arguments Argued and Adjudged in the Court of King's Bench…*, London, 1720, p 258–261 at p 260. The word 'copy-right' occurs in the account of *Mayo v Hill* (1672) given in Shower's report of *Company of Stationers v Lee*, but it is not clear whether the use of this word should be credited to a judge in *Mayo v Hill*—which would make this the earliest known use of the term—or to a lawyer in *Company of Stationers v Lee* (1683), or to Shower, or to Shower's anonymous posthumous editor (who claimed not to have changed Shower's text).

[3] See G[eorge] E[dward] Briscoe Eyre, H[enry] R[obert] Plomer and C[harles] R[obert] Rivington, *A Transcript of the Registers of the Worshipful Company of Stationers from 1640–1708 A.D.*, London, 3 volumes, 1913–1914.

considered important. But by the late seventeenth century the Company was losing its grip on publishing: the Licensing Act had made newspapers subject to a Controller of the Press, illegal presses had become impossible to stamp out, and illegal book imports flourished. While the licensing system delayed publication of mostly unexceptionable books in London, unlicensed books (like the English version of Thomas Hobbes's *Leviathan*) could simply be printed in Holland. Nor was it only unlicensed books that were produced offshore: Dutch printers held a major share of the lucrative Bible market, one of them reputedly bragging that every ploughboy and servant girl in England had one of his Bibles.[4]

At the same time, successful writers were becoming restive as the size and profitability of the book market grew and the gradual decline of literary patronage made publication an increasingly important source of income for them. John Dryden, who as a Catholic lost his official positions after the Revolution of 1688, had a series of disagreements over money with his publisher Jacob Tonson I in the 1690s, at one stage writing 'Upon triall I find all of your trade are Sharpers [swindlers] & you not more than others; therefore I have not wholly left you.'[5]

Parliament renewed the Licensing Act in 1664 and 1665, let it lapse in 1679, then renewed it in 1685 during James II's brief political honeymoon. But when the Act came up for renewal again in 1694, John Locke submitted a memorandum to Parliament attacking 'lazy Stationers' and their grip on the book trade, and advocating use of the criminal law rather than trade regulation to deal with unacceptable publications.[6] Both Houses of Parliament recorded the memorandum in their journals, and the Licensing Act lapsed for good in 1695.

---

[4] C[harles] R[alph] Boxer, *The Dutch Seaborne Empire, 1600–1800*, London, 1965, p 169.

[5] Dryden→Tonson, December 1694 or January 1695, in Charles E[ugene] Ward (ed.), *The Letters of John Dryden*, Durham, North Carolina, 1942, p 80.

[6] See E[smond] S[amuel] de Beer (ed.), *The Correspondence of John Locke*, v 5, Oxford, 1979, p 785–791.

6.2 THE ENGLISH LEGAL SYSTEM

Until 1695 most book-trade disputes were dealt with by the Court of Assistants of the Stationers' Company, but a few went before the law courts. Some decisions made by the courts were significant for the future development of copyright law and had a special bearing on a form of copyright protection that would be sought by some eighteenth-century composers and music publishers. But before describing these decisions it is necessary to describe the legal system, which would remain largely unchanged throughout the Georgian period and whose structure affected the development of copyright law in the eighteenth century.

The abolition of the prerogative courts in 1641 left the three common-law courts—the King's Bench, Common Pleas and Exchequer—without serious rivals in either public or private law. Each of these courts had four judges: the King's Bench and Common Pleas each had a Chief Justice and three puisne justices, Exchequer a Chief Baron and three puisne barons. The jurisdictions of the three courts, once distinct, had become largely coextensive as a result of legal fictions that the courts had invented in times past in attempts to extend their jurisdictions and take business and fees away from one another. The common-law courts administered two bodies of law: the written law embodied in acts of Parliament; and the unwritten common law—the age-old, theoretically unchanging body of traditional law which applied to everyone everywhere in England. The common-law courts did not make or change the law; only Parliament could do that. If a new legal question or a new set of facts came before a common-law court, the judges dealt with the case in accordance with established law, taking into account not only any relevant statute law or established common law doctrine but any precedents set by judicial decisions in similar cases.

The Court of Chancery, presided over by England's highest judicial officer, the Lord Chancellor, or his deputy, the Master of the Rolls, complemented the common-law courts. It had developed independently of them and was regarded as a court not of law but of equity because it mitigated the common law's rigour by recognising rights, and providing remedies, that were not available at common law. In particular, if a statutory or common-law right was infringed,

Chancery could order specific performance of an action or grant an injunction forbidding a certain action, whereas the common-law courts could only award damages. But it was the common-law courts that interpreted statutes and decided what the common law was: if a Chancellor encountered a question about the common law or statute law to which he did not have a clear-cut answer, he would consult the common law judges, or have one or two of them sit with him as 'assessors' (sitters-in), or refer the matter to a common-law court, or perhaps make no order—the decision about what he should do was entirely his. Conversely, although the common-law courts paid due attention to Chancery decisions, they were not bound by them as they were by common-law judicial precedent.

Chancery was not the only court in which equity proceedings could be brought or injunctions or orders for specific performance sought. Exchequer had, as well as its common-law jurisdiction, an equity jurisdiction identical with the Chancellor's. Exchequer's equity jurisdiction would be much used by musical litigants in the late eighteenth century.

Exchequer Chamber was an appellate court originally created by statute to hear appeals from Exchequer and the King's Bench, with appeals from Exchequer being heard by the eight judges of the King's Bench and Common Pleas, presided over by the Lord Chancellor and Lord Treasurer, and appeals from the King's Bench being heard by the four judges of the Common Pleas and the four barons of the Exchequer. In addition, all twelve common-law judges, perhaps joined by the Chancellor, sometimes met as a non-statutory Court of Exchequer Chamber to consider difficult legal questions currently before one or another of the common-law courts.[7]

The final court of appeal was the House of Lords, presided over by the Lord Chancellor.[8] Although it was the apex of the judicial system and heard counsel when an appeal came before it, it consisted mostly of non-lawyers and functioned less as a judicial tribunal than as a kind of extra-judicial last resort that decided not what the law was but what it should be. The House of Lords made decisions by

---

[7] See Robert Maugham, *Outlines of the Jursidiction of all the Courts in England and Wales*, London, 1838, p 105.

[8] The House of Lords lost its original common-law jurisdiction in the 1660s.

majority vote. Since few lords were lawyers, and as the lords who spoke in debate were often concerned more with matters of policy than with strictly legal issues while other lords voted without giving reasons for their votes or even necessarily having reasons, a House of Lords decision, although final, was less helpful as a statement of legal principle than the judgements given by the common-law judges or the Chancellor. In practice, however, it was rare for the House of Lords not to confirm the judgement of a lower court.

The role of precedent in the legal system made it important for lawyers to know not only what decisions judges had made in earlier cases, but also why they had made those decisions and what they had said about matters of legal principle. However, although the official archives held records of court orders as well as pleadings and other documents submitted by litigants, there was no official law reporting. What judges said about the reasons for their decisions was recorded, if at all, by individual lawyers who happened to be in court; and case reports were published, if at all, in collections which were not necessarily supervised by their authors or alleged authors, and which often came out long after many of the cases had been heard. House of Lords proceedings were never reported, since to report parliamentary proceedings was a breach of parliamentary privilege.[9]

Published case-report collections were licensed by judicial officials in accordance with the Licensing Act, but a licence was no guarantee of quality. No reports were verbatim; some were detailed, some were cursory, some were mere jottings. Some omitted basic facts like litigants' names or the date or even the outcome of a case. Some reports were garbled and some partisan; and some reporters were unreliable. Some cases were described in the reports of other cases rather than being reported in their own right. A number of cases which were known to contemporary lawyers may be unknown today because the reports of those cases circulated only in manuscript. Conversely, some cases may have remained unknown to most contemporary lawyers until the reports were published years after the cases were heard.

---

[9] The accounts of House of Lords cases quoted in the next section do not report parliamentary proceedings.

Law reporting improved greatly during the eighteenth century, and reports of parliamentary proceedings began to be published in the 1770s, but the old problems were not completely eliminated until the nineteenth century, when it became the norm for verbatim reports of all important cases to be published soon after they were heard.[10] Nevertheless, the published law-report collections provide most of what is now known about the legal standing of various forms of copyright in the late seventeenth century.[11]

6.3 Seventeenth-century Copyright: Royal Grants, Registration and the Common Law

Section 3 of the 1662 Licensing Act referred to 'any Book or Books, the Right of Printing whereof doth solely and properly belong to any particular Person or Persons', but did not make clear the legal basis of this right. Section 6 identified two bases for it: royal letter patent, and entry in the register book of the Stationers' Company or the universities.[12] A third, more shadowy, basis was ignored by the

[10] For instance, reports of the same cases in the 1770s by Henry Cowper, a lawyer, and Capel Lofft, a journalist, often differed markedly. No report was published of the important musical-copyright cases *Rennett v Longman* and *Rennett v Thompson* (1785). When discussing an incorrect report by John Dickens of a 1783 case, a judge in *Electric Telegraph v Nott* (1847) remarked that 'it is rare that Dickens is altogether right', adding however that 'it is also rare that he is altogether wrong' (reported in Charles Purton Cooper, *Reports of Cases in Chancery decided by Lord Cottenham; commencing 7th July, 1846*, v 2 part 1, London, 1848, p 61–62 at p 62).

[11] Each legal case mentioned in this chapter is described in the Summary of Legal Cases starting at page 507 of this book, where references are given to case reports reproduced in *The English Reports* volumes or, for unreported cases, to other relevant documentation. In this chapter modern legal terminology ('appeal', etc.) has been used where nothing is to be gained by using the old terms ('writ of error', etc.). Likewise, the former terminological distinction between a lawsuit (an action brought in a common-law court) and a Chancery suit has been ignored.

[12] Section 6 referred to 'any Copy or Copies, Book or Books, or Part of any Book or Books … which any Person or Person by force or virtue of any Letters Patents granted or assigned, or which shall hereafter be granted or assigned to him or them, or (where the same are not granted by any Letters Patents) by force

Licensing Act—the possibility that copyright existed at common law. Royal grants, the Stationers' register and common-law copyright would all figure in the history of copyright law in the eighteenth century.

The royal letter patent granting exclusive printing rights was a survival from the time when Tudor and Stuart monarchs, exercising the royal prerogative power, had granted trade monopolies to raise money without reference to Parliament or to buy or reward political support. This practice was strongly opposed by common lawyers and the House of Commons. In *The Case of Monopolies* (1602) the King's Bench declared an 'odious' monopoly over the trade in playing cards invalid, and in *The Clothworkers of Ipswich Case* (1615) it held that the king had no power to grant a monopoly over a common trade. Finally, in return for parliamentary support for his foreign policy, James I assented in 1624 to the Statute of Monopolies, 21 James I c.3, which abolished most of the king's power to grant monopolies. Under section 6 of that Act, however, the king retained the power to grant inventors exclusive rights to their inventions for up to fourteen years—twice the statutory length of an apprenticeship—and under section 10 he retained the power to grant monopolies in a few trades over which royal control was evidently deemed necessary in the interests of security and public order. One such trade was printing:

> Provided also, and be it enacted, That this Act, or any Declaration, Provision, Disablement, Penalty, Forfeiture or other Thing before mentioned, shall not extend to any Letters Patents or Grants of Privilege heretofore made, or hereafter to be made, of, for or concerning Printing.

When the bill that became the Licensing Act was before Parliament, some printing grants made before the Interregnum had not yet expired. Parliament had to clarify the status of such grants, and the result was section 22 of the Licensing Act, which provided that

---

or virtue of any Entry or Entries thereof duly made in the Register-Book of the said Company of Stationers, or in the Register-Book of either of the Universities respectively, have or shall have the Right, Privilege, Authority or Allowance, solely to print'.

> neither this Act, nor any Thing therein contained, shall extend to prejudice the just Rights and Privileges granted by His Majesty, or any of His Royal Predecessors, to any Person or Persons, under His Majesty's Great Seal, or otherwise; but that such Person or Persons may exercise and use such Rights and Privileges as aforesaid, according to their respective Grants; any Thing in this Act to the contrary notwithstanding.

Presumably because Parliament was unwilling to risk having its book-trade legislation ignite a parliamentary dispute over the divisive subject of the royal prerogative power, this endorsement of royal printing grants was equivocal. Section 22 could be taken to mean that all royal grants which predated the Licensing Act were intrinsically just and therefore valid; but it could also be read as saying that in order to be valid, such grants had to be just—whatever that meant. Moreover, although this section suggested that the king retained whatever power his predecessors had had to make printing grants, it said nothing about his successors, as if they might not retain that power. Thus all Members of Parliament, whatever their views on the prerogative, could support this section, leaving its interpretation to the future and the law courts.

Seventeenth- and eighteenth-century monarchs made two kinds of grants of printing rights, both by letter patent. The first kind was made to authors—that is, to content creators of all kinds, including writers, editors, translators and engravers—or to authors' assignees, executors, heirs or the like. Such grants could apply to anything that could be printed—to verbal material on any subject in any language, or to non-verbal material such as engravings. Grants of this type usually applied to one or more specified works or to the work of one author, and the rights such grants conferred were exclusive and had a relatively short duration, which by 1695 was normally fourteen years, the maximum term of patents granted to inventors under the Statute of Monopolies.

Grants of the second kind were made only to booksellers, the Stationers' Company or the universities, and they lasted longer than those of the first kind, forty years being typical. Such grants applied only to a limited number of works and types of material, all of them entirely verbal in content and many of them connected in some way with the Church or the State. With some material, such as the Bible, the Crown acted as if it owned the printing rights, except that it customarily granted these rights for a limited time by letter patent, rather than assigning them permanently by contract of sale. Moreover, where the Bible was concerned the rights were not necessarily exclusive: the Crown might grant Bible-printing rights to more than one patentee at a time. With other material the Crown acted as if exercising a general supervisory role over some types of publication. Thus the law patentee was the sole authorised publisher not only of official material such as statutes, which the Crown could reasonably claim to own, but of all law books, including those by private authors. And in some cases the material did not have a strong connection with Church or State: almanacs, for which the Stationers' Company had held a patent since 1603, contained, along with the feasts of the Church, a great deal of material with which the Crown had nothing to do.

Both types of royal printing grant were called patents in the eighteenth century, but the first type was also called a licence by around the middle of that century[13] and is often called a licence to print today. However, in contexts where both types of grant need to be distinguished from a licence issued under the Licensing Act as well as from each other, it seems best to call the first type of grant a 'privilege'[14] and the second type a 'book patent', and to reserve the word 'licence' for a permit issued under the Licensing Act.

According to section 6 of the Licensing Act, the right to print a book could be owned not only by virtue of a royal letter patent, but by virtue of an entry in the Stationers' register or another authorised register. Perhaps the Star Chamber had taken the view that a register entry created a property right, but in 1662 there was no Star Chamber and there was no support for this view in any recorded judicial decision or in any statute—unless the words of section 6 were interpreted as creating such a right, not just as taking it for granted.

Ever since Star Chamber's abolition in 1641, the Stationers' Company had wanted Parliament or the courts to provide a secure legal basis for ownership of printing rights. In 1643, when the Long Parliament was about to consider a book-trade measure which would replace Star Chamber's 1637 decree, the Company petitioned

---

[13] See William Warburton's 1759 letter quoted on page 278 below.

[14] The French term for a similar grant is *privilège générale*.

Parliament to secure 'propriety of Copies'. Taking care to point out that what it wanted did not constitute a monopoly, the Company argued *inter alia* that 'there is no reason apparent why the productions of the Brain should not be as assignable and their interest and possession … held as tender in Law, as the right of any Goods or Chattells whatsoever'.[15]

Parliament's response was the Printing Ordinance of 1643, revised and renewed in 1649. It provided that 'no person or persons shall hereafter print or cause to be reprinted … any Book or Books lawfully licensed and entred in the Register of the said Company for any particular member thereof, without the license and consent of the Owner or Owners thereof'.[16] This did not satisfy the Company, and it claimed in 1655, during a dispute with the University of Oxford, that printing rights had been unprotected since 1641.[17]

The Company changed its tactics a few years later, though not its aim of having a legal basis for ownership of printing rights established beyond all possible doubt. In a direct challenge by the Company to the law patent, a Stationer published a law book after having paid the author's heir for the right to print it. The law patentees obtained an injunction ordering not just the offending Stationer but all Stationers not to publish the book, and the Company appealed from Chancery to the House of Lords.[18] In a printed summary of their case, presumably intended for distribution to the peers who were about to hear *Stationers v Patentees about the Printing of Rolle's Abridgment* (1666), the Company argued not that Parliament should protect 'productions of the brain' but that the

---

[15] Edward Arber (ed.), *A Transcript of the Registers of the Company of Stationers of London, 1554–1640*, London, 1875–1894, v 1 p 587–588. The author of this petition was Henry Parker, secretary to the Parliamentary Army and later to the House of Commons (Cyprian Blagden, *The Stationers' Company: a history, 1403–1959*, London, 1960, p 146).

[16] C[harles] H[arding] Firth and R[obert] S[angster] Rait (eds), *Acts and Ordinances of the Interregnum*, London, 1911, v 1 p 185 (the 1643 ordinance) and v 2 p 247–249 (the 1649 ordinance, which has different wording).

[17] Blagden, *op cit.*, p 196.

[18] For background to the legal cases *Stationers v Patentees* and *Roper v Streater* see Adrian Johns, *The Nature of the Book: Print and knowledge in the making*, Chicago, 1998, p 304–318.

House of Lords should find that such productions were already protected by the common law:

> It is humbly conceived, first, that the Author of every *Manuscript* or *Copy* hath (in all reason) as good right thereunto, as any Man hath to the Estate wherein he has the most absolute property; and consequently the taking from him the one (without his own consent) will be equivalent to the bereaving him of the other, contrary to his Will.
>
> Secondly, Those who purchased such Copies for valuable considerations, having the Authors right thereby transferred to them (and a due Licence and Entrance according to Law) 'twill be as prejudicial to deprive them of the benefit of their Purchase, as to Disseise them of their Freehold.[19]

The common law had long recognised rights that did not involve physical possession. Some, such as the advowson (the right to make an ecclesiastical appointment), were closely related to land law; others were not, such as alimony and the corrody (types of entitlement to money support). By the late seventeenth century the proliferation of such rights was such that the term *chose in action*—which had once referred only to the right to bring a legal action—had come to be used as a catch-all term for any right not involving physical possession. According to Blount's 1670 law dictionary:

> *Chose in Actin* [sic] is a thing incorporeal, and onely a right, as an Annuity, Obligation for Debt, a Covenant, Voucher by Warranty, and generally all Causes of Suit, for any Debt or Duty, Trespass or Wrong, are to be accounted *Choses in Action.* And it seems *Chose in Action* may also be called *Chose in Suspence*; because it hath no real existence, or being, not can properly be said to be in our possession.[20]

The incorporeality of the alleged right to print was therefore no reason why it should not be recognised at common law. However,

---

[19] *The Case of the Booksellers and Printers Stated: with answers to the objections of the patentee*, London, 1666, single sheet (copy at BL C.18.e.1.(52)).

[20] Thomas Blount, *Νομο-λεξικον: a law-dictionary*, London, 1670 (unpaginated), article 'Chose'. Choses in action have proliferated since Blount's time: see v 7 of William S[earle] Holdsworth, *A History of English Law*, London, 1903–1972, and v 6 of *Halsbury's Laws of England*, 4th ed., London, 2003.

because past disputes over printing rights had normally been dealt with by the Stationers' Company Court of Assistants or, until 1641, by Star Chamber, the law courts had not considered whether the common law recognised such a right as the right to print a book. Hence lawyers for the Stationers' Company were unable to cite legal precedent in support of their argument in *Stationers v Patentees* and instead had to rely on Magna Carta—which provided that no man should be disseised of his free tenement, that is, wrongfully dispossessed of his freehold estate—and high principle.

Before looking at the outcome of *Stationers v Patentees* and other late-seventeenth-century copyright cases, three points are worth mentioning. First, in the absence of statutory copyright, common-law copyright was the only possible legal basis for the assumption, routinely indicated in Stationers' register entries, that printing rights constituted a form of lasting property. This assumption—that the sums that the former paid to the latter were not just gratuities—was also the only possible legal basis for booksellers' dealings with authors. Secondly, if common-law copyright existed, it had a major advantage over printing rights granted by privilege: common-law rights lasted forever, whereas a privilege protected a book only for a limited period, usually fourteen years. Thirdly, if there was such a thing as common-law copyright, privileges were not merely pointless but without any legal basis. Common-law real and personal property rights were indefeasible: not only could no man be disseised of his free tenement, but section 5 of the Act abolishing Star Chamber, 16 Charles I c.10, provided:

> That neither His Majesty, nor His Privy Council, have or ought to have any Jurisdiction, Power or Authority, by *English* Bill, Petition, Articles, Libel or any other arbitrary Way whatsoever, to examine or draw into question, determine or dispose of the Lands, Tenements, Hereditaments, Goods or Chattels of any the subjects of this Kingdom; but that the same ought to be tried and determined in the ordinary Courts of Justice, and by the ordinary Course of the Law.

Thus if printing rights constituted a form of property at common law, and the right to print a particular book had an undisputed legal owner, the king had no power to make that right the subject of a royal grant, even if only to grant the right back to its owner.

6.4 Patents, Privileges and Common-law Copyright: Seventeenth-century Cases

Most reported late-seventeenth-century lawsuits about printing rights concerned book patents. None of the litigants was an author and none of the cases was directly concerned with authors' rights. Despite this, and notwithstanding the limitations of the reports, the reported cases indicate fairly clearly what the courts might have said about privileges, and one case hints at what they might have said about common-law copyright.

Eighteen reported cases from the period between the Restoration and the time of the first copyright act in 1710 concerned royal printing grants.[21] Most of these cases involved the Stationers' Company, and about half were decided between 1679 and 1685, when the Licensing Act was inoperative and the Company, lacking the statutory power to seize imported English-language books, had to go to court to deal with imports. The most significant cases were *Stationers v Patentees about the Printing of Rolle's Abridgment* (1666), *Streater v Roper* (1675), *Company of Stationers v Seymour* (1677) and *Company of Stationers v Partridge* (1712).

The earliest decision was made by the House of Lords in *Stationers v Patentees*. The law-book patentee,[22] who had been granted the exclusive right to produce books 'touching or concerning

[21] See R[obert] C[ecil] Bald, 'Early copyright litigation and its bibliographical interest', *Papers of the Bibliographical Society of America*, v 36 (1942) p 81–96. An annotated 'Register of Copyright Infringement Suits and Actions from *c*1560 to 1800', prepared by H. Tomás Gómez-Arostegui, which dates many cases on the basis of cited documentary evidence, can be found at http://www.oldcopyrightcases.org .

[22] King James I granted the law-book patent to John More *or* Moore in 1618. In 1629 More assigned it to Miles Flesher and his partners in return for an annual sum of £60 and a third of the profits. More died in 1638 and bequeathed this annuity etc. to his daughter Martha Acheson. In 1640 she married Richard Atkyns and he then became patentee by right of his wife. The Stationers' Company bought the remainder of the lease of the patent from Flesher and his son James in 1661, and several lawsuits followed between the Company and Atkyns and his associates. See Henry R[obert] Plomer, *A Dictionary of the Booksellers and Printers who were at work in England, Scotland and Ireland from 1641 to 1667*, Oxford, 1907, p 8–9, p 76 and p 131–132.

the common or statute law',[23] enjoyed an old-fashioned trade monopoly of the kind declared illegal by the King's Bench in *The Case of Monopolies* and then banned by the Statute of Monopolies in most trades other than printing. Authors of legal texts, unless they could find publishers prepared to pay the patentee for permission to publish a law book, were forced to publish with the patentee, to take whatever terms they were given and to give up control over how their writings were adapted for publication. The patent also turned the legal profession into a captive market for the patentee's products, however unsatisfactory those products were. But the Statute of Monopolies did not apply to book grants, and in *Stationers v Patentees* the House of Lords, presumably interpreting the Licensing Act as confirming the validity of old patents, and possibly seeing in the case an opportunity to uphold an aspect of the royal prerogative power, upheld the validity of the law-book patent.

The decision had no obvious effect: it was not recorded in the *Journals of the House of Lords*, and in 1668, as if there had been no such decision, ten common-law judges stated in an Exchequer Chamber opinion submitted to the Lord Chancellor:

> that such new Law Books as have been imprinted since *Moor*'s [sic] Patent, and acquired by any particular Person or Persons, are not by Law restrained by *Moor*'s Patent. But notwithstanding that Patent, those Men who have acquired them may print; but as to those Law Books that were printed before that Patent, there are among us Diversity of Opinions.[24]

That is, some judges considered the law-book patent invalid, and none of them considered that it applied to recent law books.

In 1672 the King's Bench overlooked or ignored *Stationers v Patentees*, deciding in *Roper v Streater* that the law-book patent was invalid on the grounds 'that this patent tended to a monopoly; that it was of a large extent; … that it was difficult to ascertain what should

---

[23] M[athew] Bacon, *A New Abridgement of the Law*, 7th ed., London, 1832, v 6 p 507.

[24] This opinion, given in the unreported case *Atkyns v Stationers*, is quoted in the report of *Company of Stationers v Lee* (1681). It is perhaps abridged, like the *Roper v Streater* ruling reproduced in the same source (see below).

be called a law-book; [and] that the words in the patent, *touching or concerning the common or statute law*, were loose and uncertain'.[25]

The bookseller John Streater and his associates, who paid the law-book patentee Richard Atkyns £100 a year for permission to publish under that patent,[26] appealed to the House of Lords, which in *Streater v Roper* (1675) followed *Stationers v Patentees*, reversing the King's Bench decision and holding 'that the Letters Patents pleaded in Bar of the Action brought in the King's Bench were and are good in Law'.[27] The reasons for this decision are said to have included

> that this privilege had always been allowed, which was a strong argument in its favour; that it concerned the state, and was matter of public care; that it was in the nature of a proclamation, which none but the king could make [i.e., was an exercise of the royal prerogative and beyond the reach of the common law]; that the king had the *making* of judges, serjeants and officers of the law; [and] that as to the uncertainty, these words ... were ... not to be extended to a book containing a quotation of law, but where the principal design was to treat on that subject...[28]

The only peer who voted against the decision was the Earl of Anglesey, a lawyer. The decision bound the common-law courts, despite their opposition to monopolies, but there are signs of dissatisfaction with it in the reports of a couple of later cases.

Stationers v Patentees and *Streater v Roper* were the only reported late-seventeenth-century copyright cases decided by the House of Lords. All other such cases were heard by Chancery and the common-law courts, which upheld patents for law books, Bibles, psalm books, primers (prayer books or devotional manuals) and

---

[25] Quoted in *Company of Stationers v Lee* (1681).

[26] See David Stoker, 'Atkyns, Richard', in *The Oxford Dictionary of National Biography*.

[27] *Journals of the House of Lords*, v 12 p 704 (26 May 1675).

[28] Bacon, *loc. cit.* Bacon's sources for this statement, written in the 1730s, are not known.

almanacs.[29] Some reports indicate that Chancery was reluctant to support patents solely on the grounds that the House of Lords had upheld the law patent. In *Company of Stationers v —* (1681), the Lord Chancellor distinguished statute books from other books on the grounds that 'the Printing of the Laws was Matter of State, and concerned the State'. The Bible patent came under scrutiny after having been upheld in a few Chancery cases. In an anonymous 1682 case about Bibles the Lord Keeper (the interim Chancellor) said: 'though the patent for law-books has been adjudged good in the *House of Lords*, yet that is not exactly the same case with this, though near it'.[30] In *Hills v University of Oxford* (1684) the Lord Keeper ordered the parties to test the validity of the Bible patent at common law.

Of the patents upheld in these cases all but one had some obvious connection with Church or State, the conspicuous exception being the almanac patent. Almanacs could be said to have a connection with the Church to the extent that they contained the Christian calendar, complete with the feasts of the Church. But they also contained material—phases of the moon, prognostications, etc.—that had no such connection. Nevertheless, the Court of Common Pleas upheld the almanac patent in *Company of Stationers v Seymour* (1677), heard two years after the decision of the House of Lords in *Streater v Roper*.

---

[29] The courts upheld patents for Bibles or psalm books or both in *Mayo v Hill* (1672); almanacs in *Company of Stationers v Lee* (1681); statute books in *Company of Stationers v —* (1681); Bibles and statute books in *Company of Stationers v —* (1682); 'primers, psalters, psalms and almanacks' in *Company of Stationers v Skynner* (1682 or 1683); almanacs in *Company of Stationers v Marlow* (1683); one or more of 'primers, psalters, almanacks, and singing psalms' in *Company of Stationers v Lee* (1683); psalm books in *Company of Stationers v Wright* (1683 or 1684); and possibly psalm books or primers in *Company of Stationers v Parker* (1685). (The report of *Company of Stationers v Parker* does not identify the books involved, but see Blagden, *op cit.*, p 197–198.) No reported cases dealt with other patents.

[30] The Chancellor, as well as being head of Chancery, was a senior member of the government and chairman of the House of Lords, which had both judicial and legislative functions. A government lacking a suitable appointee might appoint a Lord Keeper of the Seal to do the Chancellor's work until a Chancellor was appointed.

In *Company of Stationers v Seymour* the Company's barrister, Sir Francis Pemberton, who might have been expected to claim that the king's power to grant printing rights was unlimited, conceded that that power extended only to certain kinds of book: 'the question here is not, whether the King may, by law, grant the sole printing of all books; but of any, and of what sort of books?'. But he then argued that the Common Pleas should not strain at a gnat when the House of Lords had swallowed a camel:

> The sole printing of *law-books* is not now in question; that seems to be a point of some difficulty, because of the large extent of such a patent, and the uncertainty of determining what should be accounted a *law-book*, and what not; and yet such a patent has been allowed to be good by a judgement in the House of Peers.

One judge seems to have agreed about the camel, saying, 'This is a stronger case than that of *law-books*'; and one said, as if rebutting criticism of the law-book patent decision: 'We ought to be guided in our opinions by the judgement of the House of Peers ... the ultimate resort of law and justice being to them'. But whatever their reservations about the law-book patent, the judges could hardly reject a case which was stronger than one which had been accepted by the House of Lords. The judges therefore had no choice but to uphold the almanac patent—a decision followed in other cases over the next few years.[31]

The reasons given by the Common Pleas for upholding the almanac patent included the fact that such patents had been granted for many years and that almanacs contained the Christian calendar.

---

[31] *Company of Stationers v Lee* (1681), *Company of Stationers v —* (1682) and *Company of Stationers v Marlow* (1683). According to Joseph Keble's report of *Company of Stationers v Seymour* (as *Corporation of Stationers v Seymor*), the Common Pleas said that by 14 Charles II c.33 § 6 'it is impliedly granted that the printing of all books is restrainable, or grantable, by the Kings patent'. But Keble's reports are notoriously unreliable (see John William Wallace, *The Reporters arranged and characterized with incidental remarks*, 4th ed., Boston, 1882, p 315–326), and this one is inconsistent with the drift of the other reported cases as well as with the *Company of Stationers v Seymour* report. (Keble perhaps attended only the first part of the hearing and then, when working from his notes years later, mistook the arguments of John Seymour's barrister for the court's remarks.)

But one judge took up an idea that had nothing to do with the royal prerogative power. Pemberton had argued that 'the book which this defendant has printed, has no certain author; and then, according to the rule of our law, the King has the property; and by consequence may grant his property to the Company'. According to the report, which seems to have been written by Pemberton or someone associated with him,[32] one judge, probably the Chief Justice, Sir Francis North,[33] accepted this argument, saying 'there is no particular author of an almanack; and then, by the rule of our law, the King has the property in the copy'.

Pemberton and the judge were referring to the common-law rule that derelict land and derelict goods such as treasure trove are the property of the king. Consistently with this, the judge used the language of property when referring in his judgement to what would happen 'if a man should claim a property in another man's copy, by reason of some inconsiderable additions of his own'. If the report is correct, North saw the right to print a book as a common-law right.

A generation after the cases of the 1680s, the King's Bench heard an almanac patent case which had been referred from Chancery. If the report of *Company of Stationers v Partridge* (1712) is a reasonable summary of what was said from the bench, the court treated the law-book patent decision in *Streater v Roper* as a special case irrelevant to the almanac patent, disregarded the *Company of Stationers v Seymour* analogy between the calendar and derelict property, and suggested that for the almanac patent to be valid the monarch needed to be more than just owner of the calendar by default. The court is reported as saying:

> The patent for the sole printing of law books is not now to be shaken, having had the sanction of the House of Lords: monopolies are

[32] The reporter gives a clear account of Pemberton's arguments but conflates the judges' comments and ignores the opposing barrister's arguments altogether.

[33] This passage occurs at the end of the remarks attributed to 'The Court' in the case report. Since judges conventionally gave their views in ascending order of seniority, with the Chief Justice speaking last, the speaker is likely to have been North. As a barrister North had addressed the House of Lords in *Stationers v Patentees* in 1666, and as Lord Keeper he would refer two Bible cases from Chancery to the common-law courts in the early 1680s.

> odious; this case, therefore, is to be distinguished [from a monopoly], by deriving to the Crown some special interest in *almanacks*.
>
> No opinion was given; but the case was ordered to be spoken to again.

According to the report's editor the further hearing did not take place.

These four cases indicated that a royal printing grant was valid when the king by virtue of his position as head of the Church or head of State had some 'special interest' in the books that were the subject of the grant. They also indicated that the books in which the king had such a special interest included the Bible, the statutes and the Book of Common Prayer. It seemed, too, that if the king did not have a special interest in a book, he did not have the power to grant the right to print it, if only because such a grant would constitute a monopoly. It is true that in *Streater v Roper* the House of Lords upheld the law-book patent. But some judges in *Company of Stationers v Seymour* felt that *Streater v Roper* went too far, even though it could not be questioned; and in *Company of Stationers v Partridge* the court wanted to quarantine *Streater v Roper* by treating it as a special case.

Nothing in these cases, or in any other cases from this period, suggested that the king might have a general power to grant privileges.

Although Francis North may have accepted the idea of common-law copyright, there is little else to suggest that this idea was in the air around 1670—unless the phrase 'men who have acquired them [new law-books]' in the 1668 Exchequer Chamber opinion quoted above is interpreted as referring to Stationers' purchase of authors' common-law rights. But in 1679 a plaintiff in an unreported lawsuit which had nothing to do with a royal grant apparently did rely upon the common law: Nathaniel Ponder brought a Common Pleas action stating that he 'was and yet is the true proprietor of the copy of a certain book, intitled *The Pilgrim's Progress*' by John Bunyan, and that Thomas Braddill had printed this book 'without [Ponder's] licence and consent'.[34] In a newspaper

[34] John Lilly, *A Collection of Modern Entries: or select pleadings in the Courts of King's Bench, Common Pleas, and Exchequer*, 5th ed., London, 1791, v 1 p 66–67. Frank Mott Harrison, 'Nathaniel Ponder: the publisher of *The Pilgrim's Progress*', *The Library* 4th ser. v 15 no. 3 (December 1934) p 257–294, describes (p 268) Lilly's translation (from Latin, the language of legal

advertisement in 1680 Ponder described himself as the proprietor of *The Pilgrim's Progress* and indicated that the lawsuit was still active.[35] But it seems that nothing more happened.

At the end of the seventeenth century two lawyers expressed the view that copyright existed at common law. In 1695, when John Locke suggested to his friends John Freke and Edward Clarke that any new book-trade legislation should protect the 'Author's property in his copy', they replied that

> there needs noe new care to be taken about property for tis a rule in Law that wherever there is *damnum* and *injuria* I may be recompensed in damages in an action on the case and whoever prints my Coppy injures me and endammages me so that I have the same security for this property that anyone has for any other.[36]

Some of the petitioners requesting new book-trade legislation after the Licensing Act lapsed also seem to have believed that common-law copyright existed. In 1696 the Stationers' Company and some printers petitioned Parliament asking that presses be regulated again, claiming that the protection to printing rights provided by common law was inadequate:

> it being no easy matter for [the owner of the rights to a book] to prove out a stol'n Impression of a Thousand Books ... that One hundred of them have been sold; and besides, if this should happen to be prov'd, yet even Then they cannot expect suitable Costs and Damages.[37]

---

pleadings until 1731) as 'free'. This dispute is not among those for which the Stationers' Company is known to have given permission for proceedings to be brought in the law courts (see Gómez-Arostegui, *op. cit.* in note 2 above, p 1259). Ponder may have sued because the Licensing Act had lapsed in 1679, removing the legal basis of the Stationers' Company's power over its members.

[35] *The True Domestick Intelligence, or, News from both City & Country*, 3 January 1680, p 2.

[36] E[smond] S[amuel] de Beer (ed.), *The Correspondence of John Locke*, v 5, Oxford, 1979, p 295.

[37] *Reasons humbly offer'd to the Consideration of the Honourable House of Commons. Shewing the great Necessity of having a Bill for the Regulating of Printing and Printing-Presses*, London, *c*1696, p 1. For the dating of this two-page document see Ronan Deazley, *On the Origin of the Right to Copy*, Oxford, 2004, p 17–18.

A 1709 submission by the book trade to the House of Commons took the same line:

> For whereas, by Common Law, we can recover no more Costs, than we can prove Damage; and the Damage we sustain, being always vastly more than we can prove; We desire you will assign such Punishment upon Delinquents, as in Your Great Wisdom You shall think fit.[38]

But there had as yet been no judicial decision which explicitly confirmed the existence of copyright at common law.

6.5. Composers and Music Publishers in the late Seventeenth Century

There seems to have been no discussion or even thought of copyright in music in the late seventeenth century. One reason for this was that music publications were generally not entered in the Stationers' register. The Licensing Act and the measures which preceded it were designed to prevent the publication of objectionable ideas; and since music could not express such ideas unless it had objectionable words or perhaps some kind of objectionable association, governments and the Stationers' Company ignored it. Music publishers were usually not members of that Company, and in practice Stationers' copyright was not used to protect music: all twenty-nine music publications entered in the Stationers' register between 1640 and 1708 contained significant amounts of verbal text, being either instruction books, vocal music or, in one case, a novel which happened to contain some music.[39] John and Henry Playford, the leading music publishers of the late seventeenth century, were represented in the register by only eleven of their numerous music publications, plus three produced in

---

[38] *More Reasons humbly offer'd to the Honourable House of Commons, for the Bill for Encouraging Learning, and for Securing Property of Copies of Books to the Rightful Owners thereof*, London, 1709.

[39] See Eyre, Plomer and Rivington, *op. cit.* in note 3 above, and William P. Williams (ed.), *Index to the Stationers' Register, 1640–1708*, La Jolla, California, 1980.

collaboration with other publishers, and all fourteen were either tutors or settings of religious words.

In any case, music notation was not disseminated only in printed form, nor were publishers the only agents of dissemination. Because of the low and unpredictable demand for many musical works, publishers mainly printed short compositions which were suitable for amateur performance and therefore had a relatively large potential market. Less popular works were copied by hand on demand. Thus

> a business in what might be called 'manuscript publication' appears to have flourished up to the end of the seventeenth century, serving a number of different purposes: through such manuscript circulation, specialized and earlier repertoires could be maintained; the market for modern music could be tested; and as the 1697 [Henry Playford] catalogue shows, copies superior to available prints could be produced.[40]

Moreover, manuscript publication was only the tip of a copying iceberg. A great deal of music was routinely copied by professional musicians as part of their work, by trainee professionals as part of their education, or by amateur musicians.

Because copying played a large part in the dissemination of music, and because each manuscript copy of a piece of music was the direct product not of the composer's labour but of a copyist's, there was little room in the music trade for the idea that the composer retained some kind of proprietary right over a piece of music once it was composed, and that this right was worth money. Indeed, musicians and publishers alike may well have seen music publishing as something like a partly mechanised copying service.

There were two other obstacles to the development of the idea of musical copyright. One was that composers generally wrote their music to fulfil a commission or as part of their work as performers or teachers, so that it was easy to see the music they produced as a by-product of their paid work, not as something that had monetary value, no matter how valuable it might be in other ways. The other was that the Playfords were on very good terms with their composers, whom

---

[40] Robert Thompson, 'Manuscript music in Purcell's London', *Early Music* v 23 no. 4 (1995) p 605–618 at p 617.

they seem to have regarded not as suppliers of raw material so much as colleagues in a common enterprise. John Playford was himself a composer and writer on music, often styling himself 'Philo-musicus' on his title pages, and he was a strong supporter of English music and musicians, writing in the preface to the third book of his collection *Choice Ayres and Songs* (1681):

> I am sorry that it is (in this age) so much the vanity of some of our English gentry to admire that in a foreigner, which they either slight or take little notice of in one of their own nation; for I am sure that our English masters in music (either for vocal or instrumental music) are not in skill and judgement inferior to any foreigners whatsoever.[41]

This collection contains several pieces by the young Henry Purcell, two of which John Playford may have commissioned.[42]

Composers seem to have been as appreciative of the Playfords as the Playfords were of them. In the preface to the fourth book of *The Theatre of Music* (1687) John Playford wrote that 'most of these songs and dialogues were composed by the eminent Dr John Blow and Mr Henry Purcell, my ever kind friends, and several other able masters, from whom I received true copies, which were by them perused before they were put to the press'.[43]

Purcell worked with the Playfords throughout his career. The connection survived two deaths: John Playford mentioned Purcell in his will, Purcell composed an elegy for him, and in 1696 Henry Playford published a Purcell collection, *A Choice Collection of Lessons for the Harpsichord or Spinnet*, for Purcell's widow Frances. Given such close and cordial relations with their publishers, even the most successful composers were unlikely to become restive about differences between the interests of composer and publisher. In the light of the Playfords' support for English music and musicians, publishers and composers may have seen the publishers' work as a service provided to composers as well as to consumers of music, though at the consumers' expense.

---

[41] Quoted from Franklin B[ersher] Zimmerman, *Henry Purcell, 1659–1695: His life and times*, London, 1967, p 79.

[42] *ibid.*, p 80.

[43] *ibid.*, p 151.

Nevertheless, Purcell decided to do some publishing on his own account. He had had an early self-publishing success in 1683, when he published his trio sonatas by subscription, using John Playford as one of the distributors. In 1690, managing the project and assuming the business risks himself, and adopting a bolder strategy than the Playfords', Purcell organised subscription publication of music from his semi-opera *Dioclesian*. The venture was intended to complement the first performance of *Dioclesian*, exploiting public interest in the work and publicising Purcell's skills as a theatre composer; but it may also indicate that he was dissatisfied either with the returns, whatever they were, from his dealings with the Playfords, or with being represented in print mostly by short pieces in popular collections, or with both. Perhaps, too, this move towards authorial independence was encouraged by the author of the words of *Dioclesian*, John Dryden, who had had to resume writing for the stage when he lost his official appointments after the Revolution of 1688, and who was discontented with what he was being paid by his publisher. Whether or not John Playford encouraged Purcell to publish *Dioclesian*, he supported the venture at least to the extent of acting as a distributor.

Subscriptions were advertised in June 1690, when *Dioclesian* was first performed. But publication was delayed until the following May, for reasons Purcell described in his postscript 'advertisement' to the score:

> In order to the speedier Publication of this Book, I employed two several Printers; but One of them falling into some trouble, and the Volume swelling to a Bulk beyond my expectation, have been the Occasions of this Delay.
>
> It has been objected that some of the Songs are already common;[44] but I presume that the Subscribers, upon perusal of the Work, will easily be convinc'd that they are not the Essential Parts of it.
>
> I have, according to my Promise in the Proposals, been very careful in the Examination of every Sheet, and hope the Whole will appear as Correct as any yet Extant.
>
> My desire to make it as cheap as possibly I cou'd to the Subscribers, prevail'd with me so far above the consideration of my own Interest, that

[44] Four items from *Dioclesian* were published before Purcell's publication came out. See Franklin B[ersher] Zimmerman, *Henry Purcell 1659–1695: An analytical catalogue of his music*, London, 1963, p 487.

> I find, too late, the Subscription-money will scarcely amount to the Expence of compleating this Edition.[45]

Purcell had made the novice entrepreneur's mistakes of underestimating the size and difficulty of the project, overestimating sales and underestimating what he needed to charge in order to cover costs and get a reasonable return. The episode showed that the Playfords' policy of concentrating on small-scale works suitable for amateur performance was sound. Purcell did not repeat his experiment, nor were music publishers or other composers quick to do so. In 1702, in the introduction to the score of the winning entry in a competition to set William Congreve's masque *The Judgement of Paris*, the music publisher John Walsh referred to 'the ill success which Publishers of Musick have mett with in other approved pieces', and cited 'the celebrated Dioclesian of Mr Henry Purcell' as 'an instance of that Nature, which found so small Encouragement in Print, as serv'd to stifle many other Intire Opera's, no less Excellent.'[46]

As the leading English music publisher of the first quarter of the eighteenth century, John Walsh would be involved in events that helped to bring the idea of musical copyright into focus. But this would happen only after Parliament radically changed the legal framework of publishing by enacting the first Copyright Act.

6.6 The Copyright Act of 1710

The lapsing of the Licensing Act in 1695 removed barriers to entry to the book publishing business, allowing newcomers to set up presses without reference to the Stationers' Company and to print whatever they liked, including books which booksellers had formerly been able to treat as their exclusive property. With their business interests threatened, established booksellers and printers called on Parliament to institute penalties for unauthorised reprinting. As the petitions

---

[45] Henry Purcell, *The vocal and instrumental Musick of The Prophetess, or The History of Dioclesian*, London, 1691, following p 173.

[46] Quoted from Jonathan Keates, *Purcell: A biography*, London, 1995, p 206.

quoted in section 6.4 above indicate, booksellers now believed that the common law gave them the property right which their seventeenth-century predecessors had unsuccessfully sought from Parliament, but they also believed that the only remedy provided by the common law—namely, damages—did not deal adequately with the problem of unauthorised reprinting. However, since no court had confirmed the existence of common-law copyright, booksellers ideally needed Parliament to put the matter beyond doubt, either by declaring that common-law copyright existed or by legislating to create a statutory right indistinguishable from it.

Writers, too, wanted new legislation. Uncontrolled printing, as well as reducing their incomes—why should a bookseller pay well for material that someone else could reprint without permission and without payment?—eliminated what little control writers had over reprints and second editions of their work, and made the use of pseudonyms all too easy, allowing unknown authors to publish their work under well-known names and helping them to evade prosecution for writings which were against the law.

Moreover, successful writers were increasingly dissatisfied, as Dryden had been, with their share of the legitimate profits made from their books. In 1709 the young Alexander Pope wrote to the literary veteran William Wycherley:

> When once a Man has appear'd as a Poet, he may give up his Pretensions to all the rich and thriving Arts: Those who have once made their court to those Mistresses without Portions, the Muses, are never like to set up for Fortunes. ... *Jacob* [the publisher Jacob Tonson I] creates Poets, as Kings sometimes do Knights, not for their honour, but for money. Certainly he ought to be esteem'd a worker of Miracles, who is grown rich by Poetry.
>
> What Authors lose, their Booksellers have won,
> So pimps grow rich, while Gallants are undone.[47]

(Pope would work miracles on his own behalf in years to come.) However, writers needed a firm legal basis for any claim they made to a share of booksellers' profits. They therefore needed security with respect to printing rights just as much as booksellers did.

---

[47] George Sherburn (ed.), *The Correspondence of Alexander Pope*, London, 1956, v 1 p 60–61.

Other groups with an interest in the book trade also wanted aspects of the pre-1695 regime restored or preserved. The Stationers' Company wanted to run the book trade and to exclude outsiders from it; the bishops wanted the government to license books and control newspapers; holders of patents and privileges wanted to keep the rights they had been granted; and major libraries wanted a legal deposit scheme.

Those who had lost nothing with the lapsing of the Licensing Act included musicians and music sellers. They took no part in the discussion of new book-trade legislation and probably regarded it as irrelevant to them. Although disputes about piracy occurred—notably a 1709 row between John Walsh and his former apprentice Luke Pippard—music sellers relied upon claim and counter-claim and price cutting to defend their business interests and not on legal action or the threat of it.[48]

Those who wanted legislation had diverse aims, for most of which Parliament had little sympathy. It is fair to say that Parliament was largely unconcerned about Stationers or the Stationers' Company, was uninterested in restoring government control of printing, was wary of creating anything which might be called a monopoly—monopolies being 'odious', as the King's Bench put it in *Company of Stationers v Partridge*—and was disinclined to give high priority to dealing with the problems of the book trade. The result was that new book-trade legislation was enacted only in 1710, after a series of earlier book-trade bills had lapsed.[49]

---

[48] For instance, Walsh advertised in *The Post-Man; and the Historical Account, &c.*, 30 April–3 May 1709, p 2, 'To all Lovers of Musick, *⁎* There being lately printed a spurious Edition of the Symphonies of the Opera of Thomyris [composed by Alessandro Scarlatti and others], by L. Pippard with many Faults, and sold at 1 s. 6 d. and insinuates in an Advertisement of this Paper of Saturday last, that the cause of his low'ring the price was Mr Walsh's reprinting a set of Italian and English Airs for 2 Flutes, which Mr Walsh did only by way of Reprizal for the said Pippards Copying his Symphonies of Thomyris, in which the said Pippard was the first Agressor…'. See also William C[harles] Smith, *A Bibliography of the Musical Works published by John Walsh during the years 1695–1720*, [London], 1968, p 102–103.

[49] For a detailed account of the genesis of the Copyright Act of 1710 see Deazley, *On the Origin of the Right to Copy*, *op. cit.* in note 37 above, p 1–50.

Writers, unlike most other interest groups, lacked any formal organisation or strong political presence. But some writers had excellent political connections, especially those who worked for Sir Robert Harley, 1st Earl of Oxford and Mortimer, who was the head of Queen Anne's government from 1704 to 1708 and Lord Treasurer from 1711 to 1714, and the first politician to make systematic use of newspapers for propaganda purposes. More than most politicians of the day, he would have had some sympathy for writers' claims, needing not just to pay them but to retain their goodwill. Harley also had a personal interest in books and writing: he was a notable collector of manuscripts, and in 1714 he often attended meetings of the Scriblerus Club.[50]

Daniel Defoe, perhaps the most trusted of Harley's stable of writers, was a strident critic of book licensing and advocate of writers' rights. In his 1704 *Essay on the Regulation of the Press* Defoe denounced 'a certain sort of Thieving' called 'Press-piracy' as an injustice to authors 'every jot as unjust as lying with their Wives, and breaking-up their Houses.'[51] And in 1705 he wrote in his *Review*:

> Books are Printed by no body, and Wrote by every body; one Man Prints another Man's Works, and calls them his own; again, another Man Prints his own, and calls them another Man's ... continual Roberies, Piracies, and Invasions of Property range among the Occupation [of publishing]. One Man Studies Seven Year, to bring a finish'd Peice into the World, and a Pyrate Printer, Reprints his Copy immediately, and Sells it for a quarter of the Price. ... These things call for an Act of Parliament, and that so loud, as I hope will not be deny'd; that so Property of Copies may be secur'd to Laborious Students to the Encouragement of Letters and all useful Studies'.[52]

This book is the most detailed history of eighteenth-century copyright and contains much material from previously unexplored sources.

[50] See Valerie Rumbold, 'Scriblerus Club [Scriblerians] (act[ive] 1714)', in the 'theme' section of the online *Oxford Dictionary of National Biography*.

[51] Daniel Defoe, *An Essay on the Regulation of the Press*, London, 1704, p 19–21.

[52] [Daniel Defoe,] *A Review of the Affairs of France: with observations on transactions at home*, v 2 no. 106 (8 November 1705) p 424.

According to Ronan Deazley, Defoe 'for the first time in this debate ... drew an explicit link between the benefit to society as a whole that comes with the encouragement of learning, and the provision of some sort of statutory protection for books as a way to achieve this end'.[53]

Defoe was not the last to make this connection. The Stationers' Company took up the idea, using society's interests as a stalking horse for its own, as it had used authors' interests in 1643 and 1666. The idea would be incorporated in the title of the bill which Parliament eventually passed in 1710.

A striking instance of how Defoe's ideas foreshadowed the legislation that was finally enacted is his remark in the *Essay*, when discussing a proposed law to re-regulate the press, that

> every author being obliged to set his Name to the Book he writes, has, by this [proposed] Law an undoubted exclusive Right to the Property of it. The Clause in the Law is a Patent to the Author and settles the propriety of the work wholly in himself, or in such to whom he shall assign it[54]

It is a short step from this to the idea of 'a general standing Patent to Authors', the apt phrase used in 1750 by Lord Chancellor Hardwicke to describe a central provision of the measure that finally became law (see section 6.9 below).

Defoe evidently discussed writers' rights with Harley. On 25 March 1707, when he was in Scotland drumming up support for the Union with Scotland at Harley's behest, he wrote to Harley: 'I hear the bill for Secureing the Right of printed Coppyes is stopt. I beg of you Sir in your respect to Encouragement of Letters and Dilligence in Learning to give it your help.'[55]

That bill failed, but Defoe outlined a proposed book-trade bill of his own in 1709. It had two major provisions: one, that unauthorised reprinting should be subject to damages and penalties; the other, that authors should publish under their own names. The omission of any reference to the nature of the right to print probably

---

[53] Deazley, *op. cit.*, p 32.

[54] Defoe, *An Essay on the Regulation of the Press*, *op. cit.*, p 21.

[55] George Harris Healey (ed.), *The Letters of Daniel Defoe*, Oxford, 1955, p 212.

indicates that he assumed that copyright existed at common law. Defoe then gave vociferous support to the copyright bill presented to Parliament in 1710, railing against 'the miserable Havock that is made in this Nation, with the Property of the Subject, with Relation to Books'.[56] Joseph Addison gave more measured support to authors' rights in *The Tatler* and after his election to Parliament in March 1710 he served on the committee dealing with that bill.[57]

After much alteration the bill was passed by Parliament as *An Act for the Encouragement of Learning, by Vesting the Copies of Printed Books in Authors or Purchasers of such Copies, During the Times therein Mentioned*, 8 Anne c.19., the Copyright Act of 1710.[58] Most of its provisions had some bearing on the subsequent development of musical copyright.

---

[56] [Daniel Defoe], *A Review of the State of the British Nation*, v 6 no. 29 (2 February 1710) p 515.

[57] *The Tatler*, v 2 no. 101 (1 December 1709) p 270–273. Articles in this periodical were written under the pseudonym 'Isaac Bickerstaff'.

[58] The Act, reproduced at http://www.copyrighthistory.com/anne.html, is discussed in Harry Ransom, *The First Copyright Statute: An essay on* An Act for the Encouragement of Learning, *1710*, Austin, Texas, 1956; in Deazley, *op. cit.*; and in John Feather, 'The book trade in politics: the making of the Copyright Act of 1710', *Publishing History* no. 8 (1980) p 19–44. It has been given several names and two dates. The word 'copyright' is not in its title or text, and while in force it was called the 'Act of Anne', the 'Statute of Anne' or the 'Act for the Encouragement of Learning'. But in the standard book on modern British copyright law it is called both 'the first Copyright Act' and 'the Statute of Anne' (Kevin Garnett and Gillian Davies (eds), *Copinger and Skone James on Copyright*, 15th ed., London, 2005, v 1 p 34–36). Although the Act was passed, received royal assent and took effect in 1710, British legal sources customarily date it 1709, because until 1793, when the Acts of Parliament (Commencement) Act, 33 George III c.13, took effect, an act commenced (and, in the absence of provision to the contrary, took effect) not on the actual day that it received royal assent (the rule since 1793) but retrospectively, on the first day of the Parliamentary session in which it was passed, because of the legal fiction that a session of Parliament lasted one day (see *Halsbury's Laws of England*, 4th ed., London, 1995, v 44 part 1 p 760–761). This book follows the practice of bibliographic historians such as Ransom, Feather, and contributors to Michael F. Suarez and Michael L. Turner (eds), *The Cambridge History of the Book in Britain v 5: 1695–1830*, Cambridge, 2009, and refers to the Act as the Copyright Act of 1710.

The Copyright Act began as a fairly simple bill brought in in January 1710.[59] By the time it was enacted in April it had grown from six to eleven sections and had undergone so much tinkering that its assumptions were no longer clear. The original title of the bill described it as 'Securing the Property of Copies in Books'. Its preamble spoke of authors 'in whom the undoubted Property of such Books and Writings, as the Product of their Learning and Labour, remains', and referred to 'Persons, to whom such Authors, for good Considerations, have lawfully Transferred their Right and Title'. Unauthorised printing was described as 'a Notorious Invasion of the Property of the Rightful Proprietors of such Books and Writings'.[60] And the bill put no time limit on authors' rights, clearly assuming that perpetual copyright existed at common law. However, Parliament watered down this aspect of the bill, possibly because it saw common-law copyright as a kind of monopoly. But the watering-down was inconsistent.

The phrase 'vesting the copies' in the title of the Act seemed to suggest that copyright did not exist at common law: one cannot vest a power or a right in someone who already possesses it. The Act's preamble, however, appeared to assume the prior existence of a non-statutory right, stating that:

> Printers, Booksellers, and other Persons have of late frequently taken the Liberty of Printing, Reprinting, and Publishing, or causing to be Printed, Reprinted and Published, Books, and other Writings, without the Consent of the Authors or Proprietors of such Books and Writings.

And the body of the Act seemed to make both assumptions. It created a statutory right for the benefit of authors and those who had 'Purchased or Acquired the Copy or Copies of such Book or Books', but it referred also to 'the property in every such book, as is intended by this Act to be secured to the proprietor or proprietors thereof'. Section 1 of the Act provided, with respect to books already published, that the author, or else whoever had 'purchased or acquired the copy or copies of any book or books, in order to print or reprint the same', was to have exclusive printing rights—which

[59] For the text of the original bill see Deazley, *op cit.*, p 38–39.

[60] *ibid.*, p 41.

various parts of the Act refer to in various ways, such as 'the sole Right and Liberty of Printing', 'the sole Liberty of Printing and Reprinting' and 'the sole Right of Printing or Disposing of'—for twenty-one years from 10 April 1710. With respect to books published after that date, the author or his or her assignee was to have exclusive printing rights for fourteen years from the date of publication. As Lord Chancellor Hardwicke succinctly put it forty years later, this provision was 'a general standing patent to authors'.

Section 1 further provided that if anyone should 'print, reprint or import, or cause to be printed, reprinted, or imported' a book without written authorisation attested by two witnesses, or 'sell, publish, or expose to sale' a book knowing that it had been published without authorisation, the legal proprietor was entitled to confiscate and deface the offending edition. In such cases a penalty of one penny per page applied, half to go to the Crown and the other half to the person who initiated legal action over the breach of the Act. But Section 2 provided that these 'forfeitures or penalties' were to apply only if a book had been entered in the Stationers' register before publication. This section also specified the fee payable to the Company for an entry and for a certificate of entry and contained provisions to ensure that the register was publicly accessible. Section 3 provided that the Company could not refuse to register a book or to issue a certificate of entry.

After details—irrelevant in the present context and later repealed—dealing with control of book prices,[61] the Act provided in Section 5 that, after 10 April 1710, 'Nine Copies of each Book or Books, upon the best Paper, that … shall be Printed and Published … or Reprinted and Published with Additions' were to be delivered to the warehouse keeper of the Stationers' Company before publication for the 'use' of nine named major libraries in England and Scotland. And like a few other statutes enacted shortly after the Union of 1707, the Act made special mention of 'that part of Great Britain called Scotland', providing that penalties for offences committed there were recoverable by action in the Court of Session there.

---

[61] Wanting religious books to be reasonably priced, governments had been concerned since the time of Henry VIII to prevent profiteering in the book trade.

The final sections of the Act had no counterparts in the original bill but, as was common practice with additional provisions, were parliamentary afterthoughts tacked on in no special order. Section 7 returned to the subject of imports, providing 'That nothing in this Act contained do extend, or shall be construed to extend, to Prohibit the Importation, Vending or Selling of any Books in Greek, Latin or any Foreign Language Printed beyond the Seas'. (The Licensing Act had also prohibited the importation only of English-language books, so that scholars were not denied access to foreign-language material printed overseas.)

Section 8 was intended to discourage litigation by increasing the risks that plaintiffs took in actions brought under the Act and the costs that they incurred if such actions were unsuccessful. The Act provided 'that if any Action or Suit shall be Commenced or Brought against any Person or Persons whatsoever, for doing or causing to be done anything in pursuance of this Act, the Defendants in such Action may plead the General Issue, and give the Special Matter in Evidence'. This allowed defendants to reserve the details of their defence until the hearing.

Section 9 dealt with royal printing grants without saying so. The royal prerogative power was now a less politically sensitive matter than it had been when the Licensing Act was passed, but Parliament still skirted around it, leaving the courts to decide questions about the validity of individual grants. Section 9 provided that 'nothing in this Act contained shall extend, or be construed to extend, either to Prejudice or Confirm any Right that the said Universities, or any of them, or any Person or Persons have, or claim to have, to the Printing or Reprinting any Book or Copy already printed, or hereafter to be Printed'.

Section 10, like section 8, was intended to discourage litigation. It provided that 'all Actions, Suits, Bills, Indictments, or Informations for any Offence that shall be committed against this Act, shall be Brought, Sued, and Commenced within Three Months next after such Offence Committed, or else the same shall be Void and of none Effect'.

Finally, section 11 provided that 'after the Expiration of the said Term of Fourteen Years, the sole Right of Printing or Disposing of Copies shall Return to the Authors thereof, if they are then living, for another Term of Fourteen Years'. This may have been included to remove an anomalous effect of the first section, under which a book published in 1711 would be protected only until 1725, but a book published in 1709 would be protected until 1730. In getting rid of this anomaly, this clause created another: a book published in 1711 by an author who died in 1726 would be protected until 1739, but a book published by the same author in 1713 would be protected only until 1727. But this new anomaly affected not the book's author but whoever owned the copyright after the author's death—which is consistent with Ronan Deazley's hypothesis that this section was 'intended to benefit the author and only the author',[62] and suggests that MPs expected the new Act to work to the advantage of authors in their dealings with booksellers.

Parliament enacted some notably forward-looking measures in the years after the Revolution of 1688, and in some ways the Copyright Act was one of them: it was the first book-trade measure not to impose government control over the trade, and the first not to support an oligopoly. On the other hand, what now seems the most innovative feature of the Act—the creation of limited-term statutory rights for authors—was a 'standing patent for authors' modelled upon the old privilege, with an extension added to the term of protection as an apparent afterthought.

Moreover, the Act undoubtedly was, or would prove to be, a severe disappointment to most of the groups that had been lobbying for book-trade legislation. Parliament's lack of enthusiasm for perpetual copyright no doubt disappointed booksellers in the short term and would have major unforeseen consequences for them many years later. Booksellers and printers alike would have been disappointed that the Act did not protect them against provincial competitors, although London booksellers managed to dominate the trade for many years to come without legislative backing, using what were orthodox business methods. Moreover, booksellers would have been unhappy that Parliament had made the penal provisions of the Act almost unusable. The Stationers' Company, although the Act gave it a central role in the book trade and an income stream from its register, would have been disappointed that it could no longer exclude

---

[62] Deazley, *op cit.*, p 43.

non-members from the trade by refusing to register their books, and it would soon find that the income stream was much lower than it might have expected. And writers, once any initial euphoria had worn off, would have found that the Act left their position unchanged, for it neither helped them to negotiate better terms with publishers nor gave them more say in what happened to their work once they had sold it. In addition, the Act had various shortcomings discussed in section 6.8 below: it did not define its key terms; the relationship between some of its provisions was obscure; and it added a measure of confusion to the uncertainty about common-law copyright.

Yet the Act represented the future: limited-term copyright would become the basis of copyright law in Britain and other nations, and the Act would become the lineal ancestor of later copyright legislation in Britain and many other parts of the world. In the short term, however, the Act's shortcomings would make it a fruitful source of uncertainty, conflict and, inevitably, litigation.

6.7 Protecting Music, 1710–1770: Registration, Music Publishing, Privileges and Parliament

After the Licensing Act lapsed in 1695 the Stationers' register became almost dormant. Nothing was added to it between 7 March 1708/1709 and 28 April 1710.[63] Stationers had evidently used the register because the law required it, not because they felt any great need to record who owned which book. But when the Copyright Act became law in 1710 the register came back to life, with 163 works entered from 28 April to the end of December 1710 and 258 in 1711.[64] The revival was brief: the annual numbers fell sharply from 1712 to 1717 (when only thirty-four works were entered) and

[63] See *MESH* p xv fn 6.

[64] The number of entries in the register in each year between 1709 and 1826, including both literary works and music, was tabulated for the House of Commons by George Greenhill, warehouse keeper of the Stationers' Company, and published as *Copyright. Return of literary works and books of prints entered at Stationers' Hall, 1709–1826*, House of Commons Parliamentary Paper no. 322, 9 May 1827.

remained low. The 1711 total would not be exceeded for over seventy years.

The relatively high levels of registration in 1710 and 1711 were probably due mainly to publishers' general awareness of the new Copyright Act and of the fact that it made registration mandatory. Indeed, some books published before the Act came into effect were registered unnecessarily. One reason why the level of registrations was generally low until the late 1760s is that registration, although mandatory, was largely pointless. It enabled registrants to invoke the Act's penal provisions—provided that registration took place before publication, that registrants launched proceedings within three months of an alleged infringement, and that registrants were not deterred by not knowing the details of the other side's defence. Otherwise registration was worthwhile only if works published after 1710 had to be registered in order to be protected by the Act—a point on which the Act was silent. And works could be registered late, if need be, as there was no penalty for late registration or for failing to register a publication.

In any case, the upper levels of the book trade had developed their own kind of protection against piracy. Government policy up to 1695 had created a trade which as well as being concentrated in London was quite close-knit and remained so even when the Stationers' Company no longer had the power to control it. Major publishers routinely worked together—as buyers and sellers of printing rights, as collaborators on large publishing projects, and in 'congers' (copyright-owning syndicates). Anyone who did not comply with trade practice with respect to printing rights ran the risk of exclusion from potentially valuable trade activities and perhaps of a concerted counter-attack. Such considerations no doubt helped to limit the incidence of book piracy and to produce the casual attitude of London publishers to the Stationers' register both before 1710 and for much of the eighteenth century.

Of a total of 3383 entries in the Stationers' register from 1710 to 1770 inclusive, only 143 were music entries, including entries for instruction books, librettos, books about music and so on.[65] The

---

[65] These figures are based upon the numbers given in *MESH* p xxv–xxviii, for music entries and total entries in the register for each year from 1710 to 1818,

annual figures for music entries followed much the same pattern as those for the total number of entries. An initial peak in 1710 and 1711 (eleven and nine music entries) was followed by a steep decline: from 1722 to 1727 the five-year average number of music entries was less than one. The annual number of music entries first exceeded the 1710 total only in 1769, when it reached twelve.

However, the Stationers' register was less important for music than even these low figures suggest. Music was seldom registered in its own right: just nineteen of the 143 music publications registered between 1710 and 1770 consisted of instrumental music; the others contained vocal music—sometimes older music fitted with new words—or substantial amounts of verbal text, with or without music notation. Most music registrants were printers and book publishers; music publishers ignored the register almost completely. John Walsh, the leading English music publisher from around 1710, registered only six country-dance collections (which contained both music and descriptions of the dance steps) and a collection of anthems in the years 1710 to 1717 and nothing thereafter. John Walsh Jr, who succeeded his father about 1730,[66] and who in turn dominated the trade until the 1760s, registered nothing at all. Many rivals of the Walshes—including Richard Meares Sr and Jr, John Cluer, William Smith, John Wilcox and John Johnson—also registered nothing.

All nineteen instrumental-music publications entered between 1710 and 1770 were registered by the composers or, in Jeremiah Clarke's case, by the late composer's brother-in-law. Only one of these composers registered more than one work: William Corbett registered two. (Some musicians, of course, only ever published one work: one publication could be enough for someone who wanted

---

and use Michael Kassler's 'inclusive' definition of a music entry. Nancy A. Mace, 'The market for music in the late eighteenth century and the entry books of the Stationers' Company', *The Library* 7th ser. vol. 10 no. 2 (June 2009) p 157–187, identified a shortfall of about 3% in Kassler's list of entries for the years 1751 to 1800 (caused by the omission of some pages of the register from a microfilm used by one of his sources), but because this shortfall does not affect the present argument, his figures have been used in this chapter for the sake of consistency.

[66] See William C[harles] Smith, *A Bibliography of the Musical Works published by John Walsh during the years 1695–1720*, [London], 1968, p viii–ix. Walsh Jr introduced several changes to the firm's practices about this time.

simply to advertise his skills as an executant or teacher.) And although instrumental music by Clarke, John Ernest Galliard and Johann Mattheson was registered in the years 1710 to 1714, none by such prominent English-resident composers as Giovanni Bononcini, Handel, Geminiani, Veracini, Greene, Thomas Arne, Boyce, John Stanley, Abel or J. C. Bach was registered in later years.

One reason for the low level of registration of music was that there was no reference to it in the 1710 Copyright Act. Also, much printed music filled only a few pages and was sold cheaply, and so was not worth enough money to justify the trouble and expense of legal proceedings if piracy occurred. Moreover, music sellers were used to operating without rules: their trade had never been subject to legislation or a licensing regime, and very few of them belonged to the Stationers' Company. Their situation was similar to that of the printers and book publishers who had set up shop in the years after the lapsing of the Licensing Act, and the business practices of music sellers often were not far removed from the 'continual Roberies, Piracies, and Invasions of Property' denounced by Defoe—a point illustrated by the piracy of one leading composer's music.

On 16 April 1733, four days after Daniel Wright, his son Daniel II and Thomas Wright advertised their forthcoming publication of *A Choice Book of Lessons for the Harpsichord or Spinnet, Composed by the famous Dr Green,*[67] Maurice Greene, professor of music at Cambridge, organist of St Paul's Cathedral, and organist and composer to the Chapel Royal, placed the following notice in a newspaper:

> Whereas Daniel Wright, Instrument-Maker, in Holbourn, has publish'd Lessons for the Harpsichord, or Spinnet, under my Name, and has asserted, that they have been carefully corrected by me; this is to acquaint the Publick, That those Lessons have been publish'd without my Knowledge or Consent; that many of them were not compos'd by me; and that those few which are mine, were composed many Years ago, and are very uncorrect.[68]

---

[67] *The Grub-Street Journal*, 12 April 1733, p 3.

[68] *The St James's Evening Post*, 21–24 April 1733, p 2.

Nevertheless, Wright readvertised the collection. Having been denied the title of music seller, he returned the compliment by demoting Greene to 'Mr' and went on to claim that the music had been 'carefully revised and corrected by the best Masters, from the many gross Errors contained in the manuscript'.[69]

John Walsh Jr promptly intervened. On 19 May there came out under his imprint *The Lady's Banquet 2d Book*, a cheaper, better engraved and more correct version of *A Choice Book of Lessons*, from which it was evidently copied. Greene was not named in the book. No doubt to Greene's great satisfaction, *The Lady's Banquet* killed off *A Choice Book of Lessons*: Wright did not readvertise his publication and he omitted it from his 1734 catalogue. It is not known whether Walsh intervened in the hope of earning Greene's goodwill; whether Greene was grateful for the intervention; whether he helped with *The Lady's Banquet*; or whether he felt, after seeing what happened to *A Choice Book of Lessons*, that it would be prudent to publish with Walsh rather than with someone else. But 'thereafter, nearly all his major works came out under Walsh's imprint'.[70]

Piracy of published material, piracy of unpublished material, misattribution, lack of attribution and publication of corrupt editions were not restricted to the Walshes or to the 1730s. Nor were they restricted to music publishing: the same practices were endemic in newspaper and magazine publishing—another branch of publishing which was peripheral to the business of book publishing, which had never been controlled by the Stationers' Company, and in which piracy was easy and the money value of what was pirated at any one time was often too small to warrant legal action. Even though it could plausibly be argued that a magazine was a book, or an article in a magazine a writing, within the meaning of the Copyright Act, newspapers and magazines routinely reprinted one another's material verbatim and without acknowledgement. Just as a music seller might make a set of three trios by pirating some that had been previously published by someone else, a newspaper publisher might fill an empty

[69] See H[arry] Diack Johnstone, 'Greene and *The Lady's Banquet*: a case of double piracy', *The Musical Times* v 108 no. 1487 (January 1967) p 36–39, upon which the present account of this case is based.

[70] *ibid.*, p 38.

column with an item from another newspaper. Publishers had to accept, perhaps grudgingly, that some of the material they paid for might be pirated; but in return they could carry out piracy of their own without any qualms and whenever they liked.

Authors suffered most from casual piracy. It reduced their income and limited their bargaining power; and corrupt, misattributed or unattributed versions of their work misrepresented them and affected their reputations. Composers suffered more than writers. Music sellers intent on reducing production costs and maximising sales might truncate a piece and omit or alter its parts, might assign parts to instruments for which they were not written, or might arbitrarily rescore whole works—say, by making a keyboard arrangement of an orchestral composition.[71] Music composed for performance or for teaching purposes was frequently copied for the benefit of performers or students, so that a composition which had served its immediate purpose often remained unpublished but extant in multiple manuscript copies, increasing the risk of piracy.

Composers and writers alike occasionally made public protest, as Greene did, about piracy of their work. In 1759 Samuel Johnson published an advertisement fulminating against those who 'with the most shameless rapacity' had pirated essays from *The Idler*, and threatening that in future 'those who have been thus busy with their sickles in the fields of their neighbours' were to expect 'that we shall vindicate our due, by the means which justice prescribes, and which are warranted by the immemorial prescriptions of honourable trade.'[72] But no legal action followed; instead, Johnson attempted to spike the pirates' guns by republishing *The Idler* complete in 1761. Oliver Goldsmith adopted the same strategy: in 1765 he published a collection of his essays, remarking in the preface that he had seen most of them regularly reprinted two or three times a year without permission, and some as many as sixteen times.[73]

---

[71] Examples of all these practices are given below.

[72] James Boswell, *Life of Johnson* ed. R[obert] W[illiam] Chapman and J[ohn] D[avid] Fleeman, Oxford, 1980, p 244.

[73] Arthur Friedman (ed.), *Collected Works of Oliver Goldsmith* v 3, Oxford, 1966, p 1.

Writers could threaten to invoke the Copyright Act, as Johnson did: 'We shall lay hold, in our turn, upon their copies, degrade them from the pomp of wide margin and diffuse typography, contract them into a narrow space, and sell them at an humble price'.[74] But it was less clear that the Act protected music than that it protected essays. Some composers, a few music publishers and an editor therefore attempted to protect their music against piracy by recourse not to the Act but to a form of copyright protection not explicitly referred to in the Act—namely, a privilege.

The validity of privileges was doubtful, at best: the Licensing Act had been equivocal about them and the Copyright Act was agnostic; they were inconsistent both with the idea of common-law copyright and with the intent of the act which abolished Star Chamber; and in 1712 the King's Bench had suggested in *Company of Stationers v Partridge* that the king had a right to make printing grants with respect only to publications in which he had a 'special interest'. But as far as is known, the question of just what printing grants the king had the power to make remained dormant from the time of *Stationers v Partridge* until the 1770s. The authorities, however, overlooked or simply ignored any legal uncertainties: about 168 privileges were granted to authors, publishers and others between 1710 and 1760.[75] And privilege holders made much of their privileges, using them to promote new publications, reproducing them in those publications, threatening to use them against anyone

[74] Boswell, *loc. cit.*

[75] Shef Rogers, 'The use of royal licences for printing in England, 1695–1760: a bibliography', *The Library* 7th ser. v 1 no. 2 (June 2000) p 133–192, lists, chronologically numbers and indexes 189 privileges granted from 1695 to 1760, of which twenty-four were granted before 1710. (No. 9 in Rogers's list is not a privilege, being a grant of money rather than of printing rights.) Three music privileges not in Rogers's list bring the post-1710 tally to 168. They were granted to William Corbett on 4 March 1742 (see David Hunter, letter to the editor, *The Library*, 7th ser. v 1 no. 4 (December 2000) p 442), to Domenico Paradies on 28 November 1754 (reprinted in his *Sonate di gravicembalo*), and to Pieter Hellendaal on 23 April 1758 (reprinted in his concertos opus 6). Music privileges granted after 1760 include those obtained by J. C. Bach (1763), Joseph Kelway (1764), John Burton (1766) and John Worgan (1771). On the latter two see David Hunter, 'More musical privileges', letter to the editor, *Music & Letters* v 68 no. 2 (April 1987) p 210.

who reproduced the protected material without authorisation, and invoking them in legal proceedings. But no copyright litigant is known to have won a legal action on the basis only of a privilege.

By the middle of the century some writers recognised that privileges added little or nothing to what the law already gave: Richard Rolt observed in 1756 that 'at present privileges are not only seldom required, but by the late act for securing the properties of books, seem needless'.[76] But a privilege was useful as an advertising tool, because it gave the impression that a book had the king's endorsement. Malachy Postlethwayt, who attacked this practice in 1755, believed that this was the main reason that booksellers obtained privileges:

> However meritorious some books may be that have been thus printed [with a privilege], I cannot but think, in the general, such practices are highly impositions and deceitful upon the mass of the people, who are weak enough to imagine, that a book with a patent to it, has the sanction and authority of his majesty, or those officers of state, who are delegated to grant such powers and privileges; when the truth is, that neither the attorney or solicitor-general, any more than the secretaries of state, or the public, have ever seen a single sheet of such book; and the king knows no more of the merits thereof, than the emperor of China; nay, it is frequent, if I am rightly informed, to obtain patents for books, before any part of them has begun to be written. And what is still more extraordinary, there are numbers of books published in this nation, with these words annexed to them, PRINTED AND PUBLISHED ACCORDING TO ACT OF PARLIAMENT, or BY THE KING'S AUTHORITY: and numbers are made to believe, that the parliament have really made an act to encourage and propagate these works throughout the nation, which are generally in the greatest contempt, and only in esteem by the ignorant and deluded multitude.[77]

William Warburton agreed with both Rolt and Postlethwayt, writing in 1759:

---

[76] Richard Rolt, *A New Dictionary of Trade and Commerce*, London, 1756 (unpaginated), article 'privilege'.

[77] Malachy Postlethwayt, *The Universal Dictionary of Trade and Commerce, translated from the French of the celebrated Monsieur [Jacques] Savary [des Brûlons], ... with large additions and improvements*, London, v 2, 1755, p 425.

> A royal patent or Licence may be obtained on very easy terms, and without wasting your interest to obtain it. You may have it for asking, and at the moderate expense of 10*l*. But I know of no service it is, to the protection of any Author's property. If the work was written within fourteen years, the property is secured by Act of Parliament; when that time is elapsed, it is then claimed by common Law. In this latter case the right has been broke into, by rascally booksellers, from time to time; and so has the right in the former; but both one and the other is, upon the whole, tolerably well preserved. They fright you with stories of the invasion of literary property, in order, I suppose, to get yours the cheaper. But whether the property be within, or without, the fourteen years, the Patent gives the proprietor no additional security. The *use* of a Patent is for new inventions in medicine or mechanics, which gives the inventor an exclusive right to make and vend his inventions or improvements for fourteen years. But with regard to books, it is of no real or material use. You will ask then how it comes to pass that you see every newspaper full of advertisements of Books printed & printing, recommended by the King's patent to all his good Subjects? This is another of the Booksellers' roguerys, whereby they impose upon the Common people, who seeing the King's patent, think in good earnest, that he is solicitous to recommend the book which he thus honours, to their special notice, and they have no conception that he would thus recommend any thing that was not very good in its kind.[78]

Nevertheless Warburton, as Pope's literary executor, obtained a privilege for Pope's works a few months later, on 24 July 1759.

The use of privileges for promotion and publicity was nothing new: those granted to Richard Blome in 1669 for *A Geographical Description of the Four Parts of the World* and in 1683 for *The Gentleman's Recreation* were unabashed sales pitches, calling on the king's subjects to subscribe. However, the deficiencies of the Copyright Act may have constituted another reason for seeking the protection of a privilege in the eighteenth century. The Act did not protect foreign-language publications against imports, and seemed not to protect publications which were not books, or did not have an

---

[78] Warburton→Mercy Doddridge, 8 March 1759, quoted in Rogers, *op cit.*, p 140–141. The cost of a privilege was £8/1/– including stamp duty (*ibid.*, p 143). Until 1852 'it cost about £100 to obtain an English patent for an invention' (Stephen van Dulken, *British Patents of Invention, 1617–1977: A guide for researchers*, London, 1999, p 24); for the steps and the various costs involved see Alan Gomme, *Patents of Invention: Origin and growth of the patent system in Britain*, London, 1946, p 16–19 and p 35.

author, or did not contain only writing. Many publications for which privileges were granted between 1710 and 1760 fell into one or more of these categories. Some were wholly or partly in a foreign language, a few were not books—a set of uncut sheets, a set of engravings, a map and a set of cards—and some perhaps could be said not to be books, being published in parts or in several volumes. Several publications for which privileges were granted did not have an author in the conventional sense: some were translations, in which the author of the English words was not the creator of the content; some—among them reference works, magazines and a newspaper—had multiple authors whose individual contributions might have been difficult to identify; some were compilations or editions of the work of a deceased author; and the content of some overlapped with that of other publications and could not properly be said to belong to any one author (the reference works, the map). Other publications seemed not to be books because they contained a significant amount of material that was not obviously writing: maps; books which contained a large number of plates; and of course music.

The first person to obtain a music privilege, George Frideric Handel, arrived in London in November or December 1710, some seven or eight months after the Copyright Act became law. He had immediate, immense success with his first London opera, *Rinaldo*, and after a brief visit back to his employers in Hannover he returned to London in 1712 and settled there.

London music publishing had changed since John Playford's day. The English market for printed music had expanded, and ambitious projects like Purcell's edition of *Dioclesian* had become more feasible—partly, no doubt, because of growth in population, literacy and disposable incomes, combined with improvements in transport; but partly, too, because of the enterprise of John Walsh Sr. He cut production costs by printing music from engraved plates instead of moveable type and by using pewter plates instead of copper ones. (Copper plates produced prints of higher quality but were more difficult to engrave.) Rather like Robert Harley, Walsh advertised his products in the newspapers which proliferated after 1695, the year he began to publish music. He was quick to see and to exploit opportunities, bringing out a collection of music from *Rinaldo* soon after its first performance in 1711, and he continued to be Handel's main publisher for the next nine years, no doubt doing well from this, given the popularity of Handel's music.

Their arrangement came to an end in 1720. On 14 June Handel was granted a privilege giving him exclusive printing rights to 'several works, consisting of vocal and instrumental musick ... for the term of fourteen years'.[79] On 2 July Richard Meares Sr advertised a forthcoming edition of Handel's latest opera *Radamisto*, stating that it was being engraved on copper and would be corrected by the composer—the implication being that in these respects it would be superior to Walsh's editions of Handel's operas.[80] And on 1 November Handel's friend John Christopher Smith Sr advertised a forthcoming collection of Handel keyboard music, to be printed from copper plates and obtainable from Smith and Meares.[81]

A major reason for Handel's starting to use music sellers other than Walsh seems to have been the publication, apparently in the second half of 1719 or early in 1720, of a collection of his keyboard music—the first such collection to be published.[82] The title-page of *Pieces à un & Deux Clavecins* [sic] bore the imprint of Jeanne Roger of Amsterdam, whose publications Walsh sometimes sold with his own label pasted over her imprint. However, in this instance, the music was printed from Walsh-style plates and some of the pieces had English-language titles. Its publication may have been the product of a business arrangement between Walsh and Roger; but this seems unlikely, since another print with a 'Roger' title-page but with music printed from Walsh-style plates—a collection of twelve sonatas for solo wind instruments and keyboard, including ten by Handel—came out some years after her death in 1722.[83] Walsh's

---

[79] This privilege is reproduced in Otto Erich Deutsch, *Handel: A documentary biography*, London, 1955, p 105–106.

[80] *The Weekly Journal or Saturday's Post*, 2 July 1720, p 497.

[81] *The Evening Post*, 1–3 November 1720, p 3.

[82] For the early publication history of Handel's harpsichord suites see Terence Best, preface to *Hallische Händel-Ausgabe* ser. 4 v 1 (*Klavierwerke I*), Kassel, 1993.

[83] Terence Best, 'Handel's chamber music: sources, chronology and authenticity', *Early Music* v 13 no 4 (November 1983) p 476–499, demonstrates (p 481–482) that the 'Roger' print of these sonatas did not appear before 1724.

reason for using an 'Amsterdam' title-page for the sonatas was probably that he thought that it would help sales; and this may have been the case with the keyboard collection as well.

Whatever its origin, *Pieces à un & Deux Clavecins* evidently angered Handel. On 9 November 1720 a revised advertisement for the Smith/Meares Handel collection noted that 'The Author has been obliged to publish these Pieces to prevent the Publick being imposed upon by some Surreptitious and Incorrect Copies of some of them that has got abroad'.[84] John Cluer subsequently published in London 'for the composer' a work entitled *Suites de Pieces pour le Clavecin.* The eight engraved suites include sixteen pieces that had appeared in the 'Roger' collection, and the publication reproduced the text of Handel's privilege after the title-page, followed by a prefatory note in which Handel again referred to 'surreptitious and incorrect copies'. The first 'Roger' print thus seems to have prompted Handel to terminate his business arrangement with Walsh, to manage publication of his music for himself from then on, and to protect his music against unauthorised publication by obtaining a privilege, presumably because he was advised that the Copyright Act did not protect music.

Forty-one music privileges are known to have been granted from 1720 to 1760. Other than Handel's, only three privileges were granted in the 1720s: to Andrew Roner in 1721 for his *Melopeia Sacra*; to William Croft in 1724 for 'several anthems'; and to Francesco Geminiani in 1728 for 'several works consisting of vocal and instrumental musick'. The Roner and Croft collections resembled many non-musical publications for which privileges were granted, in that both were published in two folio volumes. But from 1730 onwards there was a marked rise in the number of music privileges, many of which were used with more modest publications. The recipients included, along with less well-known musicians, Michael Christian Festing in 1730, and again in 1744 when his first privilege expired; 'John' (i.e., Giovanni) Bononcini in 1731, as if in rejoinder to the charges of plagiarism made against him a few months earlier; 'Joseph San Martin' (Giuseppe Sammartini) in 1736; Geminiani again in 1739, perhaps to protect music composed after his first

---

[84] *The Daily Courant*, 9 November 1720, p 2.

privilege was granted; Thomas Arne in 1741; William Corbett, Maurice Greene and John Stanley in 1742; Francesco Veracini in 1744; William Boyce in 1745; and Felice de Giardini in 1751.

Handel's privilege appears to have served as a template for subsequent music privileges. Abel's privilege, granted forty years later and transcribed in *Figure 6.1*, is almost identical, apart from the names and dates.[85] Some privileges departed further from the template. John Worgan's first privilege and Thomas Vincent Jr's were signed by officials other than a Secretary of State.[86] Worgan's was granted in the name of a group of officials. Those of Roner, Bononcini, Henry Symonds, Greene, Veracini and Corbett echoed the Copyright Act, stating that the music was written 'in order to be printed and published'. But most music privileges shared most of the distinctive features of Handel's.[87]

The differences between the typical music privilege and the typical book privilege can be seen by comparing Abel's privilege with the one granted in 1743 to the publishers of the third edition of Thomas Salmon's *Modern History: Or, the Present State of All Nations*.[88] Instead of naming and describing one or more items, as book privileges usually did, Abel's privilege refers only to 'divers Works, consisting of Vocal and Instrumental Musick'. One reason for this vagueness is that more detailed description, to the extent that it

---

[85] It was printed in some editions of Abel's 'Six sonatas for the harpsicord with accompanyments for a violin or German flute, and violoncello', op. 2, and is transcribed from the copy of this work at BL h.3055.(4).

[86] Letters patent were normally signed by one of the two Secretaries of State. If a head of government—not officially called the Prime Minister until the mid-eighteenth century—signed a privilege, it was in his capacity as a Secretary. But the head of government was not necessarily a Secretary: Sir Robert Walpole, head of government from 1721 to 1742, was a Secretary only briefly (see Mark A[lméras] Thomson, *The Secretaries of State 1681–1782*, Oxford, 1932, p 185).

[87] This conclusion is based upon a perusal of thirty-one of the forty-one music privileges known to have been granted between 1695 and 1760, and also John Christian Bach's privilege, granted in 1763 and transcribed (together with his French *privilège générale* granted in the same year) in Ernest Warburton (ed.), *The Collected Works of Johann Christian Bach 1735–1782* v 48 part 2 ('Sources & Documents'), New York, 1999, p 555–556.

[88] This privilege is transcribed in Rogers, *op cit.*, p 134–135.

George R.

George the Second, by the Grace of GOD, King of GREAT-BRITAIN, FRANCE and IRELAND, Defender of the Faith, &c. To all to whom these Presents shall come, Greeting.

WHEREAS Our Trusty and Well-beloved CHARLES FREDERICK ABEL, Gent. has by his Petition humbly represented unto Us, that he hath with great Study, Labour and Expence, composed divers Works, consisting of Vocal and Instrumental Musick, and being desirous to print the same, and apprehending, unless he can obtain Our Royal Licence and Protection, other Persons may be induced to Print and Publish the said Works, and so invade his Property therein, he hath therefore most humbly prayed Us to grant him Our Royal Licence and Protection for the sole Printing and Publishing the abovementioned Works, for the Term of fourteen Years, agreeable to the Statute in that Case made and provided; We being willing to give all due Encouragement to this his Undertaking, are graciously pleased to condescend to his Request, and We do therefore, by these presents, so far as may be agreeable to the Statute in that Behalf, made and provided, grant unto him the said CHARLES FREDERICK ABEL, his Executors, Administrators and Assigns Our Licence, for the sole Printing and Publishing the said Works for the Term of fourteen Years; to be computed from the date hereof; strictly forbidding all Our Subjects within Our Kingdoms and Dominions; to reprint, abridge, copy out in Writing for Sale, or Publish the same, either in the like or any other size, or manner whatsoever, or to import, buy, vend, utter, or distribute and Copy or Copies thereof reprinted or written for Sale beyond the Seas, during the aforesaid Term of fourteen Years, without the Approbation or Consent of the said CHARLES FREDERICK ABEL, his Executors, Administrators or Assigns under their Hands and Seals, first had and obtained, as they will answer the contrary at their Perils; whereof the Commissioners and other Officers of Our Customs; the Master Wardens and Company of Stationers are to take Notice, that due Obedience may be rendered to Our Will and Pleasure, herein declared. Given at Our Court, at *St. James's*, the Fifteenth Day of *April*, 1760, in the Thirty-Third Year of Our Reign,

By His Majesty's COMMAND,
W. PITT.

Figure 6.1 Text of the privilege granted by King George II to Charles Frederick Abel in 1760

was possible, was not useful: the descriptions in Giardini's privilege—for example, 'Six Sonatas, for the Violin and Bass; Six Duets, for two Violins', and so on—do not distinguish these sonatas or duets from one another or from other compositions of the same kind by Giardini or anyone else. The best way to identify an untitled piece of instrumental music with reasonable precision is to quote its incipit, as Breitkopf's thematic catalogues did from the 1760s. But even if this approach had been familiar in England in the first half of the eighteenth century, music notation might well have seemed inconsistent with the dignity of a royal letter patent and would certainly not have been popular with musically illiterate officials. The majority of music privileges, then, used some such phrase as 'divers works' or 'several pieces of musick', although Festing's first privilege and Symonds's privilege specified only instrumental music, while the privileges granted to Greene, Veracini, Worgan and the editor and translator John Garth referred to specific writings or compositions and also to 'divers works'.

The 'divers works' formula also made it easy to continue to use a privilege long after it had expired. Privileges were worded so that they applied only to material which was allegedly complete or well advanced at the time of the grant, but a privilege protecting 'divers works' could be printed together with music composed years later, perhaps giving potential pirates the impression that the new publication was protected or partly protected by that privilege. Handel's privilege, granted in 1720, was published with several of his subsequently composed operas, the last being *Rodelinda* (1725).[89] Worgan's 1752 privilege for 'diverse works consisting of vocal and instrumental musick and … a number of new sonatas for the harpsichord composed by Signior Dominico Scarlatti' appeared not only in Worgan's 1752 edition of twelve Scarlatti sonatas but also in Vauxhall song collections that he published in 1754 and 1757.

Abel's privilege also differs from the *Modern History* privilege in tone. The latter's preamble describes the book in glowing terms and records the publishers' belief that the book 'may be of great

---

[89] William C[harles] Smith and Charles Humphries, *Handel: A descriptive catalogue of the early editions*, Oxford, 1970, p 61. Their index entry 'Privileges' (*ibid.*, p 376) refers to additional instances of the use of this privilege.

service not only to the publick in general but to all persons concerned in trade and navigation'—to which the king responds by being 'most graciously inclined to give encouragement to all works that may be of publick use and benefit'. In some book privileges the king became almost effusive: in the privilege of the bookseller Stephen Austen for the second edition of Thomas Stackhouse's *A New History of the Holy Bible*, the king is 'graciously inclined to give encouragement ... especially to those [books] of this kind, which tend so much to the advancement of religion, and the general good of mankind'.

In Abel's privilege, by contrast, the preamble is about a third as long as the *Modern History* preamble and is silent about the intrinsic merits or public benefits of his music, while the king is merely 'willing to give all due encouragement to this his undertaking'. The reserve displayed in most music privileges about the works they protected reflects the fact that music was regarded as a mere pastime rather than a serious pursuit. Even Charles Burney described music in his *General History of Music* as 'being, at best, but an amusement', 'an innocent luxury, unnecessary, indeed, to our existence, but a great improvement and gratification of the sense of hearing'.[90] Only a few music privileges were more fulsome than Abel's. The petition of the music seller Benjamin Cooke in one of his privileges stated that he had purchased a collection of vocal and instrumental music by Domenico Scarlatti and others 'and with great labour and expence, has engrav'd, printed, and fitted some of the said works ... in such a manner as will render them very useful and entertaining to all performers on the harpsichord, or organ, or any other instruments'.[91] But the king, austerely, remained merely 'willing to give all due encouragement to this his undertaking'.

As Rogers points out, many music privileges forbade anyone to 'copy out in writing for sale'[92]—a protection not provided in the

---

[90] Charles Burney, *A General History of Music, from the Earliest Ages to the Present Period*, v 1, 1776, p xviii and p xiii. Some non-music privileges are as reserved as Abel's, and presumably for similar reasons—for example, Bernard Lintot's privilege for Pope's translation of *The Iliad* and Warburton's for Pope's works.

[91] According to the restatement of this petition in the text of the privilege.

[92] Rogers, *op cit.*, p 139.

Copyright Act. Copying was particularly important in the dissemination of music: of the thirteen privileges listed by Rogers which forbade copying, twelve were for music. Moreover, manuscript publication was slow to die out and still flourished on the continent: much of the music sold by Breitkopf of Leipzig from the 1750s onwards was in manuscript.[93] Hence, unlike the *Modern History* privilege, Abel's privilege and some earlier ones such as that granted to John Stanley, forbade the importation not just of music 'reprinted for sale beyond the seas'—the words of Handel's privilege—but of music 'reprinted or written for sale beyond the seas'.

Whereas book privileges usually granted both 'privilege' (exclusive right to print) and 'licence' (permission to print), music privileges usually granted only 'licence', regardless of what the petitioner may have requested. Stanley, however, was granted 'licence and protection', and John Jones 'privilege and licence'. The omission of the word 'privilege' from most music privileges may be due to the fact that privileges were granted 'so far as may be agreeable to the statute in that behalf, made and provided'—a hazy phrase which perhaps become standard in privileges only after the Revolution of 1688. The Copyright Act left room for the king to make grants of printing rights, but this was in a section of the Act that referred only to 'books', while the reference in the Act's preamble to 'books and other writings' suggested that for a publication to count as a book within the meaning of the Act its contents had to count as 'writing'. From this it was easy to conclude that publications consisting mainly of music could not legally be the subject of a royal grant of exclusive printing rights—a point which the authorities seem to have observed while ignoring more general questions about the validity of all privileges. It is true that in the standard music privilege the king still went on to order his subjects not to reproduce the music described in the privilege unless authorised to do so, 'as they will answer the contrary at their perils'. But anyone who wanted to take legal action against a pirate solely on the basis of a privilege that

---

[93] See Yoshitake Kobayashi, 'On the identification of Breitkopf's manuscripts', in George B. Stauffer (ed.), *Bach Perspectives* v 2, *J. S. Bach, the Breitkopfs, and the Eighteenth-Century Music Trade*, Lincoln, Nebraska, 1996, p 107–121, and George R. Hill, 'Identifying Breitkopf house copies produced by the firm's own scribes: a preliminary survey', *ibid.*, p 123–141.

omitted the word 'privilege' would have found that the privilege did not even purport to grant a property right, and that the only option available was to petition the king to act against the offending parties. And it is not clear what the king could have done, imprisonment in the Tower at the king's behest having gone out of fashion.

Shef Rogers, pointing out that some musicians who were granted privileges were affiliated with the court and that many music privileges were granted after the accession in 1727 of George II, 'a greater patron of music than his predecessors', suggests that privileges 'functioned as a form of relatively inexpensive patronage'.[94] But this is not supported by Warburton's comment that a privilege could be obtained 'without wasting your interest to obtain it. You may have it for asking'.[95] And the fact that many privileges were granted to musicians who worked at court may simply be due to the fact that the court employed many leading musicians. The rise in the number of music privileges from 1730 onwards may have owed less to George II's accession than to John Walsh Jr's taking over from his father at about that time. But there is no clear connection between publishing with Walsh Jr and obtaining a privilege: some of his composers did not obtain privileges, and some privileges were granted to composers who did not publish with him. Greene obtained his privilege only in 1742, nine years after the Wright episode, when Walsh Jr was about to publish Greene's *Forty Select Anthems* in two folio volumes. The most that can be said is that Walsh Jr may have influenced the rise in the number of music privileges by suggesting that his composers obtain privileges, thus indirectly encouraging other publishers to have their composers do the same.

A few music privileges were granted to music publishers. The first of these was granted on 20 July 1737, after Parliament had passed the Engravers' Act in 1735 to protect prints and two attempts had been made to extend statutory copyright to music (see section 6.8 below). That privilege was granted to Benjamin Cooke, who had been a victim of Walsh Sr's piracies, for 'about twenty original concertos ... by John Humphries decd.'. In 1739 Cooke and Walsh Jr both obtained privileges.

---

[94] Rogers, *op. cit.*, p 139 and p 147.

[95] See page 278 above.

Even before the latter privilege—for 'several [Handel] works consisting of vocal and instrumental music'—was granted on 31 October, Walsh used it to promote Handel's *Concerti Grossi* op. 6, advertising '*This Day are Publish'd,* PROPOSALS *for Printing by Subscription, With His Majesty's Royal Licence and Protection.* TWELVE Grand Concerto's ... *by Mr* HANDEL'.[96] However, Walsh may not have obtained this privilege simply to promote op. 6. If, as seems probable, he took an interest in copyright law, he would have known that the maximum term of protection provided by the Copyright Act was twenty-eight years. Thus his 1739 privilege may have been intended to protect works by Handel that the Act, if it protected music at all, was ceasing to protect, the first being *Rinaldo*, which Walsh Sr had published in 1711.

Like Handel's 1720 privilege, Walsh Jr's 1739 privilege was printed with works composed after it was granted: it appeared not only with op. 6 (published in 1740), but also with numerous oratorios up to *Solomon* (1749). Walsh obtained a further Handel privilege when he was about to bring out two major Handel publications after the composer's death in 1759.

On 17 June 1760 a privilege for 'several pieces of musick never yet published within our dominions' was granted to John Adolph Hummel, soon after he settled in Soho and began publishing music from St Anne Street, Soho.[97] The protection of material previously published abroad strongly suggests that John Adolph Hummel was connected with the brothers Johann Julius Hummel and Burchard Hummel, who moved in the 1750s from Waltershausen near Gotha to Amsterdam and The Hague respectively, where they established a joint music-publishing business and became major exporters of printed music.[98] The continental Hummels developed close links with London—so close that in 1773, when Burchard Hummel published under his own imprint J. C. Bach's symphonies op. 9, he also printed

[96] *The London Daily Post, and General Advertiser*, 29 October 1739, p 2.

[97] The earliest known reference to him records the baptism of his daughter Anne at St Anne's, Soho, on 19 February 1760 (IGI). His stock-in-trade was auctioned in October 1772 (advertisement, *The Daily Advertiser*, 2 October 1772, p 4).

[98] See Cari Johansson, *J. J. & B. Hummel: Music-publishing and thematic catalogues*, Stockholm, 1972.

copies for the London music publishers Longman, Lukey & Co. complete with their title-page 'in pursuance of previous advise sent by the said Hummell to [Longman, Lukey & Co.] and without [their] giving orders for the same'.[99] It may be that John Adolph Hummel acted as the London agent of the other Hummels, and that his privilege was intended to protect them and some English music sellers against piracy of music printed in Holland and sold in England, perhaps with London given on the title-page as the place of publication.

How effective were music privileges as a defence against piracy? The limited evidence available indicates that Handel's privilege and Worgan's first privilege achieved little or nothing, but that Geminiani's and Thomas Arne's helped keep some pirates at bay.

After obtaining his privilege in 1720, Handel seems to have tried for a few years to get the best publishing terms and conditions he could, regardless of who offered them. His opera *Radamisto* was published 'by the author' and 'printed and sold' by Richard Meares Sr and John Christopher Smith Sr (1720), but *Floridante* (1722), *Ottone* (1723) and *Flavio* (1723) were printed for Handel by Walsh Sr.[100] After this the printer John Cluer, who had engraved and printed Handel's *Suites de Pieces pour le Clavecin* in 1720, became his principal music seller, printing and issuing with associates the operas *Giulio Cesare* (first performed 1724), *Tamerlano* (1724), *Rodelinda* (1725), *Scipione* (1726) and *Alessandro* (1726). Handel's privilege was reproduced in the first three of these, as it had been in the Meares and Walsh editions from 1720 to 1723. After Cluer's death in 1727 his widow Elizabeth published *Admeto* (1727), *Riccardo Primo* (1728), *Siroe* (1728) and *Lotario* (1729). When *Admeto* was delayed by Cluer's death, Benjamin Cooke issued a flute arrangement of music from *Admeto* 'by authority of the patentee [Handel]'.[101]

Although Walsh Sr reproduced Handel's privilege in *Floridante*, *Ottone* and *Flavio*, he ignored it when other music sellers

---

[99] According to the sworn affidavit by James Longman and Charles Lukey quoted on page 341 below.

[100] See Smith and Humphries, *op. cit.*, p xiv–xv and the subsequent entries for these operas.

[101] *ibid.*, p 6.

reproduced it, and he responsed to the Meares, Cluer and Cooke editions by bringing out competing editions. From 1724 until the end of 1729 he published selections and arrangements of music from each new Handel opera almost as soon as the Cluers did. He also reused plates originally engraved for the operas to produce several volumes of operatic selections under the general title *Apollo's Feast*. Nor did the privilege discourage Walsh from publishing music which Handel might have composed before 1720: as mentioned, at some time between 1726 and 1730, he brought out a collection of sonatas, mostly by Handel, with a spurious Jeanne Roger title-page.[102] And in 1727 Walsh may even have had a win against Benjamin Cooke. When Cooke advertised the *Admeto* arrangement, along with two collections—one of overtures and one of songs—of material from six operas, of which five were by Handel, Walsh promptly advertised his own *Admeto* arrangement and '18 [Handel] Overtures ... also several of them curiously done for the Harpsicord'.[103] Cooke published the song collection but seems to have had second thoughts about the overtures, for no copy of that collection has been found.

Unlike the casual, small-scale piracies which were typical of the trade, Walsh's Handel piracies were systematic and large scale, almost inviting a response. Yet Handel's authorised music sellers seem to have done nothing. Perhaps the Cluers were discouraged by the legal uncertainties associated with privileges. Perhaps Handel had a financial interest in the Walsh editions, as William Smith suggests.[104] In any case, it seems that for reasons now unknown Handel and the Cluers simply put up with the Walsh publications, perhaps unwillingly.

About the beginning of 1730, the year before the Cluers' foreman Thomas Cobb married Elizabeth Cluer and took over the

---

[102] Walsh's reason for falsely attributing this publication to Roger is unlikely to have been a desire to avoid legal action: it would not have deceived a law court, because she had died in 1722. Perhaps Walsh hoped to tempt uninformed purchasers to buy an edition that purported to come from what was still a major publishing centre.

[103] Deutsch, *op. cit.*, p 209.

[104] Smith and Humphries, *op. cit.*, p xv. The introduction to this book is written solely by Smith.

business, and about when John Walsh Jr took over from his father, Handel and the music sellers seem to have reached a settlement. Cluer printed and sold Handel's *Lotario*, completed on 16 November 1729, but Walsh printed and sold Handel's next opera, *Partenope*, completed on 6 February 1730.[105] Walsh also acquired the Cluer stock of *Lotario* and other Handel operas and of *Suites de Pieces pour le Clavecin*, selling them with a Walsh label pasted over the Cluer imprint. From then on, Walsh was Handel's principal music seller. When Handel's privilege expired in 1734 he did not obtain a new one, and it was in response to his petition that a privilege for his music was granted to Walsh Jr in 1739, three years after Walsh Sr's death.

Like Handel's privilege, the first of Geminiani's two privileges was obtained in response to perceived piracy by Walsh Sr. According to Sir John Hawkins, writing some forty years later,

> The manuscript of [Geminiani's] Opera seconda had been surreptitiously obtained by Walsh, who was about to print it, but thinking it would be better for the corrections of the author, he gave him the alternative of correcting it, or submitting it to appear in the world with such faults as would have reflected indelible disgrace on the author.
>
> An offer of this kind was nothing less than an insult, and as such Geminiani received it. He therefore not only rejected it with scorn, but instituted a process in the court of chancery for an injunction against the sale of the book, but Walsh compounded [i.e., settled] the matter and the work was published under the inspection of the author.[106]

No record of such a Chancery action has been traced, but the dispute must have occurred in 1728, when Geminiani, after being introduced to a Secretary of State, obtained a privilege with great speed. On 20 March his patron and pupil the Earl of Essex wrote to the Duke of Newcastle:

> Mr Geminiany who has the honour to bring your grace this, is the gentleman you promised me the patent for the sole printing of his own music, which if your grace will be so good to order him, I shall take it as

---

[105] Deutsch, *op. cit.*, p 247, p 252 and p 253.

[106] John Hawkins, *A General History of the Science and Practice of Music*, London, 1776, v 5 p 247.

> a particular favour, the sooner he has it the more service it will be to him.[107]

Newcastle signed Geminiani's privilege six days later.

The dispute described by Hawkins was evidently about Geminiani's second set of arrangements of Corelli violin sonatas as violin concertos, which came out under the Walsh imprint in 1729 and again in the early 1730s. The outcome of this dispute raises again the question of how Walsh Sr was able to print Handel material with impunity. If Geminiani could successfully protect his music against Walsh, why did the Cluers fail to protect Handel's?

John Worgan's first privilege, granted in 1752, seems to have been quite ineffective in protecting his Vauxhall songs, for although it appeared in his 1754 collection of songs, he complained about piracy when advertising his 1755 collection (see section 6.9 below). Nevertheless, a second privilege granted to Worgan on 13 June 1771 appeared in a new collection of his Vauxhall songs and in his second collection of Scarlatti sonatas.

Thomas Arne, who had been apprenticed to an attorney, was difficult to do business with. Burney recorded that all the theatre managers, 'knowing him to be a more regular bred attorney than musician, took care to tie him neck and heels in all contracts otherwise he would not have been kept honest by his own principles and probity'.[108] Shortly after Arne obtained his privilege for 'several works of vocal and instrumental musick' on 29 January 1741, he reproduced it in *The Songs in the Comedies called As You Like It, and Twelfth Night*. In March he advertised the collection with the warning that 'Whereas the Author has procur'd His Majesty's Royal Licence for the sole printing and publishing of his works, whoever shall print or sell any Work of the Author's, without his Approbation or Consent, will be prosecuted according to Law'.[109]

---

[107] William Capell→Thomas Pelham-Holles, 20 March 1728, TNA SP 36/5 f 220, this sentence quoted in the on-line TNA catalogue.

[108] Slava Klima, Garry Bowers and Kerry S[cott] Grant (eds), *Memoirs of Dr Charles Burney 1726–1769*, Lincoln, Nebraska, 1988, p 103.

[109] *The London Daily Post, and General Advertiser*, 9 March 1741, p 1.

This threat seems to have had some effect. In 1743 Thomas Kitchin printed the verses of 'When daisies pied' (from Shakespeare's *Love's Labour's Lost*) in *The English Orpheus* with a note saying, 'The music can't be put to this song, Mr Arne having a patent for it'. And in 1744, in *The Agreeable Amusement*, Jacob Bickerstaff (perhaps a pseudonym), without bothering to explain, published the words of Sir John Vanbrugh's 'Advice to Sylvia' with empty space where Arne's music should have been.[110] Nevertheless, Arne still considered it necessary to threaten legal action against piracy when seeking subscribers in 1746 to a proposed publication of 'eighteen intire new songs and ballads':

> As Mr Arne, has his Majesty's Royal Patent for the Sole printing and publishing of his Works, he humbly Hopes no Gentlemen or Ladies, will give any Encouragement to pirated Copies, written or printed, such Persons who deliver them acting in open contempt of his Majesty's Authority and greatly injuring the Author in his Property. And as Mr Arne can offend no honest Shop-keeper, in maintaining his Right; he gives this publick Notice, that whosoever shall offer to write or print any of his Works, shall be Prosecuted according to Law.[111]

Arne was not bluffing, as Kitchin and Bickerstaff probably knew when they decided not to print his music—for he had taken legal action against two publishers in 1741. These actions are described in section 6.10 below.

6.8 The Engravers' Act; two failed bills; judicial decisions

A major deficiency of the Copyright Act was its failure to define the terms 'author', 'book', 'writing' and 'publish'.[112] These words had not needed definition when the Stationers' Company ran the book trade; and Parliament, dealing with the demands of lobby groups and the immediate problems of the book trade, saw no need to define them in

---

[110] John A. Parkinson, 'Pirates and publishers…', *Performing Right* [Performing Right Society, London] v 58 (1972) p 20–22 at p 20.

[111] Advertisement, *The General Advertiser*, 22 May 1746, p 2.

[112] Deazley, *op cit.*, p 47–49, discusses the poor drafting of the Act.

1710. But the Act would subsequently be interpreted by the law courts, where the precise meaning of a word was often important and where decisions that might have been made by, say, Star Chamber or the Company's Court of Assistants about the meaning of terms that were central to the Act had no standing.

A further inadequacy of the Act was that its ramshackle structure, combined with its haphazard use of phrases like 'provided that' and 'provided always that' to connect its clauses, left the relationship between some of its provisions obscure. In particular, the Act did not make clear whether the publication right it created was dependent on compliance with its registration provisions, with its legal-deposit provisions or with both.

A final major deficiency of the Copyright Act was that although its preamble and the first two sections seemingly assumed the existence of a common-law right, nothing was said about the relationship between this right and the new statutory right created by the Act. In general, if the common law and statute law were in conflict, statute law prevailed; but it was not clear how this principle applied where copyright was concerned. If copyright existed at common law, did the right created by the Act simply coexist with the common-law right during the statutory copyright period, or did the statutory right replace it? If the statutory right replaced it only with respect to books, was a work that was not a book within the meaning of the Act protected by the common law? If the statutory right replaced the common-law right, did it do so only for the term of the statutory right, or did it put an end to the common-law right forever? And was unpublished material, with which the Act did not deal, protected at common law?

The legal system addressed unresolved legal questions piecemeal, when they were raised in the course of litigation, and for a couple of decades few important judicial decisions were made about the book trade. One reason for this was that the Copyright Act discouraged use of its own penal clauses; furthermore, it protected books published before 1710 for twenty-one years. Also, the book trade remained close-knit and concentrated in London, the Stationers' Company remained well-off, influential and worth belonging to, its Court of Assistants continued to deal with book-trade disputes, and the book trade therefore managed to operate for some time much as it had done before 1695, dealing with internal disputes without much reference to the legal system.

Moreover, although it was true—as booksellers had argued before 1710—that the remedies for book piracy available from the common-law courts were inadequate, a satisfactory legal remedy existed in the form of an injunction issued by Chancery or by Exchequer acting in its equitable jurisdiction. If obtained soon enough, an injunction ordering an end to the production and sale of an offending edition penalised its publisher by rendering unsold stock worthless, and the plaintiff had little reason to continue the action. In 1769 Justice Edward Willes of the King's Bench remarked in the case of *Millar v Taylor* that 'few bills against pirates of books are ever brought to a hearing. If the defendant acquiesces under the injunction, it is seldom worth the plaintiff's while to proceed for an account [of the defendant's proceeds]; the sale of the edition being stopped.'

The net result was that it was only decades after the Copyright Act became law, when the publishing trade had expanded significantly, when the number of publishers who were not Stationers had grown, when the power of the Stationers' Company had declined, when the number of book-trade disputes and the sums of money at stake in them had become much greater, and when a serious threat to London's dominance of the book trade had emerged, that many of the questions left open in 1710 received definitive answers.

Significant developments occurred in the 1730s. Some of this took place in Parliament, which in 1735 extended copyright to a kind of publication which the Copyright Act had not mentioned. A petition from William Hogarth and other engravers was presented to the House of Commons on 5 February and, after amendments, became law on 25 June.

As its title suggests, *An Act for the Encouragement of the Arts of Designing, Engraving, and Etching historical and other Prints, by vesting the Properties thereof in the Inventors and Engravers, during the Time therein mentioned*, 8 George II c.13, known as the Engravers' Act or Hogarth's Act, was based to some extent on the Copyright Act.[113] But its provisions were much simpler: the

[113] See Ronald Paulson, *Hogarth: His life, art, and times*, New Haven, Connecticut, 1971, v 2 p 59–62.

proprietors of any 'historical or other print or prints' were to have the 'sole right and liberty' of publishing them for fourteen years from the date of publication; each print was to bear the name of its proprietor and the date of publication; and if during that fourteen years a print made from the same design, in whole or in part, was published without the proprietor's consent, the plates and unsold copies of the pirate print were to be destroyed, and anyone found in possession of the pirate print was to be fined five shillings per copy, half to go to the Crown and half to the injured proprietor. Like the Copyright Act, the Engravers' Act provided that action had to be taken within three months of the offence and that the defendant could reserve his defence until the hearing.

This act did not help composers or music publishers. A music publication did not depict anything and was therefore not a 'historical or other' print, regardless of whether it was issued as a single sheet bearing the name of the proprietor and the date of publication. However, the expeditious passage of the Engravers' Act may have encouraged composers and music publishers to think that Parliament would be ready to protect their interests when it dealt with another bill then before it.

On 3 March 1735, a month after Hogarth's petition had been presented, the House of Commons received

> A Petition of several Proprietors of Copies of Books … on behalf as well of the Authors and Compilers of such Books … and a great Number of others, concerned in the Manufacture of Printing ... alledging, That the Expence of printing and publishing learned and useful Books, frequently obliges the Authors thereof to transfer their Property therein; and that the Property of the Authors of such Books, and their Assignees, hath, of late Years, been, and still continues to be, injured by surreptitious Editions and Impressions made as well in *Great Britain* as in foreign parts, where Paper is purchased at Half the Expence that it can be provided for in *England....*[114]

The bookseller petitioners, perhaps taking their cue from the engravers, prayed 'that a bill may be brought in for making [the Copyright Act] more effectual; and for the better preventing the

[114] *Journals of the House of Commons* v 22 p 400 (3 March 1734/1735).

surreptitious printing or importing [copies of printed books] from foreign parts'.[115]

The bill improved the Copyright Act without remedying its worst deficiencies.[116] The copyright period was extended to twenty-one years from day of publication, and the time within which penalties for unauthorised publication could be sought was extended to twelve months. The bill provided that penalties were to be paid in full to the offended proprietor instead of being shared with the Crown, and that anyone who succeeded in an action for penalties was to be paid the costs of the action and the profits made from the unauthorised publication. The bill increased the penalties for illegally importing books, increased the number of books which were to be deposited, and made compliance with the deposit provisions a condition of copyright protection. It attempted to protect consumers' interests, allowing a book to be freely reprinted if its proprietor had let it go out of print and become scarce, and discouraging booksellers from producing 'new' editions which were the same or almost the same as the old ones.

On 29 April the House instructed the committee considering the bill that they had power to receive two clauses. The first concerned the duty on paper used in printing foreign-language books; the second ordered 'that it be an instruction to the said committtee, that they have power to extend the provisions of the said bill to the author or authors of any book or books of musick, or any compositions in musick whatsoever, whether printed or engraved'.[117]

The bill was passed by the Commons on 5 May with a provision that would have given, for the first time, statutory copyright protection to music compositions. Its text read 'That this Act shall

---

[115] *ibid.*

[116] A copy of the 1735 bill is in Bodleian ms Carte 114 f 391–396. For discussion of the bill see Deazley, *op. cit.*, p 94–103.

[117] *Journals of the House of Commons* v 22 p 479 (29 April 1735). The word 'printed' refers to typeset music, which at this time had largely been superseded by engraving. The 1737 instruction (see below) has 'written' instead of 'printed', perhaps taking account both of the continuing importance of manuscript publishing and the death in 1735 of William Pearson, the most important printer of music type in recent decades, although his widow Alice Pearson, who succeeded him, continued to use music type in the 1740s.

extend, and be construed and taken to extend to the Author or Authors of any Book or Books of Musick whatsoever, or any Composition in Musick whatsover, whether printed or Engraved'.[118] But while the bill was before Parliament the bookseller Edmund Curll advertised a newly published collection of letters in terms suggesting that it included, without authorisation, letters written by members of the Lords. Called before the House of Lords, he gave an assurance that the collection contained no such letters. However, according to Alexander Pope, some of the Lords 'thought it very unfitting such a bill should pass, without a clause to prevent such an enormous license for the future'.[119] In any case, the Lords had not passed the bill by the time Parliament was prorogued later in the month, and the bill lapsed.

Much the same happened in 1737. On 11 February the House of Commons, without receiving a petition, approved the introduction of 'a bill for the better encouragement of learning'. This time the House gave the committee appointed to prepare and bring in a bill only one order, identical to the first of the two orders of 29 April 1735. That the House did not repeat the second 1735 order, which was about music, suggests that MPs were not greatly interested in music publishing and that music sellers had not known that another bookseller's bill was about to be introduced and therefore had done no lobbying.

The 1737 bill was designed to replace the Copyright Act and addressed some matters untouched by the 1735 bill, giving authors or their assigns exclusive printing rights for a minimum of twenty-one years, and entitling an owner of such rights to bring a Chancery action for profits made on the sale of a pirate edition. Another provision permitted the importation of foreign-language books. Music publishers apparently responded quickly to the new bill's introduction, for on 15 March the House issued an instruction identical with the second instruction of 29 April 1735, except that 'written' replaced 'printed'.[120] The bill, with amendments that

[118] Bodleian ms Carte 114 f 396.

[119] George Sherburn (ed.), *The Correspondence of Alexander Pope*, London, 1956, v 3 p 64.

[120] *Journals of the House of Commons* v 22 p 803 (15 March 1736/1737).

included an extension to books of music,[121] was passed by the Commons on 4 April, but was still before the Lords and lapsed again when Parliament was prorogued on 21 June. The reason for the Lords' dilatoriness this time is not clear. Deazley suggests that the delay in the Lords may have been due to the book trade objecting to amendments that favoured the interests of authors and book purchasers rather than those of the trade.[122]

Although the background to these attempts to have Parliament extend statutory copyright to music is unknown, it is likely that John Walsh Jr had something to do with them. Although he had not hesitated to pirate Wright's publication, as Handel's publisher he had more to lose from musical piracy than anyone else did. Another publisher who may have been involved was Benjamin Cooke, who obtained a privilege for concertos by John Humphries—the first granted to a music publisher—on 20 July 1737, about a month after the 1737 bill failed. Since the normal waiting time for a privilege seems to have been about a month, Cooke may have petitioned for this privilege only after learning that the bill would not become law.

The only concrete result of this round of efforts to change copyright law came in 1739 with *An Act for Prohibiting the Importation of Books reprinted abroad and first composed or written and printed in Great Britain and for limiting the Prices of Books*, 12 George II c.36. As well as protecting booksellers against imported reprints, this Act repealed the Copyright Act's provisions about the control of book prices.

Many proprietors of engraved books sought the protection of the Engravers' Act.[123] However, the only person known to have tried

---

[121] Deazley, *op. cit.*, p 105.

[122] *ibid.*, p 108.

[123] See David Hunter, 'Copyright protection for engravings and maps in eighteenth-century Britain', *The Library* ser. 6 v 9 no. 2 (June 1987) p 128–147 at p 141. In *A Concise & Easy Method of Learning the Figuring Part of Country Dances* by the dancing master Nicholas Dukes, the words 'Publish'd according to Act of Parliament April 23 1752 Nicholas Dukes' are engraved at the bottom of each page of the text and a couple of pages of the front matter. Taking no chances, Dukes also obtained a privilege for this book and entered it at Stationers' Hall.

to use the Engravers' Act to protect music was William Tans'ur, who published collections of sacred music from the 1730s onwards. The second edition of his *The Royal Psalmodist Compleat: or, the Universal Harmony*,[124] which appeared in 1748, included the notice transcribed in *Figure 6.2*. Its title-page, stating that the work was 'Published according to Act of Parliament', reinforced the message of the notice.

Although Tans'ur took care to make his notice look like a privilege, putting it on a page of its own opposite the title-page, heading it with the royal coat of arms, and filling it with official-sounding language, the notice had no official or legal standing. And its content was pure bluff. For one thing, the pages of a book were not prints, nor were sheets of music 'historical or other prints', within the meaning of the Engravers' Act. In any case, that Act did not protect 'any Print or Prints', as his notice claimed, but only prints that bore the name of the proprietor and the date of publication—a requirement which was not met by putting the proprietor's name and the publication date in a notice at the front of a book.

Whether Tans'ur's misuse of the royal arms drew criticism is unknown, but *The Royal Psalmodist Compleat* was the only publication of his in which anything like this notice appeared. Later in 1748, when he published *A New Musical Grammar*, he had the book entered in the Stationers' register.

A notable feature of the two failed booksellers' bills was that they contained no suggestion that copyright existed at common law. Their proposed extension of the term of protection may indicate that the book trade now felt that limited-term copyright worked well enough and that there was little point—perhaps because of parliamentary opposition to monopolies—in campaigning for statutory recognition of perpetual copyright. But even if this is correct, some Chancery decisions made in the 1730s would have brought common-law copyright back into the trade's calculations and help explain why booksellers made no further attempts to replace the Copyright Act after the second bill failed.

[124] Tans'ur's name is spelt without an apostrophe in this publication.

To the PUBLICK.

WHEREAS several Persons, by their Genius, Industry, and great Expence, have *Compos'd, Invented,* and *Engraved,* various Works on *Plates,* in hopes to have reaped the sole *Benefit* of their Labours: And whereas several Persons have immediately taken an unlawful Liberty to *Copy* and *Engrave* the same; to the great Prejudice and Ruin of such *Inventors,* and *Proprietors;* and for a *Remedy* thereof, it hath pleased the King's most excellent Majesty, by, and with the Advice and Consent of the Lords Spiritual and Temporal, and Commons, then assembled in Parliament, to set forth *an Act* to this Effect, *viz.*

> **'That whosoever shall** Invent, **and** Engrave **any** Print **or** Prints, **shall have the sole Benefit of Printing, and Reprinting the same for** 14 Years; **to commence from the Day of Publication thereof; which Date shall be printed before the Work, &c — And that whoever shall** Copy **or** Engrave, **or cause to be** Copied, **or** Engraved, **any such** Print **or** Prints, **either by taking the whole, or any part thereof, by altering any of the same, shall forfeit** Five Shillings **for every Page as shall be found within his Custody; one half of which to the King's most excellent Majesty, and the other to the Person who shall sue for such a Property, and shall also forfeit the Plates whereon such Copies shall be engraved, &c. &c. &c,'**

On what is before hinted, I do hereby give Notice, That whosoever shall *Copy* or *Engrave* any Part of the following Book, (intitled, *The New Universal Harmony,* which contains above 100 *Plates,* 8vo,) shall be prosecuted according to the above, and late *Act of Parliament,* in that Case made and provided. *Witness my Hand this 25th Day of March,* 1748,

WILLIAM TANSUR.

Figure 6.2 Text of notice published by William Tans'ur in 1748 in his The Royal Psalmodist Compleat

Between 1710 and about 1730 most Chancery copyright actions were connected with the law-book patent.[125] The only legally significant point reported from any of these actions was the remark of the Lord Chancellor in *Burnet v Chetwood* (1720) that 'a translation might not be the same with the reprinting the original, on account that the translator has bestowed his care and pains upon it, and so not within the prohibition of the Act'.[126] But this case was decided on grounds unconnected with copyright law.

In the 1730s, however, after the expiry of the twenty-one-year period of protection that the Copyright Act gave to books published before 1710, Chancery dealt with several disputes about old material. Four decisions would assume great significance decades later. In *Eyre v Walker* (1735) the book in question was Richard Allestree's *The Whole Duty of Man*, published anonymously in 1657; in *Motte v Faulkner* (1735), it was a new collection which, however, contained some material which had been published in 1701 and 1702; in *Walthoe v Walker* (1737) it was Robert Nelson's *A Companion for the Festivals and Fasts of the Church of England*, published in 1703; and in *Tonson v Walker* (1739) it was Milton's *Paradise Lost*, published in 1667.[127] In all four actions Chancery granted an injunction ordering the defendant not to publish the book. The decisions were not reported at the time, but the three actions against the printer Robert Walker probably 'represent no more than actions in which the court routinely granted injunctions to a complaining party' in order to prevent any damage that might be caused by further infringement of the plaintiff's alleged rights while proceedings were ongoing.[128] In the fourth case, *Motte v Faulkner*, the collection, despite the age of some of its contents, may well have been regarded as a new publication which was protected by the Copyright Act. However, in the absence of reliable law reporting, legal mythmaking took over. Since some or all of the material in these books was not

---

[125] See Deazley, *op. cit.*, p 50–85, and 'Register of Copyright Infringement Suits and Actions from *c*1560 to 1800' cited in note 21 above.

[126] The Lord Chancellor then was Thomas Parker, 1st Earl of Macclesfield of the second creation.

[127] For detailed discussion of these actions see Deazley, *op. cit.*, p 74–79.

[128] Deazley, *op. cit.*, p 78.

protected by the Copyright Act, the decisions would later be cited, rightly or wrongly, as proof that the Chancellors of this period considered that copyright existed at common law.[129]

The same construction may have been placed on another Chancery decision, *Baller v Watson* (1737), which concerned the words of John Gay's *Polly*, published in 1729. Even though the work was still protected by the Copyright Act, the Lord Chancellor issued a perpetual injunction when the action came to an end.[130]

The reaction of the book trade to these decisions is not recorded. But with Chancery granting injunctions, seemingly on the basis of a common-law right, to protect material unprotected by the Copyright Act, the trade may have decided that it was better off with a combination of common-law copyright—which would confer perpetual ownership of rights to old books—and flawed legislation than with better legislation that provided only a limited term of protection and ignored common-law copyright. Or the trade may have felt that to request new copyright legislation for a third time would be to risk having Parliament turn its attention to the Chancery decisions and decide that common-law copyright was a monopoly that should be abolished. In any event, the Importation Act of 1739 was the last new book-trade measure that Parliament would consider for decades.

In the meantime, as London booksellers sought to advance their legal interests by going to law rather than to Parliament, such developments as there were in copyright law arose from decisions of the courts.[131] Many of these decisions were made in Chancery, whose decisions of course were not authoritative statements of the common law. But Chancery's decisions were respected, especially those of Lord Hardwicke, Chancellor from 1737 to 1756, who had a high reputation as a lawyer and had previously served as Chief Justice of the King's Bench.

---

[129] *Webb v Rose* (1732) was another case which was later misunderstood or misrepresented. It was consistently referred to as a copyright case until 2004, when Deazley (*op. cit.*, p 69–70) showed that the dispute was actually about ownership of papers.

[130] For detailed discussion of *Baller v Watson* see Deazley, *op. cit.*, p 65–69.

[131] All the cases described here, and many others, often unreported, are discussed in Deazley, *op. cit.*

Some cases from the 1730s onwards had particular relevance to malpractices common in the music trade. Although these cases were not about music, the principles they established would be there, ready to be applied, when music became subject to copyright law many years later. For instance, in *Rivington v Cooper* (1740) the Lord Chancellor considered the question of selection and adaptation. According to the report:

> The Defendant, under Pretence and Title of an Extract, printed part of the Book, and was printing the Rest in a Pamphlet called 'The Gentleman's Magazine'.—Demurrer, for that an Extract such as this was not within the Stat. 8 Ann. for then all Extracts in the Memoirs of Literature would be so. But by Lord Chan. *Hardwicke*, It is not *material* what Title you give the Book, nor whether you print all at once or not.

The notion of fair dealing was a long way off, but Hardwicke's comment made it clear that making extracts from a text was different from copying it wholesale.

Pope v Curll (1741) was concerned with the same collection of unpublished letters that had led to Edmund Curll's appearance before the House of Lords in 1735. Alexander Pope wanted to publish a collection of his own letters—an action which would have been attacked as evidence of vanity if it had been unprompted. He tricked Curll, whom he loathed, into publishing a collection of letters that gave Pope grounds for suing him, thereby not only injuring Curll but enabling Pope to publish his letters to set the record straight. In this case Chancery dealt with the author's rights in unpublished material. Pope obtained an injunction preventing the further sale of the book, and Curll asked that the injunction be dissolved, arguing that letters were not within the scope of the Copyright Act. Hardwicke is reported as saying:

> I think it would be extremely mischievous, to make a distinction between a book of letters, which comes out into the world, either by the permission of the writer, or by the receiver of them, and any other learned work.
>
> The same objection would hold against sermons, which the author may never intend should be published, but are collected from loose papers, and brought out after his death.
>
> Another objection has been made by the defendant's counsel, that where a man writes a letter, it is in the nature of a gift to the receiver.

> But I am of opinion that it is only a special property in the receiver, possibly the property of the paper may belong to him; but this does not give a licence to any person whatsoever to publish them to the world, for at most the receiver has only a joint property with the author.

Hardwicke here made two important points. First, an author owns the publication rights to unpublished material, regardless of whether it was intended for publication. Secondly, the right to publish that material is not the same as the right to possession of a manuscript of the material: one person may own the manuscript and another the right to publish its text.

Both points made explicit the legal principles underlying what was already familiar practice. While it had always been true that much material that appeared in print had been written specifically for publication, the author's intentions with respect to publication had never been relevant to the law or to trade practice. As Hardwicke pointed out, it was common for material to be published posthumously, when it was not possible to know whether the author had intended it to be published. An author's intentions when creating a text had no bearing on the question of whether the author retained the publication rights to that text.

Likewise, publication rights had never been identical with, or associated with, possession of a manuscript, whether under the Licensing Act, or under the Copyright Act, or in any reported judicial decision, or in trade practice. Nor did the failed bills of 1735 and 1737 hint at any such connection. And neither the loss or destruction of a manuscript, nor the existence of multiple manuscripts, had ever been seen as having any bearing on the copyright owner's right to publish a work: booksellers had long routinely bought and sold shares in the rights to Shakespeare's plays and other material of which the manuscripts had vanished. The facts in *Pope v Curll* allowed Curll's counsel to call these principles into question—but only to the extent of making it necessary for Hardwicke to state for the first time what had not previously needed to be said.

In *Gyles v Wilcox* (1740) and *Tonson v Walker* (1752)—the second case being between the same parties as in 1739, but over a different matter—adaptation was considered again, the question this time being whether, and if so at what point, adaptation amounted to infringement of copyright in the adapted work. *Gyles v Wilcox* settled the principles to be applied in such cases, and *Tonson v Walker* (1752) confirmed them. In the former case Hardwicke is reported to have said:

> Where books are colourably shortened only, they are undoubtedly within the meaning of the act of Parliament, and are a mere evasion of the statute, and cannot be called an abridgement. But this must not be carried so far as to restrain persons from making a real and fair abridgement, for abridgements may with great propriety be called a new book.[132]

In *Tonson v Walker* (1752) Hardwicke is reported as saying: 'In *Gyles v Wilcox*, the abridgement contained 35 sheets, the original 275; it was referred to an award, and held a fair abridgement, and not within the statute'.

Gyles v Wilcox established that the question whether an adaptation consituted a breach of copyright was a question of fact which, in a complicated case, needed to be dealt with by experts. In *Tonson v Walker* (1752), however, the facts were clear and Hardwicke had no hesitation in giving a decision without expert advice. John Marchant had prepared an edition of Milton's *Paradise Lost* with notes by others and himself, and the question arose whether Marchant was entitled to print notes written by Rev. Thomas Newton. According to the case report, 'there were 28 notes by Marchant, and ... the rest [of the notes] were 1500', which led Hardwicke to comment that 'a fair abridgement would be entitled to protection, but this is a mere evasion', and to issue an injunction.

Duke of Queensberry v Shebbeare (1758) confirmed *Pope v Curll*, on the basis of different facts. When John Shebbeare published the Earl of Clarendon's *History of the Reign of Charles II*, a descendant of the author who owned the original manuscript sought an injunction. Shebbeare stated that his co-defendant Francis Gwynne had claimed that Clarendon had given the manuscript to Gwynne's father 'that he might take a copy thereof, and make use of the same as he should think fit, of which a copy was taken'. However, Robert Henley, the Lord Keeper, 'said, that it was not to be presumed that

---

[132] The two published reports of this case agree as to the outcome but report Hardwicke's words differently. The report quoted here is by Thomas Barnardiston (*ER* 27: 682).

Lord Clarendon, when he gave a copy of his work to Mr Gwynne, intended that he should have the profit of multiplying it in print; that Mr Gwynne might make every use of it, except that'.

The principles established in these cases were important and were relevant to practices common in the music trade. But it was still not clear that copyright law applied to music; and by the time a court considered this question a major dispute had developed over common-law copyright.

6.9 England and Scotland; the Battle of the Booksellers; *Millar v Taylor*

At the end of the seventeenth century few books were produced in Scotland. But the free-trade area created by the Union, combined with the relatively low cost of skilled labour in Scotland, fostered the development of a Scottish book trade with strong connections to the increasingly accessible English book market. By the 1740s it was common for English and Scottish booksellers to collaborate on major publications, producing books in Scotland under joint English and Scottish imprints for sale on both sides of the border. But increased contact brought conflict as well as collaboration, and by the 1740s cheap unauthorised Scottish editions of books to which English booksellers had bought the copyright had become much more than a nuisance to the English book trade. In 1741 a group of English booksellers took legal action in Scotland over Scottish reprints of various works.

Scottish law and legal institutions were quite different from England's. Instead of England's confused, archaic system of superior courts, Scotland had just one, the Court of Session, from which since the time of the Union it had been possible to appeal to the House of Lords. One result of this was that where England had both common law and equity, Scotland had one indivisible body of law. Scottish law, an amalgam of Scottish traditional law and Roman law, differed radically from English law. Legal precedent was important in Scottish law, but legal theory tended to have more importance in Scotland than it did in England—especially as embodied in the work of the 'institutional' writers, which combined Roman and Scottish law with ideas derived from natural-law theory. Although these differences between the legal systems had no direct bearing on the question of whether copyright existed independently of statute, it is not surprising that judges of the two countries answered this question differently.

The action begun in 1741 followed a circuitous path and produced a decision only in 1747, when the Lords of Session concluded unanimously in *Midwinter v Hamilton* that copyright did not exist independently of statute.[133] Perhaps in response, William Warburton published in 1747 a defence of non-statutory copyright, the first isolated shot in what later became a major pamphlet war. After the 1747 decision was formally confirmed in 1748, the London booksellers appealed to the House of Lords, which began to hear the case in 1750. Following the initial hearings Lord Chancellor Hardwicke wrote an opinion in which, after stating that the appeal should fail because of faults in the drafting of the original bill, he discussed substantive matters raised by the Scottish booksellers. He was quoted as saying that:

> the Statute of Queen Anne, as to the Property of Authors and Books, might be considered as a general standing Patent to Authors, for the Term of Years mentioned in that Statute, ... but he doubted whether the Statute was declaratory of the Common Law, or introductive of a new Law for the Encouragement of Learning, and to give learned Men a Property, which they had not before .... But whatever might have been the Law of England before the Statute, he said, it was material to consider how the Common Law of Scotland was before the Statute, for that might be very material.[134]

Hardwicke's views were significant not just because of his standing and his position, but because in 1739 he had issued the injunction in *Tonson v Walker*, the last of the Chancery decisions of the 1730s which had come to be seen as evidence of the existence of copyright at common law in England. A summary of his opinion was widely circulated, and the phrase 'a general standing patent for authors' was often quoted in later discussion of the Copyright Act.

---

133 Deazley, *op. cit.*, p 115–132.

134 [John MacLaurin], *Considerations on the Nature and Origin of Literary Property...*, Edinburgh, 1767, p 26–27.

The immediate result of Hardwicke's opinion was that the London booksellers abandoned their action. More significantly, his opinion cast doubt on the idea that copyright existed in English common law, questioned whether the Copyright Act supported the idea of common-law copyright, and suggested that even if copyright existed in English common law it might not exist in Scottish law. This opinion marked the beginning of over twenty years of confusion in British copyright law.

Many London booksellers had bought the rights to works that were no longer protected by the Act but which the booksellers believed were protected by the common law. With this belief now called into question, the London book trade needed a judicial decision which confirmed the existence of common-law copyright in England and preferably in Scotland as well. But there was a significant risk that any legal decision would go against them, and it was not until 1761, in *Tonson v Collins*, that a dispute about common-law copyright first came before the King's Bench.

Leading lawyers of the day were engaged in this case, some of whom played important roles in later copyright cases. The legal scholar William Blackstone, the first Vinerian Professor of English Law at Oxford, appeared for the plaintiffs, the booksellers Jacob Tonson II and Richard Tonson, to present the case for common-law copyright. The defendant, the bookseller Benjamin Collins, was represented by Edward Thurlow and Joseph Yates. Thurlow was not an outstanding lawyer but had become a leader of the London bar by virtue of his imposing presence, his quick mind and his immense oratorical skills. His limitations as a lawyer were more than offset by the legal skills of Yates, who was regarded as one of the best lawyers of his generation.

William Murray, Lord Mansfield, the Chief Justice of the King's Bench, was the foremost lawyer of his day and one of the most important figures in English legal history. Before his appointment to the bench he had acted in many copyright cases, always acting for parties who wanted copyright to be perpetual. His interest in the subject was not exclusively legal—when a young man he displayed gifts as a poet and won a prize for Latin verse at Oxford. Alexander Pope, who is said to have coached him in public speaking, deplored Mansfield's decision to concentrate on law rather than literature ('How sweet an Ovid was in Murray lost'), but they remained friends and Murray became Pope's legal adviser and represented him in court. As Chief Justice, Mansfield had brought innovation and reform to many areas of the law, and his legal learning, his intellectual powers, and his remarkable persuasiveness even when arguing a bad case, had given him such ascendancy over his judicial colleagues that since his appointment as Chief Justice in 1756 every judgement of the King's Bench had been unanimous.

The arguments for and against common-law copyright, discussed at length in *Tonson v Collins* and later cases and in the extensive controversial literature, involved four main issues, three of which were strictly legal. The first concerned legal precedent: had there ever been such a thing as common-law copyright? There was no authoritative case law about this, but Chancery's decisions in the 1730s in *Eyre v Walker*, *Motte v Faulkner*, *Walthoe v Walker* and *Tonson v Walker* (1739) were taken to be the next best thing. The second issue was the effect of the Copyright Act upon the common law. The major difference between the right conferred by the Act and the contentious common-law right was that statutory copyright lasted no more than twenty-eight years. But once the term prescribed by the Act expired, did common-law copyright continue, or had the Act put an end to it? The third issue was the one that generated most argument: could something incorporeal such as a literary work be property at common law? The corrody and advowson and other choses in action were evidence that property could be incorporeal, but this did not deter opponents of common-law copyright from arguing against it. Finally, there was the question of whether common-law copyright was desirable public policy. Opponents of common-law copyright argued that it would act as a permanent restraint on the free dissemination of ideas and of works of literature or scholarship, and that the term of protection provided by the Act was long enough to give authors a reasonable return for their work. Against this it was argued that copyright did not inhibit traffic in ideas but only in the form of words in which ideas were expressed, that fourteen years might not be long enough to ensure an adequate return from works which took years to achieve success, and that the returns from a successful work should not be cut off after an arbitrary fixed term.

Tonson v Collins, which was expected to settle these issues, was referred to Exchequer Chamber, where it ended in anticlimax. The judges discovered that the parties, unknown to their lawyers, had colluded in an action which they hoped would result in a decision in favour of common-law copyright. Accordingly, the judges decided to do nothing more about the case.

However, this case had one unintended and, from the London book trade's viewpoint, most unwelcome effect: Chancery stopped issuing injunctions on the basis of common-law copyright. In 1764 the Edinburgh bookseller Alexander Donaldson opened a retail outlet in London to sell his cheap editions of books which the London booksellers considered were protected by common-law copyright. In 1765 Thomas Osborne and Andrew Millar obtained injunctions against Donaldson, but when Donaldson contested the matter the Lord Chancellor dissolved the injunctions, observing in *Osborne v Donaldson* that 'it was a point of so much difficulty and consequence, that he should not determine it at this hearing, but should send it to law [i.e., to a common-law court] for the opinion of the judges'.

But the case was never heard by a common-law court; instead, Millar brought a King's Bench action in 1766 against another bookseller, Robert Taylor, over a pirate edition of James Thomson's poetical work *The Seasons*, to which Millar had bought the rights in the 1730s. He may have hoped that Taylor would put up less of a fight than Donaldson, but the Scottish book trade backed Taylor, the case was strenuously contested, and the legal issues were argued at length at hearings in 1767 and 1768. Most of the lawyers involved in *Tonson v Collins* also had leading roles in *Millar v Taylor*. Mansfield chaired a full panel of four judges, among them Joseph Yates, who had had been appointed to the bench in 1764. Millar was represented by Blackstone, and Taylor by Thurlow and by Samuel Johnson's friend Arthur Murphy. Millar died after the second hearing, but a consortium of London booksellers headed by Thomas Becket bought the rights to *The Seasons* from the estate and continued the action brought in his name.

Judgement was delivered in April 1769, and for the first time in the thirteen years that Mansfield had been Chief Justice one of the judges sitting with him delivered a dissenting judgement. The dissenter was Yates, who argued from the bench, as he had from the bar, that copyright did not exist at common law. His main argument was that property is essentially corporeal:

> The claim is to the style and ideas of the author's composition. And it is a well-known and established maxim, (which I apprehend holds as true now, as it did 2000 years ago,) 'that nothing can be an object of property, which has not a corporeal substance'. There may be many different rights, and particular distinct interests, in the same subject; and the several persons intitled to these rights may be said to have an interest in them: but the objects of them all, the principal subject to which they relate, or in which they enjoy, must be corporeal. And this, I apprehend, is no arbitrary ill-founded position: but a position which arises from the necessary nature of all property. ...
>
> But the property here claimed is all ideal; a set of ideas which have no bounds or marks whatever; nothing that is capable of a visible possession, nothing that can sustain any one of the qualities or incidents of property. Their whole existence is in the mind alone; incapable of any other modes of acquisition or enjoyment, than by mental possession or apprehension; safe and invulnerable, from their own immateriality: no trespass can reach them; no tort affect them; no fraud or violence diminish or damage them. Yet these are the phantoms which the author would grasp and confine to himself: and these are what the defendant is charged with having robbed the plaintiff of.[135]

Having rejected common-law copyright on these grounds, Yates had no trouble in disposing of the arguments in its favour from legal precedent and public policy.

Mansfield's main argument in favour of common-law copyright was based upon considerations of natural justice:

> From what source, then, is the common law drawn, which is admitted to be so clear, in respect of the copy before publication? From this argument—because it is just, that an author should reap the pecuniary profits of his own ingenuity and labour. It is just, that another should not use his name, without his consent. It is fit that he should judge when to publish, or whether he ever will publish. It is fit he should not only choose the time, but the manner of publication; how many; what volume; what print. It is fit, he should choose to whose care he will trust the accuracy and correctness of the impression; in whose honesty he will confide, not to foist in additions: with other reasonings of the same effect. ... But the same reasons hold, after the author has published. He can reap no pecuniary profit, if, the next moment after his work comes

---

[135] *ER* v 98 p 233. The source quoted by Yates has not been identified.

> out, it may be pirated upon worse paper and in worse print, and in a cheaper volume. ... The author may not only be deprived of any profit, but lose the expence he has been at. He is no more master of the use of his own name. He has no control over the correctness of his own work. He cannot prevent additions. He cannot retract errors. He can not amend; or cancel a faulty edition. Any one may print, pirate and perpetuate the imperfections, to the disgrace and against the will of the author; may propagate sentiments under his name, which he disapproves, repents and is ashamed of. He can exercise no discretion as to the manner in which, or the persons by whom his work shall be published. For these and many more reasons, it seems to me just and fit, 'to protect the copy after publication'.[136]

Even though Mansfield had been involved in the Chancery cases of the 1730s, he also argued in favour of common-law copyright on the basis of legal precedent and rejected Yates's argument against it on the grounds of its incorporeality. In his view, the strongest argument—which Yates did not discuss—against common-law copyright was that it had been extinguished by the Copyright Act:

> I always thought the objection from the Act of Parliament, the most plausible. It has generally struck, at first view. But, upon consideration, it is, I think, impossible to imply this Act into an abolition of the common-law right, if it did exist; or into a declaration 'that no such right ever existed'.[137]

The validity of royal printing grants was not at issue in *Millar v Taylor*. Nevertheless, both Mansfield and Yates, in their detailed discussions of copyright law, discussed book patents. The century-old decision of the House of Lords in *Stationers v Patentees* in favour of the law patent was 'not to be shaken', and both judges concluded that the Crown had the power to grant exclusive printing rights to certain books.[138] But the logic of their views on common-law copyright

---

[136] *ER* v 98 p 252.

[137] *ER* v 98 p 256.

[138] By this time an increasing number of law books were being issued by publishers other than the law patentee. In 1769 the King's Printer bought the half share of the law patent which he did not already own, thus in effect merging the roles. The outcome was that the King's Printer published only official legal

brought Mansfield and Yates to this conclusion for quite different, and in each case somewhat uncharacteristic, reasons.

Yates, despite his Whig sympathies, based the validity of the patents for some classes of books on a prerogative power derived from, and limited by, the King's constitutional position:

> The books are Bibles, Common-Prayer Books, and all extracts from them, (such as primers, Psalters, Psalms,) and almanacs. Those have relation to the national religion or Government, or the political constitution. Other compositions to which the King's right of publication extends, are the statutes, Acts of Parliament, and State-papers. The King's right to all these is, as head of the Church, and of the political Constitution. ... it appears to me, that the right of the Crown to the sole and exclusive printing of what are called prerogative copies, is founded on reasons of religion or State.[139]

Mansfield, although a legal innovator, was a political conservative. But he denied that the Crown's power to grant book patents was connected with the royal prerogative, and he based the validity of privileges on common-law copyright:

> The King can not, by law, grant an exclusive privilege any book which does not belong to himself. Crown-copies are, as in the case of an author, civil property: which is deduced, as in the case of an author, from the King's right of original publication. ...
>
> The copy of the Hebrew Bible, the Greek Testament, or the Septuagint does not belong to the King: it is common. But the English translation he bought: therefore it has been concluded to be his property. ... His whole right rests upon the foundation of property in the copy by the common law.[140]

Mansfield also pointed out that *Company of Stationers v Partridge*, the last case in which the almanac monopoly had been discussed, had never been decided.

Both Yates and Mansfield considered that the Crown could grant patents for only a few kinds of publication. But their comments

---

material, leaving books about the law to be published by others. See Wilfred Prest, 'Law books', *The Cambridge History of the Book in Britain*, v 5, Cambridge, 2008, p 791–806 at p 802–803.

[139] *ER* v 98 p 243–244.

[140] *ER* v 98 p 254 and p 256.

drew attention to the fact that the Stationers' Company's almanac patent was in an uncertain legal position. Mansfield said in effect that the patent had no legal basis. And neither judge said anything to suggest that the Crown's power to make printing grants might extend as far as being able to grant privileges for music.

Where the main issue in *Millar v Taylor* was concerned, the other two judges concurred with Mansfield, so that the decision of the King's Bench was three to one in favour of common-law copyright. This constituted a victory for the English booksellers, but it was a less decisive victory than they needed, for it affected the law only in England. To ensure that the law was in their favour in Scotland as well, they needed a favourable decision from the House of Lords or the Court of Session. But it was some years before the issue came before either of these courts, and in the meantime *Millar v Taylor* had highlighted the differences in legal opinion about common-law copyright, had damaged the façade of judicial concord that the King's Bench had acquired under Mansfield, had encouraged the Scottish booksellers, and had provided a large stock of ammunition to the parties in the pamphlet war. Nevertheless, this case affirmed the existence of common-law copyright and settled the law in England, for the time being.

6.10 Musical Copyright Litigation to 1770

Only a few musical copyright lawsuits are known to have taken place before the early 1770s, and none was considered worth recording by contemporary law reporters. Newspaper advertisements made a few threats of legal action, but whether these led to anything is in most instances unknown.

The earliest documented legal action for breach of musical copyright was brought by Thomas Arne. As noted on page 292 above, after obtaining his privilege in 1741 he published a warning that 'whoever shall print or sell any Work of the Author's, without his Approbation or Consent, will be prosecuted according to Law'. Two music sellers disregarded this warning. Henry Roberts continued to sell his collection *Calliope, or English Harmony*, which contained several songs from Arne's *Comus* and *As You Like It* and which had first appeared before Arne's privilege was granted. And John Johnson, who had published two single sheets containing songs from *Comus* before Arne's privilege was granted, brought out two more sheets containing songs from *As You Like It*. Arne launched Chancery proceedings (*Arne v Roberts*) against both sellers by lodging a bill of complaint (a petition to the Chancellor) on 12 November 1741 outlining his case and requesting relief.[141]

Arne and his lawyers were in unexplored legal territory and left nothing to chance. Besides referring to his privilege, the Copyright Act and the Engravers' Act, his bill hinted that the common law gave him 'sole property' in any music that he wrote:

> Your Orator, having with great Study, Labour and Expense Composed several works Consisting of Vocall and Instrumentall Musick, became Intitled thereby to the sole property therein, and the same ought not to have been Printed, Published, uttered or sold without your Orator's Leave. And ... the better to Establish his property to the same, your Orator did upon his Humble Representation to his Majesty obtain his Majesty's Royall Priviledge and Lycence under his sign Manual....
>
> And your Orator ... did Cause his said Musical Compositions to be Engraved on Copper Plates at a Great Expense, and from them did print and Publish the same, and hoped that he should Quietly have Enjoyed the Benefitt arising from the sale thereof, and that no other person Whatsoever would have published the same or any part thereof without your Orator's Leave, the same being prejudicial to your Orator and contrary to the said Sign Manual, and also to a certain Act of Parliament made in the Eighth year or her late Majesty Queen Anne, intitled an Act for the Encouragement of Learning..., and also to another act of Parliament made in the Eighth year of his present Majesty's Reign, entitled an Act for the Encouragement of the Arts of Disigning, Engraving and Etching Historical and other Prints

The bill went on to claim that Roberts and Johnson had printed, published and sold music written by Arne for productions of one or more of *Rosamond* (an opera first performed in 1735), *Comus* (first performed 1737) and *As You Like It* (1741). It asked that the court

[141] See Ronald J. Rabin and Steven Zohn, 'Arne, Handel, Walsh, and music as intellectual property: two eighteenth-century lawsuits', *Journal of the Royal Musical Association* v 120 no. 1 (1995) p 112–145 at p 117–125, upon which the following description is based. Arne's bill and the defendants' answer (both at TNA C11/2260/7) are transcribed on p 135–140 of this article.

order Roberts and Johnson to respond to the charges, and that it forbid them to print, publish or sell Arne's music without his consent. Echoing the privilege and the two Acts, the bill requested that the term of the injunction be fourteen years.

In their answer, lodged on 3 December, Roberts and Johnson admitted hearing 'that the complainant was the composer of several musical works or pieces of musick which he adapted or set to some old songs made by Shakespear and other authors'—in particular, songs in *Rosamond*, *Comus* and *As You Like It*—'but whether the complainant was the real author, inventor or composer of the said several pieces of musick, or any of them, they cannot say'. Roberts admitted having published four songs from *Comus* and one from *As You Like It* before Arne obtained his privilege, and having sold since then about twenty-four copies of songs from *Comus*, engraved by Johnson, and no more than six handwritten copies of 'Blow, blow' from *As You Like It*. However, Roberts denied that his publications had caused Arne any loss. Johnson admitted that he had printed six songs from *Comus* before the privilege was issued and three more since then, that he had sold the Arne songs printed by Roberts, and that he had arranged for copies of 'Blow, blow' to be made by hand.

Roberts and Johnson then jointly denied that 'Musick and songs published by the complainant' were books within the meaning of the Copyright Act and argued moreover that Arne had failed to comply with the Act because he had neither registered his publications, nor deposited nine copies of them at Stationers' Hall, nor brought his action within three months of the defendants' publications. Roberts and Johnson also denied that music and songs were prints within the meaning of the Engravers' Act, and argued that, by not having his name engraved on each plate and by not bringing his action within three months, Arne had failed to comply with that Act as well. Finally, the defendants suggested—but delicately, perhaps so as not directly to challenge a document issued in the king's name—that the exclusive printing rights claimed by Arne, whether by virtue of his privilege or on other grounds, amounted to a monopoly and were therefore illegal:

> And as to the said grant or Licence under the Great Seale…, these Defendants submit to the Judgement of this Court what right or Benefit could thereby accrew to the Complainant for securing to him an

> exclusive Right to the Works and Musick by him printed or published, or in Case he acquired such sole right or Interest therein (which these Defendants do not admit).

They added that anything that either of them might have done before the privilege was granted could not have infringed any rights that the privilege conferred upon Arne.

This dispute seems to have ended at this point, for no further records of the action have been located. Having traversed most of the legal issues that could have been raised with respect to printed music, the parties must have come to some agreement.

Arne was involved in further copyright litigation in 1752 as co-defendant with the actor and singer Thomas Lowe in an action brought by Thomas Holt, the librettist of Arne's opera *Henry and Emma*.[142] Holt is otherwise unknown—perhaps justly, for even after Lowe and Arne had made major changes to the libretto the opera was performed just once, on 31 March 1749. Arne claimed in his and Lowe's answer that *Henry and Emma* 'would have been utterly damned and hissed off the stage' if the performance had not been a benefit for Lowe, with Lowe's friends in the audience. Nevertheless, the composer and the impresario salvaged a few items: Arne used a song from *Henry and Emma* in another unsuccessful opera, *Don Saverio*, which ran for three nights in 1749; and Lowe performed songs from *Henry and Emma* at a benefit concert in 1750. But Holt, who had published the song texts from *Henry and Emma* and had entered that work at Stationers' Hall on 16 February 1749, objected to the use of his words by Arne and Lowe and brought proceedings against them in the Court of Exchequer acting in its equitable jurisdiction.

Holt's claim was based on an agreement under which he and Arne, instead of selling their libretto and music to Lowe, as was usual, agreed to share the profits from the second and later performances of *Henry and Emma* with him. In other words, Holt and Arne would have received performance royalties, something unheard

---

[142] The description that follows is based upon Judith Milhous and Robert D. Hume, 'Librettist versus composer: the property rights to Arne's *Henry and Emma* and *Don Saverio*', *Journal of the Royal Musical Association* v 122 no. 1 (1987) p 52–67.

of at the time. But the agreement was unsigned and Lowe and Arne denied having consented to such an arrangement, and the action seems to have gone no further than the bill and answer.

Arne continued to campaign against piracy and misattribution. In a 1761 advertisement for the forthcoming edition of his *Thomas and Sally* he made threats similar to those that he had made in 1741 and 1746, invoking not his privilege, which had expired, but the Copyright Act, which contained penal provisions, and the common law, which he seems to have thought provided the only basis for an injunction:

> Whereas two or three Songs have been imposed on the Public, pretended to belong to [*Thomas and Sally*], the Town is hereby assured that they were not the Doctor's Music, but Things vilely trumped up for the Unskilful.
>
> All his future Works (single Songs excepted) will be published in Books or Pamphlets, and entered with the Company of Stationers, as the Act of Parliament directs; such Method being under the immediate Protection of the Common Law, and he will prosecute with the utmost Severity, any one, who shall presume to vend, or copy for Sale, any Part or Parts of his Works whatever.[143]

And in April 1762 Arne published the following advertisement:

> ARTAXERXES.
>
> *This Day is published,*
>
> ALL the Songs and Duetto in the first Act of that English Opera. Compos'd by Dr ARNE. Price 7 s.
>
> The Second and Third Acts will be published with all possible Expedition.
>
> ☞ Actions at Law are commenced against several Music-Sellers, for unlawfully procuring stolen Copies of favourite Songs and exhibiting them to Sale, to the unspeakable Damage of the Author; and as the above Book or Pamphlet is, and the other two will be entered with the Company of Stationers, as the Act of Parliament for the securing of the Property of Authors directs; whoever (in Defiance of Law and Equity) shall presume to print, publish, or copy for Sale, any Part of the said Opera, will be prosecuted with the utmost Rigour.—'Tis necessary to inform the Public, that whoever purchases any Song, &c. of those daring

[143] *The Public Advertiser*, 27 January 1761, p 1. Arne entered *Thomas and Sally* at Stationers' Hall on 31 January 1761.

> Th—s, so unlawfully obtained, and sold, is an Encourager of Dishonesty, and a Receiver of Stolen Goods.[144]

However, *Artaxerxes* was not entered at Stationers' Hall until 24 October 1768 and, quite unusually, no proprietor's name for this work was recorded in the Stationers' Company register.[145]

John Parkinson has suggested that the contraction 'Th–s' in the above advertisement stood both for 'Thieves' and 'Thorowgoods', a music-selling partnership of Henry Thorowgood and Robert Horne that began trading in January 1762.[146] The suggestion is plausible, for in November 1762 Thorowgood and Horne, undeterred by Arne's advertisement, advertised their publication of 'All the Airs with their Symphonies in the Opera called ARTAXERXES. Taken from the Score and Set for the German Flute, Violins and Guittar'.[147] Nothing more is known about the 'actions at law' that Arne said he had commenced.

In 1765, the year after Thorowgood ceased to work in partnership with Horne and went into business on his own, he was involved in a dispute with Isaac John Bickerstaff over the successful opera *The Maid of the Mill*, for which Bickerstaff had written the words to music by Samuel Arnold and other composers and claimed to have arranged the music for German flute.[148] Knowing that material from the opera was likely to be published without authorisation, Bickerstaff had the following warning printed on the title-page of an edition published for him by Robert Bremner:

---

144 *The Public Advertiser*, 28 April 1762, p 4.

145 *MESH* p 23.

146 Parkinson, *op. cit.* in note 110 above, p 21.

147 *The Public Advertiser*, 27 November 1762, p 3. For the guittar see note 90 on page 29 above. Thorowgood & Horne also published 'The Overture in Artaxerxes'.

148 I am grateful to Nancy Mace, who discovered this dispute, for supplying her transcripts of court documents in *Bickerstaff v Thorowgood*. When *The Maid of the Mill* was registered at Stationers' Hall on 31 January 1765 (*MESH* p 21) Bickerstaff held one-quarter of the copyright; the rest was shared among seven booksellers.

> N.B. That none may pretend ignorance, notice is here given, that who ever presumes to print, or write out for Sale, any Songs in this Opera; will be prosecuted by the Author and the Proprietor with the utmost rigour of the Law.

At Easter 1765, after Thorowgood had published an unauthorised flute arrangement of music from this opera, Bickerstaff sought an Exchequer injunction to forbid that publication. Thorowgood, in reply, pointed out that Bickerstaff had not written the opera's music but had fitted his words to music by other people who were named in the Bremner edition. Thorowgood further alleged that Bickerstaff being 'intirely ignorant of Musical Composition' could not have arranged the music for flute. At the last known hearing of this case, in June 1766, the court ordered that Bickerstaff's bill be dismissed and that he pay Thorowgood's costs.

Other disputes over music in the 1750s and 1760s led to advertisements hinting at or threatening legal action. John Worgan, who had obtained a privilege in 1752, inserted the following note in a 1755 advertisement for his 'The new Vauxhall ballads, sung there this summer by Mr Lowe and Miss Stevenson':

> ☞ No single Ballad can be wrote out or printed from this Book, the Author having been at the Expence of obtaining the King's Royal Licence, to prevent the Music Shop-keepers and others doing him so great an Injury, it being no less than robbing him of his Property.[149]

Evidently Worgan's attempt to protect his 1754 *A Collection of New Songs and Ballads* by printing his privilege in this work was unsuccessful.[150] It is not known whether he took legal action on this occasion.

The successful opera *The Padlock*, with words by Bickerstaff and music by Charles Dibdin Sr, was first performed in 1768. Bickerstaff bought the music rights from Dibdin,[151] and placed the following advertisements in July and September 1769:

---

[149] *The Public Advertiser*, 26 June 1755, p 1.

[150] A copy with the privilege is at RCM D838/8.

[151] Jon A. Gillaspie, 'Dibdin, Charles', in *Oxford Dictionary of National Biography*.

PADLOCK.

SOME of the Songs in the Comic Opera of the PADLOCK having been pirated in a Collection of Vocal Music; a Bill was last Week filed against the Publisher, who has paid the Costs, and entered into a Bond to offend no more: And the Proprietor has given Orders to prosecute one FOUGHT, a Foreign Printer, in what he calls Musical Types, for an Offence of the like Nature; which he is determined, for the Sake of Musical Property in general, to carry as far as the Law will admit: And in the mean Time it is hoped that no Music Shop will encourage, by their Countenance, such unjust and infamous Piracies.

To the Dealers in MUSIC.

THE Proprietor of the Music of the PADLOCK has commenced a Suit against one HENRY FOUGHT, a foreign Music-Printer, for pirating some of the Songs of that Opera, and against SAMUEL FORES, Stationer, for vending the same; which he is determined, for the Good of the Trade, to prosecute with Effect: And it is wished that the Dealers in Music would appoint a Place of Meeting, to consider of Means to put their Property on a more permanent Footing than it is at present.[152]

Immediately below the latter advertisement another was published relating to music piracy:

SHAKESPEARE.

This Day is published,

THE Music of the ODE composed by Dr ARNE, on dedicating a Building and erecting a Statute to Shakespeare, at Stratford upon Avon. Also the Music of Shakespeare's Garland, composed by Mr Dibdin. ...

Printed and sold by John Johnston, Music Printer, at Number 11, York-street, Covent Garden.

Whereas one of the Songs in the above Garland has been lately pirated, as also some Songs in the Opera of Cymon [with music by Michael Arne and Dibdin], the Publisher hopes that the Gentlemen in the Musical Business will discountenance this Attack on private Property, as there is a Suit now commenced against the Printer and Publishers of the

[152] *The Public Advertiser*, 20 July 1769, p 1, and 23 September 1769, p 1. 'Fought' refers to Henry Fougt. Bickerstaff's bill of complaint against the music seller Henry Roberts regarding *The Padlock* was lodged on 6 July 1769 (TNA C12/1026/3). Bickerstaff's bill of complaint against Fougt was lodged on 24 November 1769 (TNA C12/1026/2). See 'Register of Copyright Infringement Suits and Actions from *c*1560 to 1800' cited in note 21 above. Neither action went further.

> above Songs, which by it's [sic] being vigorously prosecuted may establish a Precedent of the utmost Utility to the Trade in general.[153]

This lawsuit has not been traced.

The hope that music sellers might unite against piracy was unrealistic: piracy was endemic to the trade. Moreover, copying was still important in the dissemination of music—a fact that the attention given to print publication tends to obscure, but which undermined attempts to prevent piracy. Thomas Arne, Worgan and Johnson had all complained about copying. Many music sellers offered a copying service and were probably not fussy about what was copied. And—what is much the same thing—music not in high demand was still published in manuscript. In 1761 the music-loving clergyman Thomas Twining wrote to a friend:

> I have met with some fine cantatas in the Scarlatti style, by great masters: two of the Baron D'Astorga, one of Marc Antonio Bononcini, ... one of Handel's, one of Marcello, & one of Antonio Lotti. You would have laugh'd to see me buy these: where did I buy them of all places but at Walsh's music shop. He was revenged upon me for the many laughs I have had at him. He found out my taste, & flung a whole bundle of the MS music before me: he did not say, 'Indeed, you shou'd have this', but I said so myself for him; & so he got the money out of my pocket as easily as if I had been a lady of quality & had come in a coach.[154]

In any case, it was still not clear how, if at all, the law protected music. But as disputes about music became more common and concern about piracy became more widespread, the likelihood that the law would be clarified increased. The critical legal decisions would be made in the 1770s.

---

[153] *The Public Advertiser*, 23 September 1769, p 1.

[154] Thomas Twining→John Hey, 29 July 1761, transcribed in Ralph S. Walker (ed.), *A Selection of Thomas Twining's Letters 1734–1804*, New York, 1991, v 1 p 27–29 at p 29. The reference presumably is to Alessandro Scarlatti. Both Alessandro Marcello and Benedetto Marcello composed cantatas.

6.11 THE BEGINNING OF *PYLE V FALKENER*

A significant legal action for breach of musical copyright began on 10 May 1771. Two Chancery bills, the second a revision of the first, were lodged on behalf of John Pyle, the surviving executor of the will of John Walsh Jr, who died in 1766.[155] The revised bill listed Walsh's purchases of rights to works by Handel, Greene, Arne and Bickerstaff, and noted that Walsh's 1760 privilege had granted him and his executors sole printing and publishing rights to Handel's 'Six Concertos for the Harpsichord and Organ ... Entitled a third set and a Selected Collection of Songs from his Operas and Oratorios for the Harpsichord and Concerts, never before Collected & Published together'. Walsh had evidently obtained this privilege to protect Handel's concertos op. 7, issued in 1761, as well as an unspecified collection of songs, but the privilege was phrased so that it protected that collection as a whole rather than the individual songs therein.

Pyle alleged that the London music seller Robert Falkener had published works owned by the Walsh estate, and requested an injunction ordering Falkener not to publish them, as a first step to having him hand over his profits from them to Walsh's estate. Misuse of others' property may have been characteristic of Falkener, for later in 1771 the harpsichord maker Jacob Kirkman tried to sue him for £500 over the alleged sale of six bogus Kirkman harpsichords, two of them made by Falkener.[156]

The music over which Pyle sued Falkener comprised a song from *Love in a Village* and the overture and a duet from *Thomas and*

---

[155] TNA C12/2082/42. The following description is based upon Rabin and Zohn, *op. cit.*, p 125–133, and their transcript (*ibid.*, p 140–145) of the Chancery record of the final hearing (in TNA C33/442), which summarises Pyle's bill and Falkener's answer. Presumably Pyle was given leave to lodge an amended version of his original bill.

[156] Lance Whitehead, 'Robert Falkener: an eighteenth-century harpsichord builder, music publisher and malfeasant?', *The Galpin Society Journal* v 55 (2002) p 310–331, transcribes (p 326–328) a document (at RCM) apparently drafted by Kirkman's lawyer John Skirrow in preparation for a King's Bench action. The action may not have gone ahead, for no record of any King's Bench proceedings has been located. The document gives Falkener's address as the Marshalsea debtors' prison, but this might have been just wishful thinking on Kirkman's part.

Sally—both works with music by Arne and words by Bickerstaff; two songs by Maurice Greene; ten vocal selections from Handel's *Acis and Galatea*; eight vocal items, plus a march and two overtures, from various Handel oratorios; and a three-movement version of the first movement of Handel's D-major *Water Music* suite.[157]

To the extent that the Act protected music, and that privileges protected anything, it could be claimed that most of this music, when Falkener published it, was protected by Walsh's Handel privilege or was still protected by the Act. Several items—Greene's songs, the march from Handel's *Judas Maccabeus* and the piece from the *Water Music*—were not protected in either of these ways, but this does not prove that Pyle's lawyers had the common law in mind. At the start of proceedings they may have believed that an injunction would quickly bring Falkener to heel, regardless of how the individual compositions listed in Pyle's bill were protected, or of how dependable the various forms of protection were.

However, Falkener lodged an answer. After denying any knowledge of the business transactions detailed in the bill—litigants customarily denied all knowledge of whatever they could not be proved to have known—Falkener pointed out that Greene's songs and many of the works from which the Handel songs came had been published long ago, claimed that 'in consequence of such publications such parts of the said several compositions as any one liked were copied and sold by those who make it their business to copy music for sale', and argued that he had the right to publish

> such Extracts out of the said Oratorios as he thought proper, not only as it has been the Custom, Usage and practice for all persons who thought proper so to do, but as most of the said Music has been published more than 30 years and the whole thereof more than 20 years, and because Musical Compositions are not a Subject of Literary property

Regarding Walsh's privilege, Falkener's reply submitted

> that if the said John Walsh did obtain any such licence, that such licence is an imposition on his late said Majesty and a fraud upon the public in

---

[157] See Rabin and Zohn, *op. cit.*, p 143 for Pyle's description of the items published by Falkener and p 127–129 for Rabin and Zohn's identification of them. The suit also concerned an unidentified piece entitled 'I thirst'.

> General, and is void in Law and not within the protection of the Statute [of Monopolies] made in the 21st year of the reign of His Majesty King James the first[158]

Assuming that letters patent could be granted only to protect new inventions, Falkener asserted that the Handel songs 'cannot be deemed a new invention or such as ought to have entitled him to have applied for his late Majesty's Royal Licence' and that 'in case such application to the Crown for the said Licence had been public and notorious it would have been opposed and would not have been granted'.[159]

Where *Thomas and Sally* and *Love in a Village* were concerned, Falkener pointed out that Bickerstaff had registered each opera—Falkener said opera, not libretto—with the Stationers' Company but, according to the register, had never transferred the rights to Walsh or Pyle. Falkener then in effect denied that the Arne songs identified by Pyle as being from *Love in a Village* had anything to do with the opera as it was staged, claiming that the songs performed were usually sung to traditional tunes. After again denying 'that any person whomsoever can acquire to himself any sole or distinct right or property in or to Musical Composition, and [asserting] that the same are not as he insists an object of distinct property', Falkener submitted:

> that untill the plaintiff has Established his distinct right to the said two Operas by a Tryal by law [i.e., in a common-law court], that he [Falkener] shall [not] be restrained by Injunction of this Court from printing such Musical Extracts therefrom or such Songs as have been public many Years before *Love in a Village* was wrote by the said Isaac Bickerstaff, the same having all along both before writing and since and now being copied and publickly sold by every person who usually sells Musical Notes without any interruption.

Falkener's argument was that Bickerstaff, not Pyle, owned the rights to the operas, that the purported *Thomas and Sally* and *Love in a Village* material was not in fact part of those operas, that any legal questions about ownership of the operas should be resolved by a

---

[158] Rabin and Zohn, *op. cit.*, p 143.

[159] *ibid.*, p 130, evidently quoted from Falkener's original answer.

common-law court, and that regardless of how these matters were determined Falkener should be free to publish the traditional tunes used in the operas.

Falkener thus raised several lines of defence. His claim that some of the music had been published too long ago to be protected by the Copyright Act was correct. However, his statement 'that musical compositions are not a subject of literary property' was true only to the extent that music was not explicitly protected by the Act. Although the question of whether music was protected by any form of copyright was yet to be determined by a court, the decision in *Millar v Taylor* suggested that the common law protected music even if the Copyright Act did not. Falkener's argument that Walsh's privilege was inconsistent with the 1624 Statute of Monopolies was incorrect, for that statute specifically permitted 'grants of privilege … made … of, for or concerning printing'. His assumption that letters patent could legally be granted to protect only something new was also wrong: if they were valid at all, privileges could as easily protect published material as unpublished. And in any case, Walsh's privilege described the Handel songs not as unpublished but as 'never before Collected & Published together': that is, the selection and arrangement could be said to be new, even if the individual compositions were not.

The part of Falkener's answer dealing with *Thomas and Sally* and *Love in a Village* raised or threatened to raise awkward questions. It seemed that Pyle regarded Arne's music as having been included in Bickerstaff's sale of the rights to the operas to Walsh. If so, how was this consistent with the alleged fact that *Love in a Village* was performed to traditional tunes, and how had Bickerstaff acquired the rights to Arne's music in the first place? Did Pyle claim that the rights registered in Bickerstaff's name at Stationers' Hall included the rights to the music? If he did, and music was the kind of thing that should be registered at Stationers' Hall—a question which would have to be decided by a common-law court—then why had the transfer of the rights to the operas, and to all the other music which the estate claimed to own, not been registered at Stationers' Hall? Again, was registration a condition of protection by the Act? (This too was a question which would have to be decided by a common-law court.) If it was, Pyle could not claim the protection of the Copyright Act for the works purchased from Bickerstaff.

Another awkward aspect of Falkener's answer from Pyle's point of view was its insistence that it was 'the custom, usage and practice for all persons who thought proper' to print previously published music. This threatened to complicate the legal issues and make the litigation more expensive by raising the question of what constituted accepted practice in the music-selling trade.

Until the 1750s courts had generally decided commercial disputes on the basis of the evidence given in each case about common practice. However, Lord Mansfield had begun to treat commercial cases as opportunities to clarify the legal principles that applied to commercial transactions. To ensure that the law stayed in touch with commercial reality Mansfield consulted experts and made extensive use of special juries to decide what the accepted practice was in particular cases. Under an act of 1730 either party to a case was entitled to a special jury at his own expense, while an act of 1754 provided that a judge could order a special jury to be empanelled, the additional cost to be paid by the unsuccessful party. Mansfield established a panel of jurors prepared to serve in commercial cases, instructing them in the law and personally consulting them on doubtful matters. When the special jury in a commercial case determined what commercial practice was, that practice became part of the common law.

Mansfield's work was of great benefit to lawyers and business people: it made commercial litigation less of a gamble and laid the foundations of commercial law in common-law jurisdictions. But if a King's Bench case happened to raise issues which had not yet been authoritatively dealt with, the special juries made proceedings even slower and greatly increased the costs of the losing party. Whether music was customarily treated as being in the public domain after it was first published was not the kind of question that the special juries normally dealt with; their role was usually to determine questions about the meaning and effect of commercial documents. But Falkener's claim that music-trade practice was on his side threatened to increase the risks and the costs of the case.

Falkener's lawyers probably hoped that by making *Pyle v Falkener* a potentially very complicated and drawn-out business, and a costly one for the loser, they would make Pyle more disposed to settle. And perhaps Falkener himself, faced with two major legal actions, felt that he might as well fight both of them on every possible front. But there seems to have been no talk of settlement just yet. In February 1772 Arne and other witnesses gave depositions verifying the signatures on the agreements that Pyle had cited in his bill. And on 8 June 1773 the case was adjourned, at Pyle's request, until the House of Lords dealt with a forthcoming case 'of a similar nature'.

6.12 THE BEGINNING OF *BACH V LONGMAN*

Three months before *Pyle v Falkener* was adjourned, two leading London musicians who perhaps were unaware of that case launched Chancery actions for breach of copyright against another music publisher. John Christian Bach, the youngest son of Johann Sebastian, studied in Berlin with his brother Carl Phillipp Emanuel after their father's death, and then in Bologna with Padre Martini. After working in Milan as cathedral organist, Bach had success with operas written for Turin and Naples, was engaged to work for a season at the King's Theatre in London in 1762, and stayed on in England as music master to Queen Charlotte. Charles Frederick Abel, a versatile instrumentalist whose speciality was the obsolescent viola da gamba, had worked in Dresden until the outbreak of the Seven Years War. Moving to London in the late 1750s, he rapidly became a musical celebrity and was appointed a member of the Queen's Chamber Band some time after her arrival in England in 1761. Bach and Abel were greatly admired as composers and executants: the annual concert series which they jointly directed from 1765 onwards was a notable success, and many editions of their music were published in London.

As recounted in Chapter 1, the music seller James Longman began to trade in Cheapside in 1768 and Charles Lukey joined him as a partner in 1769. In his thirty years in business Longman established a reputation for 'superior sagacity and strength of intellect',[160] but his sagacity was at least equalled by his litigiousness, for during that time

[160] According to his obituary in *The Gentleman's Magazine* v 123 (December 1803) p 1183–1184. This obituary is quoted on page 85 above.

he was involved in numerous legal actions—of which, as far as is known, those brought by Bach and Abel were the earliest.

Bach and Abel were well aware of the need to protect their music against piracy: within a year or so of arriving in England, each of them obtained a royal privilege protecting his music. Nevertheless, many London publishers produced editions of their works, and many of those editions must have been unauthorised. Bach published his op. 1 with Walsh Jr but brought out his trios op. 2 and symphonies op. 3 under his own name, after which he left the publication of his music to others and it is difficult to see a pattern in his dealings with London music publishers. Abel published his op. 1 and op. 2 with Walsh Jr, but thereafter seems to have dealt exclusively with Robert Bremner, whose title-pages stated that some Abel works were 'printed and sold by R. Bremner' while others were 'printed for the Author, and sold by R. Bremner'. It can be assumed that most prints of Abel's music by other London music sellers were unauthorised.

One such unauthorised print led to a public dispute between Abel and Longman in August–September 1769. After Longman, Lukey & Co. published 'C. F. Abel's Six favourite Overtures adapted for the Harpsichord or Organ' Abel issued the following protest:

> WRONG MUSIC.
>
> WHEREAS J. Longman has lately published in my Name, my first Set of Overtures, set for the Harpsichord as he calls it: I not only declare my having no Hand in the Performance, but that the whole is quite false and improper for that Instrument. How far the Laws of the Land allow one Man to lessen the Reputation of another, by spoiling his Works shall soon be enquired into. In the mean time, to prevent the Success of so gross an Imposition on the indulgent Public, I have with Care adapted these Overtures for the Harpsichord myself. They are now in the Hands of the Engraver, and shall be ready within three Weeks at furthest.
>
> C. F. ABEL.
>
> N. B. It is my Intention also to adapt my other Overtures, viz. Operas 4th and 7th, to the Harpsichord, as soon as Time will permit.[161]

Longman counterattacked, prefacing an advertisement for Longman, Lukey & Co.'s latest music publications with the claim that any

[161] *The Public Advertiser*, 10 August 1769, p 1. Abel also placed this advertisement in *The Gazetteer and New Daily Advertiser*, 10 August 1769, p 1.

shortcomings in the arrangement of the overtures were Abel's fault, and challenging him to take legal action:

> RIGHT MUSIC.
> ABEL's Six Favourite Overtures,
> adapted to the Harpsichord, 4s.
>
> Whereas C. F. Abel has published an Advertisement, accusing me of spoiling his Works, by printing his first Set of Overtures, set for the Harpsichord; the Public shall judge of the Falsity of this Accusation: These Overtures, as adapted for the Harpsichord, and published by me, are taken from a Set in eight Parts, originally printed in Holland, and are so compiled, that they not only serve as Lessons for the Harpsichord, but are purposely contrived still to be played together with all the Parts; yet C. F. Abel, does not blush to say, they are improper for the Instrument, and also that the whole is quite false; what Faults there are (Errors of the Press excepted) must be in his Copy originally printed in Holland, from which they are carefully done. He says he has adapted them himself, we shall see in what Manner he has, to render them more proper for that Instrument, without altering the original Composition.
>
> J. LONGMAN.[162]

Abel responded by republishing his 'Wrong Music' advertisement (changing only its last line to announce that his own adaptation of his overtures 'will be ready on Saturday next') and adding the following postscript:

> ☞ Mr. Longman calls these Overtures in his Advertisement Right Music. If he thinks them right, it is an evident Sign they are wrong.[163]

Longman then issued a lengthy reply:

> ABEL's Six Favourite Overtures, adapted for the harpsichord or organ; calculated also to be played with the instrumental parts, price only 4s. printed on a fine super-royal.
>
> Whereas C. F. ABEL has advertised 'Wrong Music', published by me (meaning the above Overtures), giving, as his reason, that 'if I think them Right, it is an evident sign they are wrong'! A mode of reasoning unanswerable indeed, because unintelligible. I beg leave to inform the

---

162 *Lloyd's Evening Post, and British Chronicle for 1769*, 18–21 August 1769, p 172.

163 *The St James's Chronicle; or, British Evening Post*, 29–31 August 1769, p 2; repeated in *The Public Advertiser*, 30 August 1769, p 1.

> public, and Mr Abel, that they were adapted by an eminent ENGLISH MASTER, and have been greatly approved by persons, whose judgments are allowed to EQUAL those of Mr ABEL. Did I stand in need of any additional proof of their being adapted with propriety, I may mention the GREAT DEMAND for them, which is alone a convincing one, and sufficient to overturn the malicious insinuations of said Abel.
>
> In my former advertisement, I asserted, they were properly adapted to the instrument; and that care had been taken, not only to preserve the original composition, as lessons, but so to adapt them, as to be able to play them with all the parts. If a liberty had been taken with the original composition, Abel might justly have complained; yet he accuses me of having published a wrong composition: though he cannot support his accusation, otherwise than by altering, essentially, the original, to adapt them merely as harpsichord lessons.
>
> Had Mr Abel suspended his advertisements, till he made the ENQUIRIES he hints at, I apprehend he would not have recourse to threats; concerning which, I feel the most perfect indifference: conscious of having taken no step to injure his reputation, and equally confident of having incurred no violation of A PROPERTY, which he parted with in Holland (where the set of Overtures I refer to, were originally published), previous to his coming into this kingdom. J. LONGMAN.[164]

The dispute appears to have ended here, but Longman had raised an awkward legal question. His claim that Abel could not be the owner in Britain of something he had sold in Holland would obviously have been correct if the right to publish a work had resembled a tangible item of personal property that always had a definite location and remained the same regardless of where that location was. But publishing and printing measures and the rights they created were effective only within national boundaries: British copyright law had no effect in France; the French *privilège générale* had no effect in Britain. Whatever property rights there were in a work published in one country did not exist in another. What was the legal effect in Britain of the sale of publication rights elsewhere? This question would not be addressed until the nineteenth century, after other countries had introduced their own copyright legislation (see section 6.16 below).

Abel was not the only composer to complain about Longman's firm or to get a defiant public response. Joseph Tacet's 1771 argument with Longman, Lukey & Co. has been described in Chapter

---

[164] *The Gazetteer and New Daily Advertiser*, 8 September 1769, p 3.

1.[165] Ten years later 'Appolo' complained about a different aspect of music publishing:

> NEW FAVOURITE ADVERTISEMENT.
>
> The Composers of Music, in London, most respectfully acquaint the nobility and gentry, that henceforth their new music will be sold at their own dwelling houses; the reason of this is, because the music-shop keepers take so much advantage over the composers, viz. 1st when a set of music sells for 10s. 6d. the music shops take half a crown for their trouble of selling it. I think sixpence or a shilling profit is sufficient for a copy, as the only trouble is to sell it to the person that asks for it in the shop.—N.B. As it is customary with the booksellers. 2dly, the music-shop keepers take the seventh copy for their profit, which they call allowance; consequently there remains only 6s. 3d. out of the half guinea to the composer for his performance, and he is obliged to pay the engraving, printing, paper and other expences. The composers of music will refer to the impartial judgement of a generous public, if it is just, that when a good composition appears, and is accepted by the public, that the music-shop keepers, take the money, and for the composer remains only the honour, by which he is to live. Consequently the shop keepers live by the sweat and labours of the composers, and are, into the bargain, very insolent and impertinent towards them. Thus much from APPOLO[166]

The god of music did not stoop to name the offending shopkeepers but one of his targets may have been Longman & Broderip, who at about this time had described their premises as 'At the King's Arms and Apollo, No. 26 Cheapside'.[167]

No press publicity preceded the outbreak of James Longman's dispute with Bach and Abel. On 18 March 1773 a Chancery bill was lodged in Bach's name, naming Longman, Lukey & Co. as defendants.[168] Signed, in accordance with Chancery practice, by

---

[165] See pages 28–29 above.

[166] *The Morning Herald, and Daily Advertiser*, 2 March 1781, p 1.

[167] Charles Humphries and William C[harles] Smith, *Music Publishing in the British Isles*, 2nd ed., Oxford, 1970, p 216.

[168] Most but not all surviving records (at TNA) of Bach's actions against Longman, Lukey & Co. have been transcribed and edited by Ann van Allen-Russell on p 577–582 of Ernest Warburton (ed.), *The Collected Works of Johann Christian Bach 1735–1782* v 48 part 2 ('Sources & Documents'), p 557–582. The transcriptions in this chapter are mine but do not differ significantly from hers.

Bach's counsel, Charles Robinson,[169] it stated that 'about twelve years ago' Bach 'Composed and wrote a certain Musical Composition for the Harpsichord called a Sonata'; that in 1763 he obtained a fourteen-year privilege granting him exclusive publication rights to the music he had composed up till then; that 'about four years ago' he 'Composed and Wrote another musical composition for the Harpsichord called a Sonata together with an accompanyment for the Viol da Gamba'; and that 'notwithstanding the said two several musical Works or Compositions and Accompanyment ... were solely of your orators Composing and Writing and his absolute and Exclusive Right and property' James Longman, Charles Lukey and unknown associates had 'by undue means' obtained copies of the compositions and published them 'for a very large profit' without Bach's permission, 'with the said Accompanyment Ignorantly changed or varied ... by putting the Viol da Gamba part for the flute or fiddle and Violoncello'. The bill stated that Bach had 'frequently in a friendly manner' tried to get the defendants to settle with him; that they had comprehensively denied all his allegations and continued to sell these publications; and that Bach has no adequate remedy at common law. The bill requested that the Chancellor order the publishers to answer the charges and hand their profits over to Bach, and that the Chancellor issue an injunction ordering Longman, Lukey & Co. not to sell the offending publications.

Bach's bill, although not exactly 'a volume of notorious lies',[170] had its share of formalities and fictions. The allegation of collusion with persons unknown gave the plaintiff the option of joining other parties as defendants later in proceedings—which in this instance would be unnecessary. Plaintiffs in Chancery actions had to claim that fraud had occurred, that the sum involved was over £5, and that the plaintiff was taking legal action only as a last resort—hence the statements that Longman, Lukey & Co. had acquired the sonatas 'by undue means', that their profits were 'very large' and that Bach had

[169] Details of Chancery procedure are taken from Robert Hinde, *The Modern Practice of the High Court of Chancery...*, London, 1785.

[170] Jeremy Bentham's famous description of a Chancery bill, given in his *An Introductory View of the Rationale of Evidence...*, reprinted in *The Works of Jeremy Bentham*, Edinburgh, v 6 (1843) p 1–187 at p 43.

tried 'frequently and in a friendly manner' to settle the dispute. In fact, Bach probably did not know how the manuscripts had been acquired and could not have known what the firm's profits were. (The total profits on both prints would be found to have been less than £5.) And the purely formal assurance about frequent and friendly attempts to settle would probably have been given regardless of how infrequent and unfriendly any recent dealings with the firm had been.

Bach would have lodged, in addition to his bill, a petition requesting a hearing. Although Chancery was notorious for its dilatory procedures and its bloated, inefficient bureaucracy, it could move quickly enough when an injunction was sought, and it responded to such petitions without delay, in ways that worked to the defendant's disadvantage. The defendant was served with a subpoena ordering him to attend the injunction hearing; but to learn what the proceedings were about he had to pay, and wait, for Chancery clerks to make an exact copy of the bill, which could easily run to over 2000 words even in relatively simple cases. Moreover, Chancery allowed plaintiffs to petition for an injunction without having lodged a bill. Plaintiffs therefore customarily ambushed defendants by first petitioning for a hearing, and then lodging the bill only shortly before the return date for the subpoena.

The injunction hearing took place on 23 March, five days after Bach's bill was lodged. Bach was represented by Edward Thurlow, who since appearing in *Millar v Taylor* had become Attorney-General but continued to practise at the bar, as was the custom. He was a music-lover—he went to the trouble of studying figured bass some years later—but is not known to have had anything to do with Bach or Abel apart from this appearance. Thurlow's engagement was probably only for this hearing, to ensure that Bach had the strongest possible courtroom representation. But there was no need for a Thurlow, for Longman, Lukey & Co. were not represented. Thurlow submitted an affidavit signed by Bach and the German keyboard player John Daniel Benser, reciting the facts described in Bach's bill, identifying the offending publications as 'a new Lesson for the Harpsichord or Piano Forte composed by J. C. Back [sic] of London' and 'a new Sonata for the Harpsichord', and stating that Benser had bought copies of both at Longman, Lukey & Co.'s shop.[171] That was all that was needed and the Chancellor granted the requested injunction.

If any negotiations took place at this point, they were brief and fruitless, for the next recorded move in the proceedings was the lodging of two more Chancery bills, one in Bach's name and another in Abel's, six weeks later. Bach's second bill, lodged on 6 May, is practically identical with his first, except that the works involved were a symphony for strings with pairs of oboes, clarinets, horns and bassoons, written about ten years earlier, and two symphonies for strings with pairs of clarinets and horns and a bassoon, respectively written about six and five years earlier. The bill did not say whether the works had been adapted. When Lord Chancellor Apsley heard an application for this injunction four days later, Bach was represented by John Hotchkin, who is not known to have had any further involvement in the litigation and was probably standing in for Robinson. Hotchkin presented an affidavit signed by Bach and John Sharp, described as a gentleman of Long Court, Saint Martin in the Fields, who had bought a copy of the offending publication at Longman, Lukey & Co.'s shop. (Bach's lawyers had a different person buy the music each time, presumably to keep the defendants in the dark about forthcoming proceedings.) The affidavit names the publication as 'three Simphonies in Eight parts for Violins Hoboys Horns Tenor and Bass composd. by Sigr. Bach' and states—what Bach apparently did not know when the bill was drafted—that the music by the plaintiff 'having been carefully Examin'd evidently appear'd to have been taken & Copied from the sd three several Simphonies before mentd to have been Compos'd and wrote by the plt [plaintiff] but very ignorantly & much to the discredit of the plt as a Composer adapted to & for Instruments not intended by the plt'.

---

171 'A new Sonata' has not survived, but 'A new Lesson' has. It is a two-movement work whose first movement is a significantly different version—Stephen Roe considers it to be an earlier version—of the first movement of Bach's sonata op. 17 no. 4, while the second movement is the last movement of op. 17 no. 1, less the final variation. See Stephen Roe, 'Introduction', in Ernest Warburton (ed.), *The Collected Works of Johann Christian Bach 1735–1782* v 42, New York, 1989, p vii–xiii at p xi.

The defendants were again not represented and the Chancellor duly granted an injunction.

Abel's bill, lodged on 7 May, is much the same as Bach's bills except for its description of the music.[172] It states that 'about fourteen years ago ... your Orator composed and wrote a certain musical work or composition for one Violin one Violincello and a Bass called a Trio', and, after giving details of Abel's privilege, that 'about ten years ago ... your Orator composed and wrote two other musical works called Trios each being composed for a Flute Viol di Gamba and a Bass'. At a hearing on 10 May—the same day as the Bach symphony hearing—Robinson appeared for Abel and presented an affidavit from him and one John Wells. This affidavit stated that on 24 April Wells had bought at Longman, Lukey & Co.'s shop a copy of a publication identified as 'Les Suites des Trois Primieres [sic] Trios pour le Violin & Violoncello et Basso composees par Charles Frederick Abell', in which the three trios are 'contrary to the plts intention publish'd for instruments not intended by the plt ... togr. with 3 other Trios of the sd. plts'.[173] Longman, Lukey & Co. were still unrepresented and the Chancellor granted a third injunction.

The second and third injunctions stirred Longman and Lukey into something like action, and on 17 June the Master of the Rolls gave them a month's further time to plead in all three cases. Defendants were entitled to three such extensions—the first for a month, the second for three weeks and the third for two weeks—but Longman and Lukey obtained only the first of these, after which proceedings in all three actions stood still for five months. Finally, on 16 November, Chancery issued a writ returnable on 26 November directing the sheriffs to arrest the defendants. Longman and Lukey were apparently inclined to ignore even this, for their answers were lodged only on 1 December, five days after the deadline. A handful of corrections and a couple of serious errors ('say' instead of 'deny', the omission of 'not') suggest that the answers were drafted and lodged in haste after Longman and Lukey realised that the threat of imprisonment was real.

---

[172] TNA C12/71/6, *Abel v Longman*, 1773.

[173] Quotations are from the account of the affidavit given in the Chancery record of the hearing (in TNA C33/439 part 1).

A Chancery bill was a petition seeking redress for an alleged wrong, but an answer was sworn evidence by a party to a dispute. The three bills were signed by Robinson and the notations on them record merely the date lodged and other administrative details; but Longman and Lukey as well as their lawyer, Maurice Bernard, signed the answers, which are endorsed, 'Both sworn at the Public Office the 30th Novr. 1773 before P. Holford' (presumably Peter Holford, Master in Chancery). But Chancery answers, although they were sworn documents, were never strictly veracious: they were designed to outline a defence while making as few admissions as possible.

Longman and Lukey's answer in the sonata action began by reserving the right to object to errors, uncertainties and insufficiencies in Bach's first bill, and denying any knowledge of his privilege or of whether he had actually composed the sonatas referred to in the bill. The answer went on to state:

> that on or about the month of December last One Adolphus Hummel late of Nassau Street Soho a very intimate Acquaintance of the said Complainants John Christian Bach and at whose House the said Complainant had formerly lodged as he at that time suggested applied to them these Defendants … and informed them these Defendants that the said Complainant John Christian Bach had made him a present of two Harpsichord Sonatas for the many Services he had done him the said Complainant at Sundry times and had also given him the said Adolphus Hummell full and free Liberty to sell and dispose of the said two Sonatas or to print them himself for his own Benefit And he at the same time told them these Defendants that he thought the said Sonatas too trifling to be at the expence of printing them himself and therefore requested them these Defendants to become the purchasors thereof and which they accordingly agreed to do for the Sum of Two pound and two shillings

The answer also noted that Francis Fane Broderip had become a partner in the defendants' firm since the action was initiated.

The defendants then stated that they would not have bought the sonatas if they had known of Bach's privilege. They pointed out that Bach had never published the sonatas himself. They admitted to publishing the sonatas, but denied that they knew Bach to be the composer of the sonatas or that they had made changes to the music. And they denied that Bach had made any attempt to get them to account to him for the 'very trifling' proceeds of sales or to stop selling the publications, other than by taking legal action.

As noted in section 6.7 above, Adolphus (i.e., John Adolph) Hummel had obtained a privilege in 1760 for 'several pieces of musick never yet published within our dominions'. Nothing is known about his dealings with Bach, and Chancery pleadings which might have thrown light on the matter, such as Bach's replication—a document joining issue with Longman and Lukey without raising any new matters of fact—have not been located. Hummel published a couple of works by Bach—his 'Canzonette with variations' for piano, and 'six sonates or nottornos for two violins with a thorough bass for the harpsichord'—but this proves nothing, for many London music sellers issued prints of Bach's music.

Why would Bach take legal action over the publication of two sonatas that he had given away? Were Longman and Lukey telling the truth? The detail about Bach's having lodged with Hummel at some stage is probably correct: it seems to have been meant to add verisimilitude, it is irrelevant to the proceedings, and Bach could have disproved it if it was untrue. The rest of the publishers' story is impossible to verify, and may have been so at the time. Hummel had gone out of business in the second half of 1772;[174] if he had died or left London—say, for Holland, to help reorganise the Hummel publishing business in preparation for Johann Julius Hummel's move to Berlin—Longman and Lukey could have invented the story of their dealings with him with little risk of being found out. Of course, if their story was an invention they could have designed one which seemed to give them a better right to publish the sonatas—one in which they had bought the sonatas from Hummel who had said that he had bought them from Bach. But they could have believed that a scenario in which the sonatas were gifts eliminated any claim that Bach might have had to the publication rights. (Such a defence would have failed, for it had been held in *Duke of Queensberry v Shebbeare* that lending a manuscript to someone 'that he might take a copy thereof, and make use of the same as he should think fit' did not confer publication rights.) So the possibility that Longman and Lukey

[174] 'All the genuine household furniture, china, plate, and stock in trade of Mr Hummel, musick-printer, at his house in King Street, opposite Nassau-Street, St Ann's, Soho' was auctioned on 6–7 October 1772 (advertisement, *The Daily Advertiser*, 5 October 1772, p 4).

were lying cannot be ruled out completely. And even if Longman and Lukey were telling the truth, Hummel might not have been.

On the other hand, the publishers' story could well be true. If so, the reason that Bach took legal action over the sonatas may be that he had never intended to let Longman, Lukey & Co. publish them, and that when their edition came out, with the viola da gamba part 'ignorantly changed or varied', and with Hummel no longer around to explain what had happened, Bach decided that this was just another of Longman's unauthorised publications—indeed, one too many. And Robinson may have advised Bach that *Duke of Queensberry v Shebbeare* had established that his gift to Hummel had transferred only the manuscript, not the publication rights.

Longman and Lukey claimed that Bach had given Hummel not just the manuscript but also publication rights to its contents—'full and free Liberty to sell and dispose of the said two Sonatas or to print them himself'—and that they had bought those rights. The publishers may have wanted to invoke the legal rule that a purchaser in good faith is not obliged to return goods to their original owner if it later emerges that the goods were not the vendor's property. Such a defence might once have been open to the objection that printing rights were not property at common law; but that possibility had been eliminated by the decision of the King's Bench in *Millar v Taylor*.

The symphony answer begins in the same style as the sonata answer, reserving the right to object to the errors and insufficiencies in Bach's second bill, and denying any knowledge of his privilege. It states that Bach may have composed the three symphonies referred to in his bill

> but whether the said Three Symphonys were the same as is hereinafter mentioned or whether the said John Christian Bach is the Sole proprietor thereof and absolutely Intitled to the entire Interest therein they these Defendants know not nor can they set forth having never seen the Licence or read the Manuscripts of such Musick or if they had so done are they in the least Capable of forming any Judgement with respect thereto they or either of them not being acquainted with the Manner or Stile of the said Complainants Musical handwriting or Composition so as to be able particularly to set forth the same or to form any Competent knowledge with respect thereto
>
> But these Defendants Severally say that at the time the said Symphonys were sent to these Defendants by [erased] Hummell as hereinafter mentioned they did not know or believe the same to be the

> Composition of the Complainant They then and until the time of their being served with the Injunction hereinafter mentioned believing the same to have been composed either by the Complainants Uncle Mr Bach of Berlin or another Mr Bach who lives somewhere in Germany ...
>
> And these Defendants Jointly and severally further Answering Say that they and each of them deny that they or either of them have or hath ever printed or published or caused to be printed or published in England or elsewhere the said three Several Symphonys in the said Complainant's said Bill mentioned or any part or parts thereof ... but they these Defendants Severally Admit that the said Three Symphonys entitled as follows Three Simphonies in 8 parts for Violins Hoboys Horns Tenor and Bass were printed at the Hague by [erased] Hummell and that seventy Setts thereof were sent from thence to these Defendants in England in pursuance of previous advise sent by the said Hummell to these Defendants and without these Defendants giving Orders for the same ...
>
> And these Defendants further Jointly and Severally Answering say that it is a Constant Uniform and well known Custom and practice as to Musical Compositions and so hath long since been understood to be as well by the Authors thereof as the Purchasers and Sellers of their said Works (and so have been Used and Accustomed to be from the first Establishment of Musick printing in England) that the English Musick Printers might reprint without Interruption any Work of any Musical Author printed at the Hague Amsterdam France or any other Foreign parts and also sell the same so printed in England and in return that the same right Usage and Custom Appertains and prevails in England with respect to the Works of All English Musical Authors printed at the Hague Amsterdam France or any other Foreign parts and sent over to England

This answer concludes along the same lines as the sonata answer, denying that Bach had approached the publishers before having them served with the injunction, hoping that the court will not order them to come to terms with Bach or continue to prevent them from selling the symphonies, and denying any suggestion of conspiracy.

'Mr Bach of Berlin' was Carl Phillipp Emanuel, who was twenty-one years John Christian's senior and therefore old enough to be taken for his uncle, but who had left Berlin for Hamburg in 1767. Longman and Lukey's claim that they thought that he or some Bach other than John Christian had written the symphonies may well be correct, for if Longman and Lukey were lying or making a purely formal disclaimer they would probably have included the same sort of statement in their other answers and would not have named the supposed composer of the symphonies. Perhaps the omission of such a statement from the other answers was the result of haste, but on the face of things the publishers seem to have thought that the composer of the symphonies lived in Germany, notwithstanding the correct attribution to John Christian Bach on the title-page of the print they received. Perhaps John Christian's visit to Mannheim in the latter part of 1772 for the production of his new opera *Temistocle* led to some misunderstanding between London and The Hague (Burchard Hummel might have written something like 'Here are some symphonies by Mr Bach who is in Germany'). In any event, it seems that Longman and Lukey were ready both to believe that Hummel had misattributed a complete set of symphonies to John Christian Bach and to let the misattribution stand when selling the symphonies under their own imprint.

The Longman, Lukey & Co. publication has survived, along with three other editions of the same three symphonies, now known as Bach's op. 9, the opus number of an edition published by Burchard Hummel in The Hague. The Hummel edition supports Longman and Lukey's account of how they came by their edition: apart from the title-pages, both editions were printed from the same plates.

Bach's second bill stated that the symphonies in the Longman & Lukey edition had been written about twelve, five and four years earlier, but does not say which symphony was written when. However, symphony no. 3 in the set had already been published by Walsh, twice in full score and once in a harpsichord arrangement, as the overture to Bach's opera *Zanaida*, first performed at the King's Theatre on 7 May 1763. Thus symphony no. 3 was written about twelve years before the bill was lodged, and the other two symphonies about 1768–1769. Bach's dating of symphony no. 3 to two years before *Zanaida*'s first performance might simply be a mistake: the imprecision of the composition dates given by Bach indicates that he did not keep a dated catalogue of his works. But he may have used as overture to *Zanaida* a work composed in Italy two years earlier and not previously heard in England. In May 1763 Bach had been in London for less than a year, and in that time had composed and directed *Orione* and *Zanaida*, contributed to and directed four other operas, and published a set of harpsichord concertos at least one of which, with a last movement based on 'God

Save the King', must have been written in England. Given this workload, he may well have reused some music written in Italy.

Bach was apparently unaware when his second bill was drafted that the Longman, Lukey & Co. edition of the symphonies altered his music, substituting pairs of horns and oboes for pairs of clarinets, oboes, bassoons and horns in one symphony, and for pairs of clarinets and horns and a bassoon in the other two. This edition's title-page also said that the oboes could be replaced by flutes and that the horns were optional. This drastic simplification of the wind scoring—in particular, the elimination of clarinets, which were relatively unfamiliar in England—and the introduction of performing options no doubt increased the edition's appeal to amateur players. But the changes created a legacy of confusion: later scholars, not knowing which of the various printed and manuscript versions of the symphonies were Bach's own, were inclined to give the Longman, Lukey & Co. edition some credence. But Ann van Allen-Russell has established that Bach's instrumentation of these works is preserved in manuscript copies of symphonies 2 and 3 and in the Walsh editions of the full score of the overture to *Zanaida*.[175]

The answer of James Longman and Charles Lukey to Abel's bill is much the same as their symphony answer, except that they do not suggest that someone other than Abel composed the trios. Their account of how they came by the music is also different:

> And they these Defendants severally admit that the said three Trios entitled as follows Les Suites des Trios pour le Violon Violoncello et Basso were on or about the midst of the year one thousand seven hundred and seventy two Engraved and printed by one Markordt of Amsterdam who sent the same to them these defendants in England and these Defendants sold the same in England

In the Longman, Lukey & Co. print (RISM AA130 and AA130a) the trios are numbered 4 to 6.[176] The other three trios referred to by Abel may be those in a Siegfried Markordt publication

---

[175] Ann van Allen-Russell, '"For instruments not intended": the second J. C. Bach lawsuit', *Music & Letters* v 83 no 1 (February 2002) p 3–29.

[176] RISM AA130 has a Longman, Lukey & Co. title-page, but RISM attributes the publication to Markordt.

'Trois trios pour le violon, violoncello et basso' (RISM A129), which are numbered 1 to 3. Trio 6 is identical with the fifth of Abel's six trios op. 9 for violin, cello and continuo, which were published by Abel in London.[177] This trio, then, is the one written in about 1759, while numbers 4 and 5 are the ones originally written for flute, viol da gamba and continuo in about 1763. Apparently Markordt acquired manuscripts of trios 4 and 5 and completed the set of three by pirating a suitable previously published third work.

Unlike Burchard Hummel, Markordt seems not to have sent his prints to Longman, Lukey & Co. without notice. Otherwise, the circumstances under which the trios were published are unclear: there is nothing to indicate whether Markordt or Longman, Lukey & Co. first acquired the manuscripts of trios 4 and 5, at whose initiative Markordt produced the Longman, Lukey & Co. print, or whether he published either set of trios under his own imprint.[178]

The four Longman, Lukey & Co. publications involved in this litigation do not inspire confidence in the firm's products. None of the four editions was completely correct. Moreover, although all four publications carried London imprints, two were produced in Holland with English title-pages;[179] and copies of the symphony print were sent to Longman, Lukey & Co. without advance notice, as if the firm was simply the Hummels' London distributor. And even though Longman and Lukey claimed to think that the attribution of the symphonies to John Christian Bach was incorrect, they went ahead and sold the edition regardless, with his name on the title-page.

The symphony and trio answers raised two lines of defence: that the editions had been produced not by Longman, Lukey & Co. but by Hummel and Markordt, and that it was a long-standing and

[177] Walter Knape, *Bibliographisch-thematisches Verzeichnis der Kompositionen von Karl Friedrich Abel*, Cuxhaven, 1972, p 145.

[178] Rudolf Rasch, 'How did publishers make up their catalogues?', *Revue de Musicologie* v 84 (1998) p 287–289, suggests (p 288–289) that Markordt and Johann Julius Hummel may have worked 'in such a way that if one of the pair was "fully booked", works offered to him were passed to the other one'.

[179] As the title-pages of the Bach symphonies and Abel trios were not engraved or printed in England, the costs given by Longman and Lukey in their answers to these cases list only payments for buying copies of the music in Holland and freight and custom-house fees paid for importing these copies.

well-known practice for English music sellers to sell or to reprint music published abroad, including music by English composers. The latter defence, in particular, threatened to complicate the legal issues and make the litigation more expensive by raising, as Falkener had done, the question of what constituted accepted practice in the music trade. But it was not clear that the courts would be well-disposed to the kind of practices described in the symphony and trio answers, however firmly established such practices were, for in *Pope v Curll* (1741) Lord Hardwicke had pointed out that they could be used to evade the Copyright Act:

> The second question is, whether a book originally printed in Ireland is lawful prize to the booksellers here.
>
> If I should be of that opinion, it would have very pernicious consequences, for then a bookseller who has got a printed copy of a book, has nothing else to do but to send it over to Ireland to be printed, and then by pretending to reprint it only in England, will by this means intirely evade the act of parliament.

Nevertheless, Longman and Lukey's claim that they acted in accordance with music-trade practice created a new legal obstacle for Bach and Abel, making it necessary for them to establish that this did not override whatever right they had to print the symphonies or trios.

To the extent that Longman and Lukey's legal tactics can be deduced from their answers, it seems that they were ready to defend themselves by claiming in the sonata action that they had acquired the printing rights in good faith, and in the symphony and trio actions that they had the right to sell the prints by virtue of well-established practice in the music trade. Perhaps their lawyers were simply giving every conceivable argument an airing. However, Longman and Lukey might have been advised that they could not succeed by claiming that music was not subject to English copyright law—that regardless of whether the Copyright Act applied to it, music was probably protected by common-law copyright, the existence of which had been confirmed by the decision of the King's Bench in *Millar v Taylor*.

But shortly after Longman and Lukey lodged their answers, that decision was reversed.

6.13 HINTON V DONALDSON; DONALDSON V BECKET; PETITIONS TO PARLIAMENT

In 1773 the Court of Session had an opportunity to reconsider its decision in *Midwinter v Hamilton.* The London bookseller John Hinton had acquired the rights to Thomas Stackhouse's *History of the Bible*—first published in 1740 and so no longer protected by the Copyright Act—through Hinton's marriage to the widow of its first publisher. In 1770 Hinton brought an action against Alexander Donaldson in Scotland over the latter's reprint of Stackhouse's book, but in 1773 the Court of Session rejected Hinton's case, upholding its earlier rejection of common-law copyright in *Midwinter v Hamilton.* The vote was eleven to one, and the lone dissenter was the eccentric Lord Monboddo, who had recently impaired his chances of being taken seriously in this forum, or any other, by publishing a book in which he advanced the outlandish idea that mankind was related to the orang-outang. James Boswell, one of Donaldson's lawyers, published a report of *Hinton v Donaldson* shortly before the House of Lords considered the question of common-law copyright early in 1774.

In some ways *Donaldson v Becket*, the case that ended the dispute over common-law copyright, was a repeat performance of earlier litigation. A consortium of London booksellers led by Thomas Becket had bought the rights to *The Seasons* from Andrew Millar's estate and obtained an injunction against Alexander Donaldson over his cheap edition of that work. When this injunction, granted by Lord Chancellor Apsley, was made perpetual in 1772, Donaldson appealed to the House of Lords. This made the stakes much higher than in *Millar v Taylor*: a decision of the Lords would settle the question of common-law copyright conclusively in both England and Scotland.

In February 1774 eleven of the twelve common-law judges appeared before the House of Lords to give their opinions on five questions. The absentee was Mansfield, perhaps because he knew that a legal decision with which he was closely identified was about to be attacked by another senior judicial officer. All these questions were strictly legal, making no reference to natural justice or public interest:

> 1. Whether, at Common Law, an Author of any Book or Literary Composition, had the Sole Right of first printing and publishing the same

> for Sale, and might bring an Action against any Person who printed, published and sold the same without his Consent?
>
> 2. If the Author had such Right originally, did the Law take it away upon his printing and publishing such Book or Literary Composition, and might any Person afterward reprint and sell, for his own Benefit, such Book or Literary Composition, against the Will of the Author?
>
> 3. If such Action would have lain at Common Law, is it taken away by the Statute of 8th *Anne*; and is an Author, by the said Statute precluded from every Remedy except on the Foundation of the said Statute, and on the Terms and Conditions prescribed thereby?
>
> 4. Whether the Author of any Literary Composition, and his Assigns, had the Sole Right of printing and publishing the same, in Perpetuity, by the Common Law?
>
> 5. Whether this Right is in any Way impeached, restrained, or taken away, by the Statute 8th *Anne*?[180]

The judges were not unanimous and the published reports of their answers are inconsistent; but it was the House of Lords, not the judiciary, which would decide whether the Chancery injunction should be upheld.[181]

The arguments against common-law copyright were again presented by Edward Thurlow and Arthur Murphy. Thurlow opened his address with an attack on literary property as being 'of so abstruse and chimerical a nature that it can hardly be defined', and ended with a grandiloquent defence of authors' rights:

> The notion of a perpetual privilege and monopoly was, within these few years, hatched among the booksellers, who under a pretence of serving literature, mean only to get the fruits of genius into their hands for ever. The consequence of this new doctrine would be fatal to the interest of letters and to the fame of every valuable author. ... in the emphatic words of Dryden, 'It will continue to be the ingratitude of mankind that they who teach wisdom shall generally live poor and unregarded, as if they were born only for the public and had no interest in

---

180 *Journals of the House of Lords* v 34 p 21 (9 February 1774).

181 Ronan Deazley concludes (*op. cit.*, p 197–205) that six judges supported the common-law right and held that it was not extinguished by publication or by the Copyright Act, that four judges recognised only a pre-publication common-law right to print belonging to the owner of the manuscript, and that one judge considered that the Act put an end to common-law copyright.

their own well-being, but were to be lighted up like tapers and waste themselves for the benefit of others.'[182]

Remarkably, when speeches were given by some of the Lords themselves, the former and current Lord Chancellors both strenuously attacked a decision closely identified with the Chief Justice of the King's Bench. The Lords were not noted for their attentiveness to legal argument, but they would have found the speech of Apsley's predecessor Lord Camden, an old legal adversary of Mansfield's who had been Chancellor from 1766 to 1770, and before that Chief Justice of the Common Pleas, as hard to ignore as Thurlow's. Camden dismissed the legal precedents cited in support of common-law copyright as a 'heterogeneous heap of rubbish ... calculated to confound your Lordships, and mislead the argument'. He claimed that if the injunction was upheld 'all our learning would be locked up in the hands of the Tonsons and the Lintots [bookselling families] of the age', enabling them to demand whatever price 'their avarice chose to demand, till the public became as much their slaves, as their own hackney [i.e., hired] compilers are'.[183] He characterised the purported common-law right as 'odious and selfish', and matched Thurlow's grandiloquence in his peroration, arguing in favour of the complete freedom of science and learning. Lord Chancellor Apsley, who had been bound to grant the injunction against Donaldson because of the King's Bench decision in *Millar v Taylor*, now stated that he favoured Donaldson's case, and gave a detailed examination—reported only in general terms—of the legal arguments in favour of common-law copyright, firmly rejecting all of them.

Camden and Apsley clearly had planned their tactics in advance, and their united opposition to common-law copyright was designed to impress lawyers and non-lawyers alike.[184] These tactics worked. Although the House of Lords when acting as an appeal court

---

[182] *ER* v 1 p 837 and p 845–846.

[183] William Cobbett (ed.), *The Parliamentary History of England, from the earliest period to the year 1803* v 17, London, 1813, p 993–994.

[184] Apsley was a mediocre lawyer who as Chancellor was careful to take advice from the common-law judges (see the next section). Since he and Camden had obviously worked out their tactics beforehand, it is likely that Camden advised Apsley on his speech.

usually followed the judges' advice, it was not obliged to do so and on this occasion it did not. On 22 February the Lords voted to reverse the Chancery order against Donaldson.

Donaldson v Becket was a disaster for the London book trade, which stood to lose its whole investment in the rights to works no longer protected by the Copyright Act, and some of its investment in the rights to works that the Act still protected. But the London booksellers had prepared for the worst, and they promptly mounted a campaign for legislation that would defer the effect of the Lords' decision. On 28 February the House of Commons received a booksellers' petition stating that 'many Thousand Pounds have been, at different Times, invested in the Purchase of ancient Copy Rights, not protected by the Statute of Queen Ann, so that the Support of many Families does in a great Measure depend upon the same', and 'praying the House, to take their singularly hard Case into Consideration'. The House referred the petition to a committee which met for the first time the next day.

Parliamentary committees appointed to deal with petitions were normally composed of MPs sympathetic to the petitioners. The parliamentary record names three members of the committee—Paul Feilde (the chairman), Edmund Burke and Alderman Thomas Harley—but it is likely that its membership was much the same as that of another committee which succeeded it a few weeks later. One member of the latter committee was the MP for Salisbury, James Harris. As well as being a lawyer and a writer on philosophical matters, he was an amateur composer, a writer on music and a patron of music and musicians.[185] He was acquainted with Bach and Abel, both of whom had performed in Salisbury, and he might have had something to do with their next move.[186]

---

[185] For his life and work see Clive Probyn, *The Sociable Humanist: The life and works of James Harris*, Oxford, 1991. He was nicknamed 'Hermes' after his book *Hermes: or, a philosophical inquiry concerning language and universal grammar*, London, 1751.

[186] James Harris kept a parliamentary diary, but the volume dealing with this period has not survived. I am grateful to the Hampshire County Archivist, Rosemary Dunhill, for information about Harris's papers.

The committees provided an opportunity for anyone interested in the Copyright Act to attempt to have it amended. The Commons proceedings for 15 March recorded that:

> A Petition of *John Christian Bach*, and *Charles Frederick Abel*, on Behalf of themselves and several other Composers and Proprietors of Books, Works, and Compositions in Music, was presented to the House, and read; Taking Notice of the Petition of the Booksellers of *London* and *Westminster*, on Behalf of themselves and others, Holders of Copy Right; and reciting Part of an Act, made in the Eighth Year of the Reign of Queen *Anne*, for the Encouragement of Learning, by vesting the Copies of printed Books in the Authors or Purchasers of such Copies; and Setting forth, That a Doubt has arisen, whether the sole Right granted by the said Act, to the Author of any Book or Books, extends to the Author of any Book, Writing or Composition in Music: And therefore praying, that Provision may be made, for obviating such Doubt; and that they may have such Relief in the Premises as to the House shall seem meet.
>
> *Ordered*, That the said Petition be referred to the Consideration of the Committee, to whom the Petition of the Booksellers of *London* and *Westminster*, on Behalf of themselves and others, Holders of Copy Right, is referred: And that they do examine the Matter of this Petition: and report the same, as it shall appear to them, to the House.[187]

The petition of Bach and Abel, if the report in the *Journals of the House of Commons* gives a fair account of it, seems to have been drafted in a hurry.[188] That they were its only signatories may indicate that they were so well known and reputable that more signatures were deemed unnecessary. But the petition is remarkably vague: having drawn attention to the uncertainty about whether the Copyright Act protected music, it says nothing about how the uncertainty arises, who it affects, how it affects them, what amendments are needed to the legislation, how those amendments could improve things, or what matters of policy or principle are at stake. It is as if whoever drafted the petition intended to discuss the matter further with Bach and Abel and perhaps other interested parties and then to prepare a detailed case to present to the committee.

---

[187] *Journals of the House of Commons* v 34 p 562–563 (15 March 1774).

[188] Bach's and Abel's original petition would have been among the records lost when the old Palace of Westminster burnt down in 1834.

Parliamentary petitioners normally appeared before Commons committees in person or were represented by a barrister. But it was not Bach or Abel or Robinson who appeared before the committee, but Robinson's brother-in-law Augustine Greenland, Bach and Abel's attorney.[189] This is surprising: attorneys did not appear before Commons committees, any more than they appeared before the King's Bench. Greenland's presence is even more remarkable because, more than most attorneys, he was well placed to know, or to find out whatever he did not know, about parliamentary procedure. In 1757 he had been appointed to the post of what would now be called Permanent Secretary to the new Attorney-General Charles Pratt,[190] and he had worked for Pratt and the Pratt family continuously since then—throughout Pratt's time as Attorney-General, as Chief Justice of the Common Pleas, as Lord Chancellor Camden, and after Camden's resignation as Chancellor in 1770. When their attorney had this kind of background, why were Bach and Abel not represented by counsel before the Commons committee?

The two reports quoted here are not quite consistent, making it difficult to reconstruct what happened. According to *The General Evening Post (London)*:

> A petition was then presented to the Committee from the composers of music.
>
> Mr Augustine Greenland was about to be examined, but as he was instructed only to inform the Committee that the musical composers

---

[189] Greenland practised at 15 Newman St, London; see [William Gilbert], *Gilbert's Law Directory for ... 1775* (London, 1775, p 31, where he is called 'Greedland') and *Browne's General Law List* for later years. His name is on the backing sheets of documents filed on Bach's behalf, noted in section 6.15 below. Robinson married Greenland's widowed sister (Edward Hasted, *The History and Topological Survey of the County of Kent* v 9, Canterbury, 1800, p 80).

[190] Greenland was appointed as 'a Clerk to take the Management of his Office to receive and Account for the fees, which were not inconsiderable, [and] draw up reports on referrences to him singly & on referrences to him in Conjunction with the Sollicitor General' (Augustine Greenland, *A Narrative of Facts Official and Political which Occurred during the Time Augustine Greenland had the Honor to be in the Service of the late Charles Earl Camden* (CKS U840 F159/A3, f 1)). The *Narrative* contains nothing of musical significance.

> entertained a doubt whether they had or not the same claim to a copy-right as booksellers.
>
> Mr B—ke and several other Members said, 'they should report this petition to the House with the other, but could say nothing as to any facts being proved, only that the petitioners entertained doubts.'[191]

The bulk of the committee's report, presented to the House of Commons on 24 March, consisted of an account of evidence given to the committee by William Johnston, a former London bookseller who had spent thirty-five years in the trade, a member of the consortium led by Becket and a knowledgeable and articulate witness who gave evidence mainly about the London booksellers' understanding of the law and practices associated with the sale of rights. The account of his evidence and of other material supporting the booksellers' petition fills over four folio columns in the *Journals of the House of Commons*. The composers' petition is dealt with in a single paragraph:

> Mr *Augustine Greenland*, informed your Committee, That Doubts have arisen, whether the Right granted by the Act of the Eighth of Queen *Anne*, to the Authors of Books, extends to the Authors of Books or Compositions in Music: That Mess. *Longman*, *Lukie*, and Company [sic], and one *Thoroughgood*, have published the compositions of Masters in Music, apprehending such Compositions were not within the Intention of the said Act of the Eighth of Queen *Anne*; but that the Witness had not taken the Opinion of Counsel upon it.[192]

Following the dispute with Isaac Bickerstaff in 1765, Henry Thorowgood had been in business on his own until *c*1780.[193] He is not known to have published anything by Bach or Abel, but Greenland's mention of him to the committee suggests that he had a reputation for piracy and that Greenland knew of this.

---

[191] *The General Evening Post (London)*, 17 March 1774, p 1. 'Mr B—ke' presumably was Edmund Burke rather than the less prominent William Burke.

[192] *Journals of the House of Commons* v 34 p 590 (24 March 1774).

[193] Humphries and Smith, *op. cit.* in note 167 above, p 310. In 1791 a Henry Thorowgood—presumably the same man or a close relative—worked for Longman & Broderip. See pages 55–56 above.

How Greenland came to appear before the committee is not clear. What happened may have been something like this: Greenland attended Parliament to assist Robinson and found that he was not there; the committee, impatient to finish its work, decided to examine Greenland; he was unprepared for this, having no first-hand knowledge of the music trade, no written opinion from counsel that he could speak from or submit to the committee, and no knowledge of what Robinson might have wanted to say; Greenland therefore, after mentioning a few instances of piracy, told the committee that although there was a question about whether music was protected by the Copyright Act, he was not equipped to give evidence or to speak authoritatively on the matter; and as a result the committee decided to ignore the composers' petition.

Unsurprisingly, the composers' petition achieved nothing. After the committee reported, the Commons ignored the unfamiliar, relatively unimportant matters raised by Bach and Abel and gave its attention to the much-publicised effect of *Donaldson v Becket* on the book trade, resolving 'That Leave be given to bring in a Bill for Relief of Booksellers, and others, by vesting the Copies of printed Books in the Purchasers of such Copies from Authors or their Assigns, for a Time therein to be limited'. The new bill, prepared by a new committee, did not mention music, nor was music mentioned in the ensuing parliamentary debate. The Commons passed the bill on 27 May, but the Lords allowed it to lapse, leaving *Donaldson v Becket* as established law—although an Act that received the royal assent on 22 May 1774 gave the universities and three public schools perpetual copyright in books given or bequeathed to them for educational purposes, and reaffirmed the provisions of the Copyright Act relating to the deposit of books with the Stationers' Company.

As Ronan Deazley emphasises, the House of Lords did not decide in *Donaldson v Becket* that common-law copyright did not exist. It simply decided, without giving reasons, to dissolve the injunction against which Donaldson had appealed. Nevertheless, the case was seen at the time, and has been seen since, as marking the end of common-law copyright. However, the transformation of copyright into a wholly statutory right remained incomplete while long-standing legal questions about the scope of the Copyright Act and the validity of privileges remained unanswered. These questions were about to be addressed by the courts.

6.14 THE OUTCOME OF *PYLE V FALKENER*; *COMPANY OF STATIONERS V CARNAN*

In June 1773 *Pyle v Falkener* had been adjourned until the House of Lords dealt with a case 'of a similar nature'. That case was undoubtedly *Donaldson v Becket*—indicating that Pyle's lawyers had decided by mid-1773 that common-law copyright could, and perhaps should, be the basis of at least part of the claim against Falkener. However, the Lords' ruling in *Donaldson v Becket* meant that some of the material published by Falkener now had no copyright protection, while the rest was protected, if at all, by the Copyright Act, or by Walsh Jr's privilege, or by both. Thus the outcome of Pyle's action would depend on how the word 'writings' in the preamble to the Act was to be interpreted, and on whether privileges provided valid copyright protection. *Donaldson v Becket* had turned *Pyle v Falkener* into a test case on the meaning of the Copyright Act and the validity of privileges.

Lord Chancellor Apsley dealt with *Pyle v Falkener* with great dispatch when it came before him on 21 April 1774. After summarising earlier pleadings, the record of the hearing concludes:

> Whereupon and upon debate of ye matter and hearing an Order dated the eighth day of June last, whereby this Cause by Consent of Counsel for the Defendant Stands adjourned to this day, the probate of the will of the Testator John Walsh, the Letter Patent dated the 19th day of August 1760, a Deed Poll of Assignment dated the 20th day of January 1762, signed Thomas Augustine Arne, the Memorandum of Agreement dated the 6th day of December 1762, signed Isaac Bickerstaff, and the proofs taken in this Cause read and what was alleged by the Counsel on both sides, The Lordship doth order, that so much of ye plaintiff's Bill as prays an Injunction to Stay the Defendant from ye printing, publishing, abridging, vending, uttering or distributing the Six English Songs and Six Overtures for Violins in eight parts composed by Maurice Green, Doctor of Music, mentioned in the proceedings, and that the Defendant may Account with and pay the plaintiff the profits arising from the sale of the said Six Songs and Six Overtures, do Stand dismissed out of the Court with Costs to be taxed ..., and that an

> Injunction be Awarded to Stay the Defendant, his Servants, Workmen and Agents from reprinting, publishing, abridging, vending, Uttering and distributing the Other Musical Compositions mentioned in the Bill or any of them during the Continuance of ye plaintiff's right therein or thereto.
>
> And His Lordship doth order and Decree that it be referred to ye said Master to take an Account of ye profits Arising from the sale of ye said other Musical Compositions received by the Defendant or by any other person or persons by his order or for his use. And It is ordered that the Defendant do pay what shall be found due from him or such Account to ye plaintiff, and for better taking the said Account the parties are to produce before the said Master upon Oath all Books, papers and writings in their Custody or power relating thereto, and are to be Examined upon Interrogatories as the said Master shall direct, whom taking the said Account is to make unto the parties all Just Allowances. And it is further Ordered that the Defendant do pay unto the plaintiff his Costs of so much of this Suit as is not dismissed, to be taxed by the said Master, and any of ye partys are to be at Liberty to Apply to this Court as there Shall be Occasion.[194]

Apsley thus confirmed the injunction that prevented Falkener from publishing the Handel and Arne music and awarded Pyle damages and costs for this part of his claim, but dismissed his case with respect to the songs by Greene.

The reasons for this ruling are not recorded, but on the face of things Apsley may seem to have cut two Gordian knots with one stroke, holding both that music was within the scope of the Copyright Act and that privileges were legally valid, and hence that Falkener was not entitled to publish music protected in either of these ways. But this view of Apsley's ruling is hard to accept for various reasons, of which the fact that neither of these forms of protection extended to the instrumental pieces from Handel's *Water Music* and *Judas Maccabeus* is only the most obvious.

For one thing, these two unresolved legal issues were properly for a common-law court to decide. When such issues arose in a Chancery action, Apsley's practice, which he followed in a dozen or more cases in his time as Chancellor, was to submit a summary of the case to a common-law court and ask for a ruling. Chancery needed to be particularly careful about doing this where copyright was concerned: not only was copyright a hotly debated area of the law,

---

[194] TNA C33/442 f 309^{v}–311, transcribed in Rabin and Zohn, *op. cit.* in note 141 above, p 140–145 at p 145.

but the long-running dispute over common-law copyright had been in part a product of Chancery decisions of the 1730s.

Also, Apsley had recently referred to a common-law court a question very similar to one of the two questions seemingly dealt with in *Pyle v Falkener*, and he later referred the other question in *Pyle v Falkener* to a common-law court as well. On 1 March, less than two months earlier, he had referred the question of the validity of the Stationers' Company's almanac monopoly to the Court of Common Pleas, in the case of *Company of Stationers v Carnan*. This question was of course similar to the question of the validity of Walsh Jr's privilege, but the Stationers' Company's grant was much older than Walsh's and had been upheld by the Common Pleas a century before. Why would Apsley give a definitive ruling on Walsh's privilege when he was waiting for the Common Pleas to rule on the validity of a grant for whose validity there seemed to be a stronger case? Again, a few years later Apsley asked the King's Bench to decide whether the Copyright Act applied to music (see page 363 below). Why would he have done this if he had already ruled on the matter?

Further, a ruling that Walsh's privilege was valid would have put Apsley at odds with both Mansfield and Yates, who had agreed in *Millar v Taylor*, despite their opposing views on the legal basis of royal printing grants, that the Crown had the power to make such grants with respect only to a certain limited class of publication. And nothing that either judge had said could be construed to suggest that the Crown's power extended to the point of being able to grant exclusive printing rights to Handel's music.

Moreover, Apsley was perhaps the least likely of all Chancellors to fail to seek a ruling from a common-law court or to ignore the views of common-law judges. A political appointee and an undistinguished lawyer, he knew his limitations: 'in weighty cases he was in the habit of calling in the assistance of Common Law Judges, and being governed by their advice'.[195] In at least two cases he revived the practice of having common-law judges sit with the Chancellor as assessors. In some judgements he mentioned that he

---

[195] John Campbell, *The Lives of the Lord Chancellors and Keepers of the Great Seal of England, from the earliest times till the reign of King George IV*, London, v 5, 1846, p 448. See also Holdsworth, *op. cit.*, v 12 p 314.

had consulted the common-law judges—something which other Chancellors almost never felt the need to say publicly that they had done.

In addition, Apsley often took time over his decisions. For him to have ruled on two significant issues without first retiring to consider his decision would have been completely uncharacteristic. Finally—although this is less persuasive, since law reporting was still fairly haphazard, despite some reforms supported by Mansfield—*Pyle v Falkener* was ignored by the legal profession. No one published a report of the case, even though one reporter of 1770s Chancery cases, John Dickens, was Apsley's Senior Register (i.e., Registrar). And no barristers or judges are known to have referred to *Pyle v Falkener* when cases that raised the same legal issues came before common-law courts during the next few years.

Thus, if Apsley ruled in *Pyle v Falkener* that the Copyright Act applied to music and that Walsh's privilege was valid, he departed from character, disregarded standard Chancery practice, ignored the views of senior common-law judges, overlooked the fact that he had recently asked another court to rule on a similar matter, and made with uncharacteristic speed two major decisions which were not his to make, both of which were ignored by the legal profession.

Such things can happen. But the outcome of *Pyle v Falkener* was not due to a fit of judicial capriciousness and forgetfulness, charitably ignored by other lawyers. Obviously, Pyle and Falkener had agreed to settle, and Apsley's order was a consent order, made at the request of the parties' lawyers. There is no documentary evidence of why Pyle and Falkener settled, but since the settlement took place two months after the House of Lords decision on which they had apparently been waiting, there can be little doubt that it was *Donaldson v Becket* that prompted the settlement.

Since *Donaldson v Becket* was widely considered to mean the end of common-law copyright in published material, there was now good reason to think that if Apsley were to consider *Pyle v Falkener* again he would refer it to a common-law court for a ruling on a series of questions. Was music protected by common-law copyright? If not, was it protected by the Copyright Act? And if a piece of music was protected neither by the common law nor by the Copyright Act—either because the Act did not protect music or because the statutory protection period for that piece had expired—but was the subject of a privilege, was that piece validly protected and, if so, what kind of remedy was appropriate for a violation of that privilege? Thus if Pyle and Falkener did not settle, the costs of the case would rise considerably and the outcome would be uncertain. Costs may not have been a primary concern for Pyle, who would have been defending the Walsh estate's valuable assets, or for that matter for Falkener, who might have become insouciant about debt. But neither party would have wanted to see the legal questions dealt with.

If *Pyle v Falkener* had been referred to a common-law court, the chances were that the court would rule that music was not protected by the common law, thus extending *Donaldson v Becket* to music and wiping out the value of any music not protected by the Copyright Act or by privilege. If Pyle did not settle, he risked having the Walsh estate lose most of its value. Falkener, on the other hand, might have welcomed a ruling that music was unprotected by the common law, but he would have been less enthusiastic about a ruling that music was protected by the Copyright Act, since such a ruling would have provided a firm legal basis for swift and effective legal action against him by anyone whose music he subsequently pirated.

Whatever the precise considerations were on either side, and whatever bluffing was done or threats made or inducements held out, *Pyle v Falkener* was settled on terms favourable to Pyle, who got most of his costs and an assurance that Falkener would not publish the pieces by Handel and Arne. And Falkener was allowed to publish the pieces by Greene, which were probably the least valuable of all the music that he had pirated. The spirit of legal compromise and conciliation—in other words, fear, greed and the glorious uncertainty of the law—had prevailed, leaving the legal questions raised by the case unresolved.[196]

---

[196] Falkener came to judicial attention again on 2 May 1776, when the Lord Chancellor considered an application from the music sellers Charles & Samuel Thompson for an injunction ordering him to stop publishing the words (by Richard Brinsley Sheridan) and music (mainly by Thomas Linley Sr and Thomas Linley Jr) of the comic opera *The Duenna* (*The Morning Chronicle, and London Advertiser*, 3 May 1776, p 2). The Lord Chancellor granted the injunction.

Company of Stationers v Carnan, the case that answered the question whether privileges were valid, was already under way. The discussion of patents in *Millar v Taylor* had been followed by an increase in the number of almanacs issued without the authorisation of the Stationers' Company, the main offender being Thomas Carnan, who brought out a series of publications that were almanacs in all but name.[197] In 1772 the Company issued a warning against such publications. In November 1773 Carnan challenged the almanac monopoly by issuing 'A Diary for the Year of Our Lord 1774', and the Company immediately obtained an injunction preventing him from selling the publication. When the case came before the Chancellor on 1 March 1774 and Carnan argued that the Crown had no power to grant a monopoly over the publication of almanacs, the Chancellor withdrew the injunction and referred the question of the validity of the Company's monopoly to the Court of Common Pleas.

This question was obviously similar to the question of the validity of privileges granted to authors or publishers. But the almanac monopoly was much more defensible than privileges were. It had first been granted to the Stationers' Company in 1603; it was perpetual; it had been granted for a charitable purpose—namely, benefitting the Company's dependants—and it had been confirmed by the Common Pleas.[198] And it could be argued that the king had the power to grant printing rights to certain material contained in almanacs: to the feasts of the Church, because he had a 'special interest' in that material by virtue of his position as head of the Church of England; and to the phases of the moon and the calendar because, as head of state, he was the default owner of derelict property and therefore, by extension, of literary material which had no identifiable author or owner. But since no such case could made for the validity of privileges, a finding that the almanac monopoly was invalid would entail that privileges, too, had no legal basis.

Carnan's arguments echoed Yates' and Mansfield's remarks:

---

[197] For a full account of this episode see Cyprian Blagden, 'Thomas Carnan and the Stationers' Company', *Studies in Bibliography* v 14 (1960) p 21–39.

[198] In *Company of Stationers v Seymour* (1677), followed by decisions in *Company of Stationers v Lee* (1681), *Company of Stationers v Skynner* (1682 or 1683), *Company of Stationers v Marlow* (1683) and possibly *Company of Stationers v Lee* (1683).

> Codes of religion and of law ought to be under the inspection of the executive power, to stamp an authenticity upon them. Therefore Bibles, Common Prayer Books, and statutes are proper objects of exclusive patents. But almanacks are not of this kind. Neither is the Crown at the expense of making the calendar, as it was of translating the Bible. ... If there is no solid ground of prerogative in the case of almanacks, there is still less ground for any pretence of copyright; and, had there been any, copyright is now exploded by the late determination of the House of Peers.

The court accepted these arguments, and on 29 May 1775 held:

> 1. That the grant made to the plaintiffs, the Stationers' Company, was restrained to such almanacs and prognostications as should be licensed by the Archbishop of Canterbury, the Bishop of London, or either of them, for the time being.
>
> 2. We are of opinion, that the Crown had not a prerogative or power to make such grant to the plaintiffs, exclusive of any other or others.

This judgement destroyed the Stationers' Company's oldest and most valuable single asset. It was the most severe legal blow the Company had suffered since the lapsing of the Licensing Act. The Company lobbied to have the law changed, but a bill to restore the almanac monopoly was defeated in 1779. Two years later, legislation was passed to pay annual compensation to the universities of Oxford and Cambridge for their shares of the almanac monopoly, but no compensation was paid to the Company. The Company had to accept defeat, and from then on it concentrated on having its register retained at the centre of any system of copyright administration.

6.15 The outcome of *Bach v Longman*

Company of Stationers v Carnan ended any hope that Bach and Abel may have had of succeeding against Longman on the basis of their privileges, and left them with whatever legal rights were left to them by *Donaldson v Becket*. If musical compositions were books or writings within the meaning of the Copyright Act then Bach and Abel owned the publishing rights to their music for the statutory term of protection. But if the Copyright Act did not protect music, their music was protected either by the common law, if *Donaldson v Becket* applied only to material protected by the Act, or else not at all, if that case meant that there was no such thing as common-law copyright in any kind of published material.[199]

Some music sellers might have welcomed statutory copyright in the absence of common-law protection. The shelf life of much published music was shorter than the statutory term of protection, so the Copyright Act would have provided many music sellers with as much security as they needed. But Longman's public exchanges with Abel and Tacet suggest that his position was not far from Falkener's—which, along with his disinclination to back away from a fight, combined with what seems from the newspaper items quoted above to have been a certain disdain for composers, was probably why the actions brought against him by Bach and Abel were not settled at this point.

From the point of view of composers, common-law copyright probably looked more desirable than the protection by the Copyright Act, since it might have enabled them to get more money for the rights to publish their music—though not much more, for it was impossible to know for how long a new piece of music would be in demand and what it would be worth in years to come. But as the House of Lords seemed to have put an end to common-law copyright, it was in the interests of composers for printed music to be protected by the Copyright Act.

It would be interesting to know what attitudes other music sellers had to the litigation against Longman, Lukey & Co., what support or opposition the parties encountered in the music trade, what financial or other backing they received, what attempts were made to get them to settle, what attempts they themselves made to settle, and just why they decided instead to go ahead with a lengthy, expensive test case. But of these matters nothing is known.

Various formalities preceded the determination of the legal issues. The first was the lodging of Bach's and Abel's replications,

---

[199] Whether *Donaldson v Becket* meant the end of common-law copyright in unpublished as well as published material—that is, whether the effect of *Donaldson v Becket* was to reverse *Pope v Curll* and *Duke of Queensberry v Shebbeare* as well as *Millar v Taylor*—seems never to have been judicially discussed.

which had to be done within three law terms.[200] After this Longman and Lukey had to enter rejoinders—formal replies to the replications—and raise any legal issues by means of demurrers. On 4 February 1775 the following order was issued in all three cases:

> Upon Motion this day made unto this Court by Mr Robinson being of the plts Council It was alledged that the plt hath replyed to the Defendants Answer and therefore It was pray'd that a supboena to rejoin returnable immediately may be Awarded agst. the Defendants and the Service thereof on their Councel in Court may be deemed good service which is ordered accordingly

This order was simply a formality: 'a rejoinder is seldom or never filed, the *subpoena* to compel the defendant to rejoin, being merely to put the matter in issue, and to give the parties an opportunity of examining witnesses to the facts alledged on the one side, and sworn to on the other'.[201] Another set of orders made on the same day specified an unrecorded date on which Longman and Lukey were to produce their witnesses for examination by Chancery officials.

The next orders in all three cases were made nine months later, on 3 November:

> Upon the humble Petition of the Defendants this day preferred to the Right Honourable the Master of the Rolls for the Reasons therein contained It is orderd that Publication in this Cause be enlarged till the last day of the next Term but this is not to hinder the plts setting down the Cause in the mean Time & hereof Notice is to be given forthwith.

Longman and Lukey's petitions have not survived and it is not known why they wanted the court to postpone making the evidence public. Bach and Abel did not oppose postponement at this time, but on 10 November Charles Robinson obtained orders setting a date for Longman and Lukey to show cause why publication should not go

[200] The law terms were Michaelmas (September to Christmas), Hilary (January to Easter) and Trinity (post-Easter to July).

[201] Robert Hinde, *The Modern Practice of the High Court of Chancery*, *op. cit.* in note 169 above, p 291.

ahead in all three actions.[202] However, Longman and Lukey managed to stall for a few months more. On 28 November publication was enlarged 'till the first day of next Term', on 19 January 'till the last Day of Hilary Term', on 22 February 'for ten days from this day' and on 2 March 'for a fortnight'. All orders followed the same pattern, except that the petitions for the enlargement of 22 February were supported by affidavits, which have not been located.

The final orders for enlargement, for three weeks, were made on 15 March 1776 in Abel's case and in one of Bach's cases—presumably the symphony case, which in many ways was similar to Abel's. From then on, the only case referred to in the court records for some time was Bach's sonata case, indicating that after 15 March this case, by agreement between the parties and their lawyers, was treated as a test case on the central legal issue of whether the Copyright Act applied to music.

The hearing of the sonata case took place before Lord Chancellor Apsley on 13 May 1776. After summarising the petition and answer, the record of the hearing continues:

> WHEREUPON upon debate of ye Matter & hearing the proofs taken in this Cause read & of what was alledgd by the Counsel on both sydes HIS LORDSHIP Doth Order that a Case be made for the Opinion of the Judges of His Majestys Court of King's Bench & that the Question therein be whether a Musical Composition is within the Statute of the 8th year of Queen Ann Intitl'd an Act for the Encouragement of Learning by Vesting the Copies of Printed Books in the Authors or Pchasers of such Copies during the times therein mentd. & that affidavits for Facts necessary to bring that Matter in Question be Stated in the said case and if the parties Differ it is hereby Refered to Mr. [William] Graves one of the Masters of the Court to Settle the same & it is Orderd that the Judges of the Court of King's Bench be attendd with the said case & his Lordship doth reserve the consideration of all further Directions until after the Judges of the Court of King's Bench shall have made their Certificate & any of the parties are to be at Liberty to Apply to this Court as there shall be Occasion.

It was another year until the King's Bench hearing. This was due partly to the formalities that had to be observed by Chancery and

---

[202] TNA C33/445/1. I am grateful to Nancy Mace for the reference to these orders, not transcribed by Ann van Allen-Russell (see note 168 above).

the King's Bench and to the heavy workload of the latter court, but it may also be connected with Bach's absence from London from July to December 1776, a period when his bank account was inactive. In November he was in Mannheim for the production of his new opera *Lucio Silla*. Also, Charles Lukey died in July 1776, and his firm was soon afterwards restyled 'Longman & Broderip'.

Chancery seems to have kept no copies of the documents prepared for the King's Bench, presumably because they were simply copies or summaries of the Chancery records; and the King's Bench seems to have kept no records of the case, presumably because it was a Chancery matter. The existence of an account of the King's Bench hearing is due to two innovations by Mansfield: his encouragement of officially sanctioned court reporting, and his policy of having the King's Bench publicly state its rulings on common-law questions referred to it from Chancery. In 1774 he had said in *Wright v Holford*:

> I found it a custom, in cases sent by the Court of *Chancery* for our opinion, to certify it privately to the Lord Chancellor in writing, without declaring in this court either the opinion itself, or the reasons upon which it is grounded. But I think the custom wrong, as well as unsatisfactory to the bar: and therefore in the two cases that now wait our certificate, and for the future, we shall declare our opinion in this court.

As a result, a report of the King's Bench hearing in *Bach v Longman* would appear, like *Wright v Holford*, in a collection of King's Bench case reports prepared by Henry Cowper and published in 1783.[203]

The hearing took place on 10 June 1777. Robinson appeared for Bach and 'Mr Wood' for Longman & Broderip. There were several Woods at the bar at this time, and it is not known which of them this was. Over seventy years later a judge in *Jefferys v Boosey* referred to 'Mr Wood' as 'Baron Wood'—that is, George Wood, later a baron of the Exchequer and a knight. This identification is plausible: George Wood was a Chancery pleader with a reputation for great meticulousness, the kind of man who might have been engaged in a Chancery matter that involved a fine legal point. He was called to

---

[203] Henry Cowper, *Reports of Cases adjudged in the Court of King's Bench; from Hilary Term, the 14th of George III, 1774, to Trinity Term, the 18th of George III, 1778...*, London, 1783. *Wright v Holford* is reported on p 31–35 (the paragraph above is on p 34); *Bach v Longman* on p 623–624.

the bar only in 1792, but may have been given leave to appear before the King's Bench because the case had originated in Chancery.

The case was heard by a single judge whose decision would be sent to the full King's Bench for later ratification unless one of the parties appealed. On this occasion the judge was one who had long taken a close interest in copyright law, who had been counsel or judge in many copyright cases, and who had played a leading part in the copyright litigation of the past decade—namely, Lord Mansfield.

Although *Donaldson v Becket* was widely seen as having settled the question of whether copyright existed at common law with a definitive 'no', *Bach v Longman* gave Mansfield an opportunity to reopen that question. If he were to decide that music was not protected by the Copyright Act, it would be necessary at some stage, not necessarily in the case now before him, for a superior court to consider whether publications unprotected by the Copyright Act were covered by whatever remained of common-law copyright after *Donaldson v Becket*. However, it was unlikely that such a decision would lead to a limited resurrection of common-law copyright, because if the House of Lords were to revisit the question, common-law copyright would once more face stiff opposition from current and former judicial officers. In any event, there is no sign in Mansfield's judgement of any desire to have the question reconsidered:

BACH *versus* LONGMAN *et al.*

THIS was a case out of *Chancery* for the opinion of this court, stating, that the plaintiff about twelve years ago composed and wrote a certain musical composition for the harpsichord, called a *Sonata*; and that being desirous of publishing the said work or composition, together with other musical works, compositions and writings, he did apply for and obtain his Majesty's licence, dated the 15th day of *December*, 1763, whereby his Majesty did grant unto the plaintiff, his executors, administrators and assigns, his royal licence for the sole printing and publishing the said works mentioned in the said licence, for fourteen years from the date of the same, as appears by the said licence; and that about four years ago the plaintiff composed and wrote another musical composition for the harpsichord, called a *Sonata*; together with an accompaniment for the *Viol di Gamba*; and that the defendants, being music sellers and copartners, had lately obtained copies of the two several *Sonatas*, musical works, or compositions before mentioned, together with the said accompaniment to the latter: and had lately in the name of the said *John Christian Bach*, but without his licence or consent, printed, published, and sold for profit, divers copies of the said two several compositions and

> accompaniment. And it likewise appeared, that it was possible to know the musical compositions of any master or composer of musick, who had composed any quantity thereof. The question was, Whether a *musical composition* is within the statute of the 8th of *Ann. c.* 19, intitled an act for the encouragement of learning, by vesting the copies of printed books in the authors, or purchasers, of such copies during the times therein mentioned.
>
> Mr *Robinson* for the plaintiff—Mr *Wood* for the defendant.
>
> Lord *Mansfield* called on Mr *Wood* to begin; and without hearing Mr *Robinson* in answer, said, the case was so clear and the arguments such, that it was difficult to speak seriously upon it. The words of the act of parliament are very large: '*Books* and *other writings*'. It is not confined to language or letters. Music is a science; it may be *written*; and the mode of conveying the ideas, is by signs and marks. A person may use the copy by playing it; but he has no right to rob the author of the profit, by multiplying copies and disposing of them to his own use. If the narrow interpretation contended for in the argument were to hold, it would equally apply to algebra, mathematics, arithmetic, hyeroglyphics. All these are conveyed by signs and figures. There is no colour for saying that music is not within the act.[204]—Afterwards, on *Monday June* 16th, the court certified in these words, 'Having heard counsel and considered this case, we are of the opinion, that a musical composition is a *writing* within the Statute of the 8th of Queen *Ann*, intitled an act for the encouragement of learning, by vesting the copies of printed books in the authors or purchasers of such copies, during the times therein mentioned'.[205]

This report of Mansfield's judgement may well be a summary. Even so, it is clear that he dealt with the Longman firm's case in a particularly swift and dismissive fashion: he did not bother to hear Bach's counsel, he began by saying that it was 'difficult to speak seriously' about the matter, and he concluded by saying that there was not even the slightest argument to support the view that music was not protected by the Copyright Act. It would be hard to find a more emphatic judicial rejection of an unsuccessful legal argument.

A few words in Cowper's summary constitute the only known remnant of the pleadings after Longman and Lukey had lodged their answers—the statement that 'it was possible to know the musical

[204] 'colour' here means 'an apparent or *prima facie* right' (Oxford English Dictionary).

[205] Cowper, *op. cit.*, p 623–624. *The English Reports* (see the Summary of Legal Cases) reproduces a slightly different version of this report.

compositions of any master or composer of musick, who had composed any quantities thereof'. In the sonata action Longman and Lukey had claimed that they had no way of being sure that Bach was the composer of the sonatas. Bach's replication evidently said something to the effect that the composer of a piece of music could be identified from its style if the composer were well known, and that Longman and Lukey were therefore able to identify the composer of the sonatas. This response was apparently recorded in the document prepared by Chancery for the King's Bench, but was condensed almost to the point of opacity in Cowper's published report.

No further legal issues were raised in court in any of the composers' three actions, which indicates that the only legal issue that Longman had raised in the pleadings in any of the actions was the question of whether music was within the scope of the Copyright Act. His only recourse now was to appeal from Chancery to the House of Lords in the hope that it would decide that music was not 'writing' within the meaning of the Copyright Act, and that Bach, if he then did not simply give up, would fail in any attempts he made to establish that music was protected by the common law. This would have been a good outcome for some music sellers, as it would have left music unprotected by any form of copyright. However, Longman's chances of success were slight. Mansfield's authority was still great, notwithstanding his differences with Yates and the Lords over common-law copyright, and there was no reason to think that the Lords would not support his decision on this point. Moreover, the House of Lords had displayed little sympathy towards publishers in *Donaldson v Becket*. And some Lords opposed to the idea of common-law copyright might have favoured an extended scope for the Copyright Act almost regardless of the merits of Longman's case.

There were two further legal arguments which Longman might have advanced in future actions to support his argument that the Copyright Act did not apply to his Bach and Abel prints. First, he could have argued that these prints were not big enough to count as a book within the meaning of the Copyright Act. But this argument would be raised and considered only many years later, in *Hime v Dale* (1803) and *Clementi v Goulding* (1809); see section 6.17 below.

Alternatively, or as well, Longman & Broderip could have argued that the Copyright Act did not apply to the Bach symphonies and Abel trios because of the Act's provision 'That nothing in this Act contained do extend, or shall be construed to extend, to Prohibit the Importation, Vending, or Selling of any Books in Greek, Latin, or any other Foreign Language Printed beyond the Seas'. He might have argued that, if musical notation constitutes a form of writing within the meaning of the Act, then it must record a language that is a foreign language within the meaning of the Copyright Act. In support of that argument he could have cited Mansfield's views on the function of writing, expressed in the Lockean terminology of ideas and impressions, and perhaps the fact that music notation was not of British origin. Or, in a later era when music came to be regarded as more than a diversion, Longman & Broderip might have argued that musical notation records not instructions to performers but the sounds that performers are required to produce, and that musical sounds constitute not a kind of protolanguage from which natural language had developed, as some eighteenth-century theorists of language held, but some transcendental language conveying things inexpressible in words—again, a foreign language within the meaning of the Act. But neither of these exotic arguments seems ever to have been raised—which might perhaps be regarded as a pity by modern connoisseurs of fine legal argument.

The full King's Bench confirmed Mansfield's ruling on 16 June, and Bach promptly reactivated the Chancery proceedings. A certificate of the King's Bench ruling was filed in Chancery,[206] and on 3 July the Chancellor ordered that the case be set down for hearing. At the hearing, on 8 July, the Lord Chancellor ordered that the 1773 injunction forbidding sale of the sonatas by Longman, Lukey & Co. be made perpetual, that a Master in Chancery assess the profits made from their sale of the sonatas, taking evidence from the defendants and examining all the relevant records, and that the defendants pay Bach damages as assessed by the Master, plus costs as taxed by the Master. At no stage was there any sign of an appeal.

Before the Master's hearing took place there was some activity in Abel's case. An order of 11 November 1777 records that:

---

[206] TNA C38/678. I am grateful to Nancy Mace for the reference to this document, which is not transcribed by Ann van Allen-Russell (see note 168 above). 'Greenland 5/6' is written on the backing sheet, indicating that Bach's attorney had to pay five shillings and sixpence to obtain this copy of the order.

> UPON the Petition of the Plaintiff this day Preferred to the Right Honourable the Lord High Chancellor of Great Britain for the Reasons therein Contained It is Ordered that this Cause be Restored to His Lordships Paper of Causes next after those Already Appointed but the same is to be set down in 4 Days or else this order is to be of no effect & hereof notice is to be givn. forthwith.[207]

It is not known why Abel's action came to life at this stage. The hearing seems not to have taken place, and from then on the only case of which any records have been located is Bach's sonata case.

The Master's hearing in that case took place on 1 April 1778; the reason for the delay is not known. Bach was represented by Greenland but no one appeared for Longman & Broderip. The Master reported:

> I do not find that any Profits were made by the Defendants from the Sale of the Sonata for the Harpsichord ..., but I find that the Defendants gained from the Sale of the Sonata for the Harpsichord with Accompanyment for the Viol di Gamba ... the Sum of Four pounds and three pence halfpenny, and I also find that two hundred copies of the said last mentioned Sonata with the Accompanyment remain in the hands of the Defendants, which I conceive ought to be delivered up by the Defendants to the Plaintiff the expence of printing and publishing the same having been allowed to the Defendants in their Account, And I have considered of the Plaintiffs Bill of Costs of this Suit amounting to the Sum of Ninety one pounds nine shillings and four pence and have taxed the same at the Sum of Seventy two pounds fourteen shillings and eleven pence[208]

The Master ordered the defendants to pay these sums to Bach, but allowed a discount of £8/4/8 if the damages and costs were paid without his having to take further legal action. Bach thus became the first composer to be awarded damages for breach of musical copyright.

The Master's assessment of the profits on the sonatas does not differ from the sworn evidence given by Longman and Lukey in 1773, when they said in their answer that they had made a loss of 6/3

---

[207] TNA C33/449 part 1 f 39.

[208] TNA C38/675. I am grateful to Nancy Mace for the reference to this document, not transcribed by Ann van Allen-Russell. The words 'Aug. Greenland / Newman Street' are on the backing sheet.

on the unaccompanied sonata and a profit of £4/0/3½ on the accompanied one, and still had 200 unsold copies of the accompanied one.[209] (Longman, Lukey & Co. had printed only 100 copies of the unaccompanied sonata—not enough to recoup the production costs. Apparently these sold out unexpectedly quickly, and the firm did not have time to restock before the injunction was granted.) Since the sales figures in the sonata case, given in multiples of ten, are probably estimates, the Master may well have discovered that stock control over cheap, locally printed items was not very careful, and that such documentation as Longman & Broderip could produce was not detailed enough for the Master to be able to arrive at his own figure.

Longman & Broderip seem to have paid promptly, for no further proceedings are known to have eventuated in the sonata case. And since no further proceedings are recorded in the other two cases, it is likely that the parties came to an agreement about what the firm should pay, using the Master's decision in the sonata case as a guide. The answers lodged by Longman and Lukey in 1773 state that they had lost £2/3/– on the Bach symphonies and had thirty-four unsold copies left from the seventy they had imported, and that they had made £1/17/6 on the Abel trios, with four copies unsold out of 100 imported.[210] Even before the legal proceedings ended, Bach and Longman & Broderip may have reached a business agreement, for Longman & Broderip published a Vauxhall song by Bach in 1777 and a new collection of his Vauxhall songs in 1779.[211]

6.16 Change, Consolidation and New Legislation

In *Bach v Longman* Lord Mansfield defined 'writings' in very broad terms, stating that the protection of the Copyright Act was 'not

[209] Their income and expenses in publishing the Bach editions under consideration appear in schedules to their answers (in TNA C12/71/22).

[210] They had bought 100 sets of Abel's trios from Markordt at a total cost of £10 and had paid 8/– for freight and other costs. They sold fifty copies at 2/3, thirty-six at 3/–, and ten at 2/6.

[211] Ernest Warburton, 'Introduction', in Ernest Warburton (ed.), *The Collected Works of Johann Christian Bach 1735–1782* v 25, New York, 1990, p vii–xv at p xiii.

confined to language or letters' but extended to music because 'music is a science; it may be written; and the mode of conveying the ideas, is by signs and marks'. Mansfield did not restrict the scope of the Act to signs and marks which recorded a natural language, or which could be understood readily, or were in current use: he explicitly referred to 'algebra, mathematics, arithmetic, hieroglyphics', the last then being still undeciphered. 'All these are conveyed by signs and figures.' That is, all signs, marks or figures used to convey ideas constituted writing within the meaning of the Copyright Act, regardless of their nature or meaning or whether many people, or anyone now living, understood them.

This broad definition of 'writings' eliminated what could have been a fruitful source of legal dispute in the decades after *Donaldson v Becket*. It seems never to have been questioned and is still referred to in dictionaries of legal terms and occasionally in legal proceedings. Likewise, the corollary that the Act protected music was accepted so completely and swiftly that judges of the day seem to have taken it for granted when disputes about music came before their courts. The only reported reference to *Bach v Longman* in an English court for many years was in *Hime v Dale*, when a barrister, not a judge, referred to the case. But Georgian writers on copyright routinely cited *Bach v Longman* as the basis of copyright protection for music,[212] and it remained a leading case in copyright law for over sixty years.

The decision in *Bach v Longman* influenced various events which took place in the music trade during the following decade or so. One episode involved the attorney Charles Rennett, who became a kind of robber baron of the music trade.[213] When the music seller John Welcker went bankrupt in 1778, Rennett took over his business, engaged a manager to run it while Welcker was in debtors' prison, and began buying the rights to musical compositions that had been published under the Welcker imprint. In 1780 Rennett sued Longman

---

212 E.g., Charles [Erdman] Petersdorff, *A practical and elementary Abridgment of the Cases argued and determined in the Courts of King's Bench, Common Pleas, Exchequer, and at Nisi Prius…*, London, v 6, 1827, p 537–538.

213 This outline of Rennett's activities is based upon Nancy A. Mace, 'Charles Rennett and the London music-sellers in the 1780s: testing the ownership of reversionary copyrights', *Journal of the Royal Musical Association* v 129 no. 1 (spring 2004) p 1–23.

& Broderip over alleged piracy of some of these works but, remarkably, he discontinued the action in return for becoming Longman & Broderip's attorney. For a time he did well, supplying the firm with Welcker prints and suing publishers who brought out music to which Longman & Broderip owned the rights. But Longman & Broderip objected both to Rennett's demand to be paid for some prints on nonstandard terms, and to the cost, both in money and to the firm's reputation, of the numerous lawsuits that he launched on their behalf. In 1784 Broderip wrote to Rennett directing him not to start any more actions and complaining that Longman & Broderip were being abused by other members of the trade, that Longman was having to spend too much time on the firm's legal affairs, and that Rennett's treatment of some defendants was oppressive. Rennett responded by terminating his association with the firm, reviving his 1780 legal action against them, and extending the action to another twenty-two instances of alleged piracy.

In 1783, at Longman's request, Rennett had obtained an opinion from Charles Ambler, a King's Counsel and Attorney-General to Queen Charlotte, about the effect of the Copyright Act upon composers. Prior agreements for the sale of rights to a musical composition had made no mention of the Act. But if a composer who had sold a piece of music published in 1769 was still alive fourteen years later, who owned the rights during the second fourteen-year term provided by the Act—the composer or the purchaser of the rights? Ambler's opinion was that the rights for the second term belonged to the composer. Rennett reported this opinion to Longman & Broderip, but advised them not to pay for the second fourteen years if a composer claimed to own the rights to those years—that is, to call any such composer's bluff. But after the breach with Longman & Broderip, Rennett bought from the composers Charles Dibdin Sr and John Garth the rights for the second fourteen years for several of their compositions. Rennett's aim, he told Dibdin, was to sue Longman & Broderip and other publishers for infringement of these rights.

Ambler's opinion no doubt made Rennett confident of success, and some music sellers paid up. But Samuel, Ann & Peter Thompson and Longman & Broderip did not, and Rennett brought Exchequer actions against them. The firms defended the actions, and claim and counterclaim followed, none of the litigants being obsessive about strict veracity. Rennett lost both actions, even though in the Longman & Broderip action Ambler's opinion was before the court. This episode was significant legally, for the decisions in *Rennett v Longman* and *Rennett v Thompson* determined that, when the agreement between an author and a purchaser of the rights to a book or a piece of music did not explicitly refer to the second fourteen-year term, the rights for those years belonged to the purchaser. But these cases, although they affected all authors and publishers, were never the subject of published law reports.

This episode illustrates how greatly music publishing had changed since John Playford's time. The parties to earlier disputes over the right to publish music had been composers and music sellers. But Rennett was an entrepreneur who saw and exploited an opportunity in the music trade, using a combination of legal skills, business knowhow, low cunning and access to capital. His only music-seller allies were Welcker and, for a time, Longman & Broderip, and he did not so much earn the trust of these allies as make himself useful to them on his own terms and for his own reasons. But entrepreneurs need to have the law on their side: if the decision in *Bach v Longman* had gone the other way, leaving it uncertain whether the Copyright Act protected music, Rennett might have decided to exercise his talents in some field unconnected with music or publishing.

Another development which may have been influenced by *Bach v Longman* was an agreement among some music sellers about 1781 to stop making manuscript copies of one another's published music. In his deposition in *Longman v Babb* (1784), Richard Bride, a clerk employed by Longman & Broderip, said that

> he has been employed in the service of the said Complainants for the space of nine years and during that time has wrote out and copied for them divers Songs Airs Tunes and Passages from other musical publications some of which may have been for sale And saith he knows that the said Complainants till within about three years last past during this Deponent's employment in their service hired engaged and employed divers persons at divers times to write out and copy for them

> for sale divers Songs Airs Tunes and Passages from divers musical publications....[214]

However,

> about three years ago to the best of his remembrance and belief he was informed and believes that there was an Agreement then entered into and made between several of the publishers and sellers of music for the purpose of putting a stop to the practice of writing and copying any parts of new publications the property of other persons but the particular purpose of such Agreement this Deponent saith he cannot set forth....[215]

The details of this agreement are not known. The parties to it are likely to have included substantial firms with much to lose from unrestricted copying of their music, and it is plausible that Rennett, who at that time owned Welcker's business and was Longman & Broderip's attorney, was involved in these negotiations. But it is not known whether the agreement dealt with matters other than copying—for example, by formalising the understanding in the trade that extracts from works which had been published for over a year could be used as examples in teaching aids and lesson books.[216] Nor is it known to what extent the attempt to manage copying of published material was a direct response to *Bach v Longman*, attempting to eliminate a practice which, apart from damaging the trade's interests, could now give rise to litigation based on the Copyright Act.

The outbreak of amity among music sellers may have not lasted long. In the reciprocal actions *Forster v Longman* and *Longman v Forster* (1791), which concerned piracy by Longman & Broderip and William Forster & Son of each other's publications, the music engraver and music seller James Freeman deposed that

---

[214] Deposition of Richard Bride in *Longman v Babb*, 15 September 1784, TNA E133/82/26. I am grateful to Jenny Nex for her transcript of this passage.

[215] *ibid.*

[216] Deposition of the musical instrument maker Peter Thompson II (of the firm of music sellers Samuel, Ann & Peter Thompson) in *Longman v Babb*, 15 September 1784, TNA E133/82/26. I thank Jenny Nex for this information.

> when the Def[endan]t Broderip gave this Dep[onen]t the printed Book to engrave from[,] this Dep[onen]t observed that it was Forster's property[.] to which he [Broderip] answered to the best of this Dep[onen]ts remembrance that he did not care as he Forster had printed opus 43 which was his property[217]

Whatever the details of the music sellers' agreement were, it did not commit the parties to registering their publications at Stationers' Hall. The numbers of music entries in the Stationers' register remained low: from 1775 to 1782 they were 3, 2, 4, 5, 7, 17, 8 and 9.[218] But there was a steep rise thereafter: from 1783 to 1789 the numbers were 37, 55, 69, 109, 176, 130 and 142.[219] After falling to 95 in 1790 and 1791, the numbers resumed their rise, with another downturn at the end of the decade: from 1792 to 1800 the numbers registered were 142, 184, 219, 227, 250, 241, 203, 214 and 171. The two downturns probably reflected conditions in the publishing industry generally, for the total numbers of registrations, musical and non-musical, fell in about the same proportion at about the same time. But there was no long-term decline in the number of entries. And the rise in the number of music entries from 1783 onwards was much faster than the rise in the total number of entries, even though the book trade registered its products with increasing frequency after the decision in *Donaldson v Becket* in 1774. Indeed, music entries constituted over thirty per cent of all entries in the mid- and late 1790s and over forty percent in most years from 1799 to 1813. After 1813 the number of non-music entries rose and the proportion of music entries therefore fell.

---

[217] Deposition of 24 June 1791, TNA E133/54/55.

[218] For these numbers see note 65 above.

[219] In a submission dated 3 June 1818 to the House of Commons Select Committee on the Copyright Acts, George Greenhill, warehouse keeper of the Stationers' Company, commented that 'very little, if any, Music was entered at Stationers['] Hall till 1776–7, when some legal dispute arose respecting the Copyright of Music [undoubtedly a reference to *Bach v Longman*]; and single Songs do not appear to have been entered till April 1783: since that period, Music, particularly single Songs, has formed a considerable portion of the articles entered' (*Report from the Select Committee on the Copyright Acts*, House of Commons Parliamentary Paper no. 402, 5 June 1818, p 6).

Although they were not legally required to do so, music publishers began about 1785 to print the phrase 'Entered at Stationers' Hall' on their title-pages, perhaps adding a reference to the Copyright Act. There was some initial confusion and uncertainty. The title-page of John Bland's edition of Haydn's *Three Sonatas for the Piano Forte or Harpsichord*, Op. 41, registered on 4 May 1785, states: 'NB. This Work is Real Property [sic] & Entered at Stationers Hall according to Act of Parliament'. And although the title-page of Bland's print of Samuel Arnold's *Anacreontic Songs*, registered on 7 June 1785, says nothing about registration, the omission seems to have been inadvertent, for the words 'Published as the Act Directs June 4th 1785' were written in ink on the title-page of one copy.[220]

The rise in the number of music entries from 1783 and the addition of the phrase 'Entered at Stationers' Hall' to title-pages undoubtedly owe something to the publication on 26 November 1783 of Henry Cowper's collection of case reports, which included the report of *Bach v Longman* that brought Lord Mansfield's decision in this case to public notice.[221] As lawyers became aware of this judgement they presumably advised their clients to register music in order to comply with the Copyright Act. However, the increase in music entries had started earlier in 1783, for thirty of the thirty-seven music entries that year were made before 26 November. Of these thirty entries, seventeen were made by just two music sellers: John Preston and Samuel, Ann & Peter Thompson; the latter first registered music on 23 July 1783. Nancy Mace notes that these two firms were responsible for about half of all 1783–1784 music entries and that both 'had been parties to the litigation initiated by Longman & Broderip and their attorney Charles Rennett, who began vigorously defending their copyrights in the courts from 1780 onward'.[222] Although she concludes that this actual or threatened litigation prompted other 'major music sellers to establish their rights to copies

[220] Now BL H.1652.(1.).

[221] See note 203 above. The book's publication date is advertised in *The Morning Herald, and Daily Advertiser*, 24 November 1783, p 2; it was registered at Stationers' Hall on 25 November 1783. My suggestion of this connection was noted by Michael Kassler in *MESH* p xxv fn 39.

[222] Mace, 'The market for music…', *op. cit.* in note 65 above, p 163.

legally by entering them at Stationers' Hall',[223] the question remains why the increase in music registrations did not start until several years after Rennett initiated his lawsuits.

Longman & Broderip were slow to start registering music at Stationers' Hall but subsequently became the leading music registrant.[224] They and their two successors—Broderip & Wilkinson and Longman, Clementi & Co.—registered 27.7% of all music entries made between 1771 and 1800.[225] The next most frequent music registrant in these years, Joseph Dale, accounted for only 8.5% of music entries. James Longman had changed his position with respect to the Copyright Act: in the 1770s he had argued that it did not protect music, but in the 1780s he wanted to be sure that it protected his firm's music.

Mace remarks that 'the rapid increase in registrations by Longman & Broderip was almost certainly the result of their own experience of defending their rights to profitable works in the courts'.[226] But why were they so slow to move? And why did other firms register little or nothing? In particular, why, from the early 1760s, when William Forster set up his business, until 1809, when he died, did he and his son William II register only the three works that had been at the centre of a dispute with Longman & Broderip?[227]

The answers to these questions are unknown. But it is conceivable that the legal advice given to Forster and initially to Longman & Broderip differed from the advice that Longman &

---

[223] *ibid.*

[224] They registered three items in 1779, one in 1780 and nothing from 1781 to 1784, but registered thirty publications from May to December 1785, and from 1786 to 1790 registered (including a couple of joint registrations) 68, 132, 87, 57 and 21 publications.

[225] Mace, 'The market for music…', p 162. She notes, however, that 34.7% of registrations during this period were made by composers for works whose copyrights had not been acquired by music sellers.

[226] *ibid.*, p 163.

[227] The dispute is discussed in Nancy A. Mace, 'Haydn and the London music sellers: Forster v. Longman & Broderip', *Music and Letters* v 77 no. 4 (November 1996) p 527–541; for the registrations see p 539. The three works were registered on 13 January 1794 (*MESH* p 216).

Broderip followed from 1785 onwards. The Copyright Act required publications to be registered, but it imposed no penalty for non-registration. Although it made registration a precondition for recovery of the penalties prescribed by the Act, it did not explicitly make the right of ownership created by the Act conditional on registration. It was therefore uncertain whether unregistered publications were protected by the Act, and Longman & Broderip may have decided in 1785 to play safe and to register publications in order to be sure of the Act's protection.

The question of whether the Act protected unregistered publications was dealt with by an English court only in 1798, in *Beckford v Hood*, in which the King's Bench decided that 'an author whose work is pirated … may maintain an action ... for damages against the offending party, although the work was not entered at Stationers' Hall'. But registration was still mandatory, and although a report of the decision was published soon after the hearing,[228] it had no obvious effect on registration numbers.

The most important effect of *Bach v Longman* was to end the distinction between musical copyright and copyright in literary material: thereafter, the Copyright Act applied to words and music in exactly the same way. Accordingly, legislators in the late eighteenth and early nineteenth centuries did not differentiate between the two. The Act of 1801, 41 George III c.107, which extended British copyright law to Ireland—then newly part of the United Kingdom—restated the main provisions of the Copyright Act of 1710 without changing them. (The 1801 Act omitted any reference to writings, but as far as is known there was no attempt to argue that it did not apply to music—which is no surprise, given the terms of Mansfield's judgement.) More substantial change to copyright law came in 1814 with 'An Act to amend the several Acts for the Encouragement of Learning', 54 George III c.156, which provided that copyright was to last for twenty-eight years from the date of publication, or until the author's death, whichever was later, and that any legal action against offences under the Act had to be brought within twelve months of the

---

[228] In Charles Durnford and Edward Hyde East, *Reports of Cases argued and determined in the Court of King's Bench, from Michaelmas Term 37 George III. 1796, to Trinity Term 38 George III. 1798...* v 7, London, 1798, p 620–629.

alleged offence. This Act also changed the legal deposit and registration provisions but did not make registration a precondition for recovering damages. Music was affected by these Acts in exactly the same way as other kinds of published material.

It was a different matter with case law, for various reasons. One was that music sellers were slow to adapt to the new legal environment and persisted in some practices which were unknown in the book trade. Moreover, music publishing had characteristic features which gave rise to characteristic disputes. In particular, the size of music publications was often quite small: many comprised just one printed sheet. Also, it was common to publish arrangements and adaptations of popular material, some of them quite elaborate. And single sheets and arrangements often needed to be published quickly, while demand was strong. Further, the number of potential stakeholders in even a small publication could be quite large: those with a potential interest in a single-sheet arrangement of a song from an opera could include the composer, the librettist, the theatre management, the arranger, the publisher of the full opera, the publisher of the single sheet, and anyone with whom any of these parties had had relevant business dealings. These features of music publishing were disincentives or obstacles to the making of detailed written contracts. One result of all this was that disputes about published music were often a product of inadequately documented business arrangements;[229] another consequence was that disputes over adaptations and arrangements were more common with music than with books. Chancery was equipped to handle the latter kind of dispute: as it had done in *Gyles v Wilcox* (1740), it could empanel experts to decide whether copyright had been infringed.[230]

---

[229] For example, Bland & Weller paid Francis Tatton Latour £31/10/– in 1812 for the right to publish his piano piece *La Retour de Windsor*, but when the firm reissued it in 1816 he sued for breach of copyright. In *Latour v Bland* (1818) the court heard that the only documentation that the publishers ever had of the 1812 transaction was the composer's receipt, which had been destroyed. The judge held that, under Section 1 of the Copyright Act, copyright had to be formally assigned in writing and that the assignment had to be attested by two witnesses. Latour was awarded £100 and the publisher received the rights.

[230] See page 305 above.

A number of legal issues with particular significance for musical copyright were dealt with in the decades after *Bach v Longman*. One was considered in 1803 by the Chief Justice of the King's Bench—Edward Law, 1st Baron Ellenborough—in *Hime v Dale*:

> This was an action for pirating the words of a song ... published on a single sheet of paper. Lord Ellenborough was inclined to think that such a publication was not protected by 8 Ann. c.19, as the word *book* not only means in common acceptation a plurality of sheets, but is decidedly used in this sense in one clause of the statute itself. He therefore nonsuited the plaintiff, but reserved the point for the opinion of the Court. [Before the full court, Thomas] Erskine for the plaintiff ... contended that the legislature could never have meant to make the operation of the statute depend upon the type in which any composition is printed, or the form in which it is bound up. The song might easily have been extended over several sheets, and rendered a duodecimo volume. In *Back* [sic] v. *Longman* ... it was decided that music is within the Act; and musical compositions most often appear in this fugitive form.[231]

The question of whether a single sheet counted as a book was referred to the full court, but the hearing never took place.

The same question came up in *Clementi v Goulding* (1809). Clementi & Co., which owned the copyright to William Shield's opera *Two Faces Under a Hood*, brought out a single-sheet version of one of the opera's songs. 'Under a conception which generally prevailed among music-sellers, that by doing so the plaintiffs had lost their exclusive property in this air', the defendants, Goulding, Phipps, d'Almaine & Co., 'likewise published an edition of it in the same form, which had a considerable sale'.[232] Clementi & Co. sued them and

> obtained a verdict with damages against the defendant in this action, tried at the sittings before Lord Ellenborough C.J., for pirating a sheet of music of which the plaintiff had the copyright; and the only question

[231] *ER* v 170 p 1069 (2 Camp. 29). This case is further described on pages 417–418 below.

[232] *ER* v 103 p 998–999 (11 East 244–245). This case is further described on page 171 above.

> was, whether this being a single sheet were within the protection of the stat. 8 Ann. c. 19.

When the full King's Bench considered this question

> Lord Ellenborough then said, that though he had leant in favour of the objection at the trial, yet on further consideration he was now disposed to consider that a sheet was a book within the meaning of the Act: and he recollected that when the same question was made in a cause [i.e., *Hime v Dale*] a few years ago, the Court were disposed to think that the case was within the statute. And such appeared to be the opinion of the other judges.[233]

The defendants then agreed to accept Lord Ellenborough's original judgement and, although no formal ruling was made, it became accepted law that 'an action is maintainable on the stat. 8 Ann. c.19, for pirating a single sheet of music'.[234] Such publications often sold well: the parties to *Clementi v Goulding* had each printed 1000 copies of the disputed song.

The courts also considered matters relating to music performance. In *Bach v Longman* Lord Mansfield had stated that 'a person may use the copy by playing it; but he has no right to rob the author of the profit, by multiplying copies and disposing of them to his own use'. But this case had been about two sonatas, and Mansfield may not have considered music expressly composed for public performance. Who owned the publication rights to a piece of music commissioned by and performed in a theatre? In *Storace v Longman* (1788)

> the declaration stated that the plaintiff [Stephen Storace] was composer of a musical air, tune and writing, and that it was reprinted by the defendant [Longman & Broderip] within the fourteen years limited by the Act, &c. [Thomas] Erskine for the defendant examined the plaintiff's sister ['Nancy' Storace], to shew that the song was composed to be sung by her at the Italian Opera; and that all compositions so performed were the property of the house, not of the composer. Lord Kenyon [Lloyd Kenyon, Chief Justice of the Court of King's Bench] said, that this defence could not be supported; that the statute vests the property in the

---

233 *ibid.*

234 *ibid.*

> author; and that no such private regulation could interfere with the public right.[235]

Storace v Longman was a Chancery case, and strictly speaking Lord Kenyon's interpretation of the law was therefore not authoritative. But his opinion was followed in another Chancery case, *Skillern v Longman* (1793), and was never seriously questioned thereafter.

Also associated with performance was the question of what later came to be called 'performing rights'. Could a person who owned the right to publish a work successfully claim damages from someone who gave an unauthorised public performance of it? This question arose in a King's Bench case, *Colman v Wathen* (1793), which was concerned not with music but with a play-script:

> This was an action for the penalty under the statute 8 Ann c. 19, for publishing an entertainment called, The Agreeable Surprise. The plaintiff [the theatre manager George Colman Sr] had purchased the copy-right from [John] O'Keeffe, the author: and the only evidence of publication by the defendant [the theatre manager George Wathen] was the representation of this piece upon the stage at Richmond.

But after the full King's Bench had heard Thomas Erskine argue the plaintiff's case, the Chief Justice, Lord Kenyon, stopped the defendant's case, saying:

> There is no evidence to support the action in this case. The statute for the protection of copyright only extends to prohibit the publication of the book itself by any other than the author or his lawful assignees. But here was no publication.

And another judge, Sir Francis Buller, commented:

> Reporting anything from memory can never be a publication within the statute. Some instances of memory are very surprising: but the mere act of repeating such a performance cannot be left as evidence to the jury that the defendant had pirated the work itself.[236]

---

[235] *ER* 170: 1069 (2 Camp. 27) in the report of *Clementi v Goulding*.

[236] *ER* 101: 137 (5 TR 245).

Colman v Wathen in effect endorsed Mansfield's view that publication and performance were different things, and put an end to any hope that authors or composers might have had of using the Copyright Act as a basis for being paid for performances of their work. It would be up to Parliament to create performing rights—which it did in 1833, in 3 William IV c.15, but only for plays.

Another unresolved question of relevance to composers and music sellers concerned copyright in works first published abroad. National copyright laws were enacted in the United States and France before the end of the eighteenth century, and the French law became a model for similar laws in other parts of Europe in the nineteenth century. However, these laws applied only within national boundaries. Although books written in a living language were for the most part produced and sold in the country of that language, pirate editions of a successful book could always be produced in another country whose government, however solicitous it might be about the rights of its own nationals, might not want to interfere with a profitable foreign-language reprint industry.[237] Where instrumental music was concerned, national copyright laws were even less effective, for music knew no linguistic boundaries. The international trade in printed music was well developed in the late eighteenth century,[238] and became even more so in the nineteenth.

The ownership of British rights to music written by a foreigner living abroad was the subject of a series of cases that extended well into Queen Victoria's reign and will be described here only summarily. In *D'Almaine v Boosey* (1835) the plaintiff had bought the British publishing rights to Daniel Auber's opera *Lestocq* under an agreement which complied with English law, and had published and registered the full opera and some pieces from it. The defendant published a set of quadrilles and waltzes based on airs from the opera. The court decided that 'the English assignee of the copyright of a

---

[237] See William Briggs, *The Law of International Copyright*, London, 1906.

[238] See Sarah Adams, 'International dissemination of printed music during the second half of the eighteenth century' in Hans Lenneberg (ed.), *The Dissemination of Music: Studies in the history of music publishing*, Lausanne, 1994, p 21–41.

foreign musical composer is within protection of the statutes relating to copyright'.

But Parliament wanted international reciprocity for any such right. It enacted the International Copyright Act, 1&2 Victoria c.59, in 1838, and that Act's successor, 7&8 Victoria c.12, in 1844. Under the latter Act a foreign country could be made the subject of an Order in Council giving authors of books published in that country exclusive British publication rights to those books, subject to compliance with the provisions of the British copyright law other than the legal deposit requirement. This measure had only limited success. Orders in Council were promulgated for some sixteen countries that agreed to reciprocity of copyright, but no agreement was reached with other countries.

In 1842 the Copyright Act of 1710 and the thicket of case law and statutory amendments and extensions that had grown up around it were completely replaced by a new Copyright Act, 5&6 Victoria c.45. Section 2 of this Act explicitly extended the definition of 'book' to sheets of music:

> And be it enacted, That in the construction of this act, the word 'book' shall be construed to mean and include every volume, part or division of a volume, pamphlet, sheet of letter-press, sheet of music, map, chart, or plan separately published....

And section 20 extended performing rights and statutory copyright to music: 'be it therefore enacted, that the provisions of the said act [3 William IV c.15] of his late Majesty [the 1833 Act which created performing rights], and of this act, shall apply to musical compositions'.

The Copyright Act of 1842 marked the end of the early history of musical copyright as far as domestic publication was concerned. However, reciprocal copyright arrangements with other countries, as envisaged by the Act of 1838, were not always easy to establish, and questions about British copyright for foreign authors and for works published abroad continued to be considered in a series of cases concerning music.

Chappell v Purday (1845) confirmed that 'a foreign author, residing abroad, has not at common law' or under British copyright legislation 'any copyright in this country'. But since other national copyright laws, like Britain's, did not protect material first published outside the nation's borders, an obvious solution—which many English music sellers had already adopted or had endeavoured to adopt—was to publish a work in several countries on the same day.[239] *Cocks v Purday* (1848) gave judicial backing to this practice: 'a foreigner resident abroad may acquire copyright in this country in a work that is first published by him ... in this country, which has not been made *publici juris*[240] by a previous publication elsewhere'.

Far-flung networks of co-publishers or distributors developed. For instance, when Louis Antoine Jullien published his *The English Quadrille* in London *c*1843, the title-page named eight publishers: Jullien (London), Troupenas (Paris), Schott (Antwerp), Simrock (Bonn), Peters (Leipzig), Lucca (Milan), Mechetti (Vienna) and Paez (St Petersburg).[241]

English courts were divided over the question whether foreign composers' works were protected in Britain in the absence of reciprocal national copyright laws. In January 1849 the Queen's Bench decided in *Boosey v Davidson* that 'a foreigner, though resident abroad, may have copyright in this country, if the first publication is in this country'. But five months later Exchequer held in *Boosey v Purday* that 'a foreign author residing abroad, who composes a work abroad, and sends it to this country, where it is first published under his authority, acquires no copyright therein'.

In *Boosey v Jeffereys* (1851) Exchequer Chamber endorsed the King's Bench view. But the House of Lords held on appeal in *Jefferys v Boosey* (1854) that:

> The object of 8 Anne, c.19, was to encourage literature among British subjects, which description includes such foreigners as, by residence here, owe the Crown a temporary allegiance; and any foreigner, first publishing his work here, is an 'author' within the

---

[239] As noted in Chapter 4, Clementi advised in 1807 that British and European editions of a work 'must appear on the same day' and took steps to ensure that London, Paris and Leipzig editions of each volume of his *Gradus ad Parnassum* would be published simultaneously. See pages 81 and 185–186 above.

[240] Of public right, i.e., in the public domain.

[241] Copy at BL h.62.p.(5).

meaning of the statute, no matter where his work was composed, or whether he came here solely with a view to its publication.

Copyright commences by publication; if at that time the foreign author is not in this country, he is not a person whom the statute meant to protect.

An Englishman, though resident abroad, will have copyright in a work of his own first published in this country.

B[ellini], a foreign musical composer, resident at that time in his own country, assigned to R[icordi], another foreigner, also resident there, according to the law of their country, his right in a musical composition [*La Sonnambula*] of which he was the author, and which was then unpublished. The assignee brought the composition to this country, and, before publication, assigned it, according to the forms required by the law of this country, to an Englishman. The first publication took place in this country.

It was held, reversing the judgment of the Court of Exchequer Chamber, that the foreign assignee had not, by the law of this country, any assignable copyright here in this musical composition.[242]

That settled the matter. A foreign author's rights would be recognised in Britain only if a treaty existed with the relevant foreign country under which each country recognised the rights of the other country's authors. Britain maintained a number of such bilateral copyright agreements until 1887, when it became a party to the multilateral Berne Convention for the Protection of Literary and Artistic Works.

[242] *ER* v 10 p 681 (4 HLC 815).

~ IV ~

NEW TECHNOLOGIES

~ 7 ~

EARL STANHOPE'S 'LETTER-MUSIC'

Michael Kassler

7.1 INTRODUCTION

In addition to his active political career, Charles Stanhope (from 1786 third Earl Stanhope, before then Viscount Mahon) endeavoured to increase knowledge in many fields.[1] He wrote a book on electricity,[2] advanced naval architecture,[3] built a novel calculating machine and the first logic machine,[4] developed a commercially successful printing

---

[1] His principal biography is Ghita Stanhope (his great-great-granddaughter) and G[eorge] P[eabody] Gooch, *The Life of Charles Third Earl Stanhope*, London, 1914. F. M. Beatty, 'The scientific work of the third Earl Stanhope', *Notes and Records of the Royal Society of London* v 11 no. 2 (March 1955) p 202–221, gives an overview of his accomplishments in areas now called 'scientific'. K[enneth] G. Webb, *Stanhope Impressions: The life and work of Charles, third Earl Stanhope*, Oxford, 1966, provides a short biography with emphasis on Stanhope's accomplishments relating to steamboats and printing. *The Oxford Dictionary of National Biography* has a recent account of his life by G[rayson] M. Ditchfield. None of these writings mentions Stanhope's work on letter-music.

[2] Charles, Viscount Mahon, *Principles of Electricity, containing divers new Theorems and Experiments...*, London, 1779. A French translation was published in 1781; a German translation in 1789.

[3] See Edward Cuff, 'Naval inventions of Charles third Earl Stanhope', *The Mariner's Mirror* v 33 no. 2 (April 1947) p 106–121; Cynthia Owen Philip, *Robert Fulton: a biography*, New York, 1985, p 28–36; and *Papers relative to Earl Stanhope's Sailing Experiment ... ordered* [by the House of Lords] *to be printed 14th April 1813*, London, 1813 (copy in Lincolnshire Archives, RA/4/D/14).

[4] See Beatty, *op. cit.*, p 205–206; Robert Harley, 'The Stanhope demonstrator, an instrument for performing logical operations', *Mind* v 4 no. 14 (April 1879) p 192–210; and Jane Wess, 'The logic demonstrators of the 3rd Earl Stanhope (1753–1816)', *Annals of Science* v 54 no. 4 (1997) p 375–395.

press,[5] enhanced stereotype printing technology,[6] invented a telescope,[7] and received English patents for improvements in shipbuilding and for a process of burning chalk, marble and limestone into lime.[8] His innovations relating to music included a new temperament, a monochord claimed to be especially accurate, 'tuning-glasses' designed to supersede tuning forks, a piano in which each key activated a single steel string, and an apparatus that recorded the duration of every key struck by a keyboard performer.[9] Stanhope's musical instruments are described in the next chapter. His extensive work on music printing has been largely forgotten, probably because it was never published.

Amongst his papers in the Centre for Kentish Studies, Maidstone,[10] is a draft of a letter dated August 1803 from Andrew Wilson,[11] proprietor of the 'Stereotype Office' in Duke Street, Lincoln's Inn Fields, London, which had been recently established to

---

[5] See Justin Howes, *On Citizen Stanhope and his iron Hand Press*, Westerham, Kent, 2003 (privately printed, copy at NAL 608.AE.0322).

[6] Stanhope's work on printing is described in Horace Hart, 'Charles Earl Stanhope and the Oxford University Press', *Collectanea* [Oxford Historical Society], 3rd ser. (1896) p 365–412, republished by the Printing Historical Society as a booklet (retaining the original pagination), with notes by James Mosley, London, 1966. See also George A. Kubler, *The Era of Charles Mahon Third Earl of Stanhope, Stereotyper, 1750–1825*, New York, 1938.

[7] Samuel Varley, 'An account of a telescope of a new and singular construction, invented by the Right Hon. the late Earl Stanhope', *London Journal of Arts and Sciences* v 1 (1820) no. 1 p 31–51 and no. 2 p 109–129.

[8] Stanhope's four patents are listed in Bennet Woodcroft, *Alphabetical Index of Patentees of Inventions...*, London, 1854 (reprinted 1969), p 538.

[9] He described the first three of these innovations in his *Principles of the Science of tuning Instruments with fixed Tones*, London, 1806.

[10] All quotations from and reproductions of these papers in this chapter are made by kind permission of the Centre manager and the Trustees of the Chevening Estate.

[11] The draft letter (in CKS U1590/C99/2) is transcribed in Michael L. Turner, 'Andrew Wilson: Lord Stanhope's stereotype printer: a preliminary report', *Journal of the Printing Historical Society* no. 9 (1973/1974) p 22–65 at p 31–34.

Figure 7.1 Detail of portrait of Charles 3rd Earl Stanhope by John Opie, exhibited at the Royal Academy of Arts in 1803 (in a private U.K. collection, by kind permission of the owner)

develop stereotype printing for commercial use.[12] Addressed 'to the authors, booksellers, printers and schoolmasters throughout Great Britain and Ireland', the document clearly was composed for eventual publication but seems not to have been widely circulated at the time, as no contemporary printed copies of it have been found.[13]

The draft announced that Stanhope had 'lately purchased' two important 'secrets' of stereotype printing and, by experiment, had improved the process substantially.[14] Because of this Wilson—a master printer—now could make stereotype plates that were 'superior to all others in point of perfection, and yet inferior in price'.[15] In the draft he initially wrote that

> in consequence of a plan, contrived by Earl Stanhope, I shall have it in my power, some time hence, to print music, at a cheap rate, and in a manner much more beautiful than any which has ever yet appeared.

---

[12] Between spring and November 1803 Stanhope worked closely with Wilson on the development of stereotype printing and spent time 'almost every day' at the Duke Street premises (*ibid.*, p 30–31).

[13] As far as is known (*ibid.*, p 34–35), Wilson's draft letter was first printed in Hart, *op. cit.*, p 377–382.

[14] He bought these secrets from the Glasgow printers Andrew Foulis (the younger) and Alexander Tilloch, who in 1784 had jointly received an English patent (subsequently numbered 1431) for 'a method of making plates for the purpose of printing by or with plates, instead of the moveable types commonly used'. Kubler, *op. cit.*, p 22, states that Stanhope paid Foulis £800 'for his work' and that Tilloch (who had removed to London, where he established *The Philosophical Magazine* in 1797) lived 'for a time' at Stanhope's home in Chevening, Kent.

[15] According to George A. Kubler, *A New History of Stereotyping*, New York, 1941, p 63–64, the stereotype process employed by Stanhope and Wilson involved the following steps. After a page was set in a forme using conventional moveable type, and one or more proofs were pulled and read to ensure the correctness of the typesetting, a mould of the page was created using plaster of Paris. After the mould hardened it was separated from the type, which became available for reuse. The mould then was baked and afterwards was immersed in molten metal, which flowed in. When the metal cooled it formed a plate into which the typefaces had been transferred. Printing then was done from this plate rather than from the original type. Stanhope and Wilson claimed economic and other advantages for their stereotyping process, and Wilson used it to print numerous publications. However, their process was adopted by few other printers during Stanhope's lifetime.

Stanhope apparently rejected this assertion, because the draft was emended to read 'in consequence of another plan, I shall have it in my power...'. This chapter tells the story of that other plan.

7.2 STANHOPE AND BALDWIN

The plan to which Wilson referred was initiated about 1798 by the Rev. Thomas Baldwin of Chester. He is particularly remembered for having ascended from there in a balloon on 8 September 1785, and for drawing, while aloft, pictures of scenes below that he published the next year in an account of his journey.[16] As these were the first views from a balloon ever printed he is considered a forefather of aerial photography.[17]

On 1 September 1798 Baldwin penned a short document called *Music in Short Hand: or a short and comprehensive Mode of writing Music, & of printing it with common Letter-Types, on common Paper: which saves the Expence of Copper-Plates, and Engraving; also Time & Paper.*[18] As his title stated, he conceived that this 'short hand' was superior to common music notation in three ways. It was faster and more compact to write (thus saving both time and paper) and could be printed more cheaply than by the then dominant method of music printing, in which music symbols were punched into plates upon which pages larger than those ordinarily used in books were subsequently impressed. The title also reveals that Baldwin lacked

---

[16] Thomas Baldwin, *Airopaidia: Containing the narrative of a balloon excursion from Chester...*, Chester, 1786. He also wrote *Almanack and Planetary, for 1791...*, Chester, [1791].

[17] See L[ionel] T[homas] C[aswell] Rolt, *The Aeronauts: A history of ballooning 1783–1903*, London, 1966, p 75. Baldwin's ballooning achievements are described in Alan W. Waterworth, 'Baldwin's balloon', *Cheshire Life* v 47 no. 9 (September 1981) p 28–29 and p 31, and in Stephen Matthews, 'Mr Baldwin's balloon: a forgotten flight', *Transactions of the Lancashire and Cheshire Antiquarian Society* v 99 (2003/2004) p 191–204. According to Waterworth, p 28, after Baldwin resigned the curacy of Haslingden, Lancashire in 1783, he seems not to have referred to himself as a clergyman.

[18] In CKS U1590/C98.

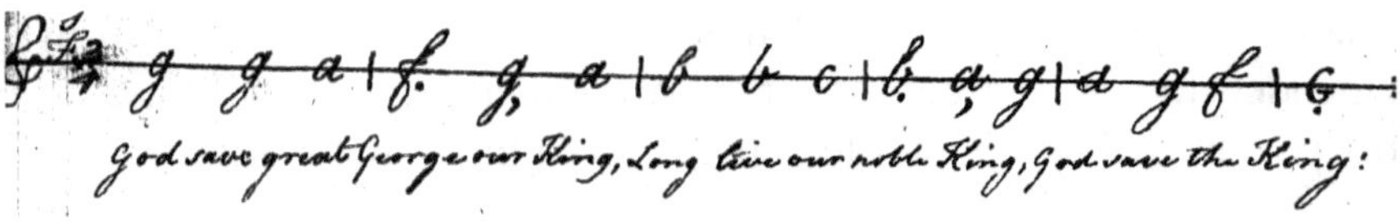

Figure 7.2 An example of Baldwin's music shorthand in 1798 (in Centre for Kentish Studies U1590/C98, by permission of the Centre manager and the Trustees of the Chevening Estate)

familiarity with this technology, as the plates into which music was engraved in England at this time generally were made of pewter rather than more costly copper.

In this document Baldwin gave examples of his new mode of writing music, of which *Figure 7.2* is an instance. The staff was replaced by a single horizontal line, through which note names were written. Upper-case letters denoted minims and lower-case letters crotchets. Quavers, semiquavers, etc. were indicated by putting one, two, etc. commas beneath a lower-case letter. Letters also were used to indicate key signatures: the '$^{S}_{F}$' after the treble clef in *Figure 7.2* specifies a signature of F sharp. The time signature, bar line and prolongation dot (that extends a note's time by half its undotted value) of conventional notation were retained. The examples he provided were of monophonic music only.[19]

---

[19] Baldwin was not the first to propose that letters and other symbols used in typesetting text be applied to typeset music. In 'New notation of music, in a letter to Francis Hopkinson, Esq.', *Transactions of the American Philosophical Society* v 3 (1793) p 139–143, Robert Patterson, professor of mathematics in the University of Pennsylvania, proposed to represent notes in four octaves by the letters 'A' to 'G' in upper- and lower-case roman and italic fonts. Punctuation marks such as comma and semicolon indicated duration, and chords were specified by setting the letters that named their constituent notes one above another. Patterson remarked (p 139) that few printers 'especially in America' had music type, and commented that print music was 'very rare among us' because of the expensiveness of 'copperplate impression' (i.e., engraving). No evidence has been found that his proposal was adopted or that Baldwin knew of it. I thank Roy E. Goodman of the American Philosophical Society for

During the next few years Baldwin developed his thoughts. In 1801, after removing from Chester to Prescot, Lancashire, he wrote a sketch entitled *Gramma Musicon; or Letter-Music* and a further manuscript on the 'advantages arising from the new mode of writing and printing music, now first presented to the public, in preference to the Scale of Guido, hitherto practised'.[20] However, until he visited London in June 1803, he seems to have confined his ideas to himself and perhaps some local acquaintances. Presumably a main purpose of this trip was to win support for his ideas from the music trade.

The path that led Baldwin to Stanhope is not known. Although Stanhope 'possessed a taste for music, was a frequent attendant at concerts, and knew most of the best performers, both in England and on the Continent',[21] Baldwin seems to have approached him because of his interests and accomplishments in printing.[22] At the time of Baldwin's trip, efforts to commercialise Stanhope's stereotyping process were known within the London printing trade,[23] and a Stanhope press was or was about to be installed at William Bulmer's printing house.[24]

---

confirming the identity of the author, who is referred to in the article only as 'R. Patterson'.

[20] Both documents are in CKS U1590/C94.

[21] According to his obituary in *The Annual Biography and Obituary for the Year 1817*, London, 1817, p 183–226 at p 203.

[22] Stanhope wrote in the preface to his undated, never completed *A New Musical Instruction Book* (CKS U1590/C92/1, transcribed in *Figure 7.5* below), 'Having been occupied, for a considerable time, in improving the invaluable Art of Printing; the late Thomas Baldwin Esq. applied to me to assist him in perfecting a Scheme, invented by him, to express Musical Sounds, by means of Letters and other simple Marks'.

[23] For instance, Wilson's order to the letter-founder Vincent Figgins to cast new type for use in stereotyping was discussed at April 1803 meetings of the London Society of Master Letter-Founders (see A[lbert] E[dward] Musson, *Trade Union and Social History*, London, 1974, p 148). Although Wilson established his Stereotype Office in 1802, the first book that he printed from stereotype plates was not published until 1804 (Turner, *op. cit.*, p 29, p 35–37 and p 47).

[24] J[ohn] Johnson wrote in *Typographia, or the Printers' Instructor...* (London, 1824, v 2 p 536) that 'the first [Stanhope] press was finished in the year 1800, and its powers were tried at the office of Mr Bulmer'. *Specimens of Typography, without the Use of Balls, executed at the printing press lately invented by Earl*

In response to Baldwin's approach, Stanhope asked him to send details of his scheme to Mrs Walburga Lackner, a pianist employed in Stanhope's household from 1802, whose musical advice he greatly valued.[25] Strikingly little has been known about her,[26] although Stanhope's biographers suggested that her presence in his household led him and his wife to separate in 1806.[27] In his will, written on 22 November 1805 and proved on 5 March 1817, Stanhope asserted:

Stanhope was 'printed by William Bulmer and Co. at the Shakspeare Printing Office, Cleveland-Row' with an imprint date of 1803 (a copy of this unpublished work is in Lincolnshire Archives, RA/4/D/5). It appeared not later than August 1803, as Wilson's draft letter refers to 'specimens … printed, with this newly invented printing press by Mr Bulmer'. The ledger of Stanhope's bank account with Coutts & Co. records his payment of £105/1/– to Bulmer on 25 August 1803, presumably for printing *Specimens* and perhaps for other trials of the Stanhope press. Only one other payment to Bulmer—of £40 on 20 August 1804—is recorded in this ledger between 1799 and 1816. I am very grateful to the Earl of Harrington and the Trustees of the Chevening Estate for permitting Stanhope's bank ledgers to be examined, and to Tracey Earl and David Luck of the Coutts archive for extracting details from Stanhope's accounts with that bank. (Traditionally, ink was transferred to the surface of type by means of ink balls: see Philip Gaskell, *A New Introduction to Bibliography*, Oxford, 1972, p 126. Stanhope's innovation was to replace them with a cylindrical roller. According to T[homas] C[urson] Hansard, *Typographia: An historical sketch of the origin and progress of the art of printing…*, London, 1825, p 622, Stanhope 'spared no expense in endeavouring to find a substance with which to cover his rollers' but did not develop a fully satisfactory way of applying ink by this method.)

[25] To pay for her services Stanhope had Coutts & Co. transfer £105 from his account to her account every four months from December 1802 to December 1816. The ledgers of her account (also at Coutts) indicate that she used this money principally to fund investments and not to pay expenses of the Stanhope household. I am grateful to David Luck for transcribing these ledgers.

[26] Stanhope and Gooch, *op. cit.* in note 1 above, said (p 252) that she was 'a foreigner of whose origin and early history nothing is known'.

[27] *ibid.*, p 252. Perhaps this is confirmed by Joseph Farington's 8 April 1806 diary entry that 'Lord Stanhopes behaviour to his wife Lady Stanhope has caused her to obtain a separate maintenance. By the management of Sir Joseph Banks, His Lordship has settled £1500 a year upon Her. — to force Him to this He was threatened with being proceeded against for adultery' (Kathryn Cave (ed.), *The Diary of Joseph Farington* v 7, New Haven, 1982, p 2711). Banks, who was a trustee of Lady Stanhope in the deed of separation dated 30 August 1806 (copies in CKC U1590/T162), knew both parties: Louisa Stanhope was his cousin (see 'A pedigree of the Banks family…', in Harold B. Carter, *Sir Joseph*

> Whereas some years ago my Wife Louisa did, with my consent and approbation, engage Mrs Walburga Lackner (born Pachmann) to give up giving Lessons in music and to agree not to play at concerts for money, and whereas that was a great sacrifice on the part of the said Mrs Lackner, on account of her extraordinary talents in the Art and Science of music, I give and bequeath unto the said Mrs Lackner the sum of Five Thousand Pounds of lawful money of Great Britain, and also all my music Books, Organs and other musical Instruments whatsoever.[28]

As recounted in the next chapter, she was born in Bohemia, probably in Prague. In England she signed her name 'Walburga Lackner',[29] and her name was so recorded in her English bank and stockbroking accounts. The inscription 'Mrs Lackner' on the inside front cover of a book published in London in 1802 appears to be in her handwriting.[30] However, she was addressed as 'Madame de Lackner' in an 1804 letter from her sister in Bohemia,[31] and was named 'Mrs de Lackner' in the porters' books of the piano maker John Broadwood & Son.[32] Stanhope's employee Samuel Varley

---

Banks, 1743–1820, London, 1988, inside front cover and following page), and from 1778 Banks was president of the Royal Society of London, of which Stanhope had been a fellow since 1772. I thank Neil Chambers for the information that no record of Banks's involvement in this settlement is found in his extant correspondence of 1805–1806.

[28] Stanhope's original will is in TNA PROB 10/4134. The court copy of this will (TNA PROB 11/1590) was inaccurately transcribed. The extracts of the will printed in *The Times*, 7 March 1817, p 3, and in Stanhope and Gooch, *op. cit.*, p 275–276, are incorrect and incomplete.

[29] For instance, on her 15 April 1817 receipt and note to Alexander Murray (of Murray & Legrice, solicitors to Stanhope's estate) in CKS U1590/E208.

[30] G[eorge] M[urgatroyd] Woodward, *The Musical Mania! for the Year 1802, delineated in six sketches of musical amateurs…*, London, 1802, copy at Harvard University Houghton Library, Harry Elkins Widener collection, catalogue no. HEW 12.12.17 F. I am grateful to Emily Walhout for advising that Mr Widener bought this copy in 1909 from the Philadelphia rare-book dealer Charles Sessler and that its prior provenance is unknown.

[31] Therese Sternfeld→Walburga Lackner, 19 September 1804, in Státní oblastní archiv v Praze [Regional State Archives in Prague]. I thank Jiří Smitka for supplying a copy of this letter and Jiří Ševčík for obtaining a transcription of it.

[32] In documentation of transfers of pianos in 1803 between Stanhope's homes in Kent and London. I thank Robert Simonson for transcribing this and other entries from the Broadwood archive in the Surrey History Centre.

called her 'Mrs De Lackner' in one letter,[33] although in other letters he named her 'Mrs Lackner'. Almost certainly she was the 'Mrs de Lackner' whose adaptation for the piano forte of a 'Second Set of Six Original German Waltz's' was 'engraved, printed & sold by E[dward] Riley' in London *c*1800.[34] Nothing is known of Mr [de] Lackner who died not later than June 1804,[35] although there is an indication that he might have been buried in England.[36]

Benjamin Silliman, the visiting American chemist who met Stanhope in London in 1805,[37] described her as German, an understandable mistake because German at that time was the administrative language of Bohemia (which was ruled by the Habsburg monarchy, based in Vienna) and therefore may have been her first language:

> There was a German lady present belonging to his [Stanhope's] family; she was performing upon the piano, and his lordship [Stanhope] informed me that such were her talents for musical composition, that she would often play the finest airs, extempore, and thus these delightful effusions of genius were irrecoverably lost, for she could never repeat them without variation. To arrest these fleeting touches of harmony, he had invented a musical instrument similar to the piano, with the keys of which he had connected a mechanical contrivance which necessarily

---

[33] Varley→Stanhope, 26 May 1809?, RI Stanhope papers v 1 p 323. Varley, a jeweller and maker of scientific instruments, was employed by Stanhope from 1801 until Stanhope's death.

[34] Copy at BL g.272.u.(7.). It presumably was printed before Riley's July 1804 bankruptcy (*The London Gazette*, 28 July 1804, p 921), after which he emigrated to New York. No 'first set' in this series has been traced.

[35] The ledger (Baring Archive, ref. 10013 f 130) recording Mrs Lackner's purchase of Louisiana stock in 1804 describes her as a widow. I am grateful to Clara Harrow for this information. The Barings bank was a principal financier of the purchase of Louisiana by the United States of America from France.

[36] See note 52 on page 448 below.

[37] Silliman noted in the 2 June 1805 entry of his 1805–1806 travel journal (Yale University Library ms 450 box 29 folder 19, p 13–17) that he was introduced to Stanhope that evening at the home of the American poet and diplomatist Joel Barlow: 'This is the first time that my plebeian hand has ever grasped the fingers of a Lord. … He is, it seems, a great mechanician & chemist; he solicited me to converse on these topicks, and took my address promising to call and take me to see his stereotype establishment' (p 15–16).

> noted down the music as fast as it was played, the same movement of the keys producing both effects.[38]

No corroboration has been found of Stanhope's intimation that she played 'at concerts for money',[39] and neither the musical instrument that he invented to record her performances nor any example of the notation it produced is known to be extant.

In a letter written in London on 5 June 1803 to 'Miss Lackner, care of Stanhope', Baldwin sent his compliments to Lord and Lady Stanhope (implying that he had met them before then) and provided examples of his current scheme 'of writing music by letters only, without the necessity of any quaver-marks'.[40] These examples were of melodies he had composed—he called one 'Baldwin's Balloon, a Country Dance'—and followed a rule that 'each detached letter is a crotchet, unless it has a line or quaver-mark below it: and two or more joined letters are quavers without any quaver-mark'. He noted the opening bars of another tune, a strathspey, in the following way:

G, 6̲: gag ḋ b̲ | ċḋċ bċb | gag ė ḋ̲ | ėċa ḋbg |

---

[38] [Benjamin Silliman], *A Journal of Travels in England, Holland, and Scotland ... in the Years 1805 and 1806*, 2nd ed., Boston, 1812, v 1 p 164–165. Silliman's name is printed at the end of his preface (p vi) but not on the title-page. Silliman omitted Stanhope's name from this book, which was published while Stanhope was alive, but a subsequent report of the same piano performance (George P[ark] Fisher, *Life of Benjamin Silliman, M.D., Ll. D.*, New York, 1866, v 1 p 149–150) identifies 'his lordship' with Stanhope. Mrs Lackner's name is not stated in either account but the reference clearly is to her. The 1812 book indicates that she performed on 2 June 1805 in the same 'private house' where Silliman met Stanhope, but as Silliman's manuscript journal entry for that day does not mention her it is conceivable that he heard her play on a subsequent occasion. Stanhope's 'contrivance' to record extempore performances is described in the next chapter.

[39] I am grateful to Simon McVeigh for advice that no one surnamed 'Lackner' or 'Pachmann' appears in his database of London performers to the year 1800.

[40] Baldwin addressed this letter (in CKS U1590/C91/1) to 2 Stratford Place, Stanhope's London residence from 1803 to 1808, which he rented from Arthur Annesley, 1st Earl of Mountnorris.

The marks before the colon signified that the work was in G major and had six quavers to the bar. Notes from Middle C to the next higher B had no marks above their names; notes an octave higher had a dot above their names.

The potential of Baldwin's ideas for music printing must have impressed Mrs Lackner and Stanhope, as he soon afterwards signed an agreement with Baldwin, described in Stanhope's 24 June letter to him as 'the Paper we made out together; & of which you have one Copy; & I, another'.[41] In this letter Stanhope said that he has 'been taking a great deal of pain about your music, since I have had the pleasure of seeing you', and proposed a number of changes to the scheme, which he had discussed with several people. He told Baldwin that 'Mr Bulmer disapproves much the double dots for the 2^d series. I have substituted this mark ı for : & T for :',[42] and added that 'Mrs Lackner, L[ad]y S[tanhope], Dr Young, & several other excellent judges approve of the *new mark*; & say it is beyond comparison, more easy to be *read quick*, which (as you know) is the *grand object* to be obtained'.[43]

It seems plausible that Stanhope, who had been elected Fellow of the Royal Society of London in 1772, got to know Bulmer and Young through Society connections. The Royal Society had appointed Bulmer in 1791 to print their *Philosophical Transactions*,[44] and the polymath Thomas Young, whose interests included music, was elected a fellow of that society in 1794.[45]

---

[41] Stanhope→Baldwin, 24 June 1803, in CKS U1590/C91/7. No copy of the actual agreement has been located.

[42] Baldwin had proposed to mark successively higher octaves with increasing numbers of dots above their note-names.

[43] In a postscript Stanhope said: 'I have been writing a tune of Mozart with the new marks. That method is really excellent. The whole appears neat and beautiful.'

[44] Bulmer was appointed because of his superior skills in printing. See Peter Isaac, *William Bulmer: The fine printer in context, 1757–1830*, London, 1993, p 140.

[45] Young studied at the University of Göttingen in 1795. According to George Peacock, *Life of Thomas Young, M.D., F.R.S., &c.*, London, 1855, p 78, Young had clavichord lessons there from the music historian Johann Nicolaus Forkel and attended his lectures at that university.

As Wilson implied in his draft letter, Stanhope's work on stereotype printing stimulated his interest in Baldwin's ideas. Stereotyping was considered especially suitable for works such as schoolbooks, of which multiple copies were expected to be required periodically. When demand for a book exceeded the number of copies on hand, an additional batch could be printed from the stereotype plates, avoiding the expense of storing formes in which the book's type had been set or storing many unsold copies of the book in anticipation of future orders. Also, if a book whose type had not been held needed to be reprinted, the cost of a new setting, which would have to be proofread and corrected, was eliminated.[46]

With greater education, and the consequential rise of literacy, the market for books, particularly schoolbooks, was expected to grow substantially. In his draft letter Wilson cited the 'ingenious and admirable System of Mr Joseph Lancaster' at whose academy 'between *three and four hundred Boys* are daily taught Reading, Writing and Arithmetic by *one* Schoolmaster only', as a result of his 'new method of teaching'.[47] Lancaster's plan to bring education at his academy 'to the industrious classes of the community' was strongly supported by Stanhope. Before March 1803 he subscribed £10/10/– towards children's accommodation there, and together with Lady Stanhope and Mrs Lackner he subsequently subscribed to the building fund for an adjacent girls' school,[48] for which he apparently

[46] In a 27 August 1801 letter (Birmingham University Information Services, Special Collections ms WP/41) to John Wyatt II, proprietor of the journal *The Repertory of Arts and Manufactures*, Stanhope said that the printer Thomas Bensley had advised him that the cost of pieces of type to print a 150-page book and 'to keep them standing for future editions' amounted to £102, 'whereas, by means of the cast [i.e., stereotyped] plates, the same object can be obtained for less than five guineas' [£5/5/–]. However, the economic advantages of stereotyping were subsequently disputed.

[47] Lancaster accomplished this feat by having older boys teach younger boys under his general supervision.

[48] See Joseph Lancaster, *Improvements in Education, as it respects the industrious classes of the community, containing ... an account of the institution for the education of one thousand poor children, Borough Road, Southwark; and of the new system of education on which it is conducted*, London, 3rd ed., 1805, p 20 and p 24.

stereotyped a prospectus.[49] He gave money to maintain schoolmasters trained at Lancaster's institution[50] and subscribed for twenty copies (more than anyone else) of the third edition of Lancaster's book *Improvements in Education.*[51]

Stanhope presumably was attracted to the idea that Baldwin's scheme would allow music to be typeset by the same compositors who set text, which would lower the cost of, and therefore increase the market for, printed music. Music engravers then charged about 5/– to engrave a plate,[52] whereas compositors were paid about 6d per thousand pieces of type set.[53] Baldwin's scheme also would enable compositors to set music next to words in hymnals and music instruction books, which at this time either were entirely engraved or

---

[49] In a 15 December 1804 letter to Stanhope (in CKS U1590/C91/9), Rev. John North wrote that he 'was greatly indebted to you for your stereotype Prospectus of your new School'. The following June Stanhope sent Joshua Gilpin 'a Specimen of *Stereotype Printing* … [which] relates to the *most admirable School*, probably in the whole World' (Stanhope→Gilpin, 5 June 1805, Historical Society of Pennsylvania, in Gilpin Papers v 53, partly transcribed in John Bidwell, 'Joshua Gilpin and Lord Stanhope's improvements in printing', *Papers of the Bibliographical Society of America* v 76 (1982) p 143–158 at p 147–148, with Bidwell's comment that this specimen 'most likely' related to a Lancaster school).

[50] Lancaster, *op. cit.*, p 27.

[51] *ibid.* Subscribers to this edition are listed in unpaginated 'Proposals' included in Joseph Lancaster, *A Letter to John Foster, Esq., Chancellor of the Exchequer for Ireland, on the best means of educating and employing the poor, in that country*, London, 1805. Stanhope and Mrs Lackner continued to support Lancaster's goal of increasing the number of educated children. On 27 October 1813 Stanhope subscribed 30 guineas (Coutts) to the West London Lancasterian Association that was formed to promote universal education in that part of London, and thereby became a member of its committee (see *Schools for All. Report of the first public meeting of the West London Lancasterian Association*, London, [1813], p 6 and *passim*, copy at Goldsmiths' Library, University of London). On 31 March 1814 Mrs Lackner subscribed £5/5/– to this Association (Coutts), and on 21 June 1814 Stanhope addressed its annual meeting (*The Baptist Magazine* v 7 (August 1815) p 350).

[52] See Michael Kassler, 'The Bachists of 1810', in Michael Kassler (ed.), *The English Bach Awakening*, Aldershot, 2004, p 315–340 at p 338–339.

[53] Ellic Howe, 'The scale of 1805', in his *The London Compositor*, London, 1947, p 84–94 at p 91–93.

had their letterpress text and engraved music examples issued in separate sections. Although music type had been used in England—notably by Henry Fougt in the late 1760s—it was not commonly employed there when Baldwin approached Stanhope.[54] Engraved music of the time generally was more attractive than typeset music, because the printing of notes, rests and other music symbols from discrete pieces of type containing staff lines to the left and right of a symbol produced breaks between adjacent staff lines and beams. Engravers, by contrast, made straight and curved lines from one music symbol to the next that could be printed without visible breaks.[55]

Following Baldwin's return to Prescot, his collaboration with Stanhope was carried out by correspondence. On 11 July 1803 Baldwin suggested simplifying the notation by eliminating flats, but Stanhope disagreed: 'as to omitting the *flats* (& substituting *sharps*) that will be quite improper. I had already talked to Salomon & others, *on that very subject*, long before I rec'd your last letter'.[56] However, Baldwin and Stanhope agreed not to put '*sharps* or *flats* at the *beginning* of the lines' (in contrast to conventional notation, which restates the key signature at the start of each system), Stanhope remarking that 'Mrs Lackner is of opinion, that *this* will be one of [the scheme's] *principal* recommendations'.[57]

---

[54] See H[erbert] Edmund Poole, 'New music types: invention in the eighteenth century', *Journal of the Printing Historical Society* no. 1 (1965) p 21–38 and no. 2 (1966) p 23–44. On 24 December 1767 Fougt received an English patent, subsequently numbered 888, for his music types.

[55] Curiously, about the time that Baldwin approached Stanhope, the Strasbourg music publisher François Reinhard printed three string quartets by Ignace Pleyel from stereotype plates that had been formed from music type. This was one of the first substantial applications of stereotype technology to music printing but no evidence has been found that Stanhope was aware of it. See 'Ueber die neuesten Erfindungen und Verbesserungen in Musikdruck', *Allgemeine musikalische Zeitung* v 6 no. 45 (8 August 1804) cols. 745–758 at cols. 748–752, and Rita Benton, 'Pleyel as music publisher', *Journal of the American Musicological Society* v 32 no. 1 (spring 1979) p 125–140 at p 126–127.

[56] Stanhope→Baldwin, 11 July 1803, in CKS U1590/C91/7. The violinist and conductor John Peter Salomon is now remembered particularly for having brought Haydn to London in the 1790s.

[57] *ibid.*

Stanhope must have remarked that the new notation had to be able to express figured-bass symbols, because Baldwin wrote to him on 16 July 1803 that ‘I have Mr Webb [sic], Mr Kollman [sic], Mr Atwood [sic], and others at my side’, and his letter of 22 July to Stanhope included an example in letter-music of a melody written above ‘$^{6}_{e}$’ and other proposed figured-bass signs.[58]

As his 21 July letter shows, Stanhope soon became irritated by Baldwin’s lack of relevant knowledge:

> Permit me to be clearly understood. I like *your ideas* in many important respects. I, every day, like *Letter music*, better & better, but every Letter I receive from you, convinces me that you cannot execute your plan *by yourself*. You see only ¼ of the subject; & be assured that the ¾ which I have *to execute for you* (if you permit me to do it,) is far more difficult than the first quarter. For, you will be so good as to recollect, that *you had no idea* of the difference that there is, between the *vivace*, the *brillante*, the *scherzando*, &c. &c. until you heard Mrs Lackner play them successively. You will be pleased to recollect that you have to teach the world, *how* to express, in your *music*, *each* of those Things.[59]

After severely criticising some of Baldwin’s suggested changes to the notation,[60] Stanhope told him in September that he could not continue to work with him, because ‘I cannot really have my name to what I do not approve’.[61] Baldwin then ceded control of the project to Stanhope, who replied, ‘I very highly approve of your declaration “that you are willing to give up every thing you have already adopted, on the appearance of a better system”’.[62]

---

[58] Both letters are in CKS U1590/C91/1. The works at Baldwin’s side probably were Samuel Webbe Sr’s *Harmony Epitomised, being a short explanation of figured basses* (entered at Stationers’ Hall on 14 May 1802), Augustus F. C. Kollmann’s *A Practical Guide to Thorough-Bass* (entered there on 14 February 1801) and—although its publication date is uncertain—Thomas Attwood’s *A Short Introduction to the Piano Forte, containing the scales in all the major and minor keys properely fingered.*

[59] Stanhope→Baldwin, 21 July 1803, in CKS U1590/C91/7.

[60] Stanhope→Baldwin, 12 September 1803, in CKS U1590/C91/7.

[61] Stanhope→Baldwin, 15 September 1803, in CKS U1590/C91/7.

[62] Stanhope→Baldwin, 27 September 1803, in CKS U1590/C91/7.

At Chevening House, his estate near Sevenoaks, Kent, Stanhope kept a printing press of his own design which he used to print a few copies of a page at a time to see how the result looked.[63] In July 1803 he printed an example of the new music notation,[64] but decided soon afterwards that a new font was needed for letter-music. Because it would appear close to words in songs, hymns, textbooks and other printed matter, performers and readers had to be able readily to distinguish the letters that denoted music from other letters on the same page. As the design and casting of a new font would have taken some time, it probably was not ready to print the examples enclosed in Stanhope's 20 August letter to Baldwin, notwithstanding Stanhope's remark nine days later that 'I am glad you are so well pleased with my new Types'.[65]

In his letter to Baldwin dated 23 November 1803, Stanhope sent a 'rough specimen of the new types for letter-music' and advised that he was going to Chevening for a few months and would 'convey the types there to make trials'.[66] By 20 January 1804 he had invested more than £80 on the new typography, telling Baldwin:

> It will give you perhaps pleasure to hear that I have been so *anxious* to do justice to your *excellent* letter music that the *new Types, Punches, Matrasses & casting moulds*, which I have had made, on my own account, on purpose to make the various trials with the letter music, have already cost above 80£; & *many more* must be made, by me, to compleat the plan, in that manner & stile in which I wish it to make it[s]

---

[63] He was required, under the Seditious Societies Act of 1799 (30 George III c.79), to register this press and did so on 30 November 1803 (Howes, *op. cit.* in note 5 above, p 7).

[64] Baldwin wrote in his 22 July 1803 letter that 'I am expecting a printed Copy of the musical Letters'—probably referring to a print of a 'Moderato' that Baldwin had written in letter-music and sent with directions 'To the Printer' in his 12 July letter to Stanhope (in CKS U1590/C91/1)—and added that 'I am extremely glad to hear y[our] own Scheme of Stereotyping goes on so smoothly'.

[65] Stanhope→Baldwin, 20 August 1803, and Stanhope→Baldwin, 29 August 1803, both in CKS U1590/C91/7. In the latter letter Stanhope mentioned that he had a new printing press that was 'inked according to a new method that I have discovered' (see note 24 above).

[66] Stanhope→Baldwin, 23 November 1803, in CKS U1590/C91/7.

> appearance in the world, where I trust, *when once well issued*, it will be permanent, & useful, not only to the *next*, (as you have said) but also to the *present* generation.[67]

It seems almost certain that Vincent Figgins was commissioned to cast the new letter-music font.[68] Stanhope knew Figgins's work for Wilson to cast the type used for preparing stereotype plates of text,[69] and the ledger of Stanhope's bank account (Coutts) records that he paid £50 to Figgins on 23 January 1804 and does not record payments to any other typefounder about this time.[70]

Figure 7.3 reproduces an undated page which contrasts the new types for letter-music with 'the common types used in printing'. It was printed by Wilson at Wild Court, where he kept his presses; his stereotype plates were made at his Duke Street premises.[71] A

---

[67] Stanhope→Baldwin, 20 January 1804, in CKS U1590/C91/8.

[68] Figgins's typographical achievements are described in James Mosley, 'The typefoundry of Vincent Figgins 1792–1836', *Motif* no. 1 (November 1958) p 29–36.

[69] See note 23 above. Turner, *op. cit.*, p 29–30, reports that Wilson engaged Figgins in June 1802 to cast type for Stanhope's stereotype experiments, and Wilson in his draft letter confirmed that Figgins had cast most of the 'original types, employed for forming ... stereotype plates'. Wilson had had prior dealings with Figgins, evidenced in *A Specimen of New Persian Types, in imitation of the Talik Character, cast by Vincent Figgins, for Wilson and Co. of the Oriental Press*, London, 1800 (copy at Goldsmiths' Library, University of London). Wilson used the business name 'The Oriental Press' in several publications relating to that part of the world that were printed at his Wild Court premises.

[70] Stanhope made further payments to Figgins in 1806 and 1809 (Coutts). The bank ledgers do not give reasons for any of these payments.

[71] Thus Stanhope's 1807 *Specification respecting Ships and Vessels* (copy at BL 8826.dd.31) bears the imprint 'London: stereotyped by A. Wilson, Duke Street, Lincoln's Inn Fields, and printed by him, in Wild Court, at the iron press of the second construction, invented by Earl Stanhope'. See also Wilson's 1808 'Plan for the Establishment of the British Stereotype Company', printed in Turner, *op. cit.*, p 45–46. Wilson advertised in *The Times*, 4 February 1804, p 1, that he was 'now prepared to undertake the printing of works by stereotype plates' according to Stanhope's improved process. The first such publication was printed in the latter part of August 1804 (*ibid.*, p 35–37; *The Times*, 16 August 1804, p 3).

The New Types made for Letter-Music.

AAAAAAAAAAAAAAAAAAAAAAAAAAAAAAAAAAAAAAAAA

BBBBBBBBBBBBBBBBBBBBBBBBBBBBBBBBBBBBBBBBB

CCCCCCCCCCCCCCCCCCCCCCCCCCCCCCCCCCCCCCCCC

DDDDDDDDDDDDDDDDDDDDDDDDDDDDDDDDDDDDDDDDD

EEEEEEEEEEEEEEEEEEEEEEEEEEEEEEEEEEEEEEEEE

FFFFFFFFFFFFFFFFFFFFFFFFFFFFFFFFFFFFFFFFF

GGGGGGGGGGGGGGGGGGGGGGGGGGGGGGGGGGGGGGGGG

A A A A A A A A A A A A A A A A A A A A A A A A A A A A A A A A A A A A A A A A A

B B B B B B B B B B B B B B B B B B B B B B B B B B B B B B B B B B B B B B B B B

C C C C C C C C C C C C C C C C C C C C C C C C C C C C C C C C C C C C C C C C C

D D D D D D D D D D D D D D D D D D D D D D D D D D D D D D D D D D D D D D D D D

E E E E E E E E E E E E E E E E E E E E E E E E E E E E E E E E E E E E E E E E E

F F F F F F F F F F F F F F F F F F F F F F F F F F F F F F F F F F F F F F F F F

G G G G G G G G G G G G G G G G G G G G G G G G G G G G G G G G G G G G G G G G G

The Common Types used in Printing.

AAAAAAAAAAAAAAAAAAAAAAAAAAAAAAAAAAAAAAAAA

BBBBBBBBBBBBBBBBBBBBBBBBBBBBBBBBBBBBBBBBB

CCCCCCCCCCCCCCCCCCCCCCCCCCCCCCCCCCCCCCCCC

DDDDDDDDDDDDDDDDDDDDDDDDDDDDDDDDDDDDDDDDD

EEEEEEEEEEEEEEEEEEEEEEEEEEEEEEEEEEEEEEEEE

FFFFFFFFFFFFFFFFFFFFFFFFFFFFFFFFFFFFFFFFF

GGGGGGGGGGGGGGGGGGGGGGGGGGGGGGGGGGGGGGGGG

Printed by Andrew Wilson, Wild Court, Westminster.

Figure 7.3 The new type font designed for letter-music (in Centre for Kentish Studies U1590/C97, by permission of the Centre manager and the Trustees of the Chevening Estate)

principal distinguishing characteristic of the letter-music types was that each letter had the same width. To achieve this, extra space was appended to smaller-sized letters and some strokes of letters were made thicker than in 'the common types'. Although fixed-width numerals had often been used in England to typeset mathematical tables, this seems to have been the first use of fixed-width letters in English typography.

Stanhope recognised that if letter-music were to have widespread appeal it could not be limited to expressing melodies such as those Baldwin had rendered into 'short hand'. Because piano music (including works in which a piano is accompanied by a voice or another instrument) was the most popular kind of music printed at this time, the notation had to be extended to express the separate parts played by a pianist's right and left hands, and also to represent chords. Stanhope and Baldwin seem to have agreed that music to be played by the right hand would be set above music for the left hand, as in conventional music notation, but that the constituents of a chord played by either hand would be set one after another, rather than (as in common notation) one above another. Stanhope's specification of a fixed-width font clearly enabled vertical alignment of the first letters in chords that both hands had to strike simultaneously.

On 28 December 1803 Stanhope sent a copy of Jan Ladislav Dussek's piano sonata 'The Farewell', op. 44, to Baldwin and asked him to 'translate' its first page, commenting that 'Salomon & others, consider it as a *difficult* piece of music'.[72] With that sonata Stanhope provided twelve paragraphs instructing how the translation should be made, including advice for representing chords. He promised, when this was done, to print the result for Baldwin's '*inspection*, altering your Translation, or not, as occasion shall require. This will be like real business'.[73]

Considerable discussion and experimentation ensued regarding the definition of a chord and how chords should be represented, as indicated in Stanhope's 7 February 1804 letter to Baldwin:[74]

---

[72] Stanhope→Baldwin, 28 December 1803, in CKS U1590/C91/8.

[73] Stanhope's copy of his instructions to Baldwin is in CKS U1590/C91/9.

[74] Stanhope→Baldwin, 7 February 1804, in CKS U1590/C91/6.

I shall now open to you the most exquisite Plan, in my opinion, for the *Chords* yet thought of. — I continue to mean by *Chords*, Notes struck at the same instant of time, whether of the same length or not.

I do not object to your expression of an *interrupted Chord*, more than to yours of a *consecutive holding Chord.* — It is the idea itself which I object to, of *confounding* by any *one* name (such as Chord), 2 ideas perfectly distinct and opposite; namely, Notes struck at the same instant, and Notes *not* struck at the same instant, whether sounded together or not.

What say you to this Case? Are these 5 Notes *one Chord* (consecutive holding) or any other name of a Chord? Or are the 2 first Notes a Chord? for they *sound together*.

Or are the 3 first a Chord? ...

You know how uniformly anxious I have always been to render your admirable Letter Music glanceable; *without which*, I continue to think it would not be worth a Straw. — I can make it *very* glanceable.[75]

Now, I must let you into the *grand Secret*, confessed to be the case by some of the first Performers in the world, of *the Method*, by means of which they can play some of the most difficult Music ... which they have never before seen; and to play it *well*, and at first sight. It is this: —

They cast the Eye on the Upper Note of each of the Chords, in the *Treble* Line; ... and they cast the Eye on the Lower Note of each of the Chords in the Bass Line; and if the Time of the Tune is *too fast* (as it often is) for them to read *quick enough*, all the *other* Notes of those respective Chords; they content themselves with *striking correctly* the said 2 Classes of Notes above described; and they then, from their knowledge of proper Chords, strike *such Chords* as will do well; whether they be the *very same* Chords which are written, or not. — This Method I hold to be exquisite. — Now, the first moment that I was informed of this fact, a luminous idea struck immediately into my mind, relative to *the best method of expressing Chords*, in your Letter Music, so as to render such Chords as glanceable as, in the nature of things, *it is possible*.

It is as follows; namely, to adapt the *Letter Chords* to the *important fact* aforesaid. — This is performed by rendering the Upper Note of each of the Chords in the *Treble* Line, and the Lower Note of each of the Chords in the *Bass* Line, as *quickly legible*, and as *easily visible*, as possible. ...

[75] I am grateful to Margot Charlton for confirming that the Oxford English Dictionary has no record of use of the word 'glanceable' at this time. The word has been revived recently to refer to displayed messages that can be understood at a glance.

> I take the liberty to wish you joy of this discovery, which Mrs Lackner and others consider as the *very best*, of all the *good* things in our Letter Music. I rejoice to be able to add my mite to your endeavours for the public good.[76]

Stanhope's idea, adopted in some later trials of letter-music, was (1) to use larger letters for the highest note of a right-hand chord and the lowest note of a left-hand chord than for the other notes in these chords, and (2) to use less space between letters of a chord than between the last letter of one chord and the first letter of the next. Baldwin earlier had proposed to signify the notes of a chord by placing a 'canopy' such as ⌒ above or below them, but Stanhope pointed out that using smaller intra-chord than inter-chord spacing would do away with two lines of canopies (for the treble and bass parts), saving room on the page. Moreover,

> Chords are of *different lengths*, especially from the *Accents* (Flats & Sharps,) which will of course require [if Baldwin's plan were adopted] Canopies of *different lengths* also. — This encreases the Number of the Types; the expence of the Fount; the Number of Boxes [in which type of the same sort—i.e., pieces used to print a character in a particular font and size—is stored]; the size of the Type Case; the difficulty to the *Printer's Compositor*; the Time of Composing [by the compositor]; and the expence of Composing. — All bad, and useless.[77]

While corresponding about chord representation Stanhope and Baldwin discussed alternative ways to mark the pitch of notes. To gather relevant data Stanhope examined 59,848 notes in 'very fair and excellent specimens' of 'difficult' piano music, recording for each note the 'set' between a C and the next higher B to which the note belonged, and whether it was to be played by the right or the left hand. In December 1803 and January 1804 he sent his summary of these data to Baldwin, observing that the 'richest set'—the one with the most instances—'deserves to be unmarked'. For the right hand,

---

[76] I have transcribed Stanhope's single, double and triple underscorings in this letter by italic letters, underlined letters and doubly underlined letters respectively. The line that Stanhope wrote between the numerator and denominator of the time-signature and the barline that he wrote after the time-signature have been suppressed.

[77] Stanhope→Baldwin, 7 February 1804, in CKS U1590/C91/6.

this set (of which the data had 18,006 instances) began an octave above Middle C. For the left hand, the richest set (with 12,146 instances) began an octave below Middle C.[78]

Sometime later, Stanhope printed and annotated the page reproduced in *Figure 7.4* on page 412 to show the distribution of instances in the sample that he had analysed. By this time he had coined the word 'septave' to refer to a set of seven diatonic and five chromatic notes between a C and the next higher B, and had changed some of the marks that he used to distinguish particular septaves of notes that were to be played by a pianist's right or left hand.[79]

Baldwin died at Prescot on 9 July 1804.[80] Soon afterwards Stanhope began to write a multi-volume book that would bring letter-music to the attention of the public and—as indicated in his draft title-page and preface, transcribed in *Figure 7.5* on pages 414–415—would provide income for Baldwin's 'orphan son'.[81] It seems likely

---

[78] Stanhope→Baldwin, 27 December 1803, in CKS U1590/C91/7, and Stanhope→Baldwin, 30 January 1804, in CKS U1590/C91/6.

[79] I am grateful to Juliet Field of the Oxford English Dictionary for advice that the word 'septave' is not known to have been published before Stanhope's 1806 *Principles* mentioned below.

[80] His death notice in *The Lancaster Gazette; and General Advertiser, for Lancashire, Westmorland, &c.*, 21 July 1804, p 3, said he was 'a man who, from gentleness of manners, highly cultivated mind, and goodness of heart, was highly esteemed by those few who really knew him'. It reported his balloon voyage but not his musical interests, and did not mention his family.

[81] The manuscript title-page and preface are in CKS U1590/C92/1. An earlier draft of this document, marked 'Not Ready for Press (~~to be fair copied~~)', is in CKS U1590/C92/2. No evidence has been found that Stanhope wrote more of this book. The epigrammatic poem on its title-page is taken, but not exactly, from Mary Monck's translation entitled 'On the invention of letters. From Brebeuf', published in her *Marinda. Poems and Translations upon Several Occasions*, London, 1741, p 41. Her reference is to Georges de Brébeuf's *c*1654 French translation of this poem from Marcus Annaeus Lucan[us]'s *Pharsalia*, written *c*61–65 AD. Baldwin is not known to have married, and his 'orphan son' may have been Benjamin Hornby, who was identified in a 4 January 1803 'order of filiation and maintenance' (Lancashire Record Office QSP 2482/83) as a bastard child of 'Thomas Baldwin ... Esquire' and Susannah Hornby, both of Prescot. The word 'Esquire' has been crossed out and 'claypotter' written in this document, but the significance of this alteration is unclear.

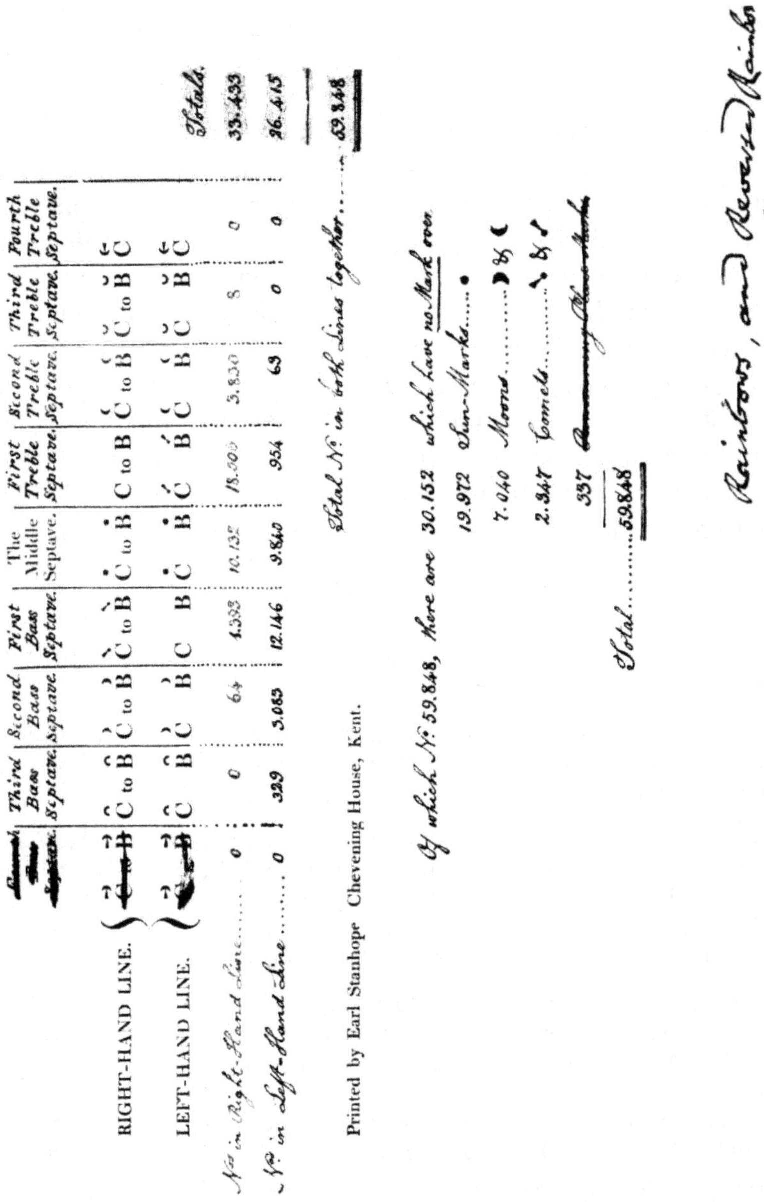

	~~Fourth Bass Septave.~~	Third Bass Septave.	Second Bass Septave.	First Bass Septave.	The Middle Septave.	First Treble Septave.	Second Treble Septave.	Third Treble Septave.	Fourth Treble Septave.	
RIGHT-HAND LINE.	~~C to B~~	C to B	C to B	C to B	C to B	C to B	C to B	C to B	C	
LEFT-HAND LINE.	~~C B~~	C B	C B	C B	C B	C B	C B	C B	C	Totals.
Nos in Right-Hand Line......	0	0	64	4.393	10.132	15.006	3.830	8	0	33.433
No in Left-Hand Line.......	0	329	3.083	12.146	9.840	954	63	0	0	26.415

Total No in both Lines together...... 59.848

Printed by Earl Stanhope Chevening House, Kent.

Of which No 59.848, there are 30.152 which have no Mark over
19.972 Sun-Marks......
7.040 Moons.......... &
2.347 Comets.......... &
337 ~~Remaining Place Marks~~
Total..........59.848

Rainbows, and Reversed Rainbows
&

Figure 7.4 Stanhope's calculation of the distribution of music into septaves (in Centre for Kentish Studies U1590/C97, by permission of the Centre manager and the Trustees of the Chevening Estate)

that these pages, dated '180 ' with no fourth digit, were drafted in 1804, as Stanhope wrote that the book's first volume would be stereotyped and printed by Wilson at Wild Court, whereas in works that Wilson stereotyped and printed between August 1804 and 1809, when his relationship with Stanhope ended,[82] only the Duke Street address appears in Wilson's imprint.[83]

7.3 'Letter-Music' after Baldwin

From 1804 Stanhope corresponded about his musical and other inventions with Rev. John North, who from 1791 was rector of Ashdon, Essex, a living of Gonville and Caius College, Cambridge, from which he had graduated B.A. and M.A.[84] The two had earlier exchanged letters regarding Stanhope's development of a machine to demonstrate logical inferences.[85] They had got to know each other in Geneva, where Stanhope lived from 1763 to 1774,[86] and had a mutual friend in Edmund Goodwyn, a medical doctor who lived at Ashdon

---

[82] Thus Stanhope's 1806 *Principles of the Science of tuning Instruments with fixed Tones* has the imprint 'Stereotyped and printed by A. Wilson, Duke Street, Lincoln's Inn Fields'. Wilson continued to use the Wild Court address in works that he printed by letterpress, e.g., *An Exposition of the Circumstances which gave rise to the Election of Sir Francis Burdett, Bart.*, London, 1807.

[83] See Hart, *op. cit.*, p 393, and Turner, *op. cit.*, p 48.

[84] John Venn, *Biographical History of Gonville and Caius College*, Cambridge, v 2, 1898, p 82.

[85] See Wess, *op. cit.* in note 4 above, p 387–394, who remarks that 'North was a very important sounding board for Stanhope' (p 387). Their correspondence on logic machinery starting in 1801 is mostly in CKS U1590/C86/3 and CKS U1590/C88.

[86] Stanhope used the sentence 'John N. of Ashdon, & John N. whom I knew at Geneva, are the same Person' as a logic example (in Stanhope→North, 17 September 1812, copy in CKS U1590/C88). In North→Stanhope, 15 December 1804 (CKS U1590/C91/9), North recalled 'the years which I passed in that city' [Geneva], and Stanhope commented (in Stanhope→North, 21 July 1806, in CKS U1590/C91/9) that North 'may remember' the 5th Earl of Rochford 'at Geneva'. Stanhope described North as 'an old friend of mine' in Stanhope→ Henry Vassall-Fox, 3rd Baron Holland, 27 January 1806 (BL Add Ms 51828, not finally foliated).

A
NEW MUSICAL
INSTRUCTION BOOK
Together with
HUNDRED
Select Tunes
in
Letter-Music

By Charles Earl Stanhope

This curious Art from Cadmus took its Rise,
Of painting Words, and speaking to the Eyes.
'Twas he who first, in magic Fetters bound
The Airy Voice, and stopt the flying Sound.
The various Figures by his Pencil wrought,
Gave Colour, and a Body to the Thought.

Vol. I
(Price Shillings each Volume.)

Printed, from Stereotype Plates, by Andrew Wilson, Wild Court, Lincolns Inn Fields, for the benefit of an Orphan Son of the late Thomas Baldwin Esq[r]. the Inventor of this Letter-Music.

LONDON
180 .

Preface.

Having been occupied, for a considerable time, in improving the invaluable Art of Printing; the late Thomas Baldwin Esq. applied to me to assist him in perfecting a Scheme, invented by him, to express Musical Sounds, by means of Letters and other simple Marks; instead of using the present common Notation, by *Staves, Notes, Cliffs*, &c.

I have examined his Plan with much care and attention; and I confess that I am struck with the great Advantages it possesses. Its Beauty, Distinctness, and Simplicity, as well as its Cheapness, will sufficiently recommend it. In the opinion of Mr Baldwin, I have been so fortunate as to have made several useful Alterations. But the principal Improvements the Letter-Music has received, are owing to the scientific Conceptions of Mrs Lackner, which are justly termed by the ingenious Inventor, in one of his last Letters to me, her '*bright ideas*'. I now submit the Plan, with confidence, to the judgment of a discerning Public.

STANHOPE.

Chevening House,
near Sevenoaks,
Kent; 180 .

Figure 7.5 Transcript of Stanhope's draft title-page and preface of the proposed first volume of his A New Musical Instruction Book *(in Centre for Kentish Studies U1590/C92/1, by permission of the Centre manager and the Trustees of the Chevening Estate)*

from at least 1795.[87] In 1805 Stanhope named Goodwyn, North and eight others the executors of his will, and Goodwyn was the sole executor of North's will written in 1816.[88]

Although North had taught singing at a prior stage of his career, he had no professional involvement with music at the time of this correspondence.[89] However, he possessed 'many books on the science of music'[90] and kept up with new publications in music theory, acquiring books by John Wall Callcott and Augustus F. C. Kollmann soon after they were published.[91]

Stanhope's work on letter-music and Mrs Lackner's presence appear to have stimulated his interest in another area of music, about which he informed North on 15 November 1804:[92]

> I have discovered a new and most delightful mode of *tuning* Instruments. — I have proved it by Mathematics & Numbers.
>
> Mr Gibbons, the tuner, has just tried it *here* [at Chevening House]. It was tried on a large Piano, against another Piano, by the same Maker, in the same (Tapestry) Room. The *same* piece was played on both Instruments alternately.

---

[87] Robert Gibson, *Annals of Ashdon: No ordinary village*, Chelmsford, 1988, p 271. Goodwyn is remembered as the author of *The Connexion of Life with Respiration* (London, 1788). Consistent with North's residing at Geneva is his friendship with the Geneva-born political writer Étienne Dumont, who lived in London between 1785 and 1814 and stayed with North at Ashdon in 1798 and 1800 (see Alexander Taylore Milne (ed.), *The Correspondence of Jeremy Bentham* v 5, London, 1981, p 372 fn 2) and again in 1804 (see North→Jeremy Bentham, 22 October 1804, and Bentham→Dumont, 30 November 1804, printed in J[ohn] R. Dinwiddy (ed.), *The Correspondence of Jeremy Bentham* v 7, Oxford, 1988, p 290–291).

[88] The court copy of North's will is in TNA PROB 11/1611.

[89] In North→Stanhope, 10 December 1804 (in CKS U1590/C91/9), North described himself as a 'poor country singing master of former days'.

[90] North→Stanhope, 11 November 1804, in CKS U1590/C91/9.

[91] North wrote to Stanhope on 28 June 1806 (in CKS U1590/C91/9) that 'I am at present engaged in reading Callcott's *Musical Grammar* [which was entered at Stationers' Hall on 29 March 1806] & have just received Kollman's [sic] new Publication' (i.e., Kollmann's *A New Theory of Musical Harmony*, entered at Stationers' Hall on 20 May 1806).

[92] Stanhope→North, 15 November 1804, in CKS U1590/C91/9.

> The other Piano was tuned in Dr Hayden's [i.e., Haydn's] Method, of *equal distribution* of the Imperfections; namely, in the method *the most* approved of by Dr Burney, by Mr [Augustus] Meves, Solomon [Salomon] &c.[93]
>
> Mrs L[ackner] tried charming pieces composed by Mozart, Hayden, Hanka [Karl Hanke], Steibelt, Pleyel, by herself &c. in the 12 major, and in the 12 minor Keys. There was *no Comparison.* My Method was found to be superior in *every* Key. And, in some, so superior that it is delightful!

In several letters to Stanhope, North pointed out problems that would have to be surmounted if letter-music were to succeed.

Copyright. Baldwin had wondered in August 1803 whether he could 'translate' a composition into letter-music without becoming liable for prosecution by its author.[94] Stanhope must have raised this question with North, who remarked in the following April that 'the Suit before Ld Ell. concerning the Property in Abraham Newland, may greatly affect the Success of your Undertaking as far as new Music is concerned'.[95]

North was referring to the case of *Hime v Dale* then under consideration at the Court of King's Bench, of which Edward Law (from 1802 first Baron Ellenborough) was Chief Justice. The Liverpool music seller Humphrey Hime had bought rights to verses by Charles Dibdin Jr entitled 'Abraham Newland'. After Hime published a song with these verses, Joseph Dale republished it in London without Hime's permission, and Hime sued him for that act. In 1803 Ellenborough declared *Hime v Dale* a 'nonsuit' because the song was printed on a single sheet and hence (he concluded) was not a book within the meaning of the Copyright Act of 1710. However,

---

93 It seems likely that both pianos were made by John Broadwood & Son. Stanhope's bank account (Coutts) shows payments to that firm of £31/12/– and £107/5/6 on 19 July 1799 and 21 July 1803 respectively, and no payments between 1799 and November 1804 to any other piano maker. An entry in one of the firm's porters' book (at Surrey History Centre, ref. 2185/JB/42/1) shows that a Broadwood grand piano, serial no. 1581, was delivered to Chevening House on 16 July 1799. Stanhope purchased another six-octave Broadwood grand piano, serial no. 2455, on 24 February 1803.

94 Baldwin→Stanhope, 10 August 1803, in CKS U1590/C91/2.

95 North→Stanhope, 27 April 1804, in CKS U1590/C91/9.

on 20 April 1804, the King's Bench set aside this nonsuit so that this particular matter could be brought for decision by a lower court.[96]

North presumably was implying that, if the courts determined (as they eventually did) that even short compositions were protected under the Copyright Act, music could not be 'translated' into and published as letter-music without permission of, and probably payment to, the copyright holder. Such a finding would greatly constrain a publisher's ability to issue popular songs or other pieces both in letter-music and in conventional music notation when the demand for them was greatest.

Combination between music sellers. North recalled hearing that

> the Revival of wooden Types would have made Music much cheaper—& that an Attempt was made not long ago for that Purpose—& that the Attempt was defeated, partly by exclusive Property in new Music—& partly by a Combination between Music Sellers.[97]

If London's leading music sellers combined to stop works whose copyright they owned from being printed in letter-music, or if they refused to sell in their shops compositions printed in letter-music, music published in the new notation would struggle to find a market.

Novelty. In March 1804, when North was beginning his acquaintance with letter-music, he wrote to Stanhope that:

> You are well aware my good Lord that the Method of Letter Music is not new. Rousseau gave up much Time to it & his System is mentioned in his Dict. & much more at large in his 'Projet concernant de nouveaux Signes pour la Musique'—lu par l'Auteur à l'Académie des

---

[96] North undoubtedly read newspaper reports of this case, e.g., in *The Times*, 21 April 1804, p 3, or in *The Morning Chronicle*, 24 April 1804, p 3. Earlier reports about this case were published in both newspapers in January 1804. No decision by a lower court has been traced. As the signature of Abraham Newland, chief cashier of the Bank of England, was printed on banknotes at this time, the phrase 'Abraham Newland' was used eponymously to refer to a banknote.

[97] North→Stanhope, 27 April 1804, in CKS U1590/C91/9. Corroboration of such a combination has not been found. However, evidence was presented in the 1784 legal case *Longman v Babb* that rival music sellers had reached agreement on another matter; see page 374 above.

> Sciences en 1742.[98] I was much pleased with it & have made much Use of it with Success in teaching a near Friend of mine to sing.... It appears plain to me however that Rousseau never knew himself what were the Reasons on which his Project was suffered to fall into Neglect.... Laudatur et alget [praise and neglect] was its History.[99]

Rousseau had used the numerals '1' to '7' to represent *ut*, *ré*, *mi*, *fa*, *sol*, *la* and *si* in any key, but—like Baldwin before he met Stanhope and Mrs Lackner—did not extend his concept to represent polyphonic music in a single part. Nevertheless, the fact that a respected philosopher's proposal to replace common music notation with linear sequences of symbols had failed to be accepted suggested that Stanhope also might find great resistance to letter-music.

Rousseau disclosed in his *Confessions* that a substantial objection to his plan was made by Jean-Philippe Rameau. When reading common music notation, one can see immediately if a passage from a high to a low note includes all the intermediate notes, but in Rousseau's notation this is not obvious at a glance: each numeral has to be considered individually.[100] Rameau's objection was

---

[98] Jean-Jacques Rousseau read his proposal for a numeric music notation to the Académie royale des sciences in Paris on 22 August 1742. It was published posthumously in Geneva in 1781 and reprinted several times. A facsimile, with commentary and an English translation by Bernarr Rainbow, is given in Rousseau, *Project concerning New Symbols for Music, 1742*, Kilkenny, Ireland, 1982. Rousseau illustrated his proposed notation on plate F of his *Dictionnaire de Musique*, Paris, 1768.

[99] North→Stanhope, 11 March 1804, in CKS U1590/C91/9.

[100] In *Les Confessions de J. J. Rousseau* (*Oeuvres complettes de J. J. Rousseau*, Paris, 1793, v 17) Rousseau wrote (p 213): 'La seule objection solide qu'il y eût à faire à mon systéme, y fut faite par *Rameau*. ... [He said:] Si deux notes, l'une très-haute, et l'autre très-basse, sont jointes par une tirade de notes intermédiaires, je vois [in common music notation] du premier coup-d'oeil le progrès de l'une à l'autre par degrés conjointes; mais pour m'assurer chez vous de cette tirade, il faut nécessairement que j'épelle tous vos chiffres l'un après l'autre; le coup-d'oeil ne peut suppléer à rien'. [The only substantial objection that was made to my system was made by Rameau. He said that if two notes, one very high and the other very low, are connected by a passage of intermediate notes in common music notation, I can see at first glance the step-by-step progression of one to the other, but to be sure of this passage in your notation it is necessary that I spell out all your numerals one after another; a glance cannot substitute for this.]

applicable to letter-music, in which melodies were presented linearly regardless of their shape.

Roman alphabet not used everywhere. North asked Stanhope 'if you reject old English Letters [so-called 'black letter' or 'Gothic' type fonts] because they could make no Part of a universal Musical Language pray tell me how are your Roman Characters to extend to Russian Musicians—I say nothing of Arabs &c.'[101]

Doubt about public acceptance of a new music notation. North's strongest criticism of letter-music was that the public were unlikely to adopt a new music notation, particularly one that did not display a melody's higher notes above its lower ones:

> Concerning the Letter Music, you will bear with me I know when I express a doubt whether you can ever bring it into general Use—Music you know my Lord is a Science of Enjoyment & its Professors are all so accustomed to Habits of Enjoyment that you must not expect I fear that any one of its great Proficients will ever trouble themselves to learn a new musical Language—there is moreover a Principle of Analogy between high & low that tho' founded ultimately in a figurative Expression runs thro' all the Cliffs [clefs] of the present Notation tho' it is interrupted in each—this Principle is seducing in itself & is become habitual in every musical Head & so congenial to the whole Mass of the musical Sort that I doubt much whether you will not one day pronounce it to be uneradicable—Your Invention is ingenious—it is simple in its Principle & you combat every difficulty as it arises with magnanimity as well as Success.
>
> Courage—Courage.[102]

Notwithstanding these critical comments, Stanhope continued to experiment with letter-music. In October 1806 he designed, and presumably had built for him, the set of three 'composing cases' shown in *Figure 7.6*, which comprised boxes in which each of the main sorts of type used to print letter-music was separately stored.[103]

---

[101] North→Stanhope, 17 April 1804, in CKS U1590/C91/9. North presumably had proposed the use of old English letters in letter-music to increase the distinction between letters denoting music and letters forming part of words.

[102] North→Stanhope, 7 March 1805, in CKS U1590/C91/9.

[103] The 'pye box' in a composing case was reserved for miscellaneous or broken pieces of type. Quadrats were nonprinting blocks used to adjust line spacing.

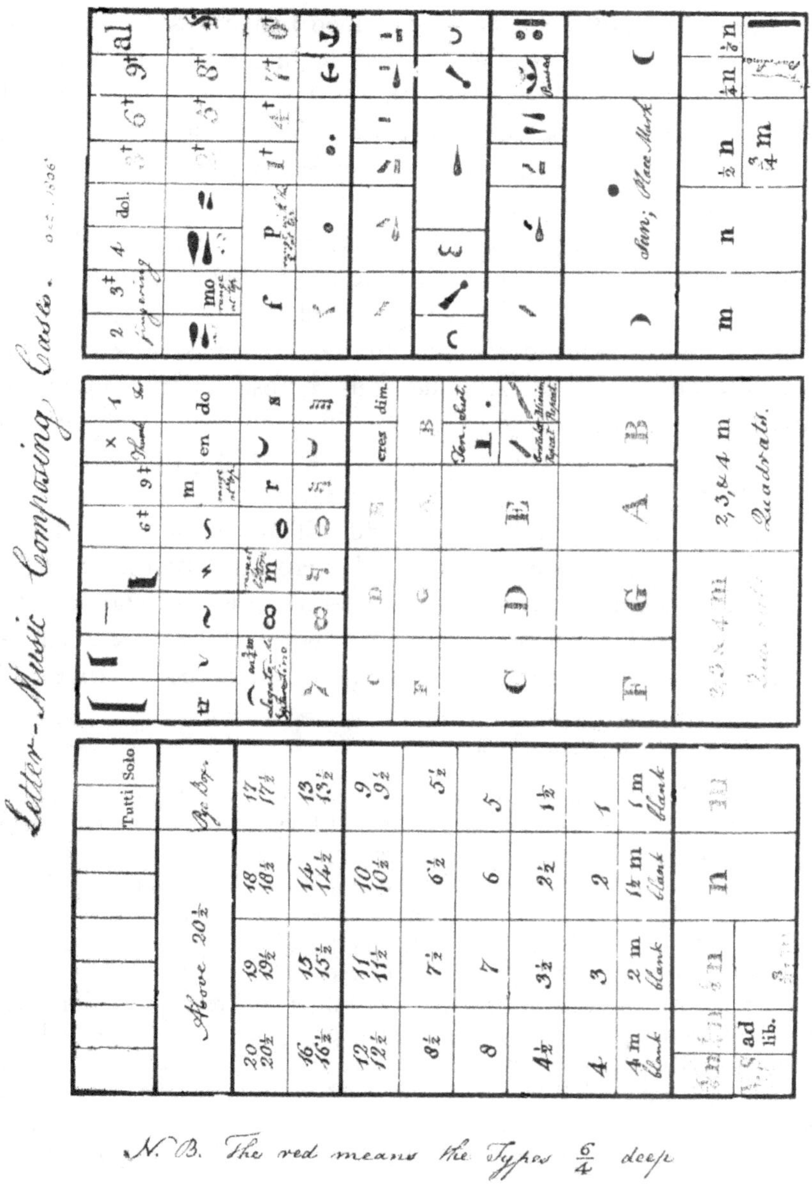

Figure 7.6 Stanhope's design of composing cases for letter-music (in Centre for Kentish Studies U1590/C97, by permission of the Centre manager and the Trustees of the Chevening Estate)

In accompanying notes Stanhope explained that boxes marked † in his diagram held type for bar rests and those marked ‡ held numerals for 'triplets'. Several boxes in these composing cases stored logotypes—sequences of frequently used letters, such as 'Tutti', 'Solo', 'cres', 'dim', 'en' and 'do', that were cast as a single piece of type to speed the compositor's work.[104]

In a complementary document also dated October 1806 and headed 'Characters for the Letter-Music',[105] Stanhope utilised three logotypes and two sizes of wedge symbols to represent long crescendos and diminuendos: e.g., 'cres ◂ ◂ ◂ en ◀ ◀ ◀ do' and 'dim ▶ ▶ ▶ en ▸ ▸ ▸ do'. Although this representation omitted the second 'c' in 'crescendo' and the 'inu' in 'diminuendo', it enabled short crescendos and diminuendos to be marked by printing just the 'cres' or 'dim' logotype followed by wedges.

At several times in 1806 and 1807 Stanhope stereotyped and printed at Chevening House pages which were composed in different variants of letter-music, presumably so that Mrs Lackner and perhaps others could play the examples, tell him how easy they were to sight-read, and suggest to him how the notation might be improved.[106]

---

[104] About this time Stanhope also designed a set of two composing cases—'upper case' and 'lower case'—for typesetters of English-language texts. These cases included boxes to store eight frequently occurring pairs of letters (such as 'th') that were cast as logotypes and replaced traditional ligatures (e.g., 'æ' and 'fl'), which Stanhope had found were comparatively underutilised. A page that he stereotyped and printed at Chevening House to illustrate these cases is reproduced in Hansard, *Typographia*, *op. cit.* in note 24 above, p 476. According to a statement printed by Andrew Wilson (and reprinted in Hart, *op. cit.* in note 6 above, p 408–409), 'a great number' of these cases were built by 'Mr [Thomas] Keeton, carpenter, in Brewer Street, Golden Square', London, for the Cambridge University Press. Wilson's efforts to introduce Stanhope's stereotyping and printing-press technologies to that press are recounted in David McKitterick, *A History of Cambridge University Press*, v 2, Cambridge, 1998, p 265–282.

[105] In CKS U1590/C97.

[106] Copies in CKS U1590/C97. The imprint 'Stereotyped and printed by Earl Stanhope' on these copies implies that he did both tasks personally, although others may have translated the music into letter-music and set the letter-music type. Persons known to have worked for Stanhope on his stereotype experiments at Chevening House include James Fergusson, a compositor who served as

Figure 7.7 Opening bars of Joseph Mazzinghi's arrangement of Handel's overture to Esther *(by permission of Jamie and Michael Kassler, Northbridge, NSW, Australia)*

Figure 7.7 shows the opening bars of a piano arrangement that Joseph Mazzinghi made of Handel's overture to his oratorio *Esther*, and *Figures 7.8* and *7.9* on pages 424–425 reproduce Stanhope's prints of two different transcriptions of this arrangement into letter-music. The 1806 example obviously proved unsatisfactory, as Stanhope marked it in ink: 'Method rejected'.

Stanhope's secretary, and Christopher ('Kit') Matthews (see Hart, *op. cit.* in note 6 above, p 387–388 and p 393, and Stanhope→Nuttall, Fisher & Dixon, 15 November 1808, BL Business & IP Centre in ms box file 1, transcribed in James Mosley's notes to Hart, *op. cit.*, p xxv–xxvi). In May 1807 Fergusson, who was then at Chevening, wrote (Fergusson→Stanhope, 18 May 1807, RI Stanhope papers v 1 p 91) that he had 'delivered the copies of the 2^{d} slip of Lewie Gordon [i.e., copies printed from the stereotype plate containing the second page of this composition in letter-music notation] to your Lordship, when I arrived in town on the 25th of March. They were rolled up into a small scroll.'

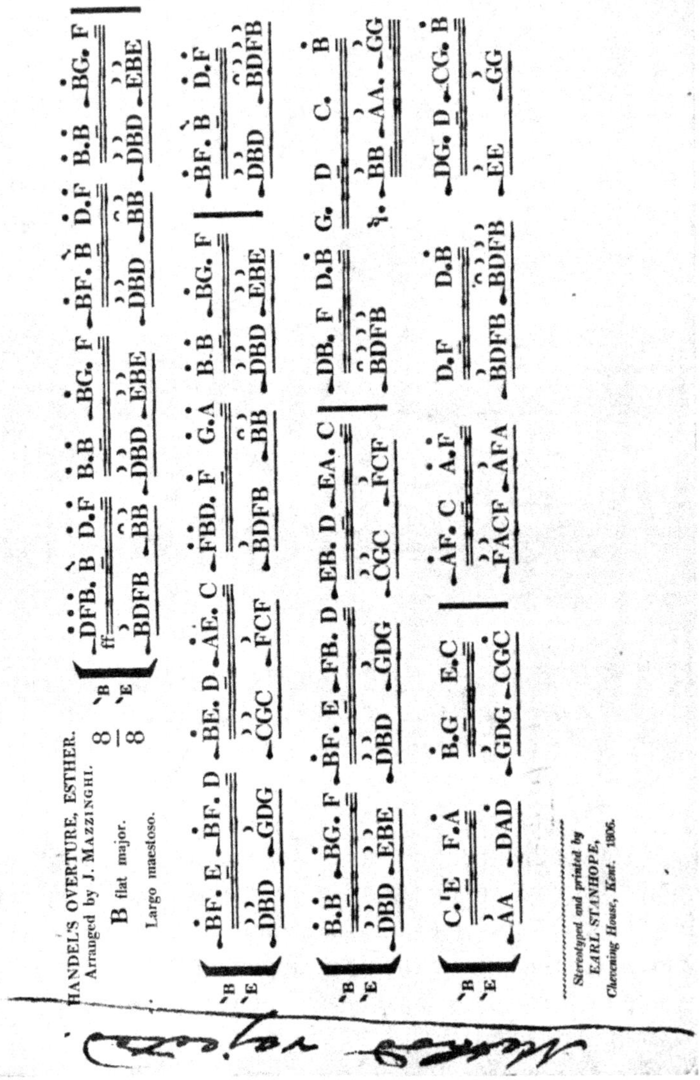

Figure 7.8 Stanhope's rejected 1806 letter-music transcription of Mazzinghi's arrangement of Handel's overture to Esther *(in Centre for Kentish Studies U1590/C97, by permission of the Centre manager and the Trustees of the Chevening Estate)*

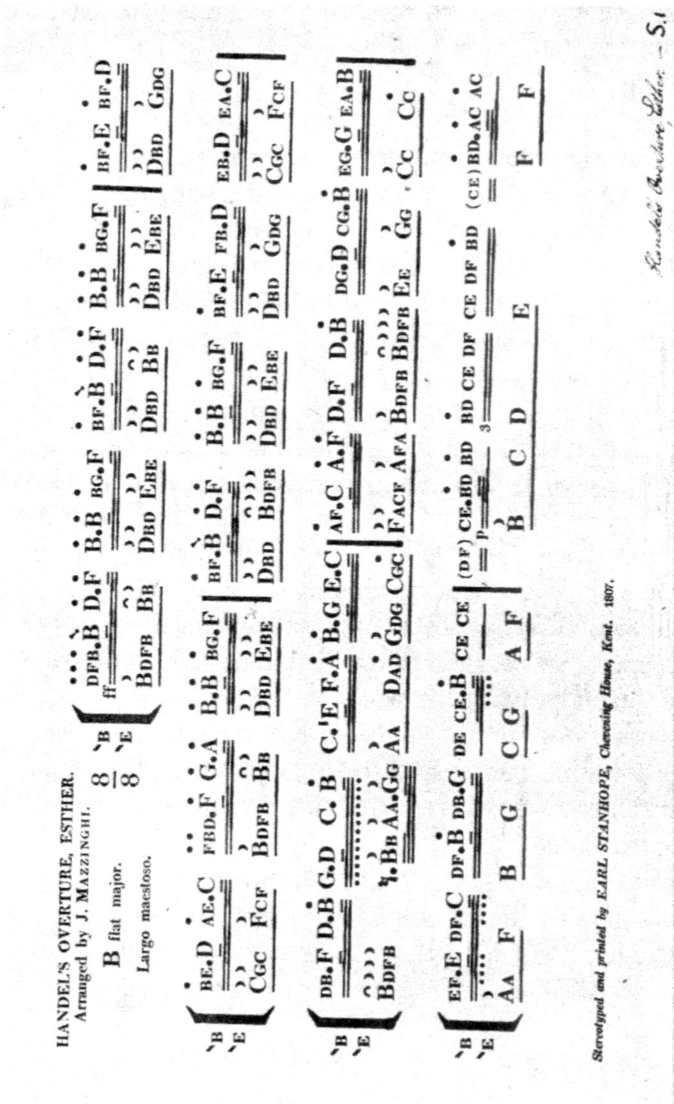

Figure 7.9 Stanhope's 1807 letter-music transcription of the same music (in Centre for Kentish Studies U1590/C97, by permission of the Centre manager and the Trustees of the Chevening Estate)

Figures 7.8 and *7.9* reveal that Stanhope had ceased to follow the method he had described as ‘exquisite’ in his 7 February 1804 letter to Baldwin.[107] The 1806 specimen used letters of a single size to name notes. In the 1807 example upper-case letters had a different meaning in right-hand and left-hand music. For the former they indicated notes not struck simultaneously with other notes in that part; for the latter, the lowest notes of chords.

One reason why Stanhope may have rejected the 1806 method was its inability to present diverse rhythms that occur simultaneously in a single part. As shown in *Figure 7.7*, the first note in the second beat of bar 4 in the right-hand part of Mazzinghi’s arrangement has two stems: the crotchet stem directs the pianist to hold the note G for the entire beat while playing the other notes in that beat. As polyrhythms such as this could not be represented in the 1806 method of letter-music, the information conveyed by that crotchet stem was lost in translation. This fault is repaired in the 1807 example, in which the sequence of dots beginning under the G means that it is to be sustained until the note above the sequence’s final dot is released.

Figures 7.8 and *7.9* show that the ‘translator’ of the music (perhaps Stanhope himself) was not a professional musician. He or she misunderstood the ‘8ve’ indication in the left-hand part of bar 6 to apply only to the first note of the passage. It is also remarkable that the time-signature **c** was rendered unconventionally as 8/8 instead of the more usual 4/4.

No evidence has been found that Stanhope pursued letter-music after 1807. Besides the problems that North had pointed out and other demands upon Stanhope’s time,[108] the following difficulties may have come to his attention and caused him to turn his inventive skills to other areas.

Further development was needed for letter-music to replicate all features of common music notation. By 1807 several facets of common music notation, such as phrase marks, slurs, pedalling, etc., remained to be implemented in letter-music. Stanhope may have

---

[107] See page 409 above.

[108] For instance, in 1807–1808 he was involved in defending a lawsuit that his eldest son Philip Henry (later 4th Earl Stanhope) had brought against him regarding family property. See Stanhope and Gooch, *op. cit.*, p 246–250.

come to realise that common music notation was more complex than he had initially thought, and that developing letter-music equivalents of all the information it conveyed would take considerable further effort and might result in pages not easy to read at sight.

Problems for the compositor. In his October 1806 document 'Characters for the Letter-Music', Stanhope prescribed that, for each system of piano music, five lines of type would be used to set the right-hand part and a further five to set the left-hand part. He named these five lines, from top to bottom, the 'High Manner Line' (in which symbols designating fingering, trills, tremolos and mordents were set, and also the logotypes 'Tutti' and 'Solo'), the 'Septave Line' (in which symbols indicating a note's octave were set), the 'Letter Line' (where letters that named notes were set, together with signs for sharp, flat and natural, rests, and prolongation dots), the 'Value Line' (for marks indicating the duration of notes, including the '3' and '6' that signalled the start of a triplet or sextuplet, and for some articulation signs), and the 'Low Manner Line' (where dynamics, crescendo and diminuendo, and fermata were indicated).

Although the names of a chord's notes were set one after another in letter-music, much letter-music type had to be vertically aligned by a compositor before it could be transferred to a forme and stereotyped into a plate. For instance, within each of the right-hand and left-hand parts of piano music, octave symbols in the Septave Line that related to note-names in the Letter Line had to be placed directly above them, and durational symbols in the Value Line that affected those note-names had to be positioned directly below them. To facilitate vertical alignment, Stanhope specified that every Septave Line, Letter Line and Value Line was to be composed of type having a single fixed (em) width, including blank type (quadrats) that had to be inserted where required. The compositor, accordingly, would place em quadrats in the Septave Line so that its octave symbols were positioned directly above the note-names in the Letter Line to which they referred (and not, for instance, above sharp signs or prolongation dots in that Line).

As mentioned, where a pianist's right hand had to strike a chord (of one or more notes) simultaneously with a chord played by the left hand, the first note-name of the treble-part chord had to be vertically aligned with the first note-name of the bass-part chord. Although the letter-music examples that Stanhope printed appear to have been only for solo piano, he would have known that each system of a song with piano accompaniment contained a third staff for the singer on top of the pianist's two staves, and that a system in an orchestral score could have more than fifteen parallel staves and fill an entire page. If such a score were translated into letter-music, type presenting a flute part near the top of a page would have to be vertically aligned with type presenting a double-bass part near the bottom of that page, in order to show where those instruments struck notes simultaneously.

At this time in England it was common practice for a compositor to set and to justify three to six lines of type in a composing stick and then to transfer this content into a wooden tray, called a 'galley'. He then proceeded to set, justify and transfer the next three to six text lines until the galley was filled with a page of type, including the headers and page numbers.[109] Following this common practice, a compositor of letter-music probably would have set type in a composing stick five lines at a time. If the work to be printed had just one staff in every system—such as a violin part—a compositor who was trained in letter-music presumably could read the first few bars of the work's common music notation, translate them mentally and proceed almost immediately to set the five lines of type that represented those bars in letter-music. He would then transfer these lines into a galley and go on to translate and set the next few bars.

However, this procedure would be inadequate for music with two or more staves in each system. A compositor setting (for example) a right-hand part of piano music needed to take into account the chord-content and rhythm played simultaneously by the pianist's left hand. Although a right-hand part of a bar of piano music might consist only of one semibreve, the number and placement of quadrats required to set that part in letter-music depended upon the number of notes, accidentals, prolongation dots and other content of the accompanying left-hand part. In general, before starting to set type representing the first staff in a system, a compositor of letter-music had to examine the content of all the staves in that system. For most music therefore he would not have been able to typeset directly from

---

[109] See Gaskell, *op. cit.* in note 24 above, p 43–51.

a score in common notation but would have needed, prior to setting, a handwritten transcription of the score that showed for each page where particular letter-music type was to be positioned on each line. This additional preparatory step—whose necessity Stanhope may have come to realise as a result of his trials—would slow the preparation of works in letter-music and increase their cost of production significantly.[110]

Lack of demand by printers. In his August 1803 draft letter Wilson expressed interest in printing music according to the new plan,[111] and he subsequently printed some letter-music specimens for Stanhope (including 'Baldwin's Balloon, a Country Dance').[112] However, Wilson's initial interest does not appear to have persisted to 1807, when he was busy stereotyping and printing books in London and also was engaged in transferring stereotype technology to the university presses at Cambridge and Oxford.[113]

Before using letter-music to write a manuscript that could be handed to a typesetter, an author had to be familiar with that notation. As no instruction-book in letter-music (such as the one Stanhope had begun) was ever published, there was no demand from composers or anyone else to learn the notation, and consequently there was no demand from printers to buy letter-music type or to learn how to set it.

Both Wilson and Stanhope printed sheets headed 'Characters which express Musical Sounds' that provided elemental information about the new notation, such as a 'Scale for beginners' showing how septaves are marked for the right-hand and left-hand parts of piano

---

[110] In addition to the cost of the handwritten transcription, compositors almost certainly would have wanted more than the standard rate to set work requiring extensive vertical alignment. The 1805 scale of prices for compositors' work had provided that unusual setting, e.g., of Hebrew, Arabic and music type, would be 'paid double' (see Howe, *op. cit.* in note 53 above, p 93).

[111] See page 392 above.

[112] In CKS U1590/C97. In contrast to Stanhope, who (as has been shown) printed letter-music examples from stereotype plates in 1806–1807, the examples of letter-music printed by Wilson appear not to have been stereotyped. Their imprints give his Wild Court address rather than his Duke Street address. See page 406 above.

[113] See Turner, *op. cit.*, p 37–43.

music.[114] However, evidence has not been found that these sheets circulated beyond Stanhope's immediate circle.

Although (as recounted in the next chapter) Stanhope approached the London music trade when he wanted prototypes built of his novel musical instruments, he would have had no reason, when contemplating the potential market for letter-music, to make contact with music engravers. They almost certainly would have defamed the new notation, not only because their skills differed substantially from those of typesetters but also because if it was widely adopted their business would be depleted.

It seems unlikely that Georg Jacob Vollweiler's introduction of music lithography to England in 1806–1807, described in Chapter 9 below, affected Stanhope's abandonment of letter-music. No indication has been found that he was aware of Vollweiler's work at this time, although they appear to have had some contact in 1814.[115]

It is curious that William Bulmer, who knew of Stanhope's early work on letter-music[116] and presumably remained acquainted with him, printed a booklet by Samuel Rootsey in 1811 that endeavoured to 'simplify' music notation by using forty-eight lower-case alphabetic letters in roman and italic fonts to stand for the forty-eight chromatic pitches in four octaves.[117] Although the proposed scheme differed fundamentally from that of Baldwin and Stanhope, about which Rootsey presumably had no information, he argued similarly to them 'that five pounds worth of music engraved and sold as it usually is, can be afforded for one shilling if printed by this notation' and remarked that 'stereotype printing could ... be applied [to his notation] with infinite advantage'.[118] His essay of more than fifty pages—which had no effect upon subsequent music printing

[114] Copies of these printed sheets are in CKS U1590/C97.

[115] See pages 488–489 below.

[116] See page 400 above.

[117] S[amuel] Rootsey, *An Attempt to Simplify the Notation of Music...*, London, 1811. The dedication page is dated 1 October 1811.

[118] *ibid.*, p 51 and p 48.

practices—had only one page with common music notation. That page was engraved and Bulmer presumably did not print it.[119]

7.4 Contemporary and Near-Contemporary Notices of Letter-Music

Only two comments about letter-music are known to have been published in the early nineteenth century. On 1 January 1812 A. F. C. Kollmann reported, in the first number of his periodical *The Quarterly Musical Register*, that:

> A few years ago a Mr Baldwin had invented a musical *notation with letters*. As far as we can recollect, the keys of the instrument were by that notation expressed by the letters of their usual denomination, over and under a single line, with marks of distinction for the different octaves, and with the addition of other characters for rests, the lengths of notes, and so forth. But as this invention was nothing more than an altered revival of what is called the ancient *tablatura*, which has been superseded by our modern notation, we suppose that the inventor has not published it.[120]

Kollmann's mention of 'a single line' (compare *Figure 7.2* on page 394 above) suggests that he saw the notation no later than Baldwin's visit to London in June 1803 and did not know of its subsequent development by Stanhope. Perhaps Baldwin had met Kollmann during that visit and had showed him a few examples of *Gramma Musicon*.

In 1819—three years after Stanhope's death—the Leipzig *Allgemeine musikalische Zeitung* recounted some of his work relating

---

[119] According to Peter Isaac, *William Bulmer*, *op. cit.* in note 44 above, p 140, 'there is no evidence that Bulmer ever printed engraved plates'.

[120] [A. F. C. Kollmann], 'A retrospect of the state of music in Great Britain, since the year 1789', *The Quarterly Musical Register* no. 1 (1 January 1812) p 6–28 at p 27, reproduced in Michael Kassler, *A. F. C. Kollmann's* Quarterly Musical Register *(1812): An annotated edition with an introduction to his life and works*, Aldershot, 2008. In the following paragraph of this article Kollmann described Rootsey's notation.

to music.[121] Its unidentified London correspondent remarked that Stanhope had

> sought to return to favour the ancient superseded (because of its incompleteness) tablature, i.e., music notation using the first seven letters of the alphabet. A few years before Earl St[anhope], a Mr Baldwin, M.A., tried to bring forward this kind of notation, which can seem suitable only to those who have insufficient knowledge of proper notation, but it is uncertain whether the Earl knew of this plan.[122]

Because both comments referred to superseded tablature it seems likely that the *Allgemeine musikalische Zeitung*'s reporter, whose article referred to Kollmann and *The Quarterly Musical Register*,[123] read about Baldwin's effort there. Although Kollmann's paragraph about Baldwin did not mention his M.A. degree (Cambridge, 1768), it is conceivable that he had told Kollmann of it during their suggested meeting and that Kollmann subsequently passed this detail on to the *Allgemeine musikalische Zeitung*'s London correspondent.[124]

---

[121] In 'Uebersicht des Zustandes der Musik in England [Review of the state of music in England]', *Allgemeine musikalische Zeitung* v 21 no. 51 (22 December 1819) col. 865–873 at col. 865–867. The article noted that the acoustician Ernst Florens Friedrich Chladni had reviewed Stanhope's *Principles of the Science of tuning Instruments with fixed Tones* in this journal's v 17 no. 3 (18 January 1815) col. 37–41.

[122] 'versuchte der Graf St., die uralte und ihrer Unvollkommenheit wegen abgeschaffte Tabulatur, oder Notenschrift mit den ersten sieben Buchstaben des Alphabets, wieder in Aufnahme zu bringen. Diese Art Notation, welche nur denen noch bequem scheinen kann, die mit den eigentlichen sogenannten Noten nicht genug bekannt sind, versuchte, einige Jahre früher als der Graf St., ein Herr Baldwin, M. A. wieder hervorzuziehen; ob aber der Graf dessen Plan gekannt habe, ist ungewiss' (*ibid.*, col. 867).

[123] *ibid.*, col. 868–869.

[124] Baldwin abbreviated his degree as 'A.M.' on the title-pages of his publications.

STANHOPE'S NOVEL MUSICAL INSTRUMENTS

Michael Kassler

Besides the new technology for music printing described in Chapter 7, Stanhope developed several novel musical instruments. In June 1804 *The Morning Chronicle* reported that he had devised a mechanism to record extempore keyboard performances:

> Earl Stanhope, it is said, has invented, and after much labour brought to perfection, a contrivance applicable to any musical machine played on by the finger; as an organ, harpsichord, or piano; by which the music is printed by the mere operation of touching the note, so that copies of the music may be multiplied as often as any tune is played over.[1]

A news item published the following month in Paris gave a few further details:

> Le comte de Stanhope a inventé une machine au moyen de laquelle un pianiste en l'adaptant à son instrument, écrit sa musique à mesure qu'il l'exécute. Le mouvement qu'il donne aux touches, se communique à la machine qui copie, et le morceau achevé, on le trouve parfaitement noté dans toutes ses parties.
>
> [Earl Stanhope has invented a machine by means of which a pianist who applies it to his instrument writes music in the way he plays it. The motion that he gives to the keys is communicated to the copying machine, and when the piece is finished one finds it perfectly noted down in all its parts.][2]

---

[1] *The Morning Chronicle*, 8 June 1804, p 3. This news was widely republished, for example in the *Mercantile Advertiser* [New York], 7 August 1804, p 3.

[2] *Journal des débats*, 5 July 1804, p 2. The Leipzig *Allgemeine musikalische Zeitung*, v 6 no. 47 (22 August 1804) col. 791, had no further information beyond reports in English and French newspapers but considered the matter so

It is not clear whether Stanhope knew of earlier similar inventions when he started to design this machine. Charles Burney, who had been elected a fellow of the Royal Society in 1773, a year after Stanhope, had written about them in his account of his tour to Germany in 1772, where he said that

> the first idea of such a contrivance being practicable, was suggested to the Royal Society of London, in a paper written by the late revd Mr Creed, and sent to the president, 1747, under the ... title ... *A demonstration of the possibility of making a* machine *that shall write* extempore voluntaries, *or other pieces of music, as fast as any master shall be able to play them....* This paper was published in the same year, in The Philosophical Transactions[3] ... and the author's idea always appeared to me so feasible, that I have long wondered at its not having been executed by some ingenious English mechanic. ... The machine was to consist of two cylinders, which were to be moved by clock-work, at the rate of an inch in a second of time; one of these was to furnish paper, and the other was to receive it when marked by pins, or pencils, fixed at the ends of the several keys of the instrument, to which the machine was applied.[4]

Burney added that [Johann Friedrich] Unger had described a similar concept in Germany, and that a machine 'which so much resembles that proposed by ... Creed' was built in Berlin by [Johann] Hohlfeld.[5]

---

significant that they wanted to share the news with their readers: 'Nach englischen und französischen öffentlichen Blättern hat der Graf von Stanhope in London eine Maschine erfunden, vermittelst welcher ein Klavierspieler, wenn er sie mit seinem Instrumente in Verbindung bringt, seine Musik, wie er sie eben spielt, niedergeschrieben erhält. Die Bewegung, die er den Tasten giebt, theilt sich der Kopirmaschine mit, und mit dem letzten angegebnen Tone ist auch das ganze Stück vollkommen auf dem Papiere. Wir haben bisher noch keine nähere Nachricht darüber erhalten können, halten aber die Sache für so bedeutend, dass wir auch diese vorläufige mit unsern Lesern theilen wollten.'

[3] v 44 no. 483 p 445–450. Nothing is known of Creed. His paper was transmitted to the Royal Society by John Freke, surgeon to St Bartholomew's Hospital, London.

[4] Charles Burney, *The Present State of Music in Germany, the Netherlands and United Provinces*, London, 1773, v 2 p 214–216.

[5] *ibid.*, p 216–218. Unger's description was written in 1752; Hohlfeld's machine was built in 1753. For their work see [Johann Georg] Sulzer, 'Description d'un instrument fait pour noter les piéces [sic] de musique, à mesure qu'on les exécute sur les clavecins', *Nouveaux mémoires de l'Academie Royale des*

Burney subsequently supported the Belgian-born mechanician John Joseph Merlin, who came to London in 1760,[6] and seems likely to have influenced Merlin's construction *c*1780 of an apparatus which resembled the one proposed by Creed and built by Hohlfeld. Hohlfeld's machine was destroyed by fire,[7] but Merlin's apparatus, restored in the twentieth century, survives in the Deutsches Museum, Munich.[8]

Although Stanhope must have realised by 1805 that he had not originated the idea of a machine to transcribe keyboard performances,[9] his plans for such a machine—as revealed in letters to

---

sciences et belles-lettres, Année 1771, Berlin, 1773, p 538–546. A recent account of these developments is given in Peter Schleuning, 'Die Fantasiermaschine', *Archiv für Musikwissenschaft* v 27 no. 3 (1970) p 192–213.

[6] According to Anne French, 'Merlin, his friends, his patrons and his portrait', in the exhibition catalogue *John Joseph Merlin: the ingenious mechanick* (London, 1985, p 17–46 at p 18), 'Dr Burney was ... arguably Merlin's greatest patron' and owned a number of his musical instruments. An advertisement in *The Morning Post and Daily Advertiser*, 26 February 1785, p 3, records that Burney performed 'in the Court of King's Bench' on an innovative instrument by Merlin that could be played both as a harpsichord and as a piano forte, in order to help him get an English patent for it. (Merlin's patent was granted on 12 September 1774 and subsequently numbered 1081.)

[7] Schleuning, *op. cit.*, p 208.

[8] Inventory no. 43872. The recording apparatus is 'mounted on a frame which fits above the soundboard' of a Merlin combined harpsichord and piano forte dated 1780 on its nameboard (see Frances Palmer, 'Merlin and music', in *John Joseph Merlin, op. cit.*, p 85–110 at p 99). The restoration is briefly described in Franz Fuchs, *Der Aufbau der technischen Akustik im Deutschen Museum*, *Deutsches Museum Abhandlungen und Berichte* v 31 no. 2 (1963) p 48–49.

[9] A letter to Stanhope dated 25 March written from 'Lansdown house' in the French language, of which only the last page and address portion survive in CKS U1590/C91/9, includes 'une passage qui peut intéresser' [a passage which may interest] Stanhope. This passage, copied from Dieudonné Thiébault, *Mes souvenirs de vingt ans de séjour à Berlin*, Paris, 1804, v 5 p 53–54, refers to Sulzer and briefly describes a machine—no doubt Hohlfeld's—that recorded keyboard performances. The writer of this letter (whose identity is confirmed by comparing its handwriting with that of his letters to Jeremy Bentham in BL Add. Ms 33543) was the Rev. John North's friend Étienne Dumont (see note 86 on page 413 above), who was then employed by William Petty *earlier* FitzMaurice, 1st Marquess of Lansdowne.

him from John North—appear to have extended the prior art significantly. North wrote on 15 December 1804 that

> I have heard of Instruments which perform some of the Functions which are included in your new Instrument—such as recording Voluntaries & Capricios [sic]—but none than [sic] have the Facility of discriminating the different Characters of Musick in so precise a Manner. In fact I do not know any Treatise in which the Terms brillante, vivace & others which denote Expression are clearly defined—So that you must get your Instrument to assist in making these Definitions—& if you could prevail on Mad^e Lackner to write a new & short Treatise at the same Time, we may send a great Deal of vague Stuff into the Vicum vendentem thus et odores[10]—as the antients did. ...
>
> The Addition to your Instrument of being never out of Tune is a Circumstance which must enhance its Value to a very considerable Degree—& is a Philosopher's Stone amongst Musicians. I heartily wish it may come within the Compass of an ordinary Man's Pocket & I should be very glad to order one to-morrow.[11]

In March 1805 North commented further:

> I have some Aperçu concerning the practicality of a recording Instrument—but a repeating one is not yet within the Limits of my Comprehension. I have a remote Idea of its transposing Power but I should perhaps be puzzled greatly to put all these Things into any intelligible Language.[12]

North's statement that the device could not go out of tune suggests that Stanhope then was designing an apparatus to record music played on an organ rather than a piano, and the remark about a 'repeating' instrument implies that it had a capability to 'read' rolls of paper on which earlier performances had been marked. The first hypothesis is corroborated by the circumstance that an organ invented by Stanhope that could 'mark off extempore music' was auctioned in 1817 (as noted below), and his bank ledger (Coutts) shows that he paid the organ builders Flight & Co. and Flight & Robson amounts

---

[10] i.e., that part of town where incense and scents are sold [and wrapped in discarded writing paper], a quotation from Horace, *Epistles*, book II, 1, 169.

[11] North→Stanhope, 15 December 1804, in CKS U1590/C91/9.

[12] North→Stanhope, 7 March 1805, in CKS U1590/C91/9.

totalling £443/13/– between May 1805 and October 1806.[13] Presumably at least part of these payments was for their work to build such an apparatus.

News of Stanhope's efforts came to the attention of the composer and writer John Wall Callcott. He was planning to lecture in autumn 1807 on 'machines invented to write down extemporary performances' and asked Stanhope for 'an account of your improvements contrasted with those of Creed and Unger'.[14] Stanhope's response has not been found, and the lecture on which Callcott was working is not known to have been delivered, perhaps because of the onset of illness that led to his admission to a private lunatic asylum on 30 May 1808.[15]

Stanhope's mechanism may have been seen by the inventor John Isaac Hawkins, although contemporary documentation of this is lacking. In 1869 Alfred Savage, who contributed frequently to the journal *English Mechanic and World of Science* using the pseudonym 'The Harmonious Blacksmith', remarked upon several endeavours to record extemporaneous keyboard performances and mentioned that

> In Lord Stanhope's apparatus the notation was on a sheet of paper as wide as the keyboard, and had to be translated into ordinary notation before it could be repeated; but in the simpler mechanism of Hawkins's, the performance was registered on a sheet of paper of the ordinary width, in his remarkably simple notation, which could be read and the performance repeated at sight.[16]

---

[13] Flight & Co. became Flight & Robson in 1805 when Joseph Robson became a partner of Benjamin Flight. For Flight & Robson and their construction of experimental organs see Rachel Cowgill, 'The London Apollonicon recitals, 1817–32: a case study in Bach, Mozart and Haydn reception', *Journal of the Royal Musical Association* v 123 no. 2 (1998) p 190–228.

[14] Callcott→Stanhope, 1 August 1807, RI Stanhope papers v 1 p 245. Earlier that year Callcott published a pamphlet (its preface is dated 15 June 1807) entitled *Plain Statement of Earl Stanhope's Temperament* and exchanged letters with Stanhope on that subject.

[15] See H. Temple Phillips, *The History of the Old Private Lunatic Asylum at Fishponds, Bristol, 1740–1859*, Master of Science thesis, University of Bristol, 1973, p 262. I am indebted to Richard Hunter for this reference.

[16] 'The Harmonious Blacksmith', 'A task for designers', *English Mechanic and Mirror of Science* [as the journal was called in 1869] v 9 no. 213 (23 April

Between May 1808 and July 1810 Hawkins opened a Museum of Useful and Mechanical Inventions in London. He said in its 1808 catalogue that he planned to introduce there, 'as fast as the public shall ... afford the inventor a prospect of compensation', an 'apparatus, to be applied to a piano forte or organ, that shall write down in a legible character, any extemporaneous music which may be played on the instrument'.[17] In the museum's 1810 catalogue he said that he had at least 'ample descriptions and drawings' of this apparatus, which he would sell for £500.[18] The proposed output of this apparatus, which he presumably developed further after then, seems likely to have been his 'new system of musical notation', in which each keyboard key was represented by a vertical column down which a line segment was drawn of length proportional to the time that the key was depressed.[19]

The London piano maker David Loeschman was engaged by Stanhope to make prototypes of two of his other musical inventions.

1869) p 111. In 1872 the same author described Hawkins as his 'late clever friend' ('Composing pianoforte', *English Mechanic and World of Science* v 16 no. 405 (27 December 1872) p 362). Both articles indicated that Hawkins's contrivance had been 'published', but no such publication has been found. The identity of the author of these articles is disclosed in 'Death of "The Harmonious Blacksmith"', *English Mechanic and World of Science* v 27 no. 680 (5 April 1878) p 85.

[17] *Plan and Catalogue of Hawkins's Museum of useful and mechanical Inventions*, London, 1808, p 11–12 (copy in Institution of Civil Engineers Library, London, catalogue no. 608 VCTV 18). Hawkins said that he had conceived this invention in 1800 but did not say in this catalogue that he had built it.

[18] *Catalogue of Hawkins's Museum, of useful and mechanical Inventions*, London, 1810, p 9–10 (copy in Wellcome Library, London, catalogue no. Closed Stores EPB/P 27939/P). This apparatus also was applicable to a violin or violoncello. Hawkins noted that 'working models or complete machines' were available for some of his inventions but does not say in this catalogue that he had produced more than descriptions and drawings of this apparatus.

[19] John Isaac Hawkins, *A New System of Musical Notation, by which any person may learn to perform the organ or piano forte in a few hours*, London, 1808 (copy in University of Kentucky Special Collections Library, catalogue no. MT35.H350 1808). I am grateful to Matthew Harris for a copy of this pamphlet, in which no reference is made to Hawkins's apparatus to transcribe extempore performances. I am particularly indebted to Michael D. Friesen for sharing his extensive knowledge of Hawkins's achievements in England and America.

Payments totalling £23 that he made to Loeschman in July 1805 and October 1806 seemingly relate to Stanhope's tuning-glasses.[20] On the back page of his *Principles of the Science of tuning Instruments with fixed Tones*, which Andrew Wilson stereotyped and printed in the latter half of 1806, Stanhope announced that:

> I have contrived a tuning instrument which is far superior [to tuning-forks, which because of beating do not yield a pure sound]. It consists of thirteen slips of plate-glass; each of which is exactly six inches long, by two inches in breadth. ... The thickness of the slip which yields the Middle C is about nine hundredths of an inch; and the thickness of the slip which yields the sound of the first treble C is about eighteen hundredths. Those two Cs are the two extremes. Each slip yields a sound which is extremely pure. The same brass support, which terminates in three pointed corks, serves for each slip in succession. Each slip is similarly placed on that support, is struck by the same cork hammer, with the same elastic force, and on the corresponding spot, each time. By means of this simple tuning apparatus, which is pitched to my NEW AND IMPROVED TEMPERAMENT, any careful person, with a moderate ear, can tune an instrument perfectly, and better perhaps than the best tuner could do without this admirable assistance, which to persons in the country may be very useful. And, to professional tuners, this permanent and portable tuning instrument will be extremely convenient.[21]

Stanhope did not assert there that his tuning-glasses were commercially available, and he continued to develop the concept in

---

[20] In the ledger of Stanhope's bank account (Coutts) one of these transactions is entered as a payment to 'Anne Loeschmann'. Callcott, *op. cit.*, p 13, called Loeschman 'Earl Stanhope's tuner', and noted that Loeschman had tuned a grand piano forte at Callcott's house according to Stanhope's temperament. It is conceivable therefore that some of Stanhope's payments to Loeschman may have been for tuning.

[21] Charles Earl Stanhope, *Principles of the Science of tuning Instruments with fixed Tones*, London, 1806, p 24. This booklet was printed so that Stanhope could send copies to friends; it was not published, although numerous copies are extant. Its content reached a wider audience by appearing in its entirety in the September 1806 *Philosophical Magazine* (v 25 no. 100 p 291–[312]) and again in the 1 October 1806 *Repertory of Arts and Manufactures* (2nd ser. v 9 no. 54, between p 440 and p 441). Andrew Wilson printed both of these inserts from the same stereotype plates he had used to print copies of the booklet (except for the first page of the *Philosophical Magazine* reprint, which was impressed from a new stereotype plate). Stanhope's text was presented to readers of both journals both for its substance and as an example of stereotype printing.

later years.[22] Although no evidence has been found that any were ever sold, his intention that Loeschman would manufacture them is expressed on a printed page preserved amongst Stanhope's papers that contains four texts identical to the one reproduced in *Figure 8.1*.[23] Each of these texts apparently was designed to be affixed to a tuning-glass to label the thirteen pitches it could produce.

On 12 February 1805 Stanhope advised John North that 'my monochord is finished'.[24] A primary innovation was that its 'wire is not made either of brass or iron, but of steel, which is very far superior. For, steel wire does not keep continually lengthening, as brass and iron wires do when they are stretched considerably'.[25] The monochord was built to accommodate a second steel wire to demonstrate the beating that arises when sounds made by two strings are not exactly in unison. After both strings were stretched so that beating between them was inaudible, a screw with 'fifty threads to the inch, and which has a micrometer head very finely divided on its edge' could be turned to shorten one of the wires by 'as little as *the one hundred and eightieth part of the one hundredth of an inch*, without altering its tension'. This small change 'invariably' produced beating that could be heard and felt.[26]

Like his tuning-glasses, Stanhope's monochords do not appear to have been sold or used beyond his immediate circle of acquaintances. However, the mathematician Olinthus Gregory remarked in 1817 that the micrometer screw that Stanhope had invented for his monochord could be applied to calibrate a rod with a standardised measure of length.[27]

---

[22] An 1811 letter to him from Samuel Varley refers to 'the large cast iron for doing the first surface of the tuning glasses' (Varley→Stanhope, 'Friday morning' [July 1811], RI Stanhope papers v 1 p 393).

[23] A copy, printed on yellow-brown paper, is in CKS U1590/C97.

[24] Stanhope→North, 12 February 1805, in CKS U1590/C91/9.

[25] Stanhope, *Principles of the Science of tuning Instruments...*, p 24.

[26] *ibid.*, italics in the original.

[27] [Olinthus Gregory], 'Weights and measures', *British Review* v 9 no. 17 (February 1817) p 159–184 at p 177; reprinted with some alterations as *A Dissertation on Weights and Measures, and the best means of revising them*, London, 1817, p 26. Although both publications were anonymous Gregory was

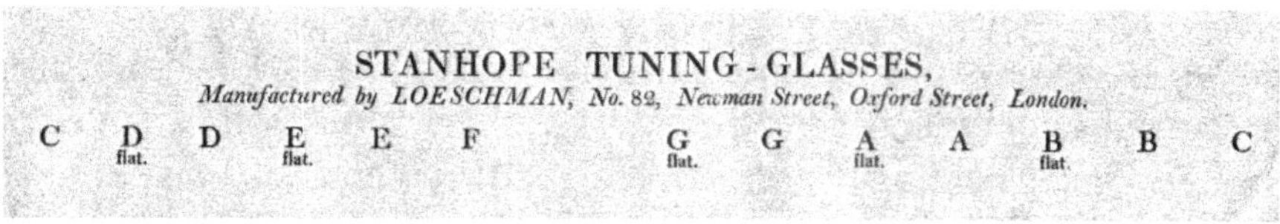
STANHOPE TUNING-GLASSES,
Manufactured by LOESCHMAN, No. 82, Newman Street, Oxford Street, London.
C D flat D E flat E F G flat G A flat A B flat B C

Figure 8.1 Label printed for Stanhope's tuning-glasses (in Centre for Kentish Studies U1590/C97, by permission of the Centre manager and the Trustees of the Chevening Estate)

By 24 January 1810 Stanhope had succeeded in having steel wires drawn that would allow pianos to be built with a single wire for each treble key in place of the usual three strings.[28] 'My principal object', he told the piano maker Thomas Tomkison, 'has been to get rid of *the three Wires*; as a want of *unison* in them, when an Instrument gets out of tune, becomes, to a good ear, very offensive'.[29] Stanhope sent his employee William Farmer, whom he had taught to draw these wires,[30] to London to discuss the proposed instrument, first with Tomkison—who showed no interest in manufacturing it—and then with other piano makers including John Broadwood, William Stodart, Joseph Dale and James Ball.[31]

---

identified as their author in *The Times*, 8 September 1819, p 3. In the reprint Gregory noted (p 35) Stanhope's death and his endeavour to have the House of Lords consider reformation of the British system of weights and measures (in May 1816; see T[homas] C[urson] Hansard, *The Parliamentary Debates from the year 1803 to the present time* v 34 (from 26/4/1816 to 2/7/1816), London, 1816, col. 305–308 and col. 771–775).

[28] Varley→Stanhope, 9 January 1808, RI Stanhope papers v 1 p 303–304, discusses some problems encountered in drawing (i.e., extending) these wires so that they had uniform consistency throughout their length and did not break.

[29] Stanhope→Tomkison, 24 January 1810, in CKS U1590/C91/9.

[30] *ibid.*

[31] See Farmer→Stanhope, 26 January 1810, 27 January 1810, 1 February 1810 and 2 February 1810, all in CKS U1590/C91/9. Farmer refers to 'Mr Broadwood' without giving a first name, but the person he met presumably was John Broadwood, then partner with his two sons (James Shudi Broadwood and

To demonstrate to prospective makers how steel wires sounded Farmer brought seven Stanhope monochords to London.[32] He also discussed with them other aspects of Stanhope's piano concept, such as its curved sounding board.[33] Broadwood recommended that Farmer see Loeschman about the proposed piano, who 'had but little business',[34] and Stanhope subsequently commissioned him to build a prototype of it, remitting £545/1/7 to him between July 1811 and July 1815, apparently for this purpose.[35]

John Farey, who wrote many articles on musical pitch and temperament, inspected the new piano on 12 May 1815 and penned the following description of it on the next day:

> Happening to have known that *Mr Loeschman* the musical-instrument maker has been long employed, under the direction of *Earl*

Thomas Broadwood) in the firm of John Broadwood & Sons. As noted in the last chapter, Stanhope had owned Broadwood pianos for many years.

[32] In the January 1805 account (CKS U1590/A146/1) of the Chevening House steward, John Brampton Jr, Farmer was listed as a valet, but Stanhope told Tomkison (Stanhope→Tomkison, 24 January 1810) that Farmer had lived 'out of livery, for many years' and might in future manufacture the new piano wires 'on his own account'.

[33] Farmer→Stanhope, 27 January 1810. This letter indicates that Mrs Lackner was involved in planning the new piano.

[34] Farmer→Stanhope, 1 February 1810.

[35] Stanhope bank ledger (Coutts). By January 1812 a correspondent of *The Philosophical Magazine* had been told that Stanhope has 'gone so far as to the manufacturing of steel wire on purpose, at his country seat [Chevening House], for the making of instruments with single strings that are to out-do those with two or three that are in common use'. The correspondent conveyed this report in a letter to the magazine's editor, Alexander Tilloch, that was published as 'On the cause of audible sound in vibrating strings …; on Earl Stanhope's proposed steel piano-forte strings, &c.', *The Philosophical Magazine* v 39 no. 165 (January 1812) p 37–39 at p 38. This appears to have been the first printed disclosure of Stanhope's planned piano. The correspondent, identified in the magazine only by the initial 'B.', conceivably might have been John Broadwood's son and partner James Shudi Broadwood. He would have heard of Stanhope's plans from William Farmer's visit; his letter refers to 'a thing pretty well understood in the trade of instrument-making'; and in the previous year he had written to another editor about 'tuning keyed stringed instruments' (James Broadwood→Editor, *The Monthly Magazine*, 11 July 1811, published in *The Monthly Magazine* v 32 no. 217 (September 1811) p 106–107).

> *Stanhope*, in constructing a new instrument, and having heard that it was at length completed, I called yesterday at his house in Newman Street, and was highly gratified by examining and hearing the novel and powerful effects of the *single steel strings* of his Lordship's invention: by which every desirable degree of loudness, more indeed than many would like in a small room, combined with a mellow sweetness of tone, seems accomplished, and the effect of an improved swell thereon, is excellent. The lower of his Lordship's *Strings*, or Wires rather, seem near or quite *a tenth of an inch in diameter*, and more resemble musical bars than strings, in their tone and effect. The chief difficulties have, as I understand, lain in effecting a construction of the instrument, to bear without alteration of form, so vast a strain as these strings collectively require, and to preserve at the same time its resonant effect; and in the construction of the hammers, for duly impelling these massive strings, without too audible a blow, and rendering the *touch* too heavy.[36]

Farey reported that the piano was not tuned in the temperament that Stanhope proposed in his 1806 *Principles*; instead, 'Mr Loeschman has been left to apply his great practical tuning skill' to the new instrument. Although the American piano maker Thomas Loud Jr said in 1833 that 'Loeschman, of London, manufactured piano fortes with cast iron frame ... after the plan of Earl Stanhope',[37] no evidence has been found that more than one Stanhope piano was ever made.

As noted on page 397 above, Stanhope bequeathed 'all my music Books, Organs and other musical Instruments whatsoever' to Walburga Lackner. On 15 April 1817 she acknowledged receiving 'all the musical instruments, left me by the will of the late Earl Stanhope',[38] and on 28 May 1817 'by order of the legatee'—i.e., Mrs Lackner—H[arry] Phillips auctioned in London:

---

[36] Farey→Editor of *The Philosophical Magazine* [Alexander Tilloch], 13 May 1815, printed in *The Philosophical Magazine* v 45 no. 205 (May 1815) p 386–387.

[37] Advertisement, *Daily Chronicle*, Philadelphia, 29 July 1833, reprinted in Keith G. Grafing, 'Alpheus Babcock's cast-iron piano frames', *The Galpin Society Journal* v 27 (May 1974) p 118–124 at p 119.

[38] Walburga Lackner→Alexander Murray [Stanhope's solicitor], pmk 21 April 1817 and docketed 25 April 1817, in CKS U1590/E208. In a postscript Mrs Lackner informed Murray that eight mahogany 'tuning-boxes, and 2 standards, belonging to the tuning-glasses' remained at Chevening House that ought to belong to her 'who has all the rest of the musical instruments, being on purpose

> The valuable and elegant original GRAND PIANO FORTE and the costly FINGER ORGAN,[39] each invented by and executed under the immediate direction of the late Earl Stanhope, and perfected at an expence [sic] of upwards of 2,000*l*. Those instruments, for power, compass, sweetness, and brilliancy of tone, have ever been esteemed superior to any known instruments of their class in Europe. The peculiar qualities of the Piano are its tone and qualities, which are superior to every other fixed toned instrument, and combines in itself the harmony of the organ, harp, and piano forte, produced by only one string. The Organ is of a peculiar fine tone, with compass of six octaves and a bird octave, a swell and of light touch, and capable of marking off extempore music and the time for the composition, &c.[40]

The term 'bird octave', which seems not to have been in common use, presumably referred to the octave immediately above the highest of the organ's other six octaves.[41] The advertisement does not say whether its keyboard compass was seven octaves (which would have been unusual at this time), whether it had two manuals—one of six octaves and another of one octave—or whether sounds in the 'bird octave' were produced by some form of octave coupling.

Although no copy of the catalogue of this auction has been located,[42] the Leipzig *Allgemeine musikalische Zeitung* reported in December 1819 that a Stanhope piano had sold at auction for about £60. This article gave additional information about the instrument and also about Stanhope's apparatus to record extemporary keyboard performances:

> Amongst newly invented musical instruments the grand pianoforte attempted by the late Earl Stanhope, with only one string for each key,

---

made, to tune them by; and not to Mr Varley, who wishes to claim them and has no right to it'.

[39] In contrast to a barrel organ, which reproduced music automatically, a 'finger organ' denoted an organ that had to be played by someone's fingers.

[40] Advertisement, *The Morning Chronicle*, 27 May 1817, p 4. Earlier advertisements (e.g., *The Morning Chronicle*, 23 May 1817, p 4) show that the auction had initially been set for 24 May but was postponed.

[41] Stanhope had used the phrase 'bird octave' in his October 1806 document 'Characters for the Letter-Music' (in CKS U1590/C97); see page 422 above.

[42] Some auctioneer's copies of Phillips sale catalogues were destroyed by fire in World War II.

deserves attention in two respects: first because of its strings, and secondly on account of the way that its hammers are constructed. As a first attempt, this instrument naturally was not yet fully developed and could be developed further under the direction of an intelligent and experienced instrument maker. According to hints of skilled instrument makers, its main mistake seems to be that the Earl, instead of using strings of different types of metal, used steel strings throughout. Certainly they have good effect in the treble and middle, and produced a beautiful full tone in the middle of the instrument, although in the lowest octave they were so thick—like the tubes of long clay tobacco pipes—that they lacked a clear body. The uncommonly strong tension of such a set of strings required a specially built frame for the instrument; many trials certainly were required to give the frame sufficient strength. The instrument accordingly was so heavy that eight men were needed to bring it in and out of the auction of the inventor's possessions after his death. This instrument at least had the advantage that no tone could be out of tune with itself, like unisons played on two or three instruments together. Of course, the overly thick strings could not be wound around wrest-pins and tuned in the usual way, so the Earl used screws to facilitate tuning.

The hammers did not strike in the customary manner, up from below between the wrest-plank and the bridge, but down onto the strings from above. This is the method applied in upright or so-called cabinet pianofortes, and a capable local piano-maker[43] produced the full treble of this instrument from the larger width of its sounding-board obtained by this means. Earl St[anhope] has mounted the hammers so that they strike up from below and protrude from the main beam [Hauptbalken] with an arch like the neck of a swan. Together with the heavy hammer, this makes the touch so difficult that the largest modern organ with full coupling is easier to play than this instrument, which does not allow quick trills with one hand. Because this piano, as your reviewer hears, has a patent, it cannot be further attempted in England for 14 years.[44] In the mentioned auction it was sold for about £60, and that was dear enough because of its present incompleteness.

Earl Stanhope has occupied himself for many years with inventions and improvements of prior inventions, of which a few belong to the field of music: first, a temperament which Dr Chladni has already correctly judged in the *musika[lische] Zeitung*;[45] secondly, an apparatus by means

---

[43] i.e., David Loeschman.

[44] The reviewer's information was incorrect, as Stanhope patented none of his musical inventions. Loeschman, however, had received an English patent in 1809 for a piano that could produce twenty-four sounds per octave.

[45] [Ernst Florens Friedrich] Chladni, review of Stanhope, *Principles of the Science of tuning Instruments with fixed Tones*, *Allgemeine musikalische Zeitung* v 17 no. 3 (18 January 1815) col. 37–39.

of which whatever is played or improvised on a pianoforte is correctly written down. This apparatus consists of long, rolled paper that unrolls during playing and on which marks are made of the length and intensity of each key played, which afterwards must be deciphered and set down as notes. With regard to this type of transcription, one should observe that although it allows us to know what someone has extemporised, there is and must be a greater difference between one performance and the next (even if the same virtuoso plays the next performance) than could be produced by universal use of this transcription. And many years of experience have confirmed this principle.[46]

---

[46] 'Unter den musikalischen Instrumenten neuerlicher Erfindung verdient das vom verstorbenen Grafen (Earl) Stanhope versuchte *Grand Pianoforte*, mit nur einer Saite zu jeder Taste, in doppelter Rücksicht Aufmerksamkeit: erstlich wegen seiner Saiten und zweytens wegen der Art, wie die Hämmer angebracht sind. Dass dieses Instrument, als erster Versuch noch nicht geworden ist, was es bey weiterem Nachdenken und under den Händen eines einsichtsreichen und erfahrnen Instrumentmachers werden kann, is natürlich. Das Hauptversehen dabey scheint zu seyn, dass der Graf nicht, dem Winke geschickter Instrumentmacher zufolge, Saiten von verschiedenen Metallarten, sondern durchgängig nur Stahlsaiten angebracht hat. Diese thaten zwar im Diskant, bis in die Mitte, gute Wirkung, und brachten in der Mitte des Instruments einen schönen vollen Ton hervor; da sie aber in der Contraoctave so dick, wie die Röhren langer thönerner Tabackspfeifen, waren, so fehlte es ihnen da an klarer Fülle. Die ungemein starke Spannung eines solchen Bezugs erforderte einen so besonders festgebauten Körper des Instruments, dass es, wie man versichert, vieler Versuche bedurfte, dem Körper genug Festigkeit zu geben. Das Instrument war daher so schwer, dass, als es nach dem Tode des Erfinders bey Versteigerung seines Nachlasses verkauft wurde, acht Männer zum Hinein- und Heraustragen desselben nöthig waren. Dieses Instrument hatte wenigstens den Vortheil, dass sich kein Ton in sich selbst verstimmen konnte, wie die Einklänge der zwey- und dreychörigen Instrumente. Da natürlich die allzudicken Saiten um keinen Stimmnagel gewunden und auf gewöhnliche Art gestimmt werden konnten, so hatte der Graf zum Stimmen Schrauben amgebracht, welche das Verfahren erleichterten. Die Hämmer schlugen nicht, wie gewöhnlich, zwischen dem Stimmstock und dem Stege, von unten hinauf, sondern von oben herunter auf die Saiten. Dies ist die Art, wie in den aufrechtstehenden oder sogenannten Cabinet-Pianofortes angebracht werden: und ein hiesiger geschickter Pianofortemacher leiten den vollen Diskant dieser Instrumente von den grössern Breite des Resonanzbodens her, welche dadurch gewonnen wird. Der Graf St. hatte aber die Hämmer so angebracht, dass sie von unten auf, vor dem Hauptbalken herum, wie ein Schwanenhals gebogen, anschlugen. Dieses, nebst dem schweren Hammer, machte den Anschlag so schwierig, dass die grösste moderne Orgel mit der vollen Kopellung noch leichter zu spielen seyn mag, als dieses Instrument, welches gar keinen prompten Triller mit Einer [sic] Hand verstattete. Da dieses Pianoforte, wie Ref.

The provenance of this Stanhope piano and organ after that auction is not known, nor whether any of his novel musical instruments is extant.[47]

Between January 1819 and May 1820 Mrs Lackner transferred more than £1,300 from her Coutts & Co. account to the Prague bankers Ballabene & Co.[48] By 1819 at the latest she left England to

---

hört, ein Patent hat, so wird es in England vor dem Verlaufe der 14 Jahre wohl nicht weiter versucht werden. In der erwähnten Versteigerung wurde es für etliche 60 Pf. Sterl. verkauft, und das war theuer genug, bey seiner damaligen Unvollkommenheit. Der Graf Stanhope hat sich seit vielen Jahren mit Erfindungen und mit Verbesserungen schon gemachter Erfindungen beschäftigt, wovon einige in das Gebiet der Musik gehören: erstlich, die schon in der musikal. Zeitung von D. Chladni richtig beurtheilte Temperatur; zweytens, eine Vorrichtung, wodurch sich das, was auf einem Pianoforte gespielt oder phantasirt wird, richtig niederschreibt: diese Vorrichtung bestand aus einem aufgerollten langen Papiere, das sich während des Spielens abrollte und auf dem jede angeschlagene Taste, nach ihrer Länge und Stärke, Zeichen machte, die nachher entziffert und in Noten gesetzt werden mussten. Ueber diese Art der mechanischen Nachschreibekunst ist zu bemerken, dass, ob sie uns gleich in den Stand setzt, zu wissen, was Jemand [sic] extemporirte, doch zwischen dem Originalspielen und dem Nachspielen (selbst wenn derselbe Virtuos der Nachspieler seyn sollte) ein zu grosser Unterschied seyn und bleiben muss, als dass je ein allgemeiner Gebrauch davon gemacht werden könnte. Und diesen Grundsatz bestätigt ja schon die vieljährige Erfahrung.' ('Uebersicht des Zustandes der Musik in England' ['Review of the state of music in England'], *Allgemeine musikalische Zeitung* v 21 no. 51 (22 December 1819) col. 865–873 at col. 865–867.)

[47] *The London Journal of Arts and Sciences* printed (v 2 no. 12 (1821) p 438–440) a letter to the editor [William Newton] by W[illiam] F[rederick] Collard with a footnote on p 439 (presumably by Newton) that asserted that 'a grand piano-forte upon his Lordship's [Stanhope's] plan is now in possession of his Lordship's legatee'. Newton's source of this information, which apparently was out of date, seems likely to have been Samuel Varley, who had contributed to the first volume of this journal and wrote a letter to its editor 'on a defect in lenses' that was printed in its v 2 no. 9 (1821) p 194–199. As a fellow employee at Chevening House and a fellow legatee of Stanhope's will, he knew Mrs Lackner well and would have known that she inherited the piano, but presumably he did not know that she had subsequently sold it at auction.

[48] The director of this firm, Ignaz Kleinwächter, was a pianist, violinist and organiser of chamber music concerts (see Michaela Freemanová, 'Prague's Society of Musicians (1803–1903/1930) and its rôle in the music and social life of the city', *Hudební Věda* v 40 no. 1 (2003) p 3–28 at p 6). He was also a close

live in Bohemia, as from that year 'Frau Walburga v. Lakner' is listed as owner of the estate 'St Johann unterm Felsen' ['St John under the Cliff', in Czech 'Svatý Jan pod Skalou'] in the Berauner Kreis [district] southwest of Prague.[49] In 1821 the Prague music seller Marco Berra published Franz Rudolph Grünwald's 'IX Walzer nebst Coda für das Pianoforte' ['Nine waltzes and a coda for the piano'], which was dedicated to 'Walburga von Lackner'.[50] The title-page noted that these waltzes had been played in the 'Brunettischen Gesellschaftsbällen', i.e., society balls of the Brunetti family, whose daughter Therese, a soprano, married the composer Jan Kalivoda in Prague that year.[51]

By 1822 Mrs Lackner had remarried.[52] Her new husband was Maximilian Berger, a student twenty–five years younger than herself

---

friend of the composer Louis Spohr (see *Louis Spohr's Autobiography*, London, 1865, v 1 p 103–104).

[49] *Schematismus für das Königreich Böhmen auf das Schaltjahr 1820*, Prague, [1819], p 311. On 8 November 1828 she purchased another property, Gut Neuhof, about 20 km away (see Johann Gottfried Sommer, *Das Königreich Böhmen; statistisch-topographisch dargestellt* v 13, Prague, 1845, p 243–244). The complex history of St John under the Cliff is briefly described in http://www.svatyjan.cz/txt_eng.htm. I am very grateful to Jiří Ševčík for information about the Berger family and their connections with Svatý Jan pod Skalou.

[50] Copy in the National Library of the Czech Republic, shelf no. *59 A 010779. I thank Jiří Ševčík for alerting me to its existence.

[51] The singer and dancer Therese Brunetti, presumably the bride's mother, was involved earlier in a relationship with the composer Carl Maria von Weber.

[52] Presumably in this connection, Coutts & Co. obtained on 27 August 1821 a certificate of burial of 'Mr C. Lackner'—the initial 'C.' is unclear in the Coutts ledger—and had this 'legalised' on 31 August by the notary public George Guillonneau. These transactions—for which deductions were made from Mrs Lackner's account with Coutts—suggest that Mr Lackner was buried in England. The registers of St Mary's German Lutheran Church in the Savoy (TNA RG4/4630 and RG4/4631) record that a copperplate engraver named Carl Lackner died on 17 July 1798 aged thirty-two and was buried there four days later. It has not been established whether he was Mrs Lackner's husband or if he was the Ig[naz] Karl von Lackner who engraved maps and drawings in Vienna in the late 1780s and early 1790s.

whose education she helped to finance.[53] From that year onwards, directories name the owner of the 'St Johann' estate as 'Frau Walburga Berger'.[54] She died on 4 April 1846 aged 75, having bequeathed 2000 Austro-Hungarian gulden to the Prague Conservatory (which opened in 1811), so that the interest it earned could be given to the neediest female student of singing there. The conservatory awarded this scholarship in her name between 1846 and 1939.[55] She also left money to support pupils in the elementary school that she had established in 1821 in the village near her estate. She left her collection of English tin medals dating from 1795, presumably acquired while she was living in England, to the National Museum (Národní muzeum) in Prague.[56]

Her sister Antonie Pachmann (*later* Lankisch von Hornitz) was the grandmother of Therese Miechura, who in 1827 married František Palacký, the Czech historian now revered as the 'father of the nation'. The recent annotated edition of his letters to Therese as fiancée and wife enabled me to recover some of Mrs Lackner's family tree and to confirm that she was born to Anton Veit Pachmann, a government official in Prague, and his wife Leopoldine *née* Katz von Katzenthal.[57]

---

[53] Their marriage was noted in a 3 May 1824 letter (in CKC U1590/C126) from Coutts & Co. to Stanhope's son Philip Henry Stanhope, the fourth Earl, informing him 'that we have received advice from Messrs Ballabene & Co, our Correspondents at Prague, stating that Mrs Lackner is still living, and is married to Mr Berger, Officer of the Custom House at Prague—and also that she sometime ago purchased an Estate called St Iwan' [i.e., St Johann unterm Felsen].

[54] For instance, in *Schematismus für das Königreich Böhmen auf das Jahr 1823*, Prague, [1822], p 307.

[55] I thank Jiří Ševčík for this information. See also Johann Branberger (translated by Emil Bezecný), *Das Konservatorium für Musik in Prag*, Prague, 1911, p 73.

[56] *Časopis Národního musea* ['Magazine of the National Museum', Prague] v 20 (1846) p 402–403. I thank Jiří Ševčík for translating this passage.

[57] Jiří Kořalka (ed.), *Briefe an Therese: Korrespondenz von František Palacký mit seiner Braut und späteren Frau aus den Jahren 1826–1880*, Dresden, 2003, p 80, 84, 136 and 251. Palacký wrote to 'tante' [i.e., to his wife's great-aunt] Walburga Berger in 1834 (*ibid.*, p 136). It is not known whether she was related to Vincenc Pachmann (1793–1878), an amateur violinist from Prague who later fathered the pianist Vladimir de Pachmann.

VOLLWEILER'S INTRODUCTION OF MUSIC LITHOGRAPHY TO ENGLAND

Michael Kassler

On 30 January 1806 Frederick Schirmer, proprietor of the German Theatre in London, entered at Stationers' Hall 'The favourite song in the celebrated opera, *Die drei Freier (The Three Suitors)*. Performed at the German Theatre. Arranged for the piano forte, with an English poetical translation of the original words'.[1] This work, which presumably was first published on that day or a few days earlier,[2] appears to have been the first music lithographed in England.

Lithography was invented about 1798 by Alois Senefelder in Munich.[3] He had printed songs by the Bavarian court composer Franz Gleißner two years earlier, from stones etched so that the areas to be printed were higher than other areas. Subsequent experimentation led Senefelder to discover that selected regions on a flat stone could be inked—and the rest of its surface stay ink-free—by applying different chemical treatments to these areas. This discovery, for which the English word 'lithography' was first used in 1813,[4] allowed paper and cloth to be printed from an even surface, in contrast both to the relief

---

[1] *MESH* p 559.

[2] For the basis of this presumption see *ibid.*, p xxi.

[3] Information about the history of lithography and its application to music printing is taken chiefly from Alois Senefelder, *A Complete Course of Lithography*, London, 1819 (reprinted New York, 1977), Michael Twyman, *Early Lithographed Music*, London, 1996, and Michael Twyman, *Breaking the Mould: The first hundred years of lithography*, London, 2001.

[4] Michael Twyman (ed.), *Henry Bankes's Treatise on Lithography*, London, 1976, p xxix–xxx.

type used in letterpress printing and to engraving, where the marks to be printed are incised into a plate.

Gleißner joined Senefelder to exploit this new chemical-printing process, and on 3 September 1799 they obtained an exclusive privilege from the elector of Bavaria, Prince Maximilian IV Joseph, to practise the art there.[5] Johann Anton André, who a few months earlier had succeeded his father Johann André as head of the family music-publishing business in Offenbach-am-Main, Hesse, learned about the invention soon afterwards and almost immediately signed a contract with Gleißner and Senefelder to establish their new printing method at his firm.[6] They both removed to Offenbach, where Senefelder introduced the technology while Gleißner proofread music and began to catalogue hundreds of Mozart manuscripts that André had purchased that year from Mozart's widow Constanze.[7] The principal initial application of lithography therefore was to music printing, including the pictorial title-pages of some music publications.

The contract placed no geographic restriction on André's right to use the new technology and he proceeded to explore opportunities to do this in France, Britain, Prussia and Austria. In July 1800 he travelled to London, where he investigated the English printing scene and met musicians.[8] After returning to Offenbach he decided to send

---

[5] A contemporary copy of the privilege is reproduced and transcribed in Gerd Vollmer, *Alois Senefelder und die 'Notenfabrique' André*, Offenbach, 1986, p 24–26. See also Karl-Heinz Döbert, 'Alois Senefelder und Johann Anton André—die Einführung der Lithographie für den Notendruck', in Jürgen Eichenauer (ed.), *Johann Anton André (1775–1842) und der Mozart-Nachlass*, Weimar, 2006, p 51–64 at p 52–53.

[6] The contract, dated 28 September 1799, is reproduced and transcribed in Vollmer, *op. cit.*, p 40–42.

[7] Senefelder, *op. cit.*, p 35, and C[ecil] B. Oldman, 'J. A. André on Mozart's manuscripts', *Music and Letters* v 5 no. 2 (April 1924) p 169–176 at p 175. In addition, André published some of Gleißner's compositions.

[8] Including the theorist Augustus F. C. Kollmann and the organist Samuel Wesley. See Michael Kassler, *A. F. C. Kollmann's* Quarterly Musical Register *(1812): An annotated edition with an introduction to his life and works*, Aldershot, 2008, p 64–67. André also investigated the commercial feasibility of using lithography to print cotton in England (Senefelder, *op. cit.*, p 36).

Senefelder to London to secure English and Scottish patents for the chemical-printing process so that André's brother Philippe Henri, who had worked in London since 1797, could establish a lithographic business upon that basis. These patents, granted to Senefelder in June 1801,[9] were sold to Johann Anton André two months later, by which time Senefelder had returned to Offenbach.[10] Shortly afterwards he and Gleißner temporarily severed their relationship with André.

In London Philippe André obtained the leasehold of two houses near Fitzroy Square, 5 Buckingham Street and 9 Buckingham Place, and a lithographic press was installed in one of them.[11] In contrast to Johann Anton André, Philippe did not use the new technology to print music but applied it exclusively to reproduce artists' drawings.[12] His efforts culminated in the first set of a series of lithographed drawings called *Specimens of Polyautography*—his name for the new printing method—which he co-published on 30 April 1803 with the historical engraver James Heath.[13] Philippe André left London about July 1804,[14] and was succeeded some eighteen months later by Georg

---

[9] The specification of the English patent (subsequently numbered 2518), granted on 20 June 1801 when Senefelder was living in Philippe Henri's house at 10 Gould Square, is printed in Carl Halbmeier, *Senefelder and the History of Lithography*, Elmhurst, New York, 1926, p 48–59. The Scottish patent was granted the day before (see Felix H. Man, 'Lithography in England (1801–1810)', in Carl Zigrosser (ed.), *Prints*, New York, 1962, p 97–130 at p 101).

[10] The deed of this sale, dated 10 August 1801, is reproduced and transcribed in Vollmer, *op. cit.*, p 57–59.

[11] I thank Hilary Davies and Tessa Forbes of Westminster Archives for the information that rate books from 1802 to 1804 name 'Philip Andre' as ratepayer for the former address and 'Philip Andre for tenants' as ratepayer for the latter address.

[12] The artist Joseph Farington wrote in his diary entry for 16 February 1802 that Samuel 'Lysons called. He had been with Mr Andre abt the engraving on stone. Andre does not seem desirous of extending it beyond artists' (transcribed in Kenneth Garlick and Angus Macintyre (eds), *The Diary of Joseph Farington* v 5, New Haven, 1979, p 1749).

[13] Man, *op. cit.*, p 116–130, provides a 'Catalogue of lithographs and polyautographs executed in England 1801–1810'.

[14] An advertisement (*The Morning Post*, 25 July 1804, p 4) for the auction on the following day of the leasehold and furniture of 5 Buckingham Street said that 'Mr Philip Andre' was 'removing into the country'.

Jacob Vollweiler,[15] who worked and presumably lived at 9 Buckingham Place.[16]

Vollweiler's career has been little investigated. He was born on 29 November 1770 at Eppingen (near Heilbronn and Karlsruhe),[17] where he attended the grammar ['lateinische'] school and learned to play the clavier. After showing a talent for music he was advised by his teacher, the schoolmaster Zimmermann, to devote himself to that subject, and in 1786 he went to Heidelberg to further his musical education. Subsequently he found employment as an orchestral cellist in Mannheim,[18] where he also instructed pupils in thorough-bass. Desiring to understand how musical compositions are structured, he read theoretical treatises by Kirnberger and Marpurg and embarked upon a lifelong effort to reduce the theory of harmony to simpler principles than these theorists had provided.[19]

---

[15] On the assumption that it took a month for Vollweiler to settle in, to meet Frederick Schirmer and convince him to use the new technology for music printing, and then to prepare and print 'The favourite song…' before it was deposited at Stationers' Hall on 30 January 1806, Vollweiler presumably arrived in London in December 1805.

[16] 'Jakob Valweiler' or a variant spelling is listed as ratepayer for 9 Buckingham Place in 1806 and 1807, but not for 1808. Following the 26 July 1804 auction of 5 Buckingham Street, Susannah Green became ratepayer of that property in 1805.

[17] I am grateful to Reinhard Ihle of Heimatfreunde Eppingen e.V. for this information. According to 'G. J. Vollweiler (Nekrolog.)', *Frankfurter Konversationsblatt: Belletrische Beilage zur Oberpostamts-Zeitung* no. 326, 26 November 1847, p 1303–1304. I thank Peter Ward Jones for sending me a copy of this obituary, which was reprinted with minor alterations in the *Wiener allgemeine Musik-Zeitung* nos 148–149 (11, 14 December 1847) p 593–594 and p 597–598. Other renderings of his name (e.g., Reinhold Sietz, 'Vollweiler, Johann Georg', *Die Musik in Geschichte und Gegenwart*, Kassel, v 14, 1968, cols. 1–2) are incorrect.

[18] Although the composer Ferdinand Hiller, who was born in 1811 and studied with Vollweiler in the 1820s, said that Vollweiler initially—'Von Haus aus'—was a 'Violoncellist in der Mannheimer Capelle' (Ferdinand Hiller, 'Frankfurter Tonkünstler vergangener Zeit', in his *Erinnerungsblätter*, Cologne, 1884, p 90–110 at p 93), this cannot have been the famous Mannheim court orchestra, which removed from Mannheim with the electoral court to Munich in 1778.

[19] 'G. J. Vollweiler (Nekrolog.)', *op. cit.*, p 1303. According to this obituary (*loc. cit.*) Vollweiler wrote a book on this subject which, at the time of his death,

In 1792 Johann Anton André, who was five years younger than Vollweiler, went to Mannheim to study music with him, and they became friends. André wrote, in an account of his life to 1800, that:

> Ich bin im Mai 1792 wieder nach Mannheim zurück, um selbst gründlich die Komposition zu erlernen; mich hierin zu unterrichten, übernahm mein Freund und Lehrer Vollweiler, der gegenwärtig hier bei mir [in Offenbach] lebt, und ihm verdanke ich hiermit endlich, daß er mich gleich anfangs richtig führte und dadurch in den Stand setze, als ich Neujahr 1793 wieder nach O[ffenbach] kam, für mich fortlernen zu können. Im Herbst 1793 ging ich zu weiterem Studium zu Vollweiler nach M[annheim], allein die damals eingetretene Kriegsunruhe verjagte die friedlichen Musen und mich mit ihnen. Von jener Zeit an bis 1796 im Oktober blieb ich, abgerechnet einige kleine Reisen, fortdauernd in Offenbach, woselbst ich nebst fortgesetztem Studium in der Komposition einige Handlungs- und Lebensarbeit in meines Vaters Haus übernehmen mußte.
> [I returned again to Mannheim in May 1792 to acquire a thorough knowledge of composition, instructed by my friend and teacher Vollweiler, who now [*c*1800] lives in my home [in Offenbach], and it is due ultimately to him that from the very beginning I was guided so correctly that I could continue to learn when I came back to Offenbach at the beginning of 1793. In autumn 1793 I went to Mannheim for further study with Vollweiler, but the war disturbances starting at that time drove away peaceful students including myself. From then until October 1796 I stayed—except for a few short trips—in Offenbach where, besides continuing my studies in composition, I had to undertake some business and family tasks in my father's house [partly as a consequence of his father's death].][20]

In 1799, the year in which Johann Anton André succeeded his father, Vollweiler removed to Offenbach to work for the André firm where he supervised the engraving and later the lithography of its music publications and took over its correspondence with

---

was beautifully finished and ready to be printed ['jetzt in schöner Vollendung und druckfertig daliegt']. However, the book was never published and its manuscript does not appear to be extant.

[20] August Hermann André, *Zur Geschichte der Familie André, Offenbach am Main*, *Offenbacher Geschichtsblätter* no. 11, Offenbach, 1962, p 21. Johann Anton André's manuscript autobiography of his early years is in the possession of the André family (*ibid.*, p 13). A 23 June 1794 letter from Vollweiler (in Mannheim) to André (in Offenbach), discussing matters of music theory, is in Stadtarchiv Mannheim, Kleine Erwerbungen, signatur 0334.

composers.[21] As part of his employment he presumably learned to write music and words on stone and to understand the lithographic process. He was a witness to the deed that transferred Senefelder's English and Scottish patents to André in August 1801.[22] He is reported to have been in Paris in December 1804,[23] where Jean Frédéric André, another brother of Johann Anton and Philippe, had received a French patent for lithography on 11 February 1802 and, with some associates, produced lithographed music soon afterwards.[24]

Vollweiler expanded the range of matter that was printed polyautographically in London. In an undated lithographed circular that appears to have been issued about February 1807, he informed

> the Nobility and Gentry, that he has undertaken the management of the art of printing from stone called Polyautography, lately under the direction of Mr P. André, and continues the publication of Specimens of Polyautography commenced by him. ... Those who already had knowledge of this art whilst under the direction of Mr André, will find it considerably improved by its application to letter- and music-printing, of which the present advertissment [sic], as well as ... the enclosed sheet of music, are specimens.[25]

---

[21] Johann Anton André 'veranlaßte ihn [Vollweiler] im Jahr 1799, in der Musikhandlung seines Vaters die Aufsicht über den Stich (später die Lithographie) der dort erscheinenden Musikalien und die Correspondenz mit den Componisten zu übernehmen', 'G. J. Vollweiler (Nekrolog.)', *op. cit.*, p 1303.

[22] See note 10 above.

[23] Joseph Farington recorded in his diary for 18 August 1806: 'Volliveiter [sic] called on me.—He was in Paris when Bonoparte [sic] was proclaimed *Emperor of the French*' on 2 December 1804 (transcribed in Kathryn Cave (ed.), *The Diary of Joseph Farington* v 8, New Haven, 1982, p 2840).

[24] See Walter Gräff, *Die Einführung der Lithographie in Frankreich*, Heidelberg, 1906, p 14–15, Elisabeth Lebeau, 'Les débuts ignorés de l'Imprimerie lithographique, Charenton, Paris, 1802–1806'; *Bulletin de la Société Archéologique, Historique et Artistique le Vieux Papier* v 20 no. 160 (July 1952) p 250–257; Elisabeth Lebeau, 'Une succursale officieuse de Johann Anton André à Paris, de 1802 à 1806', in Erich Schenk (ed.), *Bericht über den internationalen musikwissenschaftlichen Kongress Wien Mozartjahr 1956*, Graz, 1958, p 324–327; and Twyman, *Early Lithographed Music*, p 247–254.

[25] The only known copy of this circular (BM Prints and Drawings 190*.b.1 f 43, transcribed inaccurately in Emanuel Green, 'The beginnings of lithography',

This circular noted that four numbers of *Specimens of Polyautography* were now published and that 'Mr Vollweiler has had the high honour of laying the work before Her Majesty [Queen Charlotte], and their Royal Highnesses the Princesses, who honour it most graciously with their patronage'.[26] As Vollweiler advertised on 4 February 1807 that the fourth number of *Specimens* was 'just published',[27] and as this number was reviewed in that month's *Monthly Magazine*,[28] the circular presumably was printed about then.

To prepare music for printing Vollweiler followed a different procedure from that which he used for drawings. In the latter case he lent a slab of limestone and supplied ink or crayon (then called 'chalk') to an artist, who executed a drawing on the stone and

---

The Archaeological Journal v 51 = 2nd ser. v 1 (1894) p 109–119 at p 111–113) does not have 'the enclosed sheet of music', which is considered below. The misspelt word 'advertissment' suggests that the person who wrote the circular's text on stone was not an Englishman. Other items lettered in Vollweiler's Polyautographic Office also show occasional spelling or lexical mistakes: e.g., the title-page of P[eter] E[duard] Stroehling, *Original Sketches drawn upon Stone ... No 1* (copy at BM Prints and Drawings 190*.b.1 f 86) has 'recieved', and Vollweiler's 'Terms for Amateurs, who wish to draw on stone and to have impressions taken from it' (copy at BM Prints and Drawings 190*.b.1 f 42, partly reproduced in facsimile in Michael Twyman, 'Lithographic stone and the printing trade in the nineteenth century', *Journal of the Printing Historical Society* no. 8 (1972) p 1–41 at p 24) has 'forthnights' and includes the phrases 'a few prove impressions' and 'charged 1s piece' instead of 'a few proof impressions' and 'charged 1s apiece'. This lettering, whose style resembles that on lithographed music printed by Vollweiler, may have been done by Vollweiler himself.

[26] Vollweiler mentioned the patronage of the queen and princesses on the first state of his wrapper for *Specimens* (copy at BM Prints and Drawings 190*.b.1, unnumbered folio). This document—which contains the printed text 'Published May 1806 by G. J. Vollweiler, Patentee, Successor to Mr André'—was lithographed for Vollweiler's republication of the first and second numbers of *Specimens*. As noted by Man, *op. cit.*, p 129, Vollweiler changed that text to 'Published by G. J. Vollweiler, Successor to Mr André' when the fourth number of *Specimens* was issued in 1807. I am grateful to Alison Derrett for the information that no correspondence with Philippe André, Vollweiler, the Polyautographic Office or Frederick Schirmer is preserved in the Royal Archives.

[27] *The Morning Post*, 4 February 1807, p 2.

[28] *The Monthly Magazine* v 23 part 1 no. 1 = no. 153 (1 February 1807) p 75–76.

returned it to Vollweiler for printing.[29] The portrait of Vollweiler reproduced in *Figure 9.1* was made in that way.[30] For music, because there was no commercial advantage to replicate a composer's handwriting in print, another person—probably Vollweiler himself—wrote the notation and accompanying words and symbols on stone, either from a manuscript provided by the composer or from a previously printed copy. The lithographic method used by Vollweiler required that marks be written on stone in reverse, a skill that most composers would not have wanted to take the time or trouble to learn.

As discussed below and as summarised in *Table 9.1* on pages 497–501 below, the music that Vollweiler printed in London was issued either individually by his so-called Polyautographic Office or as 'embellishments' included in the monthly periodical *La Belle Assemblée*.[31] It is noteworthy that much of his individually issued music was composed by people in or associated with London's small community of German speakers, whereas the music that he prepared for *La Belle Assemblée* was not.

Vollweiler must have kept in close contact with Johann Anton André.[32] Four of the compositions that Vollweiler issued individually in London were separately lithographed and published by the André firm in Offenbach, and (as noted in *Table 9.2* on pages 502–505 below) lithographed labels bearing Vollweiler's name and address were pasted on copies of music that the André firm published and sent to London for sale.[33]

---

[29] According to Vollweiler's undated lithographed statement of terms (see note 25 above).

[30] Man, *op. cit.*, p 116–130, catalogued most artistic lithographs executed in England between 1801 and 1810, but did not list this portrait of Vollweiler.

[31] These embellishments, which included engraved portraits and fashion prints, were issued as separate sheets which owners of the periodical could have bound together with its letterpress text after a volume was published. Most extant copies of the periodical do not have all its embellishments. As noted below, if an owner sent music embellishments to be bound with the rest of the volume they would no longer be useful for performance.

[32] I am indebted to Hubert Unverricht and Axel Beer for the information that no correspondence between André and Vollweiler during the latter's stay in London from 1805 to 1807 appears in the firm's extant records.

[33] Twyman, *Early Lithographed Music*, p 209, reproduces two of these labels.

Figure 9.1 Lithographed portrait of Georg Jacob Vollweiler, London, 1807 (by permission of the Bodleian Library, University of Oxford, John Johnson Collection, in Lithography General Folder 1)

Frederick Schirmer, apparently the first to engage Vollweiler to lithograph music in London, was born in Oschatz, Saxony and came to London in 1804, intending to stage performances by his children.[34] He found, when he arrived, that he could not do this without a licence.[35] For a few months from January 1805 he exhibited 'musical, mechanical, aerostatic, acoustic and optical novelties' at the Lyceum Theatre[36] and invited prominent members of London's German community to see private performances by his children. Their abilities were so impressive that news of their talents reached Queen Charlotte,[37] who commanded them to perform before the royal family in May 1805 and afterwards instructed the Lord Chamberlain (George Legge, 3rd Earl of Dartmouth) to grant Schirmer a licence that enabled them to act and sing in public.[38] He then leased (from Charles Dibdin Sr) the Sans Souci Theatre on Leicester Place near Leicester

---

[34] A brief biography of Schirmer is given in Ursula Regener (ed.), *Joseph von Eichendorff Tagebücher Kommentar* v 11 part 2, Tübingen, 2006, p 275–276. Performances that he organised in several cities are described in Gertraude Diecke, *Die Blütezeit des Kindertheaters…*, Emsdetten, 1934 (v 8 of Carl Niessen, ed., *Die Schaubühne*), p 135–139.

[35] See 'Hr.' (i.e., John Christian Hüttner), 'Schirmer's Teutsches Kindertheater in London' (dated 16 August 1805), *London und Paris* no. 5 (1805) p 3–12, and 'Biographical sketch of Master Albert Schirmer' [Schirmer's elder son, born in 1790], *The Monthly Mirror* v 21 (February 1806) p 75–77.

[36] Schirmer conducted these exhibitions with a colleague surnamed Scholl. See their advertisements, e.g., for the 'Ergascopia' in *The Morning Chronicle*, 2 January 1805, p 1 and for 'Superb air balloon figures' in *The Morning Chronicle*, 10 April 1805, p 1; their booklet *Sketch of the Performances, at the Large Theatre, Lyceum…*, London, 1805 [their names are not on the title-page]; and Mervyn Heard, *Phantasmagoria*, Hastings, 2006, p 179–183.

[37] Queen Charlotte, whose native language was German, provided numerous benefits to the German-speaking community in London, such as giving an organ and an altarpiece painting to the Royal German Chapel at St James's Palace and patronising German schools in London. See Michael Kassler, *A. F. C. Kollmann's* Quarterly Musical Register, *op. cit.*, p 17 and p 27–28.

[38] The licence allowed Schirmer to present 'musical and dramatical interludes in the German language' at that theatre for a year from 22 June 18. See 'The Sans Souci Theatre, Leicester Place', in *Survey of London v 34: The Parish of St Anne Soho*, London, 1966, p 481–482 at p 482.

Square for a year,[39] and advertised on 1 July that 'Schirmer's children' would perform at 'Schirmer's German Theatre' three times a week, 'under the immediate patronage of Her Majesty'.[40]

One member of the German community invited to a private performance by Schirmer's children was the publisher Rudolph Ackermann.[41] He too had been born in Saxony and, after coming to England, formed 'close connections with other émigrés from Saxony',[42] which could account for his meeting Schirmer and becoming instrumental in securing the German Theatre licence for him.[43] Ackermann had published in 1803 twelve lithographed drawings printed by Philippe André,[44] and was so impressed with the chemical-printing process that he sought, unsuccessfully, to purchase its English patent.[45] He must have met Vollweiler—most likely at the

---

[39] Dibdin subsequently wrote 'expressly for the German Theatre' the words and music of a song 'A touch at the iron crown', where it was 'sung by [Schirmer's younger son] Master Frederick Schirmer' (copy at Cambridge University Library, shelfmark MRA.290.80.293).

[40] *The Morning Chronicle*, 1 July 1805, p 1. See also Robert Fahrner, 'The second Sans Souci theatre', *Theatre Notebook* v 29 no. 2 (1975) p 69–73. The company consisted of five children: two sons and two daughters of Schirmer, and Master Franz Gleisner from Saxony (who presumably was unrelated to Franz Gleißner). See 'German theatre', *The Universal Magazine* v 4 no. 20 (July 1805) p 53.

[41] Hüttner, *op. cit.*, p 6.

[42] John Ford, 'Ackermann, Rudolph', in *Oxford Dictionary of National Biography*, Oxford, 2004.

[43] Ackermann wrote (in Ackermann→Carl August Böttiger, 16 July 1805, Sächsischen Landesbibliothek – Staats- und Universitätsbibliothek Dresden, ms Dresd.h.37, 4°, Bd. 2): 'I have taken a deserving family by the hand, I mean Schirmers, a countryman of ours native of Oschatz near Leipzig and have succeeded what has often been attempted but always failed in getting them a licence to establish a German Theatre in London.... As this Juvenile Company are my children & their merits do me great honour, I naturally make all interests I possibly can for their success.' I am very grateful to John Ford for providing a transcript of this letter, written in English.

[44] Man, *op. cit.*, p 126, catalogue no. 155. See also *ibid.*, p 120, catalogue no. 58.

[45] According to the article 'Zeichnende Künste' ['Graphic arts'], in John Christian Hüttner (ed.), *Englische Miscellen* v 13 (1803) p 62–66 at p 65, translated in Man, p 105. Perhaps Philippe André was willing to sell but

urging of Philippe or Johann Anton André—soon after Vollweiler's arrival in London, because Ackermann published on 1 February 1806 a lithographed drawing that Vollweiler printed.[46] As Schirmer had entered 'The favourite song in the celebrated Opera, *Die drei Freier*' at Stationers' Hall two days earlier, it seems probable that Ackermann introduced him to Vollweiler.

The 'comic opera, never acted, called *The Three Suitors*' was first performed at the German Theatre by 'Mr Schirmer's juvenile company' on 14 August 1805. Although Vollweiler's lithograph of 'The favourite song' did not name its composer, advertisements that appeared on the opera's opening day identified him as 'Mr Holsh',[47] and a review in *The Times* on the following day said that 'the music is the production of Mr Holst, a native of Russia',[48] almost certainly a reference to Matthias von Holst, who had taught harp to the Imperial Family at St Petersburg and 'escaped' to London from Riga about 'the beginning of the nineteenth century'.[49] Additional corroboration

---

Ackermann found the price too high, as Farington recorded in his diary entry for 12 February 1802 that Josiah 'Boydell called. He had been with the man who has the patent for engraving on stone [i.e., Philippe André]. He [Boydell] thinks it might be worth while to give him £1000 for it' (transcribed in Kenneth Garlick and Angus Macintyre (eds), *The Diary of Joseph Farington* v 5, New Haven, 1979, p 1747). After the expiry in 1815 of the English and Scottish patents granted to Senefelder, Ackermann established a lithographic press in London *c*1817 (see Michael Twyman, *Lithography 1800–1850*, London, 1970, p 38) and published the English translation of Senefelder's *A Complete Course of Lithography* (London, 1819).

[46] This drawing was printed as no. 2 in the first number of Jean François-Marie Hüet-Villiers, *Rudiments of Trees*, London, 1806 (copy at Bodleian Johnson a.110). The lithographed caption of this drawing includes the text 'printed from Stone at the Polyautographic-Office, N° 9, Buckingham-Place, Fitzroy-Square, & published feb^ry 1806 at R. Ackermann's Repository of Arts 101 Strand'. The title-page of the number states 'Pub. Feb. 1st 1806', and it was noticed in *The Monthly Magazine* v 21 part 1 no. 2 = no. 140 (1 March 1806) p 257. I thank Michael Twyman and Sarah Weale for providing details of the Bodleian copy.

[47] *The Morning Chronicle*, 14 August 1805, p 1; *The Times*, 14 August 1805, p 1.

[48] *The Times*, 15 August 1805, p 3.

[49] See Imogen Holst, *Gustav Holst: A biography*, 2nd ed., Oxford, 1988, p 1. (The composer Gustav Holst was a great-grandson of Matthias von Holst.) At

of the composer's surname is found in the publication not later than July 1806 of 'Rondo for the piano forte introduced in the German comedy of *The Three Suitors.* Composed by Mr Holst'.[50]

The first page of 'The favourite song' stated that it was 'printed for the proprietor [i.e., Schirmer] by Mr Vollweiler', and that copies of this music—whose verses had been handwritten on stone both in German and in 'an English poetical translation'—were 'sold at the German Theatre', where 'a description of the polyautography' could be 'had gratis'.[51] The song, whose English words were changed from those in the bilingual edition of the opera text that had been published in London in the preceding year,[52] was printed just in time to be sold at the German Theatre on 31 January 1806, when *The Three Suitors* was performed as a benefit for the Patriotic Fund.[53]

The next musical composition individually issued by Vollweiler was 'The favourite march from the opera *La Clemenza di Tito* by Mozart, arranged for the piano forte'. This publication is undated but almost certainly was lithographed after the English premiere of *La Clemenza di Tito* at the King's Theatre on 27 March 1806, a benefit performance for the soprano Elizabeth Billington in which she and the tenor John Braham sang leading parts. Before this

---

this time Riga belonged to a predominantly German-speaking part of the Russian empire.

[50] A copy of this engraved work, 'printed & sold' by [Thomas] Preston, is in the Rare Book and Manuscript Library, University of Pennsylvania, catalogue no. Folio M312.S36 op. 6. The work bears no date but was reviewed in *The Monthly Magazine* v 22 part 2 no. 1 = no. 146 (1 August 1806) p 58. Both 'The favourite song' and 'Rondo' are in the key of G major and have similar musical style.

[51] No copies of this presumably printed description have been located.

[52] *Die drei Freier, oder Gleich und Gleich gesellt sich gern.* | *The Three Suitors, or Like loves Like.* London, printed by J[ohn] B[enjamin] G[ottlieb] Vogel … and sold at the playhouse [i.e., the German Theatre], Leicester Place, Leicester Square, 1805 (copy at BL 1343.d.10), p 11. The 'favourite song' was sung by Master Franz Gleisner (*ibid.*, p 1).

[53] Advertisement, *The Morning Chronicle*, 31 January 1806, p 1. Performances of the opera continued, for instance on 26 April 1806 (advertisement, *The Times*, 26 April 1806, p 1). After Schirmer's lease of the Sans Souci Theatre expired, his children performed *The Three Suitors* 'for the benefit of Mr Schirmer's family' at the 'private saloon theatre, Argyle Street' on 28 July 1807 (advertisement, *The Morning Chronicle*, 28 July 1807, p 1).

production—the first fully staged performance of a Mozart opera in England, which was repeated five times during that season—the march was not known in London and so presumably would not have been described as 'the favourite'.[54] On this work Vollweiler repeated the imprint 'at the new invented Patent-Polyautography' that he had used on 'The favourite song'. As this imprint differed from those on his other individually issued music, including one entered at Stationers' Hall on 12 June 1806, it seems likely that 'The favourite march' was printed before then.

The André firm published an almost identical piano arrangement of this march at Offenbach that bears no printed date but is said to have appeared in 1806.[55] Presumably Vollweiler made his edition from that source, as both are laid out in four systems and each system in Vollweiler's edition has the same number of bars as the corresponding system in the André firm's edition. An alternative hypothesis that the march was independently arranged for piano in London seems less likely.

Vollweiler's decision to lithograph a piece by Mozart—the only music he printed in London by a composer who was not alive—almost certainly was influenced by Johann Anton André's considerable investment in Mozart's music. After purchasing a large number of Mozart's manuscripts (including the autograph of *La Clemenza di Tito*), André published many editions based upon

---

[54] See William C. Smith, *The Italian Opera and Contemporary Ballet in London, 1789–1820*, London, 1955, p 80, and Rachel Cowgill, 'Mozart productions and the emergence of *Werktreue* at London's Italian opera house, 1780–1830', in Roberta Montemorra Marvin and Dowing A. Thomas (eds), *Operatic Migrations*, Aldershot, 2006, p 145–186 at p 148–152.

[55] Britta Constapel, *Die Musikverlag Johann André in Offenbach am Main*, Tutzing, 1998, p 161. The André firms's edition, which bears publisher no. 2241, was the second in a set of five editions (publisher nos. 2240–2244) entitled 'Marches pour Piano-Forte, par W. A. Mozart', and consisted of marches from *La Clemenza di Tito* and *The Magic Flute*. (Numeral sequences such as '2241' that were printed on title-pages and at the bottom of music pages published by the André firm state the number that they assigned to a work. These numbers were not plate numbers. Works published by them in more than one edition—e.g., in both 'landscape' and 'portrait' formats, or in an engraved and a lithographed edition—were assigned the same publisher number.)

them.[56] The appearance of 'The favourite march' also might indicate Vollweiler's continuing association with Schirmer, at whose German Theatre part of *The Magic Flute* was performed on 29 March 1806,[57] and who promoted, although unsuccessfully, the establishment of a German Opera in London.[58]

It is plausible that Vollweiler produced this item to give prospective clients an example of his music lithography, as the music fits on a single page and was his only individually issued piece of music on which neither a price nor an address where copies could be bought was printed. Because it appeared about the same time as his circular announcing the May 1806 publication of *Specimens of Polyautography*, 'The favourite march' might have been the 'sheet of music' he enclosed with that circular.[59]

Nina d'Aubigny von Engelbrunner was born at Kassel in 1770, where her father, Johann Conrad Engelbrunner, a prominent lawyer, had started a music society four years earlier.[60] During a trip to Mannheim with her parents in 1786 she met the court astronomer, Professor Johann Nepomuk Fischer, and she also met Johann André—father of Johann Anton and Philippe André—who had founded the family's music publishing firm at Offenbach in 1774. From 1803 to 1807 she lived in London (although not continuously)

---

[56] See Wolfgang Rehm, *Mozarts Nachlass und die Andrés*, Offenbach, 1999, p 48.

[57] Advertisement, *The Times*, 29 March 1806, p 1, in which the work is described as 'a new Musical Piece, by Mozart, called The Enchanted Flute'.

[58] See 'Hr.' (i.e., John Christian Hüttner), 'Schirmer's Project einer großen teutschen Oper in London' (dated 22 August 1806), *London und Paris* no. 7 (1806) p 189–192.

[59] I am grateful to Nicolas Bell for advising that the only extant copy of this work—BL Hirsch M.332, which shows no evidence of having been trimmed to remove printed text such as a price or an address—passed to the British Museum from the collector Paul Hirsch in October 1948. Its prior provenance is unknown.

[60] For information about her life and works see Manfred Elsberger, *Nina d'Aubigny von Engelbrunner*, Munich, 2000 (his doctoral dissertation at the Universität Passau). The family's surname also was spelt 'Engelbronner' (*ibid.*, p 20).

and wrote articles on various topics for the periodical *London und Paris* which appeared alongside those by John Christian Hüttner.

In a diary entry for February 1804 she recorded that Professor Fischer, who then also was in London, introduced her to Philippe André and his wife (Amalie, *née* Fränzl):

> führte uns Fischer zu Herrn André, dessen Bruder wir schon bei unserem Besuch in Mannheim in Jahr 1786 kennen gelernt hatten. André hat ein Patent auf dem neuen Gebiet des Steindrucks, das er uns erklärte. [Fischer led us to Mr André, with whose brother [perhaps Johann Anton André] we had become acquainted when we visited Mannheim in 1786. André has a patent in the new field of lithography, which he explained to us.][61]

Nina d'Aubigny von Engelbrunner's connections with the André family presumably led to her meeting Vollweiler and to his purchasing the English copyright of her song 'The woodland halló', which he published in June 1806.[62] Its text, written by Robert Bloomfield, appeared in his recently issued collection *Wild Flowers; or, Pastoral and Local Poetry*.[63] She dedicated this song to Bloomfield; however, no record has been found that they ever met.[64]

---

[61] I am grateful to Manfred Elsberger for supplying this extract from Dietrich Erben's transcript of Nina d'Aubigny von Engelbrunner's London diary. In 1803 Nina had accompanied her sister Susanna and Susanna's husband Carl Horstig to London, where Horstig met Philippe André and saw some of his first prints of lithographed drawings (see Carl Horstig, *Reise nach Frankreich, England und Holland zu Anfange des Jahres 1803*, Berlin, 1806, p 162–164).

[62] His ownership of this copyright is indicated by the word 'for' in the statement on the song's title-page 'printed from stone by and for G. J. Vollweiler', and by the circumstance that 'G. J. Vollweiler' is named as the proprietor of this work in the Stationers' Hall register of works entered on 12 June 1806. See *MESH* p 567, which incorrectly expands Vollweiler's middle name to 'Johann' rather than to 'Jacob'.

[63] London, 1806, p 93–94, where Bloomfield remarks that his poem is '(perhaps) adapted for music'. In Vollweiler's print of Nina d'Aubigny von Engelbrunner's song, the word 'halló' always is written 'hallò'. According to Jonathan Lawson, *Robert Bloomfield*, Boston, 1980, p 35, *Wild Flowers* was published about May 1806.

[64] Following Bloomfield's death in 1823 a two-volume book, *The Remains of Robert Bloomfield*, was published (London, 1824) for the benefit of his family.

Curiously, a month before Vollweiler published 'The woodland halló' Nina d'Aubigny von Engelbrunner entered at Stationers' Hall another of her songs, 'Weep no more', which was engraved and 'printed for the author & sold at Lynott's Library' (a circulating library) as well as at music shops. The short time between these publications suggests that she wanted to compare lithography with conventional music printing. Also in 1806 the André firm published at Offenbach two volumes comprising thirteen other songs that she composed to English and German texts.[65] It is not clear whether that publication preceded or followed the appearance of 'The woodland halló' in London.

On 2 January 1807 the following two advertisements of her works were printed on the first page of *The Morning Post*:

> NEW MUSIC, by Miss Nina d'Aubigny Von Engelbrunner, Author of The Essay on Harmony, Letters on the Art of Singing, &c.—This Day is published, in a style particularly elegant and new, Bloomfield's Woodland Hallo, composed by Miss Nina d'Aubigny Von Engelbrunner, price 1s. Also, a Collection of Songs with English and German Words, by the same Composer. Opera 8, No. 1, containing Poor Jane, The Woer [sic], Go gentle Breeze, England's Warrior, Sigh not, Fair One, Marian's Complaint. No. 2 The Silent Lover, The Emigrant, My Mother, Ode to Folly, Sympathy, The Mischievous Boy, The Smile; price of each Number 5s. Printed on stone, and sold for G. J. Vollweiler, at his

---

An unpaginated annexe entitled 'Prospectus. Bloomfield's Songs.', inserted at the end of the book's first volume, sought subscribers to a proposed publication of at least twenty-four of 'his best songs, set to music', which Goulding & Co. [i.e., Goulding & d'Almaine] would print. 'Woodland Halloo' [sic] composed by 'Miss Nina d'Aubigny' was listed as one of the items planned for inclusion in the proposed collection, but the number of subscribers presumably did not reach the hundred required, as 'Bloomfield's Songs' never appeared.

[65] Publisher nos. 2279 and 2280. According to Constapel, *op. cit.*, p 161–165, these two volumes were listed, together with several other publications issued by the André firm about the same time, in an entry dated 5 August 1806 on page 370 of a copy-book of the firm's letters preserved in their archive at Offenbach. The firm's four extant copy-books are briefly described in Hubert Unverricht, 'Vier Briefkopierbücher des Offenbacher Musikverlags André aus dem ersten Fünftel des 19. Jahrhunderts', in Georg von Dadelsen and Kurt Dorfmüller (eds), *Quellenstudien zur Musik: Wolfgang Schmieder zum 70. Geburtstag*, Frankfurt, 1972, p 161–170. The plan to edit and publish these copy-books (*ibid.*, p 161 note 3) has not yet been realised.

> Poliautographic [sic] Press, No. 9, Buckingham-place, Fitzroy-square; at Lynott's Library, No. 1, Grenville-street; and at all the principal Music Shops.[66]

> NEW MUSIC.—This Day is published, "WEEP NO MORE," price 1s. 6d.: the Music by Miss Nina d'Aubigny Von Engelbrunner: the Words from Beaumont and Fletcher.—Sold at Lynott's Library, No. 1, Grenville-street, and at all Principal Music Shops.

The simultaneous appearance of these advertisements, coupled with the circumstance that Vollweiler is not known to have paid to advertise any of his musical publications in London, suggests that these notices were placed by Nina d'Aubigny von Engelbrunner herself.[67] The first advertisement confirms that music published by the André firm at Offenbach was available for sale at Vollweiler's Buckingham Place establishment.

The two collections of songs by Nina d'Aubigny von Engelbrunner published by the André firm clearly were prepared for sale in both England and Germany. Although the price printed on their title-pages is in German gulden, the text of these title-pages is in the English language, including the imprint 'printed by John André'.

The composer and flautist Charles Saust was born at Ballenstedt, Saxony in 1773 and came to England in 1800. He associated in London with German-born musicians, studying composition with John Charles Samuel Possin and living for a time in John Peter Salomon's house.[68] The André firm had published Saust's

---

[66] 'Letters on the Art of Singing' refers to her *Briefe an Natalie über den Gesang* (Leipzig, 1803). Her essay on harmony has not been traced.

[67] The phrase 'this day is published' in the second advertisement, a common expression at the time, meant that the mentioned works were now published and does not imply that they were first published on that day. As noted on page 457 above, Vollweiler did advertise one of his non-musical publications.

[68] See Saust→Joseph Berridge (a compiler of *A Dictionary of Musicians* published by Sainsbury & Co. in 1824), pmk 23/12/1823, Glasgow University Library, Special Collections, R.d. 88/171, and Alan Tyson, 'Salomon's will', *Beiträge zur rheinischen Musikgeschichte* v 3 (1965) p 43–45 at p 45. On 19 May 1802 Salomon led the band (i.e., conducted the orchestra) at Saust's benefit concert in London (advertisement, *The Morning Chronicle*, 19 May 1802, p 1).

Variations for flute and violoncello, opus 2, before Vollweiler arrived in London,[69] and presumably suggested that he and Saust meet.

Saust's opus 5 'The favorite air *Sul Margine d'un Rio*', which Vollweiler printed for him, was composed for and dedicated to 'Miss Marianne Robarts'. Marianne Jane Robarts was the youngest child of the banker Abraham Robarts MP, and her interest in music is corroborated by the circumstance that she and other members of her family subscribed to the Philharmonic Society concerts from its first season in 1813. The dedication suggests that she may have been Saust's pupil.

Opus 5 also was lithographed and published by the André firm at Offenbach. Its publisher number, 2383, suggests that it appeared in late 1806 or in 1807,[70] perhaps after the edition printed by Vollweiler which Saust entered at Stationers' Hall on 15 October 1806.[71] The two editions differed. The London publication was printed in score, whereas the Offenbach edition was issued as separate flute and piano forte parts. Vollweiler's edition required a piano with 'additional keys' that could play an A two octaves and a sixth above Middle C, whereas the André firm's edition, which retained the dedication to 'Miss Marianne Robarts', presented music for such a piano together with an alternative that could be played on instruments lacking the additional keys. It is not known whether the person who prepared the André firm edition worked from a manuscript or a copy of the Vollweiler print.[72]

Charles Edward Horn's song, 'Fair and young or the age of love', was one of his first published compositions.[73] He and his dedicatee 'Miss Stephenson'—i.e., Mary Eliza Stephenson, eldest

---

[69] Constapel, *op. cit.*, states (p 155) that this work, publisher no. 2110, was announced in the Gotha *Reichsanzeiger* on 1 June 1805.

[70] Constapel, *op. cit.*, p 167. The copy of this work in the André firm archive is incomplete. I am grateful to Alex Nitschke for a photocopy of that copy.

[71] *MESH* p 570.

[72] About 1823 a 'second edition' of this song was published in London by R. Cocks & Co. from engraved plates.

[73] The words, by Thomas Moore, were first published in his *Odes of Anacreon, translated into English verse, with notes*, London, 1800, p 150.

daughter of his godfather Edward Stephenson[74] and an accomplished pianist[75]—were twenty years old in 1806. If Horn wrote this song to convey an amorous interest his message did not succeed, as Mary Eliza married her relation Rowland Stephenson on 23 April 1807. 'Fair and young' must have been lithographed before then, as she ceased to be Miss Stephenson on that day.

It seems likely that Horn's father, the composer Charles Frederick Horn, who was born at Nordhausen, Saxony, and came to England in 1782, suggested that Vollweiler print this song. Charles Frederick Horn was music master to Queen Charlotte from 1789 to 1793, and from 1789 to 1812 he was music master to five of the royal princesses who had honoured Vollweiler's *Specimens of Polyautography* with their patronage. From about 1801 to 1808 the Horn family lived at 13 Queen's Buildings, Brompton Road, Knightsbridge, where the song's title-page announced that copies of it could be had.[76]

Although the title-page stated that 'Fair and young' was entered at Stationers' Hall, Charles Edward Horn (in common with many other proprietors of musical compositions who made this assertion)

---

[74] For Horn's relationship with Edward Stephenson, in honour of whom Horn was given his middle name, see Michael Kassler (ed.), *Charles Edward Horn's Memoirs of his Father and Himself*, Aldershot, 2003, p 9. Horn did not mention this song in his memoirs. It was conventional at the time when referring to an eldest unmarried daughter to omit her first name.

[75] On 25 January 1806 Hester Lynch Piozzi wrote to her daughter Hester Maria Thrale that Mary Eliza Stephenson 'carries the applause away from many a fair dilletante player'. This letter is printed in Edward A. Bloom and Lillian D. Bloom (eds), *The Piozzi Letters v 4 1805–1810*, Newark, Delaware, 1996, p 95–98.

[76] See Kassler, *Charles Edward Horn's Memoirs*, p 1, p 10 and p 114. Two other connections between Charles Edward Horn and Vollweiler can be suggested. The former was principal cellist in the first London performance of Mozart's *La Clemenza di Tito* (*ibid.*, p 32) and, in consequence of this, might have seen Vollweiler's print of the March from this opera. Vollweiler lithographed Peter Eduard Stroehling's *Original Sketches...* (see note 25 above), and Stroehling later painted portraits of Charles Edward Horn (exhibited at the Royal Academy of Arts in 1825 and now in the National Portrait Gallery) and his wife Matilda (now in the possession of Martin Lloyd, Sixpenny Handley, Wiltshire). However, no evidence has been found that Stroehling (who was born in Düsseldorf) knew the Horn family in 1806–1807.

failed to do this, probably because the cost of providing eleven complimentary copies for distribution to deposit libraries, as required by the Copyright Act of 1801 (41 George III, c. 107), was considered excessive in relation to the presumably small print run of this work and a belief that no one was likely to pirate it.[77] The only surviving copy of this song was acquired by the British Museum *c*1864 from an unknown source.[78]

Nothing is known about the composer 'Potpuelsky'—conceivably a pseudonym—whose 'Polonoise for the piano-forte' was lithographed and printed 'for the author' by Vollweiler, without stating the composer's first name.[79]

Vollweiler's publication of a piano arrangement of a march from Georg Joseph Vogler's opera *Castor and Pollux* appears to reflect a long-term interest in his work, although the date of their first meeting is not known and conceivably occurred years after this publication. Vollweiler, at the suggestion of his first music teacher Zimmermann, the Eppingen schoolmaster, went to Heidelberg in 1786 to further his musical education, and Zimmerman's son, who had been Vogler's pupil, was living there then.[80] Vollweiler definitely met Vogler in Offenbach, probably in 1810,[81] where

> Of greatest value for him [Vollweiler] at that time were meetings with Vogler, often at André's house, and he soon got to know and value this native expert and ingenious thinker in this field of art [i.e., music]. The

---

[77] *MESH* p xvii–xviii.

[78] I thank Lynn Young, Corporate Archivist of the British Library, for this information.

[79] This composition is not mentioned in the catalogue of polonaises compiled by Stefan Burhardt (*Polonez: katalog tematyczny*, v 2: 1792–1830, Kraków, 1976).

[80] According to 'G. J. Vollweiler (Nekrolog.)', *op. cit.* in note 17 above.

[81] Vogler's visit to Offenbach in 1810 together with his pupil Carl Maria von Weber is recorded in J[ohn] H[enry] M[ee], 'George Joseph Vogler', in George Grove (ed.), *A Dictionary of Musicians…*, v 4, London, 1899, p 324–331 at p 327. According to Constapel, *op. cit.*, p 478 and p 194, the first Vogler composition published by the André firm—the overture to *Castor and Pollux*, publisher no. 3011—appeared in 1810 or 1811. In the absence of contrary information it is conjecturable that Vollweiler initiated Vogler's contact with André.

> two mutually exchanged their knowledge and discoveries with unlimited trust and found in this communication the richest pleasure of their learning.[82]

It seems plausible that the revival of *Castor and Pollux* in Munich in January 1806 prompted Vollweiler to publish an extract from it in England.

Vollweiler's publications of waltzes by Johann Anton André are discussed below.

Besides the music that he published individually, Vollweiler lithographed three songs for the monthly periodical *La Belle Assemblée* that were issued as 'embellishments' to its letterpress text. This journal, 'addressed particularly to the ladies', was published by the newspaper proprietor John Bell; its first number, dated February 1806, appeared on 1 March 1806.[83] As a lithographed specimen of Bell's proposed edition of 'principal pictures' in the Louvre had been printed by Philippe André in 1803,[84] it seems likely that he passed their business relationship on to Vollweiler.

In addition to these songs—the first lithographed music included in a periodical anywhere[85]—Vollweiler lithographed all the

---

[82] 'Von dem größten Werth war für ihn damals, mit Vogler öfters im André'schen Hause zusammenzutreffen, welcher bald in Vollweiler den überall auf dem Gebiete der Kunst einheimischen Kenner und scharfsinnigen Denker erkannte und liebgewann, Beide tauschten mit unbegränztem Vertrauen ihre Erfahrungen und Entdeckungen gegenseitig aus and fanden in dieser Mittheilung den reichsten Genuß ihrer Wissenschaft' ('G. J. Vollweiler (Nekrolog.)', *op. cit.*).

[83] For Bell see Stanley Morison, *John Bell, 1745–1831*, Cambridge, 1930, in which a chapter is devoted to *La Belle Assemblée*. The periodical and its context are described in Alison Adburgham, *Women in Print*, London, 1972, p 218–235.

[84] Copy at BM Prints and Drawings 190*.b.1 f 119, reproduced in Man, *op. cit.*, p 119. This publication, however, 'eventually ... appeared with copper-engraved plates' (Twyman, *Lithography 1800–1850*, p 42–43). An undated lithographed portrait of John Bell, attributed to George Arnald, is in BM Prints and Drawings 190*.b.01 f 52. The portrait is mentioned in T[homas] Fisher→'Mr [Sylvanus] Urban' [pseudonym of the editor of *The Gentleman's Magazine*], 1 February [1808], printed in *Gentleman's Magazine* v 78 = n.s. v 1 (March 1808) p 193–196 at p 196, but it is not known whether it was printed by Philippe André or by Vollweiler.

[85] Twyman, *Early Lithographed Music*, p 111.

needlework patterns that embellished each number of *La Belle Assemblée* from its first to its seventeenth number (dated May 1807 and published on 1 June 1807).[86] Although he is not named on any embellishment or elsewhere in this periodical, the work is confidently attributed to him because no other lithographic press is known to have been operating in London at the time,[87] and because the handwriting of both the music and the English words in these embellishments is similar to work explicitly printed by him.

Each number of *La Belle Assemblée* included an original music embellishment which was either lithographed or engraved. Presumably Bell or one of his employees invited composers to create new works for the magazine and, if lithography was to be used, had their manuscripts sent to Vollweiler for copying onto stone and printing.[88]

La Belle Assemblée appears to have been an immediate success. Bell advertised on 15 June 1806 that 'new editions of the first three numbers may now be had',[89] implying that their first impressions had sold out,[90] and on 27 June he asserted that 'upwards of four thousand' copies were printed of its fifth number issued on 1 July 1806.[91] His monthly order for needlework embellishments accordingly was

---

[86] On 1 January 1807 the journal published a 'supplemental' number, no. 12, in addition to the regular December 1807 number, no. 11.

[87] Twyman, *Early Lithographed Music*, p 383–385.

[88] It is not known whether Bell at this time was the journal's editor as well as its publisher. In 1809 he offered to appoint the actress Elizabeth Inchbald 'conductress' of *La Belle Assemblée*, but she declined (see James Boaden, *Memoirs of Mrs Inchbald*, London, 1833, v 2 p 130).

[89] *Bell's Weekly Messenger* (published by John Bell), 15 June 1806, p 190.

[90] When the sixth number was published in August, he announced that all the preceding numbers were now available in 'new editions' (advertisements, *The Morning Chronicle*, 2 August 1806, p 1, and *Bell's Weekly Messenger*, 3 August 1806, p 246).

[91] Advertisement, *The Morning Chronicle*, 27 June 1806, p 1. According to data compiled by Richard D. Altick and published in his *The English Common Reader* (Chicago, 1957, p 392), *The Gentleman's Magazine* had a circulation of 4,550 copies in 1797, *The Monthly Magazine* and *The Monthly Review* each had a print run of 5,000 copies in 1797, and in 1807 *The Methodist Magazine* and *The Evangelical Magazine* each had a circulation of about 18,000 copies.

Vollweiler's largest job—indeed, it appears to have been the largest print run for lithography anywhere up to that time. This job gave the Polyautographic Office steady income and would have taken about forty hours a month to finish.[92] Contrastingly, music published separately in the Georgian era (presumably including Vollweiler's separately issued lithographed music) commonly was printed in batches of fewer than 100 copies.[93]

The music embellishment in the first number of *La Belle Assemblée* was a song by D[omenico] Corri entitled 'Only tell her that I love!'. Two versions were printed—one lithographed and the other engraved—and, because of a change in Vollweiler's orthography, it seems likely that the former version was included with the first impression of the first number of *La Belle Assemblée* published on 1 March 1806, and the latter version was supplied with the 'new edition' of that number published in August 1806.[94]

In his first individually issued song (from *Die drei Freier*, published on 30 January 1806) and in the lithographed version of Corri's song, Vollweiler used both the long-'s' glyph 'ſ' and the short-'s' glyph 's' to spell English song texts: the former song has

---

[92] I am grateful to Michael Twyman for this estimate.

[93] For instance, William Forster's firm had fifty copies of a Haydn composition printed *c*1786 and a further twenty-five copies printed from the same engraved plates *c*1817. See William Sandys and Simon Andrew Forster, *The History of the Violin*..., London, 1864, p 312. Music printed lithographically by the André firm in Offenbach in the early nineteenth century generally had total print runs of at most a few hundred copies, which often were printed in more than one batch (Twyman, *Early Lithographed Music*, p 194). On 6 May 1818 Thomas Fisher told the House of Commons Select Committee on the Copyright Acts that the Polyautographic Office had printed for him, *c*1807, 120 impressions of each of eight drawings (*Report from the Select Committee on the Copyright Acts … ordered … to be printed, 5 June 1818*, parliamentary paper no. 402, p 97).

[94] Lithographed copies are at CUL MR403.a.80.1; NYPL *DA (Belle assemblée) and UNE SC052/B438; the only known engraved copy is at BL P.P. 5142. For help in retrieving and examining these copies I am very grateful to Margaret Jones (Cambridge University Library), David Christie (New York Public Library), Robyn Warwick (University of New England Library) and Michael Twyman. I thank Lynn Young for the information that the British Library's incomplete set of volume 1, which contains the engraved song, was acquired by the British Museum in 1946 to replace books damaged or destroyed during the Second World War.

'bashfulneſs'; the latter has 'ſhould', 'ſhe' and 'ſoftly'. However, in Vollweiler's later individually issued songs (by von Engelbrunner and Horn) and in the two other songs that he lithographed for *La Belle Assemblée* (by John Braham and William Reeve), only the short 's' was used to write the verses. This change is significant because Bell had decided in the 1780s to do away with the long 's', announcing in the 'Advertisement' to his edition of Shakespeare's dramatic works that

> he hath ventured to depart from the common mode, by rejecting the long ſ in favour of the round one, as being less liable to error from the occasional imperfections of the letter f, and the frequent substitution of it for the long ſ; the regularity of the print is by that means very much promoted, the lines having the effect of being more open, without really being at any additional distance.[95]

By 1801 many English printers followed Bell's example and avoided the long 's', although later instances of it can be found.[96]

It seems likely that Vollweiler was unaware of this change of practice when he arrived in England, and that Bell—after seeing the lithographed print of Corri's song—brought it to Vollweiler's attention. This would explain why he did not use the long 's' when lettering the verses of the song included with the second number of *La Belle Assemblée* published on 1 April 1806, and makes it improbable that he used the long 's' to lithograph Corri's song for the 'new edition' of the first number that was published in June.[97]

Bell clearly did not anticipate the demand for the first number of his new journal and therefore presumably did not ask Vollweiler to

---

[95] 'Advertisement' (pages unnumbered) in *Prolegomena to the Dramatick Writings of Will. Shakspere* v 1, London, printed for, and under the direction of, John Bell, 1788. Bell also asserted in this 'Advertisement' that 'Shakspere' was the correct spelling of the playwright's name.

[96] See Paul W. Nash, 'The abandoning of the long s in Britain in 1800', *Journal of the Printing Historical Society* n.s. v 3 (summer 2001) p 3–19. Nash discusses Bell's contribution to this abandonment on p 7–9.

[97] Vollweiler continued to use the long 's', though not always, when writing the English pair of letters 'ſs' in texts other than song verses.

keep Corri's song on stone after its initial print run was done.[98] It is not known why Bell chose to have this song engraved—rather than lithographed a second time—when additional copies of it were required for the first number's 'new edition' in June, nor are his reasons apparent for discontinuing lithographed music in favour of engraving after the July 1806 number (published on 1 August) while continuing with lithographed needlework patterns up to the May 1807 number (published on 1 June).

Bell's disuse of lithographed needlework patterns after then—the later needlework embellishments in *La Belle Assemblée* were engraved—clearly relates to André's decision about the middle of 1807 to close the Polyautographic Office. After finishing this task Vollweiler left London in August 1807 and returned to Offenbach where he resumed working for the André firm.[99] It is not known whether the loss of Bell's business led André to shut down the London office or if news of its planned closure forced Bell to turn to engraving to produce the journal's subsequent embellishments.

A reputed advantage of lithography was that a very large number of impressions—many more than could be taken from an engraved plate—could be obtained from a single stone without degradation of the resulting image,[100] although the process was

---

[98] After an order was completed 'most lithographic stones were ground clean and used again' (Twyman, *Early Lithographed Music*, p 62).

[99] Thomas Fisher said (in Fisher→'Mr Urban', 1 February 1808, *loc. cit.*, p 193) that Vollweiler 'returned to Germany in August last'. Lithographed drawings printed for Fisher that were dated 22 July 1807 may have been the last productions of the Polyautographic Office (see Twyman, *Lithography 1800–1850*, p 31).

[100] In 1803 John Christian Hüttner wrote (in 'Zeichnende Künste', *op. cit.* in note 45 above, p 63) that polyautography enabled an unlimited number of copies to be printed, of which the first was as good as the last ['Man kann nun Abdrücke bis ins Undendliche machen: der erste ist so gut wie der letze']. In 1807 an article in the *Morgenblatt für gebildete Stände* reported a suggestion that 10,000 to 20,000 prints of a drawing could be printed from a lithographic stone, but added that this number had not been verified (Twyman, *Lithography 1800–1850*, p 76–77), probably because no one had yet tried to print so many copies lithographically.

subject to its own hazards, such as stones breaking.[101] By contrast, each page of engraved music was printed at this time from a pewter plate, from which the maximum number of impressions obtainable was about 2,000.[102] Therefore, to print 4,000 copies of an engraved song, two plates would have had to have been engraved for each of its pages.[103]

It should be noted that extant bound volumes of *La Belle Assemblée* often lack some or all of its music embellishments. Like other contemporary periodicals, after a number of this journal was printed, its letterpress text and its separately printed other embellishments were lightly sewn into a wrapper. The number was

---

[101] See Twyman, 'Lithographic stone and the printing trade in the nineteenth century', *op. cit.* in note 25 above, p 31–32.

[102] In the pamphlet *Some Account of the Methods of Musick Printing...*, London, 1847 (reprinted in *A Century and a Half in Soho: A short history of the firm of Novello, publishers and printers of music 1811–1861*, London, 1961, p 69–75) J[oseph] Alfred Novello wrote (p 6–7, p 73–74 of the reprint): 'The cost of producing a page of musick on a Pewter Plate is comparatively small [compared to producing it from music types]; and there is the further advantage of being able to print *fifty* copies only from it as any number of hundreds, thereby saving the accumulation of useless stock, and loss of interest on the cost of paper—great advantages in a work of slow or doubtful sale, or the demand for which is likely to be limited. The disadvantages of this mode are, the early wearing out of the plates (from 1300 to 2000 impressions, according to the goodness of the workmanship), and also the comparatively high cost of the printing.' In an undated but *c*1848 pamphlet *A Day at a Music Publishers: A description of the establishment of D'Almaine & Co.* published by the firm in London (and reprinted with notes and commentary in H[erbert] Edmund Poole, '*A Day at a Music Publishers*', *Journal of the Printing Historical Society* no. 14 (1979/80) p 59–81), D'Almaine & Co. wrote (p 5) that 'Pewter Plates have long been preferred as the substance best adapted for Music-Engraving, the softness or malleability of the metal rendering it pliable to the *graver* [a tool used, for instance, to rule staff-lines], while its cost is trifling compared with copper, and its durability is considerable'.

[103] This was done for copper-plate engravings issued with other periodicals. For instance, an advertisement for the November 1761 number of *The London Magazine* (*London Evening Post*, 28 November 1761, p 4) said that 'The fine Print of her Majesty Queen Charlotte, intended for this Month, is obliged to be postponed till next; for altho' two Plates were engraved, it was impossible to work off a sufficient Number Time enough for this Publication'. I am grateful to Tim Clayton for informing me of this advertisement.

sold in this manner to the public.[104] When the last number of a volume appeared, the publisher issued an index and title-page to the volume, and interested subscribers then could have it bound, at which stage the initially supplied wrappers generally were discarded. However, because bound music could not easily be performed, as its pages would no longer lie flat, it seems likely that many owners removed the music embellishments before handing their copies to a binder.[105]

One of the German-speaking musicians whom Johann Anton André met in London in July 1800 was the theorist Augustus Frederic Christopher Kollmann, organist of the German Chapel in St James's Palace.[106] As André knew that Vollweiler and Kollmann were both interested in music theory, it seems likely that he recommended that they get together.[107] In Kollmann's *A New Theory of Musical Harmony*, which he entered at Stationers' Hall on 20 May 1806, he referred to the 'unremitted consideration' he had given to 'the science of harmony' and his 'particular study, to find out a simple method, by which every note that is useful in music, might have *as positive a*

---

[104] The sewing generally produced three holes in the central part of the left margin of each odd-numbered page that are visible in disbound parts of the journal (e.g., compendia of advertisements (in K) that were issued with *La Belle Assemblée* on 1 September 1807 and 1 October 1807). For another example of this practice see Michael Kassler, *A. F. C. Kollmann's* Quarterly Musical Register, *op. cit.*, p 189.

[105] For instance, a copy (in K) of the foldout sheet containing 'An original waltz, by Mr Kollmann, for the year 1808, composed expressly & exclusively for *La Belle Assemblée*, & to be had only with that work', which embellished the 1 December 1807 number, bears three sewing holes in the centre of its left margin but has no other sewing holes, which would have been present if the engraved sheet had been sewn into a bound volume.

[106] See note 8 above. Their subsequent relationship, which included the André firm's publication of a work by Kollmann in 1808, is described in Kassler, *A. F. C. Kollmann's* Quarterly Musical Register, p 98–99 and elsewhere.

[107] Evidence that Vollweiler met Kollmann is found in André's 22 August 1809 letter to Kollmann's brother Georg Christoph, in which André asks that Vollweiler's thanks, as well as his own, be conveyed to A. F. C. Kollmann and his son George for sending some of the latter's compositions. This letter, of which a copy is preserved in a copy-book of out-letters in the André firm archive in Offenbach, is summarised in Michael Kassler, *A. F. C. Kollmann's* Quarterly Musical Register, p 268.

rule, as it denotes a *positive sound*'.[108] A plausible consequence of their meeting is that Vollweiler introduced Kollmann to Bell, who then invited Kollmann to write music and articles about music for *La Belle Assemblée* which were published in that magazine between December 1806 and December 1807.[109]

The title-page of *La Belle Assemblée* for November 1806 (published on 1 December 1806) announced that the music embellishments issued with that number included 'two German Waltzs, by Dr Kollmann, and Mr Andre' [sic]. However, a note on the last page of that number—page 558—said that 'An original Walz, [sic] by Dr Kollmann, is composed and given in the present Number' but did not mention André, and the single sheet of engraved music that accompanied the number included Kollmann's 'General Hutchinson's Waltz' but nothing by André.[110] As Johann Anton André's compositions had not previously been printed in England, and as Vollweiler was his agent, it seems likely that Vollweiler had promised to provide Bell with copies of a waltz by André for this number but failed to do this, perhaps because the score did not arrive from Offenbach in time for Vollweiler to lithograph and print the required number of copies.

Because Vollweiler did lithograph and publish several waltzes by André, it seems likely that he decided to issue them as publications of the Polyautographic Office after the opportunity to include one in *La Belle Assemblée* had lapsed. He published one waltz by itself under the title *The Offenbach Waltz* and six others as a set entitled 'Six Waltzes for the Piano-Forte'. In both publications (and nowhere else, as far as is known), he used the imprint 'printed & Sold by G. J.

---

[108] Augustus Frederic Christopher Kollmann, *A New Theory of Musical Harmony, according to a complete and natural system of that science*, London, 1806, p 4. For Vollweiler's efforts in this area of study see page 454 above.

[109] Michael Kassler, *A. F. C. Kollmann's* Quarterly Musical Register, p 89–95 and p 238–240.

[110] So too, an initial newspaper advertisement for this number (e.g., *Trewman's Exeter Flying Post*, 27 November 1806, p 3) referred to its inclusion of 'a German waltz, by Dr Kolman; and another by Mr André', whereas the newspaper advertisement for the following number (e.g., *Caledonian Mercury*, 27 December 1806, p 1) mentioned Kollmann amongst the composers of music in the last number but did not mention André.

Vollweiler at his polyautographic office', which suggests that they were lithographed within a short interval of time. It is not known whether use of the word 'his' in these imprints, in place of the word 'the', signified that he had made a financial contribution to the London office or to the publication of these waltzes.

Figure 9.2 reproduces, as an illustration of Vollweiler's music lithography, the only known copy of his edition of *The Offenbach Waltz*. Except for small variants its music is the same as, and probably was sourced from, the first half of an André firm publication entitled 'Walze favorite du carnaval d'Offenbach arrangé pour le piano-forté', of which Vollweiler had a copy in London, as he offered it for sale.[111] He presumably omitted the second half of that composition—a coda—so that *The Offenbach Waltz* could fit on a single page and be sold for sixpence.

The André firm published 'Walze favorite...' several times. Its first edition, bearing publisher no. 1647, appeared no later than 29 January 1803, when a work with this title and publisher number which named the composer as 'Antoine André' was announced as issued by the music sellers Mme Duhan et Cie in Paris.[112] Although the relationship between André and Jeanne-Élisabeth Duhan is unclear, her company has been described as being an unofficial branch of the André firm at this time.[113] It is not known whether the first edition of 'Walze favorite...' was printed in Offenbach or in Paris or in both places, nor whether copies of it sold in Paris had the same

---

[111] A copy of 'Walze favorite…' with Vollweiler's label pasted on its title-page is in Killerton House, Broadclyst, Devon. See *Table 9.2* below on page 502. Although this edition does not name the composer, when Vollweiler lithographed *The Offenbach Waltz* he was able to identify him as André because the two were in contact.

[112] *Correspondence des Amateurs Musiciens* no. 10, 9 Pluviôse 11 = 29 January 1803, p 4. 'Walze favorite…' was noticed in this journal just above 'Symphonie à grand orchestre' by 'Antoine André', publisher no. 1586 and issued in Paris by the same music seller, which has been considered (by Elisabeth Lebeau in 'Les débuts ignorés de l'Imprimerie lithographique…', *op. cit.* in note 24 above, p 253–254) to be the oldest known lithographed music published in France.

[113] By Elisabeth Lebeau in 'Une succursale officieuse de Johann Anton André à Paris, de 1802 à 1806', *op. cit.* in note 24 above.

Figure 9.2 Johann Anton André's The Offenbach Waltz *printed by Georg Jacob Vollweiler, London,* c*1807 (by permission of Jamie and Michael Kassler, Northbridge, NSW, Australia)*

title-page as those sold in Offenbach.[114] However, the first edition apparently differed from the lithographed André firm edition that Vollweiler sold in London, as the latter edition does not state its composer's name.[115]

Its music had some popularity in the United Kingdom. The music sellers Goulding, Phipps & d'Almaine presumably acquired a copy that Vollweiler had imported and passed it to an engraver, as they published before 1810 'Favorite Waltze du Carnaval d'Offenbach', whose musical text is the same as the edition that Vollweiler imported.[116] And about 1815 that firm, now styled Goulding, d'Almaine, Potter & Co., issued 'The Offenbach Waltz, with Variations for the Piano Forte' by F. Vollrath,[117] who took the melody of his theme from the opening section of that waltz.

Vollweiler's London edition of André's 'Six Waltzes for the Piano-Forte' (which, as mentioned, does not include 'The Offenbach Waltz') presumably was sourced from the André firm's publication no. 1675. A lithographed copy of that publication, which has the French-language title 'Six walzes pour le piano-forté' and the imprint

---

[114] According to Anik Devriès and François Lesure, *Dictionnaire des éditeurs de musique français* v 1, Geneva, 1979, p 60–62, several publications of Mme Duhan et Cie in 1802 and 1803 apparently were printed from the same stones and bore the same publisher number as editions of the same music published by the André firm.

[115] A copy of another, almost certainly later lithographed edition of 'Walze favorite…', with the same title-page and publisher number but with different music (in particular, it has first and second endings, whereas *The Offenbach Waltz* and Vollweiler's presumed source do not), is preserved in the Baron collection. This edition, which also does not name the composer, seems likely to have been issued later because a copy (in the André archive) of still another edition, having publisher no. 2123, naming the composer as 'Antoine André', and marked 'quatrième édition' on the title-page, contains the same first and second endings as the copy in the Baron collection.

[116] Copy at BL g.272.i.(18). The composer's name again is not stated. The imprint advises that copies could be had not only in London but also from the firm's associates in Dublin and Glasgow. William Window Phipps retired from the Goulding partnership on 1 January 1810 (*The London Gazette*, 20–23 January 1810, p 106).

[117] Copy at BL h.1480.w.(36). I thank Lynn Young for advising that the BL copies of these two works were bought by the British Museum in the 1870s.

of Mme Duhan's company in Paris, is kept in the André firm archive in Offenbach.

After Vollweiler left London in 1807 no music appears to have been lithographed in England until the 1820s.[118] It is interesting to speculate why his efforts to introduce the new technology did not flourish. The structure of the music trade at the time offers a partial explanation. Although some composers in England dealt directly with engravers and printers, most composers who wanted their music printed contracted with a music seller. He or she arranged not only to have a composition engraved and printed but also to advertise it and to sell copies of it in his or her London shop and, through agents, elsewhere in Britain. A seller who thought that publication of a work would be profitable often bought its copyright from the composer and sold copies without further remuneration to the composer. In other cases, the seller paid the upfront expenses of publication (such as engraving and printing) and shared with the composer the income from sales, or published a work on commission from its composer, who paid the upfront expenses and received the income less an agreed fee.[119]

Vollweiler, however, set up the music part of his business not as a service to London's established music sellers but in direct competition with them. Labels pasted on title-pages show that music published by the André firm in Offenbach was sold 'by G. J. Vollweiler at the Polyautographic Printing Office, No. 9, Buckingham-Place, Fitzroy-Square', so customers could buy at his premises not only works that he had lithographed but also copies of

---

[118] See Twyman, *Early Lithographed Music*, p 386, who remarks that 'it is extraordinary how little interest was shown in the use of lithography for printing music in Britain'.

[119] See Michael Kassler, 'The Bachists of 1810', in Michael Kassler (ed.), *The English Bach Awakening: Knowledge of J. S. Bach and his music in England 1750–1830*, Aldershot, 2004, p 315–340, at p 334–340, which gives some costs of music engraving and printing at this time. These types of arrangement between composer and music seller were substantially the same as between authors of literary works and booksellers: see Theodore Besterman, *The Publishing Firm of Cadell & Davies: Select correspondence and accounts 1793–1836*, Oxford, 1938, p xxviii–xxx.

the André firm's publications.[120] As the Polyautographic Office, although nominally independent, was in effect a subsidiary of a leading German music publisher, it is not surprising that London's established music sellers declined to direct business to it.[121] Regardless of whether they liked the look of lithographed music or considered that lithography might be commercially advantageous to them in some circumstances, Vollweiler's ownership of the English and Scottish patent rights to the process meant that other British music sellers could not make use of it without paying him.

Like Philippe André, Vollweiler does not appear to have advertised or sought publicity which might have attracted inquiries from composers seeking a publisher or from members of the public wanting to buy music.[122] Aside from his own publications, and a brief report of polyautography by one of his artistic clients which mentioned in passing that 'music also has been printed from it with great success',[123] the only known contemporary reference to Vollweiler's music activities in London was published in Germany by Philipp Andreas Nemnich, who visited Britain from spring 1805 to spring 1806 to examine British industry:

> Noten oder Musikalien, womit in London vornehmlich folgende händeln: Clementi, Corry [sic], Monzani; Wilkinson; Lavenu; Dale; Kelly; Birchall. Sie lassen ihre Noten in Zinnplatten stechen. Ganz

---

[120] Publications of the André firm that were sold by Vollweiler in London are listed in *Table 9.2* on pages 502–505 below.

[121] Parallel efforts to establish an unofficial branch of the André firm in Paris—news of which probably reached the English music trade—are discussed in Elisabeth Lebeau, 'Une succursale officieuse de Johann Anton André à Paris, de 1802 à 1806', *op. cit.* in note 24 above.

[122] No contemporary reviews of music printed by Vollweiler in London have been located. It is conceivable that he did not provide review copies to periodicals such as *The Monthly Magazine* that regularly noticed new musical publications.

[123] H. B. Ker [i.e., Charles Henry Bellenden Ker], 'Some account of polyautography; a discovery lately made of printing from stone', *Philosophical Magazine* v 27 no. 105 (February 1807) p 60–61 at p 61. Vollweiler's name is misspelt 'Volwieler'. According to Man, *op. cit.*, p 122, catalogue nos 107–111, Vollweiler lithographed five drawings by Ker in 1807. Few composers seeking publishers of their music would have read the *Philosophical Magazine*.

neuerlich hat sich ein Offenbacher Namens Vollweyler [sic], aus der Andréschen Offizin, mit der Kunst, sowohl Zeichnungen, als Noten, von Steinplatten abzudrucken, in London etablirt, und sich ein Patent darüber ertheilen lassen. Er hat diese Kunst unter dem Namen von Patent Polyautography bekannt gemacht.

[Printed music is sold in London mainly by Clementi, Corri, Monzani, Wilkinson, Lavenu, Dale, Kelly and Birchall. Their music is engraved on pewter plates. Quite recently an Offenbacher named Vollweiler, from André's printing office, set up in London a business to print music as well as drawings from slabs of stone, for which a patent was granted to him. He has made this art known under the name, patent polyautography.][124]

It is remarkable that none of the composers whose music Vollweiler lithographed engaged his Polyautographic Office to prepare and print a second work. Presumably they found his product or his terms insufficiently attractive to warrant another try.[125]

Vollweiler did not run his business entirely by himself. The Offenbach artist Johann Mathias Hergenröder reportedly lived in London in the same house as Vollweiler[126] and 'practised'

---

[124] Philipp Andreas Nemnich, *Neueste Reise durch England, Schottland, und Ireland, hauptsächlich in Bezug auf Produkte, Fabriken, und Handlung* ['Recent travels through England, Scotland and Ireland, chiefly with regard to products, manufacturing and trade'], Tübingen, 1807, p 144. The period of Nemnich's British travels is stated on p vi. 'Corry' refers to Corri, Pearce & Co.

[125] Curiously, Frederick Schirmer, in association with the Austrian-born composer Joseph Woelfl who removed to London in May 1805, began a quarterly series called *Schirmer's Choice Manuscript Collection of Music*; its first number was published in December 1806. Each number (of which apparently only two appeared) comprised a printed title-page followed by handwritten piano or harp music 'arranged and partly orginally composed by' Woelfl. Extant copies of the two numbers (Beinecke OSB MSS 146 box 150 folder 802; and BL f.65.s) include Schirmer's printed prospectus dated 30 September 1806, which announced his intention to establish this quarterly 'before his return to Germany'.

[126] Thomas Fisher→'Mr Urban', 1 February 1808, wrote (*loc. cit.* in note 84 above, p 195–196) about 'The Shepherd's Boy by Mr Hergen Rodr [sic] (a German artist, who resided at the [Polyautographic] Printing-office)'. A lithograph of this drawing by Hergenröder—son of the more famous artist Georg Heinrich Hergenröder—is in BM Prints and Drawings 190*.b.1 f 78. I am grateful to Anjali Pujari of the Abteilung Archiv, Haus der Stadtgeschichte, Offenbach, for information about Johann Matthias Hergenröder.

lithography there.[127] David J. Redman, who later became a lithographic printer in London on his own account (but not of music), apparently learned that trade while employed by both Philippe André and Vollweiler 'to prepare the stones and assist in working the press'.[128] As the notation of all music printed by the Polyautographic Office was of high quality, equal to that published by the André firm in Offenbach, and as no record has been found that either Hergenröder or Redman was trained to write music on stone, it seems likely that this work was done in London by Vollweiler personally.

After Johann Anton André decided to close the London operations in 1807, Vollweiler arranged to sell Senefelder's English patent (and probably also his Scottish patent), together with the Polyautographic Office's stock (probably including its lithographic press and some stones), to the Quartermaster General of the Army for £100.[129] This purchase was recommended by Lieutenant-Colonel (later Major-General) John Brown,[130] then Assistant Quartermaster General and commander of the Royal Staff Corps.[131] In addition to his engineering achievements, Brown was a watercolourist whose 'chosen master' was the artist John Laporte.[132] Vollweiler, earlier in

---

[127] 'History of Lithography' [an anonymous review of two books], *Foreign Review* v 4 no. 7 (December 1829) p 41–58, states (p 48) that 'lithography was next practised in London [after Philippe André] by two Germans, named Volweiller [sic] and Kergenrader [sic].... Vollweiler, ... with his partner, returned to Germany in August 1807'. It is plausible that Hergenröder drew the portrait of Vollweiler illustrated in *Figure 9.1* on page 459 above.

[128] 'History of Lithography', *op. cit.*, p 48. See also H[enry] Bankes, *Lithography; or, the Art of Making Drawings on Stone*, Bath, 1813, p 4 (reproduced in facsimile in the book cited in note 4 above). Redman may have looked after the Polyautographic Office between Philippe André's departure and Vollweiler's arrival.

[129] 'History of Lithography', p 48–49. The Quartermaster General's department subsequently hired David Redman (*ibid.* and Bankes, *op. cit.*, p 4–5) and used their lithographic press to print maps and circulars but not to print music.

[130] 'History of Lithography', p 48.

[131] See *A List of All the Officers of the Army and Royal Marines…*, 55th ed., [London], War Office, 10 January 1807, p 22, and Iain Gordon Brown, 'Brown, John', *Oxford Dictionary of National Biography*, Oxford, 2004.

[132] Iain Gordon Brown, *op. cit.*

1807, had printed a landscape that Laporte had drawn on stone,[133] and Brown presumably recognised, when he saw a copy of it and heard that the technology which produced it was for sale, that lithography would be useful for printing maps and other military publications.

After returning to Offenbach, Vollweiler worked for the André firm until 1818.[134] He continued to write and to sign letters on the firm's behalf,[135] and he also taught music. Carl Arnold, who boarded with Johann Anton André between 1812 and 1815, studied piano with Vollweiler then, and André and Vollweiler jointly taught him composition.[136] The flautist Anton Bernhard Fürstenau, who played in the Frankfurt orchestra in 1817, had lessons in music theory and composition with Vollweiler in that year.[137] Wilhelm Speyer studied

---

[133] This lithograph (copy at National Gallery of Australia, Felix Man Collection, accession no. 72.509.236) has the caption '*LONDON printed from stone at the polyautographic office, Nº 9 Buckingham-Place, Fitzroy-Square. ~*'. The print is not dated but, according to Man, *op. cit.*, p 130, was included in the sixth set of *Specimens of Polyautography* that was published in 1807. After Laporte had executed his drawing on stone it is plausible that Vollweiler wrote this caption on that stone, as the lettering of the caption appears similar to the lettering of Vollweiler's imprints on music by Saust, Horn, Potpuelsky and André.

[134] The 1818 termination date of Vollweiler's employment by the André firm is given in 'G. J. Vollweiler (Nekrolog.)', *op. cit.* in note 17 above, p 1303.

[135] He signed a 16 May 1810 letter to the publisher Friedrich Justin Bertuch (Goethe- und Schiller-Archiv, Weimar, ms GSA 6/2016) 'per procura von Joh. André [on behalf of Johann André] | G. J. Vollweiler'. His June 1811 letters to Senefelder proposing publication of the latter's planned book of lithographic specimens are transcribed in Carl Wagner, *Alois Senefelder: Sein Leben und Wirken*, Leipzig, 1914, p 118–122. A 3 October 1816 letter to the Gotha music seller B[ernhard] Keil (Universität Hamburg, Zentrum fur Theaterforschung), signed by Vollweiler, included a handwritten list of selected André firm publications. I am grateful to Dr Michaela Giesing for a copy of the latter letter.

[136] I am grateful to Harald Herresthal, author of *Carl Arnold (1794–1873): ein europäischer Musiker des 19. Jahrhunderts*, Wilhelmshaven, 1993, for alerting me to this information, reported by [Heinrich Friedrich] L[udwig] Rellstab, 'Arnold, Karl' [sic], in Gustav Schilling (ed.), *Encyclopädie der gesammten musikalischen Wissenschaften, oder Universal-Lexikon der Tonkunst*, 2nd ed., v 1 (Stuttgart, 1840) p 276–279 at p 277.

[137] See F[rançois]-J[oseph] Fétis, *Biographie universelle des musiciens*, 2nd ed., v 3, Paris, 1866, p 357; and Bernhard Maria Heinrich Schneeberger, *Die Musikerfamilie Fürstenau: Untersuchungen zu Leben und Werk*, Münster, 1992,

music theory with Vollweiler about this time.[138] The composer and pianist Aloys Schmitt became acquainted with him in Offenbach and later chose Vollweiler to teach his son music.[139]

On 15 December 1811 Vollweiler married Catharina Sieffert in the Deutsch-Reformierte Kirche at Offenbach.[140] In the marriage register he was described as manager of the André music-printing works ['Director der Andreschen Musikalien Fabrik']. Their son Carl, who became a well-known composer and pianist, was born at Offenbach on 27 November 1813.[141] The Vollweilers also had two daughters, both named Carolina Ernestina. The elder daughter, born on 17 April 1816, died soon afterwards;[142] the younger daughter, nicknamed 'Lina', was born at Offenbach on 20 March 1818.

Vollweiler was back in London between May and August 1814,[143] where he apparently stayed at 20 Buckingham Place, Fitzroy Square—the street in which he had previously worked and lived.[144]

---

p 92–94. I am grateful to Dr Schneeberger for supplying an extract from this publication of his Universität Münster doctoral dissertation.

[138] Edward Speyer, *Wilhelm Speyer der Liederkomponist 1790–1878*, Munich, 1925, p 4.

[139] See Heinrich Henkel, *Leben und Wirken von Dr Aloys Schmitt*, Frankfurt, 1873, p 6–7. Henkel described Vollweiler as quiet and discreet and having a patriarchal, serious appearance and a quite opposite character to André [Vollweiler war eine ruhige, besonnene, mehr patriarchalisch ernste Erscheinung, gerade das gegentheilige Naturell von André] (*ibid.*, p 7).

[140] According to the church's marriage register. However, the register of the Evangelische Kirche Frankfurt, which recorded her death on 6 November 1829, gave her first name as Susanna and stated that she was born at Mannheim on 20 December 1785. Microfilms of both registers are in the Family History Library of the Church of Jesus Christ of Latter-day Saints, Salt Lake City, Utah.

[141] See Julius Ferdinand Georg Schuberth, *Kleines musikalisches Conversations-lexikon*, 9th ed., Leipzig, 1873, p 426. Carl's name alternatively was spelt 'Charles' or 'Karl'.

[142] 'G. J. Vollweiler (Nekrolog.)', *op. cit.*, p 1304.

[143] These dates are established by letters that the André firm sent to him in 1814 and recorded in a copy-book of out-letters preserved in the André firm archive (see note 65 above). I am very grateful to Hubert Unverricht for providing photocopies of copy-book entries relating to Vollweiler.

[144] Charles 3rd Earl Stanhope wrote this address and the note '20th July, 1814. From G. J. Vollweiler' next to examples of printing that Stanhope apparently

No evidence has been found that he resumed contact with composers whose music he had lithographed in London during his initial visit, although he presumably renewed his acquaintance with A. F. C. Kollmann, as André asked Vollweiler to introduce Myer Metz and his son Julius to Kollmann and his musical son George Augustus.[145] Myer Metz had left Offenbach to take up an appointment as 'Chazan' (conductor of services) of London's Great Synagogue in 1814, and André wrote that he could not recommend a more learned musician than Kollmann Sr to further the education of Julius, who was already an accomplished pianist.

During this trip Vollweiler is said to have helped the harp-maker Johann Andreas Stumpff, who was born in Germany but lived in London from 1790, during a serious illness.[146] As André sold at

---

received from Vollweiler that day (now in RI Stanhope papers v 2, on or between p 784–786). They included an engraved title-page of the piano arrangement of André's 'Cantate zur Geburtstagfeyer ... Fürstin Charlotte von Isenburg', a page on which 'JOH ANDRE' has been impressed in uninked raised lettering, and what appears to be an admission ticket for a concert by Aloys Schmitt. Two samples of Frankfurt printing, not obviously connected with the André firm, also are present. Presumably Vollweiler knew of Stanhope's interest in printing and presented him with recent examples from Offenbach and Frankfurt. Stanhope's archive contains (in CKC U1590/C96/2) scales and fingerings for musical instruments that were first published by Johann André (Johann Anton André's father) between 1795 and 1798, but no evidence has been found that Stanhope received these from Vollweiler. In 1814 the ratepayers of 20 Buckingham Place were Mary Manistre and Thomas Martin—presumably Vollweiler rented a room from one of them. I am grateful to Jenny Nex for transcribing these rate-book entries in the Westminster Archives.

[145] André→Vollweiler, 20 June 1814 (copy in André firm copy-book). For Myer Metz see H[ermann] Mayerowitsch, 'The Chazanim of the Great Synagogue, London', *Miscellanies of the Jewish Historical Society of England* part 4 (1942) p 85–94 at p 88, and Cecil Roth, *The Great Synagogue, London, 1690–1940*, London, 1950, p 260–261. Julius Metz went to New York City about 1819 and became a well-known pianist and composer there. I am indebted to his descendant Carol Kroeger of Moline, Illinois, for information about him.

[146] According to 'G. J. Vollweiler (Nekrolog.)', *op. cit.* in note 17 above, p 1303, Vollweiler 'besuchte während der Zeit zweimal Paris und London, machte viele bedeutende Bekanntschaften, wie die des berühmten Cramer, des trefflichen Landsmannes Stumpf [sic], welcher ihm bei einer lebensgefährlichen Krankheit, die ihn zu London im Jahr 1814 befallen hatte, mit treuer aufopfernder Freundschaft bestand' [Vollweiler 'visited Paris and London twice during this time, making many significant acquaintances, such as the famous

least five Mozart manuscripts to Stumpff in 1814,[147] it is plausible that Vollweiler assisted in this transaction.[148] However, the principal account of Stumpff's life records his travel to Germany in the spring of 1814, including a meeting with Goethe in Weimar, but makes no reference to any serious illness.[149]

On his way home from London Vollweiler stopped at Rotterdam in September 1814, apparently to visit the German-born music seller Lodewijk Plattner.[150] Plattner had introduced music lithography to the Netherlands in 1809 and had been granted a five-year patent from King Lodewijk I (i.e., Louis Napoléon Bonaparte) to use lithography there.[151]

The André firm published two compositions by Vollweiler. 'Variations d'une difficulté progressive pour le piano-forte', easy-to-play music written for his son Carl, appeared in 1818 or 1819, when

---

Cramer, the admirable countryman Stumpff, at whose life-threatening illness in London in 1814 he helped with true devoted friendship']. 'Cramer' almost certainly refers to the composer and pianist John Baptist Cramer, who was in London then.

[147] After Franz Gleißner catalogued the Mozart manuscripts that André bought from Mozart's widow (see page 452 above) André copied this catalogue and annotated it. In this copy—now in the Deutsche Mozart-Gesellschaft, Augsburg—André wrote 'Stumpff in London 1814' next to the entries for five Mozart compositions. See Ludwig Finscher, *Kritischer Bericht [Neue Mozart Ausgabe] Ser. 8 ... Werkgruppe 20 ... Abteilung 1* v 3, Kassel, 1964, p 5–6, which gives further documentation about Stumpff's purchases. Alec Hyatt King, *A Mozart Legacy: Aspects of the British Library collections*, London, 1984, records (p 35–36) that André sold a total of twenty-two Mozart manuscripts to Stumpff, but it is not clear that they were all sold at the same time.

[148] Two letters from Vollweiler to Stumpff, dated 30 May 1825 and 31 May 1826, are in Aberystwyth University, George Powell Collection, ms GP/6/3/3.

[149] Ludwig Storch, 'Ein hochherziger Mann aus dem Volke', *Die Gartenlaube*, Leipzig, 1857, no. 32 p 437–440, no. 33 p 455–457, and no. 34 p 468–470, at p 439. I thank Dr Manfred Koltes of the Goethe- und Schiller-Archiv for the information that Goethe's diary records his meetings with Stumpff in 1824 and 1829 but does not mention that they met in 1814.

[150] Vollweiler's plans to meet Plattner are mentioned in correspondence recorded in the André firm copy-book.

[151] See Jo C. Mazure, *Lodewijk Plattner, muziekuitgever en muziekhandelaar te Rotterdam (1767–1842)*, Utrecht, 1981, and Twyman, *Early Lithographed Music, op. cit.*, p 469–470.

Carl was five years old.[152] This was followed in 1821 by a 'Sonatine pour piano-forte, violon & violoncello ad libitum'.[153] In 1820 Vollweiler removed with his family to Frankfurt, where he taught piano and music theory for fifteen years[154] and where for a long time his authority was considered to be the highest in all important questions of the art.[155] One of his pupils there between 1822 and 1824 was the teenager Karl Ludwig Kayser,[156] who subsequently became a distinguished professor of philology at the University of Heidelberg.[157] He was also an accomplished musician and contributed

---

[152] The work was published in three numbers, publisher no. 3905–3907; see Constapel, *op. cit.*, p 233. I am grateful to Brian Conlon of St Olaf College Libraries, Northfield, Minnesota, for sending me a scan of no. 2 of this set.

[153] Publisher no. 4248; Constapel, p 248. This work is designated 'Let. A.' (i.e., op. 1) on its title-page, indicating that Vollweiler considered it a more mature work than his 'Variations', although its musical style—which reflects the common practice of the time—is simple. He dedicated 'Sonatine' to Mlle [Maria] Thérèse Bernus, daughter of the prominent Frankfurt businesmann Friedrich Alexander Bernus, whose career is outlined in Ralf Roth, *Stadt und Bürgertum in Frankfurt am Main...*, Munich, 1996, p 214–215. It seems likely that she was Vollweiler's pupil.

[154] Between August 1820 to May 1835 Vollweiler made applications to the senate of the free city of Frankfurt for permission to teach music at his home (Institut für Stadtgeschichte, Frankfurt am Main, Senatssuppl. 97/24). I thank Roman Fischer for this information.

[155] 'In Frankfurt hatte man sich längst gewöhnt, seine Autorität als die höchste in allen wichtigen Fragen der Kunst anzusehen' ('G. J. Vollweiler (Nekrolog.)', *op. cit.*, p 1304).

[156] In his diary entry for 24 August 1822 Kayser's father, Karl Philipp Kayser, recorded that the day finally had come for his son to go to Frankfurt for musical training under Vollweiler's direction and to continue his school studies at the Gymnasium ('Endlich kam auch der Tag, da Ludwig nach Frankfurt gebracht werden sollte, um dort unter Vollweilers Leitung seine musicalischen Übungen und auf dem Gymansium seine Schul-Studien fortzusetzen'). See Franz Schneider (ed.), *Aus gärender Zeit. Tagebuchblätter des Heidelberger Professors Karl Philipp Kayser aus den Jahren 1793 bis 1827…, Heimatblätter 'Vom Bodensee zum Main'* no. 24, Karlsruhe, 1923, p 95. Karl Ludwig Kayser returned to Heidelberg on 10 April 1824 to live with his parents, who were pleased with the musical progress he had made in Frankfurt (*ibid.*, p 96).

[157] For information about his life and works see C[arl] B[ernhard] Stark, 'Zur Erinnerung an Professor Karl Ludwig Kayser', *Heidelberger Jahrbücher der Literatur* v 65 no. 6 fascicles 26–27 (1872) p 401–422; C[arl] B[ernhard] Stark,

to the Leipzig *Allgemeine musikalische Zeitung*.[158] On 27 March 1837 he married Vollweiler's daughter Lina, a week after her nineteenth birthday.

Between 1828 and 1833 Vollweiler wrote reviews for the music periodical *Caecilia*, published in Mainz by the firm B. Schott's Söhnen. About this time Ferdinand Keßler, who had several links with that firm (including the proofreading of Beethoven's Ninth Symphony and *Missa Solemnis*, which the firm published in 1826 and 1827), studied with Vollweiler and became deeply interested in his system of harmony.[159]

In 1844 Schott published two instruction books by Vollweiler: *Elementar-Gesang-Unterricht besonders für Schulen* [*Elementary Singing Instruction, especially for schools*] and *Anleitung zum Elementarunterricht im Klavierspiel, enthaltend alle wesentliche Theile desselben in systematischer Ordnung* [*Primer of elementary Instruction in Piano Playing, comprising all essential parts in a systematic order*].[160] Vollweiler's interest in methods of teaching

---

'Karl Ludwig Kayser', in Friedrich Otto Aristides von Weech (ed.), *Badische Biographieen* v 1, Heidelberg, 1875, p 449–452; [Gottfried] Kinkel Jr, 'Kayser, Karl Ludwig', *Allgemeine deutsche Biographie* v 15, Leipzig, 1882, p 513–518 at p 513 and p 516; and F[riedrich] A[ugust] Eckstein, 'Kayser (Karl Ludwig)', in J[ohann] S[amuel] Ersch, J[ohann] G[ottfried] Gruber and August Leskien (eds), *Allgemeine Encyklopädie der Wissenschaften und Künste* section 2 part 35, Leipzig, 1884, p 45–49. In each of these memoirs Vollweiler's name has been misspelt 'Vollweyler'.

[158] The obituary of Kayser in that journal ('Nekrolog.', *Allgemeine musikalische Zeitung* v 7 no. 28 (10 July 1872) cols. 451–452) includes a list by the editor, Friedrich Chrysander, of articles that Kayser was known to have written for that periodical.

[159] See Anton Schindler, 'Ferdinand Kessler (Nekrolog)', *Neiderrheinische Musik-Zeitung für Kunstfreunde und Künstler* v 4 no. 45 (8 November 1856) p 357–359, and [Franz Rittweger], 'Zwei vergessene Frankfurter Musiker', *Frankfurter Hausblätter* no. 51 (1880) p 199–200 and p 203–204.

[160] These works are listed respectively in the March 1844 and January 1845 catalogues issued by the Hofmeister firm in Leipzig of new music publications (digitised at http://www.hofmeister.rhul.ac.uk). No copy of the former treatise has been located; a copy of the latter treatise is in the Koninklijke Bibliotheek [National Library of the Netherlands], Amsterdam, request no. NMI 72 D 133. *C[arl] F[riedrich] Whistling's Handbuch der musikalischer Literatur*, Leipzig, 3rd ed., 1845, lists (p 245) a composition by Vollweiler entitled 'Deutschlands

music is indicated also by his owning a copy of C. P. E. Bach's *Versuch über die wahre Art das Clavier zu Spielen.*[161]

Vollweiler spent his last years at Heidelberg where he taught music at the Kayserschen Institut, a school established by his son-in-law's mother Gertrud Kayser.[162] The notice in the Leipzig *Allgemeine musikalische Zeitung* that recorded his passing lamented that

> One of the most admirable German musicians has been snatched away from us by death. Vollweiler, teacher of music and composition, died at Heidelberg in the morning of 17 November [1847] in his 77th year, mourned by all his friends. ... With clear insight into the depths of the art he combined the gift of communicating at the highest level with loving devotion to his pupils. ... He has left a manuscript of a theoretical work, the fruit of more than fifty years' work. ... His main pupils include his own son in St Petersburg and Georg Aloys Schmitt Jr.[163]

After Vollweiler's death his pupil Ferdinand Keßler prepared a manuscript based upon Vollweiler's system of harmony. In 1880, after Keßler's death, this document was in the possession of Franz

---

Triumph in der Schlacht bei Leipzig, eine Fantasie', published by Baumgärtner in Leipzig. No copy of that work has been located.

[161] This copy, which bears his ownership signature 'G. J. Vollweiler', was published in two volumes (Berlin, 1759 and 1762) and is now in the Riemenschneider Bach Library, Baldwin-Wallace College, Berea, Ohio, USA. It is catalogued as no. 10 in Sylvia W. Kenney, *Catalog of the Emilie and Karl Riemenschneider Memorial Bach Library*, New York, 1960, p 2.

[162] G. J. Vollweiler (Nekrolog.)', *op. cit.*, p 1304. For the Institut see [Gottfried] Kinkel Jr, 'Kayser, Karl Ludwig', *op. cit.*, p 514. Heidelberg address directories (online at http://www.ub.uni-heidelberg.de/helios/digi/hdadressbuch.html) show that this institute operated from the Kayser family home at 19 Hauptstraße, and record that from 1840 to 1844 'Vollweiler Partikulier'—i.e., Vollweiler, private individual—lived nearby at 26 Hauptstraße.

[163] 'Einer der Trefflichsten unter den deutschen Musikern ist uns durch den Tod entrissen worden. Der Lehrer der Musik und Composition *Vollweiler* in Heidelberg starb am Morgen des 17. November im 77. Jahre seines Altes, beweint von allen seinen Freunden. … Mit klarer Einsicht in die Tiefen der Kunst verband er die Gabe der Mittheilung im höchsten Grade und der liebevollen Hingabe an seine Schüler. … Er hinterlässt das Manuscript eines theoretischen Wekes, die Frucht einer mehr als fünfzigjährigen Arbeit. … Unter seinen Schülern sind der eigene Sohn in St. Petersburg und *Georg Aloys Schmitt* jun. hauptsächlich zu nennen.' *Allgemeine musikalische Zeitung* v 49 (December 1847) no. 48 col. 836.

Rittweger, editor of the *Frankfurter Hausblätter*.[164] The manuscript was never published and its present location is not known.

The memoir of Vollweiler by the composer Ferdinand Hiller, who had studied with him in Frankfurt, is worth recollecting, even though it is entirely disconnected from his achievements as a lithographer in London:[165]

> One can think of no greater contrast than that between Vollweiler's personality and the image one generally has of a theorist. This has nothing to do with his external appearance, because he was tall and thin, grey and bald, and his features exhibited a peaceful, not very striking expression. But, as soon as he began to speak, what sparkling passion, what enthusiasm! His words stumbled over each other; his explanations, although always clear, brought him almost to breathlessness, giving his convictions a feverish expression. He had written out his lessons fully, including those to be practised on the piano, without publishing them, so students had to copy out his text. He took exceedingly great pains and many ways to keep his pupils occupied to develop their skills, particularly in harmony. I remember him presenting exercises in modulation when walking with me that I—obviously without paper or a keyboard—had to answer by naming a succession of chords exactly. Then I had to write out analyses of Bach fugues and Mozart and Beethoven sonatas. Teaching was a joy to him and, although he did nothing else all day, he seemed never tired or suffering from boredom. If one found him in the evening in a back corner of a concert hall, he eagerly conversed during each interval about what had been heard. At least with his students he was always, and above all, a teacher.[166]

---

[164] 'Zwei vergessener Frankfurter Musiker', *op. cit.*, p 200 and p 204.

[165] So too the brief article on Vollweiler by Sir George Grove in his *A Dictionary of Musicians...*, v 4, London, 1899, p 338, makes no reference to Vollweiler's time in London or his lithographic work. The *Dictionary*'s current successor, *Oxford Music Online*, has no article devoted to Vollweiler.

[166] 'Man kann sich keinen größern Gegensatz denken, als den der Persönlichkeit Vollweiler's zu dem Bilde, das man sich gemeinhin von einem Theoretiker zu machen pflegt. Zwar nicht in seiner äußern Erscheinung; denn er war lang und hager, grau und kahl, seine Züge waren von ruhigem, wenig hervorstechendem Ausdruck. Aber welch ein sprudelnder Eifer, welch eine Leidenschaftlichkeit sobald er zu sprechen begann! Seine Worte stolperten über einander, seine trotzdem durchaus klaren Auseinandersetzungen brachten ihn fast zur Athemtlosigkeit—fieberhaft gab er seinen Ueberzeugungen Ausdruck. Er hatte seine Lehre vollständig schriftlich ausgearbeitet—nicht weniger die dazu gehörigen Uebungen (auch für's Clavierspiel), ohne sie zu veröffentlichen—die Schüler mußten sich die Hefte abschreiben. Ueber die Maßen reichhaltig war

APPENDIX: MUSIC PRINTED OR SOLD BY VOLLWEILER IN LONDON

Music lithographed and printed by Vollweiler's Polyautographic Office in London is described in *Table 9.1* on pages 497–501 in the order of their estimated publication date. Music lithographed and printed by the André firm in Offenbach that Vollweiler's Polyautographic Office offered for sale in London is listed in *Table 9.2* on pages 502–505, in order of their André firm publisher number. In both tables the year given for publications of the André firm is the year when they first published a work with that publication number, according to Britta Constapel's catalogue.[167] They often reprinted works in later years and sometimes reused a publication number when a new edition of a work was prepared. Copies of music in the H. Baron Collection, University of Reading Library, have been described in detail by Michael Twyman.[168]

For each individually issued work listed in *Table 9.1*, the 'imprint' field records the phrase Vollweiler used to refer to his place of business, not the full imprint. He employed four phrases for this purpose, apparently consecutively. By contrast, he used only one phrase—'at the polyautographic office'—in all his published

die Art und Weise, wie er, namentlich in der Harmonielehre, seine Zöglinge zu beschäftigen, ihre Fertigkeit auszubilden beflissen war. Ich erinnere mich, daß er mir auf Spaziergängen modulatorische Aufgaben stellte, die ich, selbstverständlich ohne Papier und Clavier durch genau bezeichnende Nennung der sich folgenden Accorde zu lösen hatte. Dann mußte ich wieder schriftliche Analysen Bach'scher Fugen, Mozart'scher und Beethoven'scher Sonaten aufsetzen. Der Unterricht war ihm eine Lust, und obschon er den ganzen Tag nichts Anderes that, schien er nie an Ermüdung, viel weniger an Ueberdruß zu leiden. Fand man ihn dann Abends in dem hintersten Winkel eines Concertsaales, so konnte man darauf zählen, in jeder Pause den eingehendsten, eifrigsten Besprechungen des eben Gehörten lauschen zu dürfen—er war, mit seinen Schülern wenigstens, Lehrer immer und überall.' (Hiller, *op. cit.* in note 18 above, p 93–94.) A 22 April 1829 letter that Vollweiler wrote in Frankfurt to Hiller 'with all love and friendship' ['mit aller Liebe und Freundschaft'] is printed in Reinhold Seitz, *Aus Ferdinand Hillers Briefwechsel (1826–1861)*, *Beiträge zur rheinischen Musikgeschichte* v 28, Cologne, 1958, p 14.

167 *op. cit.* in note 55 above.

168 Twyman, *Early Lithographed Music*, *op. cit.* in note 3 above, p 392 and p 295–298 respectively.

drawings that have imprints.[169] For vocal music listed in this table the 's glyphs' field states whether the English-language song text has a 'long s' letter ('ſ') as well as a 'short s' letter ('s'). As shown, Vollweiler appears to have stopped using 'long s' in such texts after 1 March 1806. In both tables the 'pages' field gives the number of printed pages in the edition: blank pages are not counted.

As these tables show, the largest extant collection of music printed or sold by Vollweiler is in Killerton House, Broadclyst, Devon.[170] None of these copies bears an ownership inscription, but circumstantial evidence suggests that they were bought by or on behalf of Lydia Hoare, daughter of the banker Henry Hoare. She played the piano, organ and harp, and owned a large collection of music.[171] In anticipation of her marriage to Sir Thomas Dyke Acland, 10th Baronet, on 7 April 1808,[172] the chamber organ at Killerton House was built for her in 1807, and the couple removed there shortly after their wedding. She subsequently took lessons from Samuel Sebastian Wesley,[173] and her son Arthur Henry Dyke Acland wrote a book about music.[174]

---

[169] Man, 'Lithography in England (1801–1810)', *op. cit.* in note 9 above, p 116, records three imprints that Vollweiler used on his lithographed drawings. All of them use the phrase 'at the polyautographic office' to identify his place of business.

[170] I am grateful to The National Trust and to Penelope Cave for imagery of copies in this collection. The collection includes a few copies of André editions that do not have Vollweiler's label but which apparently were acquired about the same time as copies with his label. The former copies have been included in *Table 9.2* on the presumption that they were bought from his London shop.

[171] See Anne Acland, *A Devon Family: The story of the Aclands*, London, 1981, p 41, p 45 and p 48.

[172] The National Trust, *Killerton House, Devon*, 2000, p 10 and p 41. Apparently this organ was paid for by her father, who on the recommendation of Charles Wesley Jr chose William Gray to build it. See Samuel Wesley→Charles Wesley Jr, 15 January 1807, transcribed in Philip Olleson (ed.), *The Letters of Samuel Wesley: Professional and Social Correspondence 1797–1837*, Oxford, 2001, p 40–50 at p 47.

[173] Peter Horton, *Samuel Sebastian Wesley: A life*, Oxford, 2004, p 121. Wesley dedicated two sets of organ compositions to her.

[174] *Letters on Musical Notation and the Present State of Musical Education*, London, 1841.

A label lithographed by Vollweiler in London is pasted on the title-page of each copy listed in *Table 9.2*, with the exception of the two sets of songs by Nina d'Aubigny von Engelbrunner that were advertised for sale there and three André firm publications at Killerton that almost certainly were supplied by Vollweiler's shop.[175] These labels, apparently designed to cover the area where the price of the copy was printed in German gulden, have different dimensions but the common text: 'Sold by G. J. Vollweiler, at the Polyautographic Printing-Office'. On each label the English price of the copy has been written in ink.[176] Four works in *Table 9.2* were composed by Joseph Woelfl, a German-speaking musician who lived in London from May 1805. As Frederick Schirmer collaborated with him in London in 1806,[177] and as the André firm published several of his compositions, it seems likely that he and Vollweiler were in contact in London.

date	ESH 30/1/1806 (by Frederick Schirmer)
title	*The favourite song in the celebrated opera: Die drei Freier (The three Suitors) performed at the German Theatre, arranged for the piano-forte, with an English poetical translation of the original words*
composer	Matthias von Holst
imprint	at the new invented Patent-Polyautography
copies	Bodleian Mus. Voc. I.57(51); BL H.1250.(3.); GUL Store HQ 01063
pages	3
price	1/6
s glyphs	long and short

Table 9.1 Music lithographed and printed by Vollweiler's Polyautographic Office in London (continued overleaf)

[175] See page 467 above.

[176] Two of these labels are reproduced in Twyman, *Early Lithographed Music*, *op. cit.*, p 209.

[177] See note 125 above.

date	1/3/1806, issued with *La Belle Assemblée* v 1 no. 1 (2/1806)
title	*Only tell her that I love!*
composer	Domenico Corri
copies	CUL MR403.a.80.1; NYPL *DA (Belle assemblée); UNE SC052/B438
pages	2
s glyphs	long and short
remark	In the 'new edition' of this number published about 1/8/1806 this song was printed from engraved plates (copy at BL P.P. 5142)

date	1/4/1806, issued with *La Belle Assemblée* v 1 no. 2 (3/1806)
title	*The lover's vision*
composer	John Braham
copies	BL P.P. 5142; CUL MRA.290.80.371; NYPL *DA (Belle assemblée); UNE SC052/B438
pages	2
s glyphs	short only

date	*c*4/1806; after the first London performance of this opera on 27/3/1806
title	*The favourite march from the opera: La Clemenza di Tito by Mozart, arranged for the piano-forte*
composer	Wolfgang Amadeus Mozart
imprint	at the new invented Patent-Polyautography
copies	BL Hirsch M.322
pages	1
price	no price printed or handwritten; because of this, work perhaps not sold separately but produced as a specimen of lithographed music
remark	also published by the André firm in Offenbach, publisher no. 2241 (1806)

date	ESH 12/6/1806 (by Vollweiler)
title	*Woodland Hallò composed and inscribed to Mr Bloomfield author of The farmers boy, Wild flowers etc. etc.*
composer	Nina d'Aubigny von Engelbrunner
imprint	at the Patent-Polyautographic-Press
copies	BL H.1668.(19.); University of Virginia M1.S444 v 179 no. 24*
pages	3
price	1/–
s glyphs	short only

date	1/8/1806, issued with *La Belle Assemblée* v 1 no. 6 (7/1806)
title	*Emma of the dale*
composer	William Reeve
copies	Baron; BL P.P. 5142; CUL MR403.b.80.1; NYPL *DA (Belle assemblée); UNE SC052/B438
pages	4
s glyphs	short only

date	ESH 15/10/1806 (by Charles Saust)
title	*The favourite air Sul Margine d'un Rio, with variations for the piano-forte & flute obligato composed, & dedicated to Miss Marianne Robarts*
composer	Charles Saust (op. 5)
imprint	at the polyautographic office
copies	Baron; Bodleian JJ Lithography General Folder 1 [wmk 1805]; BL h.220.(2.); CUL MR340.a.80.2(17); Killerton
pages	11
price	3/6
remark	also published by the André firm in Offenbach, publisher no. 2383 (1807)

date	late 1806?; before dedicatee's 23/4/1807 marriage
title	*Fair and young or The age of love, a duetto for two voices respectfully dedicated to Miss Stephenson*
composer	Charles Edward Horn
imprint	at the polyautographic office
copies	BL H.1652.kk.(9.)
0pages	9
price	2/–
s glyphs	short only
remark	late 1806 suggested because imprint is the same as in Saust's work

Table 9.1 Music lithographed and printed by Vollweiler's Polyautographic Office in London (continued overleaf)

date	late 1806?
title	*A polonoise for the piano-forte*
composer	Potpuelsky [perhaps a pseudonym]
imprint	at the polyautographic office
copies	Baron [wmk 1805]; Beinecke OSB MSS 146 box 123 in folder 628[178]
pages	3
price	1/6
remark	late 1806 suggested because imprint is the same as in Saust's work

date	late 1806?
title	*Funeral march from the opera: Castor and Pollux by Vogler, arranged for the piano-forte*
composer	Georg Joseph Vogler
imprint	at the polyautographic office
copies	Killerton
pages	1
price	6d
remark	late 1806 suggested because imprint is the same as in Saust's work

---

[178] The Beinecke Library copy, part of the so-called 'Hanover Royal Music Archive', belonged to King George V of Hannover (it is recorded in the 1851–1866 'Catalog der Musikalien Sr Maj. des Königs', BL Add. Ms 57974 p 70, and again in the 1896 'Katalog der Musikalien Seiner Majestät des Königs George V', BL Add. Ms 57975 p 57). As King George V's music library included items owned by his father King Ernest Augustus of Hannover, Duke of Cumberland and son of King George III, and as Vollweiler claimed patronage of Queen Charlotte and TRH the princesses in 1806 for another publication (see page 457 above), it is conceivable that this copy was acquired in 1806 if not by the Duke then by his sister Princess Augusta Sophia, as some 5,000 volumes from her library passed to King Ernest Augustus after her death in 1840. See Karen Spicher, *Guide to the Hanover Royal Music Archive, OSB MSS 146*, New Haven, Connecticut, 2009, http://drs.library.yale.edu:8083/fedora/get/beinecke:hanover/PDF, p 7, and Ernst Hauswedell, preface to v 1 of the catalogue of his Auktion 174 (15–16 June 1970) of *Die Königliche Ernst August Fideicommiss-Bibliothek*, Hamburg, 1970, p [5]. I am grateful to Karen Spicher for advice that the Beinecke copy has been trimmed and now bears no inscriptions, and to Graham Pont for checking the entries for 'Potpuelsky' in the catalogues of King George V's music library.

date	after 1/12/1806; perhaps early 1807
title	*The Offenbach waltz*
composer	Johann Anton André
imprint	at his polyautographic office
copies	K
pages	1
price	6d
remark	probably after 1/12/1806, as the announced publication of a waltz by André in the number of *La Belle Assemblée* published that day did not eventuate. Page size approximately 295 × 240 mm; staff depth approximately 7 mm; watermark on paper indecipherable. Also published by the André firm in Offenbach and their associate Mme Duhan et Cie in Paris, publisher no. 1647 (1802).

date	after 1/12/1806; perhaps early 1807
title	*Six waltzes for the piano-forte*
composer	Johann Anton André
imprint	at his polyautographic office
copies	Killerton
pages	3
price	1/–
remark	probably after 1/12/1806, as the announced publication of a waltz by André in the number of *La Belle Assemblée* published that day did not eventuate. Also published by the André firm in Offenbach and their associate Mme Duhan et Cie in Paris, publisher no. 1675 (1802).

Table 9.1 Music lithographed and printed by Vollweiler's Polyautographic Office in London

title	*Concerto pour piano-forté avec accompagnement d'orchestre*
composer	Wolfgang Amadeus Mozart
copies	Killerton (piano part only, without Vollweiler label)
remark	André firm publisher no. 1558 (*c*1801)

title	*Trois sonates pour le piano forté & le violon, avec accompagnement d'un violoncelle ad libitum*, Op. 16
composer	Joseph Woelfl
copies	Killerton (violin part only)
pages	31 (piano part), 9 (violin part)
price	7/6
remark	André firm publisher no. 1624 (*c*1802)

title	*Walze favorite du carnaval d'Offenbach, arrangée pour le piano-forté*
composer	[Johann Anton André]
copies	Killerton[179]
pages	5
price	1/6
remark	André firm publisher no. 1647 (1802)

title	*Douze pièces de l'opera: Figaro de Mozart, arrangées pour le piano-forté avec violon ad libitum*
composer	Wolfgang Amadeus Mozart
copies	Killerton (piano and violin parts, without Vollweiler label)
remark	André firm publisher no. 1672 (*c*1802)

title	*Variations tirées d'un quatour de l'oeuvre 97 de J. Haydn, arrangées pour le piano-forté par Mr l'Abbé Gelineck*
composer	Joseph Haydn, arranged by Josef Gelinek
copies	Baron
pages	5
price	1/6
remark	André firm publisher no. 1706 (1802–1803)

[179] As mentioned in note 115 above, the copy of this work in Baron (described in Twyman, *op. cit.*, p 295, no. 9) lacks Vollweiler's label and presumably was not sold by him.

title	*Sonate pour Piano-Forté, accompagné de violon...*, Op. 24
composer	Ludwig van Beethoven
copies	Killerton (without Vollweiler label)
remark	André firm publisher no. 1764 (1803)

title	*Trois grands trios pour piano-forte, violon & basse*, Op. 23 no. 1
composer	Joseph Woelfl
copies	Killerton
pages	19 (piano part), 5 (violin part), 5 (violoncello part)
price	4/6
remark	André firm publisher no. 1771 (1803)

title	*Trois grands trios pour piano-forte, violon & basse*, Op. 23 no. 2
composer	Joseph Woelfl
copies	Killerton
pages	15 (piano part), 5 (violin part), 5 (violoncello part)
price	4/6
remark	André firm publisher no. 1772 (1803)

title	*Trois grands trios pour piano-forte, violon & basse*, Op. 23 no. 3
composer	Joseph Woelfl
copies	Killerton
pages	18 (piano part), 5 (violin part), 5 (violoncello part)
price	4/6
remark	André firm publisher no. 1773 (*c*1803)

title	*Dix variations pour le piano-forté, sur l'air: Seid uns zum zweitenmal willkommen*, Op. 5
composer	Carl Friedrich Eckhard
copies	Killerton
pages	15
price	2/6
remark	André firm publisher no. 1892 (1804)

Table 9.2 Music lithographed and printed by the André firm in Offenbach and sold by Vollweiler's Polyautographic Office in London (continued overleaf)

title	*Air varié pour le piano-forté ou la harpe*
composer	Carlo Bigatti
copies	Baron
pages	7
price	1/6
remark	André firm publisher no. 1931 (1804)

title	*Prelude pour piano-forté*
composer	Ludwig van Beethoven
copies	Killerton
pages	3
price	1/–
remark	André firm publisher no. 2146 (1805)

title	*Marche funebre pour piano-forté*
composer	Ludwig van Beethoven
copies	Baron; Killerton
pages	3
price	1/–
remark	André firm publisher no. 2174 (1805)

title	*Marches pour piano-forté, no. 5*
composer	Wolfgang Amadeus Mozart
copies	Killerton
pages	3
price	1/–
remark	André firm publisher no. 2244 (1806)

title	*Six songs with original english and translated german text*
composer	Nina d'Aubigny von Engelbrunner (op. 8 no. 1)
copies	copy in André firm archive, Offenbach; no copy located with Vollweiler's label but advertised as sold by him in *The Morning Post*, 2 January 1807, p 1
pages	23
price	5/– (in London); *fl.* 1½ (in Offenbach)
remark	André firm publisher no. 2279 (1806)

title	*Seven songs with original english and translated german text*
composer	Nina d'Aubigny von Engelbrunner (op. 8 no. 2)
copies	copy in André firm archive, Offenbach; no copy located with Vollweiler's label but advertised as sold by him in *The Morning Post*, 2 January 1807, p 1
pages	22
price	5/– (in London); *fl.* 1½ (in Offenbach)
remark	André firm publisher no. 2280 (1806)

Table 9.2 Music lithographed and printed by the André firm in Offenbach and sold by Vollweiler's Polyautographic Office in London

SUMMARY OF LEGAL CASES

The following summary, prepared by John Small with addenda by Michael Kassler, describes the legal cases mentioned in this book. Each entry has three rows.

The first row names a case,[1] the court that decided or heard it, the year when it concluded, and (at the right end) the page numbers in this book that refer to it. Court names are abbreviated as follows:

Ch	Court of Chancery
CP	Court of Common Pleas
CS	Court of Session [Scotland]
EC	Court of Exchequer Chamber
Ex	Court of Exchequer
HL	House of Lords
KB	Court of King's Bench
QB	Court of Queen's Bench

If an entire section is devoted to a case its page numbers appear in italics.

The second row cites the direct or indirect report of this case in *The English Reports* volumes, followed in parentheses by the conventional reference to the original collection of reports reproduced in *ER*. Where no such report exists, other documentation about the case is indicated.[2]

The last row briefly states the subject of the case and summarises the decision (if any) that the court made regarding

[1] As is customary in legal citations, parties to a case are cited by their surnames only, and where a party comprised more than one person (e.g., a partnership) only the first person is cited. Where known, the full name and the dates of each party have been entered in the Index of Persons at the end of this book. Misspellings of names in *ER* have been silently emended.

[2] The database 'Copyright Infringement Suits and Actions from *c*1560 to 1800', published by H. Tomás Gómez-Arostegui at http://www.oldcopyrightcases.org, gives the full names of litigants in many of the cases mentioned in this book and the location of manuscript records of these cases in The National Archives.

matters relevant to this book. Other information about some cases has been added in parentheses.

Abel v Longman — see *Bach v Longman*

Anonymous (Ch, 1682) 251
ER 23: 357 (1 Vern. 120)
Book patents; offshore printing. Chancellor refuses the patentee's request for injunction 'to stop the sale of English Bibles printed beyond sea'; notes that the Bible patent is similar to but not the same as the law patent, which the House of Lords has upheld; and directs the parties to submit the dispute to a common-law court.

Arne v Roberts (Ch, 1741) 316–318
unreported (bill of complaint and answer at TNA C11/2260/7)
Music. An injunction is granted forbidding unauthorised publication of Thomas Arne's music for *Comus* and *As You Like It*. (The defendants were the music sellers Henry Roberts and John Johnson.)

Atkyns v Stationers — see *Stationers v Patentees*

Bach v Longman (two actions) and *Abel v Longman* (one action) (KB, 1777) 19, *329–345*, *360–370*, 371, 373–376, 378, 380–381
ER 98: 1274 (2 Cowp. 623)
Music; definition of *writing*. J. C. Bach and Abel bring Chancery actions against Longman, Lukey & Co. over unauthorised publication of two Bach sonatas, three Bach symphonies and three Abel trios. Chancery refers Bach's sonata action to the KB, which holds that music notation is a form of writing within the meaning of the Copyright Act. The actions then apparently are settled.

Baller v Watson (Ch, 1737) 303
unreported (numerous Chancery documents at TNA)
Common-law copyright. The Chancellor grants a perpetual injunction protecting Gay's opera-text *Polly*, perhaps considering that common-law copyright applies after expiration of the Copyright Act's protection. (Katherine Baller, the plaintiff, was John Gay's sister and an executor of his estate.)

Beckford v Hood (KB, 1798) 378
ER 101: 1164 (7 TR 620)
Registration. 'An author whose work is pirated … may maintain an action … for damages [under the Copyright Act] although the work was not entered at Stationers' Hall.' (The author Peter Beckford took action against the bookseller Thomas Hood of Vernor & Hood.)

Bickerstaff v Fougt (Ch, 1769) 322
unreported (bill of complaint at TNA C12/1026/2)
Music; piracy. Concerns the opera *The Padlock* with words by Isaac John Bickerstaff and music by Charles Dibdin Sr, who had sold rights to this music to Bickerstaff. (The defendant was the music seller Henry Fougt.)

Bickerstaff v Roberts (Ch, 1769) 322
unreported (bill of complaint at TNA C12/1026/3)
Music; piracy. The costs of the action regarding *The Padlock* (see the case above) paid by the music seller Henry Roberts, who consented to offend no more.

Bickerstaff v Thorowgood (Ex, 1765) 320
unreported (bill and answer at TNA E112/1596/730)[3]
Music; piracy. Isaac John Bickerstaff had arranged songs in the opera *The Maid of the Mill*, with words by him and music by various composers, for German flute, and this arrangement was published by Robert Bremner. The defendant, the music seller Henry Thorowgood, allegedly pirated that edition. The case was dismissed in June 1766.

Birchall v Longman (Ch, 1818) 88
unreported (bill of complaint at TNA C13/729/6)
Music; foreign publication. Music first published abroad is not subject to copyright in England. (The parties were the music sellers Robert Birchall and Longman & Herron.)

---

[3] We are grateful to Nancy A. Mace for providing a transcript of this bill and answer.

Booksellers of London v Booksellers of Edinburgh (also called *Midwinter v Hamilton* or *Millar v Kincaid*) (CS, 1751) 308, 346
unreported; described by Ronan Deazley[4]
Common-law copyright. Court of Session (Scotland) rejects the idea of common-law copyright. (This case had different names at different times in different courts.)

Boosey v Davidson (QB, 1849) 385
ER 116: 1261 (13 QB 257)
Music; foreigners. 'There is copyright in this country for the works of a foreigner [airs from Bellini's opera *La sonnambula*] published here without having been before published abroad'. (The parties were the music seller Thomas Boosey II and the music publisher George Henry Davidson.)

Boosey v Jefferys (Ex, 1851) 385
ER 155: 675 (6 Ex. 580)
Music; foreigners. If a foreign author (Bellini) assigns his rights in a work (material from his opera *La sonnambula*), under foreign law, to a foreign assignee (G. Ricordi & Co.) who assigns the British rights, under British law, to a British subject, the British assignee has British copyright in the work if it is first published in Britain. (The defendant was the music seller Charles Jefferys.) This decision was reversed by *Jefferys v Boosey*.

Boosey v Purday (Ex, 1849) 385
ER 154: 1159 (4 Ex. 145)
Music; foreigners; foreign publication; offshore printing. 'A foreign author [Bellini] residing abroad, who composes a work [airs from *La sonnambula*] abroad, and sends it to this country, where it is first published under his authority, acquires no copyright therein. Neither does a British subject to whom such work is assigned by the foreign author gain any such right. But assuming … a foreign author and his assigns to have by law a copyright when the author means to publish contemporaneously in England and abroad, he and his assigns are not disentitled to copyright by the actual publication in one place before the other, on the same day.' 'These airs … were printed from the foreign plates.' (The defendant was the music seller Zenas Trivett Purday.)

---

[4] Ronan Deazley, *On the Origin of the Right to Copy*, Oxford, 2004, p 115–132.

Broderip v Leukfeld (Ch, 1806) 105
unreported (bill of complaint and answer at TNA C13/2415/7)
Musical instruments; breach of contract. Concerning the agreement under which Ludewig Augustus Leukfeld made pianos for the plaintiffs Francis Fane Broderip and Charles Wilkinson Jr (trading as Broderip & Wilkinson).

Burnet v Chetwood (Ch, 1720) 302
ER 35: 1008 (2 Mer. 441) in *Southey v Sherwood* [5]
Adaptation, selection and originality. 'Lord Chancellor said, that … a translation might not be the same with the reprinting the original, on account that the translator has bestowed his care and pains upon it, and so not within the prohibition of the [Copyright] Act'. The case was decided on other grounds. (The parties were George Burnet—executor of the author Thomas Burnet—and the publisher William Rufus Chetwood.)

Case of Monopolies — see *Monopolies, Case of*

Chappell v Purday (Ex, 1845) 384
ER 153: 491 (14 M. & W. 303)
Music; foreigners. 'A foreign author [Auber], residing abroad, who composes and publishes his work [the opera *Fra Diavolo*] abroad, has not, at common law, or under the [copyright acts] 8 Anne, c.19 and 54 Geo. III, c.136, any copyright in this country. Therefore, a person to whom he transfers abroad, by an instrument, not under seal, but which is valid according to the law of that country, the copyright of the work in England has no right of action against a British subject who afterwards publishes the work in England.' (The parties were the music sellers Emily Chappell and Zenas Trivett Purday.)

Clauss v Levy (Ch, 1786) 30, 53
unreported (documentation at TNA C12/154/35)
Partnership dispute. Christian Clauss (maker of English guittars) sued his former partner Joseph Levy regarding partnership assets.

Clauss v Longman (Ch, 1785) 30
unreported (documentation at TNA C217/134)
Musical instruments; patents. Christian Clauss, inventor of a musical instrument, against Longman & Broderip, for patent infringement. The outcome of this case is not known.

---

[5] That case, not included in this Summary, between the poet Robert Southey and the book publishers Sherwood, Neely & Jones, concerned the unauthorised publication of a manuscript.

Clementi v Goulding (KB, 1809) 171, 367, 380–382
ER 170: 1069 (2 Camp. 25); *ER* 103: 998 (11 East 244)
Music; definition of *book*. A single sheet of music ('Heigh-ho!', from William Shield's opera *Two Faces under a Hood*) is a book within the meaning of the Copyright Act. (The parties were the music sellers Clementi & Co. and Goulding, Phipps, d'Almaine & Co.)

Clementi v Larkin (?, 1814) 143
unreported
Musical instruments; misrepresentation. An advertisement states that legal action is being taken against M. Larkin and two other Dubliners who falsely attributed pianos to Clementi & Co. No records of this case have been found.

Clementi v Walker (KB, 1824) 171
ER 107: 601 (2 B. & C. 861)
Music; foreign publication. If a work (Frederick William Kalkbrenner's 'Introduction and variations on *Vive Henri Quatre*') first published abroad is later published in Britain without authorisation, the author's subsequent assignment of British copyright does not make continued unauthorised publication in Britain unlawful. (The defendant was the music seller George Walker Sr.)

Clothworkers of Ipswich case (KB, 1615) 242
ER 78: 147 (Godbolt 252)
Monopolies. A royal grant of a monopoly of a common trade is illegal.

Cocks v Purday (CP, 1848) 385
ER 136: 1118 (5 CB 860)
Music; foreigners. 'A foreigner resident abroad may acquire copyright in England in a work [Joseph Labitzky's *Die Elfen*] that is first published by him as author, or as author's assignee, in this country, which has not been made *publici juris* [of public right; i.e., not capable of being owned] by a previous publication elsewhere. A contemporaneous publication abroad does not defeat such right.' (The parties were Robert Cocks and Zenas Trivett Purday.)

Colman v Wathen (KB, 1793) 382–383
ER 101: 137 (5 TR 245)
Performance; definition of *publication*. 'Evidence that the defendant acted a piece upon the stage, of which the plaintiff had bought the copyright, is not evidence of a publication' within the meaning of the Copyright Act. (The parties were the theatre managers George Colman Sr and George Wathen.)

Company of Stationers v — (Ch, 1681) 251
ER 22: 854 (2 Chan. Cas. 76)
Book patents; offshore printing. The Chancellor grants the Stationers' Company a permanent injunction forbidding unauthorised importation of statute books 'printed in Amsterdam … in great bails and quantities'; 'for the printing of laws … that concerned the State. But for other books … he left them to the ordinary course.'

Company of Stationers v — (Ch, 1682) 251–252
ER 22: 862 (2 Chan. Cas. 93)
Book patents; offshore printing. The case report mentions earlier proceedings in which the Company had obtained an injunction forbidding unauthorised importation of 'many thousands' of Bibles and statute books.

Company of Stationers v Carnan (CP, 1775) 356, 359–360
ER 96: 590 (2 Black. W. 1004)
Book patents. 'The Crown hath not a prerogative or power to grant printing of almanacks to the Company of Stationers exclusive of any other.' (The defendant was the bookseller Thomas Carnan.)

Company of Stationers v Lee (Ch, 1681) 252, 359
ER 22: 849 (2 Chan. Cas. 66)
Book patents; offshore printing. Accused of printing almanacs secretly and importing almanacs from Holland, the defendant argues, evidently unsuccessfully, that the Company's almanac patent is invalid. (The defendant was the bookseller Samuel Lee. References in this book to an undated *Company of Stationers v Lee* case are to this case, not to the 1683 case of the same name.)

Company of Stationers v Lee (Ch, 1683) 236, 251, 359
ER 89: 927 (2 Show. KB 258)
Book patents; offshore printing. The Stationers' Company is granted an injunction forbidding unauthorised importation of 'some books'.

Company of Stationers v Marlow (CP, 1681) 251–252, 359
ER 89: 928 (2 Show. KB 261) in *Company of Stationers v Lee* (1683)
Book patents. Damages are awarded for a breach of the Company's almanac patent. (The defendant was the printer John Marlow.)

Company of Stationers v Wright (KB, 1683) 251
ER 90: 108 (Skinner 234) in *Company of Stationers v Parker*
Book patents; offshore printing. The Stationers' Company wins a case over psalm books imported contrary to the Company's patent. (The defendant was William Wright.)

Culliford v Longman (CP, 1796) 80
unreported; described by Jenny Nex[6]
Recovery of debts. The musical instrument makers Thomas Culliford, William Rolfe and Charles Barrow sue James Longman and Francis Fane Broderip to recover debts owed.

D'Almaine v Boosey (Ex, 1835) 383–384
ER 160: 117 (1 Y. & C. Ex 288)
Music; foreigners; adaptation, selection and originality. 'To publish, in the form of quadrilles and waltzes, the airs of an opera [Auber's *Lestocq*] of which there exists an exclusive copyright is an act of piracy. The English assignee of the copyright of a foreign musical composer is within the protection of the statutes relating to copyright.' The judge cites music entries in the Stationers' register in the 1780s as evidence that a music print counts as a book. (The parties were the music sellers Thomas d'Almaine and Thomas Boosey II.)

Darcy v Allen — see *Monopolies, Case of*

Doe dem. Tomkyns v Willan (KB, 1818) 89
ER 106: 298 (2 B. & Ald. 84)
Trusts; inheritance. Concerns property left to Elizabeth Longman *née* Tomkyns by the will of her father Packington Tomkyns.

Donaldson v Becket (HL, 1774) 346, 349, 353–354, 357–358, 360–361, 365, 367, 371, 375
ER 1: 837 (2 Bro. PC 129); *ER* 98: 257 (4 Burr. 2408) in *Millar v Taylor*
Common-law copyright. In effect, the House of Lords decides that a book that is no longer protected by the Copyright Act is not protected by common-law copyright, thus reversing *Millar v Taylor*. (The parties were the booksellers Alexander Donaldson and Thomas Becket.)

---

[6] Jenny Nex, 'Culliford and Company: keyboard instrument makers in Georgian London', *Early Keyboard Journal* v 22 (2004) p 7–48.

Duke of Queensberry v Shebbeare (Ch, 1758) 306, 339–340, 361
ER 28: 924 (2 Eden 329)
Unpublished material. An injunction is granted protecting unpublished work of which a manuscript had been given away. (The parties were Charles Douglas and John Shebbeare.)

Electric Telegraph v Nott (Ch, 1847) 241
ER 47: 1041 (2 Coop. t. Cott 42)
Law reporting. Comment on the accuracy of the law reporter John Dickens.

Eyre v Walker (Ch, 1735) 302, 310
ER 98: 213 (4 Burr. 2325) in *Millar v Taylor*
Common-law copyright. An injunction is granted protecting the anonymous work *The Whole Duty of Man*, published anonymously in 1657 and no longer protected by the Copyright Act. (The parties were the publisher John Eyre and the printer Robert Walker.)

Forster v Longman and *Longman v Forster* (Ex, 1792) 26–28, 55, 66, 110, 374
unreported; described by Nancy A. Mace[7]
Music. A complicated dispute between the music sellers William Forster & Son and Longman & Broderip regarding works by Haydn and Pleyel.

Geminiani v Walsh (Ch, *c*1728) 291
unreported
Music. The first known attempt by a composer (Francesco Geminiani) to prevent unauthorised publication (by John Walsh Sr). The action is said to have been settled. No records of it have been found.

Gyles v Wilcox (Ch, 1740) 305–306, 379
ER 26: 489, 957 (2 Atk. 141, 3 Atk. 269); *ER* 27: 682 (Barn. C 368); *ER* 22: 586 (2 Eq. Ca. Abr. 697) as *Reference to a Master in Chancery (1)*
Adaptation, selection and originality. The Chancellor says that an abridgement 'may with great propriety be called a new book'. 'When complaints have been made of a book's being printed contrary to the [Copyright Act], the single question has been, whether the second book is the same book with the former?' The Chancellor directs that a Master and two lawyers agreed on by the parties determine 'whether the book … was an Abridgement of *The* [*History of the*] *Pleas of the Crown*, or whether it was the same book shortened, and made less?' (The parties were Fletcher Gyles and the bookseller John Wilcox.)

---

[7] Nancy A. Mace, 'Haydn and the London music sellers: Forster v. Longman & Broderip', *Music and Letters* v 77 no. 4 (November 1996) p 527–541.

Hills v University of Oxford (Ch, 1684) 251
ER 23: 467 (1 Vern. 275)
Book patents. The Lord Keeper refuses to grant injunction and directs rival Bible patentees to submit their dispute to a common-law court. (The plaintiff was Henry Hills Sr, the King's printer.)

Hime v Dale (KB, 1803) 367, 371, 380–381, 417–418
ER 170: 1070 (2 Camp. 27); *ER* 103: 998 (11 East 244); both in *Clementi v Goulding*
Music; definition of *book*. The court considers whether a single sheet of music is a book within the meaning of the Copyright Act. No decision is reached. (The parties were the Liverpool music seller Humphrey Hime and the London music seller Joseph Dale.)

Hinton v Donaldson (CS, 1773) 346
unreported; described by James Boswell, 'one of the counsel in the cause'[8]
Common-law copyright. Court of Session rejects the idea of common-law copyright. (The parties were the booksellers John Hinton and Alexander Donaldson.)

Holt v Lowe (Ex, 1752) 318–319
unreported; described by Judith Milhous and Robert D. Hume[9]
Music. *Henry and Emma*'s librettist Thomas Holt sues (a) Thomas Lowe, the theatre manager who commissioned the opera, and Thomas Arne, who wrote the music, for a share of the profits from performances; and (b) Arne for allegedly using material from *Henry and Emma* in *Don Saverio*. Nothing is known about later proceedings.

Jefferys v Boosey (HL, 1854) 364, 385–386
ER 10: 681 (4 HLC 815)
Music; foreigners. British subjects, including those resident abroad, possess copyright in their works first published in Britain, as do resident foreigners. But a work (material from Bellini's *La Sonnambula*) that is owned by a foreigner (G. Ricordi & Co.) resident abroad is not protected by British law, even if it is assigned to a British subject and first published in England. This decision reversed *Boosey v Jefferys*.

---

[8] James Boswell, *The Decision of the Court of Session, upon the Question of Literary Property...*, Edinburgh, 1774.

[9] Judith Milhous and Robert D. Hume, 'Librettist versus composer: the property rights to Arne's *Henry and Emma* and *Don Saviero*', *Journal of the Royal Musical Association* v 122 no. 1 (1997) p 52–67.

Kirkman v Falkener (KB, 1771) 324
unreported; described by Lance Whitehead[10]
Musical instruments. Jacob Kirkman sues Robert Falkener over the alleged production of fake Kirkman harpsichords. Nothing is known about any later proceedings.

Latour v Bland (KB, 1818) 379
ER 171: 679 (2 Stark. 382); proceedings published separately[11]
Music; sale of rights. A composer's acquiescence in publication of a work (Francis Tatton Latour's composition *Le Retour de Windsor*) and acceptance of money from the publisher do not constitute transfer of the work's copyright. (The defendants were the music sellers Bland & Weller. The suit evidently began before 6 November 1817, when Anne Bland resigned from her partnership with Edward Weller.[12])

Longman v Assignees (Ex, 1802) 22, 80, 129
unreported (bill of complaint and answer at TNA E112/1787/6238)
Bankruptcy. James Longman disputes the financial settlement determined by the assignees of Longman & Broderip.

Longman v Babb (Ex, 1784) 28, 56, 373–374, 418
unreported (documentation at TNA E133/82/26)
Music; use of extracts from publications as examples in teaching aids and lesson books. The outcome of these proceedings is not known. (The parties were Longman & Broderip and the music seller Samuel Babb.)

Longman v Banger (Ch, 1803) 83–84
unreported (documentation at TNA C13/2333/6)
Music; ownership of rights. A dispute between James Longman and the assignees of Longman & Broderip (led by Josiah Banger) concerning ownership of rights to William Southwell's 1794 piano patent.

---

[10] Lance Whitehead, 'Robert Falkener: an eighteenth-century harpsichord builder, music publisher and malfeasant?', *Galpin Society Journal* v 55 (April 2002) p 310–331.

[11] *Musical Copyright. Proceedings on a Trial before the Hon. Mr Justice Abbott, in the Court of King's Bench, Westminster, June 13th, 1818, in the cause Latour versus Weller*, London, 1818 (copy at GUL Special Collections B.b.56).

[12] *The London Gazette*, 21 February 1818, p 358.

Longman v Blundell (Ex, 1781) 28
unreported (documentation at TNA E133/82/27)
Music; breach of contract. The case concerns the stock of print music and music plates bought by James Longman from the estate of the music seller Mary Hughes *otherwise* Welcker. (James Blundell was an executor of her estate.)

Longman v Clementi (Ch, 1803) 82–84, 133
unreported (documentation at TNA C13/29/34)
Music; breach of contract. James Longman and his creditors William Styan and Richard Hovil Sr complain that Clementi & Co. had breached agreements, particularly with respect to the right to utilise William Southwell's piano patent.[13]

Longman v Culliford (Ex, 1795) 36, 38, 68, 79
ER 145: 994 (3 Anst. 645); documentation at TNA E112/1771/5631
Musical instruments; breach of contract. Concerning the agreement between Longman & Broderip and Culliford & Co. Bill of complaint answered in 1796.[14]

Longman v Tomkyns (Ch, 1785) 22
unreported (documentation at TNA C12/1703/6)
Will administration. James Longman and his wife Elizabeth *née* Tomkyns sue her mother Elizabeth and brother John regarding bequests of Longman's father-in-law Packington Tomykns.

Mayo v Hills (KB, 1672) 236, 251
ER 89: 928 (2 Show. KB 260) in *Company of Stationers v Lee* (1683)
Book patents. The KB affirms that the Bible patent 'had always been held legal'. (The parties presumably were the printer John Mayo and Henry Hills Sr.)

*Midwinter v Hamilton (*or *v Scotch Booksellers)* — see *Booksellers of London v Booksellers of Edinburgh*

Millar v Donaldson — see *Osborne v Donaldson*

---

[13] This case and other related cases are described in George S. Bozarth and Margaret Debenham, 'Piano wars: the legal machinations of London pianoforte makers, 1795–1806', *Royal Musical Association Research Chronicle* v 42 (2009) p 45–108 at p 71–75.

[14] This case and its successors are described in Bozarth and Debenham, *op. cit.*, p 61–62 and p 83–84.

Millar v Kincaid — see
Booksellers of London v Booksellers of Edinburgh

Millar v Taylor (KB, 1769) 295, 311–315, 327, 335, 340, 345–346, 348, 356, 359, 361
ER 98: 201 (4 Burr. 2303)
Common-law copyright. With one judge dissenting, the KB holds that copyright exists at common law—a decision later effectually reversed by *Donaldson v Becket.* (The parties were the booksellers Andrew Millar and Robert Taylor.)

Monopolies, Case of (KB, 1602) 242, 249
ER 77: 1260 (11 Co. Rep. 84b); *ER* 74: 1131 (Noy 173); *ER* 72: 830 (Moore KB 671)
Monopolies. The KB holds that a royal grant of a monopoly (to Edward Darcy) of the trade in playing cards is illegal.

Moore v Watlen (CS, 1797) 35
unreported; documentation at National Archives of Scotland CS271/15736
Partnership dispute. (Concerns the four-month partnership of the music sellers Stephen Moore and John Watlen in Edinburgh.)

Motte v Faulkner (Ch, 1735) 302, 310
ER 98: 213 (4 Burr. 2325) in *Millar v Taylor*
Common-law copyright. An injunction is granted protecting in Great Britain Pope and Swift's *Miscellanies*, a recently published collection containing pieces published in the early eighteenth century and not protected by the Copyright Act. (The parties were Benjamin Motte and the Irish publisher George Faulkner.)

Osborne v Donaldson and *Millar v Donaldson* (Ch, 1765) 311
ER 28: 924 (2 Eden 327)
Common-law copyright. The Chancellor dissolves an injunction that protected a work no longer protected by the Copyright Act, and refers the question whether copyright exists at common law to a common-law court. (The parties were Thomas Osborne, Alexander Donaldson and Andrew Millar.)

Ponder v Braddill (CP, 1679) 254–255
unreported
The publisher Nathaniel Ponder brings a common-law action for alleged breach of copyright by the printer Thomas Braddill.

Pope v Curll (Ch, 1741) 304–306, 345, 361
ER 26: 608 (2 Atk. 342)
Unpublished material. The poet Alexander Pope is granted an injunction protecting his unpublished letters from publication by the bookseller Edmund Curll.

Pyle v Falkener (Ch, 1774) *324–329*, 354–358
unreported; described by Ronald J. Rabin and Steven Zohn[15]
Music. An injunction is granted forbidding unauthorised publication of works by Handel, Arne, Greene and Bickerstaff. The action is settled when the House of Lords decision in *Donaldson v Becket* turns *Pyle v Falkener* into a threat to music publishers. (The parties were the surgeon John Pyle—executor of the estate of John Walsh Jr—and the music seller Robert Falkener.)

Queensberry v Shebbeare — see *Duke of Queensberry v Shebbeare*

Reference to a Master in Chancery — see *Gyles v Wilcox*

Rennett v Longman and *Rennett v Thompson* (Ex, 1785) 56, 241, 373
unreported; described by Nancy A. Mace[16]
Music; sale of rights. Exchequer holds that an author who sells rights to a work sells all publication rights under the Copyright Act—not merely rights for 14 years from the work's date of publication, but also rights for a further 14 years, to which the author is entitled if living at the end of the first 14 years. (The plantiff was the attorney Charles Rennett, who owned music copyrights; the defendants were the music sellers Longman & Broderip and Samuel, Ann & Peter Thompson.)

Rivington v Cooper (Ch, 1740) 304
ER 22: 440 (2 Eq. Ca. Abr. 522)
Adaptation, selection and originality. Having 'printed Part of the Book', the defendant argues 'that an Extract such as this, was not within the Stat[ute] 8 *Ann.*' But the Chancellor says that 'It is not *material* what Title you give the Book, nor whether you print all at once, or not'. (The parties were the book publishers Charles Rivington and Thomas Cooper.)

---

[15] Ronald J. Rabin and Steven Zohn, 'Arne, Handel, Walsh, and music as intellectual property: two eighteenth-century lawsuits', *Journal of the Royal Musical Association* v 120 no. 1 (1995) p 112–145.

[16] Nancy A. Mace, 'Charles Rennett and the London music-sellers in the 1780s: testing the ownership of reversionary copyrights', *Journal of the Royal Musical Association* v 129 no. 1 (2004) p 1–23.

Patent rights. A dispute about whether the defendant John Longman (the organ builder) had assigned patent rights to James Longman. (The plaintiffs were the trumpet maker William Shaw and John Jeyes.)

Music. Chancery follows *Storace v Longman* by stating that copyright in a piece of music written for performance at the King's Theatre belongs to the composer. (The plaintiffs were the music sellers Thomas Skillern Sr and George Goulding; the defendant was Longman & Broderip.)

Recovery of debt. Sarah Smith seeks to recover money that she had invested with Thomas Hodgson, who may have invested some of her funds with James Longman.

Book patents. The House of Lords upholds the validity of the law-book patent.

Music; copyright in work written for performance. Copyright in a piece of music written for performance at the King's Theatre belongs to the composer. (The parties were the composer Stephen Storace and Longman & Broderip.)

Book patents. The House of Lords upholds the validity of the law-book patent (held by John Streater), reversing a KB decision (*Roper v Streater*, KB, 1672). (The defendant was the book publisher Abel Roper Sr.)

[17] Curtis Price, 'Italian opera and arson in late eighteenth-century London', *Journal of the American Musicological Society* v 42 no. 1 (1989) p 55–107 at p 94–95.

Thompson v Falkener (Ch, 1776) 358
unreported (documentation at TNA C33/446)
Music. An injunction is granted preventing unauthorised publication of the opera *The Duenna*. (The parties were the music sellers Charles & Samuel Thompson and Richard Falkener.)

Tonson v Collins (KB, 1761–1762) 309–311
ER 96: 169, 180 (1 Black. W. 301, 321)
Common-law copyright. The KB hears arguments whether copyright exists at common law, but the action is discontinued after being discovered to be collusive. (The plaintiffs were the booksellers Jacob Tonson II and Richard Tonson; the defendant was the bookseller Benjamin Collins.)

Tonson v Walker (Ch, 1739) 302, 310
ER 98: 213 (4 Burr. 2325) in *Millar v Taylor*
Common-law copyright. An injunction is granted protecting Milton's *Paradise Lost*, first published in 1667 and no longer protected by the Copyright Act. (The principal plaintiffs were the booksellers Jacob Tonson II and Richard Tonson; the principal defendant was the printer Robert Walker.)

Tonson v Walker (Ch, 1752) 305–306
ER 36: 1017 (3 Swans. App. 672)
Common-law copyright. An injunction is granted protecting *Paradise Lost* (no longer protected by the Copyright Act) and editorial notes (some no longer protected by the Copyright Act). (The principal parties were the same as in the preceding case.)

Walthoe v Walker (Ch, 1736) 302, 310
ER 98: 213 (4 Burr. 2325) in *Millar v Taylor*
Common-law copyright. An injunction is granted protecting Robert Nelson's *A Companion for the Festivals and Fasts of the Church of England*, first published in 1704 and no longer protected by the Copyright Act. (The plaintiff was John Walthoe Sr. The defendant was the printer Robert Walker.)

Webb v Rose (Ch, 1732) 303
ER 98: 216 (4 Burr. 2330) in *Millar v Taylor*
Unpublished material. An injunction is granted to the author's heir (William Webb) protecting his father's papers (about conveyancing) from publication (by Edward Rose and others).

Wood v Norman (Ch, 1803) 79
unreported (documentation at TNA C13/33/13)
Land titles. Concerns the ownership of properties in which James Longman was involved.

Wright v Holford (KB, 1774) 364
ER 98: 951 (1 Cowp. 31)
Disclosure. Lord Mansfield announces that the KB henceforth will state publicly the reasons for its decisions in matters referred to it from Chancery.

Wynne v Longman (KB, 1783) 32
unreported (documentation at Parliamentary Archives, Main Papers, HL/PO/JO/10/2/58)
Nonpayment of debts. An appeal against an unrecorded suit of Longman & Broderip to recover debts from the music seller George Wynne.

INDEX OF PERSONS

The following index lists persons mentioned in this book who were alive or—in the case of bodies corporate such as companies, government agencies, partnerships, societies and universities—were active before 1831. If an entire chapter or section is devoted to a person its page numbers appear in italics. Legal cases cited in this book are summarised in the preceding section.

For Product Safety Concerns and Information please contact our EU
representative GPSR@taylorandfrancis.com
Taylor & Francis Verlag GmbH, Kaufingerstraße 24, 80331 München, Germany

www.ingramcontent.com/pod-product-compliance
Lightning Source LLC
LaVergne TN
LVHW021003300926
849160LV00007B/232